CHEMOTAXONOMY
OF
FLOWERING PLANTS

VOLUME I

CHEMOTAXONOMY
OF
FLOWERING PLANTS

R. DARNLEY GIBBS

Emeritus Professor of Botany, McGill University, Montreal, Canada

VOLUME I

CONSTITUENTS

McGILL–QUEEN'S
UNIVERSITY PRESS

MONTREAL AND LONDON

1974

ISBN 0 7735 0098 7

Library of Congress Catalog Card No. 73-79096
Legal Deposit 2nd Quarter 1974

Printed in Great Britain
at the University Printing House, Cambridge, England
(Brooke Crutchley, University Printer)

To the memory of the late Dr E. W. R. (Ned) Steacie, friend and sometime colleague, who, as President of the National Research Council of Canada, did so much for personal research in the universities of his country.

CONTENTS

VOLUME I

VOLUME II

VOLUME III

VOLUME IV

FIGURES

VOLUME I

VOLUME II

TABLES

VOLUME I

VOLUME II

XX CHEMOTAXONOMY OF FLOWERING PLANTS

CONSTITUENTS

PREFACE

Is it usual for an author to be able to say just when his book was conceived, or what sparked the writing of it? I have been the part-author of one book, the author of another, and now write the preamble to a third. In each case I can pinpoint the occasion of conception.

Ernest J. Holmes and I were dining with our former Professor of Education and Philosophy, the late A. A. Cock. Holmes, then teaching at a secondary school, complained that no suitable textbook of biology was available for the middle school. Cock looked at us over his glasses and said, as nearly as I can remember, 'Surely you and Gibbs know enough biology to write one of your own'. We thought we did, and wrote *A Modern Biology* (1937).

About ten years later a cyclotron was built at McGill. Its construction involved the destruction of our greenhouses and effectively ruined a programme of research on which I was engaged. While I was sulking about this an agent of Blakiston's called to discuss books. When I said there was no suitable book for the type of introductory botany course that I gave, he said 'Write one'. At that moment *Botany: an evolutionary approach* (1950) was conceived.

This present book owes its origin to John Hutchinson. I was horrified to note, some time in the 1940s, that in a diagram in his *Families of flowering plants* (1926) he had what I had been led to believe is a natural order, the **Umbelliflorae** (or **Apiales**, or **Umbellales**), evolving along two lines—his 'woody' and 'herbaceous' lines. It is true that he put the pieces together again later in the book; but the damage had been done! If these two parts of the old **Umbelliflorae** had indeed evolved along separate lines, I argued, their chemistry would be different. From that moment I started to collect data on the chemistry of the *Umbelliferae*, *Araliaceae* and *Cornaceae* (s.l.). Quickly the field widened and led, almost 30 years later, to this book.

And what *is* this book? It is *not*, and could not be (since it is essentially a one-man book), an exhaustive compilation of *all* the chemistry of *all* the species that have been investigated, applied to *all* the taxonomy of *all* the plants involved. It is an attempt to gather as much information as possible from the literature, while making as many simple tests as possible on as many flowering plants as possible. The coverage is necessarily patchy. I have not been able to include much from the Russian, or the Chinese, or Japanese. I have not, while writing this book, been able to deal even with the whole of the literature in English. Travel in North America, England, Australia, New Zealand and Jamaica has made possible the study of many plants from those countries; but the plants of South America, Africa, India and much of Asia have been largely unavailable. It is true that many individuals and institutions have sent me material, often by air, from many parts of the world; and it is true that the botanical gardens to which I have had access have been generous in letting me help myself; but there are many families virtually unrepresented in even the finest gardens. And it is often the taxonomically most interesting plants that are missing!

We shall see later how important it may be to test several parts of a plant. Often I have had access only to a fragment of herbarium material —of *Malesherbia*, for example (though in that case I was looking for HCN, and found it!). Root-material was often not to be had. And this is a good place to mention the vexed question of voucher specimens. I have had great arguments with herbarists about this. Ideally, of course, it would be nice to know that one *could* check the identity of a plant reported by an investigator to have a particular constituent. But if I had made a voucher specimen for every plant I have tested there would be *thousands* (I don't exaggerate) of herbarium sheets cluttering herbaria, against the possibility that one or two people might want to check my claims—and I should have had time for *many* fewer tests. And in all too many cases I have had insufficient plant material to make a voucher specimen. When I, myself, have wanted to check other people's results I have tried to get the species they have claimed to have tested and have made tests for myself.

Early in my own work I had to decide whether to make an *intensive* study of a limited group or an *extensive* study of as many species as possible. I opted for the latter approach—see the introduction to the section on 'tests used by the author'. Had the decision been to study a few plants in depth, then I might have felt differently about voucher specimens.

I have, of course, tried to be sure of my material, but that has not always been possible. A few results are queried because of doubt as to identification. Even the best botanical gardens, one finds, have mis-labelled plants. In one or two cases the unexpected chemistry of the specimens tested has led me to query the labelling and to find it wrong!

And how does one deal with the results of early workers? Often one finds, in trying to check a name in the great *Index Kewensis*, that the name used is not recognized, or that it might apply to more than one species as recognized today. And the chemistry may be uncertain, too. Re-examination by modern methods often reveals such inadequacies. Errors crowd in, but only rarely do they mislead us at all seriously.

This book is *not* a textbook of plant biochemistry, but I hope that my lists of constituents may prove useful—they certainly took much of my time! Looking back at it I realize that I often spent far too much

time tracking down the chemistry of substances mentioned only by
trivial names; just as I wasted time over obscure references to out of the
way families.

A decision had to be made when writing was started as to the level
at which chemotaxonomy was to be discussed. Hegnauer's great work,
still incomplete, deals with *families* in alphabetical order. Could one deal
with *orders*, I wondered, and decided to try. It has become clear that
our knowledge of plant chemistry is too limited for this to be generally
successful. But I am consoled that Cronquist (1965) finds difficulties
even in defining orders:

> Still another very serious obstacle to the development of a satisfactory
> general system is that the characters which mark the families and
> orders are subject to frequent exception. Exceptions to the ordinal
> characters are indeed so numerous that it is difficult to find criteria
> sufficiently stable for even the most loose and general characterization
> of the groups. Some botanists have gone so far as to say that the
> orders of angiosperms can be defined only by the list of families to be
> included. This may be an unnecessarily pessimistic position, but it
> does point up the difficulty.

It is, of course, one of the aims of comparative chemistry to try to
find chemical characters that *are* sufficiently stable for the characteriza-
tion of groups. The reader will learn how few as yet are the chemical
characters that are of use at the *order* level. At higher levels there are
virtually none. I soon gave up the attempt to deal with super-orders,
sub-classes, and other higher categories.

ACKNOWLEDGEMENTS

The research work included here could not have been done, and this book could not have been written, without the generous help of many associates, friends, correspondents, and institutions. Some helped me but once—with a twig or even a single leaf of some much-desired plant —others have given repeated help over a long period of time. Some now are dead; some who are thanked here will not see this acknowledgement; others helped me so long ago that I have forgotten to add their names— I pray their forgiveness. Please believe, all of you, that I am sincerely grateful.

Institutions

Arnold Arboretum, Mass., U.S.A. and Dr R. Howard: for specimens.
Botanical Garden, Adelaide, Australia: for specimens.
Botanical Garden, Brisbane, Australia: for many specimens.
Botanic Gardens, Melbourne, Australia: for many specimens.
Botanical Garden, Berkeley, Calif., U.S.A.: for specimens.
British Museum (Nat. Hist.): for use of the library and much help in locating early source material.
Brooklyn Botanical Garden, N.Y., U.S.A.: for many specimens.
Cambridge University Botanic Garden, England: for many specimens.
Experimental Farm, Ottawa: for specimens.
Fairchild Tropical Garden, Florida, U.S.A.: for specimens.
Golden Gate Park, San Francisco, Calif., U.S.A.: for specimens.
Linnean Society of London, England: for bibliographic help.
McGill University, Montreal, Canada (my working home for more than 40 years) and colleagues there: for numberless favours, including (from McGill) grants for equipment.
Montreal Botanical Garden and M. Marcel Raymond: for great assistance over many years, including garden and laboratory space, and hundreds of specimens.
National Research Council of Canada: for numerous grants in aid of research; for a travel grant which made possible my second round-the-world voyage (during which I made tests on more than 700 species of plants in England, Australia, New Zealand, and Jamaica); and for grants used in the preparation and publication of this book.
New York Botanical Garden, N.Y., U.S.A.: for specimens.
Nuffield Foundation: for financial assistance in 1960-1.
Rancho Santa Ana Botanic Garden and Dr R. F. Thorne: for specimens.

Royal Botanical Garden, Edinburgh, Scotland: for many specimens.

Royal Botanic Gardens, Kew, England: for many specimens; for facilities at the Jodrell Laboratory (Dr C. R. Metcalfe—who has helped me in other ways, too); and for use of the library and assistance in tracking down early references.

Royal Botanic Gardens, Sydney, Australia: for specimens.

Royal Horticultural Society's Gardens, Wisley, England: for specimens.

University of Adelaide and Dr H. B. S. Womersley, Miss Constance M. Eardley, and others: for facilities for research, hospitality, etc.

University of Auckland, N.Z., and Professor V. J. Chapman and others: for facilities for research, hospitality, etc.

University of Canterbury, Christchurch, N.Z., and Professor W. R. Philipson: for assistance.

University of Melbourne, Australia, and Professor J. S. Turner and others: for laboratory facilities, hospitality, etc.

University of Otago, Dunedin, N.Z., and Professor G. T. S. Baylis: for help and hospitality.

University of Queensland, Australia, Professor Herbert and Dr H. T. Clifford and others: for laboratory facilities, hospitality and much assistance.

University of Southampton, England, and many friends: for my undergraduate training; for laboratory facilities in many summers; and for much generous help.

University of Sydney, Australia and Professor R. L. Crocker, Dr R. C. Carolin and others: for providing laboratory facilities, hospitality and assistance.

University of Western Australia, Nedlands and Professor B. J. Grieve and others: for laboratory facilities, hospitality and much assistance.

University of the West Indies, Mona, Jamaica and Professor A. D. Skelding, Dr C. D. Adams, Dr P. Hunt, Dr K. L. Stuart and others: for laboratory accommodation, hospitality and assistance.

Individuals

(a) Student and other laboratory assistants (mostly aided by grants from the National Research Council of Canada): Andrew Taussig and Arthur Dawson (1952); R. Buckridan (1953); Ruth L. McCulloch (Mrs J. Lowther) (1954); Eva Tobolt (1955); Irene Karpishka (1956); Brian Goodwin (1954); Marion Bourke (1958); Mrs Patsy Bahr (for several years); Dr Deirdre Edward, as an assistant and as a colleague; Elizabeth Shaw (**Hamamelidales**); Marilyn Galang (**Geraniales**);

U. N. Jha ('Amentiferae'); Monica Scott (Mrs E. Peter) (**Rhoeadales** or **Papaverales**); Maria Wehrli; G. H. N. Towers, as a student and as a colleague; Sally Liau (**Rutales**).

(*b*) Others as individuals: Mr P. E. Ballance, for analyses of fats of *Pterocarya*; Mr E. C. Bate-Smith, for help; Mr A. A. Bullock, for much help with the list of families; the late Prof. H. F. Copeland, for help with names of orders, etc.; Mr E. M. Counsell, for translations from the Latin; Dr W. L. M. Crombie, for analyses of fats of *Pterocarya*; Dr Otto Degener, for material of *Degeneria*; Mrs G. du Boulay, for specimens and for help with identifications; Professor J. T. Edward, for generous assistance over many years in matters of chemistry, etc.; Dr Joseph Ewan; Dr Clarrie Frankton, for much assistance and hospitality; Dr D. A. Fraser, for specimens; Dr Robert Goodland, for material of *Thurnia*, etc.; Dr Marjorie Harbert, for specimens, etc.; the late Dr H. H. Hatt, for help and hospitality; Dr C. Y. Hopkins, for fat analyses of *Floerkea*, and other assistance; Mr Trevor Jones; Professor R. Klibansky, for translations from the Latin; Dr Levy, for translations from the Italian; Dr Paul Maycock, for specimens; Dr McKee, for material of *Phelline*; Dr W. H. Minshall, for help and hospitality; Mr C. E. C. Nicholls, for help and hospitality; Professor J. C. Nicholson, for translations from the Russian; Dr G. T. Prance, for material of several unusual families; Professor Laurie Richardson, for help and hospitality; Dr W. W. Sanford, for data on raphides in orchids; Dr A. J. Sharp, for specimens; Professor W. L. Stern, for material of *Columellia*, etc.; Professor A. Taurins, for help in matters of chemistry; Dr Len Webb, Bill Jones and others at Brisbane, for generous help, many specimens and (Webb) for permission to use manuscript results; Professor V. C. Wynne-Edwards, for specimens.

(*c*) Those concerned with the preparation of this book: Miss Beverly Johnston and Miss M. E. Simpson of the McGill–Queen's Press, for their patience and understanding in editorial matters; David Wynne, for preparing the figures; Mrs Evelyn Fung-a-ling, Mrs Alice Holmes, Helen Caldwell and Monica Brant, for their skill in typing from a sometimes difficult manuscript; Miss Ruby Mayhew, who has helped me so often and in so many ways; and, lastly, my wife: for making many Cigarette Tests (I am not a smoker!), and some Hot-Water Tests; for helping to prepare the index; and for taking a second place to this book (and with only moderate complaint) during its long gestation!

ABBREVIATIONS

Some of the abbreviations used are too obvious to require listing here.

Names of orders are often abbreviated by dropping **-ales**; of families by dropping *-aceae*; of sub-families by dropping *-oideae*; e.g. **Ros.** for **Rosales**; *Ros.* for *Rosaceae*; *Ros.* for *Rosoideae*.

Family names not ending in *-aceae* may be variously abbreviated: *Comp.*, *Compos.* for *Compositae*; *Leg.*, *Legum.* for *Leguminosae*.

ab.-gd pts   above-ground (or aerial) parts

BH, or B. and H.   Bentham and Hooker, *Gen. pl.*

bk   bark

bl.   blue

bu.   bulb

C. and E.   Chadefaud and Emberger, *Traité de bot.*

Cig. Test   Cigarette Test

cot.   cotyledon

cv.   cultivar

dp   deep (of colour)

dry wt   dry weight

D.-S.   Dykyj-Sajfertova (Hot-Water Test)

EP1, EP2   Engler and Prantl, *Die natürlichen Pflanzenfam.*, 1st and 2nd editions

f.a.   fatty-acid

fam., fams   family, families

fl.   flower

fluor.   fluorescence

frt   fruit

fr. wt   fresh weight

herb.   herbarium

htwd   heartwood

H.-W. Test   Hot-Water Test

infl.   inflorescence

ING   *Index nominum genericorum*

lf, lvs   leaf, leaves

M.   Manske, *Alkaloids*

M. and C.   Metcalfe and Chalk, *Anat. of dicots*

M. and H.   Manske and Holmes, *Alkaloids*

mag.   magenta

mat.   material

n.c.   conserved name (after a family name)

o.r.   Oxalis reaction

p.   page, pale (of colour)

pet.   petiole
plt   plant
rhiz.   rhizome
rt   root
rtbk   rootbark
rtsk   rootstock
sap., sapog.   saponin, sapogenin
sd   seed
sdlg   seedling
spwd   sapwood
st.   stem
stbk   stembark
Syll. xi, *Syll.* xii   editions 11 and 12 of Engler's *Syll. d. Pflanzenfam.*
tu.   tuber
v.   very
v., var.   variety
v.T. and C.   van Tieghem and Constantin, *Elém. de bot.*
W. 1966   Willis, *Dict. of flow. pl. and ferns,* 7th edition, 1966 (ed.
   H. K. Airy Shaw)
yell.   yellow
yg   young

THE HISTORY OF CHEMOTAXONOMY

Some years ago I wrote (in Swain, 1963) a brief history of our subject. Here I shall attempt to give an even briefer history, adding, however, a paragraph or two about omissions from the 1963 paper.

Botany arose largely from man's efforts to describe the plants used by him for food and more particularly for medicine. Thus the root-gatherers and the herbalists began to group plants for their 'virtues' or medicinal properties. In the seventeenth century this grouping came to assume a modern look. Thus we find Nehemiah Grew (1641–1712) writing in *An Idea of a Phytological History Propounded* (1673).

> From hence likewise the Natures of Vegetables may be conjectured. For in looking upon divers Plants, though of different names and kinds; yet if some affinity may be found betwixt them, then the nature of any one of them being well known, we have thence ground of conjecture as to the nature of all the rest. So that as every Plant may have somewhat of nature individual to it self; so as far as it obtaineth any visible communities with other Plants, so far may it partake of common Nature with those also. Thus the Wild and Garden Cucumers have this difference, that the one purgeth strongly, the other not at all; yet in being Diuretick, they both agree. The Natures of Umbelliferous Plants we know are various; yet 'tis most probably that they all agree in this one, *scil.* in being Carmina-tive ... So Tulips, Lillies, Crocuses, Jacynths, and Onions them-selves, with many others in their several degrees, are all allied. If therefore Crocuses, Onions, Lillies agree in one or more faculties, then why may not all the rest? as in being anodyne. . . .

James Petiver, in a paper dated 10 May 1699, and titled '*Some* Attempts *made to prove that* Herbs *of the same* Make *or* Class *for the generallity, have the like Vertue and Tendency to work the same Effects*', starts out:

> Having by some *Persons* been asked what Method might be best proposed toward the *discovering* of the *Vertues* of *Plants*, amongst others I thought that this might not prove an altogether unsuccessful conjecture, *Viz.* That *Plants* of the same *Figure* or Likeness, have for the generallity much the same *Vertues* and *Use*: Especially if we consider, that the *Organs* or *Structure* of ye *Plants* of the same *Family* or *Class*, must have much the same *Vessels* and *Ductus's* to consum-mate that Regular formation, and consequently the *Juices* Circulated and strained thro' them cannot be very *Heterogeneous*; and that as for

[9]

the most part, the *Scent* and *Tast* have great affinity, so of course their *Vertue* likewise cannot be very *dissonant*.

He goes on to distinguish, on the grounds of 'vertue', what we would call *Umbelliferae*, *Labiatae* and *Cruciferae*, and he writes entertainingly about them.

In the same year as Petiver's paper appeared there was printed *De Convenientia Plantarum in Fructificatione et Viribus*—a thesis defended by Georg Friedrich Gmelin with Camerarius presiding. Stearn (1957), in his introduction to the Ray Society's facsimile edition of Linnaeus' *Species Plantarum* points out that theses were often primarily or entirely the work of the director, and we find that Camerarius, rather than Gmelin, is sometimes credited with this work. We may place it along-side of Petiver's as a pioneering effort in this field.

The next milestone in our history is the *Essai sur les propriétés médicales des Plantes, comparées avec leur formes extérieures et leur classification naturelle* by A. P. DeCandolle, published in 1804. The author says that Camerarius (above) was the first writer to express clearly the connections between forms and properties of plants. He gives Linnaeus some credit, too.

A second edition of the *Essai* appeared in 1816. DeCandolle notes here that differences in soils do not greatly affect the composition of plants growing in them: 'C'est un phénomene continuellement présent à notre examen, que de voir diverse plantes nées dans un sol parfaite-ment semblable, produire des matières trés-différentes, tandis que des végétaux analogues, nées dans les sols differens, y forment des produits semblables.'

Although in 1804 he did not separate the *Jasmineae* from the *Oleineae*, in 1816 he does, and notes that insects can detect the differences between the two groups: 'les cantharides attaquent d'abord les frênes, puis se jettent sur les lilas et les troènes et jusque sur les oliviers [all Oleineae] . . . Elles n'attaquent au contraire les jasmins, qu'on avais mal-à-propos réunis à la famille des Oléinées, et que forment aujourd'hui une famille particulière [Jasmineae].'

He notes, too, that experiments on grafting support the split into two families. Lindley (1830) quotes from him (but translates):

However heterogeneous the Olive tribe may appear as at present limited, it is remarkable that the species will all graft upon each other; a fact which demonstrates the analogy of their juices and their fibres. Thus the Lilac will graft upon the Ash, the Chionanthus and the Fontanesia, and I have even succeeded in making the Persian Lilac live ten years on Phyllirea latifolia. The Olive will take upon the Phyllirea, and even on the Ash: but we cannot graft the Jasmine on any plant of the Olive tribe; a circumstance which confirms the propriety of separating these two tribes.

Somewhat later we come upon further milestones in the works of Rochleder—overlooked in my earlier essay. In 1847 he published *Beiträge zur Phytochemie* and in 1854 *Phytochemie*. I quote briefly from a translation of the latter by a student of mine, Maria Wehrli (the original is in German): 'At the present time there are many more gaps in the knowledge of the chemistry of the plant kingdom than well-established and well-interpreted facts. Knowing about these deficiencies, we have done already the first step towards the solving of the problem . . . My aims in writing this book were to compile the few facts that we know and to reveal the many gaps that exist, and in doing that I hope to stimulate further investigations that [will] lead either to the support or defeat of some of my suppositions.'

I can echo Rochleder's aims in this present work!

In discussing ash analyses he says that those of members of the *Gramineae* show much more '*silicic acid*' than do those of the *Leguminosae* and *Papaveraceae*. But he says also that the ashes of two such closely related plants as *Calluna vulgaris* and *Erica carnea* differ as much as do those of wheat straw and *Aesculus hippocastanum*—an argument against facile generalization.

Rochleder gives several examples of substances which have odd distributions in plants—*caffeine*, *chrysophanic acid* and *indigo*—which might be used in arguments against correlation of 'form' and composition. But he says that all members of the *Rubiaceae* studied have similar *tannins*, as do members of the *Ericaceae*, which also have *ericolin*; and he gives further examples of correlation in a list of about 200 orders (families) of dicotyledons alone, including almost 60 from which 'no results' are available. A few of these latter could be so listed today! He concludes:

Only a number of careful and scientifically up to date plant analyses will enable us to reach our goal: to replace all the now existing classification systems by one single natural system. This can be achieved only by considering all factors, morphological and anatomical as well as chemical ones. Whoever studies the plant kingdom has to be familiar with the morphology of plants as well as with the chemical composition and biosynthesis. The botanist cannot work without a knowledge of chemistry, the chemist cannot work without a knowledge of botany, if they are to promote science.

We pass on now to the 'modern pioneers', as I have called them.

Helen C. de S. Abbott must have been a remarkable woman, writing as she did on chemotaxonomy in the 1880s. She says: 'The vegetable kingdom does not usually claim our attention for its intellectual attainments, although its members would certainly seem to possess greater chemical skill than a higher race of beings exhibit in laboratories.' And, prophetically: 'There has been comparatively little study of the chemical principles of plants from a purely botanical view. It promises to become a new field of research.'

An early centre for research in the tropics was established in the great botanical garden at Buitenzorg (now Bogor) in Java (plant anatomy and physiology, 1884; pharmacology, 1888). From these laboratories came a stream of papers, some of which are of interest here. We find Eykman (1888) discussing alkaloids and their botanical distribution, and Greshoff (1891) writing, among other things, of *laurotetanine* in the *Lauraceae*. He had found this alkaloid in several plants of that family and says: 'Dans les notes jointes à [*Hernandia, Illigera, Gyrocarpus, Cassytha*—in which he also found alkaloids] l'auteur rappelle les opinions divergentes de la place naturelle de ces quatres genres, qu'on a ranges dans les familles trés différentes. Peut-être le phytochimiste pourra renseigner le systematicien aussitot que paraîtra l'identité ou l'analogie de structure de ces alkaloïdes avec lauro-tetanine.'

A little later van Romburgh published extensively on the distribution of acetone, methyl salicylate and HCN. Treub, in several papers, and de Jong, also investigated plants for HCN—their work in this field being more reliable than that of some later workers in the tropics! Gorter's work on chlorogenic acid (1910) also came from Buitenzorg.

Greshoff, whom we mentioned above, also worked at Kew, and published (1909) a summary of tests on many plants for tannins, saponins, HCN and alkaloids. Writing of HCN in *Platanus* he brings out, in a striking way, the high concentration in the leaves: 'Indeed, in the ordinary plane-tree of the London streets (*P. acerifolia*), there is so much hydrocyanic acid present that the amount from every London plane-leaf would be enough to kill a London sparrow.' He is ambitious for chemotaxonomy, as witness: 'Strictly speaking one might demand that every accurate description of a genus or of a new species should be accompanied by ['should include' would be better] a short "chemical description" of the plant.'

If Greshoff was ambitious for his subject, McNair was perhaps overambitious in attempting to apply comparative chemistry generally to taxonomy. Twenty-six of his papers, which appeared from 1916 to 1945, have recently been reprinted (1965). In his first paper he notes that Japan 'wax' (a fat) from Asiatic species of *Rhus* is similar to the fruit-coat fats of two N. American species of the genus. He continued to be interested in fats, and in 1929 discussed those of 300 plants (from 83 families), in relation to climate and taxonomy. He concluded that fats and oils of closely related plants are closely similar, and that in general the plants of the tropics tend to store fats or non-drying oils of higher melting-points than those of plants from temperate regions.

In 1935 he is writing of alkaloids. He says that each species of a large genus, such as *Aconitum*, may have a different member of a group of closely related alkaloids; that any one alkaloid may occur in many members of one family (e.g. *protopine* in the *Papaveraceae*); but that few individual alkaloids occur in more than one family.

In 1935, too, he has a paper called 'Angiosperm phylogeny on a chemical basis'. Here he claims that plants high in the evolutionary scale have constituents with larger molecules and fats with higher iodine numbers than have those lower in the scale. He uses these 'facts' to argue that trees are more primitive than herbaceous plants. In this paper he contrasts publications by Standley and Rusby. The former had written on *Rubiaceae* in 1931, the latter—who had published on *Cinchona* in 1887—writes, in 1931-2: 'It is doubtful if any other genus of equal size has received such thorough study, as to gross and micro-scopical structure, chemistry, reproduction, embryology, horticulture, ecology and geography, as has *Cinchona* . . . [yet] In the most recent publication on the Bolivian cinchonas, Standley's *The Rubiaceae of Bolivia*, all this information is ignored, with the result of so many errors that I can regard the publication only as a misfortune to *Cinchona* literature.'

Rusby may have been unfair, but he *does* emphasize the importance to taxonomy of including data from all fields when making taxonomic judgments.

In 1945 McNair is concluding on chemical grounds that mono-cotyledons are more primitive than dicotyledons, and that in the latter group the Sympetalae are the most advanced. He has other papers, too, along similar lines.

We must applaud McNair for his courage in using comparative chemistry on such a sweeping scale, but we must question some of his assumptions and conclude that he was 'before his time' in many respects.

Now that we are well into the twentieth century with our history it is convenient to deal with some individual topics, some of which receive considerable attention elsewhere in this book.

(a) Raphides

I have myself been particularly interested in *raphides* and have looked for them in sections of many plants—more especially in the control sections when carrying out the *Syringin Test* (p. 71). Early workers, and some later ones, have included small, unoriented acicular crystals among their 'raphides'. We define them as *slender, needle-shaped crystals of calcium oxalate, arranged parallel to each other in tight bundles and occurring in special raphide-sacs*. I don't know who first used this definition, or who first used raphides as a diagnostic character. Gulliver (see below) says that Lindley used them in 1839, but Robert Brown (1773–1858) made use of presence or absence of these crystals as a diagnostic character in a paper prepared in 1831 and published in 1833. He was among many things, an authority on the *Orchidaceae* and noted the nucleus—he was the first, I think, to use the name—in cells of members of that family. He also saw raphides and wrote: 'My concluding observation on Orchideae relates to the very general existence and great abundance, in this family, of Raphides or acicular crystals in almost every part of the cellular tissue.'

In a later paper (1845) he decided that the reticulated sheath through which the flower of *Rafflesia* bursts when emerging from its host plant is part of that host because it has raphides: 'That the whole of this covering belongs to the stock, is proved by its containing those raphides or acicular crystals which are so abundant in the root of the *Vitis* or *Cissus*, and which are altogether wanting in the parasite.'

Gulliver (1804–1882), a British anatomist and microscopist, made a careful study of raphides, defining them as I have done. His many papers appeared from 1861 to 1880. He says (1866) that: 'Only 3 orders [we should say families] of British Dicotyledons can as yet be characterized as raphis-bearers, and these are—Balsaminaceae, Onagraceae, and Rubiaceae.'

He was correct in this. He knew that some non-British members of the *Rubiaceae* do have raphides. He saw that *Trapa* (not a native of Britain) lacks raphides, and therefore 'perhaps does not really belong to the order *Onagraceae*'. Today we have a family *Trapaceae* for it.

In 1880 (his last paper ?) Gulliver says that he has not seen raphides in the many members of the *Saxifragaceae* which he has examined, but that they occur in *Hydrangea*: 'Here then is a natural and sharp diagnostic between Saxifrages and Hydrangeas.'

We must not pursue this particular point further here, but see my earlier history (pp. 52–4) and our discussion of the *Saxifragaceae* (p. 1645 of this book).

Presence or absence of raphides is a character used more recently by Tomlinson (1962) in discussing the families of the **Zingiberales** (italics mine):

In contrast to the randomness just discussed, three features suggest that the eight families fall into four natural groups. These are the structure of the guard cells, *the presence or absence of raphide sacs*, and the structure of the root stele....The first of the four groups includes *Heliconiaceae*, *Musaceae*, and *Strelitziaceae*, *which have raphide sacs*, symmetrical guard cells...and anomalous root structure at least in the last two families. The second includes *Costaceae*, *Marantaceae*, and *Zingiberaceae*, which have asymmetrical guard cells...and *lack raphide sacs* and anomalous root structure....The third has *Cannaceae without raphide sacs*. The fourth group consists of *Lowiaceae with its raphide sacs*, asymmetrical guard cells, and normal root structure.

Note that some have included *Heliconiaceae*, *Musaceae*, *Strelitziaceae* and *Lowiaceae*, the only families of the eight with *raphide sacs*, in *Musaceae* (s.l.).

Tomlinson concluded that occurrence of raphides is a primitive feature. It is of interest to note that there is some evidence that raphides are primitive in the dicotyledons, too (see Gibbs, 1954).

(b) Cyanogenesis

It has long been known that many plants, but still a small minority, yield under some conditions appreciable amounts of *HCN* (*prussic acid, hydrocyanic acid*). Such plants are said to be *cyanogenic*. We deal elsewhere in this book with *cyanogenic glycosides*, but a few notes on the history of their use in chemotaxonomy are in order here.

The earliest reference that I have found is in Lindley (1830). He says that *Amygdaleae* are: 'Distinguished from Rosaceae and Pomaceae by their fruit being a drupe, their bark yielding gum, and by the presence of hydrocyanic acid; from Leguminosae by the latter character, and.. from Chrysobalaneae by their hydrocyanic acid...' Lindley also noted that cyanogenic plants may be toxic.

Endlicher (1836–40) also used presence of HCN in *Amygdaleae* to distinguish that group from the *Chrysobalaneae*.

These pioneers were followed during the next century by a host of others who tested plants for HCN. I have listed many of these, from Jorissen (1884) to Hegnauer and myself in the present. Not all reports are trustworthy—some workers have used faulty methods—but we do have a large body of information (p. 60). A weakness is the relative scarcity of *negative* records, some lists reporting only *positive* results. Another weakness is that few of the records tell us which of the dozen or more cyanogenic substances is/are responsible for cyanogenesis in particular cases. In my own very extensive testing, for example, I have dealt only with presence or absence of cyanogenesis.

In the course of my work I have noticed some atypical results (p. 59).

These suggest that further work is necessary before we can be sure that all 'positive' results are indeed due to HCN.

We must note also, as so often in this book, that only a minority of the known species of flowering plants have as yet been tested for cyanogenesis. A lot of testing remains to be done before we can say that any given taxon is non-cyanogenic. And this is made the more difficult because some plants are cyanogenic only at times, others only in some organs (p. 43).

(c) Amino-acids and proteins

Amino-acids, the building-blocks of proteins, are universally present in plants, and may be considered first. More than twenty are in all proteins; others are common constituents of plants; yet others seem to be very restricted in their distribution and these can be important taxonomic markers. Here we are concerned with the historical aspect.

The first amino-acid to be isolated was *asparagine* (Vauquelin and Robiquet, 1806), and until the work of Ritthausen (1860–72) it was the only amino-acid known to occur in plants. When E. Schulze finished *his* work (about 1906) fifteen protein amino-acids had been found. Only after the introduction of chromatography (see below) was there a very rapid increase in the number of non-protein amino-acids known. Fowden (1962) has a graph showing this, the numbers being roughly: 2 in 1915, 4 in 1930, 8 in 1940, 13 in 1950, 40 in 1955, 70 in 1960, and perhaps 100 in 1965, with no indication of a levelling off. It must be emphasized that much remains to be done, even for the known amino-acids, for we know little as yet about their distribution.

Today we have sophisticated methods for the investigation of *proteins*, and two of these may be referred to briefly here: *serology* and *amino-acid sequence determinations*.

Serology has now a rather lengthy history. Its use in taxonomy is based on the idea that each kind of living organism has its own characteristic proteins; that the proteins of nearly related organisms are closely similar; that those of organisms more distantly related are less alike; and so on. We have discussed serology elsewhere (Gibbs, 1963) and in this book (p. 384). Its history really began more than 70 years ago. It was considered by some to be the answer to the taxonomists' prayer for a certain means of determining relationships; was bitterly attacked; fell into disrepute; and only with more sophisticated modern techniques has it been restored to respectability. Perhaps it may be replaced as a tool by *amino-acid sequence determinations*, which we have also discussed elsewhere in this book (p. 383). It does seem, on the face of it, that we are here at last determining the ultimate structures of the stuffs of life, and justifying the optimism of Boulter, Laycock, Ramshaw, and Thompson (1970), quoted on p. 384. Let us hope that this optimism is not misplaced.

In discussing the history of biology with my students I have had again and again to stress the fact that progress in biology has often been hampered by lack of tools. The detailed study of anatomy had to wait in turn for the lens, the compound microscope and the electron microscope. The early student of the biogenesis of complicated substances lamented the absence of a 'flag' by which to follow elements during synthesis and/or degradation. He now has the technique of 'labelling' which gives him a set of flags.

The techniques of *chromatography* have made possible the rapid detection and estimation of very many substances important to chemotaxonomy. Let us briefly relate its history.

Pliny (A.D. 23–79) is said to have used papyrus impregnated with an extract of gall-nuts (tannins) for the detection of ferrous sulphate, essentially our *Tannin Test A* in reverse! But it was the work of Schönbein (1861), Goppelsroeder (1901) and others on 'capillary analysis' which was the real beginning of chromatography. Day (1897, 1903) used 'fractional diffusion', and he was followed by Gilpin and others (1908, 1910, 1913). While this was going on Tswett (two papers in 1906) was separating plant pigments by adsorption. We translate:

> There is a certain adsorption series by which substances can be arranged. On this law rests the following important application. If one filters a petrol–ether solution of chlorophyll through an adsorption column (I used chiefly calcium carbonate, densely packed in narrow glass tubes) the colouring matter is separated into zones from top to bottom, according to the adsorption series...This separation becomes practically complete, if after the passage of the coloured solution into the adsorption column, one then uses a stream of the pure solvent...Such a preparation I call a chromatogram and the corresponding method a chromatographic method.

How modern this sounds! But there was a long pause before chromatography 'caught on' in a big way. Martin and Synge (1941) and Consden, Gordon and Martin (1944) have been credited by Block, Durrum and Zweig (1958) with the present-day popularity of the subject. They used liquid–liquid counter-current techniques, and one-way and two-way paper chromatography.

Only a few years ago the determination of the fatty-acids from a fat was a major operation. Today, using gas-chromatography, one can get quantitative results in a very brief time. This is reflected in the rapidly increasing numbers of analyses available. In Hilditch (1st, 2nd and

3rd editions; 1940, 1947 and 1956) we find analytical data on roughly 400, 450 and 600 plant fats. In Hilditch and Williams (1964) we find 900, and in a paper by Wolff (1966) an estimate of 1000. We have referred above to the increase in our knowledge of the *amino-acids*, and we shall note the use of chromatography in the detection of the *phenolic constituents* of plants.

Illustrations could be multiplied, though not all of our increase in knowledge is due to chromatography. It is only a few years ago that the structure of the first *aucubin-type glycoside* was determined; now, in 1971, a review paper on iridoids and seco-iridoids by Plouvier and Favre-Bonvin refers to 317 papers!

We may conclude this brief essay by a reference to a remark by Alston (when, where?) that it is time for a shift in emphasis in chemotaxonomy from problem-exposing to problem-solving. This book, as we shall see, reveals that there is still a lot of the former, and not as yet a great deal of the latter!

CRITERIA USED IN TAXONOMY, AND SOME RELATED TOPICS

INTRODUCTION

Robyns, in his presidential address (1964) to the general assembly of the International Association for Plant Taxonomy (I.A.P.T.), said (the italics are mine):

All scientific taxonomists aim indeed at the best biological classification possible, by using information and data *from any and all available sources of information*, integrating them into a synthesis in order to formulate a complete knowledge of each taxon actually living or extinct, with its relationships, its origin, its variation and its chorology. As our knowledge of plants is always subject to revision in time as new and relevant data arise, the field of taxonomy is revived and increasing so that *systematics, instead of being old-fashioned and obsolete*, as is sometimes claimed, *is still and will always remain very much alive and at the same time greatly progressive, with unlimited possibilities as a most essential basis for all other branches of biological research*.

There is much that is pertinent to this section in the thoughtful review by Lincoln Constance (1964) entitled *Systematic botany, an unending synthesis*. I must content myself with a single quotation:

Every few years some new approach or technique is proclaimed which this time is going to be successfully exploited to get the stone— that is, taxonomy—over the crest of the ridge dividing intuitive art from exact science. Anatomy, paleobotany, embryology, palynology, cytology, and genetics, to name a few, have all had their try; chemistry and mathematics are chafing eagerly in the wings to have their day upon the stage. One may be reasonably sure that other actors lurk behind these, although their features are not as yet quite discernible.

The notes that follow are intended to illustrate the many criteria that have been and are being used by systematists in their search for a truly phylogenetic system of classification. We have arranged them in a more or less historical sequence—for *general morphology*, for example, obviously preceded *numerical taxonomy*—but such an apparently simple arrangement presents many difficulties.

1. General morphology

The ordinary, easily observable morphological characters of plants have been used from the beginnings of taxonomy, and have undoubted worth. Even here, however, we find that simple morphology may be misleading, and controversy still rages. Is the woody character primitive when contrasted with the herbaceous? Are numerous floral parts more primitive than few?

Sporne (1954) has tried to make a list of supposedly primitive characters (mostly morphological) which will enable him to estimate the degree of advancement of any given family. He concluded that: '...the most reliable indicators of primitiveness are: woody habit, presence of secretory cells, leaves alternate, stipules present, flowers actinomorphic, petals free, stamens pleiomerous, carpels pleiomerous, seeds arillate, two integuments, integumentary vascular bundles, nuclear endosperm, carpels free, axile placentation.'

Sporne realized that some characters which: 'are believed to have been present in ancestral dicotyledons and, therefore, are primitive in certain families...(may) have also appeared secondarily in certain advanced families. These are: unisexual flower, haplochlamydy and small number of seeds.'

He calculated, using the selected characters, 'advancement indices' for families of dicotyledons, the families with the lower values being regarded as the more primitive. He came up with the following (I give only some):

Magnoliaceae 14
Bombacaceae and *Flacourtiaceae* 15
Annonaceae, Leguminosae, Malvaceae and *Myristicaceae* 18
Rhizophoraceae 21
Guttiferae, Nymphaeaceae and *Platanaceae* 32
Medusagynaceae, Nepenthaceae, Sonneratiaceae and *Ulmaceae* 42
Proteaceae 55
Casuarinaceae and *Piperaceae* 60
Podostemonaceae 70
Brunoniaceae, Campanulaceae, Dysphaniaceae, Gentianaceae, Goodeniaceae and *Scrophulariaceae* 82
Balanophoraceae and *Phrymaceae* 92
Hippuridaceae, Hydrostachyaceae, Martyniaceae and *Valerianaceae* 100

I have tried to use Sporne's results on the arrangement of orders, and of families in orders and sub-orders, in the 11th *Syllabus* (1936) as compared with the later 12th *Syllabus* (1964). In some cases, the **Centrospermae** for example, his figures support the supposedly better system in the latter, in other cases little 'improvement' is evident.

An interesting extrapolation would be to assume that 'chemical characters' of families with low advancement indices are 'primitive' and those of families with high indices are 'advanced'. Bate-Smith and Metcalfe (1957) actually tried this out for *tannins* in dicotyledons. They found that families with tannins had advancement indices between 14 and 75; those in which few members had them were between 32 and 93; while those lacking tannins were between 36 and 100. They concluded that the capacity to synthesize tannins is a primitive character.

We could give many examples of the usefulness of even single morphological characters in taxonomy, but one must suffice here. Metcalfe and Clifford (1968) report that Festucoid grasses lack microhairs, while in Panicoid grasses they are almost universal.

2. Anatomy

We have seen that *general morphology* has been used from the beginnings of botany in classifying plants. The use of *anatomy*, except of the grossest kind, had to wait until microscopes became available, but it seems to have been slow to get under way even with their help.

Reynolds Green (1909) said that Radlkofer was the father of the use of comparative anatomy in taxonomy. He wrote:

> The founder of the method as one of general application...was Radlkofer, who gave a new impetus to it in his great monograph of the Sapindaceous genus *Serjania*, published in 1875...If Radlkofer may be regarded as the founder of this movement, the great importance which came to be attached to it towards the end of the century was in large measure due to his pupil Solereder.

As recently as 1967 Metcalfe writes:

> Two of the most important problems in systematic anatomy are these. Firstly to collect comparative histological data on a scale that is large enough to permit them to form an integral part of the descriptive matter on which taxonomy is based. The second, more exciting stage is reached when enough descriptive data have been assembled to enable us to throw further light on the interrelationships and phylogeny of the plants in which they are exemplified. One of the greatest current dangers is that some botanists may find themselves tempted to move on to the second of these 2 stages before the first has been sufficiently completed....

He applies comparative anatomy to the subject of relationship between the *Gramineae* and *Cyperaceae* and concludes that:

> The histological differences between the Cyperaceae and Gramineae are...sufficiently great to support the view that, if both families have evolved from a common prototype, it must have been very remote from the present day species of which the 2 families consist.

Metcalfe warns that parallel development may occur in anatomy, as in other characters, and that this may mislead the unwary. The occurrence of vessels in the **Gnetales** may be a case in point. It has been argued that their presence indicates relationship with the angiosperms. Some anatomists, however, say that they arise in a manner different from that leading to vessels in the latter and that this is a strong argument against relationship!

Metcalfe points out that different anatomical characters may be important in different groups:

> If we turn to *Rhododendron*, the trichomes on the leaves are at least as taxonomically interesting as the structure of the wood, whilst in a family such as the Dipterocarpaceae we cannot afford to study the structure of the wood whilst ignoring that of the bark or the fascinatingly complex vascular structure of the petioles.

In 1967(8) he writes:

> It is, however, when we turn to the Monocotyledons that the irrelevance of wood structure is most apparent, for in these plants there is little if any secondary xylem at all. Nevertheless, recent work at the Jodrell Laboratory has shown that in the taxonomically 'difficult' family Restionaceae it is often easier to identify species from characters visible in transverse sections of the stem than it is from the exomorphic characters that are normally employed for this purpose!

3. Pollen morphology and anatomy

Use of pollen characters in taxonomy is using micro-morphological and anatomical characters and is therefore comparatively modern. Nevertheless, it is said, in the *Hist. bot. en France* (I.B.C., Paris, 1954) to have been used almost 150 years ago: 'En 1825, A. Guillemin fit une étude approfondie d'un grand nombre de grains de pollen et, dans un essai de classification, souligna l'importance de l'étude des pollens pour déceler les affinités entre les familles.'

In recent years whole books have been published on pollen by Erdtman (1952), Wodehouse (1935), etc., with many examples of the usefulness of pollen characters. We shall note only a few examples from recent papers.

Thomas (1960) notes that the pollens of the three genera (*Cyrilla, Cliftonia* and *Purdiaea*) that he would include in the *Cyrillaceae* are very similar. He also says:

> Pollen studies have also added further evidence to [*sic*] a close relationship between the Cyrillaceae and the Ericales. The only

group which has pollen that closely resembles that of the Cyrillaceae is the genus *Clethra* [*Clethraceae*, included in Ericales]...In the Aquifoliaceae and the Celastraceae, on the other hand, the pollen is quite unlike that of the Cyrillaceae as was pointed out by Erdtman (1952). An examination of the pollen of *Cyrillopsis* has added further evidence for excluding this genus from the Cyrillaceae. The pollen of *Cyrillopsis* is similar to that found in some members of the Celastraceae, but quite unlike that of the Cyrillaceae.

Lewis (1961) merged the genera *Oldenlandia* L. and *Houstonia* L. with *Hedyotis* L. More recently (1965) he studied the pollens of some of these plants and concluded: 'The evidence from palynology also supports the treatment of *Hedyotis* and *Houstonia* as congeneric.'

Finally we may note that Jeffrey in 1962 proposed a new classification of the *Cucurbitaceae*. In 1964, after examining a set of pollen-slides, he concluded that they supported rather closely his classification, but he made some changes as a result of these studies.

4. Embryology

In recent times the subject embryology has come to embrace much more than study of the embryo itself. This is made clear by Maheshwari in his *An introduction to the embryology of angiosperms* (1950). There he has chapters on the microsporangium, the megasporangium, the female gametophyte, the male gametophyte, fertilization, the embryo (at last!), apomyxis, polyembryony, embryology in relation to taxonomy and experimental embryology.

His chapter on embryology in relation to taxonomy gives interesting examples. The little family *Empetraceae* has baffled the taxonomists. Don (1827) put it in or near to the *Euphorbiaceae*; Pax (1896) placed it in the **Sapindales** near *Celastraceae* and *Buxaceae*; and several authors believe it to be related to the *Ericaceae*.

Maheshwari writes: 'That this last view is the correct one and that the Empetraceae is to be classed under the Ericales have now been definitely established on the basis of the embryological data brought forward by Samuelsson (1913)...The Empetraceae show a close correspondence in all respects [with the Ericales], while the Sapindales and Celastrales differ in so many ways that there is no doubt as to the correctness of Samuelsson's view.'

We shall see that the *chemistry* of the *Empetraceae* is also in line with a position in the **Ericales**.

The *Cactaceae*, on embryological grounds, are said to be nearer to the *Portulacaceae* than to the *Passifloraceae*. This, too, is supported by the chemical evidence.

Trapa was formerly included in the *Onagraceae*. Its eight-nucleate embryo-sac, and other embryological features, mark it off from the true *Onagraceae*. It is treated today as a separate family, *Trapaceae* or *Hydrocaryaceae*, and the absence of *raphides* from *Trapa* is in line with this.

Reeder (1962) actually uses the character of the *embryo itself* in dealing with the grasses. He writes: 'Using the embryo type as the principal criterion, one may recognize 6 basic groups of grasses. These are: *festucoid, bambusoid* (including oryzoid-olyroid), *centothecoid, arundinoid-danthonioid, chloridoid-eragrostoid*, and *panicoid*...The author's previous interpretation of the bamboo embryo as distinct from the oryzoid-olyroid type is shown to be erroneous.'

We could multiply these examples, but enough has been said to make it clear that comparative embryology, as might be expected, is a valuable tool in taxonomy.

5. Biosystematics, including cytology and genetics

The nature of 'biosystematics' was discussed at the 9th International Botanical Congress held in Montreal in 1959, and an international committee on biosystematic terminology was set up. Heywood and Löve reported from this in 1961. We quote: 'biosystematics and its subdivisions, cytotaxonomy and experimental taxonomy s.str., are to be regarded as an approach to taxonomy employing the methods of cytology and genetics to its problems, and not as a replacement of classical taxonomy.'

The committee agreed that its activities embrace experimental taxonomy, cytotaxonomy, cytogeography, genecology, biometry, micro-evolutionary studies and speciation. That nearby subjects are comparative developmental physiology, comparative phytochemistry and comparative embryology. That biosystematics is not necessarily aimed at taxonomy.

There are so many examples of the use of cytology and genetics in systematic botany that we shall not bother to cite any.

6. Grafting

It has long been known that it is possible in some cases to graft successfully one plant upon another, while in other cases this proves impossible. Some years ago (1954) I wrote:

A graft may almost be likened to a parasite. The scion—the 'parasite' —grows upon the stock—its 'host', and absorbs materials from it. Unless scion and stock are 'compatible' union does not occur and the scion dies. In general scions grow only upon stocks of closely related plants and we may suppose that chemical as well as other factors are involved. Interspecific grafts are not uncommon and intergeneric grafts are possible in some cases, as in the *Cactaceae*.

Herrmann (1951) has given some examples of intergeneric grafts— *Picea* on *Abies* and vice versa, *Picea* on *Larix*, on *Pseudotsuga*, and on *Pinus*. These genera are all within the *Pinaceae*. From the dicotyledons he gives *Fagus* and *Castanea* upon *Quercus* (all *Fagaceae*); and *Halimodendron* and *Caragana* (*Leguminosae*).

Melnick, Holm and Struckmeyer (1964) grafted young fertilized ovules (7–20 days from pollination) with some placental tissue (as scion) on to the placentas of growing attached fruits of *Capsicum frutescens* L. var. California wonder (*Solanaceae*, as host), and got the following results.

Intervarietal: *C. frutescens* L. var. Wisconsin lakes—seeds germinated and grew into normal plants.

Interspecific: *C. annuum*—ditto.

Intergeneric: *Lycopersicum esculentum* Mill. var.—ditto.

        Solanum melongena L. var.—the seeds formed were dormant.

        S. pseudocapsicum L.—ditto.

Interfamilial: *Fragaria virginiana* hort. var. (*Rosaceae*)—seeds germinated and grew into seedlings.

We give these examples to show that a successful graft does not prove close relationship in every case.

Nevertheless, success in grafting is *usually* a proof of near-relationship.

We have noted elsewhere in this book the use of this in the *Oleaceae*. *Garrya* (in 'our' *Garryaceae*) has been grafted upon *Aucuba* (*Cornaceae*), and we shall see that many believe these genera to be related. *Didierea* has been grafted on members of the *Cactaceae*, and we shall see that there are other reasons, too, for believing that the *Didiereaceae* and the *Cactaceae* are related.

7. Parasites and predators

Some parasites are quite specific, each kind using a single host. Others are less so, parasitizing a few host plants. Yet others seem to be catholic in their tastes, growing on many quite unrelated hosts. One may be reasonably sure that these differences are due in large part to the differing requirements, physical and chemical, of the parasites. At the one extreme are root-parasites which grow almost independently, but which attach their roots to the roots of any, or almost any, plants they can reach. It is said that in Colorado the Bastard toadflax (*Comandra umbellata*), a member of the **Santalales**, occurs upon at least 45 different hosts. The Broomrapes (*Orobanche* spp.) are complete parasites and some of them are highly specific. We may suppose that *Comandra umbellata* needs little from its host, but that the highly specific species of *Orobanche* require many substances that they are unable to make for themselves.

We may suppose, too, that in the case of the most specialized parasitism hosts and parasites have evolved together, and this makes possible some very interesting speculation. Can we deduce the relationships within groups of parasites by noting the plants upon which they grow? Or/and can we, by noting their parasites, get clues to the relationships of the host plants?

Savile (1962) studied the rusts of *Allium* and other plants and concluded:

It appears from this evidence that *Allium* is related to, but more primitive than *Scilla* and related genera. If the inflorescence characters emphasized by Hutchinson are a reliable indication of relationship to the amaryllids, the most satisfactory disposition of Allieae seems to lie in restoring the group to family rank. Alliaceae may then be regarded as close to the immediate common ancestor of Liliaceae and Amaryllidaceae. Hutchinson's arrangement [of 1934], with Amaryllidaceae derived from Liliaceae and containing Allieae, is unrealistic, both because it denies the proximity of *Allium* to Liliaceae, and because it suggests that Allieae are more modern than Liliaceae whereas the rust relationships indicate the reverse.

In 1968 Savile considered *Filipendula* from a similar approach. It is a rosaceous genus of about 10 species which, it has been suggested, should be in the *Spiraeoideae* rather than in the *Rosoideae* (where it is usually placed). Savile noted that it is attacked by rusts of the genus *Triphragmium*. Rusts of related genera all attack members of the *Rosoideae*, and therefore: 'It appears, by inference, that *Filipendula* also belongs to this subfamily.'

Turning to predators, we find Kontuniemi (1955) arguing that a sawfly can distinguish between *Lysimachia* and *Naumburgia*, which botanists combine.

Fryxell and Lukefahr (1967) have used the presence of the boll-weevil in *Hampea* as an argument for placing the genus in a tribe *Gossypieae* of the *Malvaceae*, rather than in the *Bombacaceae*, where it is usually placed. Fryxell would include in *Gossypieae*:

Hampea Schlechtd.: the primary host of the weevil?

Gossypium L.: now the usual host.
Thespesia Corr.: some species of which are fed upon by the weevil.
Cienfuegosia Cav.: the weevil feeds on *C. affinis*.

8. Palaeontology

In attempting to assemble the phylogeny of a group for which ample fossils are available one turns to them for a trustworthy record of the history of the group. 'Primitive' characters are those appearing early: 'advanced' ones those appearing late. One can see positive evidence of parallel and convergent evolution, and so on. For some groups of organisms, plant and animal, the story is as easy as this: for the flowering plants with which we are concerned it is very different.

Darwin realized this. In a letter to Hooker, written in 1879, he wrote: 'The rapid development as far as we can judge of all the higher plants within recent geological times is an abominable mystery.'

Today, almost a century later, we may say the same. We do not know for certain from what group of plants the flowering plants arose. We cannot say with certainty that monocotyledons arose from dicotyledons: that woody plants are more 'primitive' than herbaceous ones.

If the angiosperms came from gymnosperms, then we may well conclude that some, at least, of the characters that appeared early in the gymnosperms and are to be found today in the angiosperms are indeed 'primitive', *but only if they did not arise independently in the two groups*. There are so many 'ifs' in dealing with angiosperm phylogeny that we are continually guessing. And there are still some botanists who believe the dicotyledons to be polyphyletic, while others argue for a single origin!

Because of the many uncertainties there is a grave danger that we may argue in circles. That because we believe the *Magnoliaceae*, for example, to be primitive, then any character detected in that family is necessarily a primitive one.

Only a few fossils of flowering plants are known from the Jurassic. From the Cretaceous we have many, but they include the remains of plants which represent both 'primitive' and 'advanced' families—*Magnoliaceae, Lauraceae, Nymphaeaceae, Salicaceae, Juglandaceae, Betulaceae, Fagaceae, Araliaceae, Cornaceae*, etc.

This does not mean that taxonomy gets *no* help from palaeontology. It gets relatively little.

9. Comparative chemistry

'The application of comparative plant chemistry to the solution of problems in the taxonomy of flowering plants' was a 'sort of' omnibus title for this book! We deal elsewhere (p. 9) with the history of our subject, and we deal over and over again in the following pages with problems which may well be solved by comparative plant chemistry. But we must be modest in our claims for chemotaxonomy. In its present state of development it perhaps poses more problems than it solves. One is still faced with matters of judgment, as in traditional taxonomy. How important is the presence or absence of an unusual substance or group of substances? This will vary from case to case.

The presence of *caffeine* might be relatively unimportant of itself, since it seems to occur more or less sporadically in flowering plants. But given a genus of caffeine-producers in a family not otherwise noted for the substance, the presence or absence of it in a species which might or might not be included in that genus would then loom large.

If *Picrodendron* is close to *Juglans*, as some have said, then the presence of *juglone* in it would be of great significance (I did *not* find it; but have not had sufficient material of the genus as yet).

We have several bits of chemical evidence supporting a relationship between the *Pittosporaceae* and the *Araliaceae*. Any additional evidence would be really significant. But how much chemical evidence do we need to warrant shifting the *Pittosporaceae* to an order including the *Araliaceae*?

How much more evidence do we need before we are happy in separating the *Papaveraceae* from the *Capparidaceae*, *Cruciferae*, *Resedaceae*, etc.?

The reader will find these problems, and more, in the following pages.

One more point may be discussed here. A quite eminent plant chemist has said that negative evidence—records of *absence* of substances—is unimportant. I disagree. It seems to me almost as vital to establish the complete absence of a particular substance from a group, as to establish its constant presence in another group. Let us remember our dichotomous keys, which are based very largely on presence or absence of characters. The *Theaceae* include in some interpretations plants devoid of *raphides*, in others three raphide-containing genera—*Tetramerista*, *Pelliceria* and *Trematanthera*—are included. But are *all* the rest of the family really devoid of raphides? I would be willing to bet that many members have never been examined for this character, and until all have been studied we cannot with certainty define a family *Theaceae* as raphideless. The *Chrysobalanaceae* are said to be *non*-cyanogenic: but on what evidence? I can find very little.

10. Numerical taxonomy

This would better be defined as an approach to taxonomy, for it makes use of criteria of all types—morphological, anatomical, biochemical and so on. It sometimes tries to avoid judgments by treating all characters as of equal weight, but judgments creep in. If we use 'large-leaved' as against 'small-leaved' or 'broad-leaved' as against 'narrow-leaved' (which may be good taxonomic characters) we have to judge small as against large, and broad as opposed to narrow. And we use judgment in deciding what characters we are to feed into the computer.

I am not arguing against numerical taxonomy here, but against the view that it can eliminate subjective judgments. Perhaps I am in agreement with a review by George Gaylord Simpson (1964) of a book *Principles of numerical taxonomy* by Sokal and Sneath (1963). Simpson wrote: 'The present ferment in taxonomy is a healthy sign. Eventually taxonomy will surely profit by the incorporation of a "numerical taxonomy", less rigid and less fanatical. This book by Sokal and Sneath will be a milestone in that desired development, but in the meantime I fear that its biased attitude has done not only some good but also some harm to taxonomy and, indeed, to its own basic thesis.'

Kalkman (1966) has an amusing article, resulting from a paper by Sokal and Sneath (1966) and called *Keeping up with the Joneses* in which he pokes fun at the numerical taxonomists. Much of what he says will be applauded by 'traditional' taxonomists. One important point that I have not seen made is suggested to me by the title of Kalkman's paper. Computers are expensive to buy and to operate, and botanists in the under-privileged centres must continue to do taxonomy without their help.

We may conclude this little section with a couple of examples, taken more or less at random.

Taylor has monographed the genus *Lithophragma* (*Saxifragaceae*), using traditional taxonomic methods and has also made a 'taximetric' study (1966) of it. We quote from his abstract:

> A taximetric analysis of *Lithophragma*...reveals a close similarity to the taxonomy proposed by the author...using the traditional intuitive approach. The taximetric method is based on a neo-Adansonian approach utilizing the same characters used in the intuitive study, but arbitrarily giving equal weight to all unit-characters... The conclusion is reached that taximetrics may help place plant taxonomy on an objective basis...Its application, however, must await extensive documentation of plant taxa on a broad basis.

Watson, Williams and Lance (1966) used 20 characters for 24 genera of the *Epacridaceae* and analysed these with a program of 'similarity' type. They came up with a classification which: 'seems, judged by external criteria, to represent an improvement on that of Bentham, whose scheme appears in turn to be superior to that of Drude.'

CHAOS IN TAXONOMY

I have on many occasions lectured my students on 'Chaos in taxonomy', trying to impress on them the many uncertainties which exist and the defeats taxonomists have suffered in their efforts to establish a stable system. Melchior (1959) points out that: 'Seit 1940 sind nicht weniger als 16 naturliche Systeme der Dikotyledonen und Monokotyledonen publiziert worden, von denen keines dem anderen gleicht.'

It is good for us to be reminded that our judgments are faulty, that groups that we have thought to be natural ones are often shown to be quite unnatural, that we often accept judgments by others that are based on inadequate information. Again and again in this book I point out how little we know about many of the taxonomically most interesting taxa. Here I select a very few of the problems that are as yet unsolved.

(a) Cornaceae

In *EP*1 (1897) Harms recognized a family *Cornaceae* with 15 genera. It is true that he had no less than 7 sub-families, indicating that he considered it to be a rather heterogeneous assemblage. In the notes that follow I have put together some of the views that have been expressed about the genera included by Harms.

Garrya (15–18) is usually made a family—*Garryaceae*—of its own. Some have made an order **Garryales** for it.

Nyssa (8–10) has been put in the *Santalaceae*. It is more often made the type genus of a family *Nyssaceae*, with *Camptotheca* (1) and sometimes *Davidia* (1). The family has been included in the **Myrtales**. *Davidia* has also been made a family of its own—*Davidiaceae*.

The next genus in Harms' arrangement is *Alangium* (17–18) which is often made a family *Alangiaceae*, and this has been placed in **Myrtales** and in **Santalales**. Airy Shaw (in *W*. 1966) adds a genus *Metteniusa* (3) to the *Alangiaceae*.

Mastixia (25) is yet another genus which has had a family—*Mastixiaceae*—of its own.

Curtisia (1) has also been made a family, *Curtisiaceae*. It has been placed, too, in the *Aquifoliaceae*, and has been included in the **Sapindales** and **Celastrales**.

We come now to the 8 genera which Harms considered to be sufficiently similar to form a single sub-family, *Cornoideae*. One might expect a measure of agreement here, but one is disappointed.

Helwingia (3–5) is placed by Hutchinson (1959) in the *Araliaceae*. Others have a family *Helwingiaceae* for it. This was put by Lindley

(1853) in his **Garryales** and, if Lindley was correct, *Helwingia* 'should' have *aucubin*. Does it?

Corokia (3–6) is of very doubtful position. It has been put in *Saxifragaceae* and in *Escalloniaceae*, and thus in the **Rosales** (see also below). Chemical evidence may favour its retention in the *Cornaceae*.

We come now to *Cornus* (4–45) itself. Even this genus has been placed elsewhere—in the *Hederaceae*! And what do we mean by *Cornus*? Melchior has 45 species; Airy Shaw (in *W*. 1966) has 4! Hutchinson (1959) has *Cornus*, *Afrocrania*, *Chamaepericlymenum*, *Cynoxylon*, *Dendrobenthamia* and *Thelycrania* to embrace what some call *Cornus* (s.l.). Who is right?

Torricellia (3)—which should be *Toricellia*?—has been made a family of its own, *Torricelliaceae* or *Toricelliaceae*.

Melanophylla (3) and *Kaliphora* (1) have not, I think, been pushed around.

Aucuba (3–4) has been made the type of a family, *Aucubaceae*. It has also been placed in *Loranthaceae* (and *Caprifoliaceae*?). It has been cross-grafted with *Garrya*—and both have *aucubin*!

Griselinia (6) may be related to *Melanophylla*. Philipson (1967) has suggested that it might be removed from the *Cornaceae*—but where should it go?

What a lot of problems this small group of plants proposes! We shall see that what we know of the comparative chemistry of the 'Cornaceae' by no means solves these problems.

(b) Saxifragaceae

We shall deal further with this family when we meet it in our list of familie sand again when considering the **Rosales** as an order (pp. 1645 and table 70). Here we point out only that what Schulze-Menz (in *Syll*. XII, 1964) treats as a single family of about 80/1200 has been split into at least 25 families and distributed among several orders! And the family itself has been variously placed.

(c) Musaceae

Here, to illustrate diversity of opinion, I list only a small selection of those who have recognized this family.

Pulle (1952): 6/150. Presumably *Musa*, *Strelitzia*, *Heliconia*, *Ravenala*, *Phenakospermum* and *Orchidantha* (*Lowia*).

Potztal (in *Syll*. XII, 1964): 6/220. *Musa* (60), *Ensete* (10), *Strelitzia* (4), *Heliconia* (ca. 150), *Ravenala* (1) and *Phenakospermum*. *Orchidantha* is placed in *Lowiaceae*.

Winkler (in *EP*1, 1930): 5 genera. *Musa* (incl. *Ensete*), *Strelitzia, Heliconia, Ravenala* (incl. *Phenakospermum*) and *Orchidantha* (*Lowia*).

Benson (1957): 5 genera, only 3 named.

Dumortier (1829): 4 genera. *Musa, Strelitzia, Heliconia* and *Ravenala*.

A. L. de Jussieu (1789), whose name is conserved: 3 genera. *Musa, Heliconia, Ravenala*.

Airy Shaw (in *W*. 1966): 2/42. *Musa* (35), *Ensete* (7). He has *Strelitziaceae* with *Strelitzia, Ravenala* and *Phenakospermum*; *Heliconiaceae* with *Heliconia*; and *Lowiaceae* with *Orchidantha*.

Good (1956): 1 genus. *Musa* (*ca*. 80).

Hutchinson (1959): 1 genus. *Musa* (incl. *Ensete, ca*. 45). He has *Strelitziaceae* with *Strelitzia, Ravenala, Phenakospermum* and *Heliconia*; and *Lowiaceae* with *Orchidantha*.

We find that although there are such differing opinions as to the *Musaceae* all agree that the genera mentioned are related—segregate families being retained within the same order (**Zingiberales**). It should be noted also that most modern authors—Good, Hutchinson, Airy Shaw—and some not mentioned above such as Thorne, Cronquist and Takhtajan, have a greatly restricted *Musaceae*.

At the order level we shall consider but two examples: the **Rosales** and the **Tubiflorae**.

(*a*) Rosales

Here I shall compare and contrast the systems of Rendle (1938), Hutchinson (1959) and Bessey (1915).

Rendle, who omits many small families, names 12, and describes the order as 'A very natural group, the families in which are connected by transitional forms.'

Hutchinson puts some of Rendle's families on his 'herbaceous' side: the others in his 'woody' series; with the following results. On the 'herbaceous' side:

Crassulaceae (1), *Cephalotaceae* (2) and *Saxifragaceae* (3, in part) are in his **Saxifragales** (derived from **Ranales**).

Podostemaceae (6) and *Hydrostachyaceae* (7) form his **Podostemales** (derived from **Saxifragales**).

On the 'woody' side:

Connaraceae (11) is in **Dilleniales** (derived from **Magnoliales**).

Pittosporaceae (5) is in **Pittosporales** (from **Dilleniales** through **Bixales**).

Rosaceae (10) is the *only* family of Rendle's order to appear in H.'s **Rosales** (which he derives from **Dilleniales**)! But H. adds *Dichapetal-*

aceae and *Calycanthaceae*; the former not mentioned by R., the latter in his **Ranales**.

Leguminosae (12) becomes **Leguminales** (derived from **Rosales** and consisting of *Caesalpiniaceae, Mimosaceae* and *Papilionaceae*).

Saxifragaceae (3, part) and *Cunoniaceae* (4) are in **Cunoniales** (derived from **Rosales**) as *Grossulariaceae, Philadelphaceae, Escalloniaceae, Pterostemonaceae, Baueraceae* and *Cunoniaceae!*

Hamamelidaceae (8) and *Platanaceae* (9) are in **Hamamelidales** (also from **Rosales**).

We see that Rendle's 'very natural group' is distributed over 8 orders!

Bessey was sometimes a splitter as to families but a lumper at the order level. His **Rosales** included *Crassulaceae, Cephalotaceae, Saxifragaceae* (with *Hydrangeaceae* and *Grossulariaceae* as segregates), *Cunoniaceae, Pittosporaceae, Hamamelidaceae, Platanaceae, Rosaceae* (with *Malaceae* and *Prunaceae* as segregates), *Connaraceae* and *Leguminosae* (but as *Mimosaceae, Cassiaceae* and *Fabaceae*). This is close to Rendle's order so far but B. includes five families not mentioned by R.— *Brunelliaceae, Bruniaceae, Myrothamnaceae, Crossosomataceae* and *Eucommiaceae*—as well as *Casuarinaceae* (R.'s **Casuarinales**), and *Droseraceae* (in R.'s **Sarraceniales**).

These 'extra' families are placed by Hutchinson in **Dilleniales** (*Brunelliaceae* and *Crossosomataceae*), **Hamamelidales** (*Bruniaceae* and *Myrothamnaceae*), **Casuarinales** (*Casuarinaceae*), **Urticales** (*Eucommiaceae*), and **Sarraceniales** (*Droseraceae*).

(b) Tubiflorae

I have already written to some extent upon this subject (Gibbs, 1962), but in that paper I considered only the systems of Engler and Diels (in *Syll.* XII, 1936) and Hutchinson (1959), concluding that the chemical evidence available favoured the former rather than the latter.

Let us first of all look at the later versions of these schemes—Melchior (in *Syll.*XII, 1964) and Hutchinson (1969). They are not greatly altered.

Melchior divides his order into 6 sub-orders and 26 families (add *-aceae*). Here is his system with Hutchinson's placings.

Convolvulineae

1. *Polemoni.* (*Polemoni.* in **Polemoni.**; *Cobae.* segregated and widely separated).

2. *Fouquieri.* (in **Tamaric.**)

3. *Convolvul.* (split. *Cuscut.* in **Polemoni.**; *Convolvul.* in **Solan.**)

Boraginineae

    4. *Hydrophyll.* (in **Polemoni.**)
    5. *Boragin.* (split: *Boragin.* in **Boragin.**; *Ehreti.* in **Verben.**)
    6. Lenno. (in **Eric.**)

Verbenineae

    7. *Verben.* (split: *Verben.*, *Stilb.*, and *Chloanth.* in **Verben.**)
    8. *Callitrich.* (in **Onagr.**)
    9. *Labiatae* (as *Lami.* in **Lami.**)

Solanineae

    10. *Nolan.* (in **Solan.**)
    11. *Solan.* (split: *Solan.* in **Solan.**; *Salpiglossid.* in **Person.**)
    12. *Duckeodendr.* (incl. in *Ehreti.*)
    13. *Buddlej.* (as *Buddlei.* in **Logani.**)
    14. *Scrophulari.* (split: *Scrophulari.* in **Person.**; *Selagin.* in **Lami.**)
    15. *Globulari.* (in **Lami.**)
    16. *Bignoni.* (in **Bignoni.**)
    17. *Pedali.* (in **Bignoni.**)
    18. *Martyni.* (in **Bignoni.**)
    19. *Henriquezi.* (incl. in *Rubi.* in **Rubi.**)
    20. *Acanth.* (in **Person.**)
    21. *Gesneri.* (in **Person.**)
    22. *Columelli.* (in **Person.**)
    23. *Orobanch.* (in **Person.**)
    24. *Lentibulari.* (in **Person.**)

Myoporineae

    25. *Myopor.* (in **Lami.**)

Phrymineae

    26. *Phrym.* (as *Phrymat.* in **Verben.**)

We see that families thought by Melchior to be sufficiently near each other to be placed in a single order are distributed by Hutchinson over 12 widely spread orders! We summarize:

Lignosae
  Magnoli. → **Dilleni.** → **Bix.** → **Pittospor.** → **Capparid.** →
Tamaric. (2. *Fouquieri.*)
  Magnoli. → **The.** → **Eric.** (6. *Lenno.*)
  Magnoli. → **Logani.** (13. *Buddlei.*) → **Rubi.** (17. *Henriquezi.* in *Rubi.*)

Magnoli. → **Logani.** → **Verben.** (7. *Verben.* as *V., Stilb.,* and *Chloanth.*; 5. *Boragin.* in pt and 12. *Duckeodendr.* as *Ehreti.*; 26. *Phrymat.*)

Magnoli. → **Logani.** → **Bignoni.** (1. *Polemoni.* in pt as *Cobae.*; 16. *Bignoni.*; 19. *Pedali.*; and 20. *Martyni.*)

Herbaceae

Ran. → **Caryophyll.** → **Onagr.** (8. *Callitrich.*)

Ran. → **Caryophyll.** → **Saxifrag.** → **Gerani.** → **Polemoni.** (1. *Polemoni.* in pt; 3. *Convolvul.* in pt as *Cuscut.*; and 4. *Hydrophyll.*) → **Boragin.** (5. *Boragin.* in pt) → **Lami.** (9. *Labiatae* as *Lami.*; 15. *Globulari.*; 25. *Myopor.*; 14. *Scrophulari.* in pt. as *Selagin.*)

Ran. → **Caryophyll.** → **Saxifrag.** → **Solan.** (10. *Nolan.*; 11. *Solan.* in pt; 3. *Convolvul.* in pt) → **Person.** (14. *Scrophulari.* in pt; 11. *Solan.* in pt as *Salpiglossid.*; 18. *Acanth.*; 21. *Gesneri.*; 22. *Columelli.*; 23. *Orobanch.*; and 24. *Lentibulari.*).

It is true that Hutchinson's system is an extreme one. What do 3 modern authors—Thorne (1968), Cronquist (1968) and Takhtajan (1969)—make of the families of Melchior's **Tubiflorae**? (I shall use the numbers I have assigned to M.'s families.)

Thorne has:
Superorder Malviiflorae
Solan. 11 (including 10 and 12); 1; 2; and 3.
Superorder Rosiflorae
Ros. 22 (in *Saxifrag.*)
Superorder Gentianiflorae
Gentian. 13 (in *Logani.*); 17 (in *Rubi.*)
Bignoni. 14 (including 15); 16; 18; 19; 20; 21; 23; 24; and 25
Superorder Lamiiflorae
Lami. 4; 5; 6; 7 including 26; 8; 9 as *Lami.*
He spreads M.'s families over 5 orders in 4 superorders. Three of his orders have sizeable chunks of M.'s **Tubiflorae**.

Cronquist has:
Subclass IV. Dilleniidae
Viol. 2
Subclass V. Rosidae
Ros. 22
Subclass VI. Asteridae
Polemoni. 1; 3; 4; 6; 10; 11
Lami. 5; 7; 8; 9; 26
Scrophulari. (Person.) 13; 14; 15; 16; 18; 19 (incl. 20); 21; 23; 24; 25

Rubi. 17 (in *Rubi.*)

The little family *Duckeodendraceae* (12) is not mentioned.

Again M.'s families are spread over several superorders (or sub-classes) and orders. One order—**Scrophulariales (Personales)**—is almost exactly Thorne's **Bignoniales**, and accounts for nearly half of M.'s families. All but 2 of M.'s families are in the superorder (subclass) Asteridae, but this is not matched in Thorne's system.

Takhtajan has:

Superorder V. Dillenianae

Tamaric. 2

Superorder XIV. Lamianae

Gentian. 17 (in *Rubi.*?)

Polemoni. 1; 3; 4; 5; 6

Scrophulari. 10; 11; 13; 14; 15; 16; 18; 19; 20; 21; 22; 23; 24; 25

Lami. 7; 8; 9 (as *Lami.*); 26

Duckeodendron (12 in M.) is mentioned but not placed.

Here we have almost all of M.'s families in one superorder, and 14 of them in the **Scrophulariales**—almost identical with Cronquist's order of that name, and with Thorne's **Bignoniales**—a real measure of agreement!

We could extend this discussion almost indefinitely, but enough has been said to show how confused the situation is.

Let me recall in closing this section that I once started, on a page measuring about 8 in. × 10½ in., to make a chart of the taxonomy of the **Sapindales**. Before long I stuck on a second sheet, then a third, fourth, and so on. When I had several square feet of chart I gave up!

RESTRICTION OF DISTRIBUTION OF CONSTITUENTS TO VARIOUS CATEGORIES OF PLANTS

INTRODUCTION

If one is to use comparative chemistry to distinguish between various categories of organisms one must establish facts of restriction—and this is by no means easy. A vast amount of tedious spadework must be done before one can say with any degree of confidence that a substance occurs *only* in such and such a group. Let us show how dangerous it is to jump to conclusions.

As long ago as 1954 Peters and his co-workers reported on the occurrence of *monofluoro-acetic acid* and a *fluoro-fatty-acid* in the seeds of *Dichapetalum toxicarium*. Leaves of *D. cymosum* also have the former. We might well have supposed that these remarkable fluoro-acids were peculiar to the *Dichapetalaceae* (4–5/200–250), or to *Dichapetalum* (150–225), or even to a few species of *Dichapetalum*; and it is odd that no one, I think, has examined other members of the family. More recently it has been shown that *monofluoro-acetic acid* occurs also in the poisonous Gidgie (*Acacia georginae*), in a second legume (*Gastrolobium grandiflorum*), and in *Palicourea marcgravii* (*Rubiaceae*)!

At one time *biflavonyls* were thought to be restricted to the gymnosperms. Then one of them was found in *Casuarina*, and this was hailed by some as 'proof' that *Casuarina* is near to the gymnosperms, as has been suggested. Today we know that biflavonyls occur in *Viburnum* (*Caprifoliaceae*), *Garcinia* (*Guttiferae*), *Xanthorrhoea* (a monocot.!), and other flowering plants.

Some 'vital' substances probably occur in all living organisms—the *protein amino-acids* and some *fatty-acids*, for example. Others such as the *photosynthetic pigments* may be in most plants. Let us deal with a few examples of restricted distribution, remembering the cautionary-tale examples above.

1. Plants, but not animals

The photosynthetic pigments—*chlorophylls* and *carotenoids*—occur in all (?) true plants, except where lost secondarily, as in some saprophytic and parasitic flowering plants. They are normally absent from the fungi, and from animals.

There are some substances, probably, that are normal to animals, but not to plants, but I have no knowledge of them.

2. Higher plants, but not lower ones

Pectins are very common, possibly universal in the higher plants. I believe they are absent from seaweeds, being replaced there by *alginic acid*. I don't have chapter and verse for this statement, however.

Phenol glucosylation has been studied by a number of workers including Pridham (1964), who points out: 'It would appear from the results in Table 1 [listing 23 angiosperms, 5 gymnosperms, 3 ferns, 11 mosses, 1 liverwort, 10 algae, and 2 fungi] that a marked ability to glucosylate phenols is characteristic of the majority of higher plants, but that this reaction is absent or occurs at a very slow rate in Bryophytes and Thallophytes.'

Lignins may be restricted to vascular plants, though substances resembling *lignins* occur in mosses.

3. Angiosperms, but not gymnosperms, and vice versa

Raphides, while not universal in the angiosperms, are widely spread in the group, being present in many monocotyledons and in several families of dicotyledons. I believe them to be completely absent from gymnosperms.

The cyclitol *sequoitol* (*sequoyitol*) was said by Plouvier (1960) to be confined to the gymnosperms; to be very widely spread in that group; and to prove them to be monophyletic. It has been reported (1963), however, to be formed from *meso-inositol* in leaves of *Trifolium incarnatum*. But does it occur *normally* in any angiosperm?

Rubber is virtually restricted to the angiosperms (and in those very nearly to the dicotyledons), but it has been reported from a few gymnosperms.

The chemistries of angiosperms and gymnosperms are so similar that one is convinced of a relationship, but the nature of this relationship is not clear.

4. Dicotyledons, but not monocotyledons, and vice versa

I used to think that *rubber* in the angiosperms was confined to the dicotyledons, where it is certainly widely spread. Lindley, as long ago as 1830, said that '*Limnocharis* yields milk in abundance'—but does that contain rubber? More recently rubber has been obtained, I think, from the banana.

Are *lignans* absent from monocotyledons? I have records of them from at least 26 families of dicotyledons, from *Magnoliaceae* to *Umbelliferae* and *Compositae*, but not a single record from a monocotyledon.

Plouvier and Favre-Bonvin (1971) say that *iridoids* and *seco-iridoids* are restricted to the dicotyledons. I have no record of them from the monocotyledons, but I have obtained positive reactions using the *Ehrlich Test* for *aucubin-type glycosides*, with 4 species of *Aponogeton*. Does this genus, to confound Plouvier and Favre-Bonvin, have iridoids?

Some groups of alkaloids have never been found in monocotyledons, but these are of very restricted distribution in the dicotyledons. We are looking for substances *characteristic* of one group but not the other, and they are hard to find.

5. Restriction to orders

It is hard to think of examples for this section. *Macrozamin* may be restricted to the **Cycadales** (gymnosperms).

Betalains occur only (?) in the **Centrospermae** and in *Cactaceae* and *Didiereaceae* (which some would include in the **Centrospermae**).

Some *sesquiterpenes* are confined to the *Compositae*, which some would consider to constitute an order with one family. But these substances are restricted in their distribution within the *Compositae*, they are not characteristic of the family (order) as a whole.

Derivatives of *ellagic acid* are widely spread in the **Myrtales** (table 49) and some of them are known only from families belonging to that order. Our knowledge of their distribution is still so sketchy, however, that while we can say that the order is noteworthy for the occurrence of these compounds, we cannot say that any one of them is restricted to it.

Are we on safer grounds with the **Malvales**? In this order *cyclopropenyl fatty-acids* are known to occur in *Tiliaceae*, *Malvaceae*, *Bombacaceae* and *Sterculiaceae*, at least. I have no record of them from outside the order.

6. Restriction to families

It should be increasingly easy, one would think, to find examples of restricted distribution as one considers progressively smaller groups, but we have very few cases of substances that are certainly, or even probably, restricted to individual families.

The *alkaloid protopine* comes near to this. I believe it has been found in every member of the *Papaveraceae* that has been examined for it. It has been reported, however, to occur elsewhere, and one report, at least—occurrence in *Nandina* (*Berberidaceae*)—seems to be accepted.

Several *alkaloids* occur in *Stemona* and have not been found elsewhere, but have they been looked for in the other genera—*Croomia* and *Stichoneuron*—which some, at least, would include in the *Stemonaceae*?

The *Flacourtiaceae* is noteworthy for the presence in the seed-fats of many of its members of fatty-acids of the *chaulmoogric* series. These are not known from any other source. But some members (tribes ?) of the family may not have them—so we may be dealing here with restriction to parts of a family.

7. Restriction to sub-families

We may introduce a new type of restriction here: restriction within a given family of a substance which does, however, occur also elsewhere. Is the occurrence in the *Rosaceae* of *ellagic acid* an example of this ? It is reported from the *Rosoideae*, but not from the other sub-families of that family, I believe. It does, of course, occur widely in the flowering plants.

Plumbagin is reported to occur in *Droseraceae, Ebenaceae, Apocynaceae* and perhaps *Rubiaceae*, as well as in the *Plumbaginaceae*. In the last it seems to be confined to one of the two sub-families (p. 1545).

The amino-acid *canavanine* is restricted, so far as I know, to the *Leguminosae*, and in that family to the *Faboideae*. It is not universal in that sub-family, as the following figures, now probably out of date, indicate (bracketed figures show numbers of genera in the tribes; fractions show genera/species tested).

I. *Mimosoideae. Ingeae* (10): absent from 2/2; *Acacieae* (1): absent from 1/2; *Eumimoseae* (4); absent from 2/2; *Adenanthereae* (10): absent from 2/4; *Piptadenieae* (6): absent from 1/1; *Parkieae* (2): absent from 1/2.

II. *Caesalpinioideae. Dimorphandreae* (4): absent from 1/1; *Cynometreae* (11): absent from 1/1; *Amherstieae* (25): absent from 6/6; *Bauhinieae* (3): absent from 2/5; *Cassieae* (13): absent from 2/5; *Kramerieae* (1): no record; *Eucaesalpinieae* (17): absent from 4/4; *Sclerobieae*: no record; *Tounateae* (*Swartzieae*) (7): absent from 1/1.

III. *Faboideae. Sophoreae* (33): absent from 5/7, no record of presence; *Podalyrieae* (27): absent from 5/5; no record of presence; *Genisteae* (43): absent from 10/25, *present* in 1/1; *Trifolieae* (6): *present* in 5/20; *Loteae* (8): *present* in 5/12; *Galegeae* (65): absent from 10/23, *present* in 19/41; *Hedysareae* (48): absent from 13/26, *present* in 9/20; *Dalbergieae* (27): absent from 2/3, *present* in 1/1; *Vicieae* (6): absent from 5–6/8–16, *present* in 1/5; *Phaseoleae* (47): absent from 14/38, *present* in 5/11.

8. Restriction to tribes

An examination of the figures for distribution of *canavanine* given above will reveal that it has not been found in the tribes *Sophoreae* and *Podalyrieae* of the sub-family *Faboideae*. In the *Genisteae* only one member (*Bossiaea foliosa*) of more than two dozen examined is reported to have *canavanine*. One wonders if this is correct. One might wonder, assuming it to be correct, if *Bossiaea* is properly placed. I have not tried to check opinion on these points.

There are, I am sure, some good examples of restriction of substances to tribes, but I have not noted them for this section.

9. Restriction at the genus level

I pointed out in a previous paper (1945, p. 79) that the family *Flacourtiaceae* provides an interesting example of this. In the tribe *Oncobeae* the genera *Caloncoba*, *Lindackeria*, *Mayna* and *Carpotroche* have optically active fatty-acids of the *chaulmoogric series*. The genus *Oncoba*, until split by Gilg, included *Caloncoba*. Now *Oncoba spinosa*, at least, lacks these optically active fatty-acids, differing clearly in this respect from *Caloncoba echinata*, *glauca* and *welwitschii*, all of which have been shown to have them. Gilg did not know of this chemical difference when he split *Oncoba*.

Aristolochia (350–500) of the family *Aristolochiaceae*, has several substances—*aristidinic acid* (in 1 sp.); *aristinic acid* (1); *aristolic acid* (1); *aristolochic acids I* (13), *II* (1), *III* (1), *IIIa* (1), *IV* (1), and *IVa* (1); *aristolochine* (8); and *aristolone* (1)—all but one of which have not been reported, I think, from other members of the family. *Bragantia wallichii* is said to have *aristolochic acid I*. But our sampling of the family is woefully small.

An amino-acid, *γ-hydroxy-arginine*, which had previously been found in sea animals was detected by Bell and Tirimanna (1963) in all of the 17 species of *Vicia* which they examined. Does this differentiate *Vicia* from *Lathyrus*?

If *Itea* (15–20) be included in the *Saxifragaceae* then the occurrence in at least 3 of its species of *allitol* may be a generic character. It is said to be *absent* from *Escallonia* and *Brexia*, at least; and I have no records of it from elsewhere in the family.

10. Restriction at the species level

Examples here would seem to be legion, but in the great majority of cases they are probably due to our ignorance, the substances in question occurring in other species of the genera concerned. Some of the more interesting alkaloid-yielding genera seem to have different alkaloids in each species, but closer examination often shows this to be misleading.

An interesting cautionary example is the distribution of the naphthaquinone *lomatiol* in the genus *Lomatia* (10) of the *Proteaceae*. According to Thomson (1957) *lomatiol* was known from around the *seeds* of Australian species, but not from around those of S. American species. My own tests, however, strongly suggest that it may occur in *leaves* and *bark* of both Australian and S. American species (p. 1569 and table 58). It then becomes a generic character.

11. Restriction at the infra-specific level

Detailed investigations have sometimes revealed chemical differences between plants that are considered to be members of the same species. It has been suggested that when there are no obvious morphological differences to distinguish these plants as subspecies, varieties, or forms, that they be called 'chemovars'. We shall discuss a single case.

In 1922 Penfold found the essential oil from the leaves of *Backhousia myrtifolia* growing in New South Wales to have 75–80% *elemicin*. In 1953 Penfold, McKern and Spies analysed oils from four individuals from Fraser Island, Queensland. One had about 72% *elemicin*, two had 77–78% *isoelemicin*, and the fourth had about 81% *isoeugenol methyl ether*! A third paper, by Hellyer, McKern and Willis, appeared in 1955. The authors had analysed oils from 18 individuals from S.E. Queensland. Six proved to be of the *elemicin* ('type') form and had little or no *isoelemicin*; four had *isoelemicin* as the chief constituent; one had *methyl eugenol* in preponderance; and the remaining seven had much *isoeugenol methyl ether*, with small amounts of *isoelemicin*.

RESTRICTION OF DISTRIBUTION OF CONSTITUENTS WITHIN THE INDIVIDUAL PLANT

We have considered above the restriction of distribution of substances in different taxonomic categories. Here we shall deal briefly with *restriction within the individual plant*. When studying small organisms it is possible to grind, chop, mince or pound one or more of them and to deal with the resultant material as a whole. This is, of course, the simplest possibility, though it may result in a great dilution of a substance which occurs only in a small part of each organism. When dealing with the higher plants one is obliged at times to use only a leaf (or even a part of a leaf), or a shoot, or an inflorescence, or fruit, or seed. If the choice is one's own one uses the portion most likely to have the substance one is looking for. Young shoots, for example, more often yield HCN than do older parts of the plant. We shall discuss briefly a few examples of restricted distribution.

We have referred above to *lomatiol* which occurs around the seeds of some species of *Lomatia*. Knowing this one might look for it around the seeds of other species of the genus and of other genera of the *Proteaceae*. It seems likely, however, that *lomatiol* or a nearly related naphthaquinone occurs also in the leaves and bark of *Lomatia*: it may not be as restricted as we had supposed.

Some *acetylenic compounds* are restricted to certain organs. *Pittosporum buchanani*, according to Bohlmann *et al.* (*Polyacetylenv.* 150, 1968), has at least 4 acetylene compounds in its roots, but none in its above-ground parts.

Latex provides us with some good examples. Latex ducts may occur only in certain organs, and the latex contains substances not found elsewhere in the plant. The *rubber* of *Hevea* is an example. In guayule (*Parthenium argentatum*), however, rubber occurs in cells in virtually all parts of the plant. Extraction methods on a commercial scale are necessarily quite different for the two plants. Metcalfe says that in *Decaisnea fargesii* laticifers occur only in the fruits! In *Papaver somniferum* latex tubes with *alkaloids* occur in all parts of the plant except the seeds, and these alone are free of alkaloids. *Plagiopteron*, says Metcalfe, is the only genus of the *Flacourtiaceae* with laticifers, and these contain a rubber-like substance. Airy Shaw (in *W.* 1966) has a separate family—*Plagiopteraceae*—for it. It has been placed by others in *Olacaceae*, and in *Tiliaceae*. Obviously it would repay detailed chemical investigation.

Cyanogenic glycosides may be restricted in their distribution. I have already mentioned their occurrence in young shoots. Seedlings of *Borago officinalis* yield HCN: mature plants do not. Guérin found HCN in cotyledons of the seedlings of some legumes, but not in shoots of older plants. I have confirmed some of his findings.

Smith and White obtained HCN from the inflorescence of *Grevillea banksii*, but not from the leafy shoot. With *G. sericea* I got the reverse result; but with *Lomatia tinctoria* I got HCN from the inflorescence, not from the shoot!

There are some obvious possibilities for experimental work here, and some interesting observations are accumulating. One thinks of grafting work on members of the *Solanaceae* to determine the sites of formation of alkaloids. A note by Kaul and Staba (1965) reports the formation of *visnagin* by suspension cultures of *Ammi visnaga*. They say that *digitalis glycosides* have been produced by tissue cultures of *Digitalis*, *nicotine* by *Nicotiana* cultures, *tropane alkaloids* by *Datura*, *reserpine* by *Alstonia constricta*, and *vinca alkaloids* by *Catharanthus roseus*. Suhadolnik (1964 or 1965) grew 'callous tissue' from germinated seeds of *Hippeastrum vittatum*. He did not find *hippeastrine* and *lycorine* in the tissue culture, though they *were* present in the seeds.

Some of the discordant results in the literature may be due to *faulty timing*. We have noted that HCN may in some cases be found in juvenile, but not in mature plants. A very interesting type of timing has been studied in aroids by Smith and Meeuse (1966). They point out that the often unpleasant odour of the spadix may arise rather suddenly and persist for but a few hours. It is known that this coincides with, or follows, a period of great metabolic activity, accompanied by an increase in temperature. Percival (1965) says that within the opening spathe of *Arum maculatum*, for example, there may be an increase in temperature of as much as 13 °C! This rise in temperature may be in part responsible for the volatilization of the odoriferous constituents. In the spadix of *Sauromatum* there was a 20-fold increase in the free *amino-acids* from the day before to the day after anthesis.

It is well known that the *fatty-acids* of the storage fats of mature seeds may be different from those of the unripe seeds. A whole set of highly correlated chemical changes occurs in the ripening of such fruits as bananas. *Free acids* decrease, *esters* are formed, *pectic substances* change, *starch* yields to *sugars*, the *pigments* change, *tannins* disappear or more probably are adsorbed.

Some plants have quite different youth and adult foliage, a phenomenon surprisingly prominent in New Zealand. The eucalypts of Australia provide examples. Hillis (1966) has found significant differences in composition between the youth and adult leaves of *Eucalyptus accedens*, *dives* and *ligustrina*. We have not referred specifically to restriction to individual *cells* of the plant, but this is well known to the anatomist and cytologist. Myrosin-cells, raphide-sacs, 'tanniniferous cells', come to mind; and of course only certain cells are lignified.

EXCRETION BY PLANTS

Plants in general, unlike animals, have no apparent excretory systems. Carus (1872) points out that this was recognized by Aristotle, who thought that ascidians are plant-like because they lack an excretory system: 'Auch die Ascidien, sagt Aristoteles, kann man mit Recht, pflanzlich nennen, da sie, wie die Pflanzen, keine Ausscheidung (Excremente) von sich geben.'

Yet plants, like animals, have metabolic wastes—and these are sometimes of chemotaxonomic interest.

Volatile wastes—carbon dioxide from respiration, oxygen from photosynthesis—escape to the atmosphere, largely through the stomata. Many aromatic plants are continually losing volatile organic substances to the atmosphere, and with modern techniques the mixtures can be analysed. Are these, too, to be classified as 'waste' materials, or do they have their roles in Nature? There is no doubt that strongly aromatic plants are often distasteful to animals, the odoriferous constituents in and/or on the plants discouraging attacks by predators. Escape to the atmosphere might then be considered to be accidental, or unavoidable, but there is some evidence that washing of these aromatics into the soil may be important, too (see below).

The amounts lost to the atmosphere are astonishingly large. One is familiar with the fact that plants may scent the countryside. We mention this and quote from Rasmussen and Went (1964) when discussing the *monoterpenes* (p. 772).

Muller, Muller and Haines (1964) noted apparent inhibition of growth of seedlings by aromatic shrubs in California. This was observed in the field—see the cover of *Science* for 31 January 1964—and was supported by laboratory experiments: 'Root growth of *Cucumis* and *Avena* seedlings is inhibited by volatile materials produced by leaves of *Salvia leucophylla*, *S. apiana* and *Artemisia californica*. The toxic substance may be deposited when dew condenses on affected seedlings in the field.'

More recently Muller (1970) has discussed the role of allelopathy—the control of growth, health, behaviour and population biology of organisms by chemicals produced by other organisms—on the evolution of vegetation. Even more recently Whittaker and Feeny (1971) have published a review paper—*Allelochemics: chemical interactions between species*—which shows how fascinatingly complex the subject is. They say: 'Phenolic acids released by the grass *Aristida oligantha* (and other old-field species) inhibit the nitrogen-fixing bacteria and blue-green algae of the soil. Low concentrations of available nitrogen in the soil,

[45]

to which the *Aristida* itself is tolerant, slow the invasion and replacement of this grass community by other species.'

Other substances which may be involved in similar situations include *flavonoids, terpenoids, steroids, alkaloids* and *organic cyanides*. Routes of release include fog-drip, rainwash, volatilization from leaves, excretion from roots, and decay.

Substances which may be toxic to the plant producing them may be rendered non-toxic by combination with sugars, or by deposition in dead tissues—as in bark.

Predators of some kinds are discouraged by the presence of *hypericin*, but one species of beetle, say Whittaker and Feeny: 'has further turned the evolutionary scales on the plants by using the repellant as a cue to locate its food. The beetles explore leaf-surfaces with their tarsal chemoreceptors until hypericin, present on the leaf-surface, triggers feeding.'

The *mustard-oils*, so characteristic of the *Cruciferae*, protect the plants against many predators, but some insects feed only on crucifers. An interesting development is that insects may retain toxins which they have obtained from plants, and be themselves toxic to others!

We are wandering a little from the subject of *excretion* by plants, but we cannot forbear to mention *phytoalexins* which include: 'phenolic compounds that are present in the skin of the protected organ as a first defense, and are produced in quantity in the deeper tissues surrounding a fungal penetration through the skin, as a second defense'.

Examples of these compounds are *orchinol* of orchid tubers, and *chlorogenic* and *caffeic acids* produced by potatoes.

The phenomenon of *guttation* may be mentioned briefly here. Quite large quantities of liquid are exuded under suitable conditions by many plants. Ivanoff (1963) says that this was first recorded by Munting just 300 years ago. The exudates include *water* as the chief constituent, *inorganic salts, glutamine*, etc. Modern techniques might well reveal interesting differences in composition of exudates from different species.

Guttation takes place from stomata or from hydathodes. Excretion in other ways may be discussed here.

The meal or farina on the leaves and stems of many species of *Primula* consists largely of *flavone* and related substances. It is secreted by glandular hairs. Blasdale (1947) has an interesting paper on this subject. He says:

Of the 500 or more species and subspecies of the genus *Primula*, at least one half bear minute glandular hairs which secrete a white or yellow powder, commonly designated as farina. With the exception of the closely related genus *Dionysia* I know of no other genus of flowering plants whose species yield similar secretions. Certain species of at least two fern genera, *Pitty[r]ogramma* and *Notholaena*, bear similar hairs producing similar products. Farina formation is of taxonomic importance in defining the genus [*Primula*] and the various sections into which it has been divided.

Blasdale says further that the farina is powdery rather than 'wax-like', as sometimes described. He did, however, find some wax-like material (which he did not identify) mixed with the flavonoid constituents.

More than a score of the species he studied had *flavone* as a major constituent of the farina; *P. denticulata* had *dihydroxy-flavone*; *P. verticillata* had *5-hydroxy-flavone* (reported by others from *P. imperialis* var. *gracilis*); while *P. florindae* had yet another flavonoid. Some few species bear quite different substances. Thus the skin-irritating material of the notorious *P. obconica* is said to be 'primin'.

Blasdale saw no advantage to the species of *Primula* bearing farina:

> In the absence of proof that farina is of use to the plant it becomes necessary to add these secretions to the long list of organic compounds synthesized by plants which are believed to be by-products incidental to the complex chemical reactions which take place in plant cells. They may be detrimental to the life and growth of plant cells just as the oleoresins secreted by coniferous plants are detrimental. If so, the secreting hairs may be considered part of a mechanism designed to eliminate such secretions from living tissues.

In view of the complex relations between organisms that we have discussed above we may wonder if farina is, indeed, simply a waste product.

Wax is transported from the epidermal cells to the leaf surface through micro-channels, says Hall (1967). We shall see that the waxes of different species differ in their major constituents.

Excretion from roots into the soil is hard to study. It is by no means certain that analyses under controlled conditions, as in water-culture, give an accurate picture of what happens under field conditions. Sir E. John Russell in his *The world of the soil* (1957) writes:

> Some plants can, however, excrete substances that protect them against attacks by parasitic fungi. Varieties of flax resistant to Wilt disease owe their immunity to the hydrocyanic acid which their roots secrete and which poisons the Fusarium and Helminthosporium fungi that cause the disease, but stimulates the Trichoderma that also represses these fungi. Susceptible varieties of flax on the other hand

do not excrete hydrocyanic acid and their roots become surrounded by a mixed population of fungi including those causing the disease.

Sir John notes that things do not always work out to the advantage of the higher plant. The potato, for example, secretes substances which cause spores of wart disease to germinate, and cysts of eelworms to develop. These predators then attack the potato.

ODORIFEROUS CONSTITUENTS OF PLANTS

The human nose, though far less sensitive than the noses of some animals, can still detect odoriferous materials in great dilution. Thus we find many plants have been named for their odours. Those smelling of onions or garlic (*Allium*), *Dysoxylum alliaceum*; of carraway (*Carvum*), *Lippia carviodora*, whose leaf-oil has 60% *d-carvone*; of *Citrus*, *Darwinia citriodora*, *Eucalyptus citriodora*, *Lippia citriodora*.

Sometimes the odoriferous constituents are known to us. Foetid odours, for example, are noted in the names *Coprosma foetidissima*, of which Briggs says: 'The disgustingly foetid odour of this plant has been shown by Sutherland (1946) to be due to traces of methyl mercaptan' and *Paederia foetida*, which also has a methyl mercaptan.

There are cases in which odour may reinforce impressions of relationship. Some families have quite characteristic smells. Many leguminous fruits, for example, have very similar odours. We find in LeMaout, Decaisne and Hooker (1873): '*Saurureae* [our *Saururaceae*] possess a somewhat acrid aroma, which confirms their affinity with *Piperaceae*.' I have myself noted that *Hedyosmum* (*Chloranthaceae*, also supposedly near *Piperaceae*) has a peppery smell.

Goris and Mascré (1909) observed that crushed roots of species of *Primula* have characteristic odours—anise, coriander, methyl salicylate (compare *Betula* spp. in this connection, but it is the bark that one sniffs). I do not think that this has been followed up chemotaxonomically.

Saghir and others have investigated the odoriferous constituents of *Allium* species. In 1966 they concluded:

Although in the classification of the alliums the use of morphological data is basic, information on odor may provide a valuable additional taxonomic character that will help in clarifying the systematics of this intricate genus. Inasmuch, however, as a classification based entirely on chemical characters would not only place clearly unrelated species such as *A. cepa* and *A. validum* together but separate otherwise very similar taxa like *A. campanulatum* and *A. membranaceum*, it is clear that chemical evidence must be used only in conjunction with all other pertinent evidence in determining relationships.

Some of the *sulphur-compounds* responsible for the odours were identified:

Allyl disulfide definitely has a garlic odor. Propyl disulfide... has the odor we associate with the common onion, and methyl disulfide the odor of cooked cabbage.

I have often wondered what is responsible for the characteristic smell, rather like celery, of the greengrocer's shop. Apparently *phthalides* contribute to the odour of celery, and so, perhaps, to that of the shop.

The odours of flowers may be transitory or very persistent. We note elsewhere some recent work on aroids and on orchids. A thesis by Hills (1968) may be quoted briefly here. He worked on the orchidaceous genus *Catasetum* and concluded that each species sampled that is known to have a species-specific pollinator also has a specific fragrance, and that: 'a study of the fragrances produced by the flowers of *Catasetum* is important to the taxonomy and ecology of the genus and of other genera of orchids that depend on specific attraction of euglossine bees as pollinators'.

About forty compounds are produced by *Catasetum* flowers and twelve of these were identified: *α-pinene, β-pinene, myrcene, 1,8-cineole, linalool, methyl benzoate, benzyl acetate, d-carvone, methyl salicylate, 2-phenyl ethyl acetate, 2-phenyl ethanol* and *methyl cinnamate*.

Harper, Bate-Smith and Land have produced a book on odours— *Odour description and odour classification* (1968). I have not seen it.

CHEMICAL EVOLUTION IN PLANTS

We may well believe that all evolution involves chemical changes and that the 'characters' that we use in taxonomy are the outward and visible signs of inward chemical characters: changing or evolving as the chemistry changes.

Luten (1964), in an interesting article on taxonomy in biology and chemistry, wrote: 'Certainly, as plants have become diversified, both in kind and in internal function, they have used older building blocks to assemble new chemical structures which can only be regarded as more complex.'

We should have put that somewhat differently, for evolution, as we well know, is not always towards the more complex. There can be reduction (not in the chemical sense!) and simplification: loss as well as gain (see below). There can be divergent, parallel and convergent evolution; and these are often difficult to distinguish. Let us examine one example.

The *betalains*, which seem to act as if alternative to *anthocyanins* in plants, appear to be confined to the **Centrospermae** (or **Caryophyllales**), the *Didiereaceae*, and the *Cactaceae*—all of which are grouped together by some taxonomists. But the *Caryophyllaceae*, often regarded as the type family of the order, lacks betalains: it has anthocyanins instead. How can we explain this?

Reznik (1957), who has discussed the problem, saw three possibilities:

(*a*) The *Caryophyllaceae* belongs to the order, but diverged somewhat from the line within which, at a later date, arose the ability to make betalains.

(*b*) The family belongs to the order, and *did* at one time produce betalains, but subsequently *lost* the ability to do so.

(*c*) The family does *not* belong to the order, having diverged from the ancestral stock before it produced the **Centrospermae**.

We can wonder similarly about the anthocyanins. Did the **Centrospermae**, unlike other plants, have both betalains and anthocyanins? And did the *Caryophyllaceae* lose the one and keep the other, while the remaining families did the reverse?

I am indebted to my old friend Mirov for reminding me of an interesting aspect of our work. I had asked him if his work on *terpenoid substances* in relation to the taxonomy of *Pinus* received support from the work of Erdtman on *heartwood constituents* of the same genus. He replied that there was not complete agreement but that that was to be expected since the 'evolution' of heartwood constituents might proceed quite independently of that of the terpenoid substances. Of course one then

asks which of these two groups of compounds reflects better the taxonomy of the genus.

Harborne has given much attention to the evolution of *flavonoids* in
plants. The following notes are derived from his chapter in *Comparative
phytochemistry* (ed. Swain, 1966).

In his first paragraph he agrees with me that much remains to be
done: 'The drawback is that total ascertainment has only been achieved
so far in one or two small plant groups so that the present contribution
of flavonoids to taxonomy is slight. Many more surveys at the generic
and family level are required before chemical information of this type
can be incorporated with confidence into plant classification.'

He says that the anthocyanins isolated from mosses and ferns are
biogenetically primitive in that they lack the 3-hydroxyl group of the
common anthocyanins and are derivatives of *apigeninidin* or of *luteolinidin*; and that the occurrence of the biogenetically simple *chalcones,
dihydrochalcones* and *flavanones* in ferns suggest that they are primitive
characters in plants.

Harborne makes one statement which I might query. He says (italics
mine): 'The flavonoids of the monocotyledons are more interesting
from another point of view, that of parallel evolution. If, *as is generally
accepted*, the mono and dicotyledons arose separately from a common
seed-bearing stock, then many chemical modifications in flavonoid
synthesis must have arisen independently in the two groups of plants.'
I query the 'general acceptance', not the parallel evolution.

After some detailed considerations Harborne draws up a table 'based
mainly on present ideas of evolutionary status...and on biogenetic
considerations'. According to this 3-*deoxyanthocyanidins*; *flavonols*;
leucoanthocyanidins; *chalcones, flavanones,* and *dihydrochalcones*; and
C-substitution are 'primitive characters'. 'Advanced characters' resulting from gain mutations include complex *O-glycosylation*; 6- *or* 8-
hydroxylation; *O-methylation*; and *oxidation* of *chalcones to aurones.*
'Advanced characters' resulting from loss mutations are *replacement of
flavonols by flavones*; *elimination* of *leucoanthocyanidins*; and *elimination*
of *trihydroxylation*.

A great deal that might be included in this section is to be found in
the symposium volume *Phytochemical phylogeny*, edited by Harborne
(1970).

I was flattered some years ago to be asked to contribute a paper to
the volume of the *Journal of the Linnean Society of London* (1958)
marking the centenary of the presentation to the Society of the Darwin–
Wallace papers on evolution. It seemed appropriate to make it a paper
on chemical evolution in plants. I found only a limited amount of
material on this subject, and had to say 'Organic evolution, and with it

biochemical evolution, are now generally accepted as facts, but we know all too little of the biochemical facts.'

This might be repeated today, but we have made some progress, and many more investigators are energetically digging out more facts so that speculation may be based on a wider foundation. I should like to be alive to read what will be written when the Darwin–Wallace *bicentenary* is celebrated!

TESTS USED BY THE AUTHOR

INTRODUCTION

When confronted with the vast assemblage of higher plants one is intimidated by the problems involved in the investigation for taxonomic purposes of their comparative chemistry. Very early in the present work it became evident that one must choose in one's own research between an *intensive* study of a few plants and an *extensive* investigation of all that could be made available.

Obviously the chemist, rather than the botanist, is better qualified to pursue the *intensive* course, and it is clear in the pages of this book that I have collected much information from the work of chemists. I felt myself, as a botanist, better fitted to pursue the more *extensive* course, and I have endeavoured during a quarter of a century to stick to this and not to be tempted into more intensive studies of small groups.

In following this course I have had to adopt (and adapt) simple tests which could be performed rapidly upon large numbers of specimens. The notes which follow describe the routine tests that I (and my students and assistants) have employed. As the work has developed it has become obvious that some of the tests overlap and that some are doubly or trebly useful, indicating two or three groups of chemical constituents. This will be made clear, I hope, in the notes below.

1. Raphides

This is an observation rather than a test, and it is usually made upon the control sections when carrying out the *syringin test*. In some cases, however, where the material does not lend itself to the use of the syringin test, we still look for *raphides*. These needle-like crystals, and their usefulness in taxonomy, are discussed at some length in our discussion of the history of chemotaxonomy. See also Gibbs (1963, pp. 51–5).

It is obvious that we are indebted to the plant anatomists for much information on the distribution of raphides in plants unavailable to us. Care must be taken, however, in accepting statements in early papers as to the occurrence of raphides. Many observers called unoriented acicular crystals 'raphides'. Today we restrict the term to bundles of needle-shaped crystals arranged parallel to each other and enclosed in special 'raphide-sacs'.

See individual groups for further discussion.

2. The Cigarette and Hot-Water Tests

Some years ago we came across a paper by Dykyj-Sajfertova (1958) describing two very simple tests that seemed to be of taxonomic interest. These we have designated the *Cigarette Test* (Cig. Test) and the *Hot-Water Test* (H.-W. Test). We may describe them and their use as follows:

Cig. Test. A lighted cigarette is pressed gently against the back of a mature leaf for about 3 seconds. A strongly positive reaction (I of Dykyj-Sajfertova) is the development almost at once of a *brown* to *black ring* around the heated area. A slower and weaker reaction is designated by II, a very slow (30 minutes) or doubtful reaction by III, and a negative reaction by IV.

In some young leaves (noted by us) and in leaves with acid cell-saps (as noted by Dykyj-Sajfertova), a *yellow colour* may develop around the heated spot. This was called by her the *oxalis-reaction* (O.R.) because first observed in species of *Oxalis*.

H.-W. Test. In this test a mature leaf is dipped part-way into water at about 85 °C and held steadily there for about 5 seconds (we increase the time a little for thick and/or leathery leaves). A strongly positive reaction (I) is the development almost at once of a brown or black band at the juncture of dipped and undipped areas. The dipped part may subsequently darken patchily or entirely. A slower, weaker reaction is dubbed II, a doubtful one III, and a negative one IV. Yellowing is again an oxalis-reaction.

Dykyj-Sajfertova tested in all about 1000 species. She found that some families, such as the *Compositae*, seemed always to be I for both tests. Others, such as the *Campanulaceae*, seemed always to be IV. Yet others seemed to be mixed, some members giving positive and some negative reactions, or very weak ones.

We have adopted the *Cig. Test* and the *H.-W. Test* as standard and have applied them to many plants. In general our results parallel those of Dykyj-Sajfertova, though we have found some exceptions. We have tested many plants not included in her list.

What are we testing for in these simple experiments? It seems that the heat-treatment in each case disorganizes the tissues and brings enzymes into contact with their substrates. More specifically we suppose that polyphenolases react with suitable substrates to produce dark-coloured substances. It seems likely that different materials may be involved in different families. We have noted, for example, that members of the *Boraginaceae* give a *brown* (often bright brown) colour, while those of the *Aquifoliaceae* and *Araliaceae* give a strikingly *black* reaction.

In a few cases there may be consistent differences between sub-families or between closely related families. Thus we have found the *Gentianaceae (s.s.)* to be negative; the *Menyanthaceae* to be positive. Occasionally, we have noted differences between species of the same genus. In the Australian *Anthocercis*, for example, I obtained a strikingly positive H.-W. reaction with *A. littorea* from near Perth, and a negative reaction with *A. viscosa* from Albany.

A brief note on the oxalis-reaction is in order here. This may be consistent in some groups. My student Elizabeth Shaw (see Shaw and Gibbs, 1961, and her thesis, unpublished) found that mature leaves of members of the *Hamamelidaceae* all (?) give a marked oxalis-reaction. This may be one of the 'characters' of the family. Incidentally we have not checked the acidity of the cell-saps of the *Hamamelidaceae*, and we have obtained no information on this point from the literature.

3. The HCl/Methanol ('Isenberg–Buchanan') Test

In 1945 Isenberg and Buchanan reported: 'Tests by the authors with 277 species in 56 families have shown that methanol containing a small amount of hydrochloric acid gives a purple coloration when mixed cold with the shavings of some species and not with others. The method gives promise of making it possible to identify the woods of certain species that cannot be separated on the basis of structure alone.'

Isenberg and Buchanan did not know the substances responsible for the purple coloration (a positive reaction) and we still are uncertain. Adler (1951) concluded that they are '*catechol tannins*'. The very high correlation between a positive result from this test and a positive *leuco-anthocyanin* reaction (below) makes it likely that *leucoanthocyanins* are involved. We have standardized the *HCl/Methanol Test* as follows:

A small amount of sapwood from a fresh twig (about pencil-size if possible but even smaller if no older material is available) is sliced with a pencil sharpener, or cut into small chips, and just covered in a stoppered test-tube with a few ml. of the HCl/Methanol mixture (1000 ml. methanol: 25 ml. conc. HCl). The tube is allowed to stand, with occasional shaking, for some hours. A *deep magenta* colour in the wood (4 in Isenberg and Buchanan's scale) is a strongly positive result; 3, 2, and 1 are progressively weaker reactions; and 0 a negative result in which the wood shows no magenta colour whatever.

We have noted that the supernatant liquid may also be coloured, and not always the same as the wood. In practice we decant and record the colours of liquid and of wood, using Ridgway's *Color Standards and Nomenclature* (1912). Roughly speaking positive results in the wood are often those of plate xxvi in Ridgway, 4 being 'dull magenta purple', 3 'magenta', 2 'liseran purple', 1 'rose-purple' or 'pale rose-purple'. Negative results are usually those of plate xxx of Ridgway, paler tints being 'marguerite yellow', 'ivory yellow', or 'cartridge buff'.

We have used this test on most of the woody species available to us. It soon became clear that some families are consistently positive to the test; others as consistently negative. As described in earlier papers (Gibbs, 1954, 1958, 1962) we have established a series which is HCl/ Methanol positive and another that is negative. The former includes the *Dilleniaceae, Actinidiaceae, Bixaceae, Theaceae, Clethraceae, Ericaceae, Pyrolaceae, Epacridaceae, Empetraceae,* and *Cyrillaceae*; the latter includes the *Aquifoliaceae, Salvadoraceae, Oleaceae, Loganiaceae,* woody *Boraginaceae*, and the families of the **Tubiflorae**. Taxonomists will recognize these as comprising two series in each of which the families are considered to be related one to another.

When one carries out many such tests one runs sooner or later into exceptional cases which often prove to be of great interest. We may deal briefly here with one example.

In Jamaica I tested *Euphorbia nudiflora* and, to my surprise, got a bright orangey rather than a magenta reaction ('deep chrome' and 'cadmium yellow' of Ridgway's plate iii in 2 tests). *E. heterophylla* and its var. *graminifolia* were then found to give similar results ('capucine orange', plate iii, for both). It transpired that these plants are very nearly related and that the familiar poinsettia (*E. pulcherrima*) belongs to the same group of species. It, too, gave a bright orangey colour ('bittersweet orange' of plate ii). Further research showed:

(*a*) That many other members of the *Euphorbiaceae*, including some species of *Euphorbia* less closely related to *E. nudiflora*, give typical *negative* reactions with no orange colour, while some members of the family —which is certainly a heterogeneous group—give *positive* (magenta) reactions.

(*b*) That the orange colour is very stable, remaining virtually unchanged for weeks, even with frequent changes of the HCl/Methanol mixture.

(*c*) That I had obtained a similar orange colour ('mikado orange', plate iii) years ago with *Oxyanthus tubiflorus* (*Rubiaceae*) from the Royal Botanic Garden, Edinburgh. A second species (*O. natalensis*) from the same garden, was then tested and gave 'cadmium orange' (plate iii). No other rubiaceous plant—the family is mixed in its reaction to the HCl/ Methanol test—has given anything but a normal positive or negative result.

A colleague of mine decided to study the chemistry of this 'off-beat' reaction. He and a graduate student were defeated: they failed even to extract the orange material (Gibbs, Edward, and Ferland, 1967).

And there, for the moment, the matter rests. It looks very much as if the same stable substance occurs in a closely knit group of *Euphorbia* species and in at least two species of *Oxyanthus*! I might well have considered the few species of *Euphorbia* to be unique if I had not tested *Oxyanthus*. We must be cautious indeed before we can describe a chemical character as 'peculiar' to a single group.

4. HCN (Test A)

More than a dozen *cyanogenic glycosides* are known to occur in plants (p. 632). When any one of these is hydrolysed it yields free *HCN* which may be detected very easily. We have, from the beginnings of our researches in chemotaxonomy, used a simple test which we have designated *HCN* (*Test A*), bearing in mind that we might at any time use other tests (B, C, D, etc.). This simple test is carried out as follows:

A small amount of plant material (1–2 gm., or even much less) is pounded in a mortar with a few drops of water, a tiny pinch of emulsin, and a few drops of chloroform. The resulting 'mush' is transferred at once to a glass-stoppered test-tube. The stopper has a piece of picric acid paper (filter paper dipped into a saturated aqueous solution of picric acid and then dried) fastened to its underside with melted paraffin wax. Just before insertion the paper is dipped into 10% sodium carbonate solution and gently blotted. If much HCN is released by the action of the emulsin on the glycoside in the plant material the sodium picrate turns from pale yellow to rust-red within minutes. If very little HCN is released it may require one or more days before there is obvious change. We usually leave the tubes for a week and I have some evidence that an even longer period is desirable in some cases.

In our earliest experiments we used split rubber bungs to hold the sodium picrate paper. We sometimes got positive results when we didn't expect them and experiments showed that the bungs might release (absorbed?) HCN even though they had been washed after use with truly cyanogenic material. We strongly suspect that some 'records' in the literature have been obtained by similar faulty techniques. We have never obtained positive results (using our present technique) from any member of the *Lauraceae*, for example, though others claim to have done so.

One must be cautious, however, for I have argued against the occurrence of HCN in the *Cucurbitaceae* (Gibbs, 1965). At that time I had tested 24 species belonging to 17 genera of the family without getting anything but negative results. Then, in November of 1967, material of *Xerosicyos* became available. *X. perreiri* gave a moderately strong positive reaction and *X. manguyi* a negative one! But I have *not* found HCN in other cucurbits which have been claimed to be cyanogenic by other workers.

Plants that form cyanogenic glycosides may have them in all parts, but more often than not the glycosides are restricted to certain organs, making it worthwhile to examine various parts if they are available (Gibbs, 1965). Usually we test young leafy shoots, but sometimes inflorescences have been found to be cyanogenic when leafy shoots are not. Thus we found that shoots of *Lomatia tinctoria* gave negative tests while the inflorescences yielded a positive result. We found the shoot of *L. silaifolia* to be negative, while several authors found the inflorescence to be positive for HCN. Smith and White got similar results with *Grevillea banksii*; we got the reverse with *G. sericea*! An interesting state of affairs is found in *Lotus* and its segregates. Guérin (1929) reports that *seeds* of *Dorycnium* species are negative to the test, while *seedlings* are positive and we agree. We have found older *leafy shoots* of two species to be negative. In *Tetragonolobus biflora* and probably in at least two other species there is a similar state of affairs.

While we use fresh material wherever possible there are times when small fragments of herbarium specimens are all that are available to us. A negative test from such material may be inconclusive, but a positive test is accepted as proof that the original plant had cyanogenic glycosides. See cyanogenic glycosides (p. 629) for further discussion.

Are there substances other than HCN which might emanate from plant material and might turn sodium picrate paper rust-red? We know of none. We have, however, obtained somewhat atypical results in some cases, the paper becoming rather a dull brown. Some species of *Viburnum* (*Caprifoli.*), *Velleia spathulata* (*Goodeni.*), *Mutisia coccinea* (*Comp.*), and *Casearia nitida* (*Flacourti.*) have given such results. No explanation of this is offered, but it is a pretty problem for someone.

The reader will find many references in this book to HCN as a chemotaxonomic character. See particularly *Passifloraceae*, *Malesherbiaceae*, *Turneraceae*, *Flacourtiaceae*, *Leguminosae*.

In tables 1 to 3 I record my own results and, for comparison, those of others.

A few comments upon the tables are in order:

(*a*) It would appear at first sight that I have made more tests for HCN than have all others put together! This is misleading for at least two reasons. In the first place, though I have tried hard to collect all the information available, I must have missed many records. In the second place some of the papers consulted record only the plants giving *positive* results.

(*b*) I *do* seem to have a better coverage of families than have others.

TABLE I. *Summary of Occurrence of HCN in Dicotyledons*

Families (genera/species)	Gibbs HCN (Test A) +	?	−	Others +	?	−
Acanth. (250/2600)	3/3	—	30/59	3/3	—	1/1
Acer. (2-3/152)	—	—	3/10	—	—	1/5
Achari. (3/3)	—	—	—	—	—	—
Achato. (2/8)	—	—	—	—	—	—
Actinidi. (3/320)	—	—	2/2	—	—	1/1
Adox. (1/1)	—	—	1/1	—	—	1/1
Aextoxic. (1/1)	—	—	—	—	—	—
Aizo. (131/2500)	—	—	24/27	—	—	4/5
Akani. (1/1)	—	1/1	—	—	—	1/1
Alangi. (1-2/18)	—	—	1/1	—	—	—
Alseuosmi. (3/11)	—	—	—	—	—	—
Amaranth. (60/900)	—	—	8/17	2/5	1/1	3/3
Amborell. (1/1)	—	—	—	—	—	—
Anacardi. (79/600)	—	—	8/9	4/6	—	3/3
Ancistro. (1/18)	—	—	—	—	—	—
Annon. (120/2100)	1/1	—	1/1	4/7	—	—
Apocyn. (200/2000)	1/1	—	9/10	6/6	—	6/7
Aquifoli. (3/450)	1/1[1]	—	1/3	—	—	2/2
Arali. (70/700)	—	1/1	4/6	2/2	1/2	5/6
Aristol. (7/600)	—	—	1/4	—	—	2/2
Asclepi. (250/2000)	1/1	—	12/13	2/2	—	6/8
Austrobail. (1/2)	—	—	—	—	—	—
Balanop. (1/9)	—	—	—	—	—	—
Balanoph. (18/100)	—	—	1/1[2]	—	—	—
Balsamin. (3/475)	—	—	2/5	1/1	—	—
Basell. (4/20)	—	—	2-3/2-3	—	—	—
Batid. (1/2)	—	—	1/2	—	—	—
Begoni. (5/820)	—	—	1/9	—	—	—
Berber. (14/650)	2/2	—	6/13	2/2	—	3/5
Betul. (6/100)	—	—	3/5	—	—	5/25
Bignon. (120/800)	—	—	19/20	3/3	1/1	2/2
Bix. (1/1)	—	—	1/1	—	—	1/1
Bombac. (28/200)	—	—	2/2	2/2	—	—
Borag. (100/2000)	1/1	1/1	21/39	3/3	1/1	8/8
Bretschn. (1/1)	—	—	—	—	—	—
Brunelli. (1/35)	—	—	—	—	—	—
Bruni. (12/75)	—	—	—	—	—	—
Brunoni. (1/1)	—	—	1/1	—	—	—
Buddlej. (19/160)	—	—	4/8	—	—	1/3
Burser. (18/600)	—	—	—	—	1/2	1/1
Bux. (6/60)	—	—	4/8	—	—	3/5
Byblid. (1/2)	—	—	1/1	—	—	—
Cact. (200/2000)	1/5	—	19/34	—	—	—

[1] Some *dull*.   [2] Herbarium material.

TABLE 1. (cont.)

Families (genera/species)	Gibbs HCN (Test A) +	?	−	Others +	?	−
Callitrich. (1/35)	—	—	1/1–2	—	—	—
Calycanth. (2/9)	2/4	—	—	2/4	—	—
Calycer. (6/60)	—	—	1/1	—	—	—
Campan. (70/2000)	1/4	—	15/23	1/1	—	4/6
Canell. (6/20)	1/1	—	—	1/1	—	—
Cappar. (46/800)	3/4	3/3	2/2	2/2	—	8/15
Caprifol. (15/400)	2/5[1]	1/2	7/22	2/4	2/4	11/80
Cardiopter. (1/3)	—	—	—	—	—	—
Caric. (4/45)	—	—	1/2	1/1	—	—
Caryocar. (2/25)	—	—	2/2[2]	—	—	—
Caryoph. (80/2000)	—	—	13/19	—	—	4/4
Casuar. (1/45)	—	—	1/1	—	—	1/1
Celastr. (60/850)	—	—	6/9	1/1	—	4/6
Cephalot. (1/1)	—	—	1/1	—	—	—
Ceratoph. (1/4–6)	—	—	1/1	—	—	1/1
Cercidi. (1/1–2)	—	—	1/1	—	—	—
Chenopod. (100/1500)	—	—	7/14	5/8–9	1/2	9/14
Chloranth. (5/70)	—	—	—	—	—	—
Chrysobal. (12/300)	—	—	1/1	'Absent'		
Cist. (8/175)	—	—	3/9	—	—	1/4
Clethr. (1/30)	—	—	1/3	1/2	—	1/1
Cneor. (2/3)	—	—	1/1	—	—	1/1
Cochlosp. (2/20)	—	—	—	—	—	—
Columelli. (1/4)	—	—	—	—	—	—
Combret. (18/500)	—	—	1/1	2/2	1/1	1/1
Comp. (920/19000)	2/4[3]	—	42/49	26/53	4/4	49/69
Connar. (24/350)	—	—	—	—	—	—
Convolv. (51/1600)	—	1/1[4]	3/5	3/7	1/1	3/5
Coriari. (1/12)	—	—	1/2	—	—	1/1
Corn. (12/95)	—	—	5/12	—	—	3/18
Corynocarp. (1/5)	—	—	1/1	—	1/1	—
Crassul. (30/1400)	7/11	—	18/35	3/4–5	—	2/4
Crossosom. (1/3)	—	—	1/2	—	—	—
Crucif. (350/3000)	2/2	2/2	6/8	13/17	2/2	75/120[5]
Crypteroni. (1/4)	—	—	—	—	—	—
Cucurb. (100/850)	1/1	—	18/28	5/5	—	3/3
Cunoni. (25/350)	1/1	—	3/4	—	—	4/5
Cynomori. (1/1)	—	—	—	—	—	—
Cyrill. (3/14)	—	—	1/1	—	—	—
Daphniph. (1/35)	—	—	1/1	—	—	—
Datisc. (3/4)	—	—	2/2	—	—	—
Davidi. (1/1)	—	—	1/1	—	—	—

[1] Some *dull*.   [2] Herbarium material.
[3] 1/3 dull.   [4] Dull?   [5] Honeyman (mostly seed).

TABLE 1 (*cont.*)

Families (genera/species)	Gibbs HCN (Test A) +	?	−	Others +	?	−
Davidsoni. (1/1)	—	—	1/1	1/1	—	—
Degeneri. (1/1)	1/1	—	—	—	—	—
Desfont. (1/5)	—	—	1/1	—	—	—
Dialypet. (1/1)	—	—	1/1[1]	—	—	—
Diapensi. (6/18)	—	—	2/2	—	—	—
Dichapet. (4/250)	—	—	—	1/2[3]	—	—
Didiere. (4/11)	—	—	3/3	—	—	—
Didymel. (1/2)	—	—	—	—	—	—
Dilleni. (10/350)	—	—	4/13	2/2	—	1/3
Dioncoph. (3/3)	—	—	—	—	—	—
Dipentod. (1/1)	—	—	—	—	—	—
Dipsac. (10/270)	—	—	8/10	—	—	1/1
Diptero. (22/400)	—	—	1/1	1/1	—	—
Droser. (4/93)	2/3[4]	—	1/4	3/7	—	—
Duckeoden. (1/1)	—	—	—	—	—	—
Dysphani. (1/5–6)	—	—	—	1/3	—	—
Eben. (4/450)	—	1/1	3/6	1/3	—	1/1
Elaeagn. (3/65)	—	—	3/6	—	—	1/5
Elaeoc. (10/400)	1/1	—	5/6	—	—	1/1
Elatin (2/39–45)	—	—	—	—	—	—
Empetr. (3/9)	—	—	3/3	—	1/1	1/1
Epacrid. (30/400)	3/3	—	8/18	—	1/1	9/19
Eric. (82/2500)	2/2	2/2	20/35	2/2	—	15/112[5]
Erythrox. (4/200)	—	—	1/2	1/1	—	1/1
Eucommi. (1/1)	—	—	1/1	—	—	1/1
Eucryphi. (1/5)	—	1/1	1/2	—	—	—
Euphorb. (290/7500)	6/6	1/1	21/35	28/51	2/2	12/16
Eupomati. (1/2)	—	1/1	1/1	—	—	—
Euptele. (1/2)	—	—	1/1	—	—	—
Fag. (7–8/600)	—	—	5/6	—	—	3/3
Flacour. (86/1300)	1/1	2/2	9/11[2]	9/15	4/4	4/6
Fouquieri. (1/54)	—	—	1/1	—	—	—
Frankeni. (4/50)	—	—	1/3[2]	—	—	—
Garry. (1/15)	—	—	1/6	—	—	—
Geissolom. (1/1)	—	—	—	—	—	—
Genti. (70/1100)	3/3	1/1	7/12	—	1/1	2/2
Gerani. (11/780)	—	—	3/7	—	—	3/3
Gesner. (140/1800)	—	—	8/8	—	—	1/1
Globulari. (2/27)	—	—	1/3	—	—	—
Gomorteg. (1/1)	—	—	—	—	—	—

[1] Herbarium material.
[2] Some from herbarium material.
[3] Queried by Hegnauer.
[4] 2/2 dull.
[5] About 80 from seeds of *Rhododendron* spp.

TABLE I (*cont.*)

Families (genera/species)	Gibbs HCN (Test A)			Others		
	+	?	−	+	?	−
Gooden. (14/320)	2/2	—	6/12	1/1	—	3/5
Grubbi. (1/5)	—	—	—	—	—	—
Guttif. (49/900)	—	—	4/12	3/3	—	2/4
Gyrostem. (5/16)	1/1	—	—	1/1	1/1	1/1
Haloragid. (8/160)	3/7	—	1/2	3/3	—	2/3
Hamamel. (26/110)	—	—	12/20	—	—	9/18
Henriquez. (2/13)	—	—	—	—	—	—
Hernandi. (4/65)	—	—	1/1	—	—	—
Himantand. (1/2–3)	—	—	—	—	—	—
Hippocast. (2/15)	—	—	1/4	—	—	—
Hippocrat. (18/300)	—	—	1/1	—	—	—
Hippurid. (1/1)	—	—	1/1	—	—	—
Hoplestig. (1/2)	—	—	—	—	—	—
Hydnor. (2/18)	—	—	—	—	—	—
Hydroph. (20/270)	—	2/2	3/4	—	—	1/1
Hydrostach. (1/30)	—	—	—	—	—	—
Icacin. (45/400)	1/2	—	—	—	—	—
Illici. (1/42)	—	—	1/2	—	—	—
Jugland. (8/75)	1/1	—	3/4	—	—	4/13
Juliani. (2/5)	—	—	—	—	—	—
Krameri. (1/20)	—	—	—	—	—	—
Lab. (200/3200)	3/3	1/1	39/86	3/4	—	13/17
Lactorid. (1/1)	—	—	—	—	—	—
Lardizab. (8/30)	—	—	3/3	—	—	1/1
Laur. (31/2250)	—	—	11/13	4/4	—	3/6
Lecyth. (24/450)	—	—	2/2	3/3	—	—
Lee. (1/70)	—	1/1	1/1	1/2	—	—
Legum. (600/13000)	2/26	2/4	33/64	51/121	7/7	61/119
Leitneri. (1/1)	—	—	1/1	—	—	—
Lenno. (3/4)	—	—	—	—	—	—
Lentib. (5/300)	—	—	2/4	—	—	—
Limnanth. (2/8)	—	—	2/2	—	—	1/1
Lin. (23/500)	1/3	—	2/3	1/15	—	1/4
Lissocarp. (1/2)	—	—	—	—	—	—
Loas. (15/250)	—	—	5/11[1]	—	—	3/4
Logani. (18/500)	—	1/1	3/3	1/1	1/1	2/2
Loranth. (40/1400)	—	—	1/1	—	1/1	1/2
Lythr. (22/500)[2]	—	—	5/7	1/1	—	1/1
Magnoli. (10/215)	1/2	—	4/8	1/2	—	—
Malesherb. (1/25)	1/1[1]	—	—	—	—	—
Malpighi. (65/800)	—	2/3	2/4	—	—	—
Malv. (85/1500)	—	—	17/23	4/6	—	6/9
Marcgrav. (5/120)	—	—	1/1	—	—	—

[1] Some from herbarium material.　　　　[2] Hegnauer.

TABLE I (*cont.*)

Families (genera/species)	Gibbs HCN (Test A) +	?	−	Others +	?	−
Martyni. (5/16)	—	—	1-2/1-2	—	—	—
Medusagyn. (1/1)	—	—	—	—	—	—
Medusandr. (2/6)	—	—	—	—	—	—
Melastom. (200/4000)	2/2	—	8/8	1/3	—	—
Meli. (50/1400)	—	1/1	2/2	5/5	—	2/3
Melianth. (3/38)	—	—	3/4	—	—	—
Menisper. (67/425)	—	—	5/6	4/4	—	—
Menyanth. (5/40)	—	—	2/2	—	—	1/1
Misodendr. (1/11)	—	—	—	—	—	—
Mollugin. (14/95)	—	—	1/1	1/1	—	—
Monimi. (34/450)	—	—	6/6	—	—	2/2
Mor. (61/1550)	1/1	—	8/10	7/17	—	3/5
Moring. (1/10)	—	—	1/1	1/1	—	—
Myop. (5/180)	2/2	1/1	2/10	1/1	1/1	2/2
Myric. (3/56)	—	—	2/3	—	—	1/2
Myrist. (12/150)	—	—	1/1	—	—	—
Myrothamn. (1/2)	—	—	—	—	—	—
Myrsin. (33/1000)	—	—	6/9	—	—	1/1
Myrt. (100/3000)	—	1/1	12/14	3/6	1/1	14/24
Nepenth. (1/79)	—	—	1/2	—	—	—
Neurad. (3/10)	—	—	—	—	—	—
Nolan. (2/83)	—	—	1/3	—	—	1/1
Nyctag. (30/300)	—	—	4/8	1/1	—	2/2
Nymphae. (8/65–80)	—	—	6/6	—	—	2/3
Nyss. (2/9)	—	—	1/1	—	—	—
Ochn. (28/400)	—	—	3/4	—	1/1	1/1
Olac. (27/230)	1/1	—	1/1	2/3	1/1	1/1
Ole. (27/600)	—	2/4	10/15	—	—	6/12
Olini. (1/8)	—	—	—	—	1/2	—
Onagr. (20/650)	—	—	7/9	3/4	—	4/6
Opili. (7/60)	—	—	—	—	—	—
Oroban. (13/150)	—	—	3/3	—	—	1/1
Oxalid. (8/950)	—	—	3/6	3/4	—	1/1
Paeoni. (1/33)	—	—	1/2	—	—	1/1
Pand. (1/1)	—	—	—	—	—	—
Papav. (47/700)	3/3	—	11/13	4/4	—	13/42[1]
Passifl. (12/600)	4/20	—	1/1[2]	5/28	—	1/1
Pedali. (16/55)	—	—	2/2	—	—	—
Penae. (5/21)	—	—	—	—	—	—
Pentaphrag. (1/25)	—	—	—	—	—	—
Pentaphylac. (1/3)	—	—	—	—	—	—
Peridisc. (2/2)	—	—	—	—	—	—
Phrym. (1/1-4)	—	—	1/1	—	—	1/1

[1] Mostly Honeyman (seeds).   [2] Poor material.

TABLE I (*cont.*)

Families (genera/species)	Gibbs HCN (Test A)			Others		
	+	?	−	+	?	−
Phytol. (17/120)	—	1/1	5/7	—	—	1/2
Picroden. (1/3)	—	—	1/1	—	—	—
Piper. (11/1400)	—	—	3/11	1/4	—	1/2
Pittosp. (9/240)	—	—	7/9	—	—	6/10
Plantagin. (3/265)	—	—	1/8	—	—	1/3
Platan. (1/6–7)	1/2	—	—	1/4	—	—
Plumbag. (10/350)	—	1/1	5/10	—	—	1/1
Podostem. (43/200)	—	—	—	—	—	—
Polemon. (18/320)	—	1/1	6/9	—	—	1/1
Polygal. (13/800)	—	—	2/4	—	—	2/4
Polygon. (40/800)	—	—	9/14	3/3	—	5/5
Portul. (19/500)	—	1/1	5/7	1/1	—	1/1
Primul. (28/800)	—	—	11/16	—	—	2/3
Prote. (62/1400)	8/10	2/2	12/27	11/18	—	11/34
Punic. (1/2)	—	—	1/1	—	—	—
Pyrol. (16/75)	2/2[1]	1/2[1]	1/1	—	—	—
Quiin. (3/37)	—	—	1/1[2]	—	—	—
Rafflesi. (9/55)	—	—	—	—	—	—
Ranunc. (50/2000)	7/17	5/9	16/28	5/31	—	7/12
Resed. (6/70)	2/2	—	3/5	—	—	1/4
Rhamn. (58/900)	—	—	9/11	1/1	—	5/10
Rhizoph. (16/120)	—	—	—	—	—	—
Rhoiptele. (1/1)	—	—	—	—	—	—
Roridul. (1/2)	—	—	—	—	—	—
Ros. (100/3000)	15/23	4/4	22/32	33/144	2/4	20/47
Rubi. (475/6500)	—	1/1	25/29	8/10	1/1	9/12
Rut. (150/1600)	2/3	—	12/16	4/12	—	18/25
Sabi. (4/90)	—	—	1/1	—	—	—
Salic. (2/350)	—	1/1[1]	2/3	1/1	—	—
Salvad. (3/12)	1/1	1/1	—	—	—	—
Santal. (35/400)	—	—	4/4	—	—	6/7
Sapin. (140/1500)	1/1	—	4/5	11/15	—	8/16
Sapot. (50/800)	2/2	—	4/4	4/7	1/1	1/1
Sarcolaen. (8/33)	—	—	—	—	—	—
Sarcosp. (1/8)	—	—	—	—	—	—
Sargentod. (1/1)	—	—	—	—	—	—
Sarraceni. (3/16)	—	—	1/2	—	—	—
Saurur. (4/5)	—	—	2/2	—	—	—
Saxifr. (80/1200)	5/5	1/1	21/30	5/16	3/3	21/78
Schisandr. (2/47)	—	—	2/4	—	—	1/1
Scroph. (200/3000)	1/1	—	25/43	2/5	2/4	9/9
Scyphosteg. (1/1)	—	—	—	—	—	—
Scytopet. (5/32)	—	—	—	—	—	—

[1] Dull!   [2] Herbarium material.

TABLE 1 (*cont.*)

Families (genera/species)	Gibbs HCN (Test A)			Others		
	+	?	−	+	?	−
Simaroub. (24/100)	—	—	2/3	—	—	—
Solan. (85/2300)	—	—	13/18	6/7	1/1	8/17
Sonnerati. (2/7)	—	—	—	—	—	—
Sphaerosep. (2/14)	—	—	—	—	—	—
Sphenocle. (1/1–2)	—	—	—	—	—	—
Stachyur. (1/5–6)	—	—	1/2	—	—	—
Stackhous. (3/22)	—	—	1/1	—	—	—
Staphyle. (7/50)	—	—	1/2	—	—	1/1
Stercul. (70/1000)	—	—	10/11	5/8	—	4/6
Strasburg. (1/1)	—	—	—	—	—	—
Stylidi. (6/140)	—	—	1/2	—	—	1/2
Styrac. (11/150)	—	—	1/1	—	—	1/1
Symploc. (1/350)	—	—	1/1	—	—	—
Tamaric. (4/100)	—	—	2/3	—	—	1/1
Tetracent. (1/1)	—	—	1/1	—	—	—
The. (35/600)	—	—	7/10[1]	—	—	—
Theligon. (1/3)	—	—	—	—	—	—
Theophr. (4/110)	—	—	3/3–4	—	—	—
Thymel. (48/650)	—	—	5/5	1/1	—	3/6
Tili. (47–48/400)	—	—	7/7	6/8	—	3/5
Tovari. (1/2)	1/1	—	—	—	—	1/2
Trap. (1/3–11)	—	—	1/1	—	—	—
Tremand. (3/30)	2/2	—	1/3	—	—	1/1
Trigoni. (4/35)	—	—	—	—	—	—
Trimeni. (2/7)	—	—	—	—	—	—
Trochod. (1/1)	—	—	1/1	—	—	—
Tropaeol. (2/80)	—	—	1/1	—	—	1/3
Turner. (8/120)	3/10	—	1/2[1]	2/5	—	—
Ulm. (15/150)	—	1/1	5/9	2/3	1/2	6/7
Umbell. (300/3000)	—	—	13/18	2/3	—	25/29
Urtic. (42/700)	—	—	9/12	3/3	—	4/5
Valeri. (13/360)	—	—	3/3	—	—	1/1
Verb. (100/2600)	—	—	21/46	6/8	—	5/12
Viol. (16/850)	—	1/1	5/18[1]	—	1/2	3/12
Vit. (12/700)	—	—	5/9	2/4	—	4/6
Vochysi. (6/200)	—	—	—	—	—	—
Winter. (6/95)	1/1	—	1/1	1/3	—	—
Zygoph. (30/250)	—	—	2/2	—	—	3/5

[1] Some from herbarium material.

TABLE 2. *Summary of Occurrence of HCN in Monocotyledons*

Families (genera/species)	Gibbs HCN (Test A)			Others		
	+	?	−	+	?	−
Agav. (18/560)	—	—	9/9	1/1	—	2/2
Alism. (10/70)	—	—	2/3	—	—	2/3
Amaryll. (65/860)	3/3	1/1	7/8	—	—	1/1
Aponoget. (1/40)	—	—	1/2	—	—	—
Arac. (110/1800)	7/8	—	16/18	17/50	—	14/18
Bromel. (46/1700)	—	—	9/11	—	—	—
Burmann. (22/130)	—	—	—	—	—	—
Butom. (4/13)	—	—	2/2	—	—	1/1
Cann. (1/30–60)	—	—	1/1	1/1	—	—
Centrolep. (6/38)	—	—	—	—	—	—
Commel. (40/575)	1/1	—	9/11	2/2	—	1/1
Corsi. (2/9)	—	—	—	—	—	—
Cyanastr. (1/5)	—	—	1/1	—	—	—
Cyclanth. (11/180)	—	—	2/2	1/1	—	—
Cyper. (70/3700)	—	—	9/15	3/5	—	9/34[1]
Discore. (10/650)	—	—	2/3	1/1	—	—
Eriocaul. (13/1175)	—	—	1/1	—	—	—
Flagellar. (2/6)	—	—	—	1/1	—	—
Geosirid. (1/1)	—	—	—	—	—	—
Gram. (700/8000)	3/3	—	16/16	53/106	4/5	7/9
Haemod. (22/120)	—	—	4/4	—	—	1/1
Hydrochar. (15/100)	1/1	—	5/6	—	—	3/3
Hypox. (5/140)	—	—	2/3	—	—	1/1
Irid. (70/1500)	1/1	1/1	7/7	—	—	4/6
Junc. (8/300)	—	—	2/4	1/2	—	2/5
Juncag. (4/18)	1/6	—	1/2	2/3	—	—
Lemn. (4/25)	—	—	2/2	—	—	1/1
Lili. (220/3500)	2/3	—	33/42	3/5	—	13/13
Lowi. (1/4–5)	—	—	1/1	—	—	—
Marant. (32/350)	1/1	—	2/3	2/2	—	—
Mayac. (1/9–10)	—	—	1/1	—	—	—
Mus. (6/220)	—	—	3/5	2/2	—	—
Naiad. (1/35)	—	—	—	—	—	—
Orch. (650/20000)	—	—	37/45	—	—	3/5
Palm. (236/3400)	—	—	11/13	12/12	—	—
Pandan. (3/880)	—	—	2/2	1/1	—	—
Philydr. (4/5)	1/1[2]	—	—	—	—	—
Ponteder. (7/30)	—	—	3/3	2/2	—	—
Potamoget. (5/105)	—	—	1/2	—	—	1/1
Rapate. (16/80)	—	—	—	—	—	—
Restion. (28/400)	—	—	2/2	—	—	1/1
Scheuchzer. (1/1)	1/1	—	—	1/1	—	—
Spargani. (1/20)	—	—	1/2	—	—	—

[1] Mostly seeds.   [2] Identification doubtful—should be checked.

TABLE 2 (*cont.*)

Families (genera/species)	Gibbs HCN (Test A)			Others		
	+	?	−	+	?	−
Stemon. (3/30)	—	—	1/1	—	—	—
Tacc. (2/30)	—	—	1/1	—	—	—
Thurni. (1/3)	—	—	1/1	—	—	—
Triur. (7/80)	—	—	—	—	—	—
Typh. (1/15)	1/1	—	1/1	—	—	1/1
Vellozi. (3/190)	—	—	1/1	—	—	—
Xanthorr. (8/50)	—	—	2/3	—	—	2/3
Xyrid. (4/270)	—	—	—	—	—	—
Zannichell. (5/20)	—	—	—	—	—	—
Zingib. (49/1500)	—	—	4/4	2/2	—	1/1

TABLE 3. *Occurrence of HCN in angiosperms*

	Gibbs HCN (Test A)				Others			
	+	?	−	No information	+	?	−	No information
Dicotyledons								
Families 292	58	21	143	70	93	8	62	129
Genera 9,400	135	55	1108	—	399	52	694	—
Species 166,000	232	66	1794	—	818	63	1359	—
Monocotyledons								
Families 53	11–12	0	31	10	19	0	13	21
Genera 2,500	23	2	218	—	108	4	71	—
Species 53,000	30	2	284	—	200	5	111	—

(c) Others would seem to have obtained a higher proportion of positive results than I have. There are several things that may qualify this. In the first place, as pointed out above, there is a tendency to record positive but not negative results. This is true also of records of substances other than HCN. In the second place the positive lists of others are swollen by records from legumes and grasses—plants of economic importance—which I have studied only to a very limited extent. In the third place—and Hegnauer is in agreement with me on this—a significant proportion of the positive records in the literature are of doubtful value because of faulty techniques. In the fourth place the records of others almost certainly include the results of *repeated* tests upon plants which may have HCN only at certain times, or under certain conditions, or in certain organs. This is probably only a minor factor.

(*d*) Even though large numbers of tests for HCN have been made, the coverage is still woefully poor. What do we know, for example, of the *Balanophoraceae* (18/100), of the *Connaraceae* (24/350), of the *Dipterocarpaceae* (22/400, where I have one negative record and others one positive one), or of the *Hippocrateaceae* (18/300, where I have one negative record)? I have no information at all, from my own tests and those of others, for 65 families of dicotyledons and 8 of monocotyledons!

(*e*) Despite these difficulties we *do* know enough about the distribution of HCN to use it tentatively when considering taxonomic problems. This will be clear, I hope, in the treatments of individual families and other groups.

5. Juglone Tests A–C (see also *Quinones* and *Coumarins*)

Early in the present series of investigations we became interested in the relationships of the *Juglandaceae*.

The occurrence of *juglone*, a *naphthoquinone*, in that family was supposed to be indicated by the following test, which we have designated *Juglone Test A*:

> A little (1–2 gm.) of finely chopped fresh plant material (often bark, but leaves, roots, etc. may also be tested) is steeped with occasional shaking in a few ml. of chloroform for several hours. The chloroform extract is filtered off, evaporated just to dryness over a water-bath, and the residue is taken up in a few ml. of ether. An equal volume of dilute ammonia (1 vol. conc. ammonia: 9 vols. water) is added and the mixture shaken gently. An immediate *purple colour* in the ammonia layer is considered to be a positive reaction for *juglone*. Actually it may result, too, from the presence of some other *naphthoquinones*. No purple, or the appearance of other colours than purple in the ammonia layer, is considered to be a negative reaction for *juglone*. *Lawsone*, another *naphthoquinone*, gives an *orange* reaction.

Juglone Test B

We noted that while some plants give no colour in the ammonia layer in Juglone Test A, others give a *strong yellow colour*. This may be due to flavonoid substances. The colour is recorded. In testing an extract from the bark of *Myrica cerifera*, which had given a negative reaction in Juglone Test A, we noticed that a deep *bluish-green colour* slowly developed from above down, as if something were slowly diffusing from the ether layer and reacting with the ammonia. The colour was relatively stable, remaining unchanged for several days. Further tests showed that *Myrica pensylvanica* also gives a blue-green colour, and we wondered if all members of the *Myricaceae* would behave in the same way. When *Comptonia* was tested, however, we failed to get the colour. See, however, notes under *Betulaceae, Fagaceae, Garryaceae*.

We now leave for some days all tubes in which a negative Juglone Test A has been obtained. Any colours given immediately or developing later are recorded as *Juglone Test B* (though we are not, of course, testing in this way for juglone).

Juglone Test C

While carrying out *Juglone Test A* we have noted in many cases *fluorescence* in the ammonia layer. This was first observed in testing bark of *Brunfelsia undulata*. Such fluorescence is probably due to *aesculin* or similar *coumarins*. Even where no fluorescence is visible in daylight a strong fluorescence may be seen in ultra-violet light. We now regularly look for such fluorescence, using long-wave ultra-violet light (L.W. UVL), and record it for convenience as *Juglone Test C*, though again we are not recording anything concerned with *juglone*.

Quite by chance we compared the fluorescence under L.W. UVL with that under short-wave UVL. It is clear that the long-wave light is the one that should be used. Little fluorescence is visible with the short-wave lamp.

6. Leucoanthocyanin Test A (L.A. (Test A))

Some years ago Bate-Smith showed the author a simple test for *leucoanthocyanins* which is carried out by heating fresh plant material in 2N-hydrochloric acid.

The development of a red colour which will pass into isoamyl alcohol is a positive reaction. In this test *anthocyanidins* are formed from the *leucoanthocyanins* (p. 554). Bate-Smith pointed out that the distribution of *leucoanthocyanins* is closely bound up with taxonomy, so we enthusiastically adopted his test and dubbed it for our purposes *Leucoanthocyanin Test A (L.A. (Test A))*. We carry it out as follows:

Glass-stoppered test-tubes (*ca.* 160 × 16 mm.) are marked at 5 ml. and 10 ml. levels. About 0·5 gm. of finely chopped fresh plant material (usually leaves) is placed in a tube, covered with 5 ml. of approx. 2N-hydrochloric acid, and the tube is placed in a boiling water-bath for 20 minutes. It is then cooled, 5 ml. of isoamyl alcohol are added, and then shaken. On separation of the layers the upper (isoamyl) layer may be *red* (usually near 'carmine' of plate 1 in Ridgway)—a *positive* reaction—or some other colour (usually not far from 'olive yellow' of plate xxx in Ridgway)—a *negative* reaction.

With very few exceptions our results have paralleled those of Bate-Smith as recorded in the literature. He found that in some cases a darkening of the mixture occurred during heating which made this test of doubtful or no value for *leucoanthocyanins*. We find that such darkening is almost invariably associated with the presence of *aucubin-type glycosides* (q.v.) in the plant material, and this reaction is a very useful indicator for this group of compounds. See also *Ehrlich Test A*.

We have noted above that the *HCl/Methanol Test* (which is carried out on shavings of *sapwood*) is very frequently correlated with a positive *Leucoanthocyanin Test A* (which is usually carried out on *leaf* material). This leads us to suppose that we may be testing for *leucoanthocyanins* in both cases. This is not necessarily invalidated by the few exceptions that we have found, since it is quite possible to have *leucoanthocyanins* in the leaves but not in the wood of a given plant, or *vice versa*.

We shall see that there is reason also to believe that the *magenta* colour obtained in many cases when carrying our *Ehrlich Test A* (below) is due to the presence of *leucoanthocyanins*; as may be, too, the *red* colour developing in *Syringin Test A* (below). We seem to have here again a useful overlapping of our tests.

7. Syringin Test A

The glycoside *syringin* (p. 119) seems to have been detected in relatively few plants. It is more or less general in the *Oleaceae*, and is said to occur also in *Caprifoliaceae, Leguminosae* (very rarely), and *Loranthaceae*. Tunmann (1931) says that when fresh sections of plant material are mounted in 50% aqueous sulphuric acid the development of a *blue colour* indicates the presence of *syringin*. We have adopted this test, calling it *Syringin Test A*, and we carry it out as follows:

> Freshly hand-cut sections (usually of stem material) are mounted in a drop or two of aqueous sulphuric acid (1 pt. of conc. acid: 1 pt. of water) and examined under the microscope. A *positive reaction* is recorded when a clear *bluish colour* develops in wood and/or bast-fibres. A *doubtfully positive* reaction is noted if the lignified tissues become *green*. A *negative* reaction is one in which wood and fibres are *yellow* (or yellow and partially *red*, see below).

A blue colour does not, of course, prove beyond doubt that *syringin* is present, since other substances might react similarly, but we know of none that do, and one of my students has detected syringin chromatographically in material giving a positive *Syringin Test A* (below).

Families in which we have obtained positive results include:

Oleaceae many.

Staphyleaceae Staphylea (3 spp.), *Turpinia* (1): the only members available to us so far.

Crossosomataceae 2 spp. of *Crossosoma*, the only genus. Elizabeth Shaw, one of my students, has detected *syringin* chromatographically in *Crossosoma californicum* (unpublished).

An interesting observation is that of the frequent development of a *red colour* in lignified tissues. This is closely correlated with positive reactions with the *HCl/Methanol* reagent (above), and is an example of the useful overlapping of some of our tests. In this case we can do a bit of 'extrapolation', arguing as follows: Many plants are not sufficiently woody for us to carry out an *HCl/Methanol Test*, or only young material of a plant that *does* become woody is available to us. If sections of such material when mounted in sulphuric acid develop a *red colour* in the small amount of lignified tissue present we may argue with a fair degree of safety that they 'would' give a positive HCl/Methanol reaction if they were sufficiently woody!

Another interesting observation is that some plant material subjected to this test may *darken* or develop a *pink* to *purple* colour, particularly in the cortex. We have found that this is often (always?) correlated with the presence of *aucubin* or related substances, and it points to the desirability of carrying out an *Ehrlich Test* (below).

Finally, it should be noted that we always mount 'control' sections in water for comparison with the treated material. We routinely check these control sections for presence or absence of *raphides* (above).

8. The Ehrlich Test

It was, I believe, my former student and colleague, G. H. N. Towers, who introduced me to the *Ehrlich reagent*. I have modified but slightly the test as shown to me and carry it out as follows:

A small amount (0·1 gm. or so) of freshly chopped plant material (usually leaves) is dropped into 1–2 ml. of boiling 50% aqueous ethanol and the mixture is heated in a water-bath until only a few drops of liquid remain.

Three drops of liquid are transferred on a glass rod to a marked 10 cm. filter-paper and the 3 spots are built up by further additions as evaporation proceeds. The filter-paper is then hung in a current of air until the spots are quite dry. Usually they are almost colourless: if not the colours are noted.

To spot 1 ('Ehrlich') is added one drop of the complete Ehrlich reagent (*p*-dimethylaminobenzaldehyde 1 gm.; conc. HCl 5 ml.; 95% ethanol 200 ml.).

To spot 2 ('control') is added one drop of acid alcohol (conc. HCl 5 ml.; 95% ethanol 200 ml.).

To spot 3 ('NH₃') no addition is made at this stage. Again the filter-paper is allowed to dry and any changes in colour are recorded under 'Ehrlich, cold'. The paper is now placed in an oven at 100°C for 1 minute and any changes are recorded under 'Ehrlich, hot'.

Finally a drop of *dilute ammonia* is added to spot 3 and the colour is noted.

The results obtained from this test may be summarized as follows:

Spot 1 ('Ehrlich'), cold: a bright *blue spot* is considered to be positive and indicates the presence of *aucubin* or of similar substances. A *grey* or *brown* spot may also indicate aucubin-like substances. A *magenta* spot is given (almost?) without exception by plant materials that give a positive (red) colour in *L.A.* (*Test A*) for *leucoanthocyanins*. Even if aucubin-like substances are present one can usually note this reaction, the spot being purplish with a bluey halo.

Spot 2 ('control'), cold: usually little change is noted.

Spot 1 ('Ehrlich'), hot: sometimes a *blue spot* already noted in the cold darkens somewhat. If a *magenta* colour has appeared in the cold it usually darkens.

Spot 2 ('control'), hot: if a magenta colour develops in Spot 1, then Spot 2 is usually *orange-brown*.

Spot 3 ('NH₃') may show little colour; may be *bright yellow* (flavonoids?); rarely *orange* or *orange-red* (could this indicate aurones?) see *Nuytsia floribunda, Elaeocarpus*; very rarely *green*: see *Sobralia lindleyana*.

9. The Aurone Test A (NH₃)

It has long been known that some yellow flowers if exposed to *ammonia* become *orange-red* to *red*. This generally (always?) indicates the presence of *aurone(s)*. I carry out this very simple test as follows:

A few ml. of dilute aqueous ammonia are placed in a glass-stoppered test-tube. A loose plug of tissue paper or cotton-wool is wedged just above the liquid. A yellow flower (or part of a flower) is dropped on to the plug and the tube is stoppered.

Any colour changes as the ammonia vapour penetrates the tissues of the flower are noted.

A *negative* result is indicated when no trace of red or orange-red develops (though the yellow colour may deepen).

A *doubtful* result is recorded when reddish-brown to brown coloration develops slowly.

A *positive* result is recorded when an unmistakable orange-red or red colour develops quickly.

A partial list of results from this test follows (numbers in brackets indicate numbers of species tested):

(*a*) Negative

Nyctagin. Mirabilis (1); *Aizo. Aridaria* (1), *Carpanthea* (1), *Rhombophyllum* (2).

Ranuncul. several; *Berberid. Berberis* (2).

Dilleni. Hibbertia (3), *Wormia* (1); *Guttif. Hypericum* (4, but see under 'doubtful').

Papaver. (several, but see under 'doubtful'); *Capparid. Cleome* (1); *Crucif.* several.

Crassul. Greenovia (1), *Sedum* (1); *Pittospor. Billardiera* (2); *Ros. Fragaria, Kerria, Potentilla* (some, see 'doubtful' list); *Legum.* (many, but see 'doubtful' list).

Limnanth. Limnanthes (1); *Oxalid. Oxalis* (1); *Tropaeol. Tropaeolum* (1); *Zygophyll. Tribulus* (1); *Lin. Linum* (1), *Reinwardtia* (1); *Euphorbi. Euphorbia* (1), *Dalechampia* (1).

Rut. Ruta (1); *Cneor. Cneorum* (1); *Malpighi. Galphimia* (1), see also 'doubtful' list.

Balsamin. Impatiens (2).

Tili. Tilia (1); *Malv. Althaea* (1), *Gossypium* (1), *Pavonia* (1); *Sterculi. Hermannia* (1), *Waltheria* (1).

Viol. Viola (2); *Turner. Turnera* (1); *Cist. Helianthemum* (1), see also 'doubtful' list; *Loas. Cajophora* (1), *Mentzelia* (2); *Begoni. Begonia* (1).

Cucurbit. several.

Lythr. Nesaea (1); *Onagr. Kneiffia* (1), *Oenothera* (4).

Umbell. Foeniculum (1), *Pastinaca* (1).

Primul. Lysimachia (2), *Primula* (2).

Ole. Forsythia (1).

Gentian. Chlora (1), but the stamens turned red!, *Lisianthus* (1); *Apocyn. Allamanda* (1); *Asclepiad. Asclepias* (1); *Rubi. Galium* (1), *Ixora* (1).

Boragin. Cerinthe (1), *Lithospermum* (1); *Verben. Lantana* (1); *Labi.* (several, but see 'doubtful' list); *Solan. Atropa* (1), *Hyoscyamus* (1), *Lycopersicum* (1), *Nicotiana* (2), *Solanum* (1), *Streptosolen* (1); *Buddlej. Buddleja* (1); *Scrophulari.* (several, but see also 'positive' list); *Bignoni. Tabebuia* (1), *Tecoma* (1); *Acanth.* several; *Gesneri. Besleria* (1), *Gesneria* (1); *Orobanch. Orobanche* (1).

Dipsac. Cephalaria (1).
Goodeni. Goodenia (1), *Velleia* (1); *Comp. Chrysanthemum* (1), *Helianthus*, but see also 'doubtful' list, *Tagetes* (1), etc., but see also 'positive' list.
Lili. Alstroemeria (1), *Asphodeline* (1), *Erythronium* (1), *Tulipa* (1), *Uvularia* (2); *Amaryllid. Clivia* (1); *Irid. Crocus* (1), *Freesia* (1).
Bromeli. Vriesia (1).
Orchid. Calanthe (1), *Cypripedium* (1), *Oncidium* (1).
(*b*) Doubtful
Guttiferae Hypericum (1).
Papaver. Meconopsis (1), *Papaver* (1).
Ros. Agrimonia (1), *Geum* (2), *Potentilla* (6); *Legum. Lotus* (1).
Malpighi. Stigmaphyllon (1).
Cist. Helianthemum (2 or 3).
Labi. Scutellaria (1); *Scrophulari. Linaria* (2).
Comp. Helianthus (1).
Lili. Aloe (1).
(*c*) Positive
Scrophulari. Antirrhinum (1), *Calceolaria* (2 ?), *Linaria* (2).
Comp. Bidens (2), *Coreopsis* (6), *Wedelia* (1), etc. (table 11).

10. The Mäule Test

In 1900 Mäule treated wood sections with dilute aqueous *potassium permanganate*, then (after washing) with dilute *hydrochloric acid*, and finally (after washing once more) with *ammonia*. He observed a rose-red colour (a positive reaction) in some cases, but not (a negative reaction) in others. Later workers found that in general lignified tissues of angiosperms are positive while those of gymnosperms are negative to this test.

I have adopted the Mäule test and have used it on a very large number of specimens. It is carried out by me as follows:

Hand sections (or sometimes sections cut about 45 mμ thick on a sliding microtome) of preferably fresh stem-material are soaked in freshly prepared 1% aqueous potassium permanganate for about 20 minutes. They are rinsed and placed in dilute (*ca.* 20%) aqueous hydrochloric acid for 10 minutes. They are rinsed, mounted in a drop or two of dilute aqueous ammonia, and observed under the microscope.

A *positive* reaction is the almost immediate development in lignified tissues (wood, bast fibres, sub-epidermal fibres, even stomata in a few cases) of a *bright rose-red* colour.

A *negative* reaction is the development of a *brownish*, rather indeterminate colour.

Although used by many workers, some of whom found that angiosperms in general, *Podocarpus* (a gymnosperm), and a few other non-angiospermous plants give positive reactions, the chemistry of the test was for long imperfectly known. It obviously involved a chlorination of the lignins (treatment with chlorine instead of permanganate followed by hydrochloric acid can be employed). In the early 1940s, however, Hibbert and his students were obtaining *vanillin* (fig. 143) and *syringaldehyde* (fig. 143) from lignins subjected to alkaline oxidation. When Hibbert told the present writer that he obtained both *syringaldehyde* and *vanillin* from the wood of maple, but *vanillin* only from spruce, it occurred to him that here might be the 'explanation' of the Mäule reaction—that only lignins yielding *syringaldehyde* would give the rose-red colour. This proved to be the case (Creighton, Gibbs, and Hibbert, 1944; Towers and Gibbs, 1953; Gibbs, 1958).

My 1958 paper lists results obtained up to that time. The following notes supplement that paper.

Dicotyledons (292 families)

Positive reaction, 223 families.

Negative or doubtful reaction, 8 families (*Podostem.*, *Limnanth.*?, *Elatin.*?, *Trap.*, *Hippurid.*, *Lenno.* (poor herbarium material), *Callitrich.*, *Adox.*). It will be noted that these are mostly lightly lignified plants. I am sure that most if not all of them *do* produce some *syringaldehyde*.

No information, 61 families, many of them tiny splinter families which I am prepared to bet will be found to yield *syringaldehyde*.

Didymel.

Rhoiptele.

Dipentodont., *Misodendr.*

Medusandr.

Gyrostemon., *Achatocarp.*, *Mollugin.*, *Dysphani.*

Himantandr., *Eupomati.*, *Trimeni.*, *Amborell.*, *Gomorteg.*

Sargentodox., *Ceratophyll.*

Lactorid.

Hydnor.

Eucryphi., *Medusagyn.*, *Dioncophyll.*, *Strasburgeri.*, *Ancistroclad.*

Cephalot., *Davidsoni.*, *Byblid.*, *Roridul.*, *Neurad.*, *Krameri.*

Hydrostachy.

Daphniphyll.

Akani., *Trigoni.*

Bretschneider., *Aextoxic.*

Pand., *Cardiopterid.*

Sarcolaen., *Scytopetal.*

Geissolomat.
Peridisc., Scyphostegi., Malesherbi., Achari., Sphaerosepal.
Crypteroni., Sonnerati., Olini., Theligon., Cynomori.
Alangi.
Sarcospermat., Lissocarp., Hoplestigmat.
Nolan., Duckeodendr., Henriquezi., Pedali.
Sphenocle., Pentaphragmat., Brunoni.

Monocotyledons (53 families)

Positive reaction, 36 families.

Negative or doubtful reaction, 6 families (*Aponogeton., Hydrocharit.* ?, *Lemn., Mayac.* ?, *Pontederi., Potamogeton.*).

It will be noted that these are largely aquatic plants.

Some, at least, of them *do* yield a little *syringaldehyde*. The Mäule Test is not sufficiently sensitive, it seems, in such cases.

No information, 11 families (*Scheuchzeri., Zannichelli., Najad., Triurid., Geosirid., Burmanni., Corsi., Philydr., Thurni., Rapate., Lowi.*).

Again, I predict that some or all of these will be found to yield positive results.

Most angiospermous woods yield a ratio of syringaldehyde:vanillin of about 3:1. Towers and I got some evidence that primitive angiosperms yield a lower ratio. We found a rough relationship between intensity of the Mäule reaction and the syringaldehyde:vanillin ratio. More work in this field might give interesting results.

It is clear, in conclusion, that essentially all angiosperms are likely to give *positive* Mäule reactions. We had thought that some groups might differ significantly from others in this respect. Our tests have been sufficiently numerous, however, to make it extremely unlikely that such differences will be found.

11. Tannin Test A

I cannot remember with certainty where and when I got news of this simple test, but it was almost certainly in a thesis by Miss Harney on species of *Lotus*. It involves the well-known reaction of tannins and/or tannin-like materials, with iron salts to give purple, blue, greenish, greyish, or brownish colours. I carry it out as follows:

The plant material (usually a fresh, mature leaf) is washed thoroughly.

A small filter-paper (Whatman No. 1) which has been dipped into fresh 2·5% aqueous ferric ammonium citrate is blotted gently and folded around the leaf.

The resulting 'sandwich' is squeezed with rib-nosed pliers, the paper is then opened and compared during the following few minutes with a control in which water rather than ferric ammonium citrate has been employed.

In some cases a green patch (from chlorophyll) is seen, or there may be little or no colour—a negative result.

In other cases a rapid development of a *purplish-blue* colour results.

In yet other cases a *grey* to *brown* colour is seen.

A rough scale is employed: + + +, a very strong reaction; + +, a strong reaction; +, a definite, but weak reaction; - ?, probably negative; -ve, certainly negative. In a few cases other colours may develop. It is by no means certain that all the blues to browns observed are due to *tannins*. It is very probable that these other colours are due to other substances. We record them when observed.

We have found this test, which I have used widely since November 1964, to be a useful one chemotaxonomically. Some families consistently give strongly positive results: others are as consistently negative: while some are 'mixed' in their reactions.

It is, as with other characters used in taxonomy, important to use comparable material. The amount of tannin varies widely in leaves of different ages, or in healthy and diseased specimens.

It is important, too, when comparing our results with those of others, as set out in our tables, to remember that our results are (with rare exceptions) from leaves only. The results of others may include tests on bark (often), roots, and other organs.

12. Saponin Test A (and additional tests)

It has, of course, long been known that *saponins* (and perhaps some other plant constituents) in aqueous solutions give stable foams when such solutions are shaken. The literature is full of references to 'saponins' detected by shaking a plant extract and observing a stable foam, and many of these are without doubt quite reliable.

I hesitated to use the foaming test until I could find a standardized version of it. This I got from a paper by Amarasingham *et al.* (1964) who in turn had got it from Arthur (1954). As finally adopted (November 1964) it is carried out as follows:

A small amount of fresh plant material (almost always leaves) is finely chopped, placed in a small glass-stoppered test-tube marked at 5 ml. and 10 ml., and water is added to the 5 ml. mark.

The contents are then boiled for 1 minute, cooled, shaken vigorously and set aside for 5 minutes.

A stable foam 2 cm. or more in depth is considered to be positive for saponin. A lesser amount of foam remaining after the 5-minute interval is considered to be doubtful, and no foam to be negative for saponin.

In comparing our results with those of others (as recorded in our tables) it must be remembered that theirs may stem from haemolysis tests and/or isolation of saponins, and that they may have used bark, roots, seeds, etc. as raw material.

It seemed to be wasteful to discard the tubes after observation so I have often added dilute ammonia (1 : 10 conc. ammonia : water) to the 10 ml. mark and observed any changes in colour and/or odour during 2 or 3 days (with occasional shaking while exposed to the air). I list this as 'Saponin Test B (NH₃)' though it is not actually a further test for saponin.

Results are recorded as follows:

No change in colour, 'o'.
A deep yellow colour at once, 'flavonoids?'.
A slight darkening during 2–3 days ('yellow ochre' to 'ochraceous orange', of plate xv in Ridgway), '1'.
A deeper colour ('tawny' to 'hazel' of plate xiv), '2'.
A yet deeper colour (about 'liver brown' of plate xiv), '3'.
A still deeper colour (deeper than 'liver brown'), '4'.

Occasionally the development of a foul odour is recorded. The tubes are also examined (in recent tests) under l.w. uvl, and *fluorescence* or lack of it is recorded. This may reveal the presence or absence of *coumarins* (compare the *Juglone Tests*).

We have found a close but not absolute correlation with positive tests for *tannins*. The test is chemotaxonomically useful. Members of the **Tubiflorae**, for example, tend to give o or more rarely 1 or 2 colours. Members of the *Proteaceae* when tested have all given 3 or 4 colours. Members of the *Myrtaceae* (rich in tannin) have given 3 or 4 colours.

CONCLUSION

Chemotaxonomy has many critics. Dyed-in-the-wool taxonomists have thought its claims extravagant, and they have had some justification. Many chemists have made rash taxonomic judgments that have shocked botanists, but that is happening less frequently today. The critics have seized upon examples of apparently sporadic occurrence of constituents and of chemical variability and have tended to dismiss comparative chemistry as useless; but that, too, is happening less frequently today. More and more the taxonomists are using chemical characters, as they use morphological and other ones, in their efforts to arrive at a true picture of relationships.

This book has at least one merit, and one not to be belittled. It points out, again and again, the many gaps, some little, some vast, in our knowledge of comparative chemistry.

The filling of all these gaps will never be completed, but with the development of sophisticated, rapid methods for detection of many plant constituents they can be narrowed. It is to be hoped that workers will be found to speed the process. It requires the co-operation of many from outside the laboratory, however, for one of our prime needs is the provision of living material of the hundreds of particularly interesting plants that are presently unavailable to us. I have often said, half-seriously, that if I had the disposal of a large sum of money I should use it to finance expeditions to find, collect, and bring into our botanical gardens these tantalizing species.

There is an urgency about this. Conservationists and others are alarmed at the rapid disappearance of habitats that harbour rare plants and animals. It will soon be too late to close some of the gaps that I mention in the pages above and that follow. Who knows what plants of potential medical or other value, quite apart from their scientific interest, have already gone the way of the dodo?

PLANT CONSTITUENTS

PLANT CONSTITUENTS

INTRODUCTION

Plants produce a bewildering number and kinds of substances, and just as there is no perfect taxonomic system for plants so there is no perfect taxonomy of their constituents. Many able chemists have worked on the problem. They have devised systems of nomenclature, and have tried to enforce some of them, but with only partial success. And nomenclature, of course, is only of limited use.

It has been suggested that the biosynthetic approach is the proper one—as amino-acid sequence determinations have been put forward as the ultimate answer to the problems of the taxonomy and phylogeny of living organisms—but we know little as yet about the biosynthesis of most substances and progress is slow, so we cannot wait for a biosynthetic classification. Then, too, such a classification would have its problems, comparable with those of ordinary taxonomy. How would one classify a substance produced in different organisms by different paths? How would one distinguish with certainty the primitive from the degenerate?

It will be obvious in the section on constituents which follows that I have opted for an alphabetical arrangement of groups of substances, but that in many cases I have had to decide rather arbitrarily the composition of the groups. I have a group of *acetylenic compounds*, for example, but I have put the recently discovered *acetylenic amino-acids* with the other *amino-acids*, and the *acetylenic fatty acids* with the other *fatty acids*, rather than in this group.

Perhaps the short list at the end of this introduction will help.

It will be obvious, too, that my distribution lists are not up to date in many cases. It has been quite impossible to enter recent data which have come to me since the writing of this book was started. In some cases, however, I have been able to include some of the more recent work in the section on orders.

Acetylenic compounds, excluding *acetylenic amino-acids* and *fatty acids*.

Alcohols, including *aliphatic, aromatic*, and *phenolic alcohols*, and *phenolic esters and ethers*; but excluding *phenolic glycosides* (see under glycosides), *terpenoid alcohols* (see under *terpenoids*), and *acetylenic alcohols* (see under *acetylenic compounds*).

Aldehydes, excluding *terpenoid aldehydes* and aldehydes which are *naphthalene* derivatives.

Alkaloids.

Amides, excluding amides of *amino-acids* (q.v.) and *purine bases* (see *alkaloids*).

Amines and some betaines, but see also *alkaloids*.

Amino-acids, peptides, and proteins (including enzymes).

Amino-sugars.

Betalains (betacyanins and betaxanthins).

Carbohydrates, excluding *amino-sugars* (above).

Carboxylic acids, excluding *amino-acids* (above) and obviously *terpenoid acids*.

Coumarins, including *furo-*, *chromano-*, and *benzo-coumarins*, and *isocoumarins*.

Cyclitols, including *quinic* and *shikimic* acids.

Depsides and depsidones.

α,ω-Diphenyl-alkanes.

Elements.

Fats and fatty acids.

Flavonoids.

Furan derivatives.

Glycosides, including *aucubin-type*, *cyanogenic* and *phenolic glycosides*; *glycolipids*; and *indoxyl glycosides*. Excluding *alkaloidal, anthraquinone, cardiac, coumarin, diterpenoid, flavonoid*, and *isothiocyanate glycosides*; and *saponins*.

Gums, mucilages, and resins.

Hydrocarbons, excluding *acetylenic* members, *terpenoid hydrocarbons*, and *naphthalene derivatives*.

Irritant plants, placed here for convenience, including stinging plants, those causing dermatitis, and the irritant plants of the *Anacardiaceae, Proteaceae*, etc.

Ketones, excluding *monoterpenoid* and *acetylenic ketones*, *keto-sugars* and *fatty acids*, *furan derivatives*, *chalcones* and other *flavonoids*, and the *quinones*.

Lactones, excluding α-*pyrones*, *alkaloids* which are lactones, *sesquiterpene lactones*, etc.

Lignans.

Lignins.

Melanins.

Naphthalene and some of its derivatives, excluding *naphthaquinones* and some *sesquiterpenes*.

Pyrones, excluding *coumarins, isocoumarins, furocoumarins*, etc. See also *flavonoids*.

Quinones.

Steroids, excluding *steroidal alkaloids*.

Sulfur compounds, excluding sulfur-containing *amino-acids, coenzymes, vitamins* and *acetylenic compounds.*
Tannins.
Terpenoids.
Waxes.

ACETYLENIC COMPOUNDS

GENERAL

Our knowledge of acetylenic compounds occurring in plants has increased at an astonishing speed. Johnson (1965) says: 'In 1948, a review of acetylenic acids and derivatives could list only three or four naturally occurring compounds; today, several hundred are known...The simplest polyacetylenic compounds are those derived from fungi and micro-organisms. Most of the group belong to the C_9 or C_{10} series, with a small number of C_8 compounds and a few other structures longer than C_{10}.'

Many acetylenes are elaborated by higher plants, and these are of considerable taxonomic interest. We are indebted to Bohlmann and his colleagues, who have published more than 150 papers on 'Polyacetylenverbindungen' to date, and to Sørensen and his colleagues, for much of our information. We shall not discuss in detail here the chemotaxonomy of these substances, but one or two points may be noted.

(*a*) The *Compositae* are remarkably rich in acetylenes, as the following lists show. They seem to be in most (all?) tribes of the *Asteroideae* (*Tubuliflorae*) but to be very rare in the *Cichorioideae* (*Liguliflorae*).

(*b*) The *Umbelliferae* have many acetylenes; the *Araliaceae* have some. In view of this it would be of great interest to know if they occur in the other families—*Cornaceae, Alangiaceae, Garryaceae, Nyssaceae* and *Davidiaceae*—that are associated with them by so many botanists as an order **Apiales (Umbellales, Umbelliflorae).**

(*c*) The recent discovery by Sung, Fowden, Millington and Sheppard (1969) of three *acetylenic amino-acids* in the seeds of *Euphoria* (*Sapindaceae*) interestingly extends our knowledge of acetylenes. We have included these acids with the other *amino-acids.*

(*d*) The discovery by Bohlmann *et al.* (1968) of acetylenes in *Pittosporum buchanani* raises interesting speculations.

(*e*) The *acetylenic fatty acids* have distributions of chemotaxonomic importance. We discuss this elsewhere (p. 1701).

The Biogenesis of Natural Acetylenes

This is the title of a recent review by Bu'lock (in Swain, 1966), who says that he deals with the biogenic aspect 'in the belief that an under-standing of biosynthetic mechanisms is crucial to our understanding of natural products in general and of chemotaxonomy in particular'.

While little is yet established beyond all doubt it seems that most natural *acetylenes* can be derived by reduction from *suitably unsaturated carboxylic acids*. Thus *petroselinic* and *tariric*, *oleic* and *stearolic*, and *linoleic* and *crepenynic* acids respectively 'should' be biogenetically related (fig. 1).

Of these pairs *petroselinic acid* has been found in *Picrasma* and *tariric acid* in *Picramnia* spp., members of the *Simaroubaceae*. They have not (?) been found together. It is known that *oleic acid, stearolic acid* (and other related acetylenes) *do* occur together in the *Santalaceae*. Interestingly it seems that the usual conversion of *oleic acid* to *linoleic acid* is lacking in this family. The third pair, *linoleic* and *crepenynic acids*, also are known to occur together.

Some acetylenic substances are *epoxides*, but epoxides in general are supposed to arise as in fig. 1*a* and are not, therefore, confined to plants which produce acetylenes.

Cyclopropenes might arise from acetylenes and the latter might, therefore, be looked for in the **Malvales**. Actually *sterculynic acid* (fig. 1) which *does* occur in the **Malvales**, is both a *cyclopropene* and (still) an *acetylene*!

Thiophenes, on the other hand, are supposed to arise as in fig. 1*b* and 'should' occur, if this be so, *only* in acetylene-producing plants. This assumes that they can arise by but a single route. If the parent acetylene had only two triple bonds the resulting *thiophene* would no longer be an acetylene, and there *are* some such *thiophenes* (p. 766).

Classification

I do not have sufficient knowledge of acetylenes to classify them from a chemotaxonomic viewpoint. There are so many of them, however, that I have tried to break them down into more manageable groups. I have come up with the following admittedly imperfect arrangement:

I. 'Straight-chain' or 'ordinary' acetylenes—the largest group, with about 150 members.

II. Thiophene derivatives—with about 45 members.

III. Other sulfur-containing acetylenes—with 8 members.

IV. Acetylenes with one or more phenyl groups—with about 25 members.

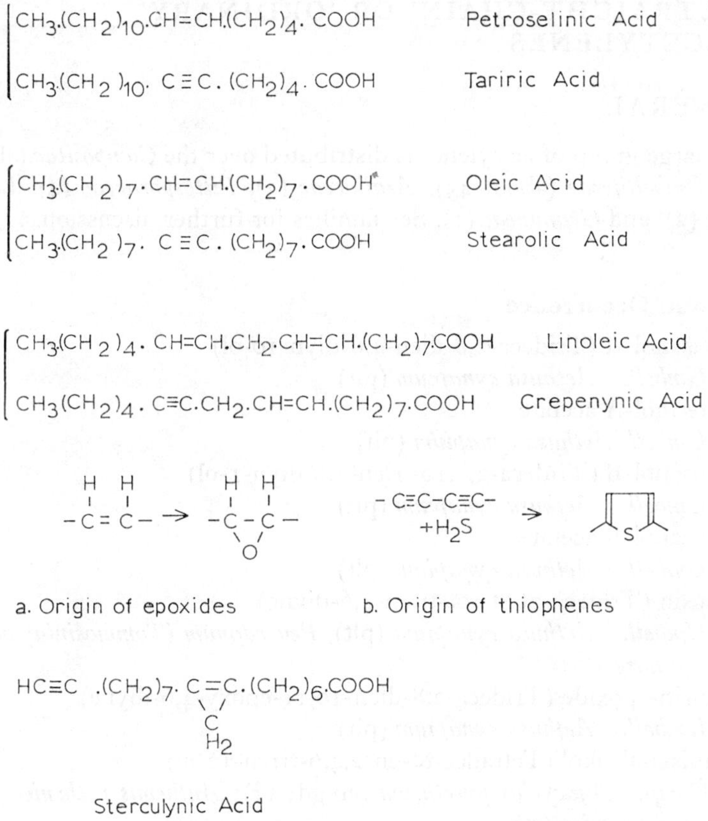

$CH_3.(CH_2)_{10}.CH=CH.(CH_2)_4. COOH$ Petroselinic Acid

$CH_3.(CH_2)_{10}. C\equiv C.(CH_2)_4. COOH$ Tariric Acid

$CH_3.(CH_2)_7.CH=CH.(CH_2)_7.COOH$ Oleic Acid

$CH_3.(CH_2)_7. C\equiv C.(CH_2)_7.COOH$ Stearolic Acid

$CH_3.(CH_2)_4. CH=CH.CH_2.CH=CH.(CH_2)_7COOH$ Linoleic Acid

$CH_3(CH_2)_4. C\equiv C.CH_2.CH=CH.(CH_2)_7.COOH$ Crepenynic Acid

a. Origin of epoxides   b. Origin of thiophenes

$HC\equiv C.(CH_2)_7. C=C.(CH_2)_6.COOH$

Sterculynic Acid

Fig. 1. The biogenesis of natural acetylenes.

V. Acetylenes with furyl groups—with about a dozen members.

VI. Acetylenes with pyran rings—with about half a dozen members.

VII. Acetylenes containing nitrogen—with about half a dozen members.

VIII. Other acetylenes—including *enol-ether spiroketals* (many) and a single *isocoumarin*.

Names

I have used some common names that occur frequently in the literature. The more scientific names have given me great trouble. Different authors use different systems and are by no means consistent. I have tried to be consistent, but some of my names are probably not acceptable to chemists.

I 'STRAIGHT-CHAIN' OR 'ORDINARY' ACETYLENES

GENERAL

This large group of acetylenes is distributed over the *Compositae* (about 95), *Umbelliferae* (about 45), *Araliaceae* (3), *Pittosporaceae* (4), *Lauraceae* (2), and *Gramineae* (1). See families for further discussion.

List and Occurrence

Aethusanol-A (Trideca-2,8-dien-4,6-diyn-10-ol)
  Umbell.   Aethusa cynapium (plt)
Aethusanol-A acetate
  Umbell.   Aethusa cynapium (plt)
Aethusanol-B (Trideca-2,8,10-trien-4,6-diyn-1-ol)
  Umbell.   Aethusa cynapium (plt)
Aethusanol-B acetate
  Umbell.   Aethusa cynapium (plt)
Aethusin (Trideca-2t,8t,10t-trien-4,6-diyne)
  Umbell.   Aethusa cynapium (plt), *Peucedanum* (*Tommasinia*) *verticillare*
Aethusin-epoxide (Trideca-2,8-dien-10,11-epoxy-4,6-diyne)
  Umbell.   Aethusa cynapium (plt)
Artemisia-alcohol (Tetradec-8t-en-2,4,6-triyn-12-ol)
  Comp.   Anacyclus pyrethrum (ab.gd; t?); *Anthemis ruthenica* (rt), *saguramica* (rt)
Artemisia-ketone (Tetradec-8t-en-2,4,6-triyn-12-one)
  Comp.   Anacyclus pyrethrum (ab.gd), *radiatus*; *Anthemis ruthenica* (rt), *saguramica* (rt); *Artemisia vulgaris* (rt); *Cotula coronopifolia* (rt)
Cicutol (Heptadeca-8,10,12-trien-4,6-diyn-1-ol)
  Umbell.   Cicuta victorinii, virosa
Cicutoxin (Heptadeca-8t,10t,12t-trien-4,6-diyn-1,14-diol;
  $CH_3CH_2CH_2CHOH.(CH{=}CH)_3(C{\equiv}C)_2CH_2CH_2.CH_2OH)$
  Umbell.   Cicuta victorinii, virosa
Cota-epoxide (Trideca-10,12-dien-8,9-epoxy-2,4,6-triyne)
  Comp.   Artemisia cota (rt)
Deca-2,6,8-trien-4-yn-1-al
  Comp.   Grindelia robusta, squarrosa
Deca-2,6,8-trien-4-yn-1-ol
  Comp.   Grindelia robusta, squarrosa
Deca-2,6,8-trien-4-yn-1-ol acetate
  Comp.   Grindelia robusta, squarrosa

Dec-8t-en-4,6-diyn-1,3-diol
   Comp. *Carthamus coeruleus* (rt)
Dec-8t-en-4,6-diyn-1,3-diol diacetate
   Comp. *Carthamus coeruleus* (rt), *tinctorius* (ab.gd)
Dec-8c-en-4,6-diyn-1-ol acetate
   Comp. *Chrysanthemum maximum* (ab.gd)
Dehydro-falcarinol (Heptadeca-1,9,16-trien-4,6-diyn-3-ol)
   Comp. *Artemisia atrata* (rt)
Dehydro-falcarinolone (Heptadeca-1,9,16-trien-4,6-diyn-8-ol-3-one)
   Comp. *Artemisia crithmifolia* (lvs)
Dehydro-falcarinone (Heptadeca-1,9,16-trien-4,6-diyn-3-one)
   Comp. *Artemisia* (3), *Cotula* (3 or 4), *Eriocephalus* (1), *Galinsoga*
      (1), *Helianthus* (5), *Iva* (1), *Lagascea* (1), *Tithonia* (1), *Tridax* (1)
cis-Dehydro-matricaria ester (Dec-2c-en-4,6,8-triyn-oic acid methyl
   ester)
   Comp. *Achillea* (5 of 10 tested in section *ptarmica*; 5/8 in *mille-*
      folium; 2/7 in *filipendulanae*; 1/4 in *santolinaidae*), *Anthemis* (3),
      Artemisia vulgaris (rt), *Chamaemelum nobile* (rt), *Chrysanthemum*
      serotinum (rt), *Cotula* (2), *Flaveria repanda* (rt)
trans-Dehydro-matricaria ester
   Comp. *Achillea* (1/10 in section *ptarmica*; 8/8 in *millefolium*; 5/7 in
      filipendulanae; 1/4 in *santolinaidae*), *Anacyclus radiatus*, *Anthemis*
      (3), *Artemisia* (l, tr.), *Chamaemelum nobile* (rt), *Chrysanthemum*,
      Cotula (3), *Echinops* (1), *Matricaria* (2)
cis-Dihydro-matricaria acid
   ($CH_3 . CH \overset{c}{=} CH . (C \equiv C)_2 . CH_2 . CH_2 . COOH$) is said to be secreted by
   a soldier beetle which may aggregate on composites (Meinwald *et al.*
   1968). It has not (?) been found in any composite, but its *methyl*
   ester (below) is common
cis-Dihydro-matricaria ester is the *methyl ester* of *cis-dihydro-matricaria*
   acid (above).
   Comp. *Amellus, Cephalophora, Felicia, Matricaria, Solidago*
2,3-Dihydro-oenanthetol (Heptadeca-8,10-dien-4,6-diyn-1-ol (t, t?))
   Umbell. *Oenanthe crocata* (ab.gd; t, t), *Opopanax chironium* (ab.gd)
2,3-Dihydro-oenanthetol acetate
   Umbell. *Oenanthe crocata* (ab.gd), *Opopanax chironium* (ab.gd)
2,3-Dihydro-oenanthotoxin (Heptadeca-8t,10t-dien-4,6-diyn-1,14-diol)
   Umbell. *Oenanthe crocata* (ab.gd, rt)
Dodeca-1,11-dien-3,5,7,9-tetrayne ($CH_2 = CH . (C \equiv C)_4 . CH = CH_2$)
   Comp. *Carthamus, Cnicus, Coreopsis, Silybum*
   Umbell. *Carum carvi, Opopanax chironium* (rt)
Dodec-4-en-6,8,10-triyn-1-ol
   Comp. *Sanvitalia procumbens* (rt)

Falcarin-diol (Heptadeca-1,9c-dien-4,6-diyn-3,8-diol
    Umbell.   Apium graveolens (rt)
Falcarin-dione (Heptadeca-1,9c-dien-4,6-diyn-3,8-dione)
    Umbell.   Carum carvi (rt), *Oenanthe pimpinelloides, Opopanax chironium* (rt), *Sium sisarum*
Falcarinol(Heptadeca-1,9c-dien-4,6-diyn-3-ol; Carotatoxin; Panaxynol) has a most interesting distribution.
    Pittospor.   Pittosporum buchanani (rt)
    Arali.   Panax schinseng
    Umbell.   Daucus carota, Falcaria vulgaris (rt), *Petroselinum sativum* (rt)
Falcarinolone?
Falcarinone (Heptadeca-1,9c-dien-4,6-diyn-3-one; $CH_3.(CH_2)_6.CH= CH.CH_2(C≡C)_2.CO.CH=CH_2$)
    Arali.   Hedera helix
    Umbell.   Apium graveolens (rt), *Carum carvi, Falcaria vulgaris* (rt), *Oenanthe pimpinelloides, Opopanax chironium* (rt), *Petroselinum sativum* (rt), *Sium sisarum*
    Comp.   Galinsoga parviflora
Falcarinone-8-ol
    Umbell.   Apium graveolens (rt)
Heptadeca-2,8-dien,4,6-diyn-1,10-diol
    Umbell.   Opopanax chironium (ab. gd)
Heptadeca-1,8c-dien-11,13-diyne
    Comp.   Chrysanthemum frutescens (rt)
Heptadeca-2t,9c-dien-4,6-diyne
    Umbell.   Oenanthe crocata (rt)
Heptadeca-8t,10t-dien-4,6-diyn-1,14-diol-1-acetate
    Umbell.   Oenanthe crocata (rt)
Heptadeca-2,9-dien-4,6-diyn-1-ol(t,c ?)
    Umbell.   Opopanax chironium (ab.gd)
Heptadeca-1,9t-dien-11,13-diyn-8-ol
    Comp.   Serratula gmelini (rt)
Heptadeca-2t,8t-dien-4,6-diyn-10-ol-1-al
    Umbell.   Oenanthe crocata (rt)
Heptadeca-8t,10t-dien-4,6-diyn-1-ol-14-one
    Umbell.   Oenanthe crocata (rt)
Heptadeca-1,9c-dien-4,6-diyn-8-ol-3-one—is this *falcarinolone* (above)?
    Arali.   Aralia nudicaulis
    Umbell.   Carum carvi, Oenanthe pimpinelloides, Sium sisarum
Heptadeca-2t,8t-dien-4,6-diyn-14-one
    Umbell.   Oenanthe crocata (rt)

Heptadeca-8t,10t-dien-4,6-diyn-14-one
  Umbell. Oenanthe crocata (rt)
Heptadeca-1,15c-dien-8,9-epoxy-11,13-diyn-10-ol
  Comp. Anthemis rudolfiana (rt)
Heptadeca-1,9t-dien-11,13,15-triyne
  Comp. Artemisia
Heptadeca-1,9t-dien-11,13,15-triyn-8-ol
  Comp. Artemisia selengensis (rt)
Heptadeca-2,8,10,16-tetraen-4,6-diyne
  Comp. Artemisia, Centaurea ruthenica and other spp.
Heptadeca-2t,8t,10t,16t-tetraen-4,6-diyn-1-al
  Comp. Carduus collinus, Tridax trilobata (ab.gd; also has 2-*cis*-)
Heptadeca-2,8,10,16-tetraen-4,6-diyn-1-ol
  Comp. Coreopsis gigantea, Isostigma peucedanifolium, Tridax trilobata (ab.gd; 2t,8t,10t,16t)
Heptadeca-1,6t,8t,10t-tetraen-4-yn-3-one
  Umbell. Falcaria vulgaris (rt)
Heptadeca-2t,8t,10t-trien-4,6-diyne
  Umbell. Oenanthe crocata (ab.gd, rt)
Heptadeca-2c,9c,16-trien-4,6-diyne
  Comp. Chrysanthemum frutescens (rt), *maximum* (ab.gd) and other spp.; *Silybum marianum*
Heptadeca-2t,8t,10t-trien-4,6-diyn-1,14-diol-1-acetate
  Umbell. Oenanthe crocata (rt)
Heptadeca-1,8,10-trien-4,6-diyn-3-ol
  Umbell. Opopanax chironium (ab.gd)
Heptadeca-2c,8,10-trien-4,6-diyn-1-ol is the *cis*- isomer of *oenanthetol*.
  Comp. Cotula plumosa (ab.gd)
Heptadeca-2c,9c,16-trien-4,6-diyn-1-ol
  Comp. Anthemis tinctoria var. (rt)
Heptadeca-2,8,16-trien-4,6-diyn-10-ol
  Comp. Anthemis cupaniana (Cousinia hystrix ?) (rts, much), *Jurinea mollis* (rt), *Serratula gmelini* (rt; 2c, 8t), *Silybum marianum* ? (2c, 8c)
Heptadeca-2t,8t,10t-trien-4,6-diyn-14-ol
  Umbell. Oenanthe crocata (rt)
Heptadeca-2t,8t,10t-trien-4,6-diyn-1-ol-14-one
  Umbell. Oenanthe crocata (rt)
Heptadeca-8,10,16-trien-2,4,6-triyne—the 8t,10t form is *centaur.* X3.
  Comp. Artemisia (t, t ?); *Centaurea cyanus, vulgaris* (both have t, t and t, c ?)
Heptadeca-8t,10t,16-trien-2,4,6-triyn-12-ol
  Comp. Artemisia selengensis (rt)

Heptadec-8t-en-4,6-diyn-1,10-diol
  Umbell. Opopanax chironium (ab.gd)
Heptadec-8t-en-4,6-diyn-1,10-diol-1-acetate
  Umbell. Oenanthe crocata (rt)
Heptadec-9c-en-4,6-diyn-1-ol
  Umbell. Oenanthe crocata (rt)
Heptadec-8t-en-4,6-diyn-1-ol-14-one
  Umbell. Oenanthe crocata (rt)
Heptadec-9-en-4,6-diyn-1-ol-3-one
  Umbell. Falcaria vulgaris (rt)
[1(Hept-6-enyl)-deca-2t,8c-dien-4,6-diynyl]-L-rhamnose occurs with other *rhamnosides* in:
  Comp. Jurinea cyanoides (rt), *mollis* (rt); *Serratula gmelini* (rt)
Hexadeca-6,8,12,14-tetraen-10-yn-1-ol
  Comp. Dahlia merckii
Hexadeca-8t,10t,15t-trien-2,4,6-triyne
  Comp. Chrysanthemum
cis-8-Hydroxy-lachnophyllum ester–angelic acid ester
  Comp. Aster novi-belgii
Lachnophyllol (Dec-2-en-4,6-diyn-1-ol)
  Comp. Cotula filicula
Lachnophyllol acetate
  Comp. Cotula filicula
cis-Lachnophyllum ester (Dec-2c-en-4,6-diynoic acid methyl ester)
  Comp. Aster novi-belgii (c or t?), *Lachnophyllum gossypinum* (and many other composites?)
trans-Lachnophyllum ester
  Comp. Bellis perennis
cis, cis-Matricaria ester (Deca-2c,8c-dien-4,6-diynoic acid methyl ester; $CH_3.CH \overset{c}{=} CH.(C \equiv C)_2 . CH \overset{c}{=} CH.COOCH_3$) is the commonest of the many acetylenic compounds of composites?
  Comp. Amellus (1), *Anthemis* (1), *Aster* (3), *Brachycome* (1), *Dimorphotheca* (1), *Erigeron* (1), *Felicia* (3), *Gaillardia* (1), *Grindelia* (2), *Saussurea* (1), *Solidago* (1), *Townsendia* (1), *Tripleurospermum* (*Matricaria* p.p.) (3). It is said to be *absent* from some tribes of the family.
trans, cis-Matricaria ester
  Comp. Amellus, Matricaria
trans, trans-Matricaria ester is said to occur in a polypore and in
  Comp. Bellis perennis
Matricarianal (Deca-2,8-dien-4,6-diyn-1-al)
  Umbell. Aethusa cynapium

Matricarianol (Deca-2t,8t-dien-4,6-diyn-1-ol)

    Comp. *Aster tripolium* (but *not* in 6 other spp.); *Erigeron* (1);
    Grindelia arenicola, stricta (free?, and as ester)

Matricarianol acetate

    Comp. *Grindelia robusta* (rt), *squarrosa* (rt)

2-Methoxy-tridec-12-yne (HC$\equiv$C.(CH$_2$)$_9$.CH(OCH$_3$).CH$_3$)

    Laur. *Litsea odorifera* (prob. present in ess. oil of bk)

2-Methoxy-undec-10-yne (HC$\equiv$C.(CH$_2$)$_7$.CH(OCH$_3$).CH$_3$)

    Laur. *Litsea odorifera* (ess. oil of bk, much; Matthews *et al.*
    1963)

Octadeca-8,10,14,16-tetraen-12-yn-3-one-1-ol acetate

    Comp. *Cosmos sulphureus* (ab.gd)

Oenanthetol (Heptadeca-2t,8t,10t-trien-4,6-diyn-1-ol)

    Umbell. *Oenanthe crocata* (ab.gd, rt), *Opopanax chironium*
    (ab.gd)

Oenanthetol acetate

    Umbell. *Oenanthe crocata* (ab.gd), *Opopanax chironium*
    (ab.gd)

Oenanthetone (Heptadeca-2t,8t,10t-trien-4,6-diyn-14-one)

    Umbell. *Oenanthe crocata* (rt), *Opopanax chironium* (ab.gd)

Oenanthotoxin (Heptadeca-2t,8t,10t-trien-4,6-diyn-1,14-diol)

    Umbell. *Oenanthe crocata* (ab.gd, rt)

16-Oxo-octadeca-9,17-dien-12,14-diyn-1-al

    Umbell. *Pastinaca sativa* (sd-oil)

Pentadeca-2t,9c-dien-4,6-diyne

    Pittospor. *Pittosporum buchanani* (rt)

Pentadeca-2t,8t-dien-4,6-diyn-10-ol

    Umbell. *Oenanthe crocata* (ab.gd, rt)

Pentadeca-9,14-dien-4,6-diyn-3-one-1-ol

    Comp. *Cotula coronopifolia* (rt)

Pentadeca-2,8,10,14-tetraen-4,6-diyne

    Comp. *Cotula bipinnata* (plt)

Pentadeca-1,8,10,14-tetraen-4,6-diyn-3-ol

    Comp. *Cotula coronopifolia* (ab.gd, rt)

Pentadeca-2t,8t,10t-trien-4,6-diyne

    Pittospor. *Pittosporum buchanani* (rt)

    Umbell. *Oenanthe crocata* (ab.gd, rt)

Pentadeca-8,10,14-trien-4,6-diyn-3-ol

    Comp. *Cotula coronopifolia* (ab.gd)

Pentadeca-2t,8t,10t-trien-4,6-diyn-12-ol

    Umbell. *Oenanthe crocata* (rt)

Pentadeca-1,8t,10c-trien-4,6-diyn-3-one

    Pittospor. *Pittosporum buchanani* (rt)

Pontica epoxide (Trideca-8,12-dien-10,11-epoxy-2,4,6-triyne)
   Comp. *Achillea ptarmica* var. and some other spp.; *Artemisia pontica* (rt) and 3 other spp.; *Chrysanthemum* (2); *Cladanthus arabicus*; *Tanacetum vulgare*
Tetradeca-4,6-dien-8,10-diyn-1,12-diol
   Comp. *Cotula coronopifolia* (ab.gd)
Tetradeca-4,6-dien-8,10-diyn-1,12-diol-1-acetate
   Comp. *Cotula coronopifolia* (ab.gd)
Tetradeca-4,6-dien-8,10-diyn-1,12-diol-di-acetate
   Comp. *Cotula coronopifolia* (ab.gd)
Tetradeca-6,12-dien-8,10-diyn-3-ol
   Comp. *Anthemis saguramica* (rt)
Tetradeca-2,12-dien-4,6,8,10-tetrayne
   Gram. *Triticum aestivum* (plt)
Tetradeca-4,6-dien-8,10,12-triyn-1-ol
   Comp. *Anthemis ruthenica* (rt), *Chrysanthemum atratum* (ab.gd)
Tetradeca-4,6-dien-8,10,12-triyn-1-ol-acetate
   Comp. *Tanacetum vulgare* (rt, little)
Tetradeca-2,4,6,12-tetraen-8,10-diynoic acid methyl ester
   Comp. *Sanvitalia procumbens* (rt)
Tetradeca-4,6,10,12-tetraen-8-yn-1-ol-acetate
   Comp. *Cotula coronopifolia* (ab.gd)
Tetradeca-4t,6t,12t-trien-8,10-diyn-1-ol
   Comp. *Cotula coronopifolia*, *Dahlia* (2)
Tetradeca-4,6,12-trien-8,10-diyn-1-ol-acetate
   Comp. *Coreopsis gigantea*; *Cotula coronopifolia*; *Dahlia merckii* (rt), scapigera
Tetradeca-2,10-13-trien-4,6,8-triyn-1-ol-acetate
   Comp. *Carlina*
Tetradec-6t-en-4,5-epoxy-8,10,12-triyn-1-ol
   Comp. *Chrysanthemum serotinum* (ab.gd)
Tetradec-6t-en-8,10,12-triyn-1,5-diol
   Comp. *Centaurea muricata* (ab.gd)
Tetradec-6t-en-8,10,12-triyn-1,5-diol-1-acetate
   Comp. *Centaurea muricata* (ab.gd)
Tetradec-5-en-8,10,12-triyn-1-ol-acetate
   Comp. *Chrysanthemum serotinum* (ab.gd)
Trideca-8t,12-dien-10,11-epoxy-2,4,6-triyne
   Comp. *Chrysanthemum serotinum* (ab.gd, rt)
Trideca-2t,10t-dien-12,13-epoxy-4,6,8-triyne
   Comp. *Carthamus* (3), *Centaurea ruthenica* (lvs; t,t ?)
Trideca-10t,12-dien-2,4,6,8-tetrayne
   Comp. *Rudbeckia* (3)

Trideca-2,12-dien-4,6,8,10-tetrayn-1-al

$(CH_2=CH.(C\equiv C)_4.CH=CH.CHO)$

> *Comp.* *Bidens* (rts of 4), *Cosmos diversifolius* (rt), *Leptosyne calliopsides*

Trideca-2,12-dien-4,6,8,10-tetrayne

$(CH_2=CH.(C\equiv C)_4.CH=CH.CH_3)$ seems to be a common acetylene. Both *cis-* and *trans-* forms occur.

> *Comp.* *Bidens* (5), *Carthamus* (rts of 3, t), *Centaurea* (in 48 spp., but *not* in 3 spp. of section *Centaurium*), *Crupina vulgaris*, *Dahlia merckii*? (rt), *Serratula* (2), and others. Bohlmann (1966) says it is in most of the *Carduinae* tested (*Arctium, Carduus, Cirsium, Cousinia, Galactites, Jurinea, Onopordon, Saussurea, Silybum*)

Trideca-2,12-dien-4,6,8,10-tetrayn-1-ol

> *Comp.* *Bidens* (5), *Cosmos diversifolius* (rt), *Leptosyne calliopsides*

Trideca-2,12-dien-4,6,8,10-tetrayn-1-ol-acetate

> *Comp.* *Bidens* (6), *Coreopsis, Cosmos diversifolius* (rt), *Leptosyne calliopsides*

Trideca-3t,11t-dien-5,7,9-triyn-2-chloro-1-ol

$(CH_3.CH=CH.(C\equiv C)_3.CH=CH.CHCl.CH_2OH)$

> *Comp.* *Carthamus coeruleus* (rt), *tinctorius* (ab.gd); *Centaurea ruthenica* (rt; t,t?); *Dicoma zeyheri* (t,t?)

Trideca-3t,11t-dien-5,7,9-triyn-2-chloro-1-ol-acetate

> *Comp.* *Carthamus* (3), *Centaurea ruthenica* (rt; t,t?), *Dicoma zeyheri* (t,t?)

Trideca-3t,11t-dien-5,7,9-triyn-1,2-diol

> *Comp.* *Carthamus lanatus* (ab.gd), *tinctorius* (ab.gd), *Centaurea ruthenica* (rt; t,t?)

Trideca-3t,11t-dien-5,7,9-triyn-1,2-diol-2-acetate

> *Comp.* *Carthamus lanatus* (ab.gd), *Centaurea ruthenica* (rt; t,t?)

Trideca-3t,11t-dien-5,7,9-triyn-1,2-diol-diacetate

> *Comp.* *Carthamus lanatus* (ab.gd), *Centaurea ruthenica* (rt; t,t?)

Trideca-1,3,5,11-tetraen-7,9-diyne

> *Comp.* *Bidens ferulaefolius* (lvs, st.), *Carthamus coeruleus* (rt), *Coreopsis, Cosmos* (rts of 2, all *-trans*)

Trideca-3,5,11-trien-7,9-diyn-1,2-diol

> *Comp.* *Centaurea ruthenica* (rt)

Trideca-3,5,11-trien-7,9-diyn-1,2-diol-di-acetate

> *Comp.* *Centaurea ruthenica* (rt)

Trideca-2c,10c,12-trien-4,6,8-triyn-1-al

> *Comp.* *Carlina vulgaris* (rt)

Trideca-2t,10t,12-trien-4,6,8-triyn-1-al

> *Comp.* *Cosmos hybridus* (rt), *sulphureus* (rt)

Trideca-2c,10c,12-trien-4,6,8-triyne
   Comp.   Bidens ferulaefolius (lvs, st.; not given as c,c), *Coreopsis*
Trideca-2t,10t-12-trien-4,6,8-triyne
   Comp.   Carthamus (ab.gd pts of 3), *Cosmos* (rts of 2)
Trideca-8t,10t,12-trien-2,4,6,triyne—not all the following are given as
t,t.
      Comp.   Achillea (26 of 29 spp. tested), *Anacyclus* (2), *Anthemis* (3),
      Artemisia, Bidens, Chrysanthemum, Coreopsis, Flaveria, Matricaria
      (*Tripleurospermum*) *oreades* (lvs, st.)
Trideca-2t,10t,12-trien-4,6,8-triyn-1-ol
   Comp.   Cosmos hybridus (rt), *sulphureus* (rt)
Trideca-2t,10c,12-trien-4,6,8-triyn-1-ol-acetate
   Comp.   Carlina
cis- and trans- Tridec-2-en-12,13-epoxy-4,6,8,10-tetrayne
   Comp.   Centaurea deusta (rt)
Tridec-12-en-2,3-epoxy-4,6,8,10-tetrayne
   Comp.   Centaurea deusta (rt)
Tridec-10t-en-12,13-epoxy-2,4,6,8-tetrayne
   Comp.   Carthamus tinctorius (ab.gd, rt), *Centaurea ruthenica* (lvs; t?)
Tridec-12-en-2,4,6,8,10-pentayne $(CH_3.(C \equiv C)_5.CH = CH_2)$ is one
of the chief acetylenes of composites. I have records from:
      Comp.   Achyrachaena (1), *Ambrosia* (3), *Arctium, Arnica* (1),
      Berkheya (1), *Bidens* (2), *Buphthalmum* (3), *Calendula* (1),
      Carduus, Carthamus (1), *Cirsium, Cousinia* (1), *Cynara* (1),
      Echinacea (2), *Flaveria* (1), *Galactites, Guizotia* (1), *Helipterum*
      (1), *Hemizonia* (1), *Jurinea, Layia* (1), *Melampodium* (2), *Ono-*
      pordon, Rudbeckia (1), *Sanvitalia* (1), *Saussurea, Serratula* (4),
      Silybum, Spilanthes (1), *Synedrella* (1), *Xanthium* (1)
Tridec-10t-en-2,4,6,8-tetrayn-12-chloro-13-ol
   Comp.   Carthamus tinctoria (ab.gd)
Tridec-10-en-2,4,6,8-tetrayn-12,13-diol
   Comp.   Centaurea ruthenica (lvs)
Tridec-12,13-epoxy-2,4,6,8,10-pentayne
   Comp.   Centaurea deusta (rt)

II THIOPHENE DERIVATIVES

GENERAL

We have seen, in discussing the biogenesis of acetylenic substances, that
the *thiophenes* appear to arise from compounds with 2 or 4 acetylenic
linkages following each other (fig. 1).

If this is the case we might expect to find both 'straight chain' poly-acetylenes and thiophenes in the same or in closely related plants, and at least 19 of the 30 or so genera listed below are known to have both.

The thiophenes seem to be confined to the *Compositae* and in that great family to the following tribes of the sub-family *Asteroideae* (*Tubuliflorae*):

4. *Inuleae—Buphthalmum, Calocephalus, Tarchonanthus*
5. *Heliantheae—Achyrachaena, Ambrosia, Bidens, Coreopsis, Eclipta, Guizotia, Hemizonia, Layia, Melampodium, Rudbeckia, Spilanthes*
6. *Helenieae—Baeria, Lasthenia, Schkuhria, Tagetes*
7. *Anthemideae—Anacyclus, Anthemis (Chamaemelum), Artemisia, Chrysanthemum, Matricaria (Tripleurospermum), Santolina*
10. *Arctoteae—Berkheya*
11. *Cardueae (Cynareae)—Atractylus, Centaurea, Echinops, Serratula*

A substance having but 2 neighbouring acetylenic linkages would, on giving rise to a *thiophene*, no longer be an *acetylene* (fig. 1). A few *thiophenes*—presumably of this type, and all from members of the *Compositae*—are listed among sulfur compounds, though they would seem to 'belong' here.

List and Occurrence

2-(Acetoxymethyl)-5'-(but-1-yn-3-ene-1)bithienyl-2,2'
    Comp. *Bidens dahlioides* (ab.gd); *Buphthalmum grandiflorum* (ab. gd), *salicifolium* (ab.gd)

2-Acetyl-3-hydroxy-5-prop-1-ynyl-thiophene (fig. 2)
    Comp. *Artemisia aborescens*

2-Acetyl-3-methoxy-5-prop-1-ynyl-thiophene
    Comp. *Artemisia arborescens* (rt)

5-(But-4-chloro-3-hydroxy-1-ynyl-1)-bithienyl-2,2'
    Comp. *Tagetes minuta* (rt)

5-(But-3-en-3-chlor-4-acetoxy-1-ynyl)-bi-thienyl-2,2'
    Comp. *Berkheya adlami* (rt)

5-(But-3-en-1-ynyl-1)-bithienyl-2,2' (fig. 2)
    Comp. *Berkheya adlami* (rt); *Echinops*; *Tagetes erecta, minuta*

2-(But-3-en-1-ynyl-1)-5-(pent-2t-en-4-yn-1-al-5)-thiophene
    Comp. *Baeria chrysostoma, coronaria*; *Coreopsis grandiflora* (rt)

2-(But-3-en-1-ynyl-1)-5-(pent-2t-en-4-yn-1-ol-5)-thiophene
    Comp. *Baeria chrysostoma, coronaria*; *Serratula radiata* (rt; t?)

2-(But-3-en-1-ynyl-1)-5-(pent-2t-en-4-yn-1-ol-acetate-5)-thiophene
    Comp. *Baeria chrysostoma, Serratula radiata* (rt; t?)

2-(But-3-en-1-ynyl-1)-5-(pent-2t-en-4-ynyl-5)-thiophene (fig. 2)
>   Comp.   Baeria (3), Bidens (2), Centaurea (rts of 4; t?), Guizotia
>   oleifera (ab.gd), Lasthenia glaberrima, Serratula radiata (rt; t?)

5-(But-4-ol-1-ynyl-1)-bithienyl-2,2'
>   Comp.   Tagetes minuta (rt)

5-(But-4-ol-1-ynyl-4-acetate-1)-bithienyl-2,2'
Occurrence?

5-(3,4-Diacetoxy-but-1-ynyl-1)-bithienyl-2,2'
>   Comp.   Echinops sphaerocephalus (rt)

5-(3,4-Dihydroxy-but-1-ynyl-1)-bithienyl-2,2'
>   Comp.   Echinops sphaerocephalus (rt)

1-(Furyl-2)-4-(5-acetoxymethyl-thienyl-2)-but-1c-en-3-yne (fig. 2)
>   Comp.   Santolina sp. (rt)

1-(Furyl-2)-4-(thienyl-2)-but-1-en-3-yne
>   Comp.   Santolina pinnata (c, and t)

5-(3-Hydroxy-4-acetoxy-but-1-ynyl)-bithienyl-2,2'
>   Comp.   Echinops sphaerocephalus (rt)

5-(4-Hydroxy-3-acetoxy-but-1-ynyl)-bithienyl-2,2'
>   Comp.   Echinops sphaerocephalus (rt)

5-(4-Hydroxy-but-1-ynyl)-bithienyl-2,2'-acetate
>   Comp.   Tagetes erecta, minuta, patula

5-(Hydroxymethyl)-5'-(but-3-en-1-ynyl-1)-bi-thienyl-2,2'
>   Comp.   Bidens dahlioides (ab.gd); Buphthalmum grandiflorum (ab.
>   gd), salicifolium (ab.gd); Echinops sphaerocephalus (rt)

2-(Methyl acrylate)-5-(prop-1-ynyl-1)-thiophene
>   Comp.   Chrysanthemum

5-(Methyl)-5'-(but-3-en-1-ynyl-1)-bithienyl-2,2'
>   Comp.   Buphthalmum grandiflorum (ab.gd), salicifolium (ab.gd);
>   Rudbeckia amplexicaulis (ab.gd)

2-(Methyl)-5-(methyl-but-α-en-γ-ynoate)-thiophene
>   Comp.   Anacyclus radiatus; Anthemis nobilis (Chamaemelum nobile?)
>   (rt; c and t), vulgaris (t)

2-(Methylpent-α-en-γ-ynoate-δ)-thiophene
>   Comp.   Anthemis fuscata (ab.gd)

2-(Nona-1,7-dien-3,5-diynyl-1)-thiophene
>   Comp.   Atractylus spp.

2-(Nona-3t,5t-dien-7-ol-1-ynyl-1)-thiophene
>   Comp.   Anthemis saguramica (rt)

2-(Nona-3,5-dien-7-one-1-ynyl-1)-thiophene
>   Comp.   Anthemis saguramica (rt; c,t and t,t) Tripleurospermum (c,t
>   or t,t?)

2-(Non-5t-en-7-ol-1-ynyl-1)-thiophene
>   Comp.   Anthemis saguramica (rt)

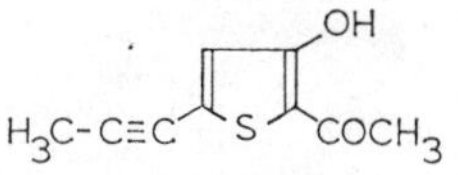

2-Acetyl-3-hydroxy-5--prop-1-ynyl-thiophene

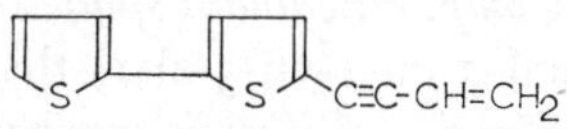

5 (But-3-en-1-ynyl-1-)--bithienyl-2,2'

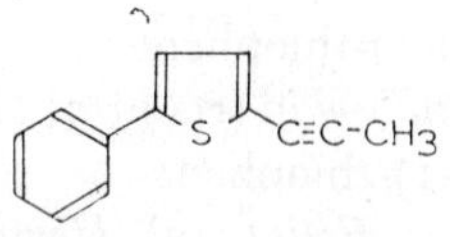

2-(Phenyl)-5(α-propynyl)--thiophene

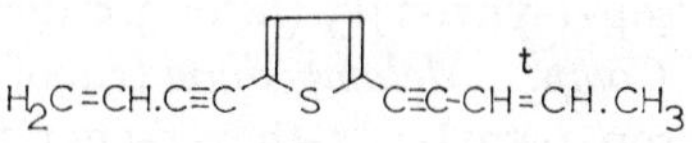

2-(But-3-en-1-ynyl-1-)-5--(pent-2t-en-4-ynyl-5)--thiophene

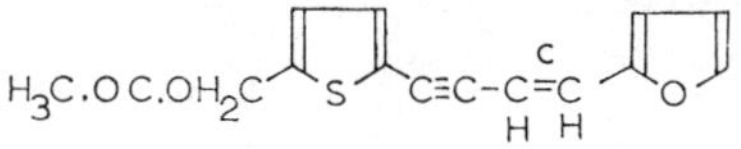

1 (Furyl-2)-4-(5-acetoxymethyl--thienyl-2)-but-1c-en-3-yne

Fig. 2. Some acetylenic derivatives of thiophene.

2(Non-3t-en-7-one-1-ynyl-1)-thiophene
 Comp. Anthemis saguramica (rt), *Matricaria (Tripleurospermum) inodora* (rt)

2-(Non-3-en-1-yn-6-ol-7-one-isovalerate-1)-thiophene
 Comp. Anthemis saguramica (rt)

2-(Non-3-en-1-yn-5-ol-7-one-isovalerate-1)-thiophene
 Comp. Anthemis saguramica (rt)

2-(Octa-3t,5t,7-trien-1-ynyl-1)-thiophene
 Comp. Matricaria (Tripleurospermum) inodora

2-(Penta-1,3-diynyl-1)-5-(4-acetoxy-but-1-ynyl-1)-thiophene
 Comp. Echinops sphaerocephala (rt)

2-(Penta-1,3-diynyl-1)-5-(but-3-en-1-ynyl-1)-thiophene
 Comp. Calocephalus citreus, Echinops sphaerocephalus (rt)

2-(Penta-1,3-diynyl-1)-5-(3-chloro-4-acetoxy-but-1-ynyl-1)-thiophene
 Comp. Echinops sphaerocephalus (rt)

2-(Penta-1,3-diynyl-1)-5-(3-chloro-4-hydroxy-but-1-ynyl-1)-thiophene
 Comp. Echinops sphaerocephalus (rt)

2-(Penta-1,3-diynyl-1)-5-(3,4-diacetoxy-but-1-ynyl-1)-thiophene
 Comp. Echinops sphaerocephalus (rt)

2-(Penta-1,3-diynyl-1)-5-(3,4-dihydroxy-but-1-ynyl-1)-thiophene
    Comp.   *Echinops sphaerocephalus* (rt)
2-(Pent-3-en-1-yn-5-al-1)-thiophene
    Comp.   *Anthemis saguramica*
2-(Phenyl)-5-(α-propynyl)-thiophene (fig. 2)
    Comp.   *Coreopsis grandiflora* (lvs, fl.)
2-(Prop-1-ynyl-1)-5'-(acetylenyl)-bithienyl-2,2'
    Comp.   *Tagetes erecta*
2-(Prop-1-ynyl-1)-5-(hexa-3,5-dien-1-ynyl-1)-thiophene
    Comp.   *Melampodium* (rts of 2; t), *Rudbeckia* (rts of 5; all t ?)
2-(Prop-1-ynyl-1)-5-(hex-5-en-1,3-diynyl-1)-thiophene
    Comp.   *Achyrachaena* (1), *Ambrosia* (3), *Eclipta* (2), *Hemizonia* (1),
        Iva (1), *Layia* (2 ?), *Rudbeckia* (1), *Schkuhria* (2), *Spilanthes* (1 ?),
        Tarchonanthus (1 ?)
2-(Prop-1-ynyl-3-ol-1)-5-(hex-5-en-1,3-diynyl-1)-thiophene
    Comp.   *Rudbeckia triloba* (rt)
2-(Prop-1-ynyl-1)-5'-(vinyl)-bithienyl-2,2'
    Comp.   *Guizotia oleifera*

III OTHER SULFUR-CONTAINING ACETYLENES

GENERAL

These, like the *thiophene derivatives*, seem to be restricted to the *Compositae* and in this case to a few species of *Anthemis* and to *Chrysanthemum segetum*. Is it significant that some other species of *Anthemis* have *thiophenes*, and that the *mercapto-acetylenes* found in *Chrysanthemum* have phenyl groups (p. 103)?

List and Occurrence

Deca-2,4-dien-4-methylmercapto-6,8-diynoic acid methyl ester
    Comp.   *Anthemis tinctoria* var. (rt; c,c and c,t)
Deca-2,6-dien-7-methylmercapto-4,8-diynoic acid methyl ester
    Comp.   *Anthemis cairica* (t,t), *carpatica* (rt; c,t and t,t), *cota* (t,t),
        ruthenica (rt; c,c and t,c), *tenuifolia* (t,t), *tinctoria* var. (rt; c,c)
Deca-2,4-dien-5-methylmercapto-6,8-diynoic acid methyl ester
    Comp.   *Anthemis carpatica* (rt, c,c)
Deca-2,8-dien-9-methylmercapto-4,6-diynoic acid methyl ester
    Comp. *Anthemis arvensis* (c,t), *carpatica* (rt; c,t), *cinerea* (c,t),
        maritima (c,t), *ruthenica* (c,t), *tinctoria* (rt; c,t), *triumfetta* (rt;
        c,t)

Deca-2,4-dien-5-methylsulfone-6,8-diynoic acid methyl ester
   Comp.   Anthemis ruthenica (rt)
Deca-2,4,8-trien-5-methylmercapto-6-ynoic acid methyl ester
   Comp.   Anthemis austriaca (rt; c,c,c and c,t,c)
Deca-2,4,6-trien-5-methylmercapto-8-ynoic acid methyl ester
   Comp.   Anthemis tinctoria var. (rt; c,c,c)
Dodeca-2,10-dien-11-methylmercapto-4,6,8-triynoic acid methyl ester
   $(CH_3 . C(SCH_3)=CH.(C≡C)_3 . CH=CH.COOCH_3)$
   Comp.   Anthemis tinctoria var. (rt; c,c)

IV   ACETYLENES WITH ONE OR MORE PHENYL GROUPS

GENERAL

Acetylenes of this type seem to be confined to the *Compositae* and in that family to a few genera of the tribes *Heliantheae* and *Anthemideae*.

List and Occurrence

7-(*m*-Acetoxyphenyl)-hept-2t-en-4,6-diyn-1-ol acetate
   Comp.   Coreopsis tinctoria cv. (rt)
Capillene (1-Phenyl-hex-2-en-4-yne)
   Comp.   Artemisia capillaris (and another sp. ?)
   Gram.   ?Agropyron (Triticum) repens. Probably *not*, says Sørensen
      (in Swain, 1963)
Capillin (1-Phenyl-hexa-2,4-diyne-1-one)
   *Comp.   Artemisia capillaris, dracunculus; Chrysanthemum frutes-
      cens; Lonas annua* (rt)
Demethyl-frutescine (Methyl-2(penta-2',4'-diynyl-1)-6-methoxy-
   benzoate)
   Comp.   Chrysanthemum frutescens (rt)
Demethyl-frutescinol acetate
   Comp.   Chrysanthemum frutescens (rt)
1,10-Diphenyl-deca-2,4,6,8-tetrayne (fig. 3)
   Comp.   Artemisia dracunculus
Frutescine (Methyl-2-hexa-2',4'-diynyl-6-methoxy-benzoate; fig. 3)
   Comp.   Chrysanthemum frutescens (rt)
Frutescinol acetate
   Comp.   Chrysanthemum frutescens (rt)
Frutescinol lactone
   Comp.   Chrysanthemum frutescens (rt)

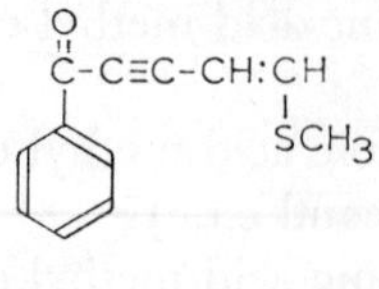

1-Phenyl-pent-4-en-
-2-yn-5-methyl-
mercapto-1-one

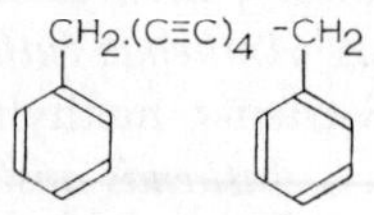

1,10-Diphenyl-deca-
-2,4,6,8-tetrayne

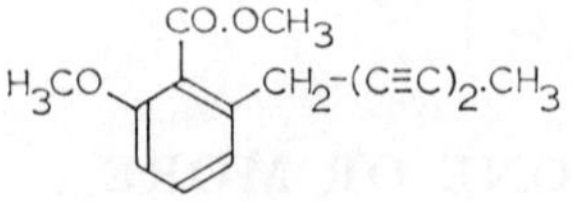

Frutescine

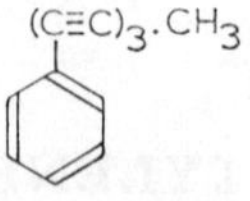

1-Phenyl-hepta-
-1,3,5-triyne

Fig. 3. Some acetylenic compounds with phenyl groups.

Frutescinone (Methyl-2-hexa-2′,4′-diynoyl-6-methoxy-benzoate)
  Comp. *Chrysanthemum frutescens* (rt)
1-Phenyl-hepta-1,3-diyn-5,6-diol
  Comp. *Dahlia* × 'Preference' (tuber)
1-Phenyl-hepta-1,3-diyn-5,6,7-triol
  Comp. *Dahlia* × 'Dolce Vita' (tuber)
1-Phenyl-hepta-1,3,5-triyn-7-ol-acetate
  Comp. *Bidens dahlioides* (ab.gd), *leucanthus* (ab.gd)
1-Phenyl-hepta-1,3,5-triyne (fig. 3)
  Comp. *Bidens* (4), *Coreopsis* (at least 3)
1-Phenyl-hept-5-en-1,3-diyne
  Comp. *Coreopsis* (tuber), *Dahlia* (tuber)
1-Phenyl-hept-5-en-1,3-diyn-7-ol
  Comp. *Bidens*
1-Phenyl-hept-5t-en-1,3-diyn-7-ol-acetate
  Comp. *Bidens pilosus* (rt), *tripartitus* (rt); *Coreopsis* sp., *leucanthus*
    (rt)
1-Phenyl-hexa-2,4-diyn-1-ol acetate
  Comp. *Lonas annua*
1-Phenyl-hexa-2,4-diyn-1-one-6-ol
  Comp. *Lonas annua* (ab.gd)
1-Phenyl-hexa-2,4-diyn-1-one-6-ol-β-methyl-crotonic acid ester
  Comp. *Lonas annua* (ab.gd)
1-Phenyl-penta-2,4-diyne (Benzyl-diacetylene)
  Comp. *Artemisia dracunculus, Chrysanthemum segetum*

1-Phenyl-pent-4-en-2-yn-5-methylmercapto
   Comp.   Chrysanthemum segetum (rt)
1-Phenyl-pent-4-en-2-yn-5-methylmercapto-1-one   (4-Benzoyl-buta-1-methylmercapto-1-en-3-yne; fig. 3)
   Comp.   Chrysanthemum segetum (rt; c and t)
1-Phenyl-undeca-7,9-dien-1,3,5-triyne—there is some doubt about this.
   Comp.   Coreopsis?

V   ACETYLENES WITH FURYL GROUPS

GENERAL

This is a small group essentially confined to the *Compositae*. One is said to occur in *Eremophila* (*Myoporaceae*), another in a legume, *Vicia faba*.

List and Occurrence

Atractylodin (1-(Furyl-2)-nona-1t,7t-dien-3,5-diyne)
   Comp.   Atractylodes sp. (rhiz.)
Carlina oxide (2-(3'-Phenyl-prop-1'-ynyl) furan; fig. 4)
   Comp.   Carlina acaulis (rt)
5-Chlormethyl-2(octa-2,4,6-triynyliden)-2,5-dihydro-furan (fig. 4)
   Comp.   Gnaphalium obtusifolium (rt; c and t)
1-(2,3-Dihydro-furyl-2)-non-1-en-3,5,7-triyne
   Comp.   Chrysanthemum leucanthemum (rt)
Freelingyne (fig. 4) has been called the 'first example of an acetylenic terpenoid'.
   Myopor.   Eremophila freelingii (wd-oil)
1-(Furyl-2)-hexa-2,4-diyne
   Occurrence?
1-(Furyl-2)-nona-1-en-3,5,7-triyne
   Comp.   Chrysanthemum leucanthemum (rt)
cis- and *trans*-5-Methoxy-2(hexa-2,4-diynylidene-1)-2,5-dihydro-furan
   Occurrence?
Methyl-3[5-(hept-4c-en-2-ynoyl)-2-furyl]-*trans*-acrylate
   Legum.   Vicia faba (shoot)
4-(Nona-6,8-dien-2,4-diynylidene)-butenolide
   Comp.   Carlina vulgaris (rt)
2-(Nona-6c,8c-dien-2,4-diynylidene)-2,5-dihydro-furan
   Comp.   Carlina vulgaris (rt)
2-(Non-1-en-3,5,7-triynyl-1)-2,3-dihydro-furan
   Comp.   Chrysanthemum leucanthemum (rt)

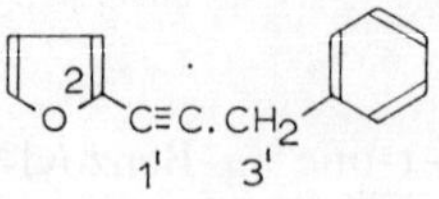

Carlina oxide

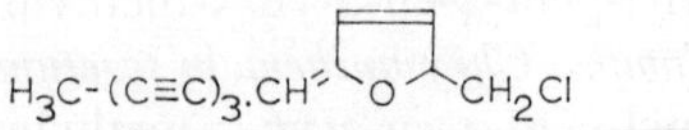

$H_3C-(C\equiv C)_3.CH\cdots O\cdots CH_2Cl$

5-Chlor methyl-2(octa-2,4,6-
triynyliden)-2,5-dihydrofuran

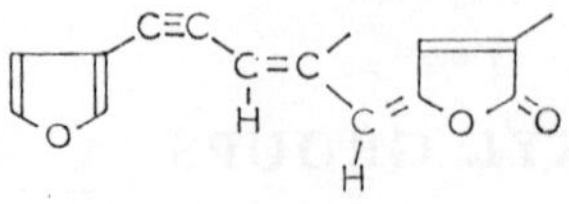

Freelingyne

Fig. 4. Some acetylenes with furyl groups.

VI ACETYLENES WITH PYRAN RINGS

GENERAL

A few acetylenes are known which have *pyran*, or rather *dihydro-* or *tetrahydro-pyran* rings. These seem to be confined to the *Compositae*, but although so few in number, they are recorded from *Inuleae* (*Anaphalis*, *Gnaphalium*); *Heliantheae* (*Dahlia*, *Ichthyothere*); *Anthemideae* (*Chrysanthemum*); and *Cardueae* (*Centaurea*).

List and Occurrence

5-Chlor-3,4-epoxy-2(octa-2,4,6-triynyliden)-5,6-dihydro-2H-pyran
  Comp. *Anaphalis triplinervis* (rt)
5-Chlor-2(octa-2,4,6-triynyliden)-5-6-dihydro-2H-pyran (fig. 5)
  Comp. *Anaphalis margaritacea, triplinervis* (rt); *Gnaphalium obtusifolium* (rt)
2e and 2a-Hydroxy-6(non-1t-en-3,5,7-triynyl-1)-tetrahydro-pyran
  Comp. *Centaurea muricata* (ab.gd)
3-Hydroxy-2(non-1t-en-3,5,7-triynyl-1)-tetrahydro-pyran
(Ichthyothereol; fig. 5)
  Comp. *Dahlia coccinea* (lvs, fl.), *Ichthyothere terminalis* (lvs)
2-(Non-1t-en-triynyl-1)-3-acetoxy-3,4,5,6-tetrahydro-pyran
  Comp. *Chrysanthemum serotinum* (ab.gd, rt)
2-(Non-1t-en-triynyl-1)-3-hydroxy-3,4,5,6-tetrahydro-pyran
  Comp. *Chrysanthemum serotinum* (rt)

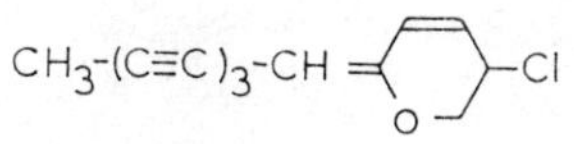

CH₃-(C≡C)₃-CH ═⟨ ⟩-Cl

5-Chloro-2(octa-2,4,6-
-triynyliden)-5,6-dihydro-
-2H-pyran

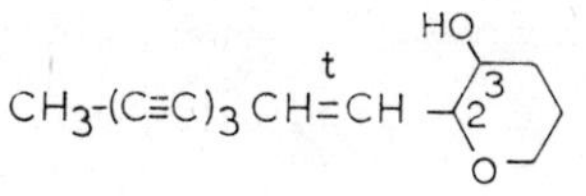

CH₃-(C≡C)₃ CH=CH ⟨ ⟩

3-Hydroxy-2(non-1t-en-3,5,7-
-triynyl)-tetrahydro-pyran

Fig. 5. Acetylenes with pyran rings.

VII ACETYLENES CONTAINING NITROGEN

GENERAL

A few acetylenes—mostly amides—are known which contain one or more nitrogen atoms. These, like so many acetylene compounds, have been recorded only from the *Compositae* and in that family only from *Heliantheae* and *Anthemideae*.

List and Occurrence

Dodeca-2c,4t-dien-8,10-diyn-1-oic acid-1-isobutylamide
    Comp. *Echinacea angustifolia* (rt), *purpurea* (rt)
Hexadeca-7,14-dien-10,12-diyn-1-ol-azobenzol-carbonic acid ester
    Comp. *Dahlia merckii*
Hexadeca-7,12,14-trien-10-yn-1-ol-azobenzol-carbonic acid ester
    Comp. *Dahlia merckii*
Tetradeca-2t,4t-dien-8,10-diyn-1-oic acid-1-isobutylamide (Anacycline)
    Comp. *Anacyclus pyrethrum* (rt)
Undeca,2,4-dien-8,10-diyn-1-oic acid-1-isobutylamide
    Comp. *Chrysanthemum frutescens* (t,t); *Echinacea angustifolia* (rt; c,t), *purpurea* (rt; c,t)

VIII OTHER ACETYLENES

A group of *enolether-spiroketals* (fig. 6)—for most of which I have no names—have been found in *Chrysanthemum* (many in 40 spp.!), *Artemisia* (several in at least 1 sp.), and *Matricaria* (at least 1 in at least 2 spp.). These are all members of the *Anthemideae*.

A single *isocoumarin acetylene—capillarin* (fig. 6)—is also to be found in two spp. of *Artemisia*.

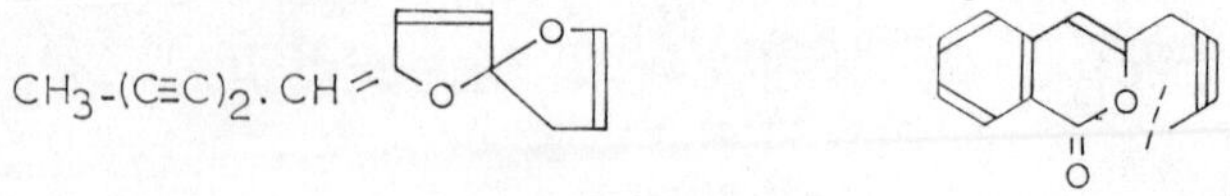

An enolether-spiroketal   Capillarin

Fig. 6. Uncommon acetylenes.

I ALCOHOLS

GENERAL

We have included here the following 'groups' of alcohols and derivatives:

I. Aliphatic
   1. Monohydric: *a*. Normal saturated; *b*. Other saturated;
     c. Unsaturated.
   2. Dihydric.
   3. Trihydric and up (Aliphatic Polyols): *a*. Trihydric;
     b. Tetrahydric; *c*. Pentahydric; *d*. Hexahydric;
     e. Heptahydric.
II. Aromatic (some are phenols)
III. Phenols
IV. Phenolic esters and ethers

We have excluded *phenolic glycosides* (p. 635), *terpenoid alcohols*, *acetylenic alcohols*, the alcohols of the *Anacardiaceae*, etc.

I.1.*a* Normal aliphatic alcohols

GENERAL

A series of *alcohols* ($C_nH_{2n+1}OH$) beginning with *methyl* (CH_3OH) and *ethyl* ($CH_3.CH_2OH$) *alcohols* is known from plant sources. The lower members of the series occur chiefly as *esters* of very varied kinds, some of which are prominent in the odoriferous mixtures of plants. The higher members of the series, with C_{20} to C_{34}, occur as *waxes* (*esters* with *fatty acids*).

An examination of the following list will show that I have little information of chemotaxonomic value. We have all too few records for most of these alcohols. It is evident, however, that the even C-number alcohols are much commoner in plants than are those with odd C-numbers. It is clear, too, that some plants appear to use higher C-number *alcohols* than do others (Table 4). This is in line with observations on *hydrocarbons* (figs. 135 and 136).

List and Occurrence

Methyl alcohol (Methanol; Wood alcohol; CH_3OH; fig. 7) occurs usually as *esters*. Is it free in any of the following?
> *Urtic.* Boehmeria
> *The.* Thea (Camellia)
> *Malv.* Gossypium
> *Umbell.* Anthriscus, Heracleum, Pastinaca
> *Verben.* Vitex

Ethyl alcohol (Ethanol; $CH_3 . CH_2OH$) occurs free and as esters
> *Fag.* Castanea sativa (wd)
> *Ros.* Fragaria (frt), Rubus idaeus (frt)
> *Rut.* Citrus (frt)
> *Myrt.* Eucalyptus spp. (ess. oil)
> *Umbell.* Anthriscus cerefolium (frt), Heracleum giganteum (frt), Pastinaca sativa (frt)
> *Solan.* Nicotiana tabacum (lvs)

Propyl alcohol (Propan-1-ol; $CH_3 . CH_2 . CH_2OH$) occurs only secondarily?

Butyl alcohol (Butan-1-ol; $CH_3 . (CH_2)_2 . CH_2OH$) occurs chiefly as esters
> *Lab.* Mentha arvensis v. *piperascens* (ess. oil; free?)

Amyl alcohol (Pentan-1-ol; $CH_3 . (CH_2)_3 . CH_2OH$) occurs only (?) as esters

Hexyl alcohol (Hexan-1-ol; $CH_3 . (CH_2)_4 . CH_2OH$) occurs free and as esters
> *Laur.* Litsea zeylanica (lvs; ess. oil)
> *The.* Thea (tea; ess. oil)
> *Ros.* Fragaria (frt)
> *Gerani.* Pelargonium (ess. oil)
> *Lab.* Lavandula spica (ess. oil), *vera* (ess. oil); *Salvia spinosa* (ess. oil)

Heptyl alcohol (Heptan-1-ol; $CH_3 . (CH_2)_5 . CH_2OH$)
> *Laur.* Litsea zeylanica (lvs; ess. oil)
> *Lili.* Hyacinthus (fl. oil?)

Octyl alcohol (Octan-1-ol; $CII_3 . (CH_2)_6 . CH_2OH$) occurs free and as esters
> *The.* Thea (tea; leaf-oil)
> *Rut.* Citrus bigaradia (oil), *paradisi* (frt-oil)

Umbell. Heracleum giganteum (villosum) (frt, free and as ester), *sphondylium* (frt, as ester); *Pastinaca sativa* (frt, as ester)

Nonyl alcohol (Nonan-1-ol; $CH_3.(CH_2)_7.CH_2OH$)

Rut. Citrus aurantium (peel-oil); *Eremocitrus glauca* (leaf-oil)?

Decyl alcohol (Decan-1-ol; $CH_3.(CH_2)_8.CH_2OH$)

Ros. Prunus amygdalus (fl.-oil)

Rut. Citrus?

Bux. Simmondsia californica (sd, as ester)

Undecyl alcohol (Undecan-1-ol; $CH_3.(CH_2)_9.CH_2OH$): no records

Dodecyl alcohol (Dodecan-1-ol; Lauryl alcohol; $CH_3.(CH_2)_{10}.CH_2OH$)

Rut. Citrus aurantifolia (oil, as ester)

Rhamn. Rhamnus purshiana (bk, as ester?)

Umbell. Ligusticum acutilobum (frt, as ester)

Agav. Furcraea gigantea (fl.)

Tridecyl alcohol (Tridecan-1-ol; Pisangceryl alcohol; $CH_3.(CH_2)_{11}.CH_2OH$)

Mus. Musa cera (wax)

Tetradecyl alcohol (Tetradecan-1-ol; Myristyl alcohol; $CH_3.(CH_2)_{12}.CH_2OH$)

Umbell. Ligusticum acutilobum (frt, as ester)

Pentadecyl alcohol (Pentadecan-1-ol; $CH_3.(CH_2)_{13}.CH_2OH$): no records

Hexadecyl alcohol (Hexadecan-1-ol; Cetyl alcohol; $CH_3.(CH_2)_{14}.CH_2OH$)

Loranth. Loranthus europaeus (frt?)

Umbell. Dorema ammoniacum (resin)

Convolvul. Ipomoea spp. (as esters)

Comp. Ambrosia artemisifolia (pollen; wax?)

Lili. Smilax spp. (rts)

Gram. Sorghum?

Heptadecyl alcohol (Heptadecan-1-ol; Margaryl alcohol; $CH_3.(CH_2)_{15}.CH_2OH$): no records

Octadecyl alcohol (Octadecan-1-ol; Stearyl alcohol; $CH_3.(CH_2)_{16}.CH_2OH$) occurs in lichens and fungi and

Piper. Piper methysticum (rt)

Comp. Ambrosia artemisifolia (pollen; wax?)

Nonadecyl alcohol (Nonadecan-1-ol; $CH_3.(CH_2)_{17}.CH_2OH$)

Ros. Rubus idaeus (frt?)

Eicosyl alcohol (Eicosan-1-ol; Arachidyl alcohol; $CH_3.(CH_2)_{18}.CH_2OH$) seems to occur widely

Fag. Fagus sylvatica (bk-wax)

Bux. Simmondsia californica (sd-wax)

Anacardi. Rhus succedanea (japan wax, free?)

Plumbagin. *Plumbago rosea* (rtbk ?)
Comp. *Artemisia vulgaris* (lf-wax)
Palmae. *Raphia*
Gram. *Triticum sativum* (oil)

Heneicosyl alcohol (Heneicosan-1-ol; $CH_3.(CH_2)_{19}.CH_2OH$): no records

Docosyl alcohol (Docosan-1-ol; $CH_3.(CH_2)_{20}.CH_2OH$)
Bux. *Simmondsia californica* (sd-wax, as ester)
Solan. *Mandragora autumnalis* (rt)

Tricosyl alcohol (Tricosan-1-ol; $CH_3.(CH_2)_{21}.CH_2OH$): no records

Tetracosyl alcohol (Tetracosan-1-ol; Lignoceryl alcohol; $CH_3.(CH_2)_{22}.CH_2OH$)
Chenopodi. *Spinacia oleracea* (as ester ?)
Malv. *Gossypium* (cotton)
Palmae. *Copernicia cerifera* (carnauba-wax, as ester)
Gram. *Dactylis glomerata* (wax)

Pentacosyl alcohol (Pentacosan-1-ol; $CH_3.(CH_2)_{23}.CH_2OH$): no records

Hexacosyl alcohol (Hexacosan-1-ol; Ceryl alcohol; $CH_3.(CH_2)_{24}.CH_2OH$) occurs free (?) and in many waxes
Chenopodi. *Spinacia oleracea* (wax ?)
Magnoli. *Michelia compressa* (lvs)
Berberid. *Epimedium macranthum* (lvs)
Aristolochi. *Aristolochia indica* (rt)
Papaver. *Papaver* (?'ceryl alcohol')
Crucif. *Brassica oleracea* (lf-wax)
Ros. *Malus* (apple-peel; wax ?)
Legum. *Gleditsia horrida* (sd, etc.)
Euphorbi. *Cluytia similis* (lf-wax)
Anacardi. *Rhus succedanea* (japan wax)
Rhamn. *Ceanothus* ('ceryl alcohol')
Onagr. *Chamaenerion angustifolium* (plt), *Epilobium obscurum* (plt)
Comp. *Chrysanthemum cinerariaefolium* (fl.-wax), *Lactuca sativa* (lf-oil)
Palmae. *Copernicia cerifera* (carnauba-wax; as ester ?)
Gram. *Dactylis glomerata* (wax), *Lolium perenne* (wax), *Triticum sativum* (wax)

Heptacosyl alcohol (Heptacosan-1-ol; $CH_3.(CH_2)_{25}.CH_2OH$)
Ros. *Malus* (apple-wax)
Cucurbit. *Citrullus colocynthis* (frt)

Octacosyl alcohol (Octacosan-1-ol; $CH_3.(CH_2)_{26}.CH_2OH$; Cluytyl alcohol)
Santal. *Santalum album* (lf-wax)
Cact. *Opuntia sp.* (wax)

> *Crucif.*   *Brassica* (lf-wax)
> *Ros.*   *Malus* (apple-wax)
> *Euphorbi.*   *Cluytia similis* (free and as ester)
> *Palmae.*   *Copernicia cerifera* (carnauba-wax), *Raphia ruffia* (wax)
> *Gram.*   *Triticum* (wax)
> *Mus.*   *Musa sapientum* (wax)

Nonacosyl alcohol (Nonacosan-1-ol; $CH_3.(CH_2)_{27}.CH_2OH$)

> *Ros.*   *Malus* (apple-wax)

Triacontyl alcohol (Triacontan-1-ol; Myricyl alcohol; Melissyl alcohol; $CH_3.(CH_2)_{28}.CH_2OH$) occurs chiefly in waxes. It is reported from conifers and

> *Santal.*   *Santalum album* (lf-wax)
> *Cact.*   *Opuntia* sp. (wax)
> *Crucif.*   *Brassica* spp. (wax)
> *Ros.*   *Malus* (apple-wax)
> *Leg.*   *Medicago sativa* (lf-wax)
> *Euphorbia.*   *Euphorbia antisyphilitica* (candelilla wax)
> *Anacardi.*   *Rhus succedanea* (japan wax)
> *Eric.*   *Arbutus unedo* (leaf)
> *Solan.*   *Mandragora* (combined)
> *Gram.*   *Saccharum* (wax)
> *Palmae.*   *Copernicia cerifera* (carnauba-wax; free and combined?),
> *Raphia* (wax)

Hentriacontyl alcohol (Hentriacontan-1-ol; $CH_3.(CH_2)_{29}.CH_2OH$): no records

Dotriacontyl alcohol (Dotriacontan-1-ol; Lacceryl alcohol; $CH_3.(CH_2)_{30}.CH_2OH$) occurs in many plant waxes

> *Eric.*   *Arbutus unedo* (leaf, free?)
> *Palmae.*   *Copernicia cerifera* (carnauba-wax, free and combined)

Tritriacontyl alcohol (Tritriacontan-1-ol; $CH_3.(CH_2)_{31}.CH_2OH$): no records

Tetratriacontyl alcohol (Tetratriacontan-1-ol; $CH_3.(CH_2)_{32}.CH_2OH$)

> *Euphorbi.*   *Euphorbia antisyphilitica* (candelilla-wax)
> *Malv.*   *Gossypium* (wax)

I.1.*b* Other saturated alcohols

GENERAL

These are few in number and seem to have no chemotaxonomic value, but several of them are known only from single sources and it is possible that increased knowledge of their occurrence will yield results useful to the chemotaxonomist. We have arranged them in alphabetical order.

List and Occurrence

Heptacosan-14-ol (Dimyristyl-carbinol; $[CH_3(CH_2)_{12}]_2.CHOH$)
    Papaver.   Corydalis aurea (combined)

Heptan-2-ol (Methyl-*n*-amyl-carbinol; 1-Methyl-hexyl alcohol; $CH_3.(CH_2)_4.C(CH_3)HOH$)
    Myrt.   Eugenia caryophyllata (oil of cloves)

Isoamyl alcohol (3-Methyl-butan-1-ol; $CH(CH_3)_2.CH_2.CH_2OH$) occurs free and as *esters*
    Ros.   Fragaria (frt), *Rubus idaeus* (frt)
    Gerani.   Pelargonium (ess. oil)
    Myrt.   Eucalyptus (ess. oil)
    Lab.   Mentha piperita (oil), *Lavandula* (oil)

Isobutyl alcohol ($(CH_3)_2CH.CH_2OH$
    Comp.   Anthemis nobilis (oil)

Methyl-diheneicosyl-methanol ($CH_3.C(C_{21}H_{43})_2.OH$)
    Gerani.   Erodium cicutarium

d-3-Methyl-pentan-1-ol ($CH_3.CH_2.CH(CH_3).CH_2.CH_2OH$)
    Gerani.   Pelargonium (ess. oil)
    Lab.   Mentha arvensis v. *piperascens* (ess. oil)

Nonacosan-10-ol (Ginnol; $CH_3.(CH_2)_8.CH(OH).(CH_2)_{18}.CH_3$) occurs in *Ginkgo* and other gymnosperms and
    Papaver.   Papaver somniferum (opium)
    Ros.   Malus (apple-wax; *d*-)

Nonacosan-15-ol
    Crucif.   Brassica oleracea v. *gemmifera*
    Eric.   Arbutus unedo (st.-wax)

Nonan-2-ol (Methyl-*n*-heptyl-carbinol; $CH_3.(CH_2)_6.CH(OH).CH_3$)
    Rut.   Ruta (oil; *l*-)
    Myrt.   Eugenia caryophyllata (oil of cloves)

Octan-2-ol (Methyl-*n*-hexyl-carbinol)
    Gerani.   Pelargonium (ess. oil)

d-Octan-3-ol (*d*-Ethyl-*n*-amyl-carbinol)
    Lab.   Lavandula vera (ess. oil); *Mentha arvensis* v. *piperascens* (ess. oil), *piperita, pulegium* (ess. oil; free and as ester)

Tricosan-12-ol (Diundecyl-carbinol; $[CH_3.(CH_2)_{10}]_2.CHOH$)
    Comp.   Artemisia vulgaris (leaf-wax)

Undecan-2-ol (Methyl-*n*-nonyl-carbinol)
    Laur.   Litsea odorifera (leaf-oil; *l*-)
    Rut.   Ruta (oil; *l*-)

I.1.c Unsaturated monohydric alcohols

GENERAL

We have excluded the *acetylenic alcohols* (see p. 85). As treated here we have a small but mixed group showing no obvious chemotaxonomic value.

List and Occurrence

Allyl alcohol (Prop-2-en-1-ol; $CH_2 = CH.CH_2OH$)
   Martyni. Martynia diandra (sd-oil)
l-n-Amyl-vinyl-carbinol (*l*-Oct-1-en-3-ol; $CH_3.(CH_2)_4.C(CH=CH_2)$ HOH) occurs in fungi, conifers and
   Lab. Lavandula vera (ess. oil); *Mentha pulegium* (ess. oil), *timija* (ess. oil)
Bixol (4,7,10,13-Tetramethyl-tetradec-3,6,9,12-tetraen-1-ol)
   Bix. Bixa orellana (sd)
But-2-en-1-ol (Crotyl alcohol; Crotonyl a.; $CH_3.CH=CH.CH_2OH$)
   Crucif. Brassica napus (sd)
But-3-en-1-ol ($CH_2 = CH.CH_2.CH_2OH$)
   Crucif. Brassica napus (sd)
1,5-Dimethyl-hex-4-en-1-ol (2-Methyl-hept-2-en-6-ol)
   Laur. Litsea zeylanica (leaf-oil?)
   Burser. Bursera delpechiana (ess. oil?)
Docos-13-en-1-ol
   Bux. Simmondsia californica (sd)
Eicos-11-en-1-ol
   Bux. Simmondsia californica (sd)
cis-Hex-3-en-1-ol ($CH_3.CH_2.CH:CH.CH_2.CH_2OH$) seems to be widely spread in leaves. Karrer (1958) says: 'Seither wurde dieser Alcohol aus vielen grünen Blättern, in denen er meist frei vorkommt, isoliert.'
   Ros. Rubus idaeus (frt)
   Rut. Citrus paradisi (frt)
1-Methyl-dec-9-en-1-ol (*l*-Undec-1-en-10-ol)
   Laur. Litsea odorifera (lvs; ess. oil)
Nona-2,6-dien-1-ol
   Viol. Viola odorata (lvs, fl.)
   Cucurbit. Cucumis sativus

TABLE 4. *Aliphatic alcohols of waxes of a few plants* (*various authors*)

Plants	Number of C atoms														
	20	21	22	23	24	25	26	27	28	29	30	31	32	33	34
Simmondsia (liquid seed-wax)	+	.	+	.	.	.	.	.	.	.	.	.	.	.	.
Copernicia (Carnauba-wax, leaf)	.	.	.	.	+	.	+	.	+	.	+	.	+	.	.
Cluytia	.	.	.	.	.	.	+	.	+	.	.	.	.	.	.
Malus (Apple-wax, fruit)	.	.	.	.	.	.	+	+	+	+	+	.	.	.	.
Euphorbia (Candelilla-wax)	.	.	.	.	.	.	.	.	.	.	+	.	.	.	+

I.2 Dihydric aliphatic alcohols

GENERAL

These are few in number. Almost all of them are α,ω-*diols*. There is some evidence that they may prove, like the *alkanes*, to be of some chemotaxonomic significance.

List and Occurrence

Ethylene glycol (Ethane-1,2-diol; $CH_2OH.CH_2OH$; fig. 7) may be considered to be the second in the series of '*sugar-alcohols*'. It is surprising, in view of the ubiquity of *fats* which are esters of *glycerol*, a *trihydric alcohol*, that no similar esters of this *dihydric alcohol* seem to be known.

I have no record of the occurrence of *ethylene glycol* in higher plants.

Dodecan-1,12-diol ($CH_2OH.(CH_2)_{10}.CH_2OH$) is known from conifers

Hexadecan-1,16-diol ($CH_2OH.(CH_2)_{14}.CH_2OH$) is known from conifers

Octadecan-1,18-diol ($CH_2OH.(CH_2)_{16}.CH_2OH$)
    Legum.   *Spartium junceum* (fl.)

Docosan-1,22-diol ($CH_2OH.(CH_2)_{20}.CH_2OH$)
    Palmae.   *Copernicia cerifera* (carnauba-wax, free?)

Tetracosan-1,24-diol ($CH_2OH.(CH_2)_{22}.CH_2OH$)
    Palmae.   *Copernicia cerifera* (carnauba-wax, free?)

Hexacosan-1,26-diol $(CH_2OH.(CH_2)_{24}.CH_2OH)$
   Legum.   *Spartium junceum* (fl.)
   Palmae.   *Copernicia cerifera* (carnauba-wax, free?)
Octacosan-1,28-diol $(CH_2OH.(CH_2)_{26}.CH_2OH)$
   Palmae.   *Copernicia cerifera* (carnauba-wax)
1-Methyl-propan-1,2-diol(Butan-2,3-diol; $CH_3.CHOH.C(CH_3)HOH)$
   is not in the above series. It is produced by micro-organisms and:
   Ros.   *Malus* (ripe and over-ripe fruit)

I.3 Aliphatic polyols (Trihydric and up)

GENERAL

These *alcohols* are often called the 'sugar-alcohols'. Actually *methyl alcohol* and *ethylene glycol* might be included as the first and second alcohols of the series. We have considered the 'polyols' to start with *glycerol*.

Hough and Stacey (1966), in a paper on the biosynthesis and metabolism of *allitol* and the sugar D-*allulose* in *Itea*, have given us a brief summary of our knowledge of some sugar alcohols. Plouvier (in Swain, 1963; and other papers) has contributed much to this knowledge.

I.3.*a* Trihydric alcohols

List and Occurrence

Glycerol (Glycerine; fig. 7) is a constituent of *fats* and *phosphatides* and
   therefore presumably of universal occurrence. It occurs free (?) and/
   or as glycosides in seaweeds. It is said to be free in
     Sterculi.   *Theobroma cacao* (sd)
     Ole.   *Olea europaea* (ripe olives)
     Palmae.   *Phoenix dactylifera* (sap)

I.3.*b* Tetrahydric alcohols (Tetritols)

List and Occurrence

Erythritol (fig. 7) occurs in algae, fungi, and lichens. It is also in:
   Gram.   ?
D-Threitol (fig. 7) is in large amount in a fungus (*Armillaria mellea*), but
   not (?) in higher plants.

I.3.*c* Pentahydric alcohols (Pentitols)

List and Occurrence

Adonitol (Ribitol; fig. 7) is universally (?) present in plants as part of *riboflavin*. It occurs free in:
>Ranuncul.   *Adonis amurensis* (to 4% of plt), *vernalis* (rt)
>Umbell.   *Bupleurum falcatum* (ıt)

D-Arabitol (fig. 7) occurs in lichens but not (?) in higher plants.

I.3.*d* Hexahydric alcohols (Hexitols)

List and Occurrence

Allitol (fig. 7) has been investigated by Plouvier (1959), and more recently by Hough and Stacey (1966) who say: 'The allitol content of *Itea* leaves increases considerably during photosynthesis whereas the converse is true during metabolism in the dark. Allitol is thought to function in a reserve capacity.'
>Saxifrag.   *Itea ilicifolia* (lvs, st.), *virginica* (lvs, st.), *yunnanensis* (lvs, 6%); but *not* in *Brexia* and *Escallonia*

Dulcitol (Dulcin; Dulcose; Euonymite; Galactite; Melampyrin; Melampyrite; fig. 7) has been studied by Plouvier (1949). It occurs in red algae, in fungi, and in
>Laur.   *Cassytha*
>Saxifrag.   *Brexia*
>Celastr.   at least 7 genera
>Hippocrate.   *Pristimera, Salacia, Tontelia*
>Scrophulari.   *Melampyrum, Rhinanthus, Scrophularia*

Plouvier did *not* find it in: *Rut., Simaroub., Meli., Rhamn.*, and *Vit.*

D-Glucitol (D-Sorbitol; fig. 7) seems to have a restricted distribution. It is said to occur in algae, fungi, oak-galls and
>Ros.   (many). Strain (1937) says: 'It thus appears that sorbitol [*glucitol*] may play the same role in the plants of the genus *Rosacae* [*sic*] that sugar alcohols play in the metabolism of some marine algae.'
>Solan.   *Nicotiana*

It has *not* been found in
>Jugland. (*Juglans*); Laur. (*Umbellularia*); Berberid. (*Berberis*); Papaver. (*Eschscholtzia*); Saxifrag. (*Astilbe*); Rut. (*Citrus*); Hippocastan. (*Aesculus*); Celastr. (*Celastrus*); Rhamn. (*Rhamnus*); Eric. (*Arbutus*); Solan. (*Physalis*); Caprifoli. (*Symphoricarpos*)

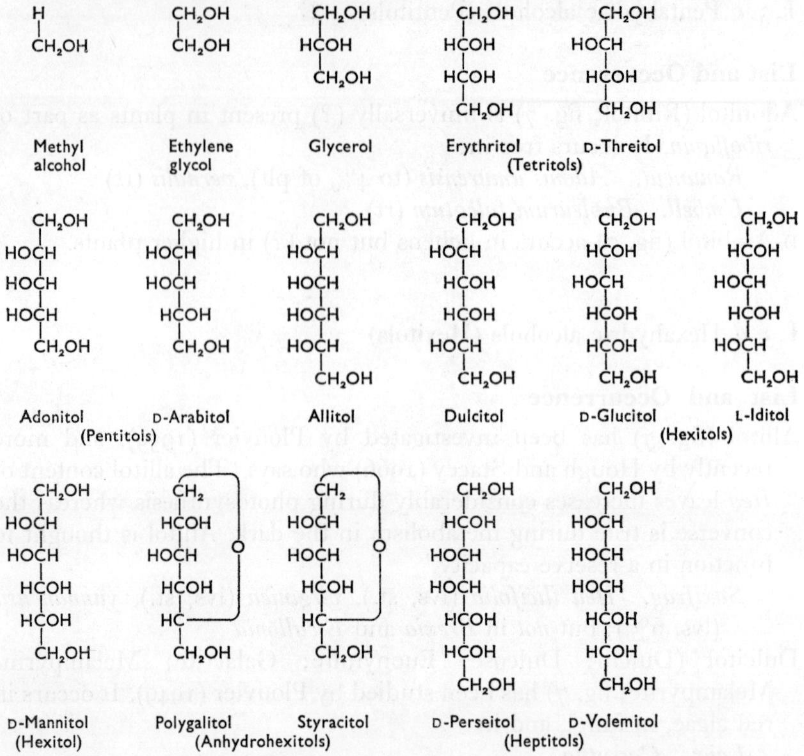

H
|
CH_2OH

Methyl
alcohol

CH_2OH
|
CH_2OH

Ethylene
glycol

CH_2OH
|
HCOH
|
CH_2OH

Glycerol

CH_2OH
|
HCOH
|
HCOH
|
CH_2OH

Erythritol
(Tetritols)

CH_2OH
|
HOCH
|
HCOH
|
CH_2OH

D-Threitol

CH_2OH
|
HOCH
|
HOCH
|
HOCH
|
CH_2OH

Adonitol
(Pentitols)

CH_2OH
|
HOCH
|
HOCH
|
HCOH
|
CH_2OH

D-Arabitol

CH_2OH
|
HOCH
|
HOCH
|
HOCH
|
HOCH
|
CH_2OH

Allitol

CH_2OH
|
HOCH
|
HCOH
|
HCOH
|
HCOH
|
CH_2OH

Dulcitol

CH_2OH
|
HCOH
|
HOCH
|
HCOH
|
HCOH
|
CH_2OH

D-Glucitol
(Hexitols)

CH_2OH
|
HCOH
|
HOCH
|
HCOH
|
HOCH
|
CH_2OH

L-Iditol

CH_2OH
|
HOCH
|
HOCH
|
HCOH
|
HCOH
|
CH_2OH

D-Mannitol
(Hexitol)

CH_2
|
HCOH
|
HOCH
|
HCOH
|
HC——
|
CH_2OH

O

Polygalitol

CH_2
|
HOCH
|
HOCH
|
HCOH
|
HC——
|
CH_2OH

O

Styracitol
(Anhydrohexitols)

CH_2OH
|
HCOH
|
HOCH
|
HOCH
|
HCOH
|
HCOH
|
CH_2OH

D-Perseitol

CH_2OH
|
HOCH
|
HOCH
|
HCOH
|
HCOH
|
CH_2OH

D-Volemitol
(Heptitols)

Fig. 7. Aliphatic alcohols.

L-Iditol (Sorbierite; fig. 7)
    Ros.   Sorbus aucuparia (frt)
D-Mannitol (Manna sugar; Mannite; fig. 7) seems to be widely distri-
    buted. It is recorded from algae, fungi, conifers, and
        Salic. (Populus); Caryophyll. (Dianthus); Cact. (Opuntia); Canell.
        (Canella, Warburgia); Laur. (Laurus, Cinnamomum); Ranuncul.
        (Aconitum); Platan. (Platanus); Legum. (at least 6 genera); Elaeagn.
        (Hippophaë); Lythr. (Lawsonia); Punic. (Punica); Umbell. (Apium,
        Daucus, Meum); Ole. (general); Rubi. (Basanacantha, Coffea,
        Genipa, Pavetta); Convolvul. (Ipomoea); Verben. (Clerodendron);
        Scrophulari. (general?); Orobanch. (Orobanche); Myopor. (Myopo-
        rum); Comp. (Scorzonera); Lili (Allium); Bromeli. (Ananas); Gram.
        (Agropyrum, Andropogon, Triticum); Palmae. (Phoenix); Cyper.
        (Carex)
    Two anhydro-hexitols (which have only 4 free -OH groups) are known
    and may be included here.

Polygalitol (Acerite; Aceritol; 1,5-Anhydro-D-glucitol; fig. 7) is known
    only (?) from:
    Prote.   *Protea* (8)
    Polygal.   *Polygala* spp.
    Acer.   *Acer* (from *acertannin*)
Styracitol (1,5-Anhydro-D-mannitol) is known only (?) from:
    Styrac.   *Styrax obassia* (frt)

I.3.e Heptahydric alcohols (Heptitols)

D-Perseitol (D-α-Mannoheptitol; D-Manno-D-*gala*-heptitol; fig. 7) is
    known only (?) from:
    Laur.   *Persea gratissima* (frt)
D-Volemitol (α-Sedoheptitol; fig. 7) is known from algae, fungi (*Lactar-*
    ius volemus), lichens, and
    Primul.   *Primula* spp.

II AROMATIC ALCOHOLS

GENERAL

As is usually the case, we have difficulties in classification. Some of the
aromatic alcohols included here, such as *coniferyl alcohol* and *salirepol*, are
also *phenols*. Where should they go?

List and Occurrence

Anethol-glycol (β-(p-Methoxyphenyl)-α-methyl-β-hydroxy-ethyl alco-
    hol)
    Rut.   *Ruta montana* (ess. oil)
Anisalcohol (4-Methoxy-benzyl alcohol)
    Umbell.   *Pimpinella anisum* (sd-oil)
    Orchid.   *Vanilla*
Benzyl alcohol (Phenyl-carbinol) is said to occur free and/or as *esters* in:

    Caryophyll.   *Dianthus*
    Annon.   *Cananga odorata* (fl.-oil)
    Legum.   *Acacia farnesiana* (fl.-oil)
    Viol.   *Viola odorata* (oil)
    Myrt.   *Eugenia caryophyllata* (clove-oil)
    Ole.   *Jasminum* (fl.-oil)

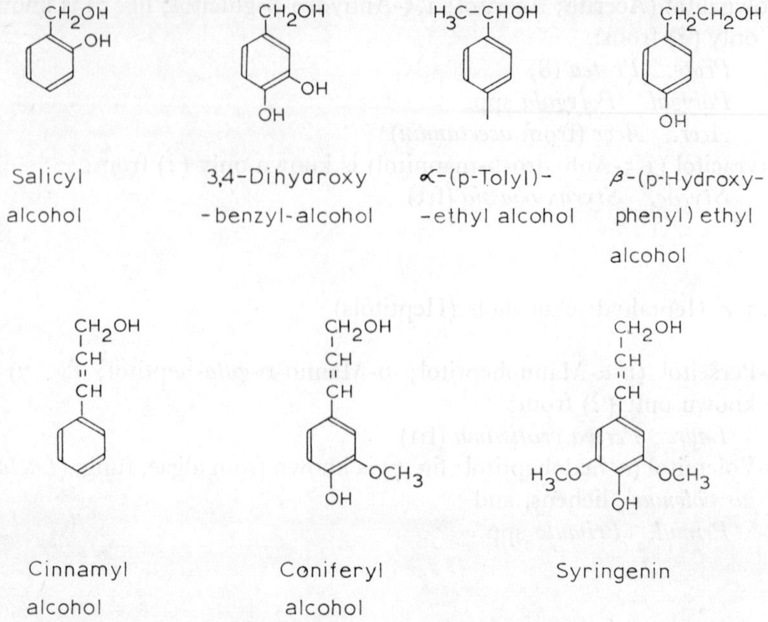

Salicyl
alcohol

3,4-Dihydroxy
-benzyl-alcohol

α-(p-Tolyl)-
-ethyl alcohol

β-(p-Hydroxy-
phenyl) ethyl
alcohol

Cinnamyl
alcohol

Coniferyl
alcohol

Syringenin

Fig. 8. Some aromatic alcohols.

Lili. Hyacinthus
Agav. Polianthes tuberosa
Amaryllid. Narcissus
Betuligenol (γ-(*p*-Hydroxyphenyl)-α-methyl-propyl alcohol; 1-*p*-Hydro-xyphenyl-butan-3-ol; Rhododendrol) is the aglycone of *betuloside*.
    Betul. Betula alba (bk; free?; to 25% of cork layer)
    Eric. Rhododendron chrysanthum (lvs)
Cinnamyl alcohol (fig. 8) occurs as *esters* in many plants.
    Salic. Populus balsamifera (buds, combined?)
    Laur. Cinnamomum zeylanicum (lvs; free and combined)
    Lili. Hyacinthus (fl.-oil; free and combined)
    Xanthorrhoe. Xanthorrhoea hastilis (resin)
    Amaryllid. Narcissus (fl.-oil)
Coniferyl alcohol (fig. 8) is the aglycone of *coniferin*. Is it a *lignin* unit?
3,4-Dihydroxy-benzyl alcohol (fig. 8) occurs (as *glycoside* only?) in:
    Ros. Prunus lusitanica (lvs), *Pyrus calleryana* (lvs)
β-(3,4-Dihydroxyphenyl)-ethyl alcohol is the aglycone of *echinacoside*.
β-Phenyl-ethyl alcohol occurs free and/or as *esters* in:

    Salic. Populus balsamifera (bud)
    Caryophyll. Dianthus caryophyllatus (fl.-oil)

Magnoli.   Michelia champaca (fl.-oil)
Annon.   Cananga odorata (fl.-oil)
The.   Thea (lf-oil)
Ros.   Rosa (fl.-oil); *Rubus idaeus* (frt ?)
Gerani.   Pelargonium (oil)
Rut.   Citrus (fl.-oil)
Lili.   Hyacinthus (fl.-oil), *Lilium* (fl.-oil)
Amaryllid.   Narcissus (fl.-oil)

γ(3)-Phenyl-propyl alcohol
Hamamelid.   Liquidambar (storax; free and as ester)
Styrac.   Styrax

Salicyl alcohol (Saligenin; Saligenol; fig. 8)
Salic.   Populus balsamifera (lvs, bk)

Salirepol (Gentisic alcohol) occurs in fungi? It is the aglycone of *salireposide.*

Syringenin (Sinapinic alcohol; fig. 8) is the aglycone of *syringin.* The syringyl group occurs in *lignins* of angiosperms and some gymnosperms. Does *syringenin* occur free in woody dicotyledons?

α-(*p*-Tolyl)-ethyl alcohol (fig. 8)
Zingiber.   Curcuma longa (rhiz.-oil, 5%)

β-(*p*-Hydroxyphenyl)-ethyl alcohol (Tyrosol; fig. 8)
Ole.   Osmanthus fragrans v. *auranticus* (fl.)

III PHENOLS

GENERAL

We have placed *phenols* here because some of the *alcohols* treated in the previous section are at the same time *phenols*, and because the *phenols* themselves resemble the true *tertiary alcohols.*

Some of the α,ω-*diphenyl-alkanes* are *phenols.*

While it may seem artificial to separate the *phenols* from the *phenol ethers* we have come across strange cases of distribution which would seem to support such separation. For example:

	Eugenol		Eugenol-methyl ether
Mor.	*Cannabis*	*Annon.*	*Cananga*
		Monimi.	*Atherosperma*
Laur.	*Cinnamomum zeylanicum,*	*Laur.*	*Cinnamomum oliveri*
	Cryptocarya, Dicypellium	*Piper.*	*Piper*
		Aristolochi.	*Asarum*
		Ros.	*Rosa*
		Legum.	*Acacia*

Myrt.	*Eugenia, Pimenta* (2)	*Myrt.*	*Melaleuca* (2), *Pimenta*
		Lili.	*Hyacinthus*
		Arac.	*Acorus calamus*

Isoeugenol	Isoeugenol-methyl ether
Magnoli. Michelia	*Aristolochi. Asarum*
Annon. Cananga	*Myrt. Backhousia, Melaleuca*
Myristic. Myristica	*Lab. Orthodon*
Laur. Cinnamomum, Nectandra	*Gram. Cymbopogon*
Ros. Prunus	
Rubi. Leptactinia	

Hydroquinone-methyl ether	Hydroquinone-dimethyl ether
Pyrol. Pyrola	*Lili. Hyacinthus*

Only in the cases of the *Lauraceae* and *Myrtaceae* are the *phenol* and its *phenol ether* found in the same family and only in the latter family is the same species involved (*Pimenta*). Do these records really reflect the distributions of these compounds or have we again examples which illustrate our ignorance? I am afraid it is the latter!

List and Occurrence

Allyl-catechol (Allyl-pyrocatechol; fig. 189)
  Piper.   Piper betle (lf-oil)
4-Allyl-2,6-dimethoxy-phenol (Methoxy-eugenol)
  Myristic.   Myristica fragrans
Antiarol (1,2,3-Trimethoxy-5-hydroxy-benzene)
  Mor.   Antiaris toxicaria (latex)
Catechol (1,2-Dihydroxy-benzene; Pyrocatechol; fig. 9) seems at first
  sight to be rather widely spread, usually in combination, but I have
  a *very* extensive list of reported absences
  Salic.   Populus (free in 7 species), *Salix* (free)
  Chenopodi.   Beta (some doubt of this)
  Guttif.   Psorospermum guineense (bk, >9%)
  Platan.   Platanus (some doubt of this)
  Rut.   Citrus paradisi (lvs, frt)
  Vit.   Ampelopsis hederacea (lvs)
  Lili.   Allium (bulb)
It has *not* been found in
  Myric. (*Myrica*); *Jugland.* (*Carya, Juglans*); *Betul.* (*Alnus, Betula*);
  Fag. (*Fagus, Quercus*); *Ulm.* (*Zelkova*); *Eucommi.* (*Eucommia*); *Mor.*
  (*Humulus, Morus*); *Loranth.* (*Viscum*); *Polygon.* (*Polygonum, Rumex*); *Caryophyll.* (*Stellaria*); *Magnoli.* (*Magnolia*); *Annon.*

(*Asimina*); *Schisandr.* (*Schisandra*); *Calycanth.* (*Calycanthus*); *Laur.* (*Lindera*); *Euptele.* (*Euptelea*); *Cercidiphyll.* (*Cercidiphyllum*); *Ranuncul.* (*Caltha*); *Berberid.* (*Berberis*); *Lardizabal.* (*Akebia*); *Aristolochi.* (*Aristolochia*); *Actinidi.* (*Actinidia*); *Guttif.* (*Hypericum*); *Papaver.* (*Chelidonium, Eschscholtzia*); *Crucif.* (*Brassica*); *Hamamelid.* (*Liquidambar*); *Saxifrag.* (*Deutzia, Philadelphus*); *Ros.* (*Amygdalus, Malus, Prunus, Pyrus*); *Legum.* (*Caragana, Lupinus, Robinia, Sophora*); *Gerani.* (*Erodium*?); *Tropaeol.* (*Tropaeolum*); *Euphorbi.* (*Euphorbia, Securinega*); *Rut.* (*Evodia*); *Simaroub.* (*Ailanthus*); *Anacardi.* (*Rhus*); *Acer.* (*Acer*); *Hippocastan.* (*Aesculus*); *Aquifoli.* (*Ilex*); *Celastr.* (*Euonymus*); *Staphyle.* (*Staphylea*); *Bux.* (*Buxus*); *Rhamn.* (*Rhamnus*); *Vit.* (*Vitis*); *Tili.* (*Tilia*); *Thymelae.* (*Daphne*); *Elaeagn.* (*Hippophaë*); *Stachyur.* (*Stachyurus*); *Tamaric* (*Myricaria*); *Davidi.* (*Davidia*); *Corn.* (*Cornus*); *Arali.* (*Acanthopanax, Hedera*); *Umbell.* (*Aegopodium*); *Eric.* (*Erica, Gaylusaccia, Rhododendron*); *Primul.* (*Primula*); *Plumbagin.* (*Armeria*); *Eben.* (*Diospyros*); *Styrac.* (*Styrax*); *Ole.* (*Fraxinus, Syringa*); *Asclepiad.* (*Periploca*); *Convolvul.* (*Convolvulus*); *Lab.* (*Elsholtzia, Lamium*); *Solan.* (*Lycium, Solanum*); *Bignoni.* (*Catalpa*); *Plantagin.* (*Plantago*); *Caprifoli.* (*Lonicera, Sambucus*); *Comp.* (*Achillea, Taraxacum*); *Lili.* (*Asparagus*); *Irid.* (*Iris*); *Gram.* (*Phragmites*); *Lemn.* (*Lemna*); *Typh.* (*Typha*)

Chavibetol (fig. 189)
> *Piper.   Piper betle* (lf-oil)

Chavicol (1-(*p*-Hydroxyphenyl)-prop-2-ene; fig. 189) is the aglycone of *lusitanicoside.*
> *Piper.   Piper* (*Chavica*) *betle* (ess. oil)
> *Rut.   Barosma venustum* (lvs)
> *Myrt.   Pimenta acris* (lvs), *racemosa* (lvs)
> *Lab.   Origanum majorana* (plt)
> *Zingiber.   Zingiber officinale*

Creosol (Homoguaiacol; 1-Methyl-3-methoxy-4-hydroxy-benzene)
> *Annon.   Cananga odorata* (fl.-oil)
> *Umbell.   Pimpinella anisum* (sd-oil)
> *Ole.   Jasminum* (fl.-oil)

m-Cresol (1-Methyl-3-hydroxy-benzene)
> *The.   Thea* (lf-oil)
> *Comp.   Artemisia transiliensis* (ess. oil)

p-Cresol (1-Methyl-4-hydroxy-benzene) has been recorded from conifers and, in small amount, from
> *The.   Thea* (lvs)
> *Legum.   Acacia farnesiana* (fl.)
> *Rut.   Citrus* (fl.)

Umbell. *Pimpinella anisum* (frt)

Eric. *Ledum palustre* v. *dilatatum* (lf-oil)

Ole. *Jasminum* (fl.-oil)

Comp. *Gnaphalium arenarium*

Lili. *Lilium candidum* (fl.)

Ethyl-guaiacol (1-Ethyl-3-methoxy-4-hydroxy-benzene)

Laur. *Cinnamomum camphora*

o-Ethyl-phenol (1-Ethyl-2-hydroxy-benzene)

Anacardi. *Schinus molle* (oil; much)

Eugenol (Allyl-guaiacol; fig. 9) occurs sometimes as acetate.

Mor. *Cannabis sativa*

Laur. *Cinnamomum zeylanicum* (lf-oil?), *Dicypellium caryophyl-latum, Cryptocarya (Cinnamomum) massoy* (bk-oil; 75%)

Myrt. *Eugenia caryophyllata* (oil of cloves; 95%); *Pimenta acris* (oil), *officinalis* (oil)

Lab. *Ocimum gratissimum* (lf-oil; 60%), *sanctum* (lf-oil; 70%)

Guaiacol (1-Hydroxy-2-methoxy-benzene; fig. 9) seems to be widely distributed (free?):

Mor. *Cannabis sativa*

Zygophyll. *Guaiacum officinale* (resin)

Rut. *Citrus* (fl.-oil), *Ruta montana* (oil)

Acer. *Acer saccharum* (sap)

Umbell. *Apium graveolens* (sd-oil)

Solan. *Nicotiana tabacum* (lf-oil)

Pandan. *Pandanus odoratissimus* (fl.-oil)

Hydroquinone (1,4-Dihydroxy-benzene) occurs mostly combined. It is the aglycone of *arbutin.*

Prote. *Protea mellifera* (lvs, 2–5%)

Saxifrag. *Bergenia; Hydrangea?*; but *not* in *Escallonia, Heuchera, Philadelphus, Ribes, Rodgersia*

Ros. *Pyrus communis* (lf-bud), *Rubus fruticosus* (lvs)

Umbell. *Pimpinella anisum* (sd)

Eric. *Arbutus unedo* (lvs), *Rhododendron* sp. (lvs), *Vaccinium vitis-idaea* (lvs, fl.)

Comp. *Xanthium canadense* (sd)

Hydroquinone-ethyl ether

Illici. *Illicium anisatum* (frt), *verum*

Rut. *Empleurum serrulatum* (lf-oil)

Hydroquinone-methyl ether (fig. 9)

Pyrol. *Pyrola secunda* (lvs)

Isoeugenol

Magnoli. *Michelia champaca* (fl.-oil)

Annon. *Cananga odorata* (fl.-oil)

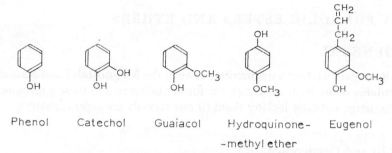

Phenol   Catechol   Guaiacol   Hydroquinone-   Eugenol

-methyl ether

Fig. 9. Some phenols.

Myristic.   Myristica fragrans (sd-oil)
Laur.   Cinnamomum, Nectandra puchury (sd-oil)
Ros.   Prunus domestica (fl.)
Rubi.   Leptactinia senegambica (fl.-oil)
p-Isopropyl-phenol (Australol)
Myrt.   Eucalyptus
Methoxy-hydroquinone is known only (?) as *glycoside.*
Phenol (Hydroxy-benzene; fig. 9) is reported from a conifer and
Salic.   Salix (bk, free ?)
The.   Thea (lvs)
Saxifrag.   Ribes nigrum (shoot, free ?)
Rut.   Ruta montana (ess. oil)
Solan.   Nicotiana tabacum (lvs)
Comp.   Artemisia annua (ess. oil)
Phloroglucin (1,3,5-Trihydroxy-benzene) is often in combination. It is
reported (free ?) from conifers and
Caryophyll.   Lychnis dioica
m-Phlorol (1-Ethyl-3-hydroxy-benzene)
Comp.   Arnica montana (rt)
Pyrogallol (1,2,3-Trihydroxy-benzene) can be obtained from many
tannins. It occurs free (?) in conifers but not (?) in angiosperms.
Pyrogallol-1,3-dimethyl ether
Comp.   Artemisia herba-alba v. *densiflora* (ess. oil)
Pyrolagenin is the aglycone of *pyrolatin.*
Sesamol (1-Hydroxy-3,4-methylenedioxy-benzene)
Pedali.   Sesamum indicum (oil)
p-Vinyl-phenol is the aglycone of *furcatin.*

IV PHENOLIC ESTERS AND ETHERS

GENERAL

Once again we find a distinction between the **Magnoliales** and **Ranunculales** (*sensu* Syll. 12, 1964), the former being rich in these substances, the latter virtually lacking them (if our records are representative).

List and Occurrence

1-Allyl-2,3,4,5-tetramethoxy-benzene
    Umbell. Petroselinum sativum (oil)
Anethole (fig. 10)
    Piper. Piper peltatum
    Magnoli. Magnolia salicifolia (lf-oil; to 73%)
    Illici. Illicium anisatum (little), *verum* (oil; to 88%)
    Rut. Clausena anisata (lf-oil; to 89%)
    Burser. Canarium commune
    Myrt. Backhousia anisata (lf-oil)
    Umbell. Foeniculum vulgare, Pimpinella anisum (sd-oil; to 85%)
    Lab. Ocimum basilicum
Apiole (1-Allyl-2,5-dimethoxy-3,4-methylenedioxy-benzene; fig. 189)
    Laur. Licaria (*Misanteca*) sp. (bk, wd), *Ocotea* sp. (bk, wd)
    Piper. Piper angustifolium (lf-oil)
    Umbell. Apium?, *Crithmum maritimum* (rt, ess. oil; to 60%),
        Petroselinum sativum
Asarone (fig. 10)
    Piper. Piper angustifolium (oil)
    Aristolochi. Asarum arifolium (rt), *caudatum* (rt), *europaeum* (rt)
    Umbell. Daucus carota (sd-oil)
    Lab. Orthodon asaroniferum (ess. oil)
    Arac. Acorus calamus, gramineus (rt-oil)
β-Asarone is the *cis-trans*- isomer of *asarone*.
    Arac. Acorus calamus (rt-oil)
Calamol ($C_6H_2 . (OCH_3)_3 . CH_2 . CH{=}CH_2$)
    Arac. Acorus calamus (rt-oil)
Coniferyl-benzoate (Lubanol-benzoate)
    Styrac. Styrax benzoin (gum, chief constit.)
p-Coumaric acid-methyl ether is the aglycone of *linocinnamarin*.
p-Cresol-methyl ether
    Annon. Cananga odorata (fl.-oil)
Crocatone (5-Methoxy-3,4-methylenedioxy-propiophenone)
    Umbell. Oenanthe crocata

Croweacin
  Rut. *Eriostemon crowei* (lf-oil)
Dill-apiole (1-Allyl-5,6-dimethoxy-3,4-methylenedioxy-benzene) is iso-
  meric with *apiole*.
  Monimi. *Laurelia serrata* (lf and st.-oil)
  Laur. an unnamed member (wd-oil)
  Piper. *Piper* (*angulatum* ?) (lf-oil)
  Umbell. *Anethum graveolens* (frt-oil), *sowa* (frt-oil); *Crithmum*
    maritimum (frt-oil); *Ligusticum scoticum* (frt-oil)
  Lab. *Orthodon formosanus* (sd-oil; to 65%)
3,4-Dimethoxy-cinnamic acid
  Scrophulari. *Veronicastrum* (*Veronica*) *virginicum* (rhiz.)
Elemicin (fig. 10) seems to be widely spread
  Laur. *Cinnamomum glanduliferum* (wd-oil)
  Rut. *Boronia muelleri, pinnata, thujona* (oils; to 90%); *Zieria*
    smithii (ess. oil)
  Burser. *Canarium commune* (resin)
  Myrt. *Backhousia myrtifolia* (ess. oil), *Melaleuca bracteata* (ess.
    oil)
  Lab. *Orthodon elemiciniferum*
  Gram. *Cymbopogon goeringii* (ess. oil; 57%), *procerus* (ess. oil;
    35%)
Esdragol (Estragol; Isoanethole; Methyl-chavicol)
  Illici. *Illicium*
  Laur. *Persea gratissima* (bk)
Ethyl-gallate
  Eric. *Arbutus unedo*
Eugenol-acetyl-salicylic acid ester
  Myrt. *Eugenia*
Eugenol-methyl ether
  Annon. *Cananga odorata* (fl.-oil)
  Monimi. *Atherosperma moschatum* (lvs)
  Laur. *Cinnamomum oliveri* (lvs)
  Piper. *Piper betle* (lvs)
  Aristolochi. *Asarum canadense* (rt; much), *europaeum* (rt; much)
  Ros. *Rosa* (fl.)
  Legum. *Acacia farnesiana* (fl.)
  Myrt. *Melaleuca bracteata* (lvs, ess. oil; to 95%), *leucadendron*;
    Pimenta
  Lili. *Hyacinthus* (fl.)
  Arac. *Acorus calamus* (Japan)
Eugenone (2,4,6-Trimethoxy-benzoyl-acetone)
  Myrt. *Eugenia caryophyllata*

Foeniculin
   Illici.   Illicium
   Umbell.   Foeniculum vulgare
Gentisic acid-benzyl ester
   Salic.   Populus
Hydroquinone-dimethyl ether
   Lili.   Hyacinthus (fl.-oil)
2-Hydroxy-4-methoxy-benzoic acid-methyl ether (Primula-camphor) occurs free (?) and as *glycoside*.
   Primul.   Primula officinalis (rt & fl.-oil), *veris* (rt), *viscosa* (rt; as *primverin*)
2-Hydroxy-5-methoxy-benzoic acid-methyl ether occurs free (?) and as *primulaverin*.
   Primul.   Primula acaulis (rt; as *primulaverin*), *auricula* (rt; free ?), *officinalis* (rt; free ?)
Iso-elemicin
   Myristic.   Myristica fragrans (sd-oil)
   Myrt.   Backhousia myrtifolia (lf-oil)
Isoeugenol-methyl ether
   Aristolochi.   Asarum arifolium
   Myrt.   Backhousia myrtifolia (lf-oil), *Melaleuca bracteata* (lf-oil)
   Lab.   Orthodon methylisoeugenoliferum (sd-oil; 53%)
   Gram.   Cymbopogon javanensis (ess. oil)
Isomyristicin
   Myristic.   Myristica
   Umbell.   Anethum graveolens (ess. oil)
Isosafrole
   Annon.   Cananga odorata
   Illici.   Illicium religiosum (frt)
   Umbell.   Ligusticum acutilobum (rt-oil)
Methyl gallate
   Anacardi.   Cotinus coggygria (lvs)
   Myrt.   Metrosideros excelsa (fl.)
Methyl salicylate (Salicylic acid-methyl ester; fig. 438) occurs usually as *glycoside*. The following list includes records of occurrence, both free and combined, largely from the early work of van Romburgh (1899) in the tropics
   Betul. (*Betula*); *Fag.* (*Quercus* (3)); *Mor.* (*Conocephalus, Ficus*); *Chenopodi.* (*Chenopodium*); *Myristic.* (*Myristica*); *Calycanth.* (*Calycanthus*); *Laur.* (*Lindera*); *Ranuncul.* (*Clematis*); *Menisperm.* (*Cocculus*); *The.* (*Camellia*); *Saxifrag.* (*Ribes*); *Ros.* (*Fragaria, Photinia, Prunus, Rubus*); *Chrysobalan.* (*Parinari*); *Legum.* (at least

22/44); *Erythroxyl.* (*Erythroxylum* (4)); *Euphorbi.* (*Bridelia* (2), *Baccaurea, Cyclostemon* (3), *Macaranga*); *Rut.* (*Atalantia, Glycosmis* (2), *Murraya*); *Burser.* (*Garuga*); *Polygal.* (*Comesperma ericinum* (rt; prob. free), *Polygala* (7), *Xanthophyllum* (2?)); *Sapind.* (at least 5–6/7–8); *Sabi.* (*Meliosma*?); *Staphyle.* (*Turpinia*); *Icacin.* (*Platea* (2)); *Rhamn.* (*Alphitonia, Ceanothus, Paliurus*); *Vit.* (*Vitis*); *Elaeocarp.* (*Elaeocarpus*); *Flacourti.* (*Homalium* (2), *Hydnocarpus* (3), *Ryparosa* (2), *Scolopia, Taraktogenos*); *Viol.* (*Alsodeia*); *Myrt.* (*Eugenia, Metrosideros*); *Lecythid.* (*Barringtonia* (2)); *Rhizophor.* (*Carallia* (1)); *Pyrol.* (*Monotropa*); *Eric.* (*Gaultheria*); *Epacrid.* (*Styphelia tubiflora* (lvs; prob. free)); *Myrsin.* (*Ardisia* (7)); *Sapot.* (*Sideroxylon*); *Eben.* (*Diospyros* (4), *Maba* (2)); *Symploc.* (*Symplocos* (2)); *Ole.* (*Linociera* (1–2), *Nyctanthes*); *Apocyn.* (*Alstonia, Chilocarpus, Hunteria*); *Asclepiad.* (*Cryptolepis, Marsdenia*); *Rubi.* (at least 10/20); *Bignoni.* (*Bignonia* (2), *Nyctocalos, Tabebuia*); *Acanth.* (*Thunbergia*); *Caprifoli.* (*Viburnum*); *Comp.* (*Stifftia, Vernonia*); *Gram.* (*Dendrocalamus*)

Myristicin (fig. 10) may be psychotropic (Shulgin, 1966)

Myristic.   Myristica fragrans (sd), and other spp. ?

Laur.   Cinnamomum glanduliferum (wd)

Umbell.   Anethum graveolens (oil), *Carum* (*Ridolfia*) *segetum* (fl.-oil; 33%), *Levisticum scoticum* (rhiz.; much), *Oenanthe stolonifera* (frt), *Pastinaca sativa* (plt; little), *Petroselinum sativum* (ess. oil), *Peucedanum graveolens* (oil)

Lab.   Orthodon asaroniferum, grosseserratum, hirtus (little)

Phaselic acid (Malic ester of caffeic acid)

Legum.   Phaseolus

m-Phlorol-isobutyrate

Comp.   Arnica montana (rt)

m-Phlorol-methyl ether

Comp.   Arnica montana (rt)

Pipataline (fig. 189)

Piper.   Piper peepuloides (frt)

Quinic acid-1,4-di-*p*-coumarate

Bromeli.   Ananas

Safrole (Shikimol; fig. 10)

Annon.   Cananga odorata

Illici.   Illicium parviflorum (oil; 90%), *religiosum* (lvs)

Monimi.   Doryphora sassafras (bk, lvs, frt ?), *Nemuaron humboldtii* (ess. oil; 99%)

Laur.   Beilsmiedia sp.; *Cinnamomum* (many); *Ocotea cymbarum, pretiosa; Sassafras albidum*

Aristolochi.   Asarum sp.

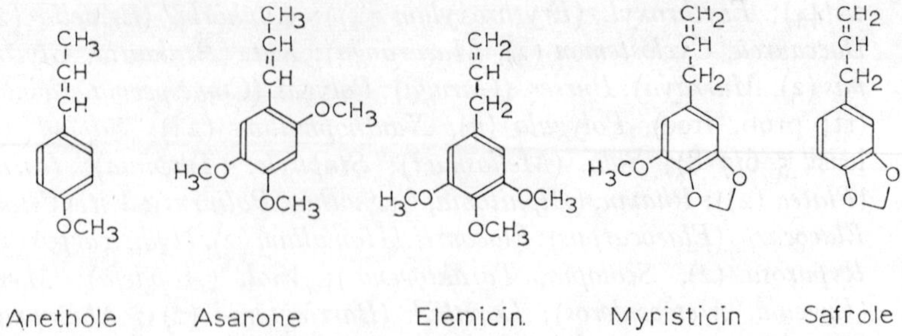

Anethole   Asarone   Elemicin.   Myristicin   Safrole

Fig. 10. Some phenolic ethers.

Sparassol (2-Hydroxy-4-methoxy-6-methyl-methyl benzoate) occurs in fungi, lichens, and
> Eric.   *Rhododendron japonicum* (rtbk)

1-Undecenyl-3,4-methylenedioxy-benzene (fig. 189)
> *Piper.*   *Piper longum* (frt)

ALDEHYDES

GENERAL

We have included here:

> I. Aliphatic aldehydes
> > 1. Saturated aliphatic aldehydes.
> > 2. Unsaturated aliphatic aldehydes.
> II. Aromatic aldehydes (mostly phenolic)

We have excluded *terpenoid aldehydes* such as *citronellal*, and aldehydes which are *naphthalene* derivatives.

I.1 Saturated aliphatic aldehydes

List and Occurrence

Formaldehyde (Methanal; H.CHO) may occur in traces in many plants
> *Chenopodi.*   *Beta* (lvs, rt)
> *Lab.*   *Monarda fistulosa, punctata* (lf-oil)
> *Comp.*   *Achillea millefolium* (ess. oil)

Acetaldehyde (Ethanal; CH_3.CHO) has been reported (free ?) in many plants
> *Betul.*   *Carpinus betulus* (lvs)

    Fag. *Quercus* (lvs)
    Laur. *Cinnamomum camphora*
    Crucif. *Brassica*
    Ros. *Rosa canina, Pyrus germanica, Sorbus aucuparia*
    Rut. *Citrus*
    Umbell. *Carum carvi* (oil), *Foeniculum vulgare* (oil), *Pimpinella anisum* (oil)
    Lab. *Mentha piperita* (oil), *Rosmarinus officinale*
    Solan. *Nicotiana tabacum* (lvs)

Propionaldehyde (Propanal; $CH_3.CH_2.CHO$) has been reported from algae and a conifer, but not (?) from angiosperms.

Butyraldehyde (Butanal; $CH_3.(CH_2)_2.CHO$) occurs (free ?) in
    Betul. *Carpinus betulus* (lvs)
    Fag. *Quercus sessiliflora* (lvs)
    Mor. *Morus* (lvs)
    Crucif. *Raphanus*
    Legum. *Acacia* (lvs)
    Myrt. *Eucalyptus globulus* (ess. oil), *Melaleuca leucadendron* (lf-oil)
    Lab. *Lavandula delphinensis* (oil), *Monarda fistulosa* (ess. oil)
    Comp. *Artemisia scoparia* (oil)

Isobutyraldehyde (Isobutanal; $(CH_3)_2CH.CHO$) is reported from algae, conifers and
    Mor. *Morus* (lvs)
    Crucif. *Raphanus*
    Legum. *Acacia* (lvs)
    Solan. *Datura stramonium* ?, *Nicotiana tabacum* (lvs)

Valeraldehyde (Pentanal; $CH_3.(CH_2)_3.CHO$)
    Betul. *Carpinus betulus* (probably in lvs)
    Fag. *Quercus sessiliflora* (lvs)
    Laur. *Ocotea pretiosa* (tr.)
    Myrt. *Eucalyptus dives, globulus*?; *Melaleuca leucadendron*?

Isovaleraldehyde (3-Methyl-butanal; $(CH_3)_2.CH.CH_2.CHO$) is a hemiterpenoid.
    Fag. *Quercus sessiliflora* (lvs)
    Laur. *Cinnamomum camphora*
    Legum. *Glycine max*
    Rut. *Citrus*
    Myrt. *Eucalyptus globulus* and other spp.
    Lab. *Lavandula delphinensis, Mentha piperita, Monarda fistulosa*
    Comp. *Helichrysum italicum* (ess. oil)

Hexanal (Caproic aldehyde; $CH_3.(CH_2)_4.CHO$) is reported from conifers and
    Fag. *Quercus sessiliflora* (lvs)

5

> *Laur. Cinnamomum camphora*
> *Myrt. Eucalyptus globulus*

Heptanal (Oenanthal; $CH_3.(CH_2)_5.CHO$)
> *Annon. Cananga odorata* (fl.-oil)
> *Lili. Hyacinthus* (fl.-oil ?)

Octanal (Caprylic aldehyde; $CH_3.(CH_2)_6.CHO$) is reported from conifers and
> *Rut. Citrus* (at least 3 spp.), *Zanthoxylum rhetsa*
> *Lab. Lavandula delphinensis*
> *Gram. Cymbopogon winterianus*

Nonanal ($CH_3.(CH_2)_7.CHO$) is reported from conifers and
> *Ros. Rosa*
> *Rut. Citrus* spp., *Eremocitrus glauca*
> *Gram. Cymbopogon*
> *Zingiber. Zingiber officinalis*

Decanal (Capric aldehyde; $CH_3.(CH_2)_8.CHO$) is said to occur in conifers and
> *Laur. Cinnamomum camphora, micranthum* (ess. oil)
> *Legum. Acacia cavenia?, farnesiana; Cassia*
> *Rut. Citrus bigaradia* (oil)
> *Umbell. Coriandrum sativum* (oil)
> *Lab. Lavandula*
> *Irid. Iris* (rt-oil)

Dodecanal (Lauryl aldehyde; $CH_3.(CH_2)_{10}.CHO$) occurs in conifers and
> *Rut. Citrus bigaradia, medica* v. *acida*

Tetradecanal (Myristic aldehyde; $CH_3.(CH_2)_{12}.CHO$) is reported from a conifer and
> *Laur. Cinnamomum* sp., *Ocotea usambarensis* (bk-oil)

Pentadecanal ($CH_3.(CH_2)_{13}.CHO$)
> *Laur. Cinnamomum micranthum*

Octadecanal (Stearyl aldehyde; $CH_3.(CH_2)_{16}.CHO$) is reported from lichens and
> *Laur. Cinnamomum* sp.

I.2 Unsaturated aliphatic aldehydes

List and Occurrence

α-Methyl-acrolein (Artemisal; Methacrolein; $CH_2{=}C(CH_3).CHO$)
> *Comp. Artemisia tridentata* (lf-oil)

Hex-2-en-1-al (α-Hexenal; $CH_3.(CH_2)_2.CH{=}CH.CHO$) has been called 'leaf-aldehyde'. Karrer (1958) says: 'Dürfte in allen chlorophyllhaltigen Pflanzen vorkommen u. bei der Assimilation eine Rolle spielen.'

Hept-2-en-1-al (β-Butyl-acrolein; $CH_3.(CH_2)_3.CH\!=\!CH.CHO$)
  Legum. Glycine max?
Oct-2-en-1-al ($CH_3.(CH_2)_4.CH\!=\!CH.CHO$)
  Zingiber. Achasma walang
8-Methyl-non-2-en-1-al
  Umbell. Coriandrum sativum
Nona-2,6-dien-1-al
  Viol. Viola odorata (lf-oil)
  Cucurbit. Cucumis sativus
Deca-2,4-dien-1-al ($CH_3.(CH_2)_4.CH\!=\!CH.CH\!=\!CH.CHO$)
  Legum. Arachis hypogaea (oil), *Glycine max* (oil)
Dec-2-en-1-al ($CH_3.(CH_2)_6.CH\!=\!CH.CHO$)
  Rut. Citrus
  Umbell. Coriandrum sativum (ess. oil)
  Zingiber. Achasma walang (oil of lvs and rt)
Dodec-2-en-1-al ($CH_3.(CH_2)_8.CH\!=\!CH.CHO$) has been found in a millipede and in
  Rut. Citrus
  Umbell. Daucus carota, Eryngium foetidum (ess. oil; much)
  Zingiber. Achasma walang, Zingiber?
2-Methyl-dodec-2-en-1-al: from an unidentified seed-oil.
Trideca-2,4-dien-1-al: see immediately above.
Tridec-2-en-1-al: see immediately above.

II AROMATIC ALDEHYDES (MOSTLY PHENOLIC)

GENERAL

Our knowledge of the distribution of *aromatic aldehydes* is so fragmentary that we can use it but little in chemotaxonomy.

It is obvious that some plants of economic value, such as *Cinnamomum* and *Vanilla*, have been studied fairly fully. Many of the occurrences recorded result, too, from the close examination of essential oils.

We may note one or two points of interest.

(*a*) The order **Magnoliales** is represented in the following list by *Magnoliaceae, Annonaceae, Illiciaceae, Monimiaceae,* and *Lauraceae*. The **Ranunculales** is without representation.

(*b*) The occurrence of *4-methoxy-salicylic aldehyde* in the order **Gentianales** might prove of real interest. It has been reported from *Apocynaceae* (1) and from *Asclepiadaceae* (several genera, mostly closely related). Is it elsewhere in the order?

5-2

List and Occurrence

3-Acetyl-6-methoxy-benzaldehyde
    Comp.   Encelia farinosa (lvs)

o-Anisaldehyde (Salicyl aldehyde-methyl ether; 2-Methoxy-benzaldehyde)
    Laur.   Cinnamomum cassia

p-Anisaldehyde (4-Methoxy-benzaldehyde) results often from oxidation of *anethole*? It is reported from algae, fungi, conifers and
    Magnoli.   Magnolia salicifolia (lf-oil)
    Illici.   Illicium
    Legum.   Acacia farnesiana (fl.-oil), *Mimosa*?
    Rut.   Pelea madagascariensis
    Burser.   Protium carana
    Eric.   Erica arborea
    Lab.   Agastache rugosa (ess. oil)
    Orchid.   Vanilla

Asaraldehyde (2,4,5-Trimethoxy-benzaldehyde)
    Aristolochi.   Asarum europaeum (rt-oil)
    Umbell.   Daucus carota
    Arac.   Acorus calamus

Benzaldehyde (fig. 11) occurs in some *cyanogenic glycosides*. It is reported free (?) from conifers and
    Annon.   Cananga odorata (fl.-oil)
    Ros.   Rosa, Rubus idaeus (frt)
    Legum.   Acacia farnesiana (fl.-oil)
    Rut.   Citrus, Ruta
    Myrt.   Eucalyptus, Melaleuca leucadendron
    Lili.   Hyacinthus (fl.-oil)
    Amaryllid.   Narcissus (fl.-oil)

Cinnamic aldehyde (fig. 11)
    Laur.   Cinnamomum (several species; to 90% of ess. oil)
    Legum.   Cassia
    Myrt.   Melaleuca
    Lab.   Lavandula, Pogostemon patchouly
    Lily.   Hyacinthus (fl.-oil)
    Amaryllid.   Narcissus (fl.-oil)

Coniferyl aldehyde (Ferulic aldehyde; fig. 11) seems to be derivable from *lignins*. Does it occur free in woods?

3,4-Dihydroxy-benzaldehyde (Protocatechuic aldehyde)
    Comp.   Cichorium intybus (free in sd and sdlg; combined later)
    Mus.   Musa ('cavendish' banana; fungistatic in green frt)

m(3)-Hydroxy-benzaldehyde: occurs in *salinigrin*.

p(4)-Hydroxy-benzaldehyde: occurs in *dhurrin*. It is reported free (?) from a moss and

    Papaver.   *Papaver somniferum*
    Xanthorrhoe.   *Xanthorrhoea australis* (resin), *hastilis* (resin)
    Gram.   *Andropogon*
    Orchid.   *Vanilla*

o(2)-Methoxy-cinnamic aldehyde
    Laur.   *Cinnamomum cassia* (oil of bk and lvs)

p(4)-Methoxy-cinnamic aldehyde
    Comp.   *Artemisia dracunculus* (ess. oil)

p(4)-Methoxy-salicylic aldehyde (fig. 11)
    Apocyn.   *Hanghomia marseillii* (rt)
    Asclepiad.   *Chlorocodon* sp. (*white?*) (rt), *Decalepis hamiltonii* (rt),
        Hemidesmus indicus (rt), *Periploca graeca* (bk), *Tylophora indica* (rt)

3,4-Methylenedioxy-cinnamic aldehyde (Piperonyl-acrolein)
    Laur.   *Cinnamomum* sp.

Parvifloral (fig. 11)
    Rut.   *Zanthoxylum parviflorum* (wd)

Phenyl-acetaldehyde
    Ros.   *Rosa*

Phenyl-propionaldehyde (Dihydro-cinnamic aldehyde)
    Laur.   *Cinnamomum cassia, zeylanicum*

Piperonal (Heliotropin; 3,4-Methylenedioxy-benzaldehyde; fig. 11)
    Monimi.   *Doryphora sassafras* (tr.)
    Laur.   *Cinnamomum* sp.
    Ros.   *Spiraea*
    Legum.   *Robinia pseudacacia* (fl.-oil; '*heliotropin*')
    Viol.   *Viola odorata* (fl.)
    Umbell.   *Eryngium poterium* (ess. oil)
    Orchid.   *Vanilla* (Tahiti; not others ?)

Salicylic aldehyde (*o*(2)-Hydroxy-benzaldehyde; fig. 11) is the aglycone of *spiraein*. It seems to be widely distributed.

    Laur.   *Cinnamomum cassia*
    Ros.   *Filipendula* (*Spiraea*) *ulmaria, Prunus avium*
    Rhamn.   *Ceanothus velutinus* (lvs)
    Flacourti.   *Homalium tomentosum*
    Apocyn.   *Rauwolfia caffra* (bk)
    Boragin.   *Cordia asperrima*
    Solan.   *Nicotiana tabacum* (lvs)

Sinapic aldehyde (fig. 11)
    Jugland.   *Juglans cinerea* (htwd), *nigra* (htwd)
    Fag.   *Quercus* (htwd)
    Acer.   *Acer saccharinum* (htwd)

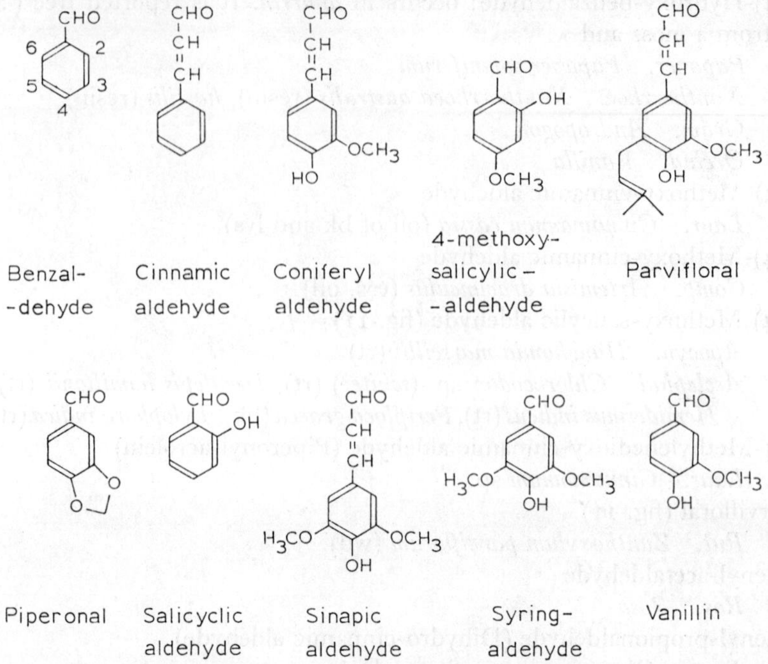

Fig. 11. Some aromatic aldehydes.

Syringaldehyde (fig. 11) can be obtained from *lignins* of all (?) angio-sperms and a few gymnosperms.

3,4,5-Trimethoxy-benzaldehyde

   Gram.   Cymbopogon (2 spp.)

Vanillin (fig. 11) can be obtained from most *lignins*, and secondarily from many plants.

   Orchid.   Nigritella suaveolens (fl.), *Vanilla planifolia* (frt; to 3%)

Veratraldehyde (3,4-Dimethoxy-benzaldehyde)

   Umbell.   Eryngium poterium

   Gram.   Cymbopogon javanensis

ALKALOIDS

GENERAL

It is hard to compile general notes for such a diverse lot of substances as the *alkaloids*. It is not even possible to define an alkaloid in a way that would please everyone, since some of the simpler alkaloids of one author would be excluded by another. The *simple amines*, for example, grade into alkaloids without an N-ring, such as the *alkaloidal amines*. It has been proposed to call these last 'proto-alkaloids'.

Alston and Turner (1963) say:

> Among nitrogenous substances of plants there is almost a continuum from the universal products of metabolism to alkaloids in the strict sense, and of course nitrogen-containing secondary compounds exist which are not classified as alkaloids. Purine and pyrimidine bases and the amino acid, histidine, are alkaloids except by the physiological criterion. Betacyanins...except for the absence of any obvious physiological effects, are clearly model alkaloids.

Mothes (1966) has reviewed our knowledge of the biogenesis of alkaloids. Even more recently Robinson has dealt generally with our subject in his *The Biochemistry of Alkaloids* (1968). We have drawn heavily upon him. Many other sources have been used in compiling the following notes and the 'list and occurrence' sections which follow. We may mention particularly the very useful, but deliberately uncritical, book *Alkaloid-bearing Plants and their Contained Alkaloids* by Willaman and Schubert (1961), which lists over 3,600 species of plants as containing 2,000 alkaloids; the now rather dated 4th edition of *The Plant Alkaloids* by Henry (1949); the long series entitled *The Alkaloids: Chemistry and Physiology* (vols 1, 1950; 2, 1952; 3, 1953; 4, 1954; edited by Manske and Holmes; and 5, 1955; 6, 1960; 7, 1960; 8, 1965; 9, 1967; 10, 1968; 11, 1968; edited by Manske); and Swan's *An Introduction to the Alkaloids* (1967).

Some surveys for distribution have been made. We may note that of Douglas and Kiang (1957), who tested 214 plants for alkaloids and found 38 strongly positive. Hegnauer (in Swain, 1963) stresses the taxonomic significance of distribution. The survey of Willaman and Li (1963) should also be mentioned, it recalls the work of McNair (1931, 1935, 1936). Efforts to relate 'size' of alkaloids to the type of plant (herb, shrub, tree) and to the habitat (tropical, sub-tropical, temperate) meet with little success. Wideness of distribution of individual alkaloids is also considered by Willaman and Li. They conclude that *caffeine* (14 families) is the most widely distributed alkaloid, followed by *trigonelline* (12), and *nicotine* (9). Less widely spread as to families but occurring in many genera and species (genera/species) are *lycorine* (30/85), *berberine* (26/89), and *protopine* (25/79). I give their figures in each case. At the other end of the scale, they say, are 1,443 alkaloids known to occur in but one species!

Schultes (1963) has something to say as to richness of individual families. He estimates that at least 10% of the species of the *Leguminosae* and *Solanaceae* have alkaloids. Recent work on the *Apocynaceae*, he points out, has tremendously increased our knowledge of that family and he concludes that about 10% of all known alkaloids occur in it! Mothes (1966) has figures to illustrate this last point. He says that in the 5 years before he writes the known alkaloids of *Vinca* (including *Catharanthus*?) have jumped from 20 to 80 and that the *Apocynaceae* (which includes *Vinca*) have more than 300 alkaloids, as many as were known from the plant kingdom 40 or 50 years ago! The plants of Australia and of Papua–New Guinea have been surveyed by Webb (1949, 1952, 1955).

As to the physical properties of alkaloids we may note that they are usually basic—hence the name *alkaloid* or 'alkali-like', proposed by Meisner a century and a half ago—but there are exceptions. They are usually colourless solids, but some (such as *berberine*) are coloured, and some (such as *nicotine*) are liquid. Most of them are optically active, and the different active forms are usually, but not always, found in different plants.

They are said to occur in the cell-sap as cations and may be associated with particular acids, but this is not always the case.

They are rare in animals. *Salamandra* is said to have some with *oxazolidine* nuclei and some with a *carbinolamine* system. An arthropod, *Glomeris marginata*, secretes *1,2-dimethyl-4-quinazolone*.

In the plant kingdom they have been found in fungi, in *Equisetum*, in *Lycopodium*, and in the higher plants. It is difficult to say just how many families of angiosperms produce alkaloids. Some of the supposed records are highly suspect. I have hundreds of names of 'alkaloids' which seem to have been recorded but once and whose existence, let alone structure, has never been confirmed.

It would be idle at this time to try to generalize as to the biogenesis of alkaloids. Much is known, but much is speculative, or based on but a few examples. It is probable that some of the widely distributed alkaloids arise in different ways in different groups; in such cases they would, chemotaxonomically speaking, be different substances! Mothes (1966) recognizes this sort of difficulty. Writing of the *quinoline alkaloids* he says:

> There are a number of other quinoline alkaloids, including fabianines, furoquinolines, isopropylquinolines, acridines, etc. We cannot presume that these quinolines represent a biosynthetically uniform group. It may be that the moieties which condense with anthranilic acid or with the opened indole nucleus are of greater taxonomic significance than the N-precursor.

Hegnauer (in Swain, 1963) too, in writing of the odd distribution of the *quinine* alkaloids, says:

Although it is impossible to speculate on the origin of the quinine alkaloids in the *Annonaceae* and *Simarubaceae* without experimental facts, it appears highly probable that they are formed in quite a different way from that in *Cinchona*.

He says that the *indole* ring in most cases arises from *tryptophan* but that in several cases (including the *betanins*) it arises from *phenylalanine*.

When we *do* know enough of the biogenesis of alkaloids it will be possible to group them more naturally and to use the distribution of the groups as an important taxonomic character. Alkaloid biogenesis and distribution even now are of considerable use as the notes which follow will show.

The grouping we have arrived at, after some abortive attempts, is as follows. We realize that it is imperfect, but we believe that a committee of alkaloid chemists would never agree on a single system, so we make no apology.

Acridines

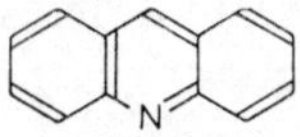

Alkaloids of
Amaryllidaceae

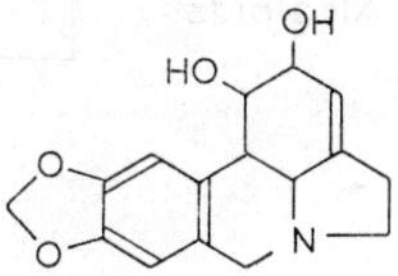

Lycorine 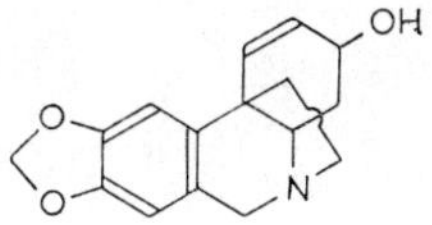   Crinine

Alkaloidal Amines

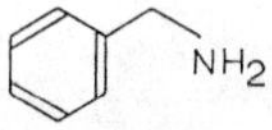

Benzylamine

Daphniphyllum Group

Dihydroquinolones

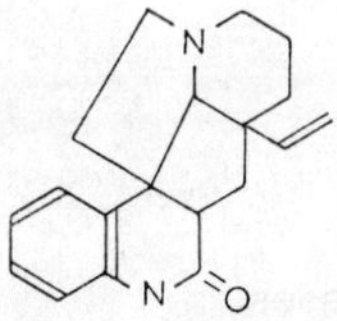

Meloscine

Diterpenoid Alkaloids

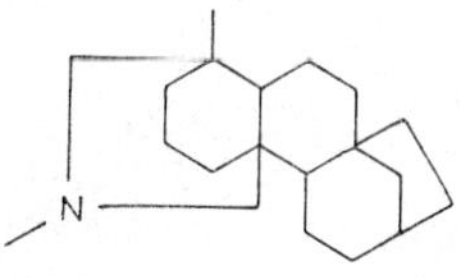

Imidazoles

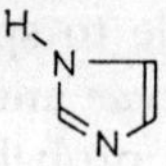

Indole Groups

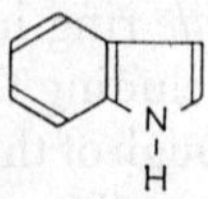

Indolizidine

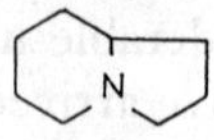

Isoquinoline Groups

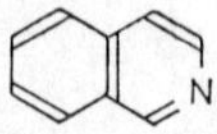

The Lunaria Group

Monoterpenoid Alkaloids   Actinidine

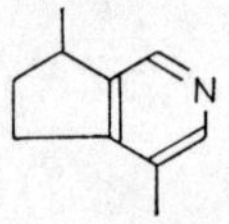

Oxazoles

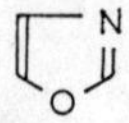

Papaverrubines

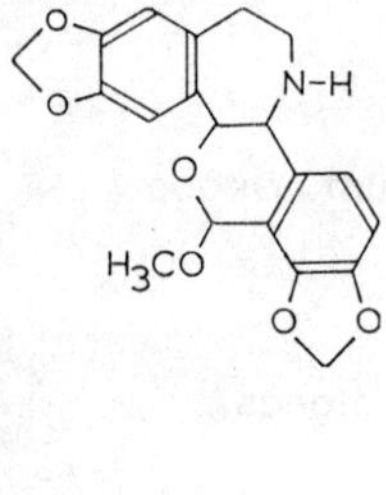

The Purine Bases

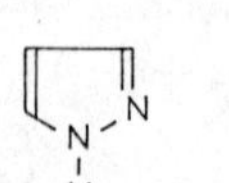

Pyrazoles

Pyridine Groups

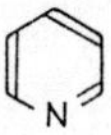

Pyrido (3,4-c) quinolines

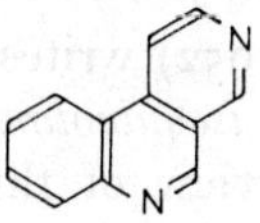

Pyrrolidines

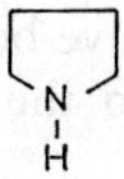

Pyrrolizidines

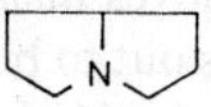

Quinazolines

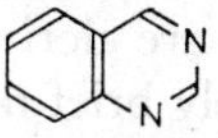

Quinolines

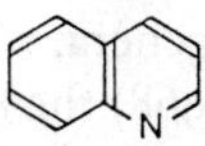

Quinolizidines

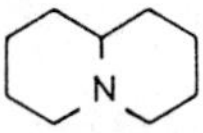

Steroid Alkaloids

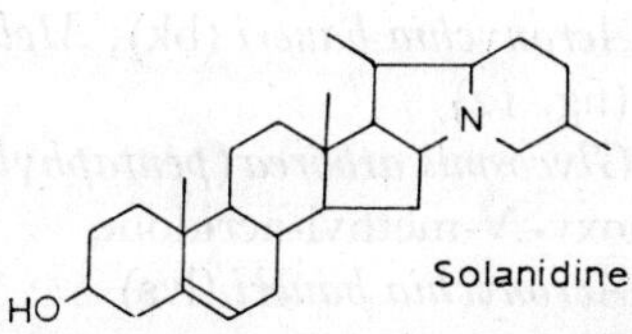

Solanidine

HO

Tropane Alkaloids

Tropolones

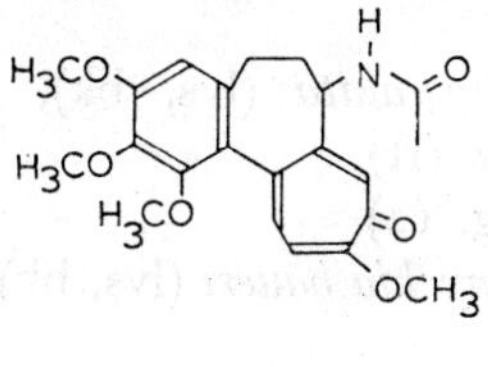

H₃CO

H₃CO

H₃CO

OCH₃

Colchicine

ACRIDINE GROUP

GENERAL

Price (in *M. & H.*, v.2, 1952) writes of the wide variety of alkaloids—
quinoline, furano-quinoline, isoquinoline, carboline, etc.—occurring in the
Rutaceae, and says: 'In view of this biogenetic versatility it seems
appropriate that the recently discovered group of acridine alkaloids
[Hughes, Lahey, Price and Webb, 1948] should occur also in the Rutaceae. Members of this group have been found in five species, belonging
to three genera, indigenous to the tropical rain forests of Northern
Australia.'

Price listed 10 alkaloids, 2 of which may arise during isolation. Openshaw (in *M.*, v.9, 1967) removes *dubamine*, which had been included in
the *acridines*, because it turns out to be a *quinoline* rather than an *acridine*.

We are indebted to Albert (1966) for a whole volume on the *acridines*,
but this deals with the chemistry of the group as a whole. The naturally
occurring *alkaloids*, which are derivatives of *acridone* rather than of
acridine (fig. 12), receive only brief mention.

To the best of my knowledge these alkaloids number about a dozen;
are restricted to the *Rutaceae*; and occur in that family in a handful of
species belonging to 6 or 7 genera.

According to Robinson (1968) the *acridines* are believed to be derived
from *anthranilic acid* and *acetate*, but there is no proof of this.

List and Occurrence

Acronycine (fig. 12)
    Rut.   *Acronychia baueri* (bk); *Melicope fareana*
Arborinine (fig. 12)
    Rut.   *Glycosmis arborea* (*pentaphylla*) (lvs); *Ravenia spectabilis* (lvs)
1,3-Dimethoxy-*N*-methyl-acridone
    Rut.   *Acronychia baueri* (lvs)
Evoprenine
    Rut.   *Evodia alata* (bk)
Evoxanthidine (Nor-evoxanthine)
    Rut.   *Evodia alata, xanthoxyloides* (lvs); *Teclea grandifolia*
Evoxanthine (1-Methoxy-2,3-methylenedioxy-*N*-methyl-acridone; fig.
    12)
    Rut.   *Evodia alata* (lvs, bk), *xanthoxyloides* (lvs, bk); *Teclea
        grandifolia* (rt)
Melicopicine (fig. 12)
    Rut.   *Acronychia baueri* (lvs, bk); *Melicope fareana* (lvs, bk)

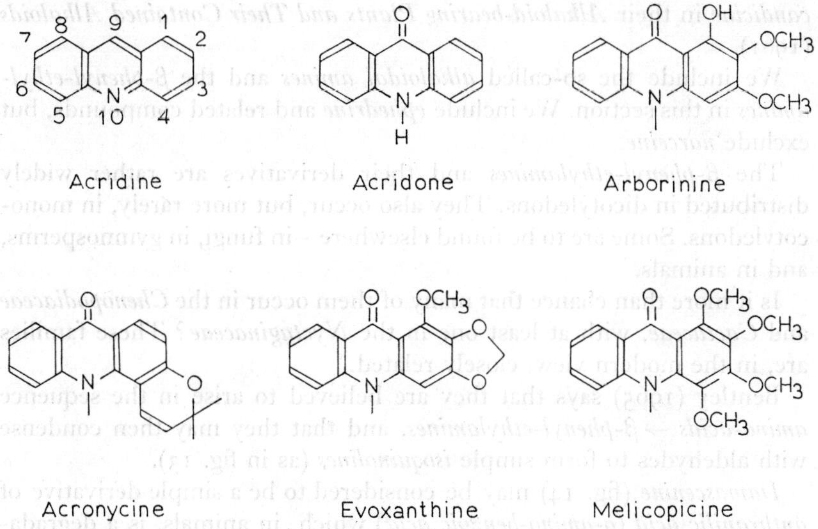

Acridine   Acridone   Arborinine

Acronycine   Evoxanthine   Melicopicine

Fig. 12. Acridine, acridone, and some acridine alkaloids.

Melicopidine

    Rut. Acronychia baueri (lvs, bk); *Evodia alata* (bk), *xanthoxyloides*
      (lvs, bk); *Melicope fareana* (lvs, bk)

Melicopine

    Rut. Acronychia acidula (bk), *baueri* (lvs, bk); *Evodia alata*,
      xanthoxyloides; *Melicope fareana* (lvs, bk)

1,2,3-Trimethoxy-*N*-methyl-acridone

    Rut. Evodia alata (lvs)

Xanthevodine (Nor-melicopidine)

    Rut. Acronychia baueri (lvs); *Evodia xanthoxyloides* (lvs)

Xanthoxoline—what is this?

    Rut. Evodia xanthoxyloides (lvs); *Zanthoxylum (Fagara) naranjillo*
      (lvs)

ALKALOIDAL AMINES (including the
β-Phenyl-ethylamines)

GENERAL

It is difficult to decide which compounds should be listed here and which
with other *amines* (p. 360). Karrer (1958), who excludes alkaloids as a
whole from his book, *does* include *anhaline* (*hordenine*) and *candicine*.
Willaman and Schubert, on the other hand, include *anhaline* and

candicine in their *Alkaloid-bearing Plants and Their Contained Alkaloids* (1961).

We include the so-called *alkaloidal amines* and the *β-phenyl-ethylamines* in this section. We include *ephedrine* and related compounds, but exclude *narceine*.

The *β-phenyl-ethylamines* and their derivatives are rather widely distributed in dicotyledons. They also occur, but more rarely, in monocotyledons. Some are to be found elsewhere—in fungi, in gymnosperms, and in animals.

Is it more than chance that many of them occur in the *Chenopodiaceae* and *Cactaceae*, with at least one in the *Nyctaginaceae*? These families are, in the modern view, closely related.

Bentley (1965) says that they are believed to arise in the sequence *amino-acids → β-phenyl-ethylamines*, and that they may then condense with aldehydes to form simple *isoquinolines* (as in fig. 13).

Damascenine (fig. 14) may be considered to be a simple derivative of *anthranilic acid* (*o-amino-benzoic acid*) which, in animals, is a degradation product of *tryptophan*. In plants *damascenine* does not arise from *tryptophan* but it can be formed from *anthranilic acid* or *shikimic acid*. Unlike *nicotine*, which is formed in the root, and many alkaloids which are formed in leaves, *damascenine* is synthesized and stored in the seed.

List and Occurrence

Adrenaline does not, I think, occur in higher plants, but *nor-adrenaline* does.

Aegeline
> *Rut.   Aegle marmelos*

o-Amino-benzoic acid (Anthranilic acid; 2-Amino-benzoic acid) occurs in bacteria, but not (?) in higher plants.

o-Amino-benzoic acid-methyl ester is said to be present in small amount in many *essential oils*.

p-Amino-benzoic acid (4-Amino-benzoic acid) occurs in fungi and bacteria, but not (?) in higher plants.

Anhaline (Hordenine; β-*p*-Hydroxy-phenyl-ethyl-dimethylamine; fig. 14)
> *Cact.   Lophophora* (*Anhalonium*) *williamsii, Mammillaria, Trichocereus*
> *Legum.   Acacia berlandieri*
> *Gram.   Avena, Hordeum* (2), *Oryza, Panicum* (2), *Phalaris, Sorghum, Zea*

Benzylamine (Moringine; Moringinine; fig. 14)
> *Moring.   Moringa oleifera* (bk)

Candicine (β-p-Hydroxy-phenylethyl-trimethyl-ammonium hydroxide)
> *Cact.* *Lophophora williamsii*; *Trichocereus candicans* and 2 other spp.
> *Magnoli.* *Magnolia grandiflora* (bk)
> *Rut.* *Fagara* (bk of 6 spp.), *Phellodendron amurense*

Coryneine (3-Hydroxy-candicine)
> *Cact.* *Stetsonia (Cereus) coryne*
> *Rut.* *Fagara hiemalis* (bk)

Damascenine (fig. 14)
> *Ranuncul.* *Nigella arvensis (aristata)* (sd), *damascena* (sd)

l-Ephedrine occurs in species of *Ephedra* (**Gnetales**). In angio-sperms it has been recorded from
> *Ranuncul.* *Aconitum napellus* (rt)
> *Papaver.* *Roemeria refracta*
> *Moring.* *Moringa oleifera*
> *Malv.* *Sida cordifolia* (lvs) and 3 other spp.
> *Celastr.* *Catha edulis*

Epinine (*N*-methyl-3,4-dihydroxy-phenylethylamine)
> *Legum.* *Cytisus*

Feruloputrescine (Subaphylline)
> *Chenopodi.* *Salsola subaphylla*
> *Rut.* *Citrus paradisi* (lvs)

Halostachine (better Halostachyine; Phenylethanol-methylamine)
> *Chenopodi.* *Halostachys caspica*

3-Hydroxy-tyramine (β-3,4-dihydroxy-phenylethylamine)
> *Nyctagin.* *Hermidium alipes* (rt)
> *Legum.* *Cytisus (Sarothamnus) scoparius*

Jaborandine—belongs here?
> *Piper.* *Piper jaborandi, reticulatum* (lvs)
> *Rut.* *Pilocarpus pinnatifolius* (lvs, fl., frt)

Jaxartine (*N*-Methyl-2-(4-hydroxyphenethyl)-amine)
> *Chenopodi.* *Anabasis jaxartica*

Kuramerine is related to *Kumokirine* (a *pyrrolizidine*).
> *Orchid.* *Liparis kumokiri, kurameri*

Macromerine (1-(3,4-Dimethoxyphenyl)-2-dimethylamino-ethanol)
> *Cact.* *Coryphantha runyonii, Thelocactus micromeris (Coryphantha macromeris)*

Mescaline (Mezcaline: β-3,4,5-Trimethoxy-phenylethylamine; fig. 14)
> *Cact.* *Gymnocalycium, Lophophora, Opuntia, Trichocereus*

Methyl-damascenine
> *Ranuncul.* *Nigella?*

N-Acetyl-mescaline
> *Cact.* *Lophophora williamsii*

N-Benzoyl-β-phenyl-ethylamine
    Legum. Oxytropis muricata
N-Benzoyl-tyramine
    Rut. Casimiroa edulis (sd)
N-Methyl-anthranilic acid
    Rut. Citrus paradisi (frt?)
N-Methyl-anthranilic acid methyl ester
    Rut. Citrus spp. (ess. oil)
    Zingiber. Kaempferia ethelae (rhiz.?)
N-Methyl-mescaline
    Cact. Lophophora williamsii
N-Methyl-β-phenyl-ethylamine
    Chenopodi. Arthrophytum leptocladum (lvs, st.)
    Legum. Acacia spp.
N-Methyl-tyramine (Andirine?; Angeline; β-p-Hydroxy-phenylethyl-methylamine; Geoffroyine; Rhatamine; Surinamine)
    Chenopodi. Anabasis jaxartica (plt)
    Cact. Lophophora williamsii
    Legum. Acacia berlandieri; *Andira* spp.?
    Gram. Hordeum
N,N-Dimethyl-4-methoxy-phenethylamine
    Rut. Toddalia (*Teclea*) *simplicifolia*
Nor-adrenaline (Arterenol; Nor-epinephrine)
    Ros. Prunus domestica
    Rut. Citrus aurantium
    Solan. Solanum tuberosum
    Mus. Musa paradisiaca, sapientum
d-Nor-iso-ephedrine (Cathine) occurs in *Ephedra* and
    Celastr. Catha edulis
l-Octopamine (l-Nor-synephrine) occurs in the octopus and other animals. It has recently been reported from
    Rut. Citrus (lemon)
O-Methyl-tyramine-N-methylcinnamide (Herclavine)
    Rut. Zanthoxylum clava-herculis
Oxy-candicine
    Cact. Stetsonia (*Cereus*) *coryne*
Oxytyramine
    Legum. Cytisus
β-Phenylethylamine (fig. 14) occurs in fungi and
    Loranth. Viscum album?
    Legum. Acacia (many spp., but see discussion under *Leguminosae*)
Pseudo-ephedrine (Iso-ephedrine) is recorded from *Ephedra* and *Taxus* and
    Papaver. Roemeria refracta

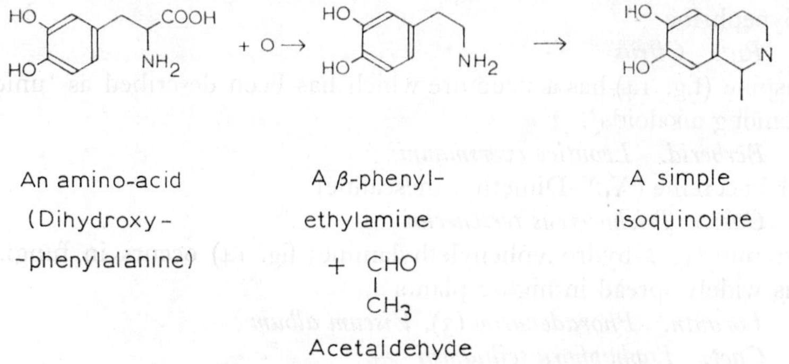

An amino-acid	A β-phenyl-	A simple
(Dihydroxy-	ethylamine	isoquinoline
-phenylalanine)	+ CHO	
	CH₃	
	Acetaldehyde	

Fig. 13. Origin of β-phenyl-ethylamines and simple isoquinolines.

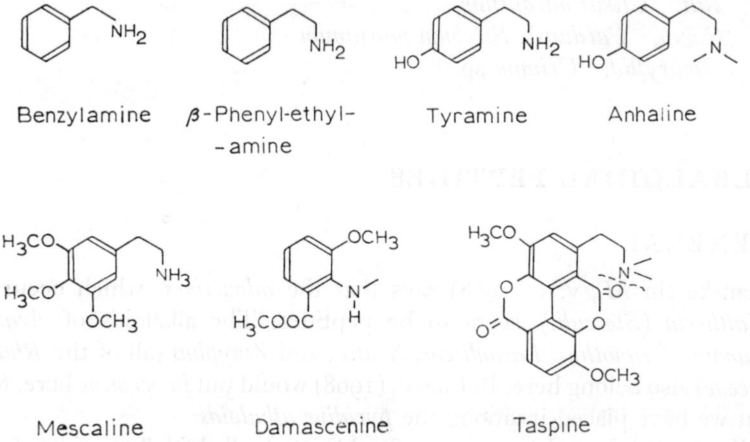

Benzylamine   β-Phenyl-ethyl-   Tyramine   Anhaline
-amine

Mescaline   Damascenine   Taspine

Fig. 14. Some alkaloidal amines.

Celastr.   *Catha edulis*
Malv.   *Sida cordifolia*
Salicifoline
     Magnoli.   *Magnolia salicifolia* (bk) and 5 other spp.
Smirnowine
     Legum.   *Eremosparton aphyllum* (st.), *flaccidum*; *Smirnowia turkes-*
       tana (lvs)
Smirnowinine
     Legum.   *Eremosparton aphyllum* (st.), *Smirnowia turkestana* (lvs, st.)
Sphaerophysine (? Isoamyl-putrescine; Spherophytine)
     Legum.   *Eremosparton flaccidum* (lvs, st.), *Smirnowia turkestana*
       (lvs), *Sphaerophysa salsula*

l-Synephrine
    Rut.   Citrus
Taspine (fig. 14) has a structure which has been described as 'unique among alkaloids'.
    Berberid.   Leontice eversmannii
Trichocereine (*N,N*-Dimethyl-mescaline)
    Cact.   Trichocereus terscheckii
Tyramine (β-*p*-hydroxyphenylethylamine; fig. 14) occurs in fungi. It is widely spread in higher plants
    Loranth.   Phoradendron (3), *Viscum album*
    Cact.   Lophophora williamsii
    Crucif.   Capsella bursa-pastoris
    Legum.   Acacia berlandieri, Cytisus (*Sarothamnus*) *scoparius*
    Gerani.   Erodium cicutarium
    Rut.   Citrus aurantium
    Comp.   Carduus?, Silybum marianum
    Amaryllid.   Crinum sp.

ALKALOIDAL PEPTIDES

GENERAL

Manske (in *M.*, v.10, 1968) says that the *adouetines*, which occur in *Waltheria* (*Sterculi.*), seem to be peptides. The alkaloids of *Araliorhamnus, Ceanothus, Lasiodiscus, Scutia,* and *Zizyphus* (all of the *Rhamnaceae*) also belong here. Robinson (1968) would put *julocrotine* here, too, but we have placed it among the *pyridine alkaloids*.

Recent workers have reported additional alkaloidal peptides from *Euphorbiaceae, Pandaceae, Rubiaceae,* and *Urticaceae,* so they are evidently widely spread.

List and Occurrence

Adouetines -X, -Y, and -Z
    Sterculi.   Waltheria indica (*americana*)
Aralionin
    Rhamn.   Araliorhamnus vaginata (lvs)
Canthiumine yields *N,N-dimethyl-*L*-phenylalanine, p-hydroxy-styrylamine,* L-*proline,* and L-*threo-*β*-phenylserine.*
    Rubi.   Canthium euryoides
Ceanothin-B
    Rhamn.   Ceanothus americana

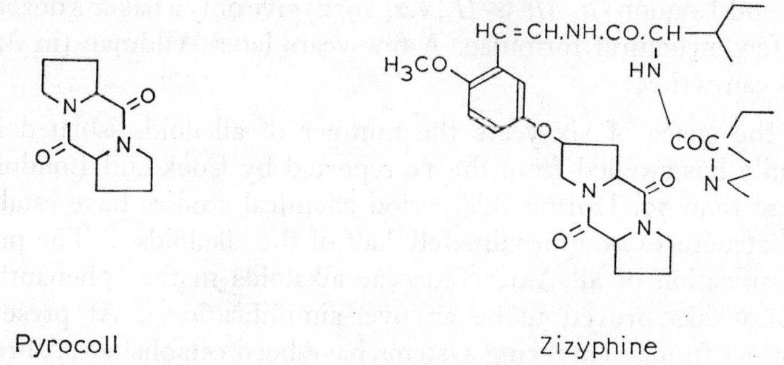

Pyrocoll   Zizyphine

Fig. 15. Alkaloidal peptides.

Hymenocardine
    Euphorbi.   Hymenocardia acida
Integerrenin
    Rhamn.   Ceanothus integerrimus (rt)
Integerressen
    Rhamn.   Ceanothus integerrimus (rt)
Integerrin
    Rhamn.   Ceanothus integerrimus
Lasioidines -A and -B
    Rhamn.   Lasiodiscus marmoratus
Myrianthines -A, -B, and -C
    Urtic.   Myrianthus arboreus
Pandamine
    Pand.   Panda oleosa
Scutianine yields *N,N-dimethyl-phenylalanine, phenylalanine, β-hydroxy-*
    leucine, proline, leucine, and *glycine*
    Rhamn.   Scutia buxifolia (bk)
Zizyphine (fig. 15) is a derivative of *pyrocoll* (fig. 15) (Zbiral *et al.* 1965).
    Rhamn.   Zizyphus oenophila (rt, bk)
Zizyphinine
    Rhamn.   Zizyphus oenophila (rt, bk)

ALKALOIDS OF THE AMARYLLIDACEAE, etc.

GENERAL

The history of this group illustrates well the remarkable increase in our
knowledge during recent years. Henry, in the fourth edition of *The Plant
Alkaloids* (1949), lists only a few alkaloids from the *Amaryllidaceae*.

Cook and Loudon (in *M. & H.*, v.2, 1952) give only a baker's dozen or so, with few structural formulae. A few years later Wildman (in *M.*, v.6, 1960) can write:

> In the space of six years the number of alkaloids isolated in this family has swelled from the 15 reported by Cook and Loudon...to more than 70. During this period chemical studies have established the structures of approximately half of the alkaloids...The previous classification of all Amaryllidaceae alkaloids in the 'phenanthridine group' has proved to be an over-simplification...At present, six distinct fundamental ring systems have been established...From the number of alkaloids remaining with undetermined structure, it seems certain that to these six ring systems several more will be added...
> To date, the alkaloids isolated from this family have been found only in the subfamily Amaryllidoideae. No alkaloids have been reported in the remaining subfamilies Agavoideae, Hypoxidoideae, and Campynematoideae.

For further taxonomic discussion see *Amaryllidaceae*.

In most cases the alkaloids have been found in the bulbs or other underground parts of the plants. In a few cases the leaves and/or seeds may yield them. Cook and Loudon (loc. cit.) speculate as to the possible functions of these compounds in the *Amaryllidaceae*, and say: 'From the demonstrated fungicidal action of lycorine, considered together with the quantity and localization of the alkaloids in the plants they [Greathouse and Rigler] concluded that the alkaloid content contributes to the immunity displayed by this plant family towards *Phymatotrichum* root rot.'

Wildman (in *M.*, v.11, 1968) brings our knowledge up to date. He says that more than 60 members of the *Amaryllidaceae* have been examined for alkaloids in the last 6 years. Unfortunately, as he points out, exchange of information and samples has not been as free as it should have been, and there may be some duplication of names.

We have followed Wildman more or less closely in our treatment of these alkaloids. They seem to fall into the following groups:

I. Lycorine type (all pyrrolo-[de]-phenanthridines?): about 25
II. Lycorenine type (all [2]-benzopyrano-[3,4g] indoles?): about 20.
   These are listed here, rather than with the other *indole* alkaloids, because their relationships are obviously here.
III. Galanthamine type (all dibenzofurans?): about 10
IV. Tazettine type: 3 only. Although *indoles* they belong here.
V. Crinine type (all 5,10b-ethanophenanthridines?): about 35
VI. Belladine type (*N*-benzyl-*N*-(β-phenethylamine)): 2 only
VII. Montanine type: 3 only

VIII. Alkaloids of unknown structure or otherwise unassigned: a rag-bag of about 40

IX. 'Amaryllidaceous' Alkaloids of the Menispermaceae—4 alkaloids which resemble *lycorine* closely

I LYCORINE TYPE (PYRROLO-[DE]-PHENANTHRIDINE ALKALOIDS)

List and Occurrence

Acetyl-caranine (Bellamarine)

> *Amaryllid. Amaryllis belladonna, Ammocharis coranica, Brunsvigia rosea, Nerine bowdenii*

Amaryllidine: is an *ar-methoxy-parkamine*?

> *Amaryllid. Amaryllis belladonna, Nerine crispa*

Caranine seems to be rather widely distributed

> *Amaryllid. Amaryllis belladonna, parkeri; Ammocharis coranica; Brunsdonna tubergenii; Brunsvigia rosea; Crinum* (3); *Hymenocallis* (2); *Nerine* (3)

Falcatine: is an *ar-methoxy-caranine*?

> *Amaryllid. Nerine falcata, laticoma*

Galanthine is widely distributed

> *Amaryllid. Amaryllis belladonna* var. *purpurea major; Brunsdonna tubergenii; Crinum* (3); *Eustephia yuyuensis; Galanthus worono-wii; Hippeastrum aulicum* var. *robustum; Hymenocallis* (3); *Narcissus* (5); *Nerine flexuosa* (pink); *Zephyranthus* (2)

Golceptine

> *Amaryllid. Narcissus jonquilla* var.

Goleptine

> *Amaryllid. Narcissus jonquilla* var.

Hippamine (2-*O*-Methyl-lycorine)

> *Amaryllid. Hippeastrum* sp.

Jonquilline

> *Amaryllid. Narcissus jonquilla* var.

Lycorine (Galanthidine; Narcissine; fig. 16) may be called the '*protopine*' of the *Amaryllidaceae*. Is it, in fact, in all members of the family?

> *Amaryllid. Amaryllis* (2), *Ammocharis, Boöphone, Brunsdonna, Brunsvigia, Calostemma, Chlidanthus, Clivia, Cooperanthes, Cooperia, Crinum* (7), *Cyrtanthus, Elisena, Eucharis, Eustephia, Galanthus* (2), *Haemanthus* (2), *Hippeastrum* (3), *Hymenocallis* (3), *Leucojum, Lycoris* (3), *Narcissus, Nerine* (6), *Pancratium* (5), *Sprekelia, Sternbergia, Ungernia* (5), *Urceolina, Vallota, Zephyr-anthes* (2)

Magnarcine may be a diastereomer of *methyl-pseudolycorine*.
   Amaryllid. Galanthus nivalis, Narcissus ×
Methyl-pseudolycorine
   Amaryllid. Amaryllis parkeri, Crinum (2), *Narcissus pseudonarcissus, Nerine bowdenii, Sternbergia fischeriana*
Narcissidine
   Amaryllid. Crinum powellii; Hippeastrum aulicum var. *robustum, brachyandrum; Hymenocallis* (3); *Ismene* × ; *Narcissus* (3); *Nerine* (2)
Nartazine (*O,O*-Diacetyl-dihydro-lycorine)
   Amaryllid. Galanthus nivalis, Narcissus tazetta
Neflexine: resembles *parkamine*?
   Amaryllid. Crinum powellii, Nerine flexuosa (pink)
Nerispine: is the 8-methoxy isomer of *falcatine*?
   Amaryllid. Nerine undulata, Zephyranthes tubispatha (bulb)
Norpluviine
   Amaryllid. Hippeastrum aulicum var. *robustum, Lycoris radiata, Pancratium maritimum*
1-*O*-Acetyl-lycorine
   Amaryllid. Crinum moorei (sd), *Nerine bowdenii*
2-*O*-Acetyl-lycorine (Aulamine)
   Amaryllid. Hippeastrum aulicum var. *robustum*
Parkacine is closely related to *pluviine*
   Amaryllid. Amaryllis parkeri
Parkamine: is 2-*methoxy-falcatine*?
   Amaryllid. Amaryllis parkeri
Pluviine
   Amaryllid. Hippeastrum × ; *Lycoris radiata, squamigera; Narcissus* (3); *Nerine bowdenii*
Poetaminine
   Amaryllid. Narcissus poeticus var. *ornatus*
Pseudolycorine
   Amaryllid. Brunsdonna tubergenii, Cooperia pedunculata, Hippeastrum aulicum var. *robustum, Hymenocallis harrisiana, Lycoris* (3), *Pancratium maritimum*
Ungiminorine
   Amaryllid. Ungernia minor, severtzovii (lvs)
Zephyranthine is α-*dihydro-2-epilycorine*
   Amaryllid. Zephyranthes candida

II LYCORENINE TYPE ([2]-BENZOPYRANO [3,4g] INDOLE) ALKALOIDS

Albomaculine
> *Amaryllid. Haemanthus albo-maculatus*

Candimine
> *Amaryllid. Hippeastrum candidum*

Clivimine: seems to be a diester involving 2 × *clivonine* and 2,6-*di-methylpyridine*-3,5-*dicarboxylic acid*!
> *Amaryllid. Clivia miniata*

Clivonine
> *Amaryllid. Clivia miniata*

9-Demethyl-homolycorine
> *Amaryllid. Lycoris radiata, Pancratium maritimum*

Hippeastrine is widely distributed
> *Amaryllid. Amaryllis, Crinum* (2), *Haemanthus* (2), *Galanthus nivalis, Hippeastrum* (2), *Hymenocallis* (3), *Lycoris squamigera, Narcissus* (2), *Pancratium maritimum, Sternbergia fischeriana, Ungernia severtzovii*

Homolycorine (Narcipoetine?; fig. 16)
> *Amaryllid. Clivia elizabethae, Hippeastrum* (2), *Hymenocallis* (2), *Leucojum vernum, Lycoris* (4), *Narcissus* (6), *Pancratium* (3)

Krigeine
> *Amaryllid. Nerine krigei*

Krigenamine
> *Amaryllid. Nerine krigei*

Lycorenine
> *Amaryllid. Amaryllis, Cooperanthes, Haemanthus* (3), *Hippeastrum, Hymenocallis, Leucojum* (2), *Lycoris* (4), *Narcissus* (6), *Nerine, Pancratium* (2), *Zephyranthes*

Masonine is the methylenedioxy analogue of *homolycorine*?
> *Amaryllid. Galanthus nivalis, Narcissus jonquilla, Nerine masono-rum*

Nerinine
> *Amaryllid. Hymenocallis* (4), *Nerine sarniensis, Zephyranthes candida*

Neronine
> *Amaryllid. Nerine krigei*

Neruscine (Deoxy-lycorenine)
> *Amaryllid. Crinum powellii; Hippeastrum aulicum* var. *robustum; Nerine corusca, flexuosa*

Nivaline (Ungerine)
>   *Amaryllid.   Galanthus nivalis; Hymenocallis occidentalis; Ungernia
>   severtzovii, trisphaera*

Nor-neronine (11-Demethyl-neronine?)
>   *Amaryllid.   Pancratium longiflorum* (bulb)

Oduline is the methylenedioxy analogue of *lycorenine*?
>   *Amaryllid.   Narcissus jonquilla, odora* var. *rugulosus*

Penarcine is a diastereomer of *homolycorine*?
>   *Amaryllid.   Narcissus* hybrids

'Radiatine' is an artefact?
>   *Amaryllid.   Lycoris radiata*?

Unsevine
>   *Amaryllid.   Ungernia severtzowii* (lvs)

Urceoline is a stereoisomer of *nerinine*?
>   *Amaryllid.   Urceolina miniata*

Urminine is a stereoisomer of *albomaculine*?
>   *Amaryllid.   Amaryllis parkeri, Urceolina miniata*

III GALANTHAMINE TYPE (DIBENZOFURAN) ALKALOIDS

Chlidanthine
>   *Amaryllid.   Chlidanthus fragrans, Haemanthus multiflorus, Hippeas-
>   trum aulicum* var. *robustum*

(+)-De-*N*-methyl-dihydro-galanthamine
>   *Amaryllid.   Narcissus*

(−)-De-*N*-methyl-galanthamine
>   *Amaryllid.   Narcissus*

Epigalanthamine (Base IX) is very like *galanthamine*.
>   *Amaryllid.   Lycoris radiata, squamigera*

Galanthamine (Lycoremine; Bodamine is ($\pm$)-G.; fig. 16) occurs in 9
of the 10 tribes of the subfam. *Amaryllidoideae.*
>   *Amaryllid.   Amaryllis, Cooperanthes, Crinum* (5), *Eustephia, Galan-
>   thus* (3), *Haemanthus, Hippeastrum, Hymenocallis, Ismene* ×,
>   *Leucojum, Lycoris* (5), *Narcissus* (6), *Nerine, Pancratium* (5),
>   *Sternbergia, Ungernia* (2), *Vallota, Zephyranthes* (2)

Irenine (Dihydro-epigalanthamine)
>   *Amaryllid.   Narcissus* × 'Irene Copeland'

Lycoramine (Dihydro-galanthamine; originally pseudo-homolycorine)
>   *Amaryllid.   Crinum powellii, Lycoris* (4), *Narcissus cyclamineus*

'Narcissamine' is a mixture.

Narwedine (? Narvedine)
>*Amaryllid.   Galanthus nivalis, Narcissus* hybrids, *Ungernia severt-*
>   *zovii* (lvs)
Nivalidine (6-*O*-Methyl-apo-galanthamine) may bc an artefact.
>*Amaryllid.   ? Galanthus nivalis* var. *gracilis*

IV TAZETTINE TYPE ALKALOIDS

Criwelline is an epimer of *tazettine*.
>*Amaryllid.   Crinum macrantherum, powellii; Galanthus nivalis*
Macronine
>*Amaryllid.   Crinum macrantherum*
Tazettine (Base VIII; Sekisanine?; Sekisanoline; Ungernine; fig. 16) is
interesting as having a spiro-structure. It seems to be a commonly
occurring alkaloid.
>*Amaryllid.   Chlidanthus; Crinum* (2 or more); *Elisena; Galanthus*
>   (3); *Haemanthus* spp.; *Hippeastrum; Hymenocallis* (3); *Ismene*
>   × ; *Lycoris* (2); *Narcissus tazetta* and other spp.; *Pancratium*
>   (4); *Sprekelia; Sternbergia; Ungernia* (4); *Zephyranthes* (2)

V CRININE TYPE
(5,10b-ETHANOPHENANTHRIDINE) ALKALOIDS

Amaryllisine
>*Amaryllid.   Amaryllis belladonna*
Ambelline
>*Amaryllid.   Amaryllis belladonna, Ammocharis coranica, Boöphone,*
>   *Brunsvigia rosea, Clivia elizabethae, Crinum* (3), *Hippeastrum,*
>   *Nerine* (4)
Annapowine
>*Amaryllid.   Hippeastrum* × 'Anna Powlowna'
Bowdensine
>*Amaryllid.   Nerine bowdenii*
Buphanamine
>*Amaryllid.   Boöphone (Buphane) disticha, fischeri; Brunsvigia* sp.,
>   *Crinum* × , *Nerine* (3)
Buphanidrine is the methyl ether of *powelline*.
>*Amaryllid.   Ammocharis coranica; Boöphone (Buphane) disticha,*
>   *fischeri; Brunsvigia* sp.; *Nerine bowdenii*

Buphanisine is the methyl ether of *crinine*.

    Amaryllid. Ammocharis coranica; *Boöphone (Buphane) disticha, fischeri*; *Nerine bowdenii*

Crinalbine

    Amaryllid. Crinum powellii var. *album*

Crinamidine

    Amaryllid. Boöphone disticha, Crinum (3), *Hippeastrum brachyandrum, Nerine* (4)

Crinamine: is the C_3-methoxy epimer of *haemanthamine*?

    Amaryllid. Amaryllis parkeri, Ammocharis coranica, Brunsvigia cooperi, Crinum (8) *Nerine bowdenii*

Crinine (Crinidine?; fig. 16) is isomeric with *caranine*.

    Amaryllid. Boöphone (2), *Calostemma, Crinum* (3), *Hippeastrum* sp., *Nerine* (3), *Zephyranthes* ×

Cripaline

    Amaryllid. Crinum powellii var. *harlemense*

Dihydro-ambelline

    Amaryllid. Nerine crispa

Dihydro-haemanthamine

    Amaryllid. Crinum powellii var. *harlemense*

Dihydro-haemanthidine (Hippawine)

    Amaryllid. Hippeastrum ×

Elwesine

    Amaryllid. Galanthus elwesii

(+)-Epi-buphanisine

    Amaryllid. Ammocharis coranica

(+)-Epi-crinine

    Amaryllid. Nerine bowdenii

Fiancine

    Amaryllid. Crinum ×, *Hippeastrum auliculum* var. *robustum, Narcissus pseudo-narcissus*

Flexamine

    Amaryllid. Nerine flexuosa

Flexine

    Amaryllid. Nerine flexuosa

Flexinine (ar-Demethoxy-crinamidine)

    Amaryllid. Galanthus elwesii, Nerine corusca, flexuosa alba

Haemanthamine (Natalensine) seems to be a common alkaloid.

    Amaryllid. Boöphone disticha, Calostemma purpureum, Crinum (4), *Elisena longipetala, Galanthus elwesii, Haemanthus* (3), *Hippeastrum* (2), *Hymenocallis* (6), *Ismene* ×, *Narcissus* (6), *Nerine* (2), *Sprekelia formosissima, Sternbergia lutea, Urceolina miniata, Vallota purpurea, Zephyranthes* (4)

Haemanthidine (Pancratine)

> *Amaryllid.* Galanthus nivalis, Haemanthus (3), Hymenocallis (2), Lycoris incarnata, Narcissus cyclamineus, Pancratium (4), Sprekelia formosissima, Sternbergia lutea, Ungernia (3), Vallota purpurea, Zephyranthes candida

Haemultine may be an artefact.

> *Amaryllid.* ? Amaryllis parkeri, Crinum powellii, Haemanthus (2)

6-Hydroxy-crinamine

> *Amaryllid.* Haemanthus natalensis

11-Hydroxy-vittatine

> *Amaryllid.* Hippeastrum(Rhodophiala)bifida,Pancratiummaritimum

Krelagine

> *Amaryllid.* Crinum powellii var. krelagei

Maritidine

> *Amaryllid.* Pancratium maritimum (only in plants from Rhodes?)

Nerbowdine

> *Amaryllid.* Boöphone disticha, Brunsvigia sp., Nerine bowdenii

3-O-Acetyl-nerbowdine

> *Amaryllid.* Boöphone disticha, Nerine crispa

Powellamine

> *Amaryllid.* Crinum powellii

Powelline (? ar-Methoxy-crinine)

> *Amaryllid.* Calostemma purpureum, Crinum powellii and other spp., Hippeastrum vars, Nerine flexuosa (white), Zephyranthes tubispatha (bulb)

Tubispathine (? Tubispacine)

> *Amaryllid.* Zephyranthes tubispatha (bulb)

Undulatine (Distichine)

> *Amaryllid.* Boöphone disticha, Crinum (3), Hippeastrum brachyandrum, Nerine undulata and 3 other spp.

Vittatine: is the optical antipode of *crinine*?

> *Amaryllid.* Hippeastrum vittatum, Hymenocallis calathina, Lycoris squamigera, Nerine corusca, Pancratium (3)

VI BELLADINE TYPE (*N*-BENZYL-*N*-(β-PHENETHYLAMINE)) ALKALOIDS

Belladine (fig. 16)

> *Amaryllid.* Amaryllis belladonna, Brunsvigia gigantea, Crinum powellii, Nerine bowdenii

O-Methyl-norbelladine

> Occurrence ?

VII MONTANINE TYPE ALKALOIDS

Coccinine is isomeric with *montanine*.
> Amaryllid.   *Haemanthus coccineus* and 3 other spp.

Manthine
> Amaryllid.   *Haemanthus amarylloides, tigrinus*

Montanine (2)
> Amaryllid.   *Haemanthus amarylloides, coccineus, montanus, multi-florus, tigrinus; Hippeastrum aulicum* var. *robustum*

VIII ALKALOIDS OF UNKNOWN STRUCTURE OR OTHERWISE UNASSIGNED

Aestivine
> Amaryllid.   *Leucojum aestivum*

Brunsdonnine
> Amaryllid.   *Brunsdonna tubergenii* (*Amaryllis belladonna* × *Brunsvigia rosea*)

Brunsvigine
> Amaryllid.   *Brunsvigia cooperi*

Brunsvinine
> Amaryllid.   *Brunsvigia cooperi*

Buphacetine
> Amaryllid.   *Boöphone* (*Buphane*) *disticha*

Buphanine
> Amaryllid.   *Ammocharis* sp. ?

Buphanitine
> Amaryllid.   *Boöphone* (*Buphane*)

Clivatine
> Amaryllid.   *Clivia miniata*

Clivianine
> Amaryllid.   *Clivia nobilis*

Coranicine
> Amaryllid.   *Ammocharis coranica*

Coruscine
> Amaryllid.   *Brunsdonna* ×, *Nerine corusca*

Crinosine
> Amaryllid.   *Crinum powellii*

Crispine
> Amaryllid.   *Nerine undulata*

Distichamine
  Amaryllid.   *Boöphone disticha*
Galanthamidine
  Amaryllid.   *Galanthus woronowii*
Haemanthine
  Amaryllid.   *Boöphone toxicaria*
Hippacine
  Occurrence ?
Hippandrine
  Amaryllid.   *Hippeastrum brachyandrum*
Hippauline
  Amaryllid.   *Hippeastrum aulicum* var. *robustum*
Ismine
  Amaryllid.   *Crinum powellii, Ismene* sp., *Sprekelia formosissima*
Isotazettine
  Amaryllid.   *Leucojum*
Luteine
  Amaryllid.   *Sternbergia lutea*
Macranthine
  Amaryllid.   *Crinum macrantherum*
Manthidine
  Amaryllid.   *Haemanthus coccineus*
Miniatine
  Amaryllid.   *Clivia miniata*
Narzettine
  Amaryllid.   *Narcissus tazetta*
Nerifline
  Amaryllid.   *Nerine flexuosa* (pink)
Nerundine
  Amaryllid.   *Nerine undulata*
O,O-Diacetyl-macranthine
  Amaryllid.   *Crinum macrantherum*
Petomine
  Amaryllid.   *Amaryllis parkeri, Crinum powellii, Narcissus* ×
Poetamine
  Amaryllid.   *Narcissus poeticus* var. *ornatus*
Poetaricine
  Amaryllid.   *Narcissus poeticus* var. *ornatus*
Poeticine
  Amaryllid.   *Narcissus poeticus*
Powellidine
  Amaryllid.   *Crinum powellii*

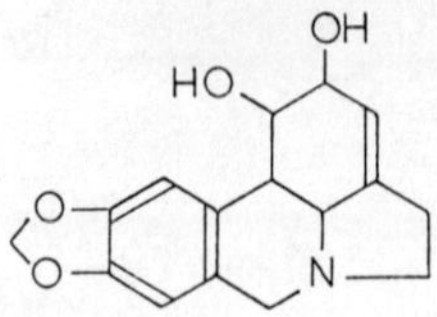

I. Lycorine

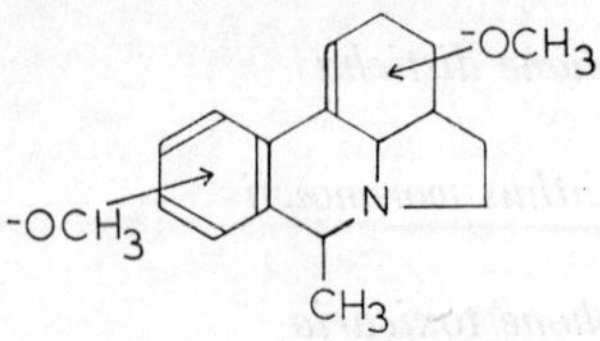

I. Cocculidine

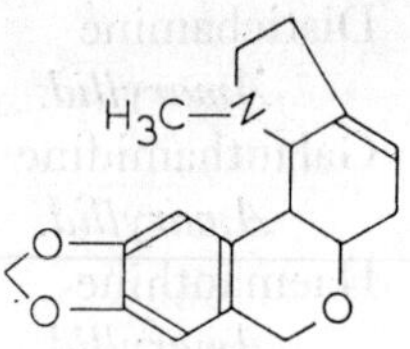

II. Homolycorine

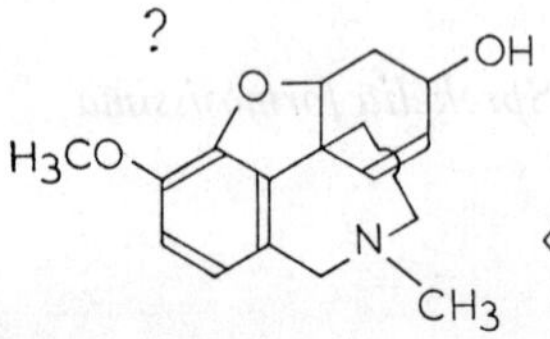

III. Galanthamine

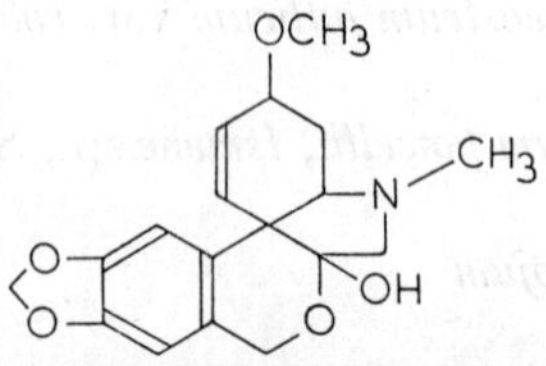

IV. Tazettine

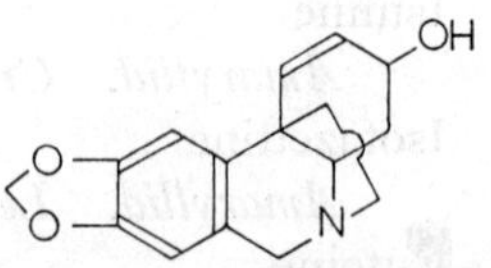

V. Crinine

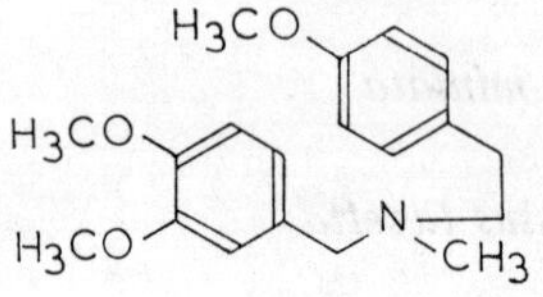

VI. Belladine

Fig. 16. Alkaloids of the Amaryllidaceae, etc.

Punikathine
    Amaryllid. *Haemanthus* ×
Sickenbergine
    Amaryllid. *Pancratium sickenbergeri* and 3 other spp.
Squamigerine
    Amaryllid. *Lycoris squamigera*
Sternidine
    Amaryllid. *Sternbergia fischeriana*
Sternine
    Amaryllid. *Sternbergia fischeriana*
'Suisenine' is a mixture.

Trispheridine
  Amaryllid.   Ungernia trisphaera
'Ungeridine' is a mixture.
'Ungerine' is a mixture.
Vallopurfine
  Amaryllid.   Vallota purpurea
Vallotidine
  Amaryllid.   Vallota purpurea
Vallotine
  Amaryllid.   Vallota purpurea
Yemensine
  Amaryllid.   Crinum yemense

IX 'AMARYLLIDACEOUS' ALKALOIDS OF THE MENISPERMACEAE

Cocculidine (fig. 16)
  Menisperm.   Cocculus laurifolius (lvs)
Cocculine
  Menisperm.   Anamirta cocculus (frt), *Cocculus laurifolius* (lvs)
Coclamine
  Menisperm.   Cocculus laurifolius (plt)
Coclifoline
  Menisperm.   Cocculus laurifolius (plt)

DAPHNIPHYLLUM GROUP

GENERAL

An alkaloid 'daphniphylline' was isolated about 75 years ago by Plugge, from *Daphniphyllum bancanum*. Recent investigations have led to the discovery of several more alkaloids from the genus. Some, at least, of them are now well known, and these are regarded by Irikawa *et al.* (1967) as having a C-skeleton consisting of 4 isoprene units and 1 acetate unit.

So far as we know they are restricted to the little family *Daphniphyllaceae* (which see for further discussion).

List and Occurrence

Codaphniphylline (Deacetoxy-daphniphylline?)
  Daphniphyll.   Daphniphyllum macropodium (bk, lvs)

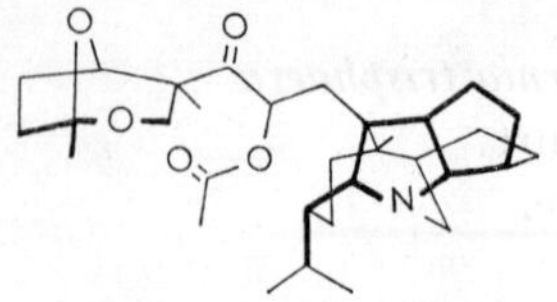

Daphniphylline

Fig. 17. Daphniphylline.

Daphnicadine ($C_{22}H_{27}O_2N$) belongs here?
  Daphniphyll. Daphniphyllum calycinum
Daphnicaline ($C_{21}H_{29}O_2N$) belongs here?
  Daphniphyll. Daphniphyllum calycinum
Daphnicamine ($C_{21}H_{31}O_2N$) belongs here?
  Daphniphyll. Daphniphyllum calycinum
Daphnimacrine ($C_{27}H_{41}O_4N$) belongs here?
  Daphniphyll. Daphniphyllum macropodium (bk)
Daphniphylline ($C_{32}H_{49}O_5N$; fig. 17) is presumably the alkaloid isolated
  by Plugge.
  Daphniphyll. Daphniphyllum bancanum (lvs, sd, bk), *macropodium*
Neodaphniphylline
  Daphniphyll. Daphniphyllum macropodium (bk, lvs)
Neoyuzurimine
  Daphniphyll. Daphniphyllum macropodium (bk, lvs)
Yuzurimine
  Daphniphyll. Daphniphyllum macropodium

DIHYDROQUINOLONES. THE MELOSCINE GROUP

GENERAL

An interesting genus of the *Apocynaceae* is *Melodinus* with about 50 spp.,
widely distributed in the Pacific area. Some species have *indole* alkaloids
of the *ajmaline-sarpagine* and *aspidospermine* groups.

Melodinus scandens has these but in addition four alkaloids have been
found in it which are *dihydroquinolones*. These constitute the *meloscine
group*, which Gilbert (in *M.*, v.11, 1968) discusses. He considers the
indole alkaloids to be the precursors of the *dihydroquinolones*.

List and Occurrence

Epimeloscine
    Apocyn.   Melodinus scandens
Melodinus scandens alkaloid-4
    Apocyn.   Melodinus scandens
Meloscandine
    Apocyn.   Melodinus scandens
Meloscine (p. 137)
    Apocyn.   Melodinus scandens

DITERPENOID GROUPS

GENERAL

We may recognize three groups here.

I. The alkaloids of *Aconitum, Delphinium,* and *Inula*

Stern (in *M. & H.*, v.4, 1954) reviewed our knowledge of the *Aconitum* and *Delphinium* alkaloids at that time and said: 'In spite of their intrinsic interest and although raw material is often available in abundance, the elucidation of structures of *Aconitum* and *Delphinium* alkaloids has not so far been possible because of the considerable practical difficulties attending the investigations.'

Although exact structures cannot be written, he said, they are clearly derived from complex polyhydric alcohols, probably based on $C_{19}H_{28}NH$, and may be considered to be *diterpenoid*. He divided them into groups based on *atisine, aconitine,* and *lycoctonine* respectively, and had a fourth group of miscellaneous alkaloids.

Only a few years later Stern (in *M.*, v.7, 1960) was able to say that 'remarkable progress has been made in the elucidation of the structures of some of these alkaloids'.

The *Aconitum* and *Delphinium* alkaloids are not quite restricted to these two ranunculaceous genera. Three of them are said to occur also in *Inula* of the *Compositae.*

II. The alkaloids of *Garrya*

It is now clear that the genus *Garrya* (*Garryaceae*) has several alkaloids which are *diterpenoid* and similar to those of Group I above.

6

Garrya is not at all closely related to *Aconitum, Delphinium*, and *Inula*. We must have here an example of the independent origin of compounds in two or three groups of plants.

III. The alkaloids of *Erythrophleum*

Dalma (in *M. & H.*, v.4, 1954) discussed the alkaloids of the leguminous genus *Erythrophleum*. Although the structures of these were not then fully worked out he concluded that they 'are alkamine esters of mono-carboxylic acids of the diterpene series...'.

Morin (in *M.*, v.10., 1968) says that the structures of these alkaloids are now known and that they: 'are in general N-alkylaminoethyl esters of diterpene acids containing a perhydrophenanthrene skeleton. It is remarkable that compounds of this general structure should have the same type of pharmacological activity as the non-nitrogenous digitalis group of steroid glycosides. The diterpene portion of the *Erythrophleum* alkaloids is devoid of this characteristic biological activity.'

The *Erythrophleum* alkaloids may be considered to be derivatives of *cassanic acid* (fig. 18). The genus has about 17 species. The alkaloids listed here have been obtained from but 5 of them. It seems highly probable that some, at least, of the remaining species will be found to have further members of this interesting group of compounds.

List and Occurrence

I. The Alkaloids of *Aconitum, Delphinium*, and *Inula*

Although it is possible now to sort out some of these alkaloids into smaller groups we have not attempted to do so here. Relationships are indicated where they seem to be well established.

Acetyl-songorine
    Ranuncul.   Aconitum

Aconine is an amino-alcohol, parent of *aconitine, benzoyl-aconine*, and *jesaconitine*.
    Ranuncul.   Aconitum (2)

Aconitine is an ester of *aconine* whose structure is still (1960) uncertain.
    Ranuncul.   Aconitum (more than 30 species)

Acsinatine ($C_{21}H_{27}O_4N$) is *acsinatidine* esterified with *acetic acid*.
    Ranuncul.   Aconitum excelsum (rt)

Acsine ($C_{21}H_{29}O_5N$) is *acsinidine* esterified with *acetic acid*.
    Ranuncul.   Aconitum excelsum (rt)

Ajacine
    Ranuncul.   Delphinium ajacis (sd)

Ajacinine
  Ranuncul.   *Delphinium ajacis* (sd), *orientale* (sd)
Ajacinoidine
  Ranuncul.   *Delphinium ajacis* (sd)
Ajaconine (Hydroxy-atisine)
  Ranuncul.   *Delphinium ajacis* (sd)
Anthranoyl-lycoctonine (Inuline)—Edwards and Rodger (1959) say that
  Inula has this alkaloid, *lycoctonine*, and *methyl-lycaconitine*. They say
  also: 'Lycoctonine and its derivatives have been found in *Aconitum
  lycoctonum* and all the *Delphinium* species which have been carefully
  examined…It seems remarkable to us that not only should an
  alkaloid as complex as lycoctonine be synthesized by a plant belonging
  to an entirely different family from the previously known sources, but
  that it should be esterified with the same complex acid.'
  Ranuncul.   *Delphinium* (2)
  Comp.   *Inula royleana* (rt)
Atidine
  Ranuncul.   *Aconitum heterophyllum*
Atisine (?Anthorine; fig. 18)
  Ranuncul.   *Aconitum anthora, heterophyllum*
Avadharine ($C_{22}H_{31}O_3N$): may be *lycaconitine*?
  Ranuncul.   *Aconitum orientale* (rt)
Benzaconine (Benzoyl-aconine; Isaconitine; Picraconitine) yields *aconine*
  and *benzoic acid*.
  Ranuncul.   *Aconitum napellus* (rt)
Benzoyl-heteratisine
  Ranuncul.   *Aconitum heterophyllum*
Bikhaconitine
  Ranuncul.   *Aconitum spicatum* (rt)
Condelphine is an acetyl ester of *isotalatisidine*. It is one of the very few
  alkaloids occurring both in *Aconitum* and in *Delphinium*.
  Ranuncul.   *Aconitum talassicum, Delphinium confusum*
Consolidine (1) yields *consoline* and *benzoic acid*.
  Ranuncul.   *Delphinium consolida*
10-Dehydro-delcosine (Shimoburo base II)
  Ranuncul.   *Aconitum* sp., *japonicum*
Delatine
  Ranuncul.   *Delphinium elatum*
Delbine is an ester of *delsonine*.
  Ranuncul.   *Delphinium biternatum*
Delcosine (Alkaloid-C; ?Delphamine; Takao base I) is very closely
  related to *lycoctonine*.
  Ranuncul.   *Delphinium consolida*

Delorine ($C_{22}H_{29}O_5N.HCl$): belongs here?
  Ranuncul. Delphinium orientale (sd)
Delpheline may be closely related to *lycoctonine*.
  Ranuncul. Delphinium elatum
Delphinine is still (1960) of uncertain structure.
  Ranuncul. Delphinium staphisagria
Delphinoidine ($C_{25}H_{42}O_4N$): belongs here?
  Ranuncul. Delphinium staphisagria (sd)
Delphisine: belongs here?
  Ranuncul. Delphinium staphisagria (sd)
Delphonine ($C_{25}H_{41}O_7N$): belongs here?
  Ranuncul. Delphinium sp.
Delsoline
  Ranuncul. Delphinium consolida (sd)
Delsonine (?Delphatine)
  Ranuncul. Delphinium consolida, ?*biternatum*
Elatine is said to be closely related to *methyl-lycaconitine*.
  Ranuncul. Delphinium elatum
Eldelidine (Deltamine)
  Ranuncul. Delphinium elatum
Eldeline (Delphelatine, Deltaline) is a monoacetyl derivative of *eldelidine*.
  Ranuncul. Delphinium elatum, ?*occidentale*
Heteratisine may be an artefact arising from *benzoyl-heteratisine*.
  Ranuncul. Aconitum heterophyllum
Hetisine
  Ranuncul. Aconitum heterophyllum
Hypaconine is the parent of *hypaconitine*.
  Does it occur naturally?
Hypaconitine
  Ranuncul. Aconitum (at least 17 species)
Hypognavine
  Ranuncul. Aconitum sanyoënse
Ignavine
  Ranuncul. Aconitum sanyoënse (and other spp.)
Indaconitine
  Ranuncul. Aconitum chasmanthus (rt)
Isoaconitine
  Ranuncul. Aconitum spp.
Isoatisine: does this occur naturally?
Isohypognavine
  Ranuncul. Aconitum japonicum (plt), *majiani*
Jesaconitine
  Ranuncul. Aconitum (4 spp.)

Kobusine
>   *Ranuncul.*   *Aconitum* (3 spp.)

Lappaconitine
>   *Ranuncul.*   *Aconitum* (4 or 5 spp.)

Lucaconine
>   *Ranuncul.*   *Aconitum lucidusculum*

Lucidusculine
>   *Ranuncul.*   *Aconitum lucidusculum*

Lycaconitine (?*Avadharine*)
>   *Ranuncul.*   *Aconitum lycoctonum, gigas, orientale* (*avadharine*)

Lycoctonine (Royline; Delsine; fig. 18) is the parent alcohol of *anthranoyl-lycoctonine, ajacine, lycaconitine, delartine, methyl-lycaconitine,* and *delsamine.*
>   *Ranuncul.*   *Aconitum lycoctonum, Delphinium barbeyi*
>   *Comp.*   *Inula royleana*

Mesaconine is the amino-alcohol parent of *mesaconitine.* Does it occur naturally?

Mesaconitine
>   *Ranuncul.*   *Aconitum* (most spp. ?)

Methyl-lycaconitine (Delartine, Delsamidine; Delsemine)
>   *Ranuncul.*   *Delphinium* (4 spp.)
>   *Comp.*   *Inula royleana* (rt)

Miyaconitine may form a link between the *atisines* and the *aconitines.*
>   *Ranuncul.*   *Aconitum miyabei*

Miyaconitinone
>   *Ranuncul.*   *Aconitum miyabei*

Monoacetyl-talatisamine
>   *Ranuncul.*   *Aconitum nemorum* (plt)

Napelline
>   *Ranuncul.*   *Aconitum napellus*

Napellonine (Songorine; Shimoburo base I)
>   *Ranuncul.*   *Aconitum napellus*

Neoline occurs in the free (unesterified) state. See *neopelline.*
>   *Ranuncul.*   *Aconitum napellus*

Neopelline: is an ester of *neoline?*
>   Occurrence?

Pseudaconine is the parent of 4 ester-alkaloids—*pseudaconitine,* α-*pseudaconitine,* α-*veratroyl-pseudaconitine,* and *indaconitine.* Does it occur naturally?

Pseudaconitine is isomeric with α-*pseudaconitine.*
>   *Ranuncul.*   *Aconitum* (4–5 spp.)

α-Pseudaconitine
>   *Ranuncul.*   *Aconitum*

Pseudanthorine
  Ranuncul.   Aconitum anthora
Pseudo-kobusine
  Ranuncul.   Aconitum lucidusculum, yezoënse
Septentrionaline
  Ranuncul.   Aconitum septentrionale
Staphisine
  Ranuncul.   Delphinium staphisagria
Talatisamine (?Isotalatisidine)
  Ranuncul.   Aconitum talassicum, nemorum; Delphinium confusum
  (isotalatisidine)
Talatisidine
  Ranuncul.   Aconitum talassicum
Talatisine
  Ranuncul.   Aconitum talassicum
α-Veratroyl-pseudaconitine may be an artefact.
  Ranuncul.   Aconitum sp.

II. The Alkaloids of *Garrya*

The four *Garrya* bases are isomers, and they are isomeric with *atisine* and *isoatisine*! Their structures may be derived from the pentacyclic skeleton shown in fig. 18. Their absolute configurations, we are told, may be correlated with the *phyllocladene* type of *diterpene*.

Cuauchichicine
  Garry.   Garrya laurifolia (bk)
Garryfoline was called *laurifoline* but that name is now used for an aporphine alkaloid from *Cocculus laurifolius*.
  Garry.   Garrya laurifolia (bk)
Garryine
  Garry.   Garrya fremontii (rt), *racemosa* (bk), *veatchii* (bk)
Veatchine
  Garry.   Garrya laurifolia, veatchii (bk)

III. The Alkaloids of *Erythrophleum*

Cassaidine ($C_{24}H_{41}O_4N$)
  Legum.   Erythrophleum guineense (bk)
Cassaine ($C_{24}H_{39}O_4N$; fig. 18)
  Legum.   Erythrophleum guineense (bk)
Cassamine ($C_{25}H_{39}O_5N$)
  Legum.   Erythrophleum guineense (bk)

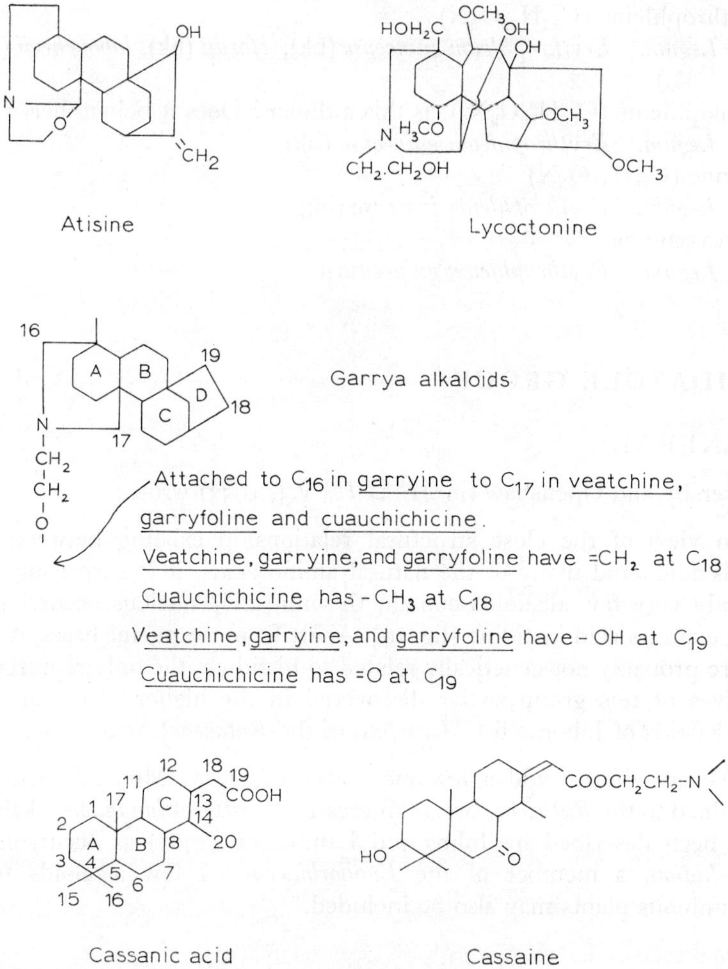

Atisine

Lycoctonine

Garrya alkaloids

Attached to C_{16} in <u>garryine</u> to C_{17} in <u>veatchine</u>, <u>garryfoline</u> and <u>cuauchichicine</u>.

<u>Veatchine</u>, <u>garryine</u>, and <u>garryfoline</u> have $=CH_2$ at C_{18}

<u>Cuauchichicine</u> has $-CH_3$ at C_{18}

<u>Veatchine</u>, <u>garryine</u>, and <u>garryfoline</u> have $-OH$ at C_{19}

<u>Cuauchichicine</u> has $=O$ at C_{19}

Cassanic acid

Cassaine

Fig. 18. Diterpenoid alkaloids.

Coumingaine
    Legum. *Erythrophleum coumingo* (bk)
Coumingidine is incompletely known but is related to *cassaine*.
    Legum. *Erythrophleum coumingo* (bk)
Coumingine (β-Hydroxy-isovaleryl-cassaine)
    Legum. *Erythrophleum coumingo* (bk)
Erythrophlamine ($C_{25}H_{39}O_6N$)
    Legum. *Erythrophleum guineense* (bk)
Erythrophleguine ($C_{25}H_{39}O_6N$) is very like *erythrophlamine*.
    Legum. *Erythrophleum guineense*

Erythrophleine ($C_{24}H_{39}O_5N$)
> *Legum.   Erythrophleum guineense* (bk), ?*fordii* (bk), *laboucherii* (lvs, st.)

Homophleine ($C_{56}H_{90}O_9N_2$): is this a dimer? Does it belong here?
> *Legum.   Erythrophleum guineense* (bk)

Ivorine ($C_{26}H_{44}O_5N$)
> *Legum.   Erythrophleum ivorense* (bk)

Norcassaidine
> *Legum.   Erythrophleum guineense*

IMIDAZOLE GROUP

GENERAL

Battersby and Openshaw (in *M. & H.*, v.3, 1953) wrote:

> In view of the close structural relationship existing between the alkaloids and many of the natural amino acids, it is surprising that only very few alkaloids contain the imidazole nucleus occurring in the amino acid histidine [fig. 19]. Apart from the purine bases, which are probably not genetically related to histidine, the only representatives of this group so far discovered in the higher plants are the alkaloids of Jaborandi [*Pilocarpus*, of the *Rutaceae*].

We are able to add a few more alkaloids now. Most of them are confined to the *Rutaceae*, but an interesting cluster of *imidazole* alkaloids has been described by Johns and Lamberton (1967) as occurring in *Glochidion*, a member of the *Euphorbiaceae*. A few alkaloids from leguminous plants may also be included.

List and Occurrence

Casimiroedine (fig. 19)
> *Rut.   Casimiroa edulis*

Chaksine, which was described as a pseudo-alkaloid by Hegnauer, belongs here?
> *Legum.   Cassia absus* (sd)

Glochidicine (fig. 19)
> *Euphorbi.   Glochidion* sp. (*philippicum?*) (lvs)

Glochidine (fig. 19)
> *Euphorbi.   Glochidion* sp. (*philippicum?*) (lvs)

Histamine (fig. 19) is dealt with as an *amine* (p. 363).

Histidine (fig. 19) is dealt with as an *amino-acid* (p. 373).

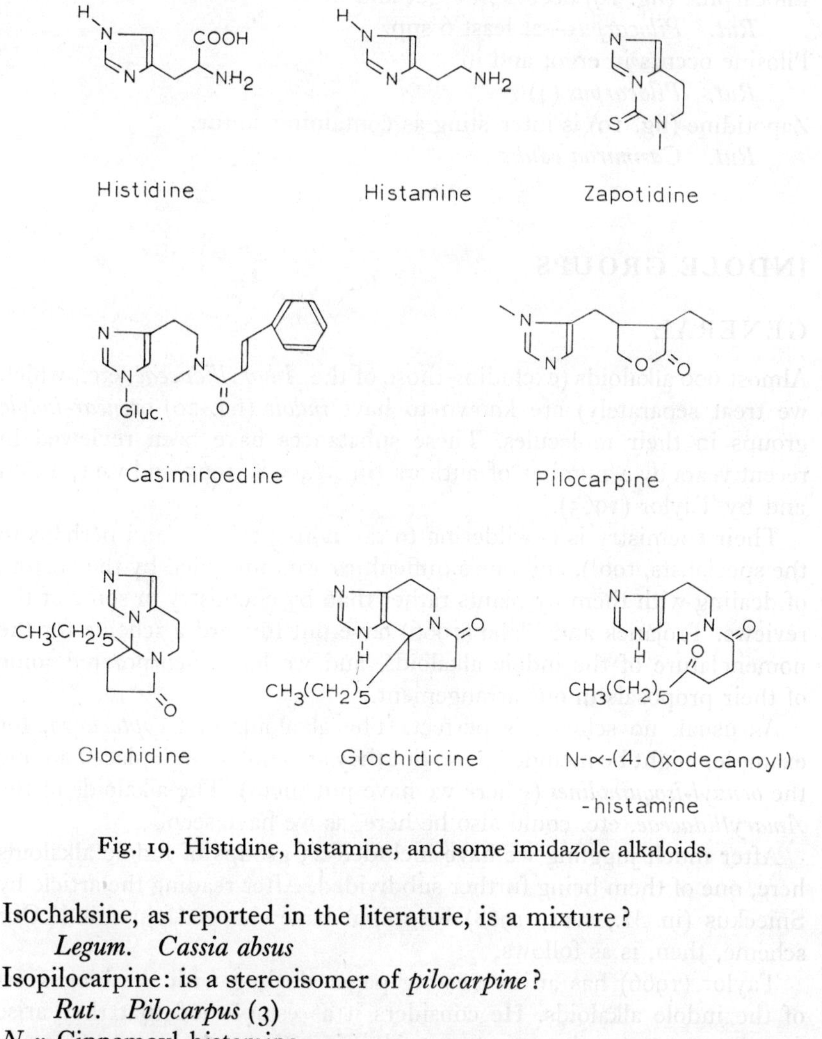

Fig. 19. Histidine, histamine, and some imidazole alkaloids.

Isochaksine, as reported in the literature, is a mixture?
>   Legum.   *Cassia absus*
Isopilocarpine: is a stereoisomer of *pilocarpine*?
>   *Rut.   Pilocarpus* (3)
N-α-Cinnamoyl-histamine
>   Legum.   *Acacia argentea, polystachya* (reported without the α-)
>   *Euphorbi.   Glochidion* sp. (*philippicum*?) (lvs)
N,N-Dimethyl-histamine
>   Chenopodi.   *Spinacia oleracea*
>   *Rut.   Casimiroa edulis* (sd)
N-α-(4-Oxodecanoyl)-histamine (fig. 19)
>   *Euphorbi.   Glochidion* sp. (*philippicum*?) (lvs)
Pilocarpidine (De-*N*-methyl-pilocarpine)
>   *Rut.   Pilocarpus jaborandi* (lvs)

Pilocarpine (fig. 19) occurs in ergot and in
  Rut. Pilocarpus—at least 6 spp.
Pilosine occurs in ergot and in
  Rut. Pilocarpus (4)
Zapotidine (fig. 19) is interesting as containing sulfur.
  Rut. Casimiroa edulis

INDOLE GROUPS

GENERAL

Almost 600 alkaloids (excluding those of the *Amaryllidaceae*, etc., which we treat separately) are known to have *indole* (fig. 20) or *near-indole* groups in their molecules. These substances have been reviewed in recent years by a number of authors (in *M.*, v.8, 1965 and v.11, 1968) and by Taylor (1965).

Their chemistry is bewildering to the non-specialist (and perhaps to the specialists, too!), and one's difficulties are multiplied by the custom of dealing with them by plants rather than by chemistry in some of the reviews. Trojánek and Bláha (1966) have put forward a scheme for the nomenclature of the indole alkaloids, and we have incorporated some of their proposals in our arrangement.

As usual, no scheme is perfect. The alkaloids of *Cryptocarya*, for example, might be included here, but they are equally well placed among the *benzyl-isoquinolines* (where we have put them). The alkaloids of the *Amaryllidaceae*, etc. could also be here, as we have seen.

After much juggling we have included 23 groups of indole alkaloids here, one of them being further subdivided. After reading the article by Snieckus (in *M.*, v.11, 1968) we might have changed our mind! Our scheme, then, is as follows.

Taylor (1966) has an interesting paper dealing with the biogenesis of the indole alkaloids. He considers it as established that they arise from *tryptophan* and a *monoterpenoid* moiety (below).

I. Simple Indole Bases -- about 20

Indole

II. Carboline Alkaloids -- nearly 20

Carboline

III. Quinazolinocarbolines -- 7

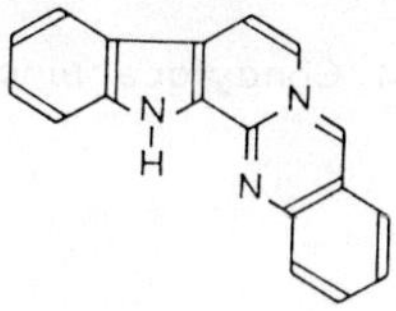

IV Hexahydro-pyrrolo (2,3b) indoles
(Alkaloids of Physostigma ,
Calycanthaceae , etc.) -- about 15

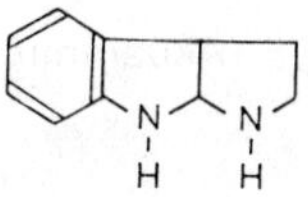

V Canthin-6-ones -- 5

Canthin-6-one

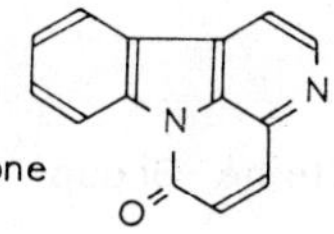

VI Eburnamine -Vincamine
Alkaloids -- nearly 40

Eburnane (Trojánek and
Bláha)

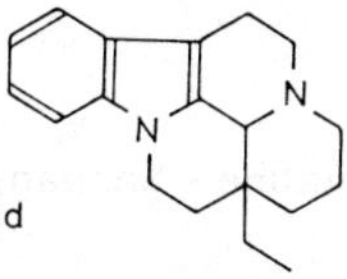

VII. Oxindoles (incl. Corynoxanes)

Oxindole

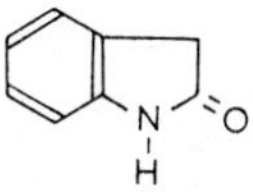

Corynoxane

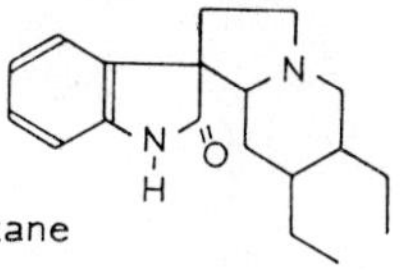

VIII Aspidosperma Groups -- about 180

1. Aspidospermine Group

Aspidospermane
(Trojánek and Bláha)

2. Aspidofractinine Group

Aspidofractinine

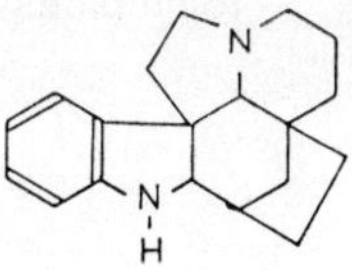

3. Aspidoalbine Group

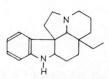

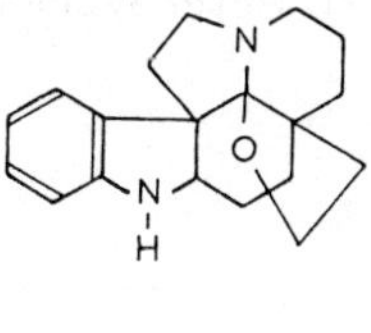

4. Condylocarpine Group

Aspidospermatidine

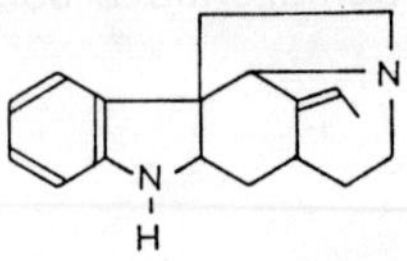

5. Akuammicine (Strychnos) Group

Akuammicine

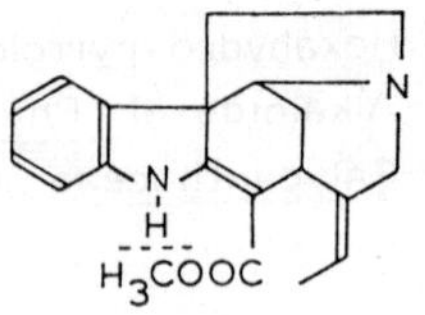

6. Uleine Group

Uleine

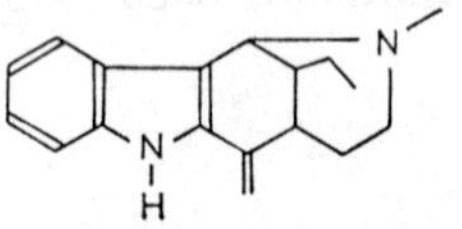

IX. Ajmaline - Sarpagine Alkaloids
       -- about 50

Ajmaline group

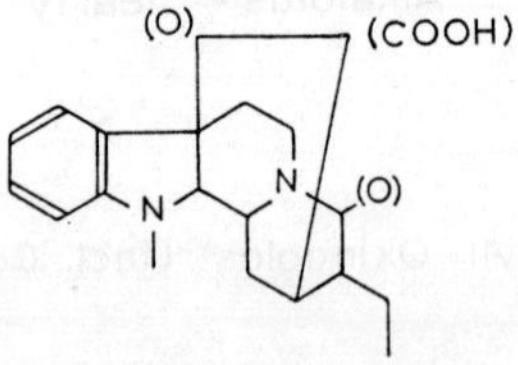

Sarpagine group

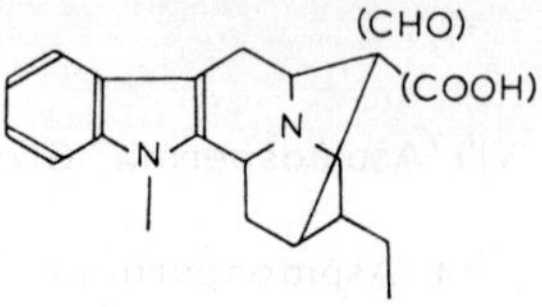

X. Yohimbanes -- more than 40
    (Yohimbines , etc.)

Yohimbane

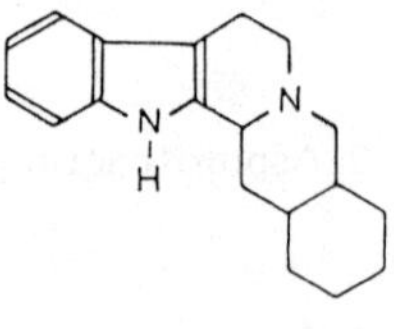

XI. Heteroyohimbanes -- nearly 30

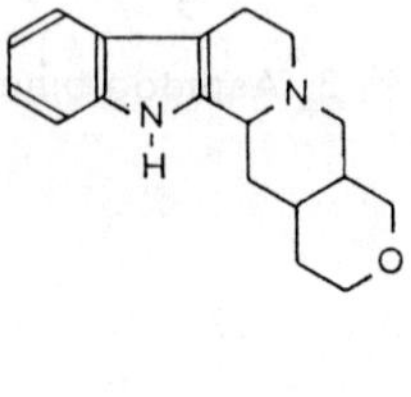

XII. Corynanes -- about 30

XIII. 2,2'- Indolyl- quinuclidines -- 5

Cinchonamine

XIV. Ergolines -- about 8

Ergoline

XV. Iboga and Voacanga
     Alkaloids -- more than 40

Ibogaine

XVI. Aspidosperma –Iboga Dimers -- about a dozen

XVII. Some <u>Alstonia</u> Alkaloids -- 5

XVIII. Erythrinanes -- about 20

Erythrinane

XIX. Indole Alkaloids of the Orchidaceae -
                         -- about 7

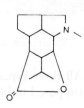

Dendrobine

XX. The Mesembrine Group -- a few

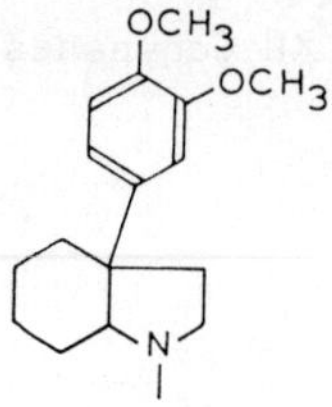

Mesembrane

XXI. The Stemona Group --about a dozen

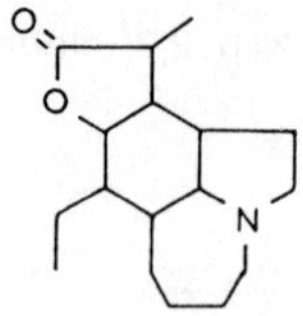

Stenine

XXII. Indolo (2,3∝) quinolizine -- 1

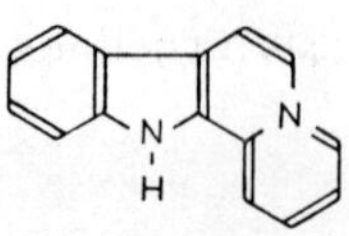

XXIII. Carbazoles -- 5

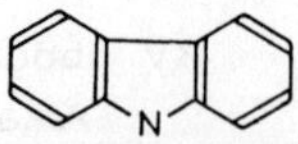

Carbazole

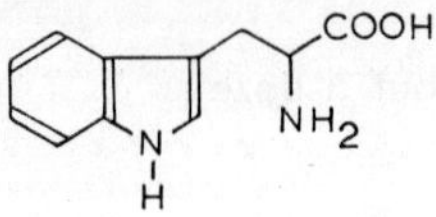

Tryptophan

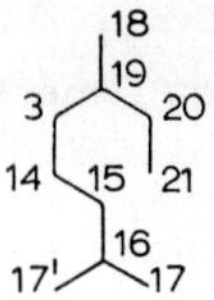

Monoterpene

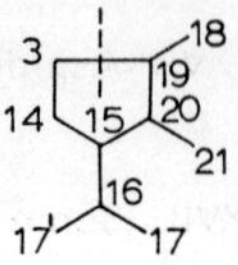

Cyclopentanoterpene

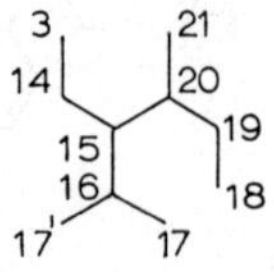

Yohimbine type

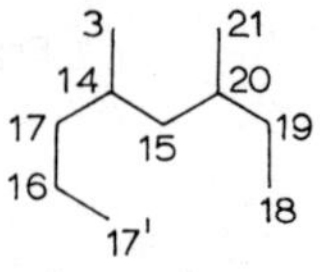

Iboga type

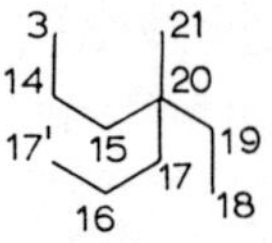

Aspidosperma type

All three types of alkaloid—yohimbine, iboga, and aspidosperma—are supposed to be formed from these precursors.

INDOLE GROUPS
I SIMPLE INDOLE BASES

GENERAL

Saxton (in *M.*, v.8, 1965) deals with the 'several simple derivatives of indole, which are presumably closely related to the routes of biosynthesis and metabolism of indoleacetic acid or tryptophan, [and which] occur widely in the vegetable kingdom'.

He reviews the group again in 1968 (*M.*, v.10).

Most of these bases occur in the *Leguminosae*, but they are rather widely distributed, as the list following will show.

List and Occurrence

Abrine
  Legum. *Abrus precatorius* (sd)
3-Aminomethyl-indole
  Gram. *Hordeum* (sdlgs)
Bufotenine (5-Hydroxy-N_b,N_b-dimethyltryptamine; fig. 20) was first isolated, as the name suggests, from a toad, *Bufo vulgaris*. It is known to occur in some fungi. Seeds containing it are used to cause hallucinations, but there is some doubt as to whether this alkaloid is the substance responsible.
  Legum. *Piptadenia excelsa* (sd), *macrocarpa* (frt); *Desmodium pulchellum* (plt); *Lespedeza bicolor* v. *japonica* (lvs, rtbk)
  Apocyn. *Prestonia amazonica*
  Gram. *Phalaris tuberosa* (plt)
Bufotenine-N_b-oxide may be an artefact in some cases. It has been found in fungi.
  Legum. *Piptadenia excelsa* (sd), *macrocarpa* (frt)
Cryptolepine (fig. 20) is not a simple indole, but where does it belong?
  Asclepiad. *Cryptolepis* (2)
Dipterine (N_b-methyl-tryptamine)
  Chenopodi. *Arthrophytum* (*Hammada*) *leptocladum*, *wakhanicum*; *Girgensohnia diptera*
  Legum. *Acacia maidenii* (bk), *confusa* (bk); *Piptadenia* spp.
Donaxarine may not belong here. It occurs with *gramine* in
  Gram. *Arundo donax*
Gramine (Donaxine; 3-Dimethylamino-methylindole; fig. 20) seems to be rather widely distributed.
  Legum. *Desmodium pulchellum*; *Lupinus luteus* (sd), *absent* from some other spp.

    Acer.   *Acer rubrum, saccharinum*
    Gram.   *Arundo donax, Hordeum, Phalaris arundinacea* (plt)
5-Hydroxytryptamine (Enteramine; ?Oxytryptamine; Serotonin; Thrombocytin; fig. 20) has been found in animals, where it plays an important but not fully understood part in the central nervous system. In plants it is widely spread and occurs particularly in irritant plants. Saxton (1965) thinks it may be responsible for the irritation caused by *Mucuna*, etc. It is said to be present in many fruits—banana, plum, tomato, pineapple, avocado, egg-plant, plantain, papaw, passion-fruit, walnut, etc. A whole volume has been written on *serotonin* by Garattini and Valzelli (1965).
    Urtic.   *Girardinia heterophylla* (lvs), *Laportea moroides* (hairs), *Urtica dioica*
    Ranuncul.   *Ranunculus sceleratus*
    Legum.   *Mucuna pruriens* (hairs), *Prosopis*
    Malv.   *Gossypium*
    Anacardi.   *Gluta renghas*
    Elaeagn.   *Hippophaë*
    Arac.   *Symplocarpus*
    Mus.   *Musa*
Hypaphorine may be called the *betaine of tryptophane.*
    Chenopodi.   *Beta* ?
    Legum.   *Erythrina* (*Hypaphorus*) spp. in seeds of all so far examined ?
Hypaphorine methyl ester
    Legum.   *Pultenaea altissima*
Indole (fig. 20) is said to occur free (?) in the flowers of some plants, but not (?) in other parts.
    Calycanth.   *Chimonanthus* (fl. ?)
    Crucif.   *Cheiranthus* (fl. ?)
    Legum.   *Robinia* (fl. ?)
    Rut.   *Citrus* (fl. ?)
    Ole.   *Jasminum* (fl. ?)
    Amaryllid.   *Narcissus tazetta* v. *chinensis* (ess. oil of fl.)
Lespedamine (N_a-methoxy-N_b,N_b-dimethyl-tryptamine)
    Legum.   *Lespedeza bicolor* var. *japonica* (lvs)
6-Methoxy-N_b-dimethyl-tryptamine
    Malpighi.   ? *Banisteriopsis* spp.
5-Methoxy-N_b,N_b-dimethyl-tryptamine has been found in fungi and in
    Legum.   *Piptadenia peregrina, Desmodium pulchellum* (plt), *Lespedeza bicolor* v. *japonica* (rt, bk)
    Rut.   *Dictyoloma incanescens*
    Gram.   *Phalaris tuberosa* (plt)

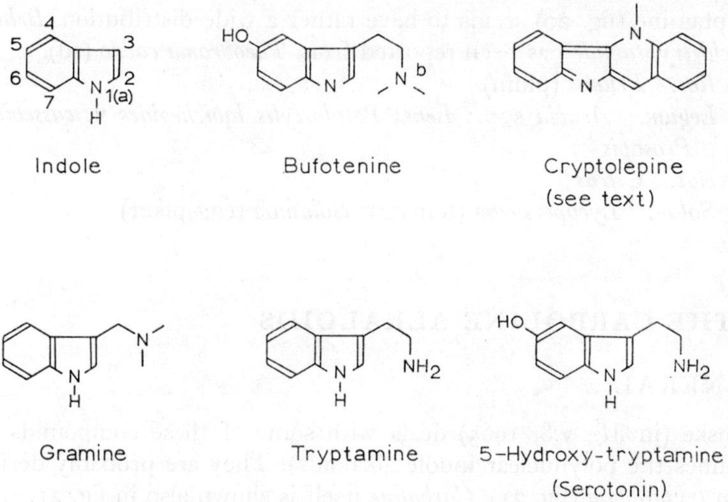

Fig. 20. Indole and some derivatives.

5-Methoxy-N_b,N_b-dimethyltryptamine-N_b-oxide
> Legum. *Desmodium pulchellum* (plt), *Lespedeza bicolor* v. *japonica* (rtbk)

5-Methoxy-N_b-methyltryptamine
> Legum. *Desmodium pulchellum* (plt); *Piptadenia macrocarpa* (bk), *peregrina*
> Gram. *Phalaris*

3-Methylamino-methylindole
> Gram. *Hordeum* (sdlgs)

N_b,N_b-Dimethyl-tryptamine (Nigerine) is said to be psychotomimetic. It has been found in fungi, and in
> Legum. *Acacia maidenii* (bk); *Desmodium pulchellum* (plt); *Lespedeza bicolor* v. *japonica*; *Mimosa hostilis* (rtbk); *Petalostylis labicheoides* v. *casseoides* (lvs, st.); *Piptadenia excelsa* (frt), *macrocarpa* (frt)
> Malpighi. *Banisteriopsis* spp. (lvs)
> Apocyn. *Prestonia amazonica*
> Gram. *Phalaris arundinacea* (plt), *tuberosa* (plt)

N_b,N_b-Dimethyl-tryptamine-oxide: may arise as an artefact?
> Legum. *Desmodium pulchellum*, *Lespedeza bicolor* v. *japonica*, *Piptadenia*

Skatole (β-Methyl-indole) is widely distributed.
> Ulm. *Celtis reticulosa* (wd)
> Laur. *Nectandra* sp. (wd)
> Arac. *Arum dioscoridis* (infl), *italicum* (infl); *Hydrosme rivieri* (infl)

Tryptamine (fig. 20) seems to have rather a wide distribution. *Behenic acid tryptamide* has been reported from *Theobroma cacao* (sd).

    Ros.   *Prunus* (plum)

    Legum.   *Acacia* spp.; *Lens*; *Petalostylis labicheoides* v. *casseoides*; *Prosopis*

    Rut.   *Citrus*

    Solan.   *Lycopersicum* (tomato); *Solanum* (egg-plant)

II THE CARBOLINE ALKALOIDS

GENERAL

Manske (in *M.*, v.8, 1965) deals with some of these compounds (he excludes the polynuclear indole alkaloids). They are probably derived from *tryptophan* (fig. 21). *Carboline* itself is shown also in fig. 21.

They seem to be distributed in a rather haphazard fashion. Several occur in the *Rubiaceae* and at least one in each of the supposedly related families *Loganiaceae* and *Apocynaceae*. Is this more than chance?

List and Occurrence

Adifoline (fig. 21)

    Rubi.   *Adina cordifolia* (htwd)

Aribine may be *harman*, but reports are conflicting.

    Rubi.   *Arariba* (*Sickingia*) *rubra* (bk)

Brevicarine is very like *brevicolline*?

    Cyper.   *Carex brevicollis*

Brevicolline (fig. 21) has an extra N-ring.

    Cyper.   *Carex brevicollis*

3,4-Dimethyl-3,4,5,6-tetrahydro-4-carboline

    Chenopodi.   *Arthrophytum* (*Hammada*) *leptocladum* (plt)

Harmaline (3,4-Dihydro-harmine; Harmidine)

    Malpighi.   *Banisteria* sp.

    Zygophyll.   *Peganum harmala*

Harmalol

    Zygophyll.   *Peganum harmala*

Harman (?Aribine; ?Loturine; Passiflorine; fig. 21) seems to be rather widely distributed.

    Passiflor.   *Passiflora* spp.

    Zygophyll.   ?*Tribulus terrestris*

    Symploc.   *Symplocos*

    Bignoni.   *Newbouldia laevis*

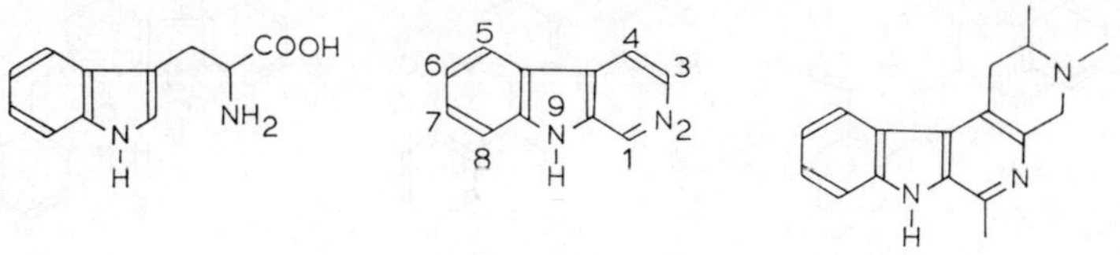

Tryptophan   Carboline   ? Brevicolline

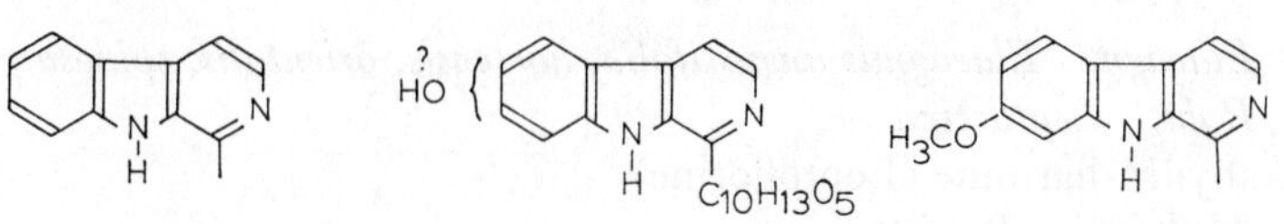

Harman   Adifoline   Harmine
(Loturine)

Fig. 21. Tryptophan, carboline, and some carboline alkaloids.

Rubi. Sickingia klugii (bk)
Cyper. Carex brevicollis
Harman-3-carboxylic acid
Apocyn. Aspidosperma polyneuron
Harmine (?Banisterine; ?Passiflorine; ?Telepathine; ?Yageine; fig. 21)
Malpighi. Banisteria spp., *Banisteriopsis, Cabi*
Zygophyll. Peganum, ?Tribulus terrestris, Zygophyllum
Passiflor. Passiflora spp. (as *passiflorine?*)
Rubi. Arariba (Sickingia) rubra
Harmol
Passiflor. Passiflora
4-Methyl-3,4,5,6-tetrahydro-4-carboline
Chenopodi. Arthrophytum leptocladum (plt)
N_b-Methyl-harman (Melinonine-F)
Logani. Strychnos
N_b-Methyl-tetrahydro-harman (Leptocladine)
Chenopodi. Arthrophyton leptocladum (lvs, st.)
Legum. Acacia complanata (lvs, st.)
N-Methyl-tetrahydro-harmol
Elaeagn. Elaeagnus
Tetrahydro-harman (Calligonine; Eleagnine)
Polygon. Calligonum minimum
Chenopodi. Arthrophytum leptocladum
Legum. Petalostylis

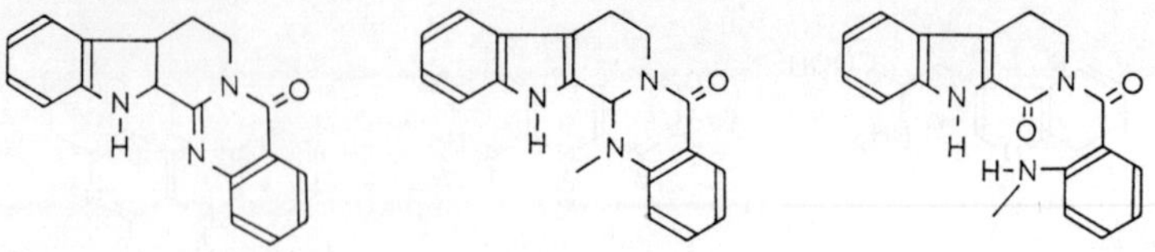

Rutaecarpine   Evodiamine   Rhetsinine

Fig. 22. Some quinazolinocarboline alkaloids.

> *Elaeagn.*   *Elaeagnus angustifolia, hortensis, orientalis, spinosa*
> *Rubi.*   *Leptactina*

Tetrahydro-harmine (Leptoflorine)

> *Malpighi.*   *Banisteria* sp.
> *Rubi.*   *Leptactina densiflora*

Tetrahydro-harmol

> *Elaeagn.*   *Elaeagnus*

III THE QUINAZOLINOCARBOLINES

GENERAL

These alkaloids are discussed by Manske (in *M.*, v.8, 1965). He points out that they contain both *carboline* (fig. 21) and *quinazoline* nuclei.

They seem to be restricted to a few genera of the *Rutaceae*.

List and Occurrence

Evodiamine (fig. 22)
> *Rut.*   *Evodia rutaecarpa, Hortia*

Hortiacine
> *Rut.*   *Hortia arborea, brasiliana*

Hortiamine
> *Rut.*   *Hortia aborea, brasiliana*

Hydroxy-evodiamine
> *Rut.*   *Evodia rutaecarpa* var. *officinalis*

Rhetsine (*dl*-Evodiamine)
> *Rut.*   *Zanthoxylum rhetsa*

Rhetsinine (fig. 22) has only 4 rings, but is obviously related to the other alkaloids of this group.
> *Rut.*   *Zanthoxylum oxyphyllum, rhetsa*

Rutaecarpine (fig. 22)
> *Rut.*   *Evodia rutaecarpa* var. *officinalis, Hortia arborea*

IV HEXAHYDRO-PYRROLO [2,3b]INDOLE
ALKALOIDS (Alkaloids of Physostigma, Calycanthaceae, etc.)

GENERAL

The unit of structure here is *hexahydro-pyrrolo [2,3 b]indole*. Some of these alkaloids, such as *chimonanthine*, are dimers.

The seeds of the Calabar bean (*Physostigma venenosum, Leguminosae*) have been used as an ordeal poison in Africa. They contain several alkaloids which have been discussed by Coxworth (in *M.*, v.8, 1965).

Manske (in *M.*, v.8, 1965) has dealt with the dimers of the *Calycanthaceae*, and with the related *hodgkinsine* of the *Rubiaceae* (which is a trimer?).

Several alkaloids of the *Apocynaceae* seem also to belong here.

List and Occurrence

Calycanthidine (fig. 23)
  Calycanth. Calycanthus glaucus
Calycanthine (fig. 23) does not appear to belong here but Manske (in *M.*, v.8, 1965) says: 'It is not an indole alkaloid, but its facile conversion to indoles and the fact that most of its congeners are indoles is justification for treating it in this volume [devoted to indole alkaloids].'
  Calycanth. Calycanthus (3), *Chimonanthus*
Chimonanthine (fig. 23)
  Calycanth. Calycanthus floridus, Chimonanthus fragrans
Corymine
  Apocyn. Hunteria corymbosa, umbellata (sd)
Echitamine (fig. 23)
  Apocyn. Alstonia (8)
Eseramine
  Legum. Physostigma venenosum (sd)
Geneserine (?Eseridine; Physostigmine-*N*-oxide)
  Legum. Physostigma venenosum (sd)
Hodgkinsine is said to be a trimer!
  Rubi. Hodgkinsonia frutescens
Isocalycanthine may not exist.
Isocorymine
  Apocyn. Hunteria umbellata (sd)
Isophysostigmine: there is some doubt as to the existence of this alkaloid. It has been said to occur in
  Legum. Physostigma venenosum (sd)

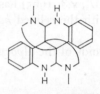

Hexahydro-pyrrolo
(2,3b) indole

Physostigmine
(Eserine)

Echitamine

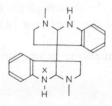

Chimonanthine
(Calycanthidine
has⁻CH₃ at x)

Calycanthine

Fig. 23. Hexahydro-pyrrolo [2,3 b]indole and some of its
alkaloids.

Nerifoline (Demethyl-echitamine) may be an artefact.
    Apocyn. Alstonia neriifolia (bk?)
N,N-Dimethyl-chimonanthine (?Folicanth(id)ine)
    Calycanth. Calycanthus (2)
O-Acetyl-corymine
    Apocyn. Hunteria umbellata (sd)
Physostigmine (Eserine; fig. 23)
    Legum. Dioclea macrocarpa, Mucuna (2), *Physostigma* (2), *Vicia
    calabarica*
    Euphorbi. Hippomane? (a doubtful record)
Physovenine is like *physostigmine* but with oxygen in place of nitrogen
in ring C, so it really should not be here.
    Legum. Physostigma venenosum (sd)

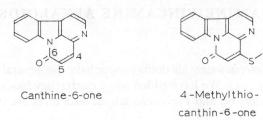

Canthine-6-one   4-Methylthio-
canthin-6-one

Fig. 24. Canthin-6-ones.

V CANTHIN-6-ONES

GENERAL

Taylor (in *M.*, v.8, 1965) deals with the small group of *canthin-6-one* alkaloids. There are a few *canthin-4-one* alkaloids which are placed by Taylor (in *M.*, v.11, 1968) in the *eburnamine-vincamine* group. We have followed him.

Apart from one occurrence in the *Amaranthaceae*, the *canthin-6-ones* seem to be confined to the *Rutaceae* and *Simaroubaceae*, families so nearly related that they are placed by Scholz (in *Syll.* 12, 1964) in the same sub-order of the **Rutales.**

List and Occurrence

Canthine-6-one (fig. 24)
    Rut.   *Pentaceras australis, Zanthoxylum suberosum*
    Simaroub.   *Picrasma ailanthoides, crenata (vellozii)*
4,5-Dimethoxy-canthin-6-one
    Simaroub.   *Picrasma ailanthoides*
4-Methoxy-canthin-6-one
    Amaranth.   *Charpentiera obovata*
5-Methoxy-canthin-6-one
    Rut.   *Pentaceras australis, Zanthoxylum caribaeum*
4-Methylthio-canthin-6-one (fig. 24)
    Rut.   *Pentaceras australis*

VI EBURNAMINE-VINCAMINE ALKALOIDS

GENERAL

The *eburnamine-vincamine* alkaloids proper have the general structure of *eburnamine* (fig. 25). We have added some quaternary bases and several alkaloids of *Hunteria* and *Pleiocarpa* whose structures are incompletely known.

Taylor (in *M.*,v.11, 1968) includes the *canthine* and *schizozygia groups* (fig. 25) here. Of the latter he says that they are obviously related both to the *eburnamine group* and to the *aspidosperma* group.

These alkaloids seem to be confined to a few genera of the *Apocynaceae*.

List and Occurrence

Caffaeoschizine is a member of the *schizozygia group*.
> *Apocyn.* *Schizozygia caffaeoides* (lvs, rt)

Eburnamenine
> *Apocyn.* *Aspidosperma quebracho-blanco*, *Hunteria eburnea*, *Pleiocarpa mutica*, *Rhazya stricta*

Eburnamine (fig. 25)
> *Apocyn.* *Amsonia tabernaemontana*, *Gonioma kamassi*, *Haplophyton cimicidum*, *Hunteria eburnea*, *Pleiocarpa mutica*, *Rhazya stricta*

Eburnamonine (Vincanorine; fig. 25)
> *Apocyn.* *Amsonia tabernaemontana*, *Hunteria eburnea*, *Rhazya stricta*?, *Vinca minor*

16-Epivincamine
> *Apocyn.* *Vinca minor*

Hunteracine-N_b-methochloride: incompletely known?
> *Apocyn.* *Hunteria eburnea*

Hunteramine: incompletely known?
> *Apocyn.* *Hunteria eburnea*

Hunterburnine-α-methochloride (fig. 25) is a quaternary base.
> *Apocyn.* *Hunteria eburnea*, *Pleiocarpa mutica*

Hunterburnine-β-methochloride is a quaternary base.
> *Apocyn.* *Hunteria eburnea*, *Pleiocarpa mutica*

Hunterine: incompletely known?
> *Apocyn.* *Hunteria eburnea*

Isoeburnamine is a diastereoisomer of *eburnamine*.
> *Apocyn.* *Amsonia tabernaemontana*, *Haplophyton cimicidum*, *Hunteria eburnea*, *Rhazya stricta*

Isoschizogaline (7-Epischizogaline) is a member of the *schizozygia group*.

   Apocyn.   *Schizozygia caffaeoides* (lvs, rt)

Isoschizogamine is a stereoisomer of *schizogamine*?

   Apocyn.   *Schizozygia caffaeoides* (lvs, rt)

Isotuboflavine is a *canthin-4-one*.

   Apocyn.   *Pleiocarpa mutica*

Isovincamine is said to be a mixture.

16-Methoxy-20-oxo-1-vincadifformine

   Apocyn.   *Vinca minor*

Neburnamine: incompletely known?

   Apocyn.   *Hunteria eburnea*

Nor-isotuboflavine is a *canthine-4-one*.

   Apocyn.   *Pleiocarpa mutica*

O-Methyl-eburnamine

   Apocyn.   *Haplophyton cimicidum*

20-Oxo-1-vincadifformine (Minovincine)

   Apocyn.   *Vinca minor*

Perivincine is said to be a mixture.

Pleiocarpamine: belongs here?

   Apocyn.   *Hunteria eburnea, Pleiocarpa mutica* (rt)

Pleiocarpinidine: incompletely known?

   Apocyn.   *Pleiocarpa mutica*

Pleiomutine is now (1968) known to be a *pleiocarpinine-eburnamine dimer*.

   Apocyn.   *Pleiocarpa mutica*

Pleiomutinine: incompletely known?

   Apocyn.   *Pleiocarpa mutica*

Schizogaline

   Apocyn.   *Schizozygia caffaeoides* (lvs, rt)

Schizogamine

   Apocyn.   *Schizozygia caffaeoides* (lvs, rt)

Schizoluteine

   Apocyn.   *Schizozygia caffaeoides*?

Schizophylline

   Apocyn.   *Schizozygia caffaeoides* (lvs only)

Schizozygine (fig. 25)

   Apocyn.   *Schizozygia caffaeoides* (lvs, rt)

α-Schizozygol

   Apocyn.   *Schizozygia caffaeoides*

β-Schizozygol

   Apocyn.   *Schizozygia caffaeoides*

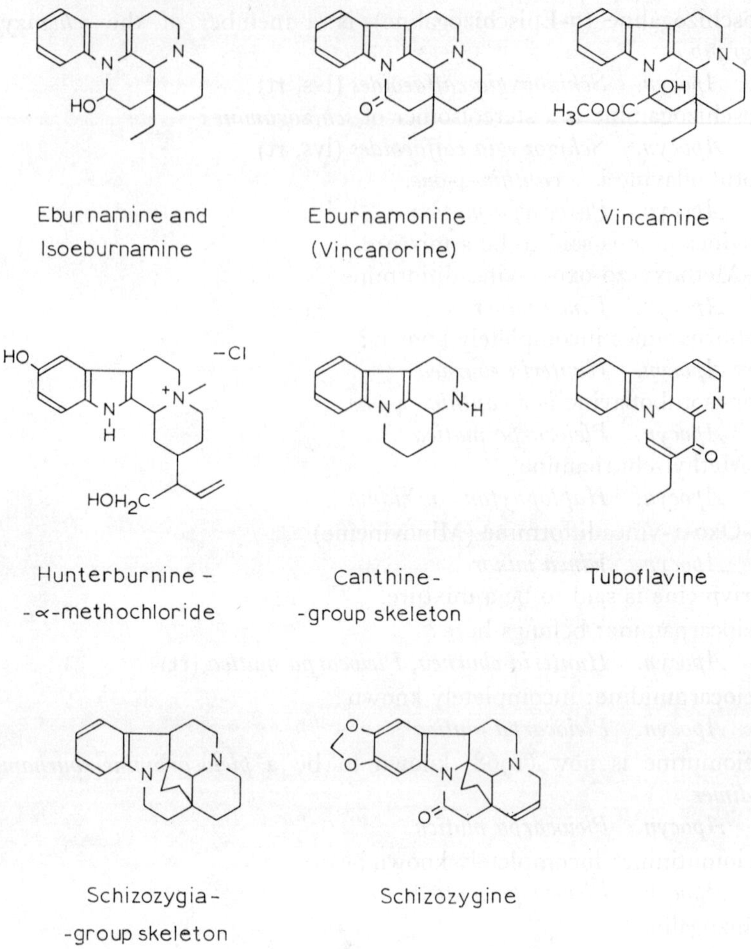

| Eburnamine and Isoeburnamine | Eburnamonine (Vincanorine) | Vincamine |

| Hunterburnine – -α-methochloride | Canthine- -group skeleton | Tuboflavine |

| Schizozygia- -group skeleton | Schizozygine |

Fig. 25. Some eburnamine-vincamine alkaloids and
related substances.

Tabernoschizine (Alkaloid-E of *Conopharyngia*; Pericalline) is, to me, of
unknown structure.

> *Apocyn.* *Catharanthus roseus* ('*pericalline*'); *Conopharyngia duris-*
> *sima* ('Alk.-E'), *holstii*; *Schizozygia caffaeoides* (lvs, rt)

Tuboflavine (fig. 25) is a *canthin-4-one*

> *Apocyn.* *Pleiocarpa mutica, tubicina*

Vincamine (Minorine; fig. 25)

> *Apocyn.* *Vinca minor* (principal alkaloid) and other spp.

Vincaminine (Vincareine)

> *Apocyn.* *Vinca minor*

Vincarodine is a dimer related to *vincine*?
  Apocyn.   Catharanthus (Vinca) roseus
Vincine (11-Methoxy-vincamine)
  Apocyn.   Vinca minor
Vincinine (11-Methoxy-vincaminine)
  Apocyn.   Vinca minor

VII OXINDOLE ALKALOIDS (Including Corynoxane Derivatives)

GENERAL

Alkaloids with an *oxindole* nucleus (fig. 26) form a distinct group. They have been discussed by Saxton (in *M.*, v.8, 1965 and v.10, 1968) and by Monteiro (in *M.*, v.11, 1968).

Like so many of the *indole* alkaloids the *oxindoles* seem to be confined to the **Gentianales** (*sensu* Wagenitz, in *Syll.*12, 1964). Fam. 1, *Loganiaceae*: 4–5 in 1 or 2 genera; fam. 5, *Apocynaceae*: 9 or so in 4 genera; fam. 7, *Rubiaceae*: 15–20 in 5 genera.

List and Occurrence

Africanine: belongs here?
  Rubi.   Uncaria (Ourouparia) africana (st)
Alstonia alkaloid-C: belongs here? It occurs (with at least 23 other alkaloids!) in
  Apocyn.   Alstonia muelleriana
Carapanaubine
  Apocyn.   Aspidosperma carapanauba, rigidum (laxiflorum) (bk);
    Vinca pubescens
Ciliaphylline: belongs here?
  Rubi.   Mitragyna ciliata (lvs)
Corynoxeine differs only slightly from *rhynchophylline*.
  Rubi.   Pseudocinchona africana
Corynoxine: an isomer of *rhynchophylline*?
  Rubi.   Pseudocinchona africana
Formosanine (Uncarine-B) is a stereoisomer of *mitraphylline*.
  Rubi.   Nauclea (Ourouparia) formosana, Uncaria kawakamii (bk, wd)
Gelsedine (11-Demethoxy-gelsemicine)
  Logani.   Gelsemium sempervirens
Gelsemicine (fig. 26)
  Logani.   Gelsemium sempervirens

Gelsemine
> *Logani.* *Gelsemium elegans, sempervirens*; *Mostuea stimulans*?

Gelsevirine (Gelseverine): belongs here?
> *Logani.* *Gelsemium sempervirens*

Herbaline (fig. 26)
> *Apocyn.* *Vinca herbacea* (lvs)

Isomitraphylline
> *Rubi.* *Mitragyna hirsuta* (lvs), *javanica* (lvs), *speciosa* (lvs)

Isopteropodine (Uncarine-E): a stereoisomer of *mitraphylline*?
> *Rubi.* *Uncaria pteropoda* (bk, st., rt)

Isorhynchophylline is a stereoisomer of *rhynchophylline*.
> *Rubi.* *Mitragyna ciliata* (lvs), *hirsuta* (lvs), *parvifolia* (lvs), *rotundi-folia* (lvs), *speciosa* (lvs); *Nauclea rhynchophylla*

'Kouminine': a mixture?

Majdine is isomeric with *carapanaubine*
> *Apocyn.* *Vinca pubescens*

11-Methoxy-mitraphylline (?Vineridine)
> *Rubi.* *Mitragyna javanica* (lvs)?

Mitragynol (Isorotundifoline)
> *Rubi.* *Mitragyna* (6); *Nauclea formosana*, (st.), *rhynchophylla*

Mitraphylline (Rubradinine; fig. 26) is probably 'the true oxindole analog of the hetero-yohimbine alkaloids'.
> *Apocyn.* *Catharanthus roseus* (lvs, rt)
> *Rubi.* *Mitragyna* (5); *Nauclea formosana*

Mitraspecine: belongs here?
> *Rubi.* *Mitragyna speciosa* (bk)

Mitraversine: belongs here?
> *Rubi.* *Mitragyna* (4), *Nauclea rhynchophylla*

Pteropodine (Uncarine-C): a stereoisomer of *mitraphylline*?
> *Rubi.* *Uncaria bernaysii, ferrea, pteropoda* (bk, st., rt)

Rauvoxine is isomeric with *carapanaubine*.
> *Apocyn.* *Rauwolfia vomitoria*

Rauvoxinine is isomeric with *carapanaubine*.
> *Apocyn.* *Rauwolfia vomitoria*

Rhynchociline: belongs here?
> *Rubi.* *Mitragyna ciliata* (lvs)

Rhynchophylline (Crossopterine?; Dihydro-corynoxeine; Mitriner-mine; fig. 26)
> *Rubi.* *Crossopteryx kotschyana* (bk, as 'crossopterine'), *Mitragyna* (at least 9 spp. ?), *Nauclea rhynchophylla*, *Uncaria tomentosa* (lvs, st.)

Rotundifoline (Stipulatine; fig. 26)
> *Rubi.* *Mitragyna* (at least 6 spp. ?), *Nauclea rhynchophylla* (st.)

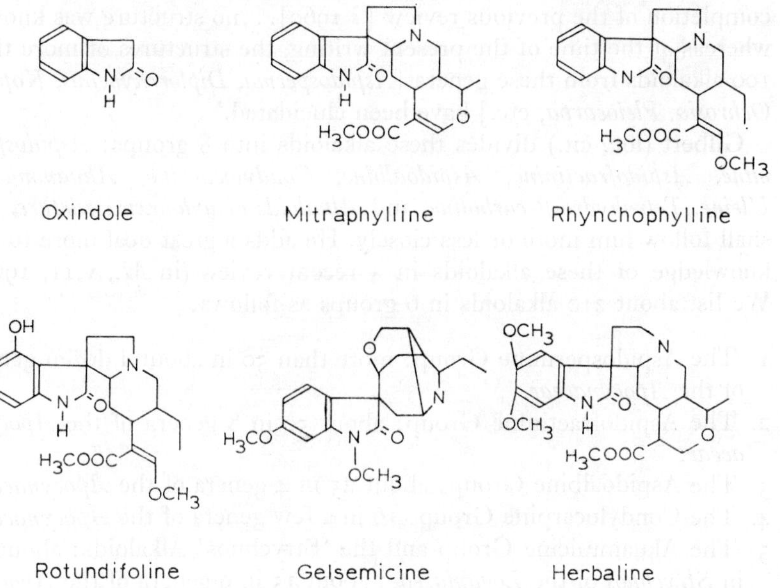

Fig. 26. Some oxindole alkaloids.

Sempervirine (?Gelseminine) is not actually an *oxindole*, but it is related to, and occurs with *oxindoles* in

Logani. *Gelsemium elegans, sempervirens*; *Mostuea buchholzii, stimulans*?

Speciofoline is a stereoisomer of *rotundifoline*.

Rubi. *Mitragyna speciosa* (lvs)

Speciophylline (Uncarine-D): an isomer of *mitraphylline*?

Rubi. *Mitragyna speciosa* (lvs)

Vineridine

Apocyn. *Vinca herbacea*

Vinerine

Apocyn. *Vinca herbacea*

VIII ASPIDOSPERMA GROUPS

GENERAL

It is only very recently, Taylor (1965) tells us, that the structures of *aspidospermine* and of related bases have been determined. Gilbert (in *M.*, v.8, 1965) says: 'The great advance in our knowledge of the chemistry of this group is indicated by the fact that at the time of completion of the previous review [? 1960]...no structure was known, whereas at the time of the present writing, the structures of more than 100 alkaloids from these genera [*Aspidosperma, Diplorrhynchus, Kopsia, Ochrosia, Pleiocarpa*, etc.] have been elucidated.'

Gilbert (loc. cit.) divides these alkaloids into 8 groups: *Aspidospermine, Aspidofractinine, Aspidoalbine, Condylocarpine, Akuammicine, Uleine, Tetrahydro-β-carboline*, and *Alkaloids of unknown structure*. We shall follow him more or less closely. He adds a great deal more to our knowledge of these alkaloids in a recent review (in *M.*, v.11, 1968). We list about 210 alkaloids in 6 groups as follows:

1. The Aspidospermine Group: more than 50 in about a dozen genera of the *Apocynaceae*.
2. The Aspidofractinine Group: about 50 in 8 genera of the *Apocynaceae*.
3. The Aspidoalbine Group: about 25 in 4 genera of the *Apocynaceae*.
4. The Condylocarpine Group: 16 in a few genera of the *Apocynaceae*.
5. The Akuammicine Group and the 'Strychnos' Alkaloids: about 30 in *Strychnos* of the *Loganiaceae*; about 15 in 9 genera of the *Apocynaceae*.
6. The Uleine Group: about 25 in a few genera of the *Apocynaceae*.

We have dealt with the *carboline* alkaloids as group II of the *indole* alkaloids.

VIII.1 The Aspidospermine Group

List and Occurrence

20-Acetoxy-tabersonine
    Apocyn. *Melodinus scandens*
Aspidocarpine
    Apocyn. *Aspidosperma megalocarpon* and several other spp.
Aspidolimine
    Apocyn. *Aspidosperma limae* (bk) and 2 other spp.
Aspidospermidine has been described as 'the parent of the aspidospermine group'.
    Apocyn. *Aspidosperma quebracho-blanco, Rhazya stricta*
Aspidospermine (fig. 27)
    Apocyn. *Aspidosperma* (7), *Vallesia* (2)
Catharosine (Deacetyl-vindorosine)
    Apocyn. *Catharanthus roseus*
Cylindrocarpidine is the N_a-acetyl analogue of *cylindrocarpine*.
    Apocyn. *Aspidosperma cylindrocarpon* (bk)

Cylindrocarpine (fig. 27)
  Apocyn. Aspidosperma cylindrocarpon (bk)
Deacetyl-aspidospermine
  Apocyn. Aspidosperma (2)
Deacetyl-(+)-pyrifolidine
  Apocyn. Aspidosperma pyrifolium, quebracho-blanco
Deacetyl-vindoline (16-Methoxy-catharosine)
  Apocyn. Catharanthus roseus
1,2-Dehydro-aspidospermidine
  Apocyn. Aspidosperma quebracho-blanco, Pleiocarpa tubicina, Rhazya stricta
Demethyl-aspidocarpine
  Apocyn. Aspidosperma album, cuspa (bk)
Demethyl-aspidospermine
  Apocyn. Aspidosperma (3)
Echitovenidine is like vincadifformine?
  Apocyn. Alstonia venenata (frt)
Echitovenine
  Apocyn. Alstonia venenata
Limapodine (*N*-Depropionyl-*N*-acetyl-limaspermine)
  Apocyn. Aspidosperma limae
Limaspermine
  Apocyn. Aspidosperma limae
Lochnericine
  Apocyn. Catharanthus (Lochnera) roseus
Lochnerinine (16-Methoxy-lochnericine)
  Apocyn. Catharanthus roseus, Vinca herbacea
16-Methoxy-limapodine (21-Hydroxy-aspidocarpine)
  Apocyn. Aspidosperma limae
16-Methoxy-limaspermine (21-Hydroxy-aspidolimine)
  Apocyn. Aspidosperma limae
16-Methoxy-minovincine
  Apocyn. Vinca minor
(−)-Minovincine (20-Oxo-*l*-vincadifformine)
  Apocyn. Catharanthus lanceus, Vinca minor
Minovine (*N*$_a$-Methyl-vincadifformine)
  Apocyn. Vinca minor
N$_a$-Acetyl-aspidospermidine (?Demethoxy-aspidospermine)
  Apocyn. Aspidosperma (4), *Vallesia dichotoma*
N$_a$-Acetyl-*N*$_a$-depropionyl-aspidoalbinol: belongs here?
  Apocyn. Aspidosperma album
N$_a$-Formyl-aspidospermidine (Demethoxy-vallesine)
  Apocyn. Aspidosperma discolor

N_a-Methyl-aspidospermidine
  Apocyn.   Aspidosperma quebracho-blanco, Vinca minor
N_a-Methyl-deacetyl-aspidospermine
  Apocyn.   Aspidosperma quebracho-blanco
N-Methyl-quebrachamine
  Apocyn.   Vallesia dichotoma (−), *Vinca minor* (±)
N_a-Propionyl-aspidospermidine (Demethoxy-palosine): is this *O-demethyl-palosine*?
  Apocyn.   Aspidosperma (2), *Tabernaemontana amygdalifolia* (as '*O-demethyl-palosine*')
10-Oxo-cylindrocarpidine
  Apocyn.   Tabernaemontana amygdalifolia
Palosine (N_a-Propionyl-deacetyl-aspidospermine)
  Apocyn.   Aspidosperma polyneuron
Pubescine: belongs here?
  Apocyn.   Vinca major
(+)-Pyrifolidine is an enantiomer of (−)-*pyrifolidine.*
  Apocyn.   Aspidosperma pyrifolium
(−)-Pyrifolidine (*O*-Methyl-aspidocarpine)
  Apocyn.   Aspidosperma quebracho-blanco
(+)-Quebrachamine
  Apocyn.   Stemmadenia donnell-smithii
(−)-Quebrachamine (?Kamassine; fig. 27)
  Apocyn.   Aspidosperma quebracho-blanco and 4 other spp.; *Gonioma kamassi*; *Rhazya stricta*
Rhazidine
  Apocyn.   Aspidosperma quebracho-blanco, Rhazya stricta
Spegazzinidine
  Apocyn.   Aspidosperma chakensis
Spegazzinine
  Apocyn.   Aspidosperma chakensis
(−)-Tabersonine (fig. 27)
  Apocyn.   Amsonia tabernaemontana, Melodinus scandens, Stemmadenia (3), *Tabernaemontana citrifolia*
Tuboxenine
  Apocyn.   Pleiocarpa tubicina
Vallesine (N_a-Formyl-deacetyl-aspidospermine)
  Apocyn.   Vallesia dichotoma, glabra
Vincadifformine
  Apocyn.   Rhazya stricta (+ and −); *Vinca difformis* (±), *minor* (−), *major* (±)
Vincadine (N_a-Demethyl-vincaminoreine)
  Apocyn.   Vinca minor

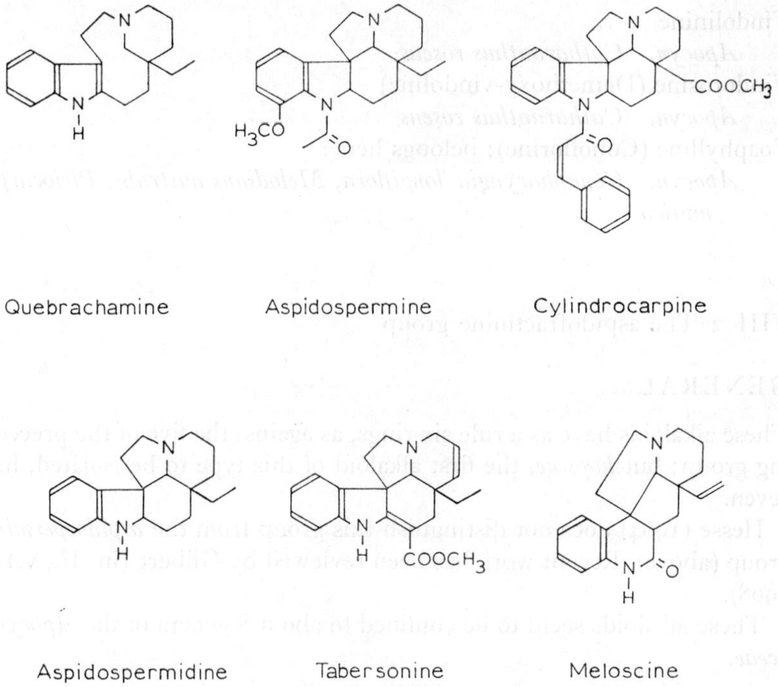

Quebrachamine   Aspidospermine   Cylindrocarpine

Aspidospermidine   Tabersonine   Meloscine

Fig. 27. Some aspidospermine alkaloids and meloscine.

Vincamidine (Strictamine): belongs here?
Apocyn. Rhazya stricta, Vinca minor
Vincaminoreine (3-Carbomethoxy-N_a-methyl-(+)-quebrachamine; N_a-methyl-vincadine)
Apocyn. Vinca minor
Vincaminoridine (16-Methoxy-vincaminorine)
Apocyn. Vinca minor
Vincaminorine is a 3-*carbomethoxy-N_a-methyl-quebrachamine*.
Apocyn. Vinca minor
Vincoridine: belongs here?
Apocyn. Vinca minor
Vincorine (16-Methoxy-*l*-vincadifformine)
Apocyn. Vinca minor
Vindolicine: is a dimer of *vindoline*?
Apocyn. Catharanthus roseus
Vindolidine: is a dimer of *vindoline*?
Apocyn. Catharanthus roseus
Vindoline
Apocyn. Catharanthus roseus

7

Vindolinine
  Apocyn.   Catharanthus roseus
Vindorosine (Demethoxy-vindoline)
  Apocyn.   Catharanthus roseus
Voaphylline (Conoflorine): belongs here?
  *Apocyn.   Conopharyngia longiflora, Melodinus australis, Pleiocarpa
  mutica*

VIII.2 The aspidofractinine group

GENERAL

These alkaloids have as a rule six rings, as against the five of the preceding group; but *kopsine*, the first alkaloid of this type to be isolated, has
seven.

Hesse (1964) does not distinguish this group from the *aspidospermine*
group (above). Recent work has been reviewed by Gilbert (in *M.*, v.11,
1968).

These alkaloids seem to be confined to about 8 genera of the *Apocynaceae*.

List and Occurrence

Aspidofiline is very like *pyrifoline*.
  Apocyn.   Aspidosperma pyrifolium
Aspidofractine
  Apocyn.   Aspidosperma populifolium, refractum
Aspidofractinine (fig. 28) is the 'unsubstituted parent' of this group.
  *Apocyn.   Aspidosperma refractum, Gonioma kamassi, Pleiocarpa
  tubicina*
1-Carbomethoxy-kopsinine (Pleiocarpine; Pleiocine)
  Apocyn.   Hunteria eburnea, Pleiocarpa (2)
Decarbomethoxy-isokopsine
  Apocyn.   Kopsia fruticosa
Decarbomethoxy-kopsine
  Apocyn.   Kopsia fruticosa
16,17-Dimethoxy-aspidofractinine
  Apocyn.   Aspidosperma populifolium
10,22-Dioxo-kopsane is included by Gilbert in his *kopsane* group.
  Apocyn.   Pleiocarpa mutica
10,11-Dioxo-pleiocarpine
  Apocyn.   Pleiocarpa mutica

Epikopsanol is included by Gilbert in his *kopsane* group.
    Apocyn.   *Aspidosperma duckei, macrocarpon*
Fruticosamine
    Apocyn.   *Kopsia fruticosa*
Fruticosine
    Apocyn.   *Kopsia fruticosa*
6(or 7)-Hydroxy-kopsinine
    Apocyn.   *Melodinus australis*
20-Hydroxy-kopsinine
    Apocyn.   *Melodinus australis*
Kopsamine
    Apocyn.   *Kopsia longiflora*
Kopsanol is included by Gilbert in his *kopsane* group.
    Apocyn.   *Aspidosperma duckei, macrocarpon, verbascifolium*
Kopsanone is included by Gilbert in his *kopsane* group.
    Apocyn.   *Aspidosperma duckei, macrocarpon*
Kopsaporine
    Apocyn.   *Kopsia singapurensis*
Kopsenine is thought to be closely related to *kopsine*.
    Apocyn.   *Kopsia longiflora*
Kopsiflorine: closely related to *kopsine*?
    Apocyn.   *Kopsia longiflora*
Kopsiforgine: closely related to *kopsine*?
    Apocyn.   *Kopsia longiflora*
Kopsilongine
    Apocyn.   *Kopsia longiflora*
Kopsine (fig. 28)
    Apocyn.   *Kopsia albiflora, fruticosa, longiflora*
Kopsingarine: belongs here?
    Apocyn.   *Kopsia singapurensis*
Kopsingine
    Apocyn.   *Kopsia singapurensis*
Kopsinic acid-methochloride
    Apocyn.   *Pleiocarpa mutica*
Kopsinilam (10-Oxo-kopsinine) is an amide.
    Apocyn.   *Hunteria eburnea; Pleiocarpa flavescens, mutica*
Kopsinine
    Apocyn.   *Aspidosperma* (2), *Kopsia* (3), *Pleiocarpa* (2), *Vinca herbacea* (lvs, st.)
Kopsinoline
    Apocyn.   *Hunteria eburnea; Pleiocarpa mutica, tubicina*
17-Methoxy-aspidofractinine
    Apocyn.   *Aspidosperma populifolium*

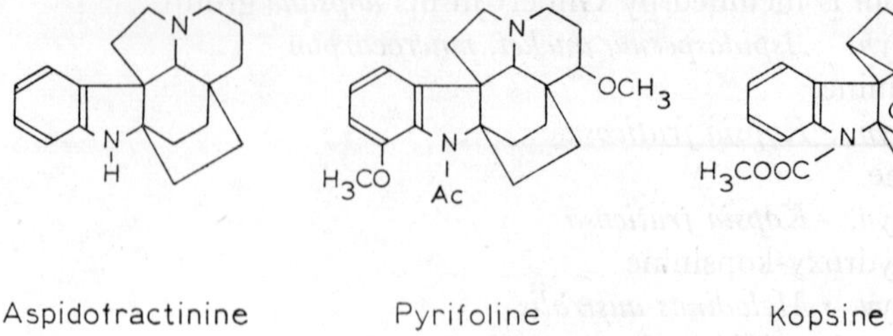

Aspidofractinine   Pyrifoline   Kopsine

Fig. 28. Some alkaloids of the aspidofractinine group.

1-Methyl-kopsinine (Pleiocarpinine; Pleiocinine)
    Apocyn.   *Hunteria eburnea, Pleiocarpa* (2)
N_a-Carbomethoxy-10,22-dioxo-kopsane is included by Gilbert in his *kopsane* group.
    Apocyn.   *Pleiocarpa mutica*
N-Formyl-16,17-dimethoxy-aspidofractinine
    Apocyn.   *Aspidosperma populifolium*
N-Formyl-17-methoxy-aspidofractinine
    Apocyn.   *Aspidosperma populifolium*
N-Formyl-O-methyl-deacetyl-aspidofiline
    Apocyn.   *Aspidosperma populifolium*
N_a-Methyl-10,22-dioxo-kopsane is included by Gilbert in his *kopsane* group.
    Apocyn.   *Pleiocarpa mutica*
O-Methyl-deacetyl-aspidofiline
    Apocyn.   *Aspidosperma populifolium*
10-Oxo-epikopsanol is included by Gilbert in his *kopsane* group.
    Apocyn.   *Aspidosperma duckei*
Δ^6-8-Oxo-kopsinene
    Apocyn.   *Melodinus australis*
Δ^6-8-Oxo-kopsinene-N_b-oxide
    Apocyn.   *Melodinus australis*
Pleiocarpinolam (10-Oxo-1-methyl-kopsinine) is an amide.
    Apocyn.   *Hunteria eburnea; Pleiocarpa mutica, tubicina*
Pleiocarpoline
    Apocyn.   *Hunteria eburnea; Pleiocarpa mutica, tubicina*
Pleiocarpolinine
    Apocyn.   *Hunteria eburnea; Pleiocarpa mutica, tubicina*
Pseudo-kopsinine
    Apocyn.   *Vinca herbacea*
Pyrifoline (fig. 28)
    Apocyn.   *Aspidosperma pyrifolium*

Refractalam
  Apocyn.   *Aspidosperma refractum*
Refractidine
  Apocyn.   *Aspidosperma refractum*
Refractine
  Apocyn.   *Aspidosperma populifolium, refractum*
Venalstonidine (6-7-Epoxy-kopsinine)
  Apocyn.   *Melodinus australis*
Venalstonine (Δ^6-Kopsinene)
  Apocyn.   *Alstonia venenata, Melodinus australis*

VIII.3 The aspidoalbine group

GENERAL

These alkaloids, the 'parent member' of which is fendleridine (fig. 29), are included by Hesse (1964) in his *aspidosperma* group. Gilbert (in *M.*, v.11, 1968) reviews recent developments. He has a sub-group which he calls *obscurinervane*.

The two dozen or so known *aspidoalbine* alkaloids are restricted, it seems, to the *Apocynaceae*, and in that family to about 4 genera.

List and Occurrence
1-Acetyl-aspidoalbine
  Apocyn.   *Vallesia dichotoma*
Aspidoalbine (fig. 29)
  Apocyn.   *Aspidosperma album, spruceanum*
Aspidofendlerine
  Apocyn.   *Aspidosperma fendleri*
Aspidolimidine
  Apocyn.   *Aspidospermum album, limae*
Aspidolrabine
  Apocyn.   *Aspidosperma spruceanum*
Beninine: may be included here?
  Apocyn.   *Hedranthera (Callichilia) barteri*
Cimicidine (16-Methoxy-cimicine)
  Apocyn.   *Haplophyton cimicidum*
Cimicine (21-Oxo-haplocine)
  Apocyn.   *Haplophyton cimicidum*
Dichotamine
  Apocyn.   *Vallesia dichotoma*

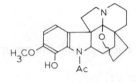

Fendleridine   Obscurinervine

Aspidoalbine   Aspidolimidine

Fig. 29. Some alkaloids of the aspidoalbine group.

Dihydro-obscurinervidine is in Gilbert's *obscurinervane* group.
    Apocyn.   Aspidosperma obscurinervium
Dihydro-obscurinervine is in Gilbert's *obscurinervane* group.
    Apocyn.   Aspidosperma obscurinervium
Fendleridine (Aspidoalbidine; fig. 29)
    Apocyn.   Aspidosperma fendleri
Fendlerine is the N_a-propionyl analogue of *aspidolimidine*.
    Apocyn.   Aspidosperma album, fendleri
Haplocidine
    Apocyn.   Haplophyton cimicidum, Vallesia dichotoma
Haplocine
    Apocyn.   Haplophyton cimicidum
Haplophytine: belongs here?
    Apocyn.   Haplophyton cimicidum
Homoneblinine is in Gilbert's *obscurinervane* group.
    Apocyn.   Aspidosperma neblinae
17-Methoxy-N_a-formyl-aspidoalbidine
    Apocyn.   Vallesia dichotoma
N_a-Acetyl-N-depropionyl-aspidoalbine
    Apocyn.   Aspidosperma album, spruceanum
Neblinine is a demethoxy derivative of *obscurinervidine*. Gilbert puts it
  in his *obscurinervane* group.
    Apocyn.   Aspidosperma neblinae

Obscurinervidine is in Gilbert's *obscurinervane group*.
   Apocyn. Aspidosperma obscurinervium
Obscurinervine (fig. 29) is in Gilbert's *obscurinervane* group.
   Apocyn. Aspidosperma obscurinervium
21-Oxo-aspidoalbine
   Apocyn. Aspidosperma exalatum
21-Oxo-*O*-methyl-aspidoalbine
   Apocyn. Aspidosperma exalatum

VIII.4 The condylocarpine group

GENERAL

Gilbert (in *M.*, v.8, 1965) says that 9 alkaloids are known to belong here: he then lists 10! Hesse (1964) has 8 of these alkaloids in his *aspidospermatine* group. Gilbert (in *M.*, v.11, 1968) reviews recent advances in our knowledge of the group and we can now list 16.

They are said to be close biogenetic relatives of the *uleine* group (below).

They seem to be confined, as are so many of the *indole* alkaloids, to a few genera of the *Apocynaceae*.

List and Occurrence

Aspidospermatidine (fig. 30)
   Apocyn. Aspidosperma quebracho-blanco
Aspidospermatine
   Apocyn. Aspidosperma quebracho-blanco
Condylocarpine (fig. 30)
   Apocyn. Diplorrhynchus condylocarpon subsp. *mossambicensis*; *Vallesia dichotoma* (lvs)
Deacetyl-aspidospermatine
   Apocyn. Aspidosperma quebracho-blanco
14,19-Dihydro-aspidospermatine
   Apocyn. Aspidosperma quebracho-blanco
14,19-Dihydro-condylocarpine (Tubotaiwine)
   Apocyn. Aspidosperma limae, Picralima tubicina (lvs), *Vallesia dichotoma* (lvs)
11,12-Dihydroxy-N_a-acetyl-aspidospermatidine
   Apocyn. Aspidosperma sp.
Limatine (12-Hydroxy-*N*-propionyl-aspidospermatidine)
   Apocyn. Aspidosperma limae

Aspidospermatidine   Condylocarpine

Fig. 30. Alkaloids of the condylocarpine group.

Limatinine (12-Hydroxy-N_a-acetyl-aspidospermatidine)
  Apocyn. Aspidosperma limae, tomentosum
11-Methoxy-14,19-dihydro-condylocarpine
  Apocyn. Aspidosperma populifolium
11-Methoxy-limatine
  Apocyn. Aspidosperma limae
11-Methoxy-limatinine
  Apocyn. Aspidosperma limae
N_a-Acetyl-aspidospermatidine
  Apocyn. Aspidosperma quebracho-blanco, Vallesia dichotoma
N_a-Methyl-aspidospermatidine
  Apocyn. Aspidosperma quebracho-blanco
Precondylocarpine
  Apocyn. Vallesia dichotoma (lvs)
Stemmadenine
  Apocyn. Aspidosperma pyricollum (frt,(+)−), *Diplorrhynchus condylocarpon* subsp. *mossambicensis, Melodinus* sp., *Stemmadenia* (3), *Vallesia dichotoma* (lvs)?

VIII.5 The akuammicine group and the 'strychnos' alkaloids

GENERAL

I find it very difficult indeed to get these alkaloids sorted out; the names seem to have been used very loosely by some authors.

Members of this group occur in two families of the **Gentianales** (*sensu* Wagenitz, in *Syll.*12, 1964): 1. *Loganiaceae*, about 30 in *Strychnos*; 5. *Apocynaceae*, about 15 in 9 genera.

List and Occurrence

Akuammicine (fig. 31)

> *Apocyn. Catharanthus roseus* (rt), *Picralima nitida* (sd), *Vinca herbacea*

Akuammicine-N_b-methochloride

> *Apocyn. Hunteria eburnea* (stbk, rtbk)

Brucine (10,11-Dimethoxy-strychnine)

> *Logani. Strychnos* (14)

Caracurines-II, -V, and -VI: are dimers?

> *Logani. Strychnos toxifera*

C-Calebassine (*C*-Toxiferine-II): essentially a dimer of *akuammicine*?

> *Logani. Strychnos* (4)

C-Curarine-I is a dimer.

> *Logani. Strychnos trinervis* (bk) and 4 other spp.

C-Curarine-III (*C*-fluoro-curarine)

> *Logani. Strychnos* sp. (calabash) and several named spp.

C-Dihydro-toxiferine-I

> *Logani. Strychnos toxifera*?

C-Mavacurine

> *Logani. Strychnos nux-vomica, toxifera*

α-Colubrine (3-Methoxy-strychnine)

> *Logani. Strychnos nux-vomica*

β-Colubrine (2-Methoxy-strychnine)

> *Logani. Strychnos nux-vomica*

Compactinervine

> *Apocyn. Aspidosperma compactinervium*

Condensamine

> *Logani. Strychnos holstii*

C-Toxiferine-I (Toxiferines V and XI) is a dimer.

> *Logani. Strychnos froesii, toxifera*

Deacetyl-diaboline (Caracurine-VII; Wieland–Gumlich aldehyde)

> *Logani. Strychnos subcordata* (bk), *toxifera*

Deacetyl-strychnospermine

> *Logani. Strychnos psilosperma*

Diaboline

> *Logani. Strychnos diaboli, chlorantha, henningsii* (bk)

2,16-Dihydro-akuammicine: does this occur naturally?

19,20-Dihydro-akuammicine

> *Apocyn. Pleiocarpa tubicina*

Echitamidine (19-Hydroxy-19,20-dihydro-akuammicine)

> *Apocyn. Alstonia scholaris*

Geissolosimine (Alkaloid-D2) is essentially a dimer of *geissoschizoline* and *vellosimine.*

   Apocyn. Geissospermum laeve (vellosii)

Geissoschizoline (Pereirine; fig. 31)

   Apocyn. Geissospermum laeve

Geissospermine (fig. 31) is essentially a dimer with a *geissoschizoline* unit.

   Apocyn. Geissospermum laeve, sericeum

Henningsamine: belongs here?

   Logani. Strychnos henningsii (bk)

Henningsoline (?12-Hydroxy-11-methoxy-diaboline)

   Logani. Strychnos henningsii (bk)

Holstiine

   Logani. Strychnos holstii

Holstiline

   Logani. Strychnos holstii

Lochnericine: belongs here?

   Apocyn. Catharanthus (Lochnera) roseus

Lochneridine (fig. 31)

   Apocyn. Catharanthus roseus

Lucidine-S

   Logani. Strychnos lucida

Methoxy-strychnine: may be a *colubrine?*

   Logani. Strychnos nux-vomica (rtbk)

Mossambine (14-Hydroxy-akuammicine)

   Apocyn. Diplorrhynchus condylocarpon subsp. *mossambicensis*

N_b,N_b-Dimethyl-caracurine-II (Toxiferine-IX)

   Logani. Strychnos toxifera

Nor-*C*-dihydro-toxiferine: is this *nordihydro-toxiferine* of *Strychnos toxifera* and calabash curare?

Nor-fluorocurarine

   Apocyn. Diplorrhynchus condylocarpon subsp. *mossambicensis*

Novacine (*N*-methyl-sec-pseudobrucine) is, says Smith (in *M.*, v.8, 1965), 'another biogenetic link between the strychnine and vomicine series'.

   Logani. Strychnos nux-vomica

Pseudo-akuammicine ((±)-Akuammicine)

   Apocyn. Picralima nitida (sd)

Pseudo-strychnine (Hydroxy-strychnine): does not occur naturally?

Retuline (Tetrahydro-neostrychnine?)

   Logani. Strychnos holstii

Rindline: belongs here?

   Logani. Strychnos henningsii (bk)

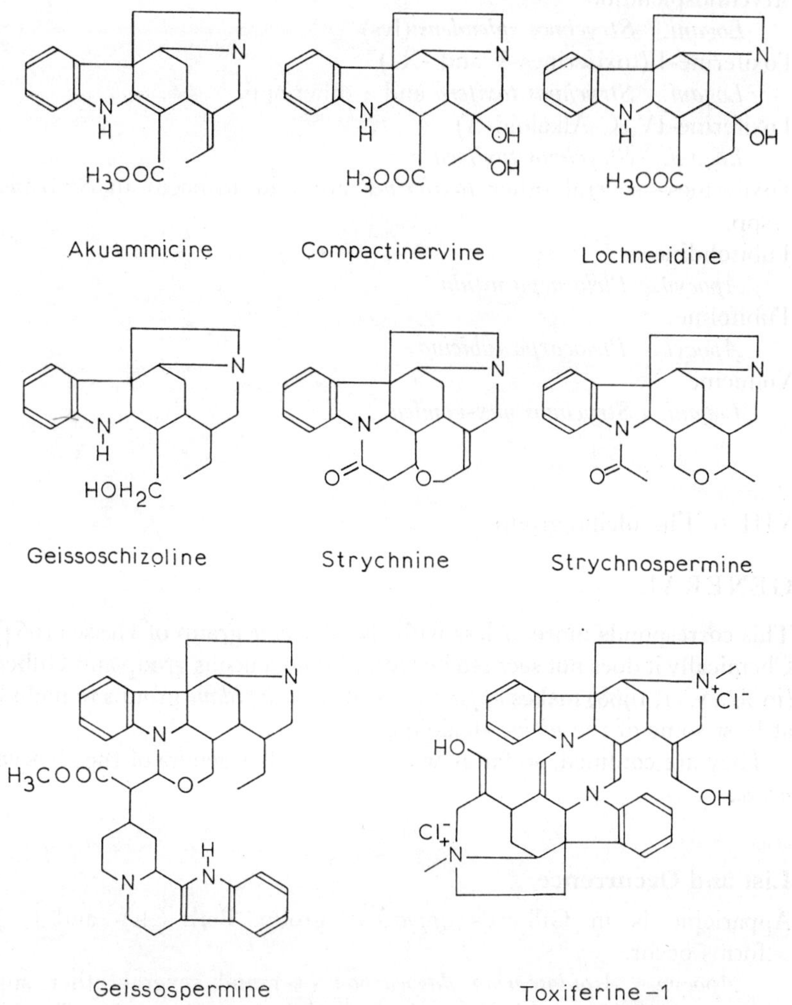

Fig. 31. Akuammicine and some related alkaloids.

Spermostrychnine (Demethoxy-strychnospermine)
  Logani.   Strychnos psilosperma
Strychnicine may be a mixture.
  Logani.   Strychnos nux-vomica (lvs), *psilosperma* (lvs)
Strychnine (fig. 31)
  Logani.   Strychnos (at least 13 spp.)
Strychnospermine (fig. 31)
  Logani.   Strychnos psilosperma

Strychnosplendine
> *Logani. Strychnos splendens* (lvs)

Toxiferine-I (toxiferines-V and -XI)
> *Logani. Strychnos toxifera* and 4 other spp.

Toxiferine-IV (C-Alkaloid-A)
> *Logani. Strychnos toxifera*

Toxiferines—several other *toxiferines* are said to occur in *Strychnos* spp.

Tubifolidine
> *Apocyn. Pleiocarpa nitida*

Tubifoline
> *Apocyn. Pleiocarpa tubicina*

Vomicine
> *Logani. Strychnos nux-vomica*

VIII.6 The uleine group

GENERAL

This corresponds more or less with the *olivacine* group of Hesse (1964). Chemically it does not seem to be a very homogeneous group and Gilbert (in *M.*, v.11, 1968) makes *apparicine* and *dasycarpidane* groups to include at least some of the *uleine* alkaloids.

They are confined, so far as we know, to a few genera of the *Apocynaceae*.

List and Occurrence

Apparicine is in Gilbert's *apparicine* group. Both (+)- and (−)- forms occur.
> *Apocyn. Aspidosperma dasycarpon* (+) and several other spp. (−); *Catharanthus lanceus* (−), *roseus* (−); *Schizozygia caffaeoides* (−)

Dasycarpidol is in Gilbert's *dasycarpidane* group.
> *Apocyn. Aspidosperma dasycarpon*

Dasycarpidone is in Gilbert's *dasycarpidane* group.
> *Apocyn. Aspidosperma australe, dasycarpon, multiflorum, pyricollum* (bk)

Dehydro-de-*N*-methyl-uleine
> *Apocyn. Aspidosperma dasycarpon*

De-*N*-methyl-dasycarpidone is in Gilbert's *dasycarpidane* group.
> *Apocyn. Aspidosperma dasycarpon*

De-*N*-methyl-uleine is in Gilbert's *dasycarpidane* group.
  Apocyn. Aspidosperma dasycarpon
1,2-Dihydro-ellipticine
  Apocyn. Aspidosperma subincanum, ulei
1,2-Dihydro-ellipticine-methonitrate
  Apocyn. Aspidosperma subincanum
1,13-Dihydro-13-hydroxy-uleine: is this the same as *1,1′-dihydro-1′
  hydroxy-uleine*?
  Apocyn. Aspidosperma dasycarpon
1,2-Dihydro-olivacine
  Apocyn. Aspidosperma ulei
Dihydro-uleine
  Apocyn. Aspidosperma nigricans
Ellipticine (fig. 32): has antitumour activity?
  Apocyn. Aspidosperma subincanum, Ochrosia elliptica and 4 other
    spp.
Ellipticine-*N*$_\text{b}$-methonitrate
  Apocyn. Aspidosperma subincanum
Elliptinine
  Apocyn. Ochrosia elliptica
3-Epi-dasycarpidone is in Gilbert's *dasycarpidane* group.
  Apocyn. Aspidosperma subincanum
3-Epi-uleine is in Gilbert's *dasycarpidane* group.
  Apocyn. Aspidosperma subincanum
Guatambuine (*N*-methyl-tetrahydro-olivacine)
  Apocyn. Aspidosperma (*d*- in 5 spp.), *australe* (*dl*- and *l*-)
9-Methoxy-ellipticine: has antitumour activity?
  Apocyn. Ochrosia (5)
9-Methoxy-olivacine: belongs here?
  Apocyn. Aspidosperma vargasii
N-Methyl-tetrahydro-ellipticine
  Apocyn. Aspidosperma (4)
N-Nor-dasycarpidone
  Apocyn. Aspidosperma dasycarpon
N-Nor-uleine
  Apocyn. Aspidosperma dasycarpon
O-Acetyl-vallesamine is in Gilbert's *apparicine* group.
  Apocyn. Vallesia dichotoma
Olivacine (Guatambuinine; fig. 32): belongs here?
  Apocyn. Aspidosperma olivaceum and 5 other spp.; *Tabernae-
    montana psychotrifolia*
Olivacine-*N*-oxide: belongs here?
  Apocyn. Aspidosperma nigricans

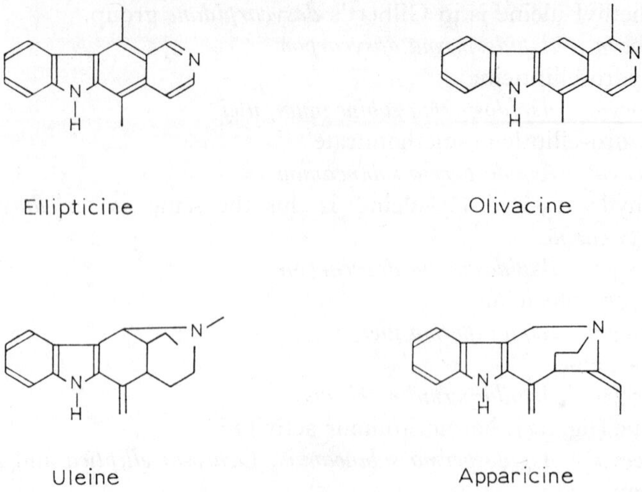

Ellipticine   Olivacine

Uleine   Apparicine

Fig. 32. Some alkaloids of the uleine group.

Uleine (fig. 32)
    Apocyn.   *Aspidosperma ulei* and at least 11 other spp.
Vallesamine is in Gilbert's *apparicine* group.
    Apocyn.   *Vallesia dichotoma*

IX AJMALINE-SARPAGINE ALKALOIDS

GENERAL

These are discussed by Taylor (in *M.*, v.8, 1965; 1966; in *M.*, v.11, 1968). He classes them as 'yohimbinoid' and gives the scheme shown in fig. 33 to indicate relationships. We follow him more or less in the list which follows.

The ajmaline-sarpagine alkaloids seem to be confined to the families *Loganiaceae* and *Apocynaceae*, both of the **Gentianales**.

List and Occurrence

Affinisine (Deoxy-ajmalol-B)
    Apocyn.   *Peschiera affinis*
Ajmalidine (Ajmaline-17-ketone)
    Apocyn.   *Rauwolfia mauiensis, sellowii*
Ajmaline (Neoajmaline; Raugalline; Rauwolfine; fig. 33)
    Apocyn.   *Aspidosperma spegazzini* (bk), *Rauwolfia* (at least 17 spp.),
        Tonduzia longifolia

Akuammenine: belongs here?
  Apocyn.   Picralima nitida
Akuammidine (16-Carbomethoxy-10-deoxy-sarpagine; Rhazine)
  Apocyn.   Aspidosperma quebracho-blanco; Melodinus australis (bk),
    scandens; Picralima nitida; Rhazya stricta; Vallesia dichotoma
    (lvs); *Vinca difformis, erecta*
Akuammiline
  Apocyn.   Picralima nitida
Akuammine (Vincamajoridine)
  Apocyn.   Catharanthus roseus; Vinca difformis, major; Picrolima
    nitida
Aspidodasycarpine: belongs here?
  Apocyn.   Aspidosperma cuspa (bk), *dasycarpon*
Deacetyl-akuammiline
  Apocyn.   Picralima nitida
Deacetyl-picraline (Burnamine)
  Apocyn.   Aspidosperma cuspa (bk), *rigidum* (*laxiflorum*); *Hunteria*
    eburnea (bk); *Picralima nitida* (sd)
Δ^1-1-Demethyl-tetraphyllicine-17-O-acetate
  Apocyn.   Rauwolfia perakensis
1-Demethyl-vincamajine (Quebrachidine?; Vincarine?)
  Apocyn.   Aspidosperma quebracho-blanco, Vinca erecta
10-Deoxy-sarpagine (Normacusine-B; Tombozine; Vellosiminol)
  Apocyn.   Aspidosperma polyneuron, Diplorrhynchus condylocarpon,
    Geissospermum laeve (*vellosii*), *Rauwolfia perakensis*
10-Deoxy-sarpagine-metho salt (Macusine-B)
  Logani.   Strychnos toxifera
  Apocyn.   Aspidosperma peroba
Iso-ajmaline (20-Epi-21-epi-ajmaline; Iso-rauwolfine)
  Apocyn.   Rauwolfia (2)
Iso-sandwicensine (17,20,21-Triepi-ajmaline)
  Apocyn.   Rauwolfia vomitoria
Lochneram (Lochnerine-metho salt)
  Logani.?   Calabash-curare (*Strychnos?*)
Lochnerine (10-Methyl-sarpagine)
  Logani.?   Calabash-curare (*Strychnos?*)
  Apocyn.   Catharanthus (*Lochnera*) *roseus*
Macusine-C: belongs here?
  Logani.   Strychnos toxifera
  Apocyu.   Aspidosperma spegazzini
Majoridine (10-Methoxy-tetraphyllicine-17-O-acetate)
  Apocyn.   Vinca major (lvs, st.)

Mauiensine (17-Epi-tetraphyllicine)
Apocyn. Rauwolfia mauiensis
10-Methoxy-vellosimine
Apocyn. Vinca major
1-Methyl-sarpagine-methochloride
Apocyn. Pleiocarpa mutica
Mitoridine (12-Hydroxy-tetraphyllicinone)
Apocyn. Rauwolfia vomitoria
Neo-sarpagine: is *sarpagine*?
Perakine
Apocyn. Rauwolfia perakensis, vomitoria
Peraksine: belongs here?
Apocyn. Rauwolfia perakensis
Pericyclivine
Apocyn. Catharanthus lanceus, Gabunia odoratissima
Perividine: is related to *perivine*?
Apocyn. Catharanthus roseus
Perivine
Apocyn. Catharanthus roseus, Gabunia odoratissima
Picralinal
Apocyn. Rhazya orientalis (lvs, st.)
Picraline
Apocyn. Aspidosperma rigidum (laxiflorum), Picralima nitida (sd)
Picrinine is related to *picraline*.
Apocyn. Alstonia scholaris, Rauwolfia vomitoria, Rhazya orientalis (lvs, st.)
Polyneuridine (16-Carbomethoxy-16-epi-10-deoxy-sarpagine)
Apocyn. Aspidosperma polyneuron
Polyneuridine-metho salt (Macusine-A)
Logani. Strychnos toxifera
Pseudo-akuammigine (Deoxy-akuammine)
Apocyn. Picralima nitida
Purpeline (12-Methoxy-tetraphyllicinone)
Apocyn. Rauwolfia vomitoria
Rauvomitine (Tetraphyllicine-17-O-trimethoxy-benzoate)
Apocyn. Rauwolfia vomitoria
Rauwolfinine, according to Lucas (1963), is *perakenine*. Taylor (in *M.*, v.8, 1965) says that it is probably impure *isoajmaline*.
Sandwicensine (?1-Demethyl-mauiensine)
Apocyn. Rauwolfia sandwicensis
Sandwicine (17-Epi-ajmaline)
Apocyn. Rauwolfia (3)

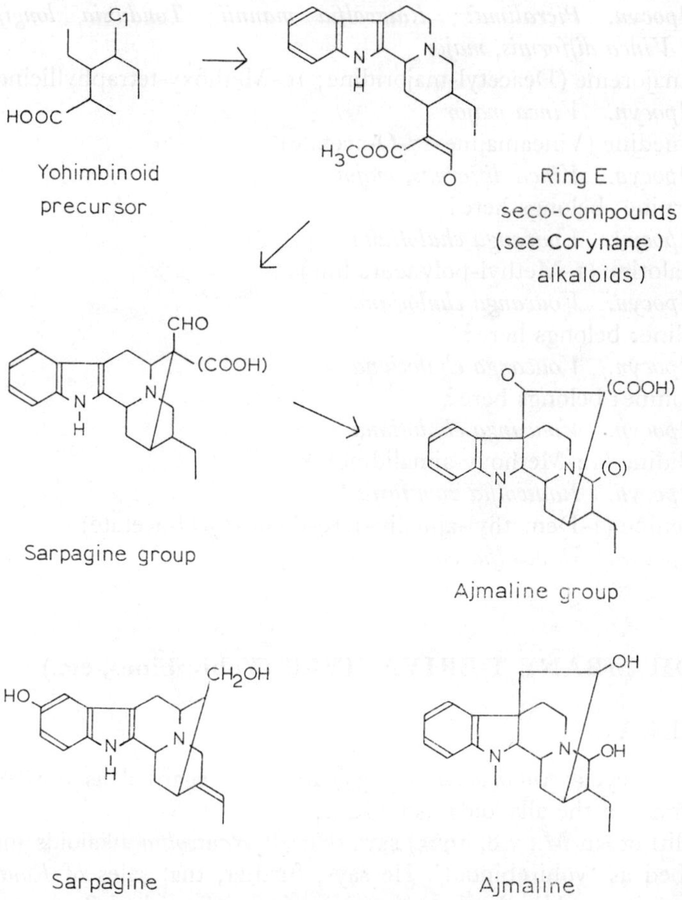

Fig. 33. Ajmaline-sarpagine alkaloids.

Sarpagine (?Neosarpagine; Raupine, fig. 33)

   Apocyn.   *Rauwolfia* (about a dozen spp.), *Vinca difformis*

Sarpagine methochloride

   Apocyn.   *Aspidosperma spegazzini*

Tetraphyllicine (21-Deoxy-ajmaline-19-ene; ?Semperflorine; Serpinine)

   Apocyn.   *Rauwolfia tetraphylla* and about 5 other spp., *Vinca?*

Vellosimine (10-Deoxy-sarpagine aldehyde)

   Apocyn.   *Geissospermum laeve (vellosii)*, *Vinca difformis*

Vellosine may not occur as such.

Vincadiffine is a 2-*acyl*-indole.

   Apocyn.   *Vinca difformis*

Vincamajine (16-Carbomethoxy-2-epi-tetraphyllicine)
Apocyn. Picralima?; Rauwolfia mannii; Tonduzia longifolia; Vinca difformis, major
Vincamajoreine (Deacetyl-majoridine; 10-Methoxy-tetraphyllicine)
Apocyn. Vinca major
Vincamedine (Vincamajine-17-O-acetate)
Apocyn. Vinca difformis, major
Voacarpine: belongs here?
Apocyn. Voacanga chalotiana
Voachalotine (1-Methyl-polyneuradine)
Apocyn. Voacanga chalotiana
Voacoline: belongs here?
Apocyn. Voacanga chalotiana
Voamonine: belongs here?
Apocyn. Voacanga chalotiana
Vomalidine (12-Methoxy-ajmalidine)
Apocyn. Rauwolfia vomitoria
Vomilenine (1-Demethyl-ajmalin-1,19-diene-17-O-acetate)
Apocyn. Rauwolfia vomitoria

X YOHIMBANE DERIVATIVES (Yohimbines, etc.)

GENERAL

The pentacyclic *yohimbane* (fig. 34) may be regarded as the 'parent substance' of the alkaloids listed here.

Schlittler (in *M.*, v.8, 1965) says that all *Rauwolfia* alkaloids may be described as 'yohimbinoid'. He says, further, that sales of *Rauwolfia* products in the U.S.A. alone may in 1961 have reached $100,000,000! Is there an error here?

A few 'new' yohimbanes have been added from the review by Monteiro (in *M.*, v.11, 1968).

These alkaloids appear to be restricted to the **Gentianales** (*sensu* Wagenitz in *Syll.*12, 1964). They are known from: fam. 1, *Loganiaceae*, if *melinonines-E* and *-M* are yohimbanes; fam. 5, *Apocynaceae* (many); fam. 7, *Rubiaceae* (a few).

List and Occurrence

Allo-yohimbine
Apocyn. Rauwolfia
Rubi. Corynanthe

Alstoniline
    Apocyn.   Alstonia constricta (bk)
Amsoniaefoline: belongs here?
    Apocyn.   Rauwolfia amsoniaefolia
Canembine: is distinct from *raunescine*?
    Apocyn.   Rauwolfia canescens
Chalcupine-B: belongs here?
    Apocyn.   Rauwolfia heterophylla
Chandrine: belongs here?
    Apocyn.   Rauwolfia serpentina
Corynanthine (Rauhimbine)
    Apocyn.   Rauwolfia (2)
    Rubi.   Corynanthe spp., *Pseudocinchona*
19-Dehydro-yohimbine
    Apocyn.   Aspidosperma pyricollum
Demethoxy-alstoniline (Ourouparine)
    Rubi.   Uncaria (Ourouparia) gambier (st.)
Deserpideine
    Apocyn.   Rauwolfia nitida
Deserpidine (Canescine; 11-Demethoxy-reserpine; Raunormine?;
  Recanescine)
    Apocyn.   Rauwolfia (several spp.), *Tonduzia*
3,14-Dihydro-gambirtannine
    Rubi.   Uncaria gambier
3-Epi-α-yohimbine (?Ajmalinine; 3-Epi-rauwolscine; Iso-rauhim-
  bine)
    Apocyn.   Rauwolfia (1–3 spp.)
Excelsinine (10-Methoxy-corynanthine)
    Apocyn.   Aspidosperma excelsum
Gambirtannine
    Rubi.   Uncaria gambier
Iso-raunescine
    Apocyn.   Rauwolfia (2)
Iso-reserpine
    Apocyn.   Rauwolfia ligustrina
Iso-venenatine (Alstovenine)
    Apocyn.   Alstonia venenata
Melinonine-E: belongs here?
    Logani.   Strychnos melinoniana (bk)
Melinonine-M: belongs here?
    Logani.   Strychnos melinoniana (bk)
11-Methoxy-yohimbine
    Apocyn.   Aspidosperma oblongum

11-Methoxy-δ-yohimbine (Alkaloid-A)
  Apocyn.   Rauwolfia serpentina (rt)
Obscuridine: belongs here?
  Apocyn.   Rauwolfia obscura
Oxy-gambirtannine
  Rubi.   Uncaria gambier
Pelirine: belongs here?
  Apocyn.   Rauwolfia perakensis
Poweridine (17-*O*-Acetyl-11-methoxy-yohimbine)
  Apocyn.   Ochrosia poweri
Pseudo-reserpine
  Apocyn.   Rauwolfia (2)
Pseudo-yohimbine (Yohimbene)
  Apocyn.   Rauwolfia (2)
Raugustine
  Apocyn.   Rauwolfia ligustrina
Raujemidine ($\Delta^{19,20}$-Reserpine)
  Apocyn.   Rauwolfia canescens
Raujemidine-*N*-oxide
  Apocyn.   Rauwolfia canescens
Raunamine: belongs here?
  Apocyn.   Rauwolfia micrantha
Raunescine may be *canembine*, but Schlittler lists both.
  Apocyn.   Rauwolfia (2)
Renoxidine (Renoxydine; Reserpoxidine; Reserpine-*N*-oxide): an arte-
  fact?
  Apocyn.   Rauwolfia spp.?
Rescidine
  Apocyn.   Rauwolfia vomitoria
Rescinnamine ('Reserpinine' of some authors)
  Apocyn.   Rauwolfia (many spp.?), *Tonduzia*
Reserpine (fig. 34) is one of the most widely distributed alkaloids of
  this group.
  Apocyn.   Alstonia, Bleekeria?, Excavatia, Rauwolfia (many spp.),
    Ochrosia, Tonduzia, Vallesia. Absent from *Catharanthus*
Seredamine: belongs here?
  Apocyn.   Rauwolfia vomitoria
Seredine (10,11-Dimethoxy-α-yohimbine; Methyl reserpate)
  Apocyn.   Rauwolfia vomitoria
Venenatine
  Apocyn.   Alstonia venenata
Venoxidine (Venenatine-*N*$_b$-oxide)
  Apocyn.   Alstonia venenata

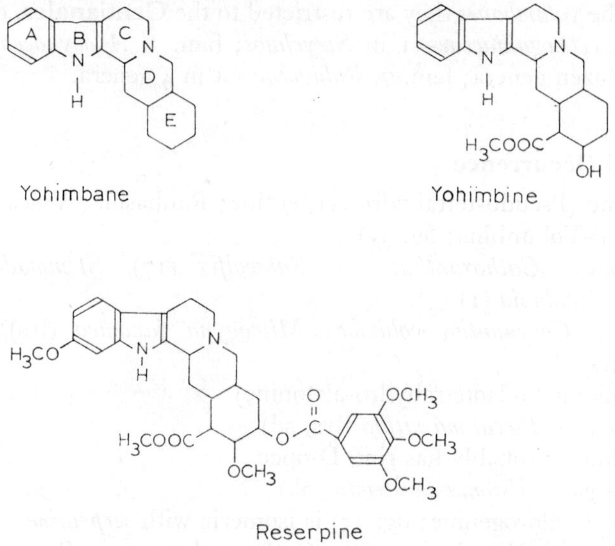

Yohimbane   Yohimbine

Reserpine

Fig. 34. Yohimbane and some related alkaloids.

Yohimbine (Isoyohimbine?; fig. 34)
  Apocyn.   *Alstonia, Aspidosperma* spp., *Rauwolfia* (several spp.),
    Vinca
  Rubi.   *Corynanthe (Pausinystalia) yohimbe, Ladenbergia hexandra*
α-Yohimbine (Chalcupine-A; Corynanthidine; Rauwolscine)
  Apocyn.   *Alstonia, Rauwolfia* (6)
  Rubi.   *Pseudocinchona*
β-Yohimbine (Amsonine)
  Apocyn.   *Amsonia, Aspidosperma pyricollum, Rauwolfia*
  Rubi.   *Corynanthe, Pseudocinchona*
'γ-Yohimbine' is a mixture.
Yohimbol-methochloride
  Apocyn.   *Hunteria eburnea*

XI HETEROYOHIMBANE DERIVATIVES (Ajmalicine and related Alkaloids)

GENERAL

These are like the *yohimbanes* (above) but have an oxygen in ring E (fig. 35). Hesse (1964) includes them in his *ajmalicine* group. Monteiro (in *M.*, v.11, 1968) discusses new members.

Like the *yohimbanes* they are restricted to the **Gentianales**, occurring in: fam. 1, *Loganiaceae*—1 in *Strychnos*; fam. 5, *Apocynaceae*—about 25 in a dozen genera; fam. 7, *Rubiaceae*—4 in 4 genera.

List and Occurrence

Ajmalicine (Pseudo-tetrahydro-serpentine; Raubasine; Vincaine; Vinceine; δ-Yohimbine; fig. 35)
  Apocyn. *Catharanthus* (3), *Rauwolfia* (17), *Stemmadenia* (1), *Tonduzia* (1)
  Rubi. *Corynanthe yohimbe*; *Mitragyna javanica* (lvs), *speciosa* (lvs)
Akuammigine (3-Isotetrahydro-alstonine)
  Apocyn. *Picralima nitida* (lvs, sd)
Alstonidine probably has ring D open
  Apocyn. *Alstonia constricta* (bk)
Alstonine (Chlorogenine; fig. 35) is isomeric with *serpentine*
  Apocyn. *Alstonia constricta, Catharanthus roseus, Rauwolfia* (3)
Aricine (Heterophylline; Quinovatine)
  Apocyn. *Aspidosperma marcgravianum, Rauwolfia* (7)
  Rubi. *Cinchona* (4)
Elliptamine
  Apocyn. *Excavatia coccinea, Ochrosia* (4)
Ervine is an isomer of *tetrahydro-alstonine*
  Apocyn. *Vinca herbacea* (*erecta*) (st., lvs)
Herbaceine (Vincaherbinine)
  Apocyn. *Vinca herbacea*
Herbaine (Vincaherbine)
  Apocyn. *Vinca herbacea*
Holeinine
  Apocyn. *Ochrosia sandwicensis*
Isoreserpiline (Elliptine)
  Apocyn. *Aspidosperma discolor, Ochrosia elliptica* and 3 other spp., *Rauwolfia* (12), *Vallesia dichotoma*
Isoreserpiline-methochloride
  Apocyn. *Ochrosia elliptica*
Isoreserpiline-pseudoindoxyl
  Apocyn. *Aspidosperma discolor, Rauwolfia* (2)
3-Isoreserpinine
  Apocyn. *Rauwolfia* (3)
Mayumbine is a stereoisomer of *ajmalicine*.
  Rubi. *Pseudocinchona* (*Pausinystalia?*) *mayumbensis* (bk) and another sp. ?

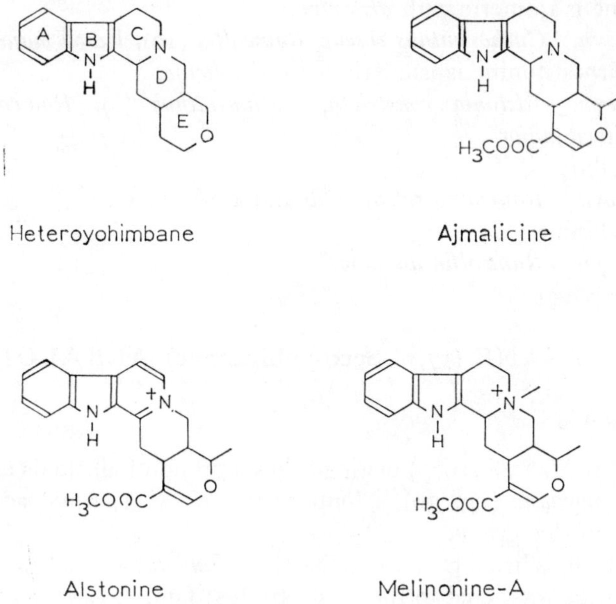

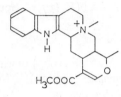

Heteroyohimbane   Ajmalicine

Alstonine   Melinonine-A

Fig. 35. Heteroyohimbane and some heteroyohimbane (ajmalicine) alkaloids.

Melinonine-A (N_b-Methyl-tetrahydro-alstonine; fig. 35)
   Logani.   Strychnos melinoniana (bk)
Mitrajavine is probably a *methoxy-ajmalicine* or an isomer.
   Rubi.   Mitragyna javanica (lvs)
Picraphylline: belongs here?
   Apocyn.   Picralima nitida (lvs)
Raumitorine is closely related to *rauvanine*.
   Apocyn.   Rauwolfia vomitoria
Rauniticine
   Apocyn.   Rauwolfia nitida
Raunitidine is a *methoxy-rauniticine*.
   Apocyn.   Rauwolfia nitida
Rauvanine
   Apocyn.   Rauwolfia vomitoria
Reserpiline (Micranthine; 10,11-dimethoxy-ajmalicine)
   Apocyn.   Aspidosperma discolor, marcgravianum (wd), *rigidum
      (laxiflorum)*; *Rauwolfia micrantha, serpentina*, and 26 other spp.
Reserpinine (Raubasinine)
   Apocyn.   Aspidosperma auriculatum, Rauwolfia (7?), *Vinca* (2)
Serpentidine (Serpentinine) is an *ajmalicine dimer*.
   Apocyn.   Rauwolfia (several spp.)

Serpentine is isomeric with *alstonine*.
>   *Apocyn. Catharanthus roseus, Rauwolfia* (10), *Vinca major*

Tetrahydro-alstonine is isomeric with *ajmalicine*.
>   *Apocyn. Alstonia constricta, Catharanthus* (2), *Rauwolfia* (2), *Vinca major*

Tetraphylline
>   *Apocyn. Rauwolfia tetraphylla* and 4 other spp.

Tetraphyllinine
>   *Apocyn. Rauwolfia discolor*

XII CORYNANE (17,18-Seco-yohimbane) ALKALOIDS

GENERAL

Manske (in *M.*, v. 8, 1965) distinguishes a group of alkaloids as derivatives of *corynane* (fig. 36). Monteiro (in *M.*, v.11, 1968) adds a few members of this group.

The alkaloids listed here seem, like the *yohimbane* and *heteroyohimbane* groups, to be restricted to the **Gentianales**: fam. 1, *Loganiaceae*—2 in *Strychnos*; fam. 5, *Apocynaceae*—about 20 in 8 genera; fam. 7, *Rubiaceae* —about 11 in 6 genera.

List and Occurrence

Antirhine
>   *Rubi. Antirhea putaminosa*

Aspexcine
>   *Apocyn. Aspidosperma excelsum*

Burnamicine: if it exists at all, belongs here?
>   *Apocyn. Hunteria eburnea*

Cathindine: related to *sitsirikine*?
>   *Apocyn. Catharanthus roseus*

Cavincidine: belongs here?
>   *Apocyn. Catharanthus roseus*

Cavincine: related to *sitsirikine*?
>   *Apocyn. Catharanthus roseus*

Corynantheidine
>   *Rubi. Pseudocinchona africana*

Corynantheine (fig. 36) has been described as '...a "missing link" between yohimbine and cinchonamine'.
>   *Rubi. Corynanthe yohimbe, Pausinystalia, Pseudocinchona* (2)

19,20-Dehydro-corynantheol
>   *Apocyn. Aspidosperma* (2)

Demethyl-dihydro-corynantheine
    Occurrence?
Dihydro-corynantheine
    Rubi. *Pseudocinchona africana, Uncaria gambier* (lvs, st.)
Dihydro-corynantheol
    Apocyn. *Aspidosperma* (2)
Dihydro-sitsirikine
    Apocyn. *Catharanthus roseus*
    Rubi. *Pausinystalia yohimbe* (bk)
Flavocarpine (fig. 36) is very similar in structure to *melinonine-G.*
    Apocyn. *Pleiocarpa mutica*
Gambirine (9-Hydroxydihydro-corynantheine)
    Rubi. *Uncaria formosana* (st.), *gambier* (lvs, st.)
Hervine
    Apocyn. *Vinca herbacea*
Hirsutine (Demethoxy-mitraciliatine)
    Rubi. *Mitragyna hirsuta* (lvs)
Huntrabrine-N_b-methochloride: belongs here?
    Apocyn. *Hunteria eburnea, Pleiocarpa mutica*
Isositsirikine
    Apocyn. *Aspidosperma oblongum?, Catharanthus roseus*
Melinonine-B (fig. 36)
    Logani. *Strychnos melinoniana*
Melinonine-G (Flavopereirine; 15-De-ethyl-flavocoryline; fig. 36)
    Logani. *Strychnos melinoniana* (bk)
    Apocyn. *Geissospermum laeve (vellosii)* (bk)
9-Methoxy-corynantheidine (Mitragynine)
    Rubi. *Mitragyna* spp., *Uncaria (Ourouparia)* spp.
10-Methoxydihydro-corynantheol
    Apocyn. *Aspidosperma* (3-4)
Methoxy-geissoschizine
    Apocyn. *Aspidosperma excelsum*
Mitraciliatine is a stereoisomer of 9-*methoxy-corynantheidine.*
    Rubi. *Mitragyna ciliata* (lvs)
N_b-Methyldihydro-corynantheol
    Apocyn. *Hunteria eburnea*
Ochrosandwine
    Apocyn. *Ochrosia sandwicensis*
Paynantheine
    Rubi. *Mitragyna speciosa* (lvs)
Pleiocarpamine (fig. 36): belongs here?
    Apocyn. *Hunteria eburnea, Pleiocarpa mutica*

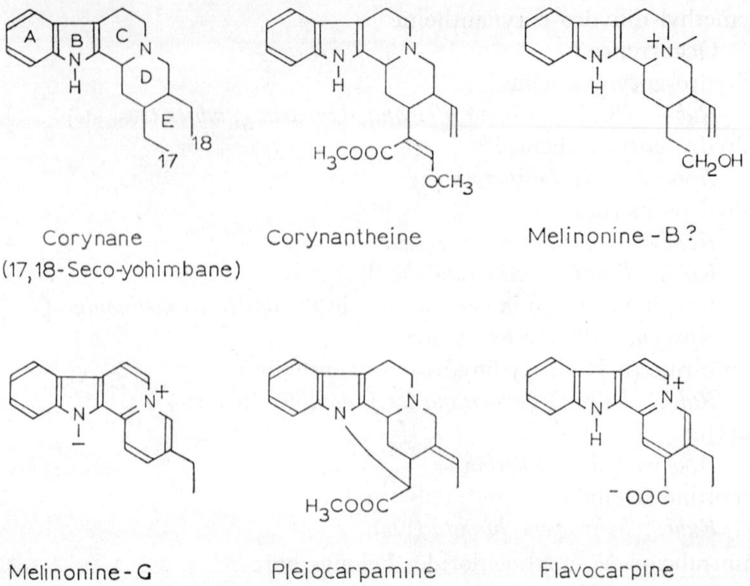

Corynane
(17,18-Seco-yohimbane)

Corynantheine

Melinonine - B ?

Melinonine - G

Pleiocarpamine

Flavocarpine

Fig. 36. Some corynane alkaloids.

Sitsirikine
  Apocyn.   Aspidosperma oblongum?, Catharanthus roseus
Speciociliatine is a stereoisomer of 9-*methoxy-corynantheidine*.
  Rubi.   Mitragyna speciosa (lvs)
Vallesiachotamine
  Apocyn.   Vallesia dichotoma

XIII THE 2,2'-INDOLYL-QUINUCLIDINE ALKALOIDS

GENERAL

Taylor (in *M.*, v.8, 1965) and Hesse (1964) list three alkaloids belonging to this group. Taylor, in a more recent review (in *M.*,v. 11, 1968), is able to add two more.

These alkaloids are confined, so far as we know, to *Cinchona*, *Isertia*, and *Remijia*—closely (?) related genera of the *Rubiaceae*.

List and Occurrence

Cinchonamine (fig. 37)
  Rubi.   Cinchona ledgeriana, Remijia purdieana

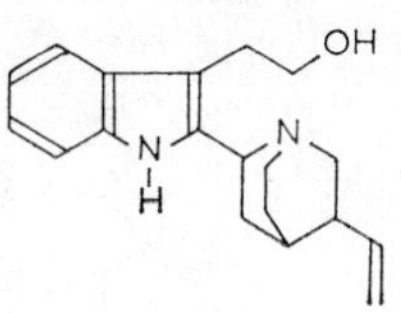

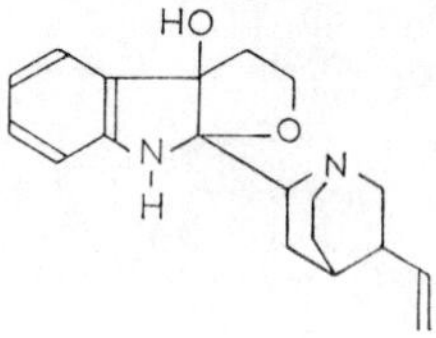

Cinchonamine   Quinamine

Fig. 37. Some 2,2'-Indolyl-quinuclidine alkaloids.

Cinchophyllamine
    Rubi.   Cinchona ledgeriana (lvs)
Conquinamine (3-Epiquinamine)
    Rubi.   Cinchona (4), *Remijia* (1)
Dihydroquinamine
    Rubi.   Isertia hypoleuca (lvs)
Iso-cinchophyllamine: is a stereoisomer of *cinchophyllamine*?
    Rubi.   Cinchona ledgeriana (lvs)
Quinamine (fig. 37)
    Rubi.   Cinchona (8), *Remijia* (1)

XIV ERGOLINE ALKALOIDS

GENERAL

Until recently *ergoline* alkaloids were known only from the fungi, but it is now clear that at least two types occur in some members of the *Convolvulaceae* (which see for further discussion).

Stoll and Hoffman (in *M.*, v.8, 1965) deal with the ergot alkaloids. They say:

> If the stereoisomer forms are regarded as a single alkaloid in each case and those bases which, though shown to exist by means of paper chromatography, have not had their structure elucidated are ignored, a total of approximately two dozen ergot alkaloids have been described to date. All these alkaloids are formed from the same tetracyclic ring system that Jacobs and Gould...named ergoline...On the basis of their structural differences, the ergot alkaloids may be divided into two main groups: one group to include all lysergic acid derivatives of the acid amide type, and the other to include the so-called clavine alkaloids.

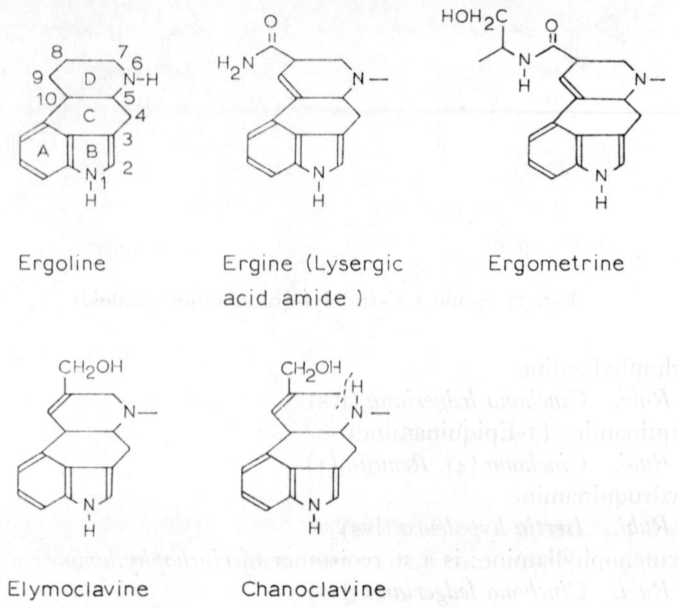

Fig. 38. Ergoline and some ergoline alkaloids.

Both types have been shown by tracer experiments to be formed from *tryptophan* and *mevalonic acid*. The *clavines* are probably precursors of the *lysergic acid* alkaloids.

Some peptides of *lysergic acid* are known to occur.

List and Occurrence

Chanoclavine (fig. 38)
    Convolvul.   *Rivea corymbosa* (sd)?
Elymoclavine (fig. 38)
    Convolvul.   *Rivea corymbosa* (sd)?
Ergine (Lysergic acid amide; fig. 38)
    Convolvul.   *Argyreia nervosa* (sd)?, *Ipomoea purpurea* (sd)?, *Rivea corymbosa* (sd)?
Ergometrine (Ergobasine; Ergonovine; fig. 38)
    Convolvul.   *Argyreia nervosa* (sd), *Ipomoea purpurea* (sd)?
Ergometrinine (Ergobasinine) is a stereoisomer of *ergometrine*.
    Convolvul.   *Argyreia nervosa* (sd)?, *Ipomoea purpurea* (sd)
Isoergine
    Convolvul.   *Argyreia nervosa* (sd)?, *Ipomoea purpurea* (sd)?, *Rivea corymbosa* (sd)?

Lysergol
    Convolvul.   Rivea corymbosa (sd)?
Penniclavine
    Convolvul.   Argyreia nervosa (sd)?, *Ipomoea purpurea* (sd)?

XV IBOGA AND VOACANGA ALKALOIDS

GENERAL

These were discussed by Taylor (in *M.*, v.8, 1965). He warns: 'Many of the alkaloids [of this group] suffer facile autoxidation to yield hydroperoxy- and hydroxy-indolenines, whose further degradation products are 4-hydroxyquinolines and pseudoindoxyls...Therefore, the isolation of these products from the plant cannot by itself be taken as proof of their natural occurrence.'

In a more recent review (in *M.*, v.11, 1968) he adds some new alkaloids, and says: 'It is now quite certain that the iboga alkaloids originate from tryptophan or its equivalent and two mevalonate residues...The latter are linked head to tail since geraniol can also function as a precursor of the hydroaromatic portion...'

The iboga and voacanga alkaloids are often treated as two groups. We prefer to combine them in one list. They seem to be confined to the *Apocynaceae.*

List and Occurrence

Affinine is a *2-acyl-indole.*
    Apocyn.   Peschiera affinis
Callichiline is a *bis-aspidosperma* alkaloid (Taylor, in *M.*, v. 11, 1968).
    Apocyn.   Callichilia barteri, subsessilis
Catharanthine is closely related to *ibogaine.*
    Apocyn.   Catharanthus roseus
Cleavamine: does not occur naturally?
Conoduramine is a *bis-indole.*
    Apocyn.   Conopharyngia durissima, Gabunia odoratissima
Conodurine is a *bis-indole.*
    Apocyn.   Conopharyngia durissima, Gabunia odoratissima
Conopharyngine: are there two alkaloids with this name? (see under *steroid alkaloids*)
    Apocyn.   Conopharyngia pachysiphon v. *cuminsii*
Coronaridine (Carbomethoxy-ibogamine; Demethoxy-voacangine; fig. 39) seems to be rather common.
    Apocyn.   Conopharyngia jollyana; *Ervatamia coronaria* and 2

others; *Gabunia odoratissima*; *Stemmadenia* (3); *Tabernae-montana* (6)

16-Decarbomethoxy-dihydrovobasine (H 100)
Apocyn. Rauwolfia discolor (Combes *et al.* 1968)

Demethoxy-iboluteine
Apocyn. Tabernanthe iboga

Dregamine is a 2-*acyl-indole.*
Apocyn. Ervatamia coronaria, Voacanga dregei

19-Epivoacorine is a *dimer.*
Apocyn. Voacanga bracteata v. *bracteata (zenkeri)*

19-Epivoacristine
Apocyn. Voacanga bracteata v. *bracteata (zenkeri)*

Gabonine is an artefact formed from *ibogaline.*

Gabunine (4'-Demethyl-conodurine)
Apocyn. Gabunia odoratissima

Heyneanine
Apocyn. Conopharyngia jollyana, Ervatamia dichotoma, Tabernae-montana heyneana

Hydroxy-indolenin-ibogaine
Apocyn. Tabernanthe iboga

Hydroxy-indolenin-ibogamine
Apocyn. Tabernanthe iboga

Ibogaine (fig. 39) was isolated more than 60 years ago.
Apocyn. Tabernanthe iboga

Ibogaline
Apocyn. Tabernanthe iboga

Ibogamine is rather common.
Apocyn. Ervatamia?; *Gabunia odoratissima*; *Stemmadenia galeot-tiana*; *Tabernanthe iboga, laurifolia, oppositifolia*

Iboluteine (Ibogaine-pseudoindoxyl)
Apocyn. Rejoua aurantiaca, Tabernanthe iboga

Iboquine (Ibogaine-4-quinolinol)
Apocyn. Tabernanthe iboga

Iboxygaine
Apocyn. Tabernanthe iboga, laurifolia

Isovoacangine
Apocyn. Conopharyngia durissima, Gabunia odoratissima, Stem-madenia donnell-smithii, Tabernaemontana laurifolia

Isovoacristine
Apocyn. Tabernaemontana laurifolia

Kimvuline may be *iboxygaine*; it occurs with it.

Kisantine is an artefact arising from *ibogaline.*

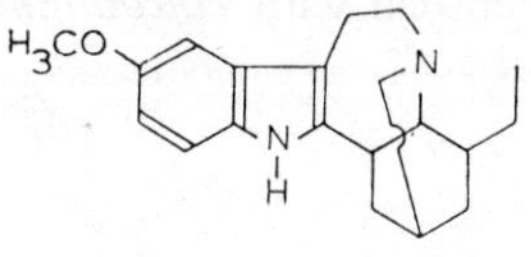

Ibogaine

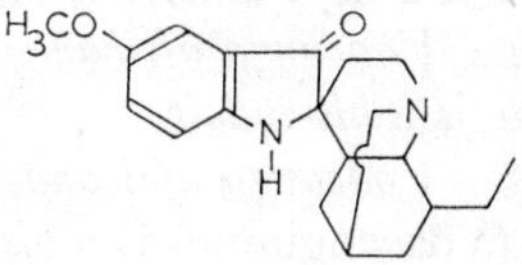

Iboluteine

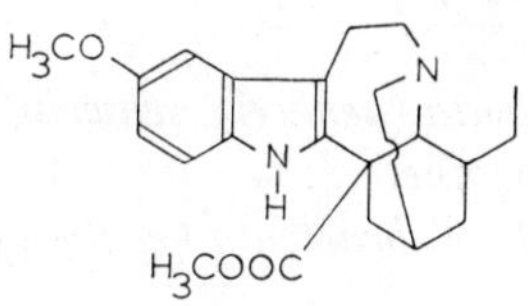

Coronaridine

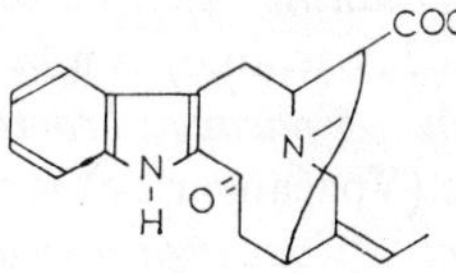

Vobasine

Fig. 39. Some Iboga and Voacanga alkaloids.

Montanine (1) (Voacangarine-pseudoindoxyl ?)
Apocyn. *Tabernaemontana rupicola*
Ochropamine is a 2-*acyl-indole*: belongs here ?
Apocyn. *Ochrosia poweri*
Ochropine is a 2-*acyl-indole*: belongs here ?
Apocyn. *Ochrosia poweri*
Periformyline is a 2-*acyl-indole*: belongs here ?
Apocyn. *Catharanthus lanceus*
Periline is a 2-*acyl-indole*: belongs here ?
Apocyn. *Rauwolfia perakensis*
Perivine (Perosine) is a 2-*acyl-indole*: belongs here ?
Apocyn. *Catharanthus roseus, Gabunia odoratissima*
Tabernaemontanine is a *dihydro-vobasine* alkaloid (and a 2-*acyl-indole*).
Apocyn. *Ervatamia coronaria, Rauwolfia discolor, Tabernaemontana salzmanni*
Tabernanthine is related to *ibogaine.*
Apocyn. *Stemmadenia donnell-smithii*; *Tabernanthe iboga, laurifolia*
Velbanamine: does not occur naturally ?
Voacafricine is a 2-*acyl-indole.* It *may* be identical with *vincadiffine.*
Apocyn. *Voacanga africana*

Voacafrine is a 2-*acyl-indole*. It *may* be identical with *vincadiffine*.
> *Apocyn. Voacanga africana*

Voacamidine is a *bis-indole*.
> *Apocyn. Voacanga africana, globosa*

Voacamine (Voacanginine) is a *bis-indole*.
> *Apocyn. Ervatamia?; Stemmadenia donnell-smithii; Tabernae-montana?; Voacanga bracteata* v. *bracteata* (*zenkeri*), *papuana* (and other spp. ?)

Voacaminine may be a mixture of *voacamine* and *voacorine*.

Voacangine is very similar to *ibogaine*.
> *Apocyn. Gabunia eglandulosa, Rejoua aurantiaca, Stemmadenia* (2), *Tabernanthe* (4), *Voacanga* (4 or more)

Voacorine (?Voacaline) is a *bis-indole*.
> *Apocyn. Voacanga bracteata* v. *bracteata* (*zenkeri*), *schweinfurthii*

Voacristine (Voacangarine) is very like *ibogaine*.
> *Apocyn. Voacanga africana, bracteata* v. *bracteata* (*zenkeri*)

Voacryptine is also very like *ibogaine*.
> *Apocyn. Voacanga africana*

Voaluteine (Rupicoline; Voacangine-pseudoindoxyl)
> *Apocyn. Rejoua aurantiaca*

Vobasine (fig. 39) is a 2-*acyl-indole*.
> *Apocyn. Gabunia odoratissima, Peschiera affinis, Voacanga africana*

Vobtusine is a *bis-indole*.
> *Apocyn. Callichilia* (3), *Voacanga* (4 ?)

XVI ASPIDOSPERMA–IBOGA DIMERS

GENERAL

Taylor (1965), in discussing the *Vinca* alkaloids, lists as occurring in *Vinca rosea* (we should say *Catharanthus roseus*) a group of *aspidosperma-iboga dimers*. They are all presumed to have structures similar to that of *vincaleucoblastine* (fig. 40) and thus to approximate to a combination of *aspidospermine* and *ibogaine*.

The possession of this group of alkaloids seems to mark off *Catharanthus roseus* as distinct from *Vinca*, but what of other species of *Catharanthus*?

List and Occurrence

Carosidine: belongs here?
> *Apocyn. Catharanthus roseus*

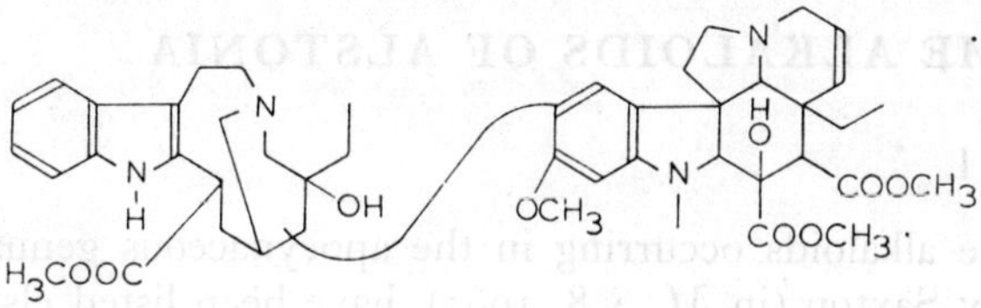

Vincaleucoblastine   (Vinblastine)

Fig. 40. An aspidosperma-iboga dimer.

Carosine
  Apocyn.   Catharanthus roseus
Catharicine
  Apocyn.   Catharanthus roseus
Catharine
  Apocyn.   Catharanthus roseus
Isoleurosine: a part of this dimer is *vindoline*.
  Apocyn.   Catharanthus roseus
Leurocristine
  Apocyn.   Catharanthus roseus
Leurosidine is related to *vincaleucoblastine*, but still imperfectly known
  (Taylor, in *M.*, v.11, 1968).
  Apocyn.   Catharanthus roseus
Leurosine: also imperfectly known?
  Apocyn.   Catharanthus roseus
Neoleurocristine
  Apocyn.   Catharanthus roseus
Neoleurosidine
  Apocyn.   Catharanthus roseus
Pleurosine
  Apocyn.   Catharanthus roseus
Vincaleucoblastine (Vinblastine; fig. 40) depresses the white cell
  count of the blood, hence the name.
  Apocyn.   Catharanthus (Vinca) roseus
Vincamicine: belongs here?
  Apocyn.   Catharanthus roseus

8

XVII SOME ALKALOIDS OF ALSTONIA

GENERAL

Some of the alkaloids occurring in the apocynaceous genus *Alstonia*, discussed by Saxton (in *M.*, v.8, 1965), have been listed elsewhere. A few remain unaccounted for and these may be considered here.

List and Occurrence

Alstonamine (?Ditaine)
  Apocyn.   Alstonia scholaris
Echitenine: is of unknown structure?
  Apocyn.   Alstonia (2)
Macralstonidine is, says Saxton, a dimer in which 'one (at least) of the
  indole nuclei may be contained in a ring of the ibogamine type'.
  Apocyn.   Alstonia (4)
Macralstonine
  Apocyn.   Alstonia macrophylla, somersetensis (and other spp. ?)
Macrophylline (1) is distinct from the *macrophylline* of *Senecio*. It *may*
  be identical with *macralstonine*.
  Apocyn.   Alstonia macrophylla

XVIII THE ERYTHRINANE ALKALOIDS

GENERAL

These alkaloids, which may be considered chemically to be derivatives of *erythrinane* (fig. 41), have been called the 'erythrina alkaloids' because they were found originally in the leguminous genus *Erythrina*. The history of our knowledge of this group is typical in that it shows the 'information explosion' which has occurred.

As recently as 1952 Marion (in *M. & H.*, v. 2) was unable to give a certain structural formula to any one of the small group of 'erythrina alkaloids'. He remarked on their great physiological activity and said: 'In a systematic investigation it has been shown that out of one hundred and five known species of *Erythrina*, the fifty which have been tested all contain alkaloids of paralyzing activity.'

Marion recognized three sub-groups: 'free' alkaloids, designated by '*erythr-*' names; 'combined' alkaloids, designated by '*erysothio-*' names; and 'liberated' alkaloids, derived from the 'combined' members by hydrolysis, never (?) occurring free in the plant, and designated by '*eryso-*' names.

Boekelheide (in *M.*, v. 7, 1960) was able to add a great deal to Marion's review. It had been established when Boekelheide wrote that the 'erythrina alkaloids' are *indole* derivatives with a *spiro-structure*. Two new alkaloids had been added, one of them occurring surprisingly in the *Menispermaceae*.

Our knowledge of this group has been brought more or less up to date by Hill (in *M.*, v.9, 1967). He writes:

> The eight years which have elapsed since then [the appearance of Boekelheide's review] have seen complete confirmation of the structures proposed, both by syntheses of most of the rearrangement and degradation products and by X-ray analysis of members of both major classes. . .
>
> Ingenious biosynthetic proposals involving oxidative coupling of tyrosine units have been put forward to account for the formation of the *Erythrina* group, and an exciting laboratory analogy for such a scheme has been realized. Tracer feeding experiments have confirmed the origin from tyrosine.

A second member of the group from the *Menispermaceae* has been added.

List and Occurrence

Cocculolidine (fig. 41) is said to have striking insecticidal properties.
    Menisperm.   *Cocculus trilobus* (lvs)
Dihydro-erysodine (fig. 41)
    Menisperm.   *Cocculus laurifolius*
Erysodine
    Legum.   *Erythrina* (at least 22 spp.)
Erysonine (3-Demethyl-erysodine)
    Legum.   *Erythrina* (4)
Erysopine (fig. 41)
    Legum.   *Erythrina* (at least 21 spp.)
Erysothiopine
    Legum.   *Erythrina* (6)
Erysothiovine
    Legum.   *Erythrina* (8)
Erysovine
    Legum.   *Erythrina* (at least 23 spp.)
Erythraline (fig. 41)
    Legum.   *Erythrina* (12)
Erythramine (Dihydro-erythraline)
    Legum.   *Erythrina* (7)

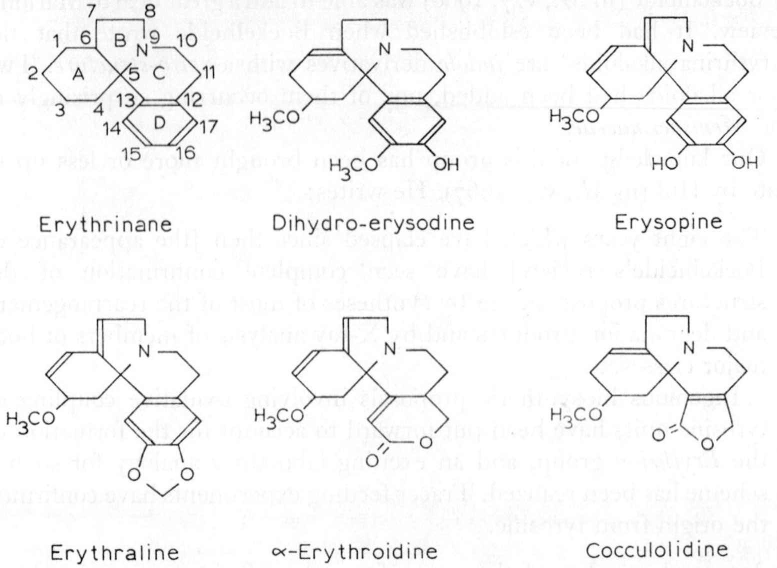

Fig. 41. Erythrinane and some related alkaloids.

Erythratidine
> *Legum.* *Erythrina falcata* (sd)

Erythratine
> *Legum.* *Erythrina* (5)

Erythratine ketone
> *Legum.* *Erythrina crista-galli*

Erythrine: what is this?
> *Legum.* *Erythrina crista-galli*

Erythroidine (fig. 41) is said to be a mixture of α- and *β-erythroidines*, which are double-bond isomers.
> *Legum.* *Erythrina* (4)

Gluco-erysodine is a glucoside of *erysodine* and perhaps the form in which it occurs (Boekelheide).
> *Legum.* *Erythrina abyssinica*

XIX INDOLE ALKALOIDS OF THE ORCHIDACEAE

GENERAL

The *Orchidaceae* is one of the largest of plant families (*ca.* 600/20,000 ?), yet very few compounds have been isolated from its members. As

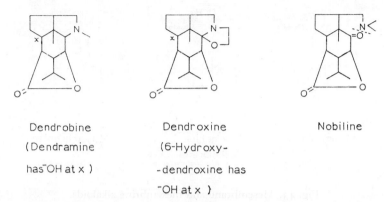

Dendrobine
(Dendramine
has⁻OH at x)

Dendroxine
(6-Hydroxy-
-dendroxine has
⁻OH at x)

Nobiline

Fig. 42. Some indole and near-indole alkaloids of the *Orchidaceae*.

recently as 1964 Lüning examined the first big batch of orchids for *alkaloids* and reported: '525 orchid species have been screened for their alkaloid content. Among these 77 species have been shown to contain more than 0·01%, and 21 species more than 0·1% alkaloids calculated on an estimated "dry weight".'

In a later (1967) communication he gives results for a further 500 species. Many more alkaloid-containing orchids, belonging to many genera, have thus been added to the list.

In his earlier paper he said that 9 alkaloids had been isolated, all (?) very sensitive to oxidation and hydrolysis. Most of these are *indole* or near-indole derivatives, but *hygrine* (a *pyrrolidine*) occurs in *Dendrobium*, as does *5,7-dimethyl-indolizidine*. The *indole* alkaloids listed in this section seem to be unique to the *Orchidaceae*, and indeed to *Dendrobium*. It seems likely, however, that further work will reveal their presence in other orchidaceous genera, and perhaps in other families.

List and Occurrence

Dendramine (6-Hydroxy-dendrobine; fig. 42)
  Orchid.   Dendrobium nobile
Dendrine
  Orchid.   Dendrobium nobile (as a minor constituent)
Dendrobine (fig. 42)
  Orchid.   Dendrobium linaweanum, monile, moniliforme, nobile
Dendroxine (fig. 42)
  Orchid.   Dendrobium nobile
6-Hydroxy-dendroxine (fig. 42)
  Orchid.   Dendrobium nobile

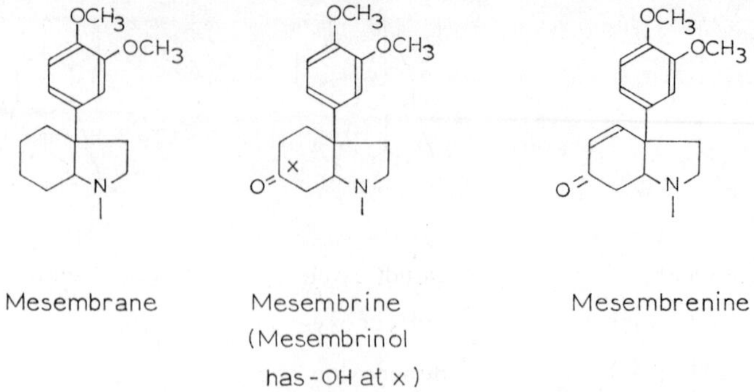

Mesembrane   Mesembrine   Mesembrenine

(Mesembrinol

has-OH at x)

Fig. 43. Mesembrane and mesembrine alkaloids.

Nobiline (fig. 42) is a near-indole.
 Orchid. Dendrobium nobile
Nobilonine: an isomer of *nobiline*?
 Orchid. Dendrobium nobile

XX THE MESEMBRINE GROUP

GENERAL

The members of this group have a *near-indole* nucleus and may be included for convenience here. They are confined, so far as we know, to the genus *Sceletium* (a segregate from *Mesembryanthemum, Aizoaceae*).

The bushmen of Namaqualand prepare a drug 'channa' by fermentation from *Sceletium* and use it as a stimulant. The first *mesembrine alkaloids* were isolated from the drug.

A recent review by Popelak and Lettenbauer (in *M.*, v.9, 1967) has been consulted. These authors point out that these alkaloids may be derived from *mesembrane* (fig. 43) and that they are thus closely related to the alkaloids of the *Amaryllidaceae* which are derived from *crinane*.

Sceletium plants fed with radioactive precursors have yielded evidence that the C_6-C_2-N part of *mesembrine* is derived from *tyrosine* and the aromatic ring from *phenylalanine*.

List and Occurrence

Channaine has been isolated from 'channa'. It may be dimeric.
Mesembrenine (fig. 43)
 Aizo. Sceletium (Mesembryanthemum) tortuosum (plt)

Mesembrine (fig. 43)

 Aizo. *Sceletium anatomicum, expansum, tortuosum*

Mesembrinol (fig. 43) has been isolated from 'channa'.

Nor-mesembrine

 Aizo. *Sceletium tortuosum?*

Sceletium alkaloid-A_4 has been isolated from 'channa'.

Sceletium alkaloid-B_3 has been isolated from 'channa'. It is isomeric with *channaine*.

XXI THE STEMONA GROUP

GENERAL

The genus *Stemona*, of the little family *Stemonaceae*, is considered to have about 25 species. Several of these are known to produce alkaloids, about a dozen of which have been isolated and named. Two, at least, of these have a peculiar structure incorporating an *indole* nucleus. The others have similar empirical formulae and may have the same type of structure.

 Edwards (in *M.*, v.9, 1967) has reviewed our knowledge of this little group.

List and Occurrence

Hodorine ($C_{19}H_{31}O_5N$)

 Stemon. *Stemona sessilifolia* (rt)

Hypotuberostemonine

 Stemon. *Stemona tuberosa* (rt)

Isostemonidine ($C_{19}H_{31}O_5N$)

 Stemon. *Stemona ovata*

Isotuberostemonine ($C_{22}H_{33}O_4N$)

 Stemon. *Stemona tuberosa* (rt)

Oxotuberostemonine ($C_{22}H_{31}O_5N$)

 Stemon. *Stemona tuberosa*

Paipunine ($C_{24}H_{37}O_4N$)

 Stemon. *Stemona sp.*

Protostemonine ($C_{20}H_{29}O_5N$)

 Stemon. *Stemona japonica* (rt), *sessilifolia* or *tuberosa* (rt)

Sinostemonine ($C_{21}H_{36}O_5N$)

 Stemon. *Stemona sp.*

Stemonidine ($C_{19}H_{36}O_5N$)

 Stemon. *Stemona japonica, ovata*

Stemonine ($C_{17}H_{23}O_4N$)

 Stemon. *Stemona japonica* (rt), *ovata, sessilifolia* (rt), *tuberosa* (rt)

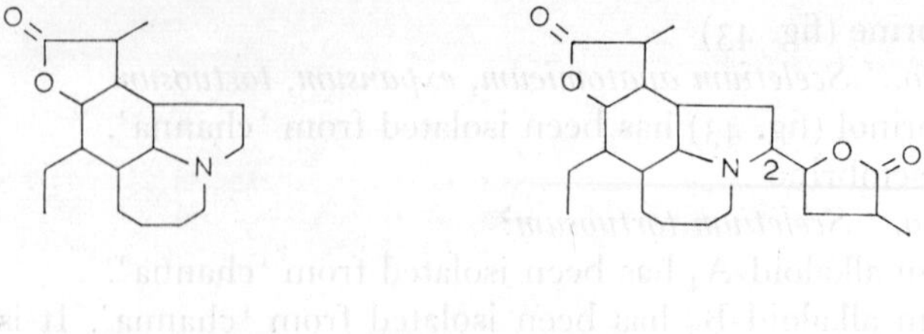

Stenine   Tuberostemonine and
                          Tuberostemonine-A

Fig. 44. Alkaloids of *Stemona*.

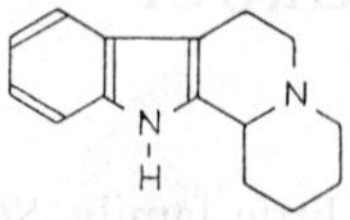

Octahydro-indolo
[2,3a] quinolizine

Fig. 45. An indole alkaloid of group XXII.

Stenine (fig. 44)
    Stemon.   *Stemona tuberosa*
Tuberostemonine (fig. 44)
    Stemon.   *Stemona tuberosa* (rt)
Tuberostemonine-A differs from *tuberostemonine* only in the stereo-
chemistry at C_2.
    Stemon.   *Stemona sessilifolia*

XXII THE INDOLO [2,3α]QUINOLIZINE GROUP

GENERAL

I believe that only one member of this group is known to occur naturally.
Others, no doubt, will be found.

According to Johns, Lamberton and Occolowitz (1966) the one alkaloid known arises from *tryptophan* and *α-ketoadipate* or *lysine*. The
yohimbine alkaloids, although they have the same ring-system, arise
from mevalonate.

List and Occurrence

(−)-1,2,3,4,6,7,12,12b-Octahydro-indolo [2,3α]quinolizine (fig. 45)
    Anacardi.   *Dracontomelum mangiferum*

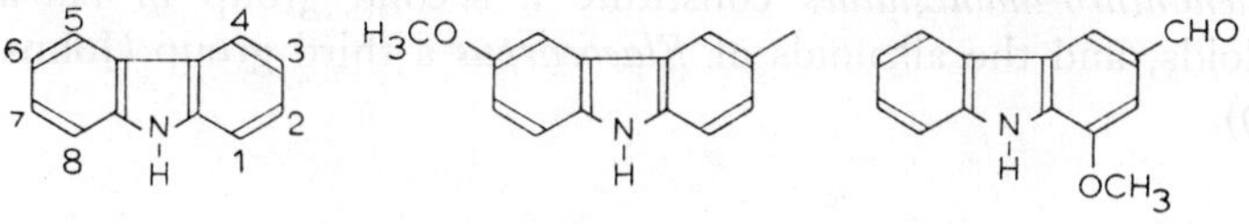

Carbazole   Glycozoline   Murrayanine

Fig. 46. Carbazole and carbazole alkaloids.

XXIII THE CARBAZOLE GROUP

GENERAL

Crude *anthracene* is said to contain small quantities of *carbazole* (*dibenzo-pyrrole*; fig. 46), an extremely stable compound. Alkaloids with a *carbazole* nucleus seem to be very rare indeed and to be confined to the *Rutaceae*.

List and Occurrence

Girinimbine ($C_{18}H_{17}ON$) is said to be a *pyrano-carbazole*.
    Rut.   *Murraya koenigii*
Glycozolidine (5,7-Dimethoxy-3-methyl-carbazole)
    Rut.   *Glycosmis pentaphylla*
Glycozoline (3-Methyl-6-methoxy-carbazole; fig. 46)
    Rut.   *Glycosmis pentaphylla* (rtbk)
Heptaphylline
    Rut.   *Clausena heptaphylla*
Murrayanine (fig. 46)
    Rut.   *Murraya koenigii* (bk)

INDOLIZIDINE GROUPS

GENERAL

Meyer and Sapianchiay (1964) used the name *indolizidine* for the ring-system shown in fig. 48. They were dealing with pure chemistry and made no reference to naturally occurring substances with this nucleus.

    It is interesting to learn that at least one orchid synthesizes a *simple indolizidine*. No doubt others will be found to do the same.

Phenanthro-indolizidines constitute a second group of *indolizidine* alkaloids, and the alkaloids of *Elaeocarpus* a third group (Johns *et al.* 1969).

I SIMPLE INDOLIZIDINES

List and Occurrence

5,7-Dimethyl-indolizidine (5,7-Dimethyl-octahydro-indolizine; fig. 48)
  Orchid. Dendrobium primulinum

II PHENANTHRO-INDOLIZIDINE ALKALOIDS

GENERAL

This small group of alkaloids—sometimes known as the 'tylophora group'—is a very interesting one. It has been reviewed for us recently by Govindachari (in *M.*, v. 9, 1967).

The members occur in the *Asclepiadaceae*, and particularly in the genus *Tylophora*, but two—*tylocrebrine* and *tylophorine*—are found also in *Ficus septica*, a member of the *Moraceae*.

Apparently the *phenanthro-indolizidine* alkaloids are powerfully vesicant. It is interesting that the *phenanthro-quinolizidine* alkaloid *cryptopleurine* (which closely resembles *tylocrebrine* and *tylophorine*) is also vesicant.

As Govindachari points out:

[If]...the phenanthroindolizidine alkaloids can be visualized as arising by the condensation of two molecules of dihydroxyphenylalanine or one molecule of dihydroxyphenylalanine and one of tyrosine (or their equivalents the corresponding benzoyl acetic and phenyl pyruvic acids) with ornithine (or its equivalent γ-amino-butyralde-hyde) [then] the joint occurrence of tylophorine and tylocrebrine with the secophenanthroindolizidine alkaloid septicine...lends support to the biogenetic scheme [fig. 47].

List and Occurrence

Antofine (Vincetoxicum alkaloid-A?)
  Asclepiad. Antitoxicum funebre (plt), *Vincetoxicum officinale* (rt)
Septicine (fig. 48)
  Mor. Ficus septica

Tylocrebrine (fig. 48)
>   *Mor.   Ficus septica* (+)
>   *Asclepiad.   Tylophora crebriflora (floribunda)* (−)

(−)-Tylophorine (fig. 48)
>   *Mor.   Ficus septica*
>   *Asclepiad.   Tylophora asthmatica, brevipes, crebriflora, fasciculata,*
>   *indica; Vincetoxicum officinale* (rt)

Tylophorinine
>   *Asclepiad.   Tylophora asthmatica, indica* (lvs, st., rt)

III ALKALOIDS OF ELAEOCARPUS

List and Occurrence

Elaeocarpidine is an *indole* but also almost an *indolizidine*. Its occurrence
places it here.
>   *Elaeocarp.   Elaeocarpus densiflorus* (lvs), *polydactylus* (lvs, little)

(+)-Elaeocarpiline ((+)-15,16-Dihydro-elaeocarpine)
>   *Elaeocarp.   Elaeocarpus dolichostylis* (lvs)

(±)-Elaeocarpine (fig. 48)
>   *Elaeocarp.   Elaeocarpus polydactylus* (lvs)

(+)-Iso-elaeocarpicine is nearly related to *elaeocarpine*
>   *Elaeocarp.   Elaeocarpus polydactylus* (lvs)

(−)-Iso-elaeocarpiline ((−)-15,16-Dihydro-elaeocarpine)
>   *Elaeocarp.   Elaeocarpus dolichostylis* (lvs)

(+)-Iso-elaeocarpine is an isomer of *elaeocarpine*
>   *Elaeocarp.   Elaeocarpus polydactylus* (lvs)

ISOQUINOLINE GROUPS

GENERAL

Bentley (1965) has monographed this group of alkaloids. He says: 'The
alkaloids of the isoquinoline group may be further subdivided into
families, all of which are clearly related structurally and by their mode
of formation in the plant.'

These bases are believed to arise by the condensation of *β-phenyl-
ethylamines* (which themselves arise from *amino-acids*) with *aldehydes*
(fig. 49). From such a base as *nor-laudanosine* could arise *aporphines,
cularine-type alkaloids* and *protoberberines* (Manske, in *M. & H.*, v.4,
1954).

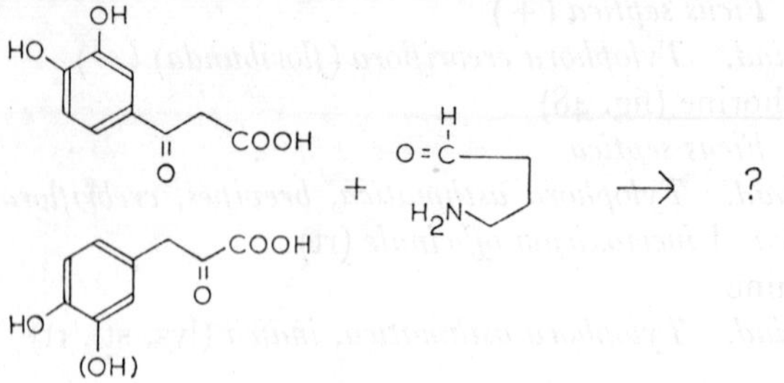

Fig. 47. Biogenesis of phenanthro-indolizidine alkaloids?

Indolizidine   5,7-Dimethyl-   Septicine
                            -indolizidine

(-)-Tylophorine   Tylocrebrine   Elaeocarpine

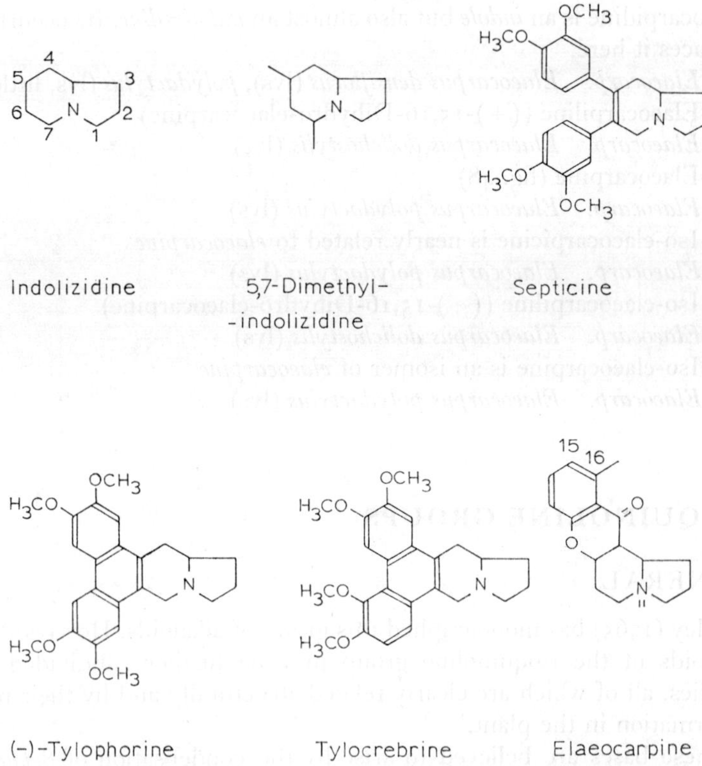

Fig. 48. Indolizidine and some indolizidine alkaloids.

Bentley (loc. cit.) has the following scheme to show probable inter-relationships. We have added our own group numbers.

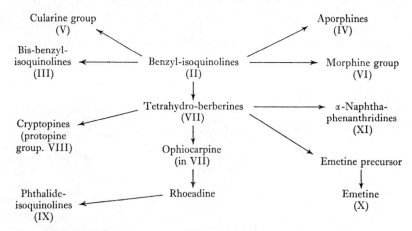

We have recognized the following groups in our treatment of the *isoquinolines*:

     I. Simple isoquinolines: about 20 alkaloids.
    II. 1,1'-Benzylisoquinolines: about 60.
   III. Bisbenzylisoquinolines: about 80.
   IV. The Aporphine group: almost 100.
    V. The Cularine group: 4.
   VI. The Morphine group: about 20.
  VII. Protoberberines: more than 50.
VIII. The Protopine group: 14.
   IX. Phthalide-isoquinolines: about 12.
    X. The Emetine group: about 17.
   XI. The α-Naphthaphenanthridines: about 18.
  XII. Miscellaneous isoquinolines: 6.

This treatment recognizes about 400 *isoquinoline alkaloids*—a very large group, but smaller than the *indole* group (about 600).

I SIMPLE ISOQUINOLINES

GENERAL

We define *simple isoquinolines* for our purpose as those alkaloids having essentially an *isoquinoline* (or more accurately a *tetrahydro-isoquinoline*) nucleus and no other rings, except in some cases one formed by a methylenedioxy group.

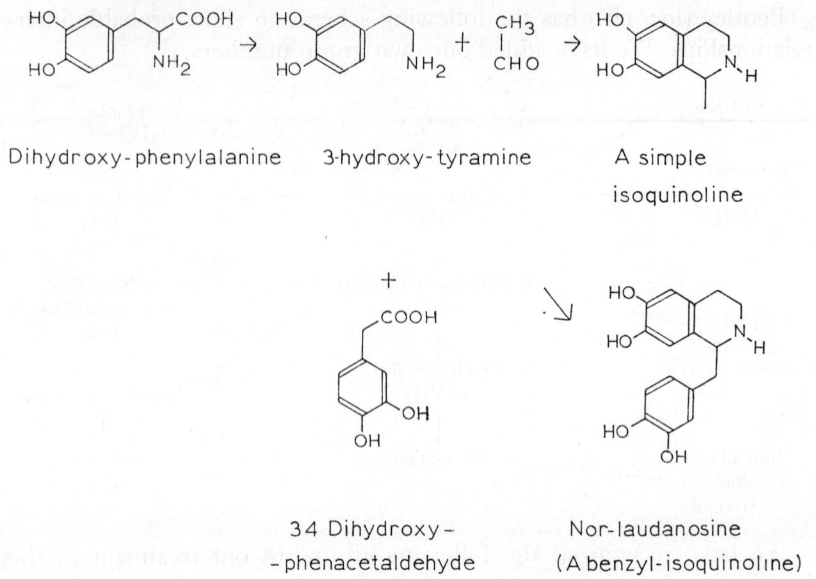

Dihydroxy-phenylalanine   3-hydroxy-tyramine   A simple
isoquinoline

3 4 Dihydroxy –   Nor-laudanosine
- phenacetaldehyde   (A benzyl-isoquinoline)

Fig. 49. Biosynthesis of isoquinolines.

Some *simple isoquinolines* occur in the *Cactaceae*; two or three in the related *Chenopodiaceae*; two in the *Leguminosae*; three (two of which may be artefacts derived from more complicated alkaloids) in the *Papaveraceae*; and one in the *Monimiaceae*.

This group has been discussed by Reti (in *M. & H.*, v.4, 1954).

List and Occurrence

Anhalamine (fig. 50)
    Cact.   Lophophora williamsii
Anhalidine (*N*-Methyl-anhalamine)
    Cact.   Lophophora williamsii
Anhalinine (*O*-Methyl-anhalamine)
    Cact.   Lophophora williamsii
Anhalonidine
    Cact.   Lemaireocereus weberi, Lophophora williamsii
Anhalonine
    Cact.   Ariocarpus sp., *Gymnocalycium gibbosum, Lophophora wil-
    liamsii, Mammillaria jourdanianum, Trichocereus terscheckii*
Calycotomine (fig. 50)
    Legum.   Calycotome spinosa (d- and *dl-), Cytisus nigricans* (plt, sd),
    proliferus (sd., *dl-*)

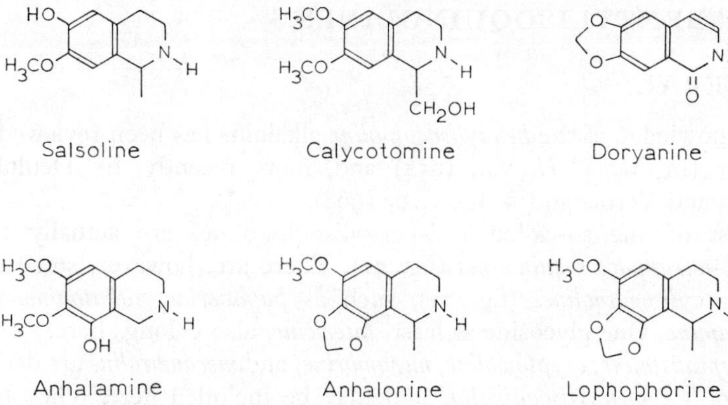

Fig. 50. Some simple isoquinoline alkaloids.

Carnegine (*O,N*-Dimethyl-salsoline; Pectenine)
    Cact. Carnegiea gigantea, Cereus pecten-aborigenum
Corypalline
    Papaver. Corydalis aurea (sd), *pallida* (plt)
Doryanine (fig. 50)
    Monimi. Doryphora sassafras
Gigantine is a *hydroxy-carnegine.*
    Cact. Carnegiea gigantea
Hydrocotarnine may be an artefact.
    Papaver. Papaver somniferum (frt)
Hydrohydrastinine may be an artefact.
    Papaver. Corydalis tuberosa (rt)
Lophocerine
    Cact. Lophocereus schottii (plt)
Lophophorine (*N*-Methyl-1-anhalonine; fig. 50)
    Cact. Lophophora williamsii
O-Methyl-*d*-anhalonidine
    Cact. Lophophora williamsii
Pellotine (*N*-Methyl-anhalonidine)
    Cact. Lophophora williamsii
Salsamine: of uncertain structure?
    Chenopodi. Salsola richleri
Salsolidine (*O*-Methyl-salsoline)
    Chenopodi. Salsola kali, richleri, ruthenica, soda
    Legum. Genista pungens (frt, sd)
Salsoline (fig. 50)
    Chenopodi. Salsola kali, richleri, ruthenica, soda

II 1,1′-BENZYLISOQUINOLINES

GENERAL

Our knowledge of the *benzylisoquinoline* alkaloids has been reviewed by Burger (in *M. & H.*, v.4, 1954) and, more recently, by Deulofeu, Comin and Vernengo (in *M.*, v.10, 1968).

Most of the so-called 1,1′-benzylisoquinolines are actually 1,1′-*benzyl-tetrahydroisoquinolines* (fig. 51). There are, however, some true 1,1′-*benzylisoquinolines* (fig. 51), such as *papaverine, takatonine,* and *escholamine.* One glycoside at least, *latericine,* also belongs here.

Cryptaustoline, cryptowoline, mecambrine, and *mecambroline* are derivatives of 1,1′-*benzylisoquinoline* and may be included here. They have been called *pro-aporphines.*

At least one *N-benzyl-tetrahydroisoquinoline* is known. This is *sendaverine* (fig. 51) which is included here for convenience.

We have seen, in discussing *isoquinolines* in general, that the 1,1′-*benzylisoquinolines* may arise from such substances as 3,4-*dihydroxy-phenylalanine* and 3,4-*dihydroxy-phenylacetaldehyde.* Deulofeu, Comin and Vernengo say: 'Not only the early assumption that the simple benzylisoquinolines originate from aromatic amino acids... has been given experimental proof but evidence has been accumulating that some of them are biogenetic precursors of more elaborated natural bases of the morphine, berberine, protopine, and benzophenanthridine groups ...'

About 60 benzylisoquinoline alkaloids are now known and these are listed in the pages that follow. They appear at first sight to be widely distributed, but they are, in fact, rather restricted in their distribution, as the following notes show.

(*a*) About half of the known members are found in the *Papaveraceae,* but there only in relatively few genera.

(*b*) They occur in 9 families of the 'Polycarpicae'—*Magnoliaceae, Annonaceae, Monimiaceae, Lauraceae* and *Hernandiaceae* of the **Magnoliales** (*sensu Syll.* 12); and *Ranunculaceae, Berberidaceae, Menispermaceae* and *Nymphaeaceae* of the **Ranunculales** (*sensu Syll.* 12). See 'Polycarpicae' for further discussion.

(*c*) A single member of the *Euphorbiaceae, Croton linearis,* yields 4 benzylisoquinoline alkaloids, all of the *crotonosine* type.

(*d*) Two genera of the *Rhamnaceae*—*Colletia* (2 spp.) and *Phylica rogersii*—yield between them 4 of these alkaloids, all of them benzyl-tetrahydroisoquinolines.

(*e*) Several species of *Fagara* (*Rutaceae*) have *tembetarine.*

List and Occurrence

Amurensine (fig. 52)
    Papaver.   *Papaver* (5)
Amurensinine (fig. 52)
    Papaver.   *Papaver* (5)
Amuroline
    Papaver.   *Papaver nudicaule* v. *amurense*
Amuronine
    Papaver.   *Papaver nudicaule* v. *amurense*
d-(−)-Armepavine
    Papaver.   *Papaver caucasicum* (*armeniacum*) and at least 4 other spp.
dl-(±)-Armepavine
    Nymphae.   *Nelumbo nucifera* (lvs), *pentapetala* (*lutea*)
Bis-nor-argemonine (Rotundine (2))
    Papaver.   *Argemone munita* subsp. *rotunda, aenea, hispida* (*mexicana*); *Eschscholtzia californica*
dl-Caryachine: belongs here?
    Laur.   *Cryptocarya chinensis* (bk, wd)
dl-Coclaurine (Machiline, fig. 51): the *d*-(–)-isomer is said to be an efficient precursor of *crotonosine*.
    Laur.   *Cryptocarya konishii* (wd); *Machilus kusanoi, macrantha*
    Menisperm.   *Cocculus hirsutus, laeba, laurifolius* (bk, wd)
l-(+)-Codamine occurs in traces in opium.
    Papaver.   *Papaver somniferum* (frt)
d-(−)-Colletine
    Rhamn.   *Colletia paradoxa, spinosissima*
Crotonosine (fig. 51) has been called a *pro-aporphine*.
    Euphorbi.   *Croton linearis*
Cryptaustoline is, like *cryptowoline*, both an *isoquinoline* and an *indole*.
    Laur.   *Cryptocarya bowiei* (bk)
Cryptowoline (fig. 51): see *cryptaustoline*.
    Laur.   *Cryptocarya bowiei* (bk)
Doryafranine
    Monimi.   *Doryphora sassafras* (lvs)
Escholamine
    Papaver.   *Eschscholtzia* sp. (prob. *oregona*)
Eschscholtzidine (d-*O*-Methyl-caryachine)
    Laur.   *Cryptocarya chinensis* (bk, wd)
    Papaver.   *Eschscholtzia californica*
Eschscholtzine (Crychine) is very like *bis-nor-argemonine*.
    Laur.   *Cryptocarya chinensis* (bk, wd)
    Papaver.   *Eschscholtzia californica*

(+)-Isococlaurine has been isolated only once—... ISOQUINOLI...
bravae.

   Menisperm.   Chondrodendron platyphyllum (microphyllum?) (rt)
Iso-nor-argemonine
   Occurrence?
Latericine (fig. 51) is a D-*xyloside* of L-(+)-*N-methyl-coclaurine*
   Papaver.   Papaver lateritium, monanthum, pilosum, californicum
l-(+)-Laudanidine
   Laur.   Machilus arisaensis, obovatifolia
dl-Laudanine (($\pm$)-Launanidine) occurs in very small amount in opium.
   Papaver.   Papaver somniferum (frt)
l-Laudanine (Tritopine; Launanidine)
   Papaver.   Papaver somniferum (frt)
l-(+)-Laudanosine (d-*N*-Methyl-tetrahydro-papaverine)
   Papaver.   Papaver somniferum (frt)
Laudanosoline may give rise to *morphine*-type alkaloids.
   Occurrence?
Leonticine is a near-benzylisoquinoline which should properly be called
   petaline-methine. It may be an artefact.
   *Berberid.   Leontice leontopetalum?, Bongardia chrysogonum (rau-
      wolfii?)*
Linearisine (*N*-Methyl-dihydro-crotonosine)
   Euphorbi.   Croton linearis
d-(−)-Lotusine
   Nymphae.   Nelumbo nucifera (embryo)
d-(−)-Magnocurarine (*N*-Methyl-coclaurine methyl hydroxide)
   Magnoli.   Magnolia (6) (bk); *Michelia fuscata*
   Rhamn.   Colletia paradoxa, spinosissima
l-(+)-Magnocurarine
   Hernandi.   Gyrocarpus americanus (bk), *jacquinii*
Mecambrine (Fugapavine)
   Papaver.   Meconopsis cambrica; Papaver fugax (and several other
      spp.)
Mecambroline (Isofugapavine; Isofungipavine)
   Papaver.   Meconopsis cambrica; Papaver caucasicum
Munitagine is very like *bis-nor-argemonine* and occurs with it.
   Papaver.   Argemone munita subsp. *rotunda, hispida, pleiacantha*
N-Acetyl-stepharine: belongs here?
   Menisperm.   Stephania rotunda (tuber)
d-(−)-*N*-Methyl-coclaurine
   Rhamn.   Phylica rogersii
l-(+)-*N*-Methyl-coclaurine is the aglycone of *latericine.* Does it occur
   free?

l-(−)-*N*-Methyl-crotonosine (Homolinearisine)
> *Euphorbi.* *Croton linearis*

N-Methyl-papaveraldinium
> *Menisperm.* *Stephania sasakii*

N-Methyl-pavine (Argemonine; fig. 52)
> *Papaver.* *Argemone aenea, hispida* (*mexicana*), *platyceras, munita, sanguinea* (white)

d-(+)-*N*-Nor-armepavine
> *Magnoli.* *Magnolia kachikachirai*
> *Laur.* *Machilus* (5)

l-(−)-*N*-Nor-armepavine (1-(−)-7-*O*-Methyl-coclaurine)
> *Laur.* *Cryptocarya konishii* (wd, *l*- and *dl*-); *Machilus* (6)
> *Nymphae.* *Nelumbo pentapetala* (*lutea*)

Nor-argemonine
> *Papaver.* *Argemone hispida* (*mexicana*), *platyceras*

Ochotensimine (fig. 52) has been described as a 'novel benzyliso-quinoline alkaloid'.
> *Papaver.* *Corydalis ochotensis* (plt)

Ochotensine
> *Papaver.* *Corydalis ochotensis* (plt), *sibirica* (plt); *Dicentra cucullaria* (tuber)

l-(+)-*O*-Methyl-armepavine
> *Magnoli.* *Magnolia acuminata*

O,O,N-Trimethyl-coclaurine-methyl-methine is a near-benzylisoquino-line.
> *Nymphae.* *Nelumbo pentapetala* (*lutea*)

(−)-Orientalinone is very like *crotonosine*.
> *Papaver.* *Papaver bracteatum* (young frt)

Papaveraldine (Xanthaline)
> *Papaver.* *Papaver somniferum*

Papaverine (Pseudopapaverine; fig. 51) has been reported to occur in the *Apocynaceae* (*Rauwolfia*), but probably it does *not* occur there.
> *Papaver.* *Papaver somniferum, commutatum, paeoniflorum, setigerum.* It is of great pharmacological interest and has been searched for, but it seems to be absent from many members of the family.

Petaline
> *Berberid.* *Leontice leontopetalum*

(+)-Pronuciferine (Miltanthine; ?*N*-Methyl-stepharine) is the *O,N*-dimethyl ether of *crotonosine*. It seems to be widely distributed.
> *Menisperm.* *Stephania rotunda* (tuber)
> *Nymphae.* *Nelumbo nucifera* (embryo)

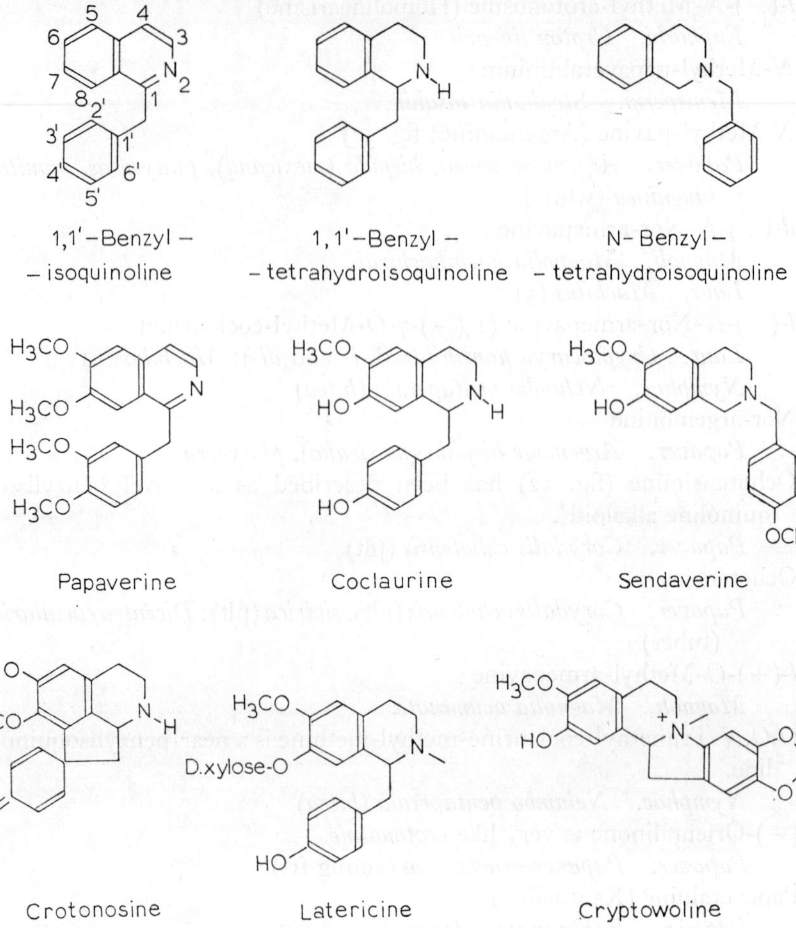

1,1'–Benzyl –
– isoquinoline

1,1'–Benzyl –
– tetrahydroisoquinoline

N– Benzyl –
– tetrahydroisoquinoline

Papaverine

Coclaurine

Sendaverine

Crotonosine

Latericine

Cryptowoline

Fig. 51. 1,1'-Benzylisoquinoline, some related compounds, and some benzylisoquinoline alkaloids.

Papaver. *Papaver caucasicum*
Euphorbi. *Croton linearis*
l-(+)-Reticuline seems to be widely distributed.
    Annon. *Annona reticulata*
    Laur. *Cinnamomum camphora*; ?*Machilus* spp.
    Papaver. *Argemone* (2), *Papaver somniferum* (+ and − forms?)
        Romneya coulteri var. *trichocalyx* (+)
    Rhamn. *Phylica rogersii*
Rhoeagenine
    Papaver. *Papaver rhoeas* and 4 other spp.

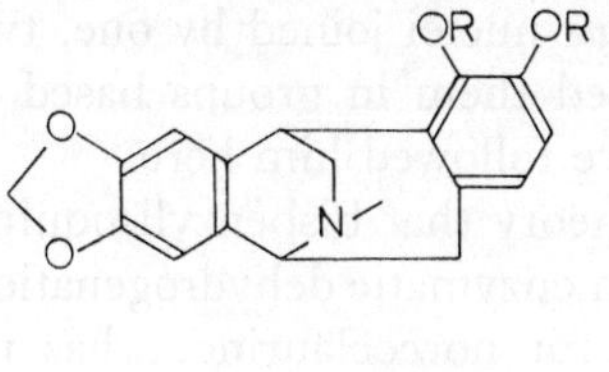

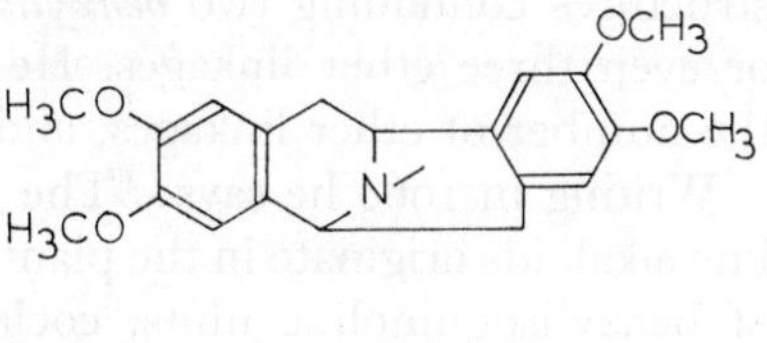

Amurensine (R+R=H+CH₃)

Amurensinine (R=R=CH₃)

N-Methyl-pavine

(Argemonine)

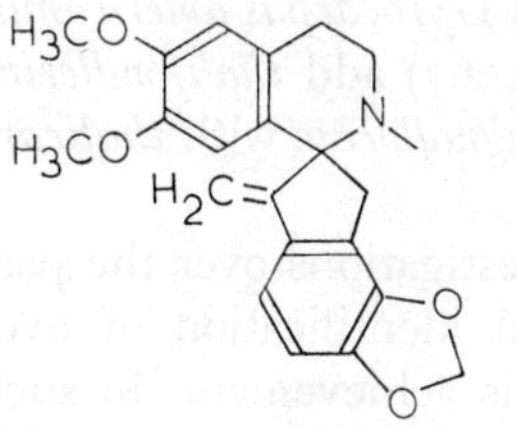

Ochotensimine

Fig. 52. Some unusual benzylisoquinoline alkaloids.

Romneine
  Papaver. Romneya coulteri v. *trichocalyx*
Sendaverine (fig. 51) is an *N-benzyl-tetrahydroisoquinoline*, included here
  for convenience.
  Papaver. Corydalis aurea
Stepharine is closely related to *crotonosine.*
  Menisperm. Stephania rotunda (tuber)
Takatonine
  Ranuncul. Thalictrum minus, thunbergii (rt)
l-(+)-Tembetarine (*N*-Methyl-*l*-(+)-reticuline)
  Laur. Phoebe porphiria
  Rut. Fagara (6)
Thalifendlerine
  Ranuncul. Thalictrum fendleri

III BISBENZYLISOQUINOLINES

GENERAL

This large series of alkaloids—more than 80 have been described—are
said by Kulka (in *M. & H.*, v.4, 1954 and in *M.*, v.7, 1960) to have

structures containing two *benzylisoquinoline* nuclei joined by one, two, or even three ether linkages. He discussed them in groups based on the number of ether linkages, and we have followed him here.

Writing in 1960 he says: 'The Faltis theory that bisbenzylisoquinoline alkaloids originate in the plant through enzymatic dehydrogenations of benzylisoquinoline units, coclaurine...or norcoclaurine...has not been disputed. Instead the theory has received support from the observation that coclaurine-type bases occur together with bisbenzylisoquinoline alkaloids in the same plant.'

As examples of this last he mentions *coclaurine* and *trilobine* in *Cocculus laurifolius* and *magnocurarine* and *phaeanthine* in *Gyrocarpus americanus.* Curcumelli-Rodostamo and Kulka (in *M.*, v.9, 1967) add *thalifendlerine* with *hernandezine* in *Thalictrum fendleri* and *magnoflorine* with *thalicarpine* in *Thalictrum dasycarpum.*

Curcumelli-Rodostamo and Kulka say: 'Investigations over the past eight years have resulted in the isolation and identification of over thirty new bisbenzylisoquinoline alkaloids. This achievement, in such a short time, can be attributed not only to increased activity in this field but also to the application of modern physical methods.'

They repeat essentially what was written about the Faltis theory by Kulka in 1960 and quoted above. They add: 'This theory has played a role in influencing researchers in their structural assignments to new alkaloids, and the assignments based on biogenetic considerations have generally proved to be correct.'

The *bisbenzylisoquinolines* are practically confined to the 'Polycarpicae' (**Magnoliales** and **Ranunculales**) (qq.v. for further discussion).

List and Occurrence

1. Alkaloids with one diphenyl ether linkage

Kulka, writing in 1954, included 4 alkaloids in this group. We can now list 13–15.

Aztequine
> *Magnoli.   Talauma mexicana* (lvs)

Berbamunine
> *Berberid.   Berberis amurensis*

Dauricine is a *dimethyl-magnoline.*
> *Menisperm.   Menispermum canadense* (rt), *dauricum* (rhiz.)

Daurinoline
> *Menisperm.   Menispermum dauricum*

Dirosine
> *Laur.   Ocotea (Nectandra) rodiei*

Foetidine (Fetidine)
  Ranuncul. *Thalictrum foetidum*
Isoliensinine
  Nymphae. *Nelumbo nucifera* (embryo)
Isorodiasine
  Laur. *Ocotea (Nectandra) rodiei*
Liensinine
  Nymphae. *Nelumbo nucifera* (embryo)
Magnolamine
  Magnoli. *Michelia fuscata* (lvs)
Magnoline (fig. 53) is one of the simplest of the *bisbenzylisoquino-lines.*
  Magnoli. *Michelia fuscata* (lvs)
Neferine
  Nymphae. *Nelumbo nucifera* (embryo)
Nor-rodiasine: has this one or two linkages?
  Laur. *Ocotea (Nectandra) rodiei*
Rodiasine: has this one or two linkages?
  Laur. *Ocotea (Nectandra) rodiei*
Thalisopine
  Ranuncul. *Thalictrum isopyroides*

2. Alkaloids with two diphenyl ether linkages

Kulka (1954) listed more than 20 alkaloids in this group. We can now list nearly 60.
Aromoline (*N*-Methyl-daphnoline; Thalicrine)
  Monimi. *Daphnandra aromatica, tenuipes*
  Ranuncul. *Thalictrum thunbergii*
Atherospermoline
  Monimi. *Atherosperma moschatum* (lvs)
Bebeerine (Buxine (2); Chondodendrine; Chondrodendrine; Curine; Pelosine)
  Laur. *Ocotea (Nectandra) rodiei* (Recent work throws doubt on this occurrence)
  Hernandi. *Hernandia ovigera*
  Menisperm. *Pleogyne, Chondrodendron* spp., *Cissampelos pareira, Tinospora*
  Bux. *Buxus sempervirens*
Berbamine is a structural isomer of *oxyacanthine.*
  Berberid. *Berberis* (13 or more); *Mahonia* (7)
  Menisperm. *Stephania* (2), *Pycnarrhena*
  Monimi. *Atherosperma moschatum*

Cepharanthine is said to be antibiotic.

> *Menisperm.* *Stephania cephalantha* (the specific name *has* been given as *cepharantha*) (rt), *sasakii* (rt)

*Chondofoline

> *Menisperm.* *Chondrodendron platyphyllum*

*d-Chondrocurine (d-Chondocurine)

> *Menisperm.* *Chondrodendron tomentosum*

l-Curine (l-Bebeerine)

> *Menisperm.* *Chondrodendron tomentosum*

Cycleanine (Methyl-isochondodendrine)

> *Menisperm.* *Cissampelos (Cyclea) insularis*; *Epinetrum cordifolium, mangenotii* (rt); *Stephania* (3); *Chondrodendron?*

Daphnandrine is related to *oxyacanthine*.

> *Monimi.* *Daphnandra micrantha* (bk), *repandula*

Daphnoline (Trilobamine?)

> *Monimi.* *Daphnandra aromatica, micrantha, repandula*
>
> *Menisperm.* *Cocculus trilobus*

Demerarine: is a diastereoisomer of *ocoteamine*?

> *Laur.* *Ocotea rodiei*

De-N-methyl-tenuipine

> *Monimi.* *Daphnandra tenuipes*

Epistephanine

> *Menisperm.* *Stephania capitata, japonica* (st.)

Fangchinoline (Menisidine is a low-melting isomorph?)

> *Menisperm.* *Cocculus trilobus* (st.); *Pericampylus glaucus*; *Stephania tetrandra, hernandifolia* (rt)

Funiferine ($C_{36}H_{40}O_6N_2$): belongs here? Manske (1968) says 'apparently not identical with either tiliacorine or with tiliarine'.

> *Menisperm.* *Tiliacora funifera* (rtbk)

Hayatidine

> *Menisperm.* *Cissampelos pareira* (rt)

Hayatine: belongs here?

> *Menisperm.* *Cissampelos pareira* (rtbk)

Hernandezine (Thaliximine)

> *Ranuncul.* *Thalictrum hernandezii* (rt), *rochbrunnianum* (rt), *fendleri*

Homoaromoline

> *Ranuncul.* *Thalictrum thunbergii*

Hypoepistephanine (Pseudo-epistephanine)

> *Menisperm.* *Stephania japonica*

---

* The genus *Chondodendron* R. & P. has been corrected by Miers to *Chondrodendron* (Airy Shaw in *W.*, 1966). Both spellings are used and the alkaloid names with and without the first 'r' may also be found.

Insulanoline (*O*-Demethyl-insularine): why is this not in group III ?
  Menisperm. Cissampelos (Cyclea) insularis (rhiz.)
Insularine
  Menisperm. Cissampelos insularis, ochiaiana; Stephania japonica
d-Isochondrodendrine (Isobebeerine)
  Menisperm. Chondrodendron (5), *Anomospermum, Cissampelos* (2),
    Pleogyne, Epinetrum (2), *Stephania hernandifolia* (rt)
  Laur. Ocotea rodiei
  Bux. Buxus sempervirens
d-Isochondrodendrine-dimethyl ether
  Menisperm. Chondrodendron
Isotetrandrine (*O*-Methyl-berbamine; Ambaline and Ambalinine were
  impure *isotetrandrine*?) is an optical isomer of *tetrandrine*
  Berberid. Berberis (5); *Mahonia* (4)
  *Menisperm. Cocculus diversifolius, japonicus; Pycnarrhena manil-
    lensis*?; *Sinomenium*?; *Stephania cephalantha, tetrandra*
  Monimi. Atherosperma moschatum
Neoprotocuridine: differs from *isochondrodendrine* only in the orientation
  of the phenolic and methoxyl groups ? It has been found in *curare*.
Norcycleanine
  *Menisperm. Chondrodendron tomentosum; Cissampelos (Cyclea)
    insularis* (rhiz.); *Epinetrum cordifolium* (rt), *mangenotii* (rt)
Nortenuipine
  Occurrence ?
Obamegine (Stepholine)
  Ranuncul. Thalictrum rugosum
  Berberid. Berberis tschonoskyana
  Menisperm. Stephania japonica
Ocodemerine: is a diastereoisomer of *otocamine* ?
  Laur. Ocotea rodiei
Ocoteamine is a methyl ether of *trilobamine (daphnoline* ?).
  Laur. Ocotea rodiei
Ocotine: belongs here ? Its structure is not yet known (1967).
  Laur. Ocotea rodiei (bk)
O-Methyl-oxyacanthine (Obaberine)
  Berberid. Berberis tschonoskyana
O-Methyl-repandine
  Monimi. Daphnandra dielsii, repandula
O-Methyl-thalicberine (Thalmidine ?)
  Ranuncul. Thalictrum minus, thunbergii (lvs, sd)
O-Methyl-thalmethine
  Ranuncul. Thalictrum minus var. (plt)
Otocamine: is this *Ocoteamine* ?

Oxyacanthine (fig 53.)

    Berberid.   *Berberis* (many); *Mahonia* (many)

    Magnoli.   *Michelia compressa*

Phaeantharine (fig. 53) is 'unique among bisbenzylisoquinoline alkaloids in that both isoquinoline rings are aromatized'.

    Annon.   *Phaeanthus ebracteolatus*

Phaeanthine (Pheanthine)

    Annon.   *Phaeanthus ebracteolatus*

    Hernandi.   *Gyrocarpus americanus* (lvs, bk), *jacquinii* (lvs, bk)

Protocuridine differs from *isochondrodendrine* only in the orientation of the phenolic and methoxyl groups. It has been found in *curare*.

Pycnamine is a diastereomer of *berbamine*.

    Menisperm.   *Pycnarrhena manillensis*

    Hernandi.   *Gyrocarpus jacquinii* (bk, lf)

Repandine is an optical isomer of *oxyacanthine*, and may be an artefact arising from it.

    Berberid.   *Berberis*?

    Monimi.   *Daphnandra repandula*

Repandinine: the racemic form of *tenuipine*?

    Monimi.   *Daphnandra dielsii, repandula*

Repanduline

    Monimi.   *Daphnandra dielsii, repandula, tenuipes*

Sepeerine

    Laur.   *Ocotea rodiei* (bk)

    Menisperm.   *Cissampelos pareira* (rt)

Stebisimine (*N*-Nor-1,2-dehydro-epistephanine)

    Menisperm.   *Stephania rotunda* (*japonica*)

Tenuipine

    Monimi.   *Daphnandra dielsii, tenuipes*

Tetrandrine is a diastereoisomer of *isotetrandrine*. *Menisine*: a low-melting isomorph?

    Magnoli.   *Michelia fuscata*

    Menisperm.   *Cocculus* (*Sinomenium*?) spp.; *Cyclea peltata* (*burmanni*); *Menispermum dauricum*; *Stephania cephalantha, tetrandra, hernandifolia* (*d*- and *dl*-, rt); *Pericampylus glaucus*

Thalfoetidine

    Ranuncul.   *Thalictrum foetidum*

Thalicberine

    Ranuncul.   *Thalictrum thunbergii* (lvs, sd)

Thalmethine

    Ranuncul.   *Thalictrum minus* var. (plt)

Thalmine

    Ranuncul.   *Thalictrum minus* (plt)

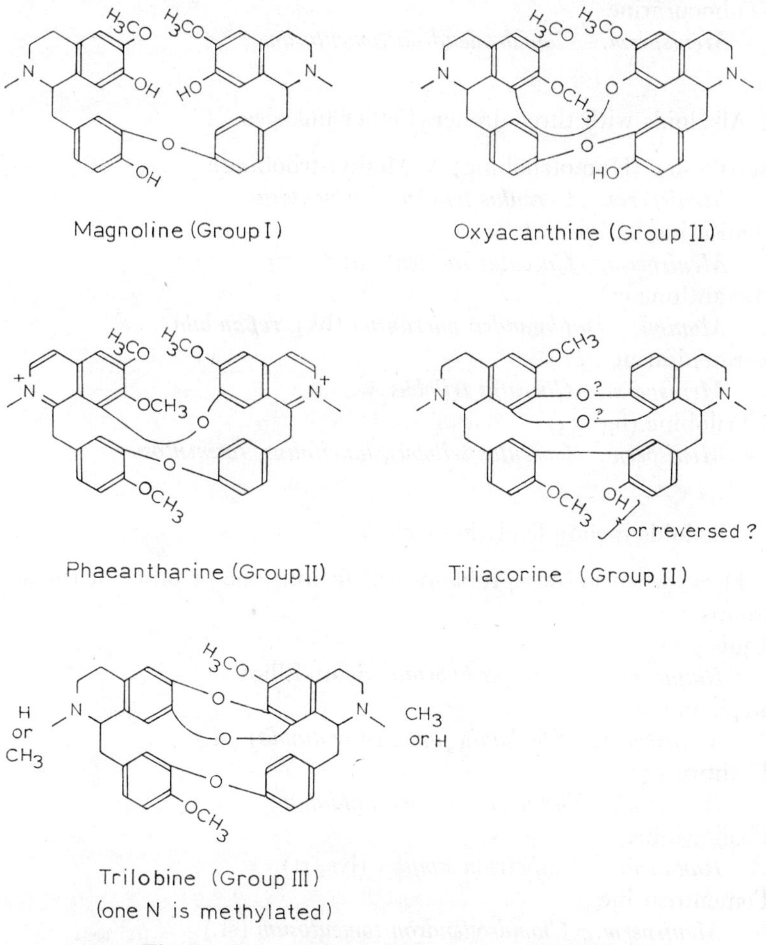

Fig. 53. Some bisbenzylisoquinoline alkaloids.

Thalsimine
    Ranuncul.   *Thalictrum simplex*
Tiliacorine (fig. 53). This alkaloid and *tiliarine* '...are the only known
    bisbenzylisoquinoline alkaloids containing a diphenyl grouping', say
    Curcumelli-Rodostamo and Kulka (1967), but Grundon (1964) says
    that *rodiasine* also has a diphenyl linkage.
    Menisperm.   *Tiliacora racemosa* (bk, rt)
Tiliarine
    Menisperm.   *Tiliacora racemosa* (rt)
d-Tubocurarine
    Menisperm.   *Chondrodendron tomentosum*

l-Tubocurarine
  Menisperm.   Chondrodendron tomentosum

3. Alkaloids with three diphenyl ether linkages

Isotrilobine (Homotrilobine; *N*-Methyl-trilobine)
  Menisperm.   Cocculus trilobus, sarmentosus
Menisarine
  Menisperm.   Cocculus sarmentosus
Micranthine (1)
  Monimi.   Daphnandra micrantha (bk), *repandula*
Normenisarine
  Menisperm.   Cocculus trilobus
d-Trilobine (fig. 53)
  Menisperm.   Cocculus trilobus, laurifolius, sarmentosus

4. Alkaloids incompletely known?

These when known probably will fit into one or other of the above groups.
Aquilegine
  Ranuncul.   Aquilegia hybrida 'Scott-Elliott'
Stephanoline
  Menisperm.   Stephania japonica (*rotunda*) (st.)
Thalibrunine
  Ranuncul.   Thalictrum rochebrunnianum
Thalictrinine
  Ranuncul.   Thalictrum simplex (lvs, rt)
Tomentocurine
  Menisperm.   Chondrodendron tomentosum (st.)

IV THE APORPHINE GROUP

GENERAL

The *aporphines*, says Bentley (1965): '...arise naturally by oxidation of phenols of the benzyl-tetrahydro [iso]-quinoline series...'.

Shamma (1967) has written a new account of this group of alkaloids. He says that 20 new *aporphine alkaloids* have been added since he and Slusarchyk reviewed them in 1964! Shamma uses the numbering shown in fig. 54.

An interesting group of '*pro-aporphines*' includes *crotonosine*, *pronuciferine*, etc. We have dealt with these as *1,1'-benzyl-isoquinolines* (qq.v.).

Hegnauer (in Swain, 1963) thinks that the alkaloids of the *Aristolochiaceae* may be related biogenetically to the *aporphines*. We have included them here.

It will be evident from the following list that the distribution of the aporphine alkaloids is of considerable taxonomic interest. We may note the following points here:

(*a*) Five families (*Magnoli.*, *Annon.*, *Monimi.*, *Laur.*, and *Hernandi.*) of the **Magnoliales** have between them many aporphine alkaloids.

(*b*) Four families (*Ranuncul.*, *Berberid.*, *Menisperm.*, and *Nymphae.*) of the **Ranunculales** have between them many aporphine alkaloids.

(*c*) Ten aporphine alkaloids (*Glaucine*, *magnoflorine*, *thalicmine*, *domesticine*, *isoboldine*, *nantenine*, *dicentrine*, *isocorydine*, *isocorydine methiodide*, and *anonaine*) are said to occur in both the **Magnoliales** and **Ranunculales**.

(*d*) Occurrence outside these two orders is comparatively rare, but they are found in *Aristolochiaceae* (*Aristolochia*, *Bragantia*), a family which some believe to be close to the above orders (p. 1584). They are numerous in the *Papaveraceae*, which, too, are not far removed from the **Ranunculales**. Many of them are found in the *Rutaceae*, a family which is able to synthesize many types of alkaloids (p. 140).

In the *Euphorbiaceae* only the genus *Croton* is known to have aporphines (*magnoflorine*, *sparsiflorine*). *Croton* also has *1,1'-benzyl-isoquinolines* ('pro-aporphines'). A single genus of the *Rhamnaceae*, *Phylica*, has *isocorydine* and *N-methyl-laurotetanine*.

Finally there are said to be at least two aporphines—*caaverine* and *isoboldine*—in *Symplocos celastrinea* (*Symplocaceae*).

List and Occurrence

Actinodaphnine (Nor-cassythicine)
>   *Laur.*   *Actinodaphne hookeri*; *Cassytha melantha*; *Laurus nobilis*?; *Notaphoebe* sp.

Anolobine
>   *Annon.*   *Asimina* (*Annona*) *triloba*

Anonaine
>   *Annon.*   *Annona* spp.
>   *Nymphae.*   *Nelumbo nucifera* (cotyledons)

Aristidinic acid ($C_{18}H_{13}O_7N$): belongs here?
>   *Aristolochi.*   *Aristolochia argentina* (rt)

Aristinic acid ($C_{18}H_{13}O_7N$): belongs here?
>   *Aristolochi.*   *Aristolochia argentina* (rt)

Aristolic acid ($C_{15}H_{11}O_7N$): belongs here?
  Aristolochi. Aristolochia argentina (rt)
Aristolochic acid-I (Aristolochine; Iso-aristolochic acid)
  Aristolochi. Aristolochia (12 or more species), *Bragantia wallichii*
Aristolochic acid-II (Demethoxy-aristolochic acid-I)
  Aristolochi. Aristolochia clematitis
Aristolochic acid-III
  Aristolochi. Aristolochia clematitis
Aristolochic acid-IIIa (Demethyl-aristolochic acid-III)
  Aristolochi. Aristolochia clematitis
Aristolochic acid-IV
  Aristolochi. Aristolochia clematitis
Aristolochic acid-IVa
  Aristolochi. Aristolochia clematitis
Artabotrinine (*O*-Methyl-anolobine?)
  Annon. Artabotrys suaveolens; Asimina triloba
Asimilobine
  Annon. Asimina triloba (wd, rt)
Atheroline
  Monimi. Atherosperma moschatum
Atherospermidine
  Monimi. Atherosperma moschatum (bk)
  Annon. Guatteria psilopus
Atherosperminine is a near-aporphine.
  Monimi. Atherosperma moschatum
Boldine
  Monimi. Peumus boldus
  Laur. Litsea?; Neolitsea sericea (bk)
Bulbocapnine
  Papaver. Corydalis bulbosa and 4 other spp.; *Dicentra* (2)
Caaverine
  Symploc. Symplocos celastrinea (bk)
Cassyfiline (Cassythine)
  Laur. Cassytha filiformis (st.)
Cassythicine
  Laur. Cassytha glabella, melantha
Cassythidine
  Laur. Cassytha filiformis
Catalpifoline
  Hernandi. Hernandia catalpifolia
Corydine (Glaucentrine)
  Papaver. Corydalis (5), *Dactylicapnos* (1), *Dicentra* (4), *Glaucium*
  (7)

Corytuberine
>   *Papaver.* *Corydalis tuberosa* and 2 other spp., *Dactylicapnos* (1),
>   *Dicentra* (2), *Dicranostigma* (1), *Glaucium* (1), *Papaver somniferum*

Crebanine
>   *Menisperm.* *Stephania capitata, sasakii*

Dicentrine (Eximine)
>   *Laur.* *Ocotea leucoxylon*
>   *Menisperm.* *Stephania capitata*
>   *Papaver.* *Dicentra eximia* (rt) and 2 other spp., *Dactylicapnos* (1)

1,10-Dihydroxy-2-methoxy-aporphine
>   *Laur.* *Ocotea glaziovii* (lvs)

3,4-Dimethoxy-1-(dimethylaminoethyl)-phenanthrene is a near-aporphine which may be included here.
>   *Laur.* *Cryptocarya* (2)

Diversine
>   *Menisperm.* *Cocculus diversifolius* (rt), *Sinomenium acutum*

Domesticine (Epidicentrine)
>   *Berberid.* *Nandina domestica*
>   *Laur.* *Cassytha pubescens*
>   *Papaver.* *Glaucium oxylobum*

Glaucine (fig. 54): the natural base is the *d*-form.
>   *Magnoli.* *Liriodendron tulipiferum* (wd)
>   *Ranuncul.* *Thalictrum minus* (sds)
>   *Papaver.* *Corydalis* (2), *Dactylicapnos* (1), *Dicentra* (2), *Glaucium*
>   (4), *Papaver* (1)

Guatterine
>   *Annon.* *Guatteria psilopus*

Hernandaline (fig. 54) is 'intermediate between aporphines and benzyl-isoquinoline-aporphine dimers...' (Shamma, 1967).
>   *Hernandi.* *Hernandia ovigera*

Hernovine
>   *Hernandi.* *Hernandia ovigera*

10-Hydroxy-1,2-methylenedioxy-aporphine
>   *Laur.* *Phoebe clemensii* (lvs)

Isoboldine
>   *Laur.* *Cassytha pubescens*
>   *Berberid.* *Nandina domestica*
>   *Menisperm.* *Cocculus trilobus* (lvs)
>   *Papaver.* *Papaver somniferum*
>   *Symploc.* *Symplocos celastrinea*

Isocorydine (Artabotrine; Luteanine; fig. 54) is a very widely distributed aporphine. I have records of it in
>   *Monimi.* *Atherosperma, Peumus*

Annon.   Artabotrys suaveolens, Asimina triloba
Laur.   Cryptocarya (2)?
Menisperm.   Legnephora moorei (Cocculus?)
Papaver.   Corydalis (5), *Dicentra* (2), *Dicranostigma* (1), *Glaucium*
  (3), *Papaver* (1), *Stylophorum* (1)
Rut.   Zanthoxylum (2)
Rhamn.   Phylica rogersii
Lili.   Camptorrhiza strumosa (all pts)
Isocorydine chloromethylate (Chakranine)
  Aristolochi.   Bragantia wallichii (rt)
Isocorydine methiodide
  Menisperm.   Menispermum dauricum
  Laur.   Cryptocarya (2)
Isothebaine
  Papaver.   Papaver (2)
Launobine (Norbulbocapnine)
  Laur.   Laurus nobilis (bk, wd)
Laureline
  Monimi.   Laurelia novae-zelandiae (bk)
Laurelliptine
  Laur.   Beilschmiedia elliptica, Cassytha pubescens
Laurepukine
  Monimi.   Laurelia novae-zelandiae (bk)
Laurifoline
  Menisperm.   Cocculus laurifolius
  Rut.   Zanthoxylum (Fagara) ailanthoides, elephantiasis; Fagara (3)
Laurolitsine
  Laur.   Cinnamomum camphora (rt), *Litsea japonica* (rt, bk, wd),
    Neolitsea sericea (lvs), *Phoebe clemensii*
Laurotetanine (fig. 54)
  Monimi.   Palmeria fengeriana
  Laur.   Actinodaphne (1), *Cassytha* (1), *Cryptocarya* (1), *Litsea* (9),
    Neolitsea (1), *Notaphoebe* (1), *Tetranthera (Litsea)* (1)
  Hernandi.   Illigera pulchra
Lindcarpine
  Laur.   Lindera pipericarpa (rt)
Liriodendron alkaloid (name?) is a tetramethoxy compound corres-
  ponding to *liriodenine*
  Magnoli.   Liriodendron tulipifera (htwd)
Liriodenine (Micheline-B; Oxo-ushinsunine; fig. 54)
  Magnoli.   Liriodendron tulipifera (htwd); *Michelia champaca* (bk),
    compressa v. *formosana* (wd); *Magnolia coco*
  Monimi.   Doryphora sassafras (lvs)

    Annon.   Asimina triloba
Magnoflorine (fig. 54). 'This is definitely the most widely distributed
  aporphine' (Shamma, 1967). I have records of it from
    Ranuncul.   Aconitum, Adonis, Aquilegia (2), *Coptis* (1), *Delphinium,*
      Nigella, Thalictrum (3), *Trollius, Xanthorrhiza* (1)
    Magnoli.   Magnolia (4), *Michelia* (1)
    Berberid.   Berberis (4), *Caulophyllum* (1), *Epimedium* (2), *Nandina*
      (1), *Mahonia* (3)
    Menisperm.   Cocculus (2), *Cissampelos (Cyclea)* (1), *Sinomenium* (1)
    Aristolochi.   Aristolochia (2)
    Papaver.   Glaucium flavum, Papaver somniferum
    Euphorbi.   Croton cumingii
    Rut.   Fagara (6), *Phellodendron* (1), *Zanthoxylum* (2)
Mecambroline (Isofugapavine; Isofungipavine; free base of Miche-
  pressine?)
    Papaver.   Meconopsis cambrica, Papaver caucasicum
Menisperine
    Menisperm.   Menispermum dauricum (rhiz.)
    Berberid.   Nandina domestica (st.)
Methoxy-atherosperminine is a near-aporphine.
    Monimi.   Atherosperma moschatum
(−)-5-Methoxy-6-hydroxy-aporphine
    Nymphae.   Nelumbo nucifera (cotyledons)
Micheline-A
    Magnoli.   Michelia compressa v. *formosana* (wd)
Michepressine: belongs here?
    Occurrence?
Moschatoline
    Monimi.   Atherosperma moschatum
Muricine: belongs here?
    Annon.   Annona muricata
Muricinine: belongs here?
    Annon.   Annona muricata
Nandigerine
    Hernandi.   Hernandia ovigera
Nantenine (Domestine)
    Laur.   Cassytha pubescens, racemosa
    Berberid.   Nandina domestica
    Papaver.   Corydalis tuberosa, Glaucium oxylobum
Neolitsine
    Laur.   Neolitsea pulchella
N-Methyl-actinodaphnine
    Laur.   Neolitsea sericea (bk)

9

(+)-*N*-Methyl-corydine
    Rut. Fagara nigrescens (bk)
N-Methyl-corydinium cation
    Rut. Fagara nigrescens (bk)
N-Methyl-isocorydine
    Laur. Cryptocarya angulata (bk)
    Rut. Fagara coco (bk) and 3 other spp.; *Zanthoxylum* (2) (bk)
N-Methyl-isocorydinium cation
    Rut. Fagara pterota, rhoifolia
N-Methyl-laurotetanine (Rogersine)
    Laur. Litsea (1), *Tetranthera* (1)
    Monimi. Palmeria fengeriana, Peumus boldus
    Papaver. Eschscholtzia californica
    Rhamn. Phylica rogersii
N-Methyl-nandigerine
    Hernandi. Hernandia ovigera
N-Methyl-ovigerine
    Hernandi. Hernandia ovigera
(−)-*N*-Nor-nuciferine
    Nymphae. Nelumbo pentapetala (*lutea*)
Nor-domesticine
    Laur. Cassytha pubescens
Nor-isocorydine
    Monimi. Peumus boldus (lvs)
Nor-ushinsunine
    Annon. Asimina triloba
(−)-Nuciferine
    Nymphae. Nelumbo pentapetala (*lutea*), *nucifera* (*speciosa*) (lvs, cot.)
    Papaver. Papaver caucasicum
(−)-Nuciferoline
    Papaver. Papaver caucasicum
Ovigerine
    Hernandi. Hernandia ovigera
Phanostenine
    Menisperm. Stephania (2)
Preocoteine
    Ranuncul. Thalictrum fendleri
Protostephanine: belongs here?
    Menisperm. Stephania japonica (st.)
Pukateine
    Monimi. Laurelia novae-zelandiae (bk)
Quaternary aporphine of Fagara tinguassoiba
    Rut. Fagara tinguassoiba, rhoifolia

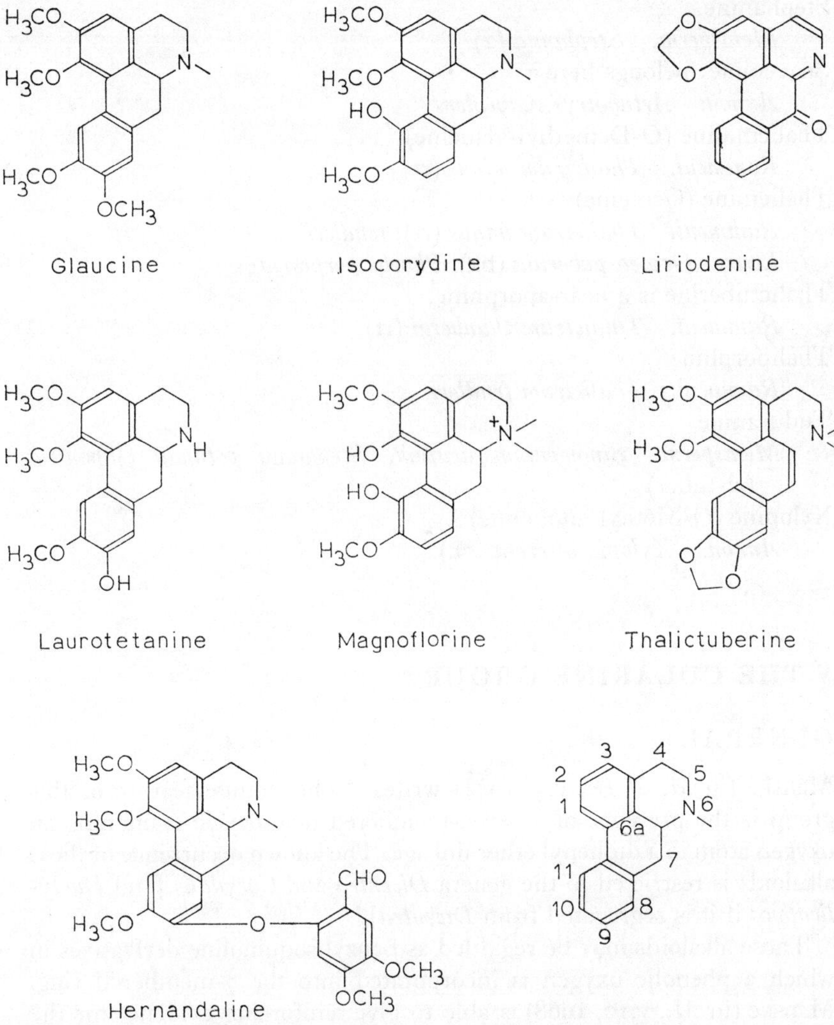

Glaucine   Isocorydine   Liriodenine

Laurotetanine   Magnoflorine   Thalictuberine

Hernandaline

Fig. 54. Some aporphine and near-aporphine alkaloids.

(+)-Roemerine (Aporheine)—the (+) is not always present in the records.

Laur. Cryptocarya (2), *Neolitsea* (1)

Nymphae. Nelumbo nucifera

Papaver. Roemeria refracta; Papaver feddei, caucasicum (+), *dubium* (+), *fugax* (+)

Sparsiflorine

Euphorbi. Croton sparsiflorus (lvs)

9-2

Stephanine
>   Menisperm.   Stephania (2)
Suaveoline: belongs here?
>   Annon.   Artabotrys suaveolens
Thalicmidine (O-Demethyl-glaucine)
>   Ranuncul.   Thalictrum minus (rt)
Thalicmine (Ocoteine)
>   Ranuncul.   Thalictrum minus (rt), fendleri
>   Laur.   Ocotea puberula (bk), Phoebe porphiria
Thalictuberine is a near-aporphine.
>   Ranuncul.   Thalictrum thunbergi (rt)
Thaliporphine
>   Ranuncul.   Thalictrum fendleri
Tuduranine
>   Menisperm.   Sinomenium acutum, Stephania rotunda (japonica)
>   (rt-tuber)
Xylopine (O-Methyl-anolobine)
>   Annon.   Xylopia discreta (bk)

V THE CULARINE GROUP

GENERAL

Manske (in *M. & H.*, v.4, 1954) writes: 'The unique feature of this group is the presence of a seven-membered heterocycle containing an oxygen atom in a diphenyl ether linkage. The known occurrence of these alkaloids is restricted to the genera *Dicentra* and *Corydalis* [and *Dactylicapnos* if it is segregated from *Dicentra*].'

These alkaloids may be regarded as benzylisoquinoline derivatives in which a phenolic oxygen is incorporated into the 7-membered ring. Manske (in *M.*, v.10, 1968) is able to give reinforcing evidence for the structures proposed earlier.

List and Occurrence

Cularicine (fig. 55)
>   Papaver.   Corydalis claviculata
Cularidine (fig. 55)
>   Papaver.   Corydalis claviculata, Dicentra cucullaria
Cularimine
>   Papaver.   Dicentra eximia

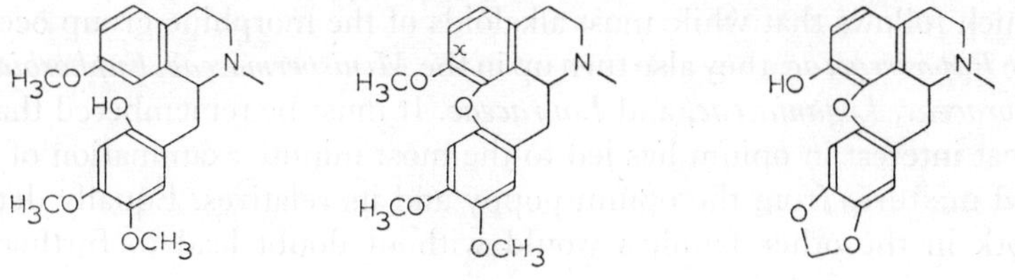

| A benzylisoquinoline | Cūlarine | Cularicine |

(Cularidine has

—OH at x)

Fig. 55. Cularine alkaloids and a possible parent.

Cularine (fig. 55)

Papaver. Corydalis claviculata (a major alkaloid); *Dactylicapnos macrocapnos*; *Dicentra cucullaria, eximia, oregona*

VI THE MORPHINE GROUP

GENERAL

Henry (1949) listed six alkaloids known from opium (from *Papaver somniferum*) as of this type—*morphine, codeine, neopine, pseudomorphine, thebaine* and *porphyroxine* (we have placed the last with the *papaver-rubines*). Recent work has increased our knowledge of this group.

A most interesting paper by Kirby (1967) deals with the biosynthesis of the *morphine alkaloids*. Kirby concludes that:

Tracer experiments, supported throughout by the analogous chemical transformations, have firmly established the biosynthetic sequence tyrosine → norlaudanosoline → reticuline → salutaridine → salutaridinol-I → thebaine → codeine → morphine in *Papaver somniferum*. In general, the further a precursor lies along this sequence, the more efficient its conversion to morphine in the intact plant...[but] Proof that morphine is made only by the reticuline-salutaridine route is still lacking.

He points out that it has been shown that the latex of *Papaver somniferum* is capable of transforming *tyrosine* into *morphine*, and says: 'Perhaps further work with opium latex will provide the key to the remaining problems of morphine biosynthesis.'

In fig. 56 we give the formulae of those of the compounds named above that have been found in *Papaver*. It will be seen from the list which follows that while most alkaloids of the morphine group occur in the *Papaveraceae*, they also turn up in the *Menispermaceae*, *Euphorbiaceae*, *Moraceae*, *Loganiaceae*, and *Lauraceae*. It must be remembered that the great interest in opium has led to the most minute examination of alkaloid mixtures from the opium poppy and its relatives. Equally detailed work in the other families would without doubt lead to further discoveries in this field.

List and Occurrence

Amurine
> *Papaver.   Papaver feddei, nudicaule* var. *amurense* and other vars.

Codeine (fig. 56)
> *Mor.   Humulus lupulus*
> *Papaver.   Argemone mexicana*; *Eschscholtzia mexicana*; *Papaver paeoniflorum, somniferum* (lvs)

Disinomenine seems to be a *morphine-dimer* which may be an artefact resulting from aerial oxidation of *sinomenine*.
> *Menisperm.   Sinomenium acutum* (rt)

Flavinine closely resembles *salutaridine*.
> *Euphorbi.   Croton flavens*

Hasubanonine
> *Menisperm.   Stephania rotunda* (*japonica*) (tuber)

Homostephanoline (fig. 56) is a near-morphine alkaloid.
> *Menisperm.   Stephania rotunda* (*japonica*) (tuber)

Isosinomenine is closely related to *salutaridine*.
> *Menisperm.   Sinomenium acutum* (plt)

Isothebaine
> *Papaver.   Papaver bracteatum* (young frt), *orientale*

Metaphanine (fig. 56) is a near-morphine alkaloid.
> *Menisperm.   Stephania abyssinica, rotunda* (*japonica*) (tuber)

Morphine (fig. 56) is the chief alkaloid of opium.
> *Mor.   Humulus lupulus*
> *Papaver.   Argemone mexicana*; *Eschscholtzia mexicana*; *Papaver rhoeas, setigerum* (frt), *somniferum* (lvs, frt)

Neopine (β-Codeine)
> *Papaver.   Papaver somniferum*

Nor-sinoacutine is a 'morphine-precursor'.
> *Euphorbi.   Croton balsamifera*

Nudaurine
> *Papaver.   Papaver nudicaule* var. *aurantiacum*

Oripavine
> *Papaver.   Papaver bracteatum, floribundum, orientale*

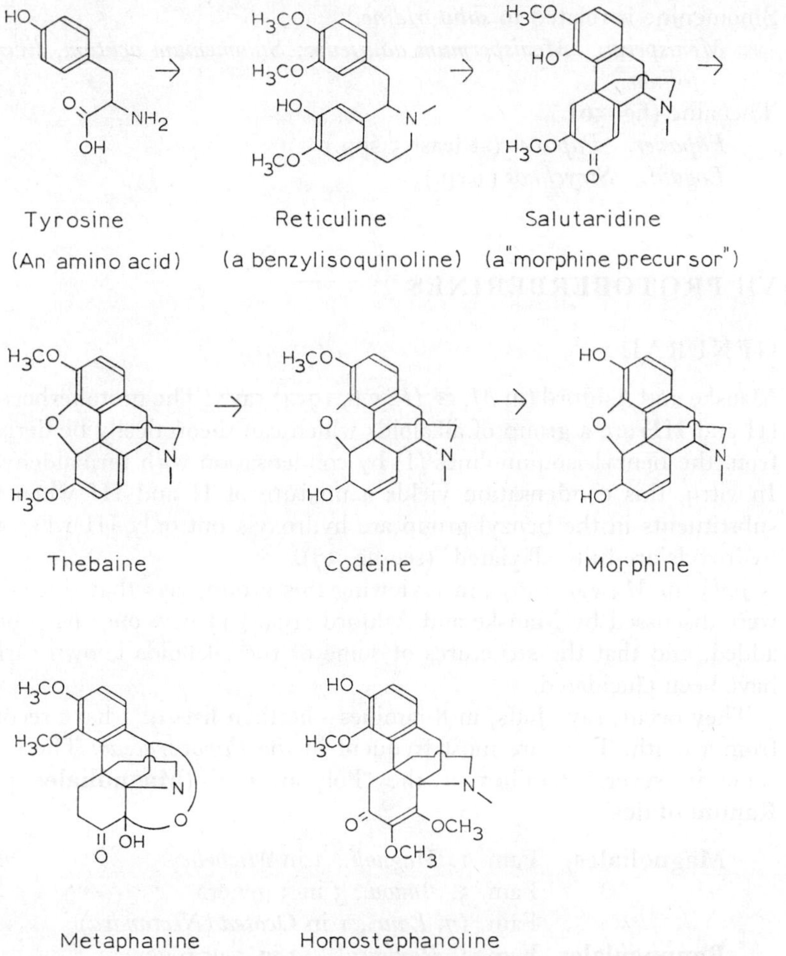

Tyrosine

(An amino acid)

Reticuline

(a benzylisoquinoline)

Salutaridine

(a "morphine precursor")

Thebaine

Codeine

Morphine

Metaphanine

Homostephanoline

Fig. 56. Some steps in the biosynthesis of morphine (above, after Kirby, 1967) and some morphine alkaloids.

Pseudomorphine (Dehydro-morphine; Oxydimorphine; Oxymorphine) is a dimer.

   Papaver.   *Papaver somniferum*

Salutaridine (fig. 56) has been called a 'morphine-precursor'. It is an intermediate in the biosynthesis of *morphine alkaloids*.

   Papaver.   *Papaver bracteatum, orientale*

   Euphorbi.   *Croton balsamifera* (plt), *salutaris*

Sinoacutine is an optical isomer of *salutaridine*.

   Laur.   *Cassytha pubescens*

   Menisperm.   *Sinomenium acutum*

Sinomenine is related to *salutaridine*.

> *Menisperm.   Menispermum dauricum*; *Sinomenium acutum, diversi-folium*

Thebaine (fig. 56)

> *Papaver.   Papaver* (at least 5 spp.)
> *Logani.   Strychnos* (1 sp.)

VII **PROTOBERBERINES**

GENERAL

Manske and Ashford (in *M. & H.*, v.6, 1954) say: 'The protoberberines (II and III) are a group of alkaloids which can theoretically be derived from the benzyl-isoquinolines (I) by condensation with formaldehyde. In vitro, this condensation yields a mixture of II and III when the substituents in the benzyl group are hydroxyls but only III when the hydroxyls are fully alkylated' (see fig. 57).

Jeffs (in *M.*, v.9, 1967), in reviewing this group, says that since they were discussed by Manske and Ashford (1954) 13 new ones have been added, and that the structures of some of the alkaloids known earlier have been elucidated.

They occur, says Jeffs, in 8 families—he then lists 9! I have records from a tenth. They are most frequent in the *Papaveraceae*. There are some in several families of the 'Polycarpicae' (**Magnoliales** plus **Ranunculales**):

> **Magnoliales**,   Fam. 1. *Magnoli.*, 3 in *Michelia*
> Fam. 5. *Annon.*, 5 in 3 genera
> Fam. 17. *Laur.*, 1 in *Ocotea* (*Nectandra*)
> **Ranunculales**,   Fam. 1. *Ranuncul.*, 12 in 5 or 6 genera
> Fam. 2. *Berberid.*, 11 in 4 or 5 genera
> Fam. 5. *Menisperm.*, 9 in 13 genera

In addition they have been recorded from *Aristolochiaceae* (related to the 'Polycarpicae'), *Rutaceae*, and *Convolvulaceae*.

List and Occurrence

Alborine may be an artefact arising from *mecambridine*.

> *Papaver.   Papaver alboroseum*

Berberastine (5-Hydroxy-berberine)

> *Ranuncul.   Hydrastis canadensis*

Berberine (Umbellatine; fig. 58) was described by Henry (1949) as 'probably the most widely distributed alkaloid'. I should query this, since its distribution is mostly in nearly related families.

Magnoli. Michelia compressa

Annon. Xylopia polycarpa

Laur. Nectandra rodiaei

Ranuncul. Aquilegia?, Caltha, Coptis (4), *Hydrastis* (2), *Thalictrum* (at least 5)

Berberid. Berberis (many), *Jeffersonia?, Mahonia* (many), *Nandina, Podophyllum*

Menisperm. Anomospermum, Archangelisia, Coscinium (2), *Menispermum, Tinospora*

Papaver. Argemone (4), *Chelidonium majus, Corydalis* (2), *Dicranostigma, Glaucium* (3), *Hunnemannia, Macleaya, Papaver*

Rut. Evodia, Fagara, Phellodendron (3), *Toddalia, Zanthoxylum*

Berberubine: belongs here?

Berberid. Berberis hauniensis, vulgaris (rt)

(−)-Bis,*O,O′*-didemethyl-tetrahydro-palmatine

Papaver. Hunnemannia fumariaefolia

Bractavine: belongs here?

Papaver. Papaver bracteatum (young frt)

Burasaine: occurs, like the nearly related *palmatine*, as the nitrate?

Menisperm. Burasaia madagascariensis (wd)

(−)-Capaurimine

Papaver. Corydalis montana, pallida

Capaurine (Capauridine is *dl-*)

Papaver. Corydalis aurea and 3 other spp. (all *dl-* ?)

Cheilanthifoline

Papaver. Corydalis cheilanthifolia and 2 others

Columbamine (fig. 58) is isomeric with *jatrorrhizine.*

Ranuncul. Coptis japonica

Berberid. Berberis (4 or more spp.)

Menisperm. Archangelisia flava, Burasaia madagascariensis, Jateorhiza palmata

Coptisine

Ranuncul. Coptis japonica, teeta

Papaver. Argemone (3), *Bocconia, Chelidonium, Corydalis* (2), *Dicentra, Dicranostigma* (2), *Eschscholtzia, Glaucium* (2), *Hunnemannia, Hypecoum* (2), *Macleaya, Meconopsis, Papaver* (10), *Platystemon, Stylophorum*

Coramine is a *tetrahydro-protoberberine.*

Papaver. Corydalis pseudoadunca

Coreximine

Annon. Asimina triloba

Ranuncul.   Coptis japonica
Papaver.   Corydalis cava, Dicentra eximia
Corybulbine
Papaver.   Corydalis (4), Dicentra (2)
Corydaline: occurs only in the d-form?
Papaver.   Corydalis (10), Dicentra (2), Fumaria officinalis?
Corydalmine: is of uncertain structure?
Papaver.   Corydalis ambigua, sp.
Corypalmine (Tetrahydro-jatrorrhizine is the dl-form)
Papaver.   Corydalis (9), Dicentra (1)
Corysamine
Papaver.   Corydalis incisa, Hunnemannia fumariaefolia
Cyclanoline
Menisperm.   Cissampelos (Cyclea) insularis, Stephania japonica
Aristolochi.   Aristolochia debilis
Dehydro-corydaline
Berberid.   Berberis floribunda
Papaver.   Corydalis (6)
Dehydro-corydalmine
Papaver.   Corydalis sp.
Dihydro-berberine (Deoxy-berberine; Lambertine)
Berberid.   Berberis lambertii (rt), thunbergii
*Discretamine (Descretamine) is a bisdemethyl-(−)-tetrahydro-palmatine, isomeric with (−)-scoulerine.
Annon.   Xylopia discreta (bk)
*Discretine (Descretine; 3-O-Demethyl-(−)-nor-coralydine)
Annon.   Xylopia discreta (bk)
*Discretinine   (Descretinine;   9(or 10)-O-Demethyl-(−)-tetrahydro-palmatine)
Annon.   Xylopia discreta (bk)
Epiberberine
Berberid.   Berberis floribunda (rt)
Hydroxy-berberine
Berberid.   Berberis amurensis (st.)
Isocorybulbine
Papaver.   Corydalis (3)
Isocorypalmine: the (±)- form is (−)-tetrahydrocolumbamine?, the (−)- form is casealutine?
Papaver.   Corydalis caseana, lutea, and 5 other spp.; Papaver somniferum

---

* Jeffs (in M., v.9, 1967) has descretamine, etc. I find no authority for Xylopia descreta. It is Xylopia discreta, hence discretamine, etc.

Jatrorrhizine (Jateorhizine) is isomeric with *columbamine*. It *may* be identical with *neprotine*.

Magnoli. *Michelia compressa*

Ranuncul. *Coptis, Thalictrum* (3), *Xanthorrhiza*

Berberid. *Berberis* (8 or more spp.), *Mahonia* (5), *Nandina*

Menisperm. *Archangelisia, Burasaia, Coscinium* (2), *Fibraurea, Jateorhiza*

Rut. *Phellodendron amurense* and vars.

Mecrambridine (Oreophiline)

Papaver. *Meconopsis cambrica, Papaver oreophilum* and several other spp.

Nandinine occurs as a molecular compound of ($+$)- and ($\pm$)- forms?

Berberid. *Nandina*

($-$)-*N*-Methyl-tetrahydroberberine chloride (α-*l*-Canadine methochloride?)

Ranuncul. *Hydrastis*

Papaver. *Corydalis*?

Rut. *Zanthoxylum brachyacanthum*?, *veneficum*

Ophiocarpine is said to represent 'the first oxidation step along the assumed biosynthetic pathway from tetrahydroberberine to hydrastine'.

Papaver. *Corydalis ophiocarpa*

Oxyberberine (Berlambine)

Berberid. *Berberis lambertii* and 4 other spp.; *Mahonia limariifolia, morrisonensis*

Palmatine (Calystegine; Gindarinine) is widely distributed.

Magnoli. *Michelia compressa*

Annon. *Enantia chlorantha, polycarpa*

Ranuncul. *Coptis, Thalictrum*

Berberid. *Berberis* (5 or so), *Mahonia* (4)

Menisperm. *Burasaia* (as nitrate in wd?), *Cocculus, Coscinium, Fibraurea, Jateorhiza palmata, Parabaena* (*Aspidocarya*), *Tinospora*

Papaver. *Corydalis, Papaver* (2)

Rut. *Fagara coco* (bk), *Phellodendron* (3?)

Convolvul. *Calystegia hydraceae*

Phellodendrine

Rut. *Phellodendron amurense* and vars.

Scoulerine occurs in ($+$)- and ($-$)-forms and as a molecular compound of ($\pm$)- and ($-$)-forms ('*aurotensine*').

Papaver. *Corydalis aurea, ochotensis* and at least 2 other spp.; *Fumaria officinalis*; *Glaucium* (3); *Hunnemannia fumariaefolia* (?) all have '*auretensine*'; *Corydalis tuberosa* ($+$), *scouleri* and 4 other spp. ($-$).

Shobakunine is a mixture of *berberine* and *palmatine*?

Sinactine (*l*-Tetrahydro-epi-berberine)

> *Menisperm.   Sinomenium acutum* (*l*- form)
> *Papaver.   Fumaria officinalis* (*dl*- and *l*-), *Papaver rhoeas* (*l*-)

Stepharotine: belongs here?

> *Menisperm.   Stephania rotunda* (tuber)

Steponine

> *Menisperm.   Stephania rotunda*

Stylopine (Diphylline; Tetrahydro-coptisine): occurs in *d*-, *dl*-, and *l*-forms?

> *Papaver.   Chelidonium majus* (*d*-, *dl*-); *Corydalis ambigua* (*d*-, *dl*-?); *cheilanthifolia, claviculata* (*d*-), *cornuta* (*d*-), *lutea, nobilis, platycarpa* (*dl*-), *solida* (*d*-), *ternata* (*d*-, *dl*-?), *thalictrifolia, tuberosa* (*d*-); *Dactylicapnos macrocapnos* (*dl*-, *l*-); *Dicranostigma franchetianum; Fumaria officinalis* (*dl*-); *Stylophorum diphyllum* (*l*-)

(−)-Tetrahydro-berberine ((−)-Canadine)

> *Ranuncul.   Hydrastis canadensis*
> *Papaver.   Corydalis ambigua?, solida?*

Tetrahydro-palmatine (Casearine; Gindarine; Rotundine (1)) occurs in *d*-, *dl*-, and *l*- forms.

> *Menisperm.   Stephania glabra* (*l*-), *rotunda* (tuber)
> *Papaver.   Corydalis ambigua* (*dl*-), *angustifolia* (*dl*-), *aurea* (*dl*-, *l*-), *caseana* (*l*-), *decumbens* (*d*-), *lutea* (*l*-), *micrantha* (*l*-), *montana* (*dl*-), *nobilis* (*d*-, *dl*-), *ochroleuca* (*l*-), *pallida* (*d*-, *dl*-), *platycarpa* (*l*-), *solida, tuberosa* (*dl*-)

Tetrahydro-shobakunine: belongs here?

> *Berberid.   Berberis thunbergii*

Thalictricavine is an isomer of *thalictrifoline*.

> *Papaver.   Corydalis tuberosa*

Thalictrifoline

> *Papaver.   Corydalis ambigua, thalictrifolia* (*d*-)

Thalictrine

> *Ranuncul.   Thalictrum* (4)

Thalidastine (fig. 58)

> *Ranuncul.   Thalictrum fendleri*

Thalifendine is closely related to *berberine*.

> *Ranuncul.   Thalictrum fendleri*

Worenine may be 13-*methyl-corveximine*.

> *Ranuncul.   Coptis japonica*

Xylopinine ((−)-Nor-coralydine)

> *Annon.   Xylopia discreta* (bk, chief alkaloid)

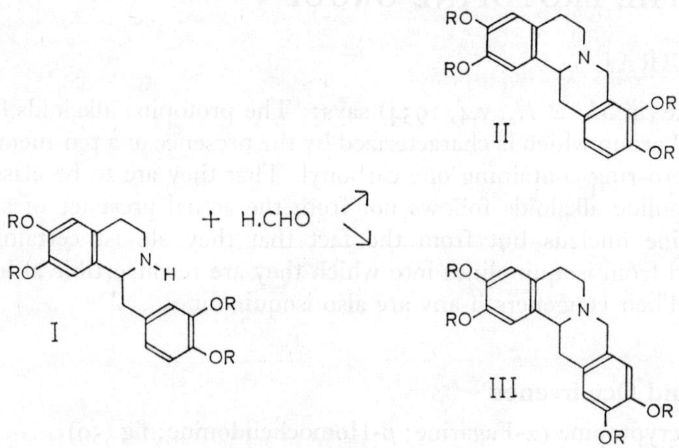

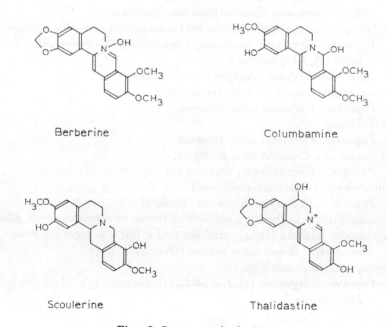

Fig. 57. Theoretical relationships of the protoberberines (see the quotation from Manske and Ashford, above).

Berberine

Columbamine

Scoulerine

Thalidastine

Fig. 58. Some protoberberines.

VIII THE PROTOPINE GROUP

GENERAL

Manske (in *M. & H.*, v.4, 1954) says: 'The protopine alkaloids form a natural group which is characterized by the presence of a ten-membered *N*-hetero-ring containing one carbonyl. That they are to be classed as isoquinoline alkaloids follows not from the actual presence of an isoquinoline nucleus but from the fact that they almost certainly are derived from isoquinolines into which they are reconvertible at least *in vitro*. Their congeners if any are also isoquinolines....'

List and Occurrence

α-Allocryptopine (α-Fagarine; β-Homochelidonine; fig. 59)

> *Papaver.* Adlumia (1), Arctomecon (1), Argemone (7), Bocconia (4), Chelidonium (1), Corydalis (8), Dactylicapnos (1), Dendromecon (1), Dicentra (2), Dicranostigma (2), Eschscholtzia (1), Glaucium (6), Hunnemannia (1), Hypecoum (1), Macleaya (2), Papaver (1), Pteridophyllum (1), Sanguinaria (1)
>
> *Rut.* Fagara coco, Zanthoxylum brachyanthum

β-Allocryptopine (γ-Homochelidonine) is an isomer of α-*allocryptopine*.

> *Papaver.* Argemone squarrosa, Chelidonium, Eschscholtzia, Macleaya (2), Sanguinaria
>
> *Rut.* Zanthoxylum brachyanthum (lvs, bk)

Corycavamine is isomeric with *corycavine*.

> *Papaver.* Corydalis cava, tuberosa

Corycavidine

> *Papaver.* Corydalis cava, tuberosa

Corycavine is a C-methylated *protopine*.

> *Papaver.* Corydalis (2), Dicentra (2)

Coulteropine (1-Methoxy-protopine)

> *Papaver.* Romneya coulteri var. trichocalyx

Cryptopalmatine is the tetramethoxy analogue of *cryptopine* and *allocryptopine*. Manske (1954) could *not* find it but it is recorded from

> *Menisperm.* Sinomenium acutum (Ovechov, 1955)

Cryptopine (Cryptocavine)

> *Papaver.* Argemone (1), Corydalis (4), Dicentra (3), Macleaya (1), Papaver (2)

Fagarine-II

> *Rut.* Fagara coco (lvs, st.)

Hunnemannine

> *Papaver.* Hunnemannia fumariaefolia

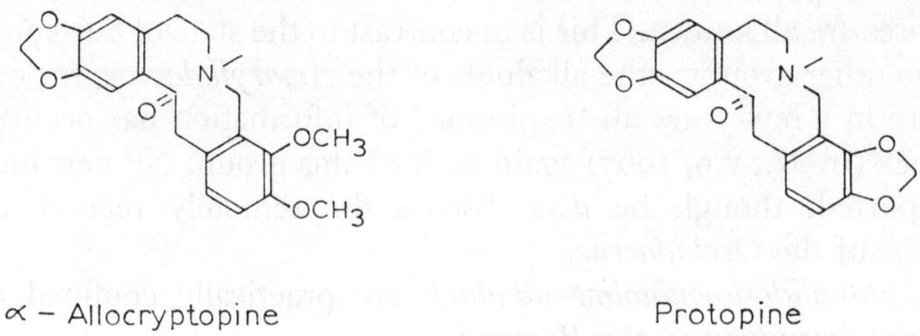

α – Allocryptopine   Protopine

Fig. 59. Alkaloids of the protopine group.

Muramine
  Papaver. *Argemone munita rotundata, Papaver nudicaule* var.
    amurense and other vars, *pilosum*
Ochrobirine
  Papaver. *Corydalis lutea* (plt), *ochroleuca* (plt), *sibirica* (plt)
13-Oxo-muramine (Alpinone (2)?)
  Papaver. *Papaver alpinum, nudicaule* var. *croceum*
Protopine (Fumarine; Macleyine; fig. 59) is the 'signature alkaloid' of
  the *Papaveraceae*. Although an Indian worker claims to have found it
  in a grass, there seems to be only one authentic record of it from outside
  the *Papaveraceae*, that of Ohta (1949) who found it in *Nandina*.
  Berberid. *Nandina domestica* (sd)
  Papaver. *Adlumia* (1), *Arctomecon* (1), *Argemone* (2), *Bocconia* (3),
    Chelidonium (1), *Corydalis* (36), *Cysticapnos* (1), *Dactylicapnos*
    (1), *Dendromecon* (1), *Dicentra* (8), *Dicranostigma* (1), *Eschscholtzia*
    (1), *Fumaria* (8), *Glaucium* (8), *Hunnemannia* (1), *Hypecoum* (3–4),
    Macleaya (2), *Meconella* (1), *Meconopsis* (6), *Papaver* (17),
    Platycapnos (1), *Platystemon* (1), *Pteridophyllum* (1), *Roemeria*
    (2), *Romneya* (1), *Sanguinaria* (1), *Sarcocapnos* (1), *Stylophorum*
    (1)

IX PHTHALIDE-ISOQUINOLINES

GENERAL

Staněk and Manske (in *M. & H.*, v.4, 1954) say: 'The term phthalide-
isoquinoline is applied to a group of eleven known alkaloids which are
all derived from the parent substance I [fig. 60] by the substitution of a
hydroxyl or methoxyl at position 8, and/or methoxyl and methylenedioxy groups at positions 6, 7, 4' and 5'.'

  Staněk (in *M. & H.*, v.7, 1960) can add little to our knowledge of
these alkaloids. No new ones have been discovered, he says, and the

structures are all known. This is in contrast to the state of our knowledge of some other groups—the alkaloids of the *Amaryllidaceae*, for example —where in a few years an 'explosion' of information has occurred.

Staněk (in *M.*, v.9, 1967) again reviews this group. No new members are reported, though he *does* discuss the remotely related alkaloid *shihunine* of the *Orchidaceae*.

The *phthalide-isoquinoline alkaloids* are practically confined to that factory of *isoquinolines*, the *Papaveraceae*.

List and Occurrence

Acutimine may belong here.
> *Menisperm.*   *Menispermum dauricum, Sinomenium acutum*

Adlumidine is isomeric with *bicuculline*.
> *Papaver.*   *Adlumia fungosa (cirrhosa)*; *Corydalis incisa* (lvs, st.), *thalictrifolia*

Adlumine (fig. 60) occurs in (+)- and (−)- forms.
> *Papaver.*   *Adlumia fungosa* (+), *Corydalis* (4, −)

Bicucine: an artefact ? (Staněk and Manske)
> *Papaver.*   *Adlumia?, Corydalis?, Dicentra?*

Bicuculline is a stereoisomer of *adlumidine* and *capnoidine*.
> *Papaver.*   *Adlumia fungosa, Corydalis* (11), *Dicentra cucullaria* and 2 other spp.

Capnoidine
> *Papaver.*   *Corydalis* (4)

Cordrastine
> *Papaver.*   *Corydalis aurea*

Corlumidine
> *Papaver.*   *Corydalis* (3), *Dicentra* (1)

Corlumine
> *Papaver.*   *Corydalis* (6), *Dicentra* (1)

Hydrastine
> *Ranuncul.*   *Hydrastis canadensis* (rhiz.)

Narceine (fig. 60) is almost a *phthalide-isoquinoline*.
> *Papaver.*   *Papaver somniferum*
> *Caprifoli.*   *Diervilla florida* (frt)

(±)-α-Narcotine (α-Gnoscopine) may be an artefact.
> *Papaver.*   *Papaver somniferum?*

(−)-α-Narcotine (Methoxy-hydrastine; fig. 60) is said to have an extraordinary distribution. One feels with Staněk (1967) that some of these records should be very carefully checked.
> *Papaver.*   *Papaver* (3)
> *Crucif.*   *Brassica oleracea* (lvs)

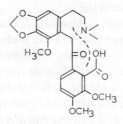

Fig. 60. Some phthalide-isoquinoline and related alkaloids.

Substance I

Adlumine

(-)-α-Narcotine

Narceine

Rut.   *Citrus aurantium, sinensis*
Logani.   *Strychnos melinoniana* (bk): queried by Staněk
Apocyn.   *Rauwolfia heterophylla*: queried by Staněk
Solan.   *Lycopersicum esculentum, Solanum tuberosum*
Narcotoline
Papaver.   *Papaver somniferum*
Nor-narceine (Hydroxy-narcotine; Oxy-narcotine) is a *near-phthalide-isoquinoline*. It may be an artefact.
Papaver.   *Papaver somniferum*

X THE EMETINE GROUP

GENERAL

Some of the compounds included here have been known as the 'ipecac alkaloids'. It has long been known that 'ipecac root', from the rubiaceous genus *Psychotria*, is emetic. More recently it has been found to be extremely valuable in the treatment of amoebic dysentery.

These alkaloids have been discussed by Janot (in *M. & H.*, v.3, 1953), by Manske (in *M. & H.*, v.7, 1960; in *M.*, v.10, 1968), and by Bentley (1965). They are known to have both *isoquinoline* and *quinolizidine* nuclei.

This interesting group of substances was thought to be confined to the *Rubiaceae* (with one doubtful record from the *Violaceae*). It now seems that they occur, too, in the *Alangiaceae*, and in the *Icacinaceae*. They have surely arisen independently in these families.

List and Occurrence

Alangicine (fig. 61) really has 2 *isoquinoline* groups.
  Alangi.   Alangium lamarckii
Alangimarckine
  Alangi.   Alangium lamarckii
Cephaeline (fig. 61) has both *isoquinoline* and *quinolizidine* groups.
  Alangi.   Alangium lamarckii (rtbk)
  Rubi.   Bothriospora corymbosa; Capirona decorticans; Cephaelis acuminata (rt), *ipecacuanha* (rhiz.); *Ferdinandusa elliptica; Hillia illustris; Psychotria emetica, ipecacuanha; Remijia amazonica; Tocoyena longiflora*
Demethyl-psychotrine
  Alangi.   Alangium lamarckii
Demethyl-tubulosine
  Alangi.   Alangium lamarckii
Deoxy-tubulosine
  Icacin.   Cassinopsis ilicifolia
  Alangi.   Alangium lamarckii (rt, frt)
  Rubi.   Pogonopus tubulosus
Emetamine
  Rubi.   Psychotria granadensis, ipecacuanha
Emetine (fig. 61) has both *isoquinoline* and *quinolizidine* groups.
  Viol.   Hybanthus indecorus (a very doubtful record)
  Alangi.   Alangium lamarckii
  Rubi.   Borreria (*Spermococe*) *verticillata* (rt)—but *not* (?) in other spp.; *Bothriospora corymbosa; Capirona decorticans; Cephaelis acuminata* (rt), *ipecacuanha* (rhiz.); *Ferdinandusa elliptica; Hillia illustris; Manettia cordifolia* (lvs, st., rt), *ignita; Psychotria granadensis* (rt), *ipecacuanha* (rt), *tomentosa* (rt); *Remijia amazonica; Richardsonia scabra* (rt); *Tocoyena longiflora*
Emetoidine
  Rubi.   Psychotria ipecacuanha
Isotubulosine: a stereoisomer of *tubulosine?*
  Alangi.   Alangium lamarckii (rt)

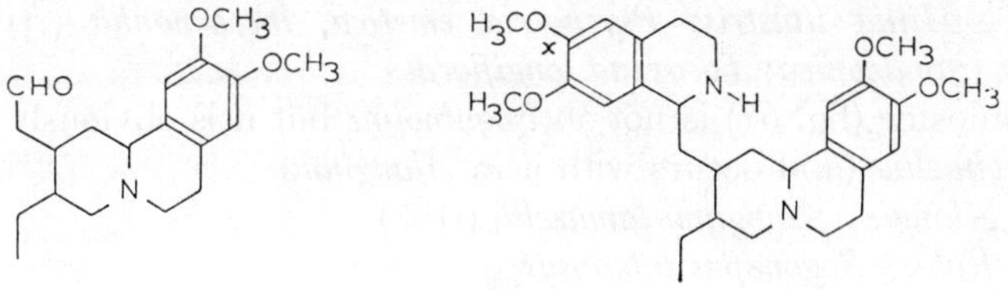

Protoemetine

Emetine

(Cephaeline has OH at x)

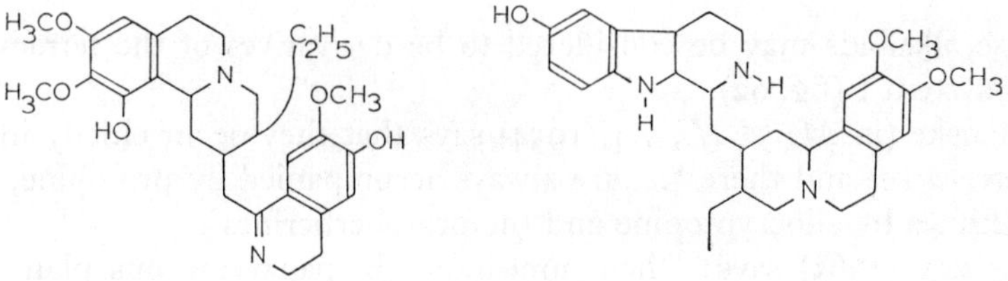

Alangicine

Tubulosine

Fig. 61. Alkaloids of the emetine group.

Lamarchinine: belongs here?
  Alangi. Alangium lamarckii
N-Methyl-cephaeline (Alamarckine)
  Alangi. Alangium lamarckii
O-Methyl-psychotrine
  Rubi. Psychotria granadensis, ipecacuanha
Protoemetine (fig. 61) should, perhaps, be put in the *quinolizidine* group.
  Manske (in *M.*, v.10, 1968) says: 'One of the most important inter-
  mediates in the synthesis of emetine is the naturally occurring
  protoemetine... The condensation of protoemetine...with 3-
  hydroxy-4-methoxyphenethylamine under mild quasiphysiological
  conditions gave cephaeline [*demethylemetine*]...and some 20% of
  isocephaeline.'
  Rubi. Psychotria ipecacuanha (rt)
Protoemetinol
  Alangi. Alangium lamarckii
Psychotrine is very nearly related to *emetine*.
  Alangi. Alangium lamarckii
  *Rubi. Bothriospora corymbosa; Capirona decorticans; Cephaelis
    acuminata* (rt), *ipecacuanha* (rhiz.); *Ferdinandusa elliptica*;

Hillia illustris; *Psychotria emetica, ipecacuanha* (rt); *Remijia amazonica*; *Tocoyena longiflora*

Tubulosine (fig. 61) is not an *isoquinoline* but it is obviously related to *cephaeline* (and occurs with it in *Alangium*).

    Alangi.   *Alangium lamarckii* (rtbk)

    Rubi.   *Pogonopus tubulosus*

XI THE α-NAPHTHAPHENANTHRIDINES

GENERAL

These alkaloids may be considered to be derivatives of the tetracyclic ring-system I (fig. 62).

Manske (in *M. & H.*, v.4, 1954) says that they occur chiefly in the *Papaveraceae* and there '...are always accompanied by protopine, and sometimes by allocryptopine and the protoberberines'.

Bentley (1965) says: 'their appearance in papaveraceous plants, to which they are almost completely restricted, makes their derivation from the tetrahydroberberine system seem probable'.

A few occur in the *Rutaceae*, and one (*sanguinarine*) is recorded from the *Sapindaceae* and the *Dipsacaceae*. Have these reported occurrences been carefully checked?

It is surprising to have no records from 'Polycarpicae' (**Magnoliales + Ranunculales**) which have so many other *isoquinolines*.

List and Occurrence

Avicine
    Rut.   *Zanthoxylum avicennae*

Chelerythrine (Toddaline; fig. 62)
    Papaver.   *Argemone* (2), *Bocconia* (3), *Chelidonium majus, Dicentra* (1), *Dicranostigma* (1 or 2), *Eschscholtzia* (1), *Glaucium* (7), *Hunnemannia* (1), *Hypecoum* (2), *Macleaya* (2), *Papaver* (1), *Platystemon* (1), *Sanguinaria* (1), *Stylophorum* (1)
    Rut.   *Fagara* (6), *Toddalia aculeata, Zanthoxylum* (2)

Chelidonine (fig. 62)
    Papaver.   *Chelidonium majus*; *Dicranostigma* (1); *Glaucium corniculatum* (l-), *flavum* (l-); *Stylophorum diphyllum* (dl- = diphylline?)

Chelilutine: belongs here?
    Papaver.   *Chelidonium majus*; *Dicentra spectabilis* (lvs, st., rt); *Eschscholtzia* (1); *Glaucium oxylobum*; *Hunnemannia fumariaefolia*; *Macleaya microcarpa* (rt), *cordata*; *Sanguinaria canadensis*

Chelirubine: belongs here?
Papaver. Chelidonium majus, Dicentra spectabilis (lvs., st., rt), *Dicranostigma* (2), *Eschscholtzia* (1), *Glaucium* (5), *Hunnemannia* (1), *Hypecoum* (2), *Macleaya* (2), *Platystemon* (1), *Sanguinaria* (1), *Stylophorum* (1)
Corynoline
Papaver. Corydalis incisa
Dihydro-chelerythrine
Papaver. Argemone hispida (*mexicana*) (rt)
Rut. Toddalia aculeata
Dihydro-sanguinarine
Papaver. Argemone hispida (plt)
Homochelidonine (formerly α-Chelidonine)
Papaver. Chelidonium majus
Macarpine: belongs here?
Papaver. Macleaya microcarpa (rt), *Stylophorum diphyllum*
9-Methoxy-chelerythrine (Angoline)
Rut. Fagara angolensis (rtbk), *leprieurii* (rtbk)
Methoxy-chelidonine
Papaver. Chelidonium majus
Nitidine is isomeric with *chelerythrine.*
Rut. Fagara (bk, 5); *Zanthoxylum hamiltonianum, nitidum*
Oxychelidonine
Papaver. Chelidonium majus
Oxynitidine
Rut. Zanthoxylum nitidum
Oxysanguinarine
Papaver. Bocconia latisepala, Dicranostigma lactucoides, Macleaya cordata, Sanguinaria canadensis (rt)
Sanguilutine: belongs here?
Papaver. Sanguinaria canadensis
Sanguinarine (Pseudo-chelerythrine) has, if the records are accurate, a queer distribution!
Papaver. Argemone (2 or 3), *Bocconia* (2), *Chelidonium majus, Corydalis* (3), *Dicentra* (1), *Dicranostigma* (2), *Eschscholtzia* (1), *Glaucium* (7), *Hunnemannia* (1), *Hypecoum* (3 or 4), *Macleaya* (2), *Meconopsis* (6), *Papaver* (5), *Platystemon* (1), *Sanguinaria canadensis*—but *not* found by recent investigators, *Stylophorum* (1)
Sapind. Sapindus emarginatus
Dipsac. Scabiosa succisa
Sanguirubine: belongs here?
Papaver. Sanguinaria canadensis

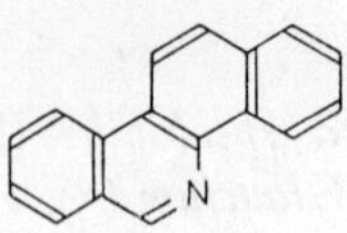

I

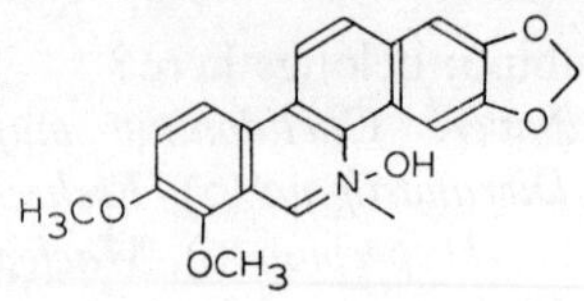

Chelerythrine

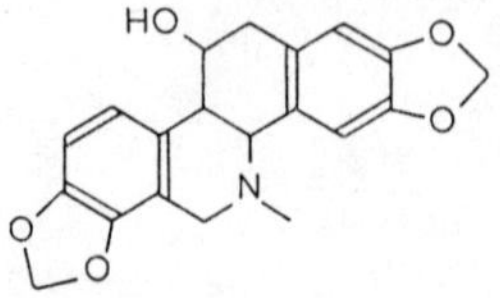

Chelidonine

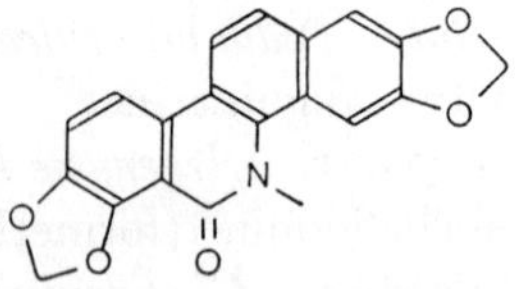

Oxysanguinarine

Fig. 62. Some α-naphthaphenanthridine alkaloids.

XII MISCELLANEOUS ISOQUINOLINES

GENERAL

We have included here a few alkaloids that do not fit easily into any of the above categories. There must be many more.

List and Occurrence

Dehydro-thalicarpine is a *benzylisoquinoline-aporphine* alkaloid.
  Ranuncul. Thalictrum minus subsp. *elatum*
Melanthioidine may be a *bis-phenylethylisoquinoline*.
  Lili. Androcymbium melanthioides var. *stricta* (lvs, corm)
Piloceredine may be an isomer of *pilocereine*.
  Cact. Lophocereus schottii
Pilocereine was thought until recently to have 2 *isoquinoline* groups. It is now said to have 3!
  Cact. Lophocereus australis, gatesii, schottii; *Pachycereus marginatus*; *Pilocereus sargentianus*
Thalicarpine is a *benzylisoquinoline-aporphine* alkaloid.
  Ranuncul. Thalictrum dasycarpum (rt), *minus* subsp. *elatum*, *revolutum* (rt)
  Hernandi. Hernandia sonorae (ovigera)
Thalmelatine is a *demethyl-thalicarpine*?
  Ranuncul. Thalictrum minus subsp. *elatum*

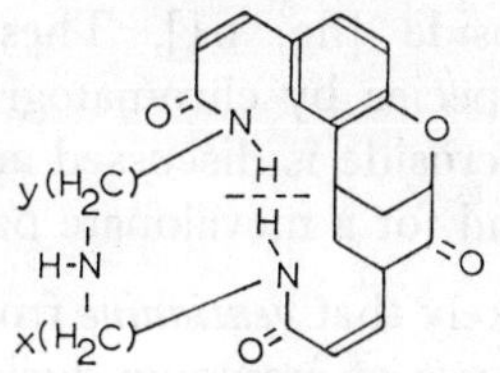

Lunarine (x=3; y=4
or x=4; y=3)

Fig. 63. An alkaloid of the Lunaria group.

THE LUNARIA GROUP

GENERAL

The *Cruciferae* are rather poor in alkaloids. Several have been found in at least 2 of the 3 species of *Lunaria*, however, and these seem to be of unique type.

List and Occurrence

Lunariamine ($C_{24}H_{33}O_4N_3$)
    Crucif. *Lunaria annua* (*biennis*) (sd), *rediviva*
Lunaridine is an isomer of *lunarine*.
    Crucif. *Lunaria annua* (sd), *rediviva*
Lunarine ($C_{25}H_{31}O_4N_3$; fig. 63)
    Crucif. *Lunaria annua* (sd), *rediviva*
Numismine ($C_{25}H_{33}O_4N_3$)
    Crucif. *Lunaria annua* (sd), *rediviva*

MONOTERPENOID ALKALOIDS

GENERAL

This is a small group of alkaloids, very similar in structure to *aucubin* and other glycosides of the aucubin-group (p. 624).

At least one of the alkaloids listed here, *gentianine*, seems to be largely, if not entirely, an artefact arising during extraction. Thus we have Floss, Mothes, and Rettig (1964) writing:

> Using ^{15}N it is shown that 91% of the nitrogen of the alkaloid gentianine isolated from *Gentiana lutea* originates from the ammonia added during the isolation. Gentianine thus is mainly an artefact which, according to chromatographic evidence, is formed from

gentiopicroside [fig. 64]. These findings are extended to other *Gentiana* species by chromatographic techniques. The biosynthesis of gentiopicroside is discussed and some evidence against an acetate pathway and for a mevalonate pathway is presented.

It seems likely that *gentianine* from *Swertia*, too, is an artefact resulting from the use of ammonia during extraction. Do other alkaloids of this group arise similarly?

List and Occurrence

Actinidine (fig. 64)
  Actinidi. Actinidia polygama
Bakankosine (fig. 64)
  Logani. Strychnos vacacoua
Boschniakine (fig. 64)—see also *boschnia-lactone* (fig. 64)
  Orobanch. Boschniakia rossica (plt, (+)-)
Boschniakinic acid
  Orobanch. Boschniakia rossica (plt, (+)-)
Dehydro-skytanthine
  Apocyn. Skytanthus acutus
Gentianine (Erythricine; fig. 64) may be an artefact, see above. It has been obtained from:
  Dipsac. Dipsacus azureus (rt), *Scabiosa succisa*
  Gentian. Centaurium umbellatum, Chlora perfoliata, Enicostema litorale (plt), *Erythraea centaurium, Gentiana* (11), *Ixanthus viscosus, Swertia* (5)
  Menyanth. Fauria crista-galli, Limmanthemum indicum, Menyanthes trifoliata (lvs, rt)
  Logani. Fagraea fragrans
Hydroxy-skytanthine-I (Alkaloid-D)
  Apocyn. Skytanthus acutus (lvs)
Hydroxy-skytanthine-II
  Apocyn. Skytanthus acutus (lvs)
Indicaine ($C_{10}H_{11}ON$): belongs here?
  Plantagin. Plantago indica (lvs, st.), *ramosa* (?lvs, st.)
Indicamine ($C_{14}H_{23}ON$): belongs here?
  Plantagin. Plantago indica (lvs, st.)
Pedicularine ($C_{11}H_{13}O_2N$): belongs here?
  Scrophulari. Pedicularis olgae
Plantagonine (fig. 64)
  Plantagin. Plantago indica (lvs, st.), *ramosa* (?lvs, st.)
Skytanthine (fig. 64)
  Apocyn. Skytanthus acutus

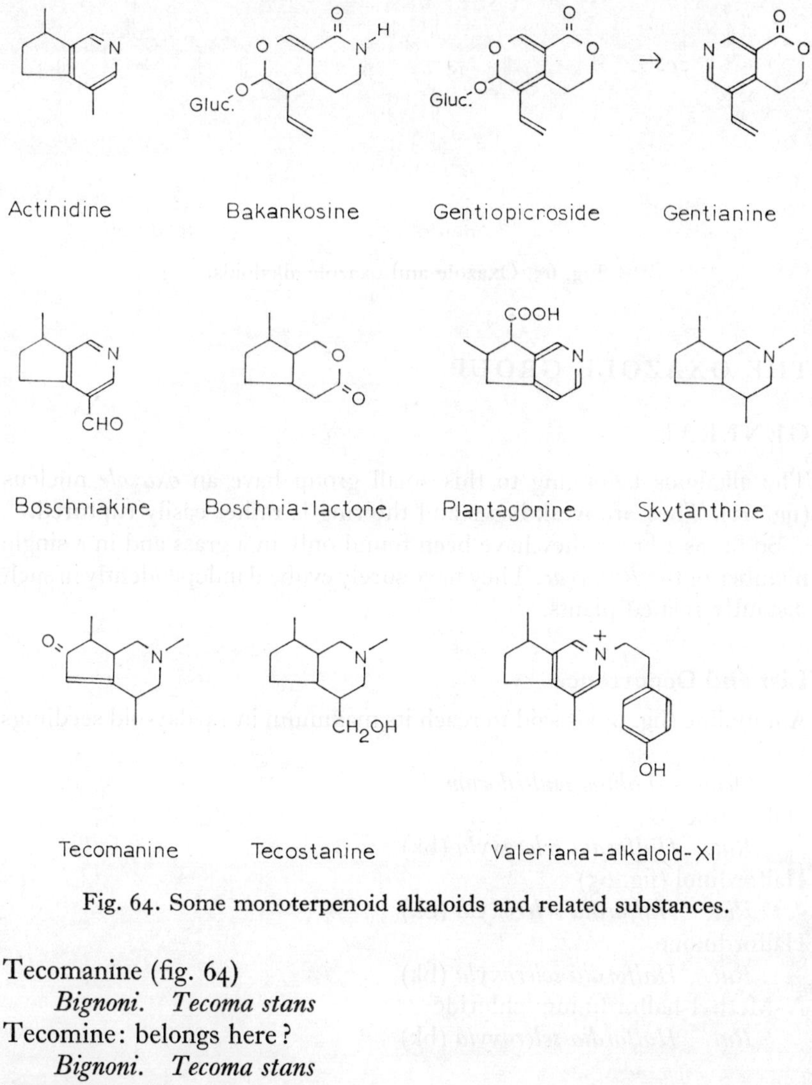
Actinidine
Bakankosine
Gentiopicroside
Gentianine
Gluc.
COOH
CHO
Boschniakine
Boschnia-lactone
Plantagonine
Skytanthine
CH_2OH
OH
Tecomanine
Tecostanine
Valeriana-alkaloid-XI

Fig. 64. Some monoterpenoid alkaloids and related substances.

Tecomanine (fig. 64)
Bignoni. *Tecoma stans*
Tecomine: belongs here?
Bignoni. *Tecoma stans*
Tecostanine (fig. 64)
Bignoni. *Tecoma stans*
Tecostidine
Bignoni. *Tecoma stans* (lvs)
Valeriana-alkaloid-XI (fig. 64) is a derivative of *actinidine* and yields it on pyrolysis.
Valerian. *Valeriana officinalis* (rt)

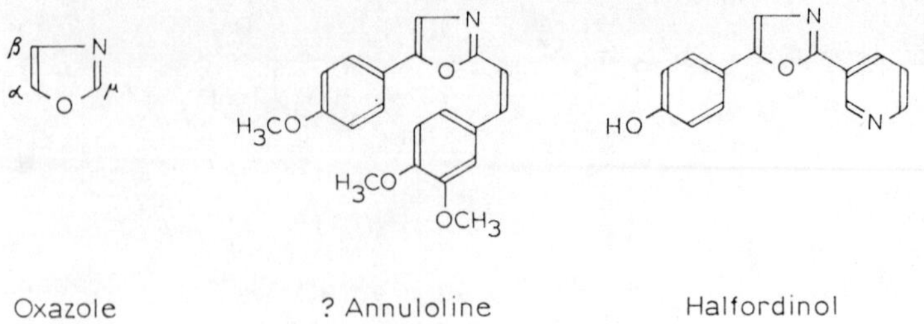

| Oxazole | ? Annuloline | Halfordinol |

Fig. 65. Oxazole and oxazole alkaloids.

THE OXAZOLE GROUP

GENERAL

The alkaloids belonging to this small group have an *oxazole* nucleus (fig. 65). They are weak bases and the ring is rather easily ruptured.

So far as I know they have been found only in a grass and in a single member of the *Rutaceae*. They have surely evolved independently in such distantly related plants.

List and Occurrence

Annuloline (fig. 65) is said to reach its maximum in 14-day-old seedlings of
  Gram.   Lolium multiflorum
Halfordine
  Rut.   Halfordia scleroxyla (bk)
Halfordinol (fig. 65)
  Rut.   Halfordia scleroxyla (bk)
Halfordinone
  Rut.   Halfordia scleroxyla (bk)
N-Methyl-halfordinium chloride
  Rut.   Halfordia scleroxyla (bk)

THE PAPAVERRUBINES

GENERAL

The *papaverrubines* closely resemble some of the *isoquinolines* but have a 7-membered ring containing nitrogen. They give an intense red colour in acid solution (hence the name?).

They are confined, I think, to the genus *Papaver* of the *Papaveraceae*.

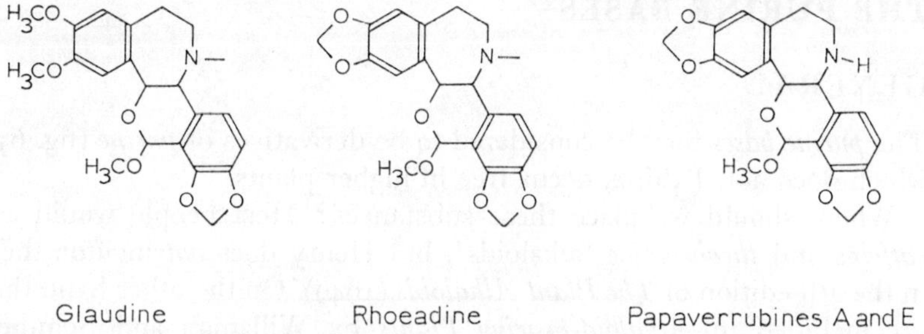

Glaudine   Rhoeadine   Papaverrubines A and E

Fig. 66. Some papaverrubines.

List and Occurrence

Dubirheine (Ethyl-rhoeagenine): belongs here?
  Papaver. Papaver dubium
Glaucamine is a stereoisomer of *oreogenine*.
  Papaver. Papaver glaucum
Glaudine (*O*-Methyl-glaucamine; fig. 66) is a stereoisomer of *oreodine*.
  Papaver. Papaver glaucum (plt), *rhoeas*
Isorhoeadine
  Papaver. Papaver oreophilum
N-Demethyl-glaudine (Papaverrubine-B)
  Papaver. Papaver glaucum
N-Demethyl-oreodine (Papaverrubine-F)
  Papaver. Papaver oreophilum
Oreodine is a stereoisomer of *glaudine*.
  Papaver. Papaver oreophilum
Oreogenine
  Papaver. Papaver oreophilum
Papaverrubine-A (fig. 66)
  Papaver. Papaver atlanticum
Papaverrubine-C
  Papaver. Papaver alboroseum, atlanticum, glaucum
Papaverrubine-E
  Papaver. Papaver atlanticum
Porphyroxine (Papaverrubine-D)
  Papaver. Papaver glaucum, setigerum (*somniferum?*)
Rhoeadine (fig. 66): Bentley (1965) says that it: 'may be regarded as an
  interesting half-way stage between the bases of the tetrahydrober-
  berine and phthalideisoquinoline groups...on treatment with
  mineral acid it is readily converted to rhoeagenine'.
  Papaver. Papaver rhoeas (fl., frt) and about 20 other species.

THE PURINE BASES

GENERAL

The *purine bases* may be considered to be derivatives of *purine* (fig. 67), which does not, I think, occur free in higher plants.

Where should we place these substances? Most people would call *caffeine* and *theobromine* 'alkaloids', but Henry does *not* include them in the 4th edition of *The Plant Alkaloids* (1949). On the other hand they *are* included in *Alkaloid-bearing Plants* by Willaman and Schubert (1961). Karrer (1958), who excludes alkaloids in general, includes the *purine bases* in his compilation of plant products, and Ulbricht (1965) deals with some of them in his *Introduction to Nucleic Acids and Related Natural Products* (1965).

We have chosen to deal with them briefly here.

List and Occurrence

Adenine (6-Amino-purine; fig. 67) is reported (free?) from fungi and from

>Chenopodi. Beta
>The. Thea
>Rubi. Coffea
>Gram. Saccharum

Caffeine (Coffeine, Guaranine; Theine; 1,3,7-Trimethyl-xanthine; fig 67) is one of the several alkaloids competing for the title of 'the most widely distributed alkaloid'. Perhaps not all of the following records are reliable.

>Nyctagin. Neea theifera (lvs)
>Phytolacc. Gallesia goranzema (lvs)
>Cact. Cereus jamacaru (sd), Harrisia adscandens (sd), Leocereus bahiensis (sd), Pilocereus gounellei (sd), Trichocereus sp. (sd)
>Annon. Annona cherimolia (sd)
>Dilleni. Davilla rugosa (lvs, sd)
>The. Camellia (Thea) (lvs—'tea')
>Gerani. Erodium cicutarium (plt)
>Aquifoli. Ilex paraguensis (lvs—'maté') and other spp.
>Sapind. Paullinia spp.
>Sterculi. Cola (4), Helicteres, Herrania, Guazuma, Sterculia (5), Theobroma cacao (sd—'cocoa')
>Icacin. Villaresia (2)
>Turner. Piriqueta ulmifolia; Turnera ulmifolia
>Celastr. Maytenus (2)

Combret.   Combretum (2)
Apocyn.   Pleiocarpa
Rubi.   Coffea (13 spp., sd—'coffee'), Genipa americana, Olden-
    landia corymbosa
Lili.   Urginea scilla
Crotonoside (Isoguanosine; Isoguanine-D-riboside)
Euphorbi.   Croton tiglium
Guanine (2-Amino-6-oxy-purine) is reported from fungi and from
deoxyribonucleic acid
Arali.   Aralia cordata (free ?)
Guanosine (Guanine-D-riboside; Vernine) has been obtained from the
nucleic acids of various plants. Does it occur free ?
Heteroxanthine (7-Methyl-xanthine; fig. 67)
Chenopodi.   Beta vulgaris (sap)
Hypoxanthine (6-Oxy-purine) occurs in fungi (free ?) and secondarily
from many plants. It is reported (free ?) from
Legum.   Lupinus luteus (sdlgs)
Solan.   Solanum tuberosum
Inosine (Hypoxanthine-riboside)
Chenopodi.   Beta
Isoguanine (2-Hydroxy-6-amino-purine) is the aglycone of crotonoside.
1,3,7,9-Tetramethyl-uric acid
The.   Camellia (Thea) (lvs—'tea' (free ?))
Theobromine (3,7-Dimethyl-xanthine: fig. 67)
The.   Camellia (Thea) (lvs—'tea')
Sterculi.   Cola, Guazuma, Herrania (3), Sterculia?, Theobroma
    cacao (sd—'cocoa')
Aquifoli.   Ilex paraguensis (lvs—'maté')
Sapind.   Paullinia cupana (lvs, bk, fl.)
Theophylline (1,3-Dimethyl-xanthine; fig. 67)
The.   Camellia (Thea) (lvs—'tea')
Aquifoli.   Ilex?
Togholamine (Alkaloid-B; fig. 67)
Apocyn.   Holarrhena floribunda
Triacanthine (3-(γ,γ-Dimethylallyl)-adenine)
Legum.   Gleditsia horrida, triacanthos (lvs)
Uric acid (2,6,8-Trioxy-purine; fig. 67) occurs free (?) in fungi and
Legum.   Melilotus officinalis (free ?)
Xanthine (2,6-Dioxy-purine; fig. 67) is reported from fungi and second-
arily (?) from many higher plants.
Chenopodi.   Beta (free ?)
Legum.   Lupinus luteus (sdlgs, free ?), Vicia
The.   Camellia (Thea) (lvs—'tea', free ?)

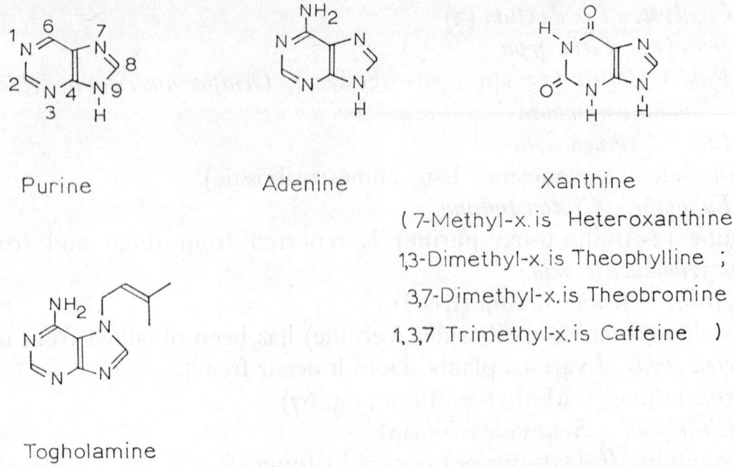

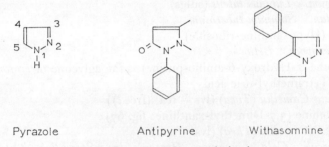

Purine   Adenine   Xanthine

(7-Methyl-x. is Heteroxanthine ;

1,3-Dimethyl-x. is Theophylline ;

3,7-Dimethyl-x.is Theobromine ;

1,3,7 Trimethyl-x.is Caffeine)

Togholamine

Fig. 67. Purine and some purine bases.

Pyrazole   Antipyrine   Withasomnine

Fig. 68. Pyrazole and some derivatives.

PYRAZOLES

GENERAL

The *pyrazole* ring is shown in fig. 68. Derivatives, such as *antipyrine* (fig. 68), are important in medicine as antifebrifuges.

I know of but two *alkaloids* of this series from higher plants, one from a dicotyledon and the other from a grass! These surely evolved independently.

List and Occurrence

Methylene-4,4'-bisantipyrine
    Gram.   *Panicum (Trichachne) vestitum*
Withasomnine (fig. 68)
    Solan.   *Withania somnifera*

PYRIDINE GROUPS

GENERAL

It is difficult to decide the limits of this group. Marion (in *M. & H.*, v.1, 1950) included *piperidine* as well as *pyridine* alkaloids in his treatment. It is also very difficult to subdivide the group. Manske classified them according to the positions of substitution and we have followed him more or less closely. Ayer and Habgood (in *M.*, v.11, 1968) summarize much of our recent knowledge and so expand our list.

Pyridine (fig. 69) is reported to occur in considerable amount in the composite *Haplopappus (Aplopappus) hartwegii*. Is it also in *Atropa* of the *Solanaceae*?

Piperidine (fig. 69) is said to occur rather widely. I have records of it from

Aizo. *Psilocaulon absimile* (plt)
Chenopodi. *Petrosimonia monandra*
Mor. *Cannabis sativa*
Piper. *Piper nigrum* (frt)
Umbell. *Conium maculatum*
Solan. *Nicotiana tabacum*

Our grouping is as follows:

Group I

a. Substitution at position 1 (alkaloids of pepper, etc.)
b. Substitution at positions 1 and 3 (alkaloids of *Areca*, etc.)
c. Substitution at positions 1 and 2, and at 1, 2 and 6 (pomegranate and other alkaloids)
d. Substitution at positions 1, 2, and sometimes 6 (alkaloids of *Lobelia, Galbulimima, Crassulaceae*, etc.)
e. Substitution at positions 1, 3 and 4; at 1, 2, 3 and 4; and at 1, 2 and 5
f. Substitution at positions 1, 2, 3 and 6

Group II

a. Substitution at position 2 (alkaloids of *Conium, Withania*, etc.)
b. Substitution at positions 2 and 6
c. Substitution at positions 2, 5 and 6

Group III

Substitution at position 3 and sometimes elsewhere (alkaloids of tobacco, etc.)

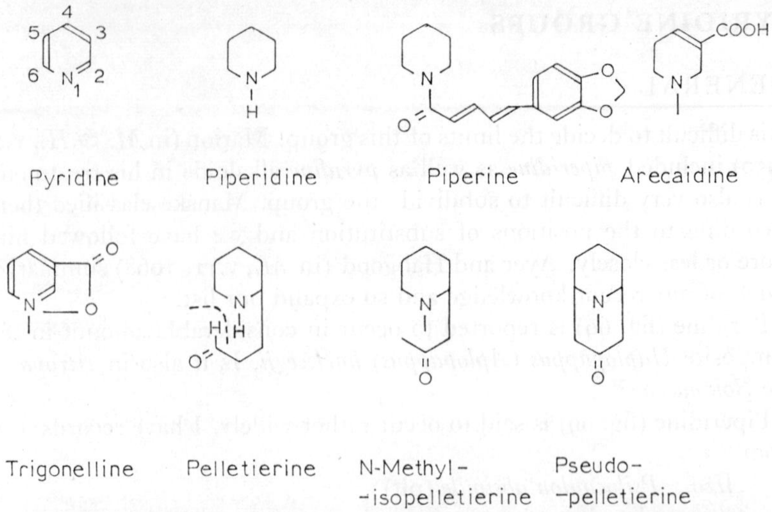

Pyridine   Piperidine   Piperine   Arecaidine

Trigonelline   Pelletierine   N-Methyl-   Pseudo-
                                  -isopelletierine -pelletierine

Fig. 69. Pyridine, piperidine, and some pyridine alkaloids of groups
Ia, Ib, and Ic.

Group IV

Miscellaneous, often imperfectly known
a. Alkaloids of *Withania* (other than those of group IIa)
b. Alkaloids of Gymnosperms
c. Alkaloids of *Celastraceae*
d. *Carpaine*, etc.

The *piperidine alkaloids* may be formed much as the *pyrrolidine alkaloids*, with *cadaverine* or *lysine* (in place of *putrescine*) as a starting-point, but at least 3 possible routes starting with *lysine* have been suggested for the synthesis of *coniine*. There is evidence, however, that *acetate*, rather than *mevalonate* or *lysine* is the best precursor for *carpaine*.

The *pyridine alkaloids*, such as *ricinine*, seem to be derived from *nicotinic acid*, but the route of synthesis of this last in plants is still not fully known. *Trigonelline* is a simple derivative of *nicotinic acid* and there is evidence that it may serve as a pool for it.

The *tobacco alkaloids*, such as *nicotine*, have two nitrogen-containing rings, and it has been shown that the *pyridine* ring is derived from *nicotinic acid* and the *pyrrolidine* ring from *ornithine*. It is interesting that *nicotine* is produced in the roots and transferred to the upper parts of the plant, where, in some species of *Nicotiana*, it may be rapidly demethylated to *nornicotine*. It may be further transformed, and there is no doubt that *nicotine* is an active metabolite and not an inert end-product.

I*a* Alkaloids with substitution at Position 1
(alkaloids of pepper, etc.)

List and Occurrence

Alangine-A (3-Anisoyl-2-piperidyl-propanol)
    Alangi. Alangium lamarckii
Alangine-B: belongs here?
    Alangi. Alangium lamarckii
Chavicine yields *piperine* and *chavicinic acid* (isomeric with *piperic acid*).
    Piper. Piper nigrum (frt)
Girgensonine (better 'Girgensohnine') is said to yield, on alkaline
    hydrolysis, *piperidine, HCN,* and *p-hydroxybenzaldehyde.*
    Chenopodi. Girgensohnia diptera, oppositiflora
N-Methyl-piperidine (1-Methyl-piperidine)
    Chenopodi. Girgensohnia diptera, oppositiflora
Piperettine: belongs here? It can be hydrolysed to *piperidine* and
    piperettic acid.
    Piper. Piper
Piperine (fig. 69) can be hydrolysed to *piperine* and *piperic acid.*
    Aizo. Psilocaulon absimile
    Annon. Xylopia brasiliensis (frt)
    Piper. Piper nigrum (frt) and at least 8 other spp.
    Eric. Rhododendron fauriae var. *rufescens*
Piperlongumine (?Piplartine; *N*-(3,4,5-Trimethoxy-cinnamoyl)-3,4-
    dihydro-2-pyridone): should be in group I*c*?
    Piper. Piper longum (rt; the st. has '*piplartine*')
Piperovatine: belongs here? It *may* be identical with, or closely related
    to, *pellitorine.*
    Piper. Piper ovatum (plt), *nigrum*

I*b* Alkaloids with substitution at Positions 1 and 3
(alkaloids of *Areca*, etc.)

List and Occurrence

Arecaidine (fig. 69)
    Palmae. Areca catechu (sd)
Arecolidine is an isomer of *arecoline.*
    Palmae. Areca catechu (sd)
Arecoline is the methyl ester of *arecaidine.*
    Palmae. Areca catechu (sd) and possibly another sp.

Guvacine (?Nor-arecaidine; De-*N*-methyl-arecaidine)
    Palmae. Areca catechu (sd)
Guvacoline is the methyl ester of *guvacine*.
    Palmae. Areca catechu (sd)
Iso-guvacine may be impure *arecaidine*.
Trigonelline (Coffearin; fig. 69) is the *methyl-betaine* of *nicotinic acid*.
    Weevers has said that it is the most widely distributed alkaloid.
    My records have it in:
        Nyctagin. Mirabilis
        Mor. Cannabis, Morus
        Legum. Acacia, Astragalus, Canavalia, Glycine, Lupinus, Medicago,
            Pisum, Trigonella
        Dichapetal. Dichapetalum
        Rut. Dictamnus
        Aquifoli. Ilex
        Cucurbit. Cucurbita
        Apocyn. Strophanthus (3)
        Rubi. Coffea
        Lab. Stachys
        Solan. Solanum
        Caprifoli. Sambucus
        Comp. Dahlia, Scorzonera
        Gram. Avena

I*c* Alkaloids with substitution at
    Positions 1 and 2, and 1, 2, and 6
    (pomegranate and other alkaloids)

List and Occurrence

(−)-Homostachydrine
    Legum. Medicago sativa (lvs, st., sd)
    Comp. Achillea atrata, moschata
Lythramine: belongs here ?
    Lythr. Lythrum anceps
Lythranidine: belongs here ?
    Lythr. Lythrum anceps
Lythranthine: belongs here ?
    Lythr. Lythrum anceps
Methyl-pelletierine
    Punic. Punica granatum (rtbk)
N-Methyl-dihydro-isopelletierine
    Crassul. Sedum sarmentosum

N-Methyl-isopelletierine (Tanret's 'methyl-pelletierine'; fig. 69)
   Crassul. Sedum sarmentosum
   Punic. Punica granatum (bk)
Pelletierine (Tanret's 'isopelletierine'; fig. 69)
   Crassul. Sedum acre
   Punic. Punica granatum (bk)
   Solan. Withania somnifera
Pseudo-pelletierine (*N*-Methyl-granatonine; fig. 69)
   Occurrence?
(–)-1,2,6-Trimethyl-piperidine
   Chenopodi. Nanophytum caspicum, erinaceum (lvs, st.)

I*d* Alkaloids with substitution at
   Positions 1, 2 and sometimes 6
   (alkaloids of *Lobelia, Galbulimima, Crassulaceae*, etc.)

GENERAL

Writing of the *Lobelia* alkaloids in 1950 Manske said that all except *lobinaline* seemed to be restricted to *L. inflata*. We know today that a few occur in other spp. of the genus, and in the family *Crassulaceae*. The alkaloids of *Galbulimima* (*Himantandra*) are also included here. The genus was called *Himantandra* when some of the alkaloids were named, but it should be *Galbulimima*. Ritchie and Taylor (in *M.*, v.9, 1967) say that although 4 species were recognized there are grounds for believing that only a single species should be 'made'. They therefore propose to label the alkaloids as from North Queensland plants (NQ) and New Guinea plants (NG) respectively and to number new alkaloids as 'G.B.1', etc. (the single provisional 'species' being *Galbulimima belgraveana*). They say that no less than 28 alkaloids have been isolated from bark material, the leaves and wood having very little alkaloid content. They comment on the variability of the species They distinguish 3 classes of *Galbulimima* alkaloids—tetracyclic lactones, highly oxygenated hexacyclic esters, and hexa- and pentacyclic bases of low oxygen content. Their fourth group consists of yet unclassifiable compounds. We make but one list.

List and Occurrence

trans-3,4-Dehydro-8,10-diethyl-lobelidiol
   Campanul. Lobelia syphilitica
trans-3,4 (or 4,5)-Dehydro-8-methyl-10-ethyl-lobelidiol
   Campanul. Lobelia syphilitica

8,10-Diethyl-lobelidiol (fig. 70)
    Campanul.   Lobelia inflata
cis-8,10-Diethyl-lobelionol
    Campanul.   Lobelia syphilitica
cis-8,10-Diethyl-nor-lobelidione
    Campanul.   Lobelia syphilitica
cis-8,10-Diethyl-nor-lobelionol
    Campanul.   Lobelia syphilitica
cis-8,10-Diphenyl-lobelidione (Lobelanine; fig. 70): after *lobeline*, the
    most abundant alkaloid of *Lobelia*?
    Campanul.   Lobelia inflata (plt), *radicans* (plt), *salicifolia* (plt)
8-Ethyl-nor-lobelol-I
    Campanul.   Lobelia inflata
Himandravine (NG) is very nearly related to *himbeline*.
    Himantandr.   Galbulimima belgraveana (bk)
'Himandreline' is a polymorph of *himandridine*.
Himandridine (NQ, NG) is a major alkaloid of
    Himantandr.   Galbulimima baccata (bk)
Himandrine (NQ, NG)
    Himantandr.   Galbulimima baccata (bk), *belgraveana* (bk)
Himbacine (NQ, NG; fig. 70)—is a major alkaloid of
    Himantandr.   Galbulimima baccata (bk), *belgraveana* (bk)
Himbadine (NQ)
    Himantandr.   Galbulimima baccata (bk)
Himbeline (NG; *N*-Demethyl-himbacine)
    Himantandr.   Galbulimima belgraveana (bk)
Himbosine (NQ, NG) has a very complex hexacyclic structure shared
    by some other *Galbulimima* alkaloids.
    Himantandr.   Galbulimima baccata (bk)
Himgaline (NQ, NG)
    Himantandr.   Galbulimima
Himgravine (NQ, NG)
    Himantandr.   Galbulimima baccata (bk)
Himgrine (NG)
    Himantandr.   Galbulimima belgraveana (bk)
    In addition the following alkaloids of *Galbulimima* are being studied:
G.B.1 (NQ, NG), 2 (NQ, NG), 3 (NG), 4 (NQ, NG), 5 (NQ, NG),
6 (NQ), 7 (NQ), 8 (NG), 9 (NG), 10 (NG), 11 (NG), 12 (NG), 13 (NQ),
14 (NG), 15 (NG), 16 (NG), 17 (NQ), 18 (NQ)
Isolobinanidine
    Campanul.   Lobelia inflata
Isolobinine
    Campanul.   Lobelia inflata

dl-Lelobanidine (fig. 70)
 Campanul. Lobelia inflata (and other spp. ?)
l-Lelobanidine-I
 Campanul. Lobelia inflata, nicotianaefolia
l-Lelobanidine-II
 Campanul. Lobelia inflata, nicotianaefolia
l-Lelobanidine-III
 Campanul. Lobelia nicotianaefolia
Lobelanidine
 Campanul. Lobelia (3)
Lobeline
 Campanul. Lobelia (12 or 13 spp., *l-* form in most; *dl-* in one ?)
Lobinaline (fig. 70) appears to be both a *pyridine* and a *quinoline* derivative. It is formed in the plant from *lysine* and *phenylalanine* ?
 Campanul. Lobelia cardinalis, elongata
Lobinanidine
 Campanul. Lobelia inflata
Lobinine
 Campanul. Lobelia inflata
Lopheline (Lophiline ?): belongs here ?
 Campanul. Lobelia syphilitica
Lophilacrine: belongs here ?
 Campanul. Lobelia syphilitica
Lurenine: belongs here ?
 Campanul. Lobelia urens
8-Methyl-10-ethyl-lobelidiol
 Campanul. Lobelia inflata
(+)-8-Methyl-nor-lobelol (Sedridine)
 Crassul. Sedum acre (Europe)
(+)-8-Methyl-10-phenyl-lobelidiol
 Crassul. Sedum acre
 Campanul. Lobelia inflata
8-Methyl-10-phenyl-lobelionol (Sedinone)
 Crassul. Sedum acre
d-Nor-lelobanidine
 Campanul. Lobelia inflata
Nor-lobelanidine
 Campanul. Lobelia inflata, nicotianaefolia, salicifolia
Nor-lobelanine
 Campanul. Lobelia inflata, tupa
(−)-8-Phenyl-lobilol ((−)-Sedamine; fig. 70)
 Crassul. Sedum acre (Canada), *sarmentosum*

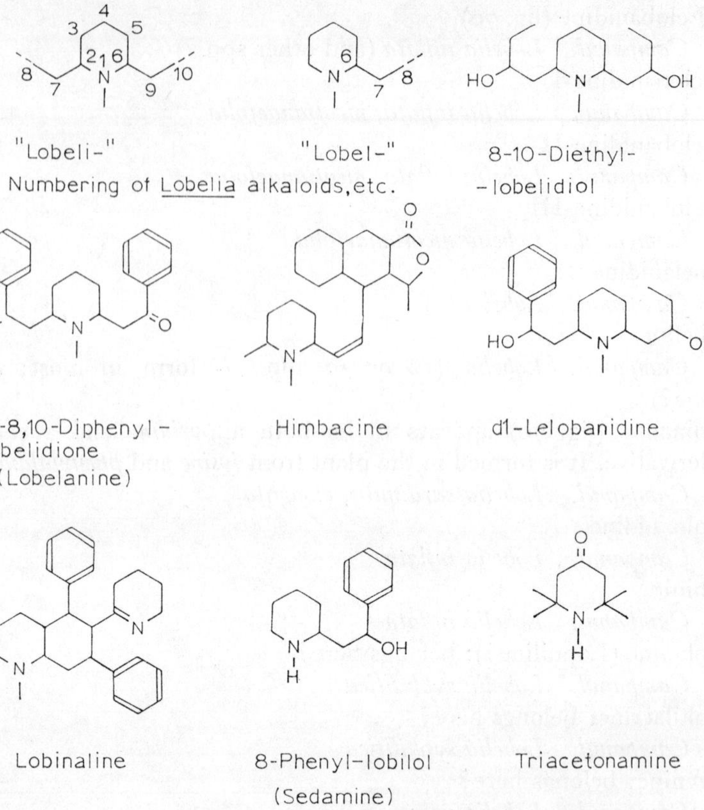

"Lobeli-"

"Lobel-"

8-10-Diethyl-
-lobelidiol

Numbering of Lobelia alkaloids,etc.

Cis-8,10-Diphenyl-
-lobelidione
(Lobelanine)

Himbacine

dl-Lelobanidine

Lobinaline

8-Phenyl-lobilol
(Sedamine)

Triacetonamine

Fig. 70. Pyridine alkaloids of group I*d*.

(−)-8-Phenyl-lobilol-I ((−)-Allo-sedamine)
   Campanul.   Lobelia inflata
(+)-8-Phenyl-norlobelol-I ((+)-Nor-allo-sedamine)
   Campanul.   Lobelia inflata
Sedinine (?8-Methyl-10-phenyl-dehydro-lobelidiol)
   Crassul.   Sedum acre
Syphilobine-A is related to *lobinaline*
   Campanul.   Lobelia syphilitica
Syphilobine-F is related to *lobinaline*.
   Campanul.   Lobelia syphilitica
Triacetonamine (Odoratine; fig. 70) is now believed to be (along with
   diacetonamine) an artefact formed during extraction (Stewart and
   Wheaton, 1967). It was reported to occur in
   Euphorbi.   Acalypha indica
   Viol.   Viola odorata

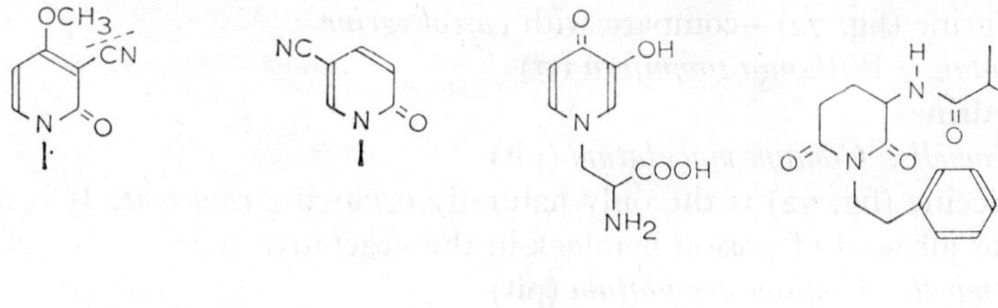

Ricinine   Nudiflorine   Leucaenine   Julocrotine

Fig. 71. Some pyridine alkaloids of groups I*e* and I*f*.

I*e* Alkaloids with substitution at
    Positions 1, 3 and 4; at 1, 2, 3 and 4;
    and at 1, 2 and 5

List and Occurrence

Ricinine (fig. 71) is one of the few naturally occurring nitriles. It is said
    to be derived biogenetically from *nicotinic acid.*
    Euphorbi. Croton tiglium (sd), *Ricinus communis* (lvs, sd) and vars
Leucaenine (Leucenol; fig. 71) is optically inactive.
    Legum. Leucaena glauca (sd)
Mimosine (*l*-Leucaenine)
    Legum. Leucaena glauca and at least 3 other spp.; *Mimosa pudica.*
        It is said to be *absent* from 10 other leguminous genera.
Nudiflorine (fig. 71)
    Euphorbi. Trewia nudiflora (lvs)

I*f* Alkaloid(s) with substitution at
    Positions 1, 2, 3 and 6

List and Occurrence

Julocrotine (Yulocrotine; fig. 71)
    Legum. Julocroton camporum?, montevidensis (rt), *subpannosus* (rt)

II*a* Alkaloids with substitution at
    Position 2 (alkaloids of Conium, Withania, etc.)

List and Occurrence

Anaferine (fig. 27)
    Solan. Withania somnifera (rt)

Anahygrine (fig. 72)—compare with *cuscohygrine*
    Solan.   Withania somnifera (rt)
Conhydrine
    Umbell.   Conium maculatum (plt)
γ-Coniceine (fig. 72) is the only naturally occurring *coniceine*. It is the
    major alkaloid of poison hemlock in the vegetative state.
    Umbell.   Conium maculatum (plt)
Coniine (fig. 72) is said to be widely distributed, and I give the records
    (queried) which I have collected. Marion (1950), however, says that
    it is known with certainty *only* from *Conium maculatum*.
    Urtic.   Parietaria officinalis?
    Mor.   Humulus?
    Punic.   Punica?
    Umbell.   Aethusa cynapium?, *Conium maculatum* (plt)
    Asclepiad.   Sarcolobus?
    Arac.   Amorphophallus?, *Arisarum?*, *Arum?*, *Caladium?*
2-Methyl-piperidine
    Umbell.   Conium maculatum
N-Methyl-coniine
    Umbell.   Conium maculatum (*d-* and *l-*)
α-Picoline (α-Methyl-pyridine)
    Polygon.   Rumex obtusifolius (lvs)
    Gram.   Lolium p renne (lvs)
Pleurospermine (fig. 72)
    Laur.   Cryptocarya pleurosperma (lvs)
2-(2-Propenyl)-Δ¹-piperideine
    Punic.   Punica granatum (lvs of young plt)
Pseudo-conhydrine (5-Hydroxy-coniine)
    Umbell.   Conium maculatum

II*b* Alkaloid(s) with substitution at
    Positions 2 and 6

List and Occurrence

(−)-2,6-Dimethyl-piperidine
    Chenopodi.   Nanophyton caspicum, erinaceum (fl., st.)

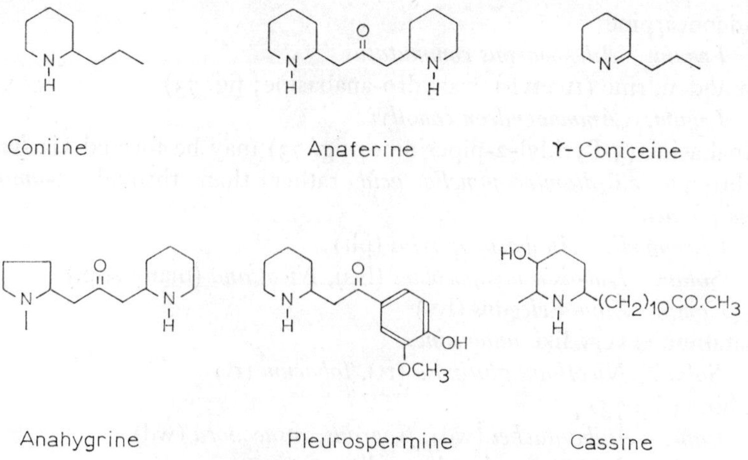

Coniine   Anaferine   γ-Coniceine

Anahygrine   Pleurospermine   Cassine

Fig. 72. Pyridine alkaloids of groups IIa and IIc.

IIc Alkaloids with substitution at
    Positions 2, 5, and 6

List and Occurrence

Carnavoline
    Legum. *Cassia carnaval*
Cassine (fig. 72)
    Legum. *Cassia carnaval, excelsa*
Prosopine
    Legum. *Prosopis africana*
Prosopinine
    Legum. *Prosopis africana*

III ALKALOIDS WITH SUBSTITUTION AT
POSITION 3 AND SOMETIMES ELSEWHERE
(the tobacco alkaloids and some others)

List and Occurrence

d-Adenocarpine (N-Cinnamyl-tetrahydro-anabasine; Teidine; fig. 73)
    Legum. *Adenocarpus anagyrus* (*viscosus*), *complicatus*, etc.; *Cytisus*
        sp. (d-?)
dl-Adenocarpine (Orensine; fig. 73)
    Legum. *Adenocarpus commutatus, grandiflorus* (lvs)

l-Adenocarpine
> *Legum.*　*Adenocarpus commutatus*

Ammodendrine (Acetyl-tetrahydro-anabasine; fig. 73)
> *Legum.*　*Ammodendron conollyi*

l-Anabasine (3-Pyridyl-2-piperidine; fig. 73) may be formed via *lysine* through 2,6-*diamino-pimelic acid* rather than through 2-*amino-adipic acid*.
> *Chenopodi.*　*Anabasis aphylla* (plt)
> *Solan.*　*Duboisia myoporoides* (lvs), *Nicotiana* (many spp.)
> *Comp.*　*Zinnia elegans* (lvs)

Anatabine is very like *anabasine*.
> *Solan.*　*Nicotiana glutinosa* (rt), *tabacum* (rt)

Anibine (fig. 73)
> *Laur.*　*Aniba duckei* (wd), *fragrans, rosaeodora* (wd)

Astrocasine (fig. 73) is related to *adenocarpine*.
> *Euphorbi.*　*Astrocasia phyllanthoides*

Astrophylline is *very* closely related to *adenocarpine*.
> *Euphorbi.*　*Astrocasia phyllanthoides*

2,3'-Dipyridyl ('Iso-nicoteine' of Noga)
> *Solan.*　*Nicotiana tabacum* (smoke)

Fontaphilline: belongs here?
> *Ole.*　*Fontanesia phillyreoides* (lvs)

Hystrine
> *Legum.*　*Genista hystrix*

Iso-ammodendrine (Sphaerocarpine) is an isomer of *ammodendrine*.
> *Legum.*　*Ammodendron conollyi*; *Genista (Retama) monosperma, sphaerocarpa* (frt)

Iso-orensine is an isomer of *dl-adenocarpine* (*orensine*).
> *Legum.*　*Adenocarpus complicatus* (lvs), *grandiflorus* (lvs); *Cytisus* sp.

3-Methoxy-pyridine is said to occur in *Equisetum* and
> *Legum.*　*Thermopsis rhombifolia*

Myosmine
> *Solan.*　*Nicotiana tabacum* (plt)

'Nicoteine' was probably a mixture.

Nicotelline (fig. 73)
> *Solan.*　*Nicotiana tabacum* (plt)

Nicotimine may not exist as such.
> *Solan.*　*Nicotiana tabacum*

Nicotine (fig. 73) is of great interest. It is now known to be widely distributed. Dawson (1960) goes so far as to say: 'Nicotine has been reported to occur more widely than any other alkaloid.' Marion (1950) says: 'It is noteworthy that nicotine is the only alkaloid that has bridged the gap between the flowering plants (Spermatophyta) and

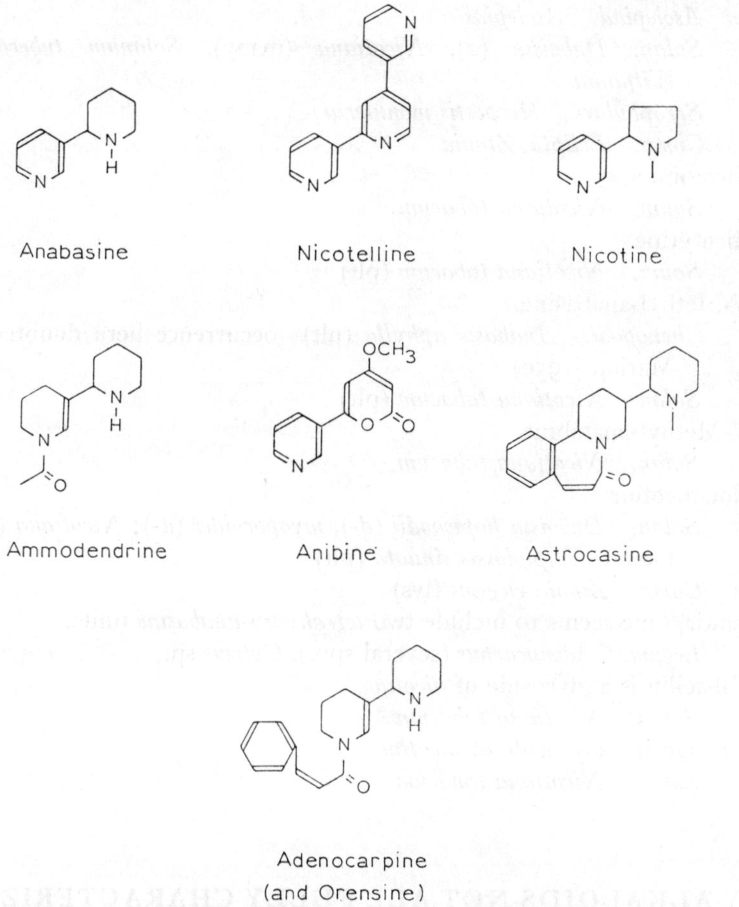

Anabasine   Nicotelline   Nicotine

OCH₃

Ammodendrine   Anibine   Astrocasine

Adenocarpine
(and Orensine)

Fig. 73. Some pyridine alkaloids of group III.

the vascular cryptogams (Pteridophyta).' We may now query this, since 3-*methoxy-pyridine*, at least, seems to do the same. Not all the following records are to be trusted.

Mor.   *Cannabis* (but *not Humulus*)
Urtic.   *Urtica dioica* (but *not urens*)
Jugland.   *Juglans regia*
Crassul.   *Echeveria, Sempervivum arachnoideum* (but *not Sedum acre*, where it had been reported)
Legum.   *Acacia, Mucuna pruriens*
Ros.   *Prunus*
Hippocastan.   *Aesculus hippocastanum*
Erythroxyl.   *Erythroxylum coca*

> *Asclepiad.   Asclepias*
> *Solan.   Duboisia* (2), *Nicotiana* (many), *Solanum tuberosum,*
>   *Withania*
> *Scrophulari.   Herpestis monnieria*
> *Comp.   Eclipta, Zinnia*

Nicotoine
> *Solan.   Nicotiana tabacum*

Nicotyrine
> *Solan.   Nicotiana tabacum* (plt)

N-Methyl-anabasine
> *Chenopodi.   Anabasis aphylla* (plt)—occurrence here doubted by
>   Marion (1950)
> *Solan.   Nicotiana tabacum* (plt)

N-Methyl-anatabine
> *Solan.   Nicotiana tabacum*

Nor-nicotine
> *Solan.   Duboisia hopwoodii* (*d*-), *myoporoides* (*d*-); *Nicotiana* (*l*- in
>   many); *Salpiglossis sinuata* (plt)
> *Comp.   Zinnia elegans* (lvs)

Santiaguine seems to include two *tetrahydro-anabasine* units.
> *Legum.   Adenocarpus* (several spp.), *Cytisus* sp.

Tabacilin is a glycoside of *nicotine.*
> *Solan.   Nicotiana tabacum*

Tabacin is a glycoside of *nicotine.*
> *Solan.   Nicotiana tabacum*

IV ALKALOIDS NOT ALL FULLY CHARACTERIZED, OR NOT ASSIGNED TO ONE OF THE PRECEDING GROUPS

List and Occurrence

(*a*) Alkaloids of *Withania somnifera*

In addition to *nicotine, withasomnine,* and some other well-known alkaloids, this plant is said to contain *pseudo-withanine, somniferine, somniferinine, somnine, withaninine, withananinine,* and *withanine.*

(*b*) Alkaloids of Gymnosperms

A very few alkaloids from *Pinus* spp., such as *pinidine* and (+)-α-*pipecoline,* are *piperidine* derivatives. They have not, I think, been found in angiosperms.

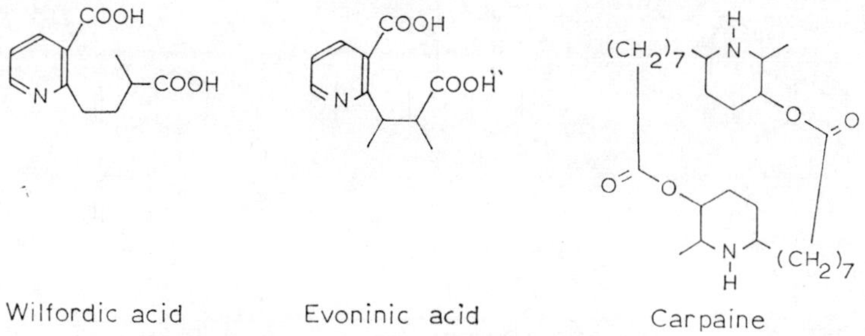

Fig. 74. Some group IV compounds.

Wilfordic acid   Evoninic acid   Carpaine

(c) Alkaloids of the *Celastraceae*

At least two members of the *Celastraceae* have complex alkaloids which are pyridine derivatives. They include

Evonine, which yields on hydrolysis *evoninic acid* (fig. 74).
    Celastr.   *Euonymus* (*Evonymus*) *europaeus* (sd)
Tripterygine
    Celastr.   *Tripterygium wilfordii*
Wilfordine yields *hydroxy-wilfordic acid.*
    Celastr.   *Tripterygium wilfordii* (rt)
Wilforgine yields *wilfordic acid* (fig. 74).
    Celastr.   *Tripterygium wilfordii* (rt)
Wilforine yields *wilfordic acid.*
    Celastr.   *Tripterygium wilfordii* (rt)
Wilfortrine yields *hydroxy-wilfordic acid.*
    Celastr.   *Tripterygium wilfordii* (rt)
Wilforzine yields *wilfordic acid.*
    Celastr.   *Tripterygium wilfordii* (rt)

(d) Carpaine and Related Alkaloids

Azcarpine is very like *carpaine.*
    Salvador.   *Azima tetracantha* (lvs)
Azimine is very like *carpaine.*
    Salvador.   *Azima tetracantha* (lvs)
Carpaine (fig. 74) has a remarkable structure, yet it has been reported from two unrelated families; and a third unrelated family has the very similar alkaloids *azcarpine* and *azimine* (above)!
    Caric.   *Carica dodecaphylla* (lvs, frt, sd), *hastata, papaya* (lvs, frt, sd)
    Apocyn.   *Cerbera ahouai*
Pseudo-carpaine differs only very slightly from *carpaine.*
    Caric.   *Carica papaya* (lvs)

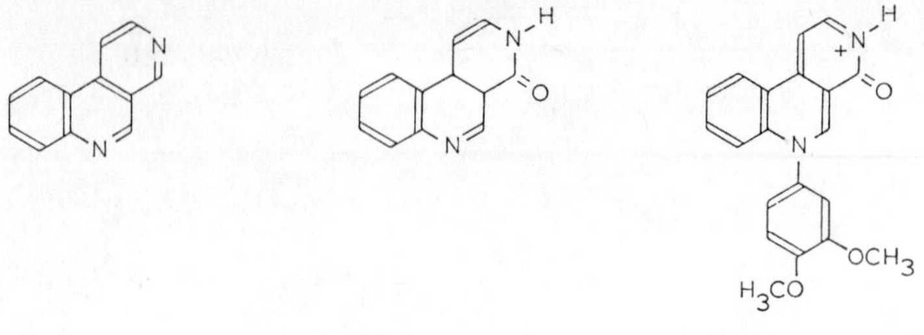

Perlolidine   Perloline

Fig. 75. Alkaloids of the *Lolium* group.

PYRIDO [3,4-c] QUINOLINES (the *Lolium* group)

GENERAL

At least two of the alkaloids of *Lolium* and some other grasses have a 3-ring system with 2 of the rings containing nitrogen (fig. 75).

List and Occurrence

Perlolidine (fig. 75)

    Gram. *Festuca* sp., *Lolium perenne*, *Setaria* sp.

Perloline (fig. 75)

    Gram. *Festuca arundinacea* (a toxic var.), *elatior* (lvs); *Lolium multiflorum* (lvs), *perenne* (lvs), *temulentum* (lvs); *Setaria lutescens* (lvs)

PYRROLIDINES

GENERAL

Some alkaloids with one or more *N*-containing rings in addition to a *pyrrolidine* ring, such as *nicotine*, have been dealt with elsewhere. The alkaloids treated here have one or two *pyrrolidine* rings.

Recently *pyrrolidine* alkaloids of unique nature have been found in *Ficus*. These yield the flavone *chrysin* when treated with alkali.

Recently, too, several sulfur-containing alkaloids have been found in the *Rhizophoraceae*. At least one of these, *gerrardine*, is a *pyrrolidine*: others may have *tropane* and *pyrrolizidine* rings.

List and Occurrence

l-Betonicine (Achilleine; fig. 76) is the *methyl-betaine* of *4-hydroxy-hygrinic acid*
    Legum.   *Canavalia ensiformis*
    Lab.   *Betonica officinalis, Marrubium vulgare, Stachys sylvatica*
    Comp.   *Achillea millefolium*

Cuscohygrine (Bellaradine; Cuskhygrine; fig. 76)
    Erythroxyl.   *Erythroxylum coca* (lvs), *truxillense* (lvs)
    Convolvul.   *Convolvulus hamadae* (rt), *lineatus*
    Solan.   *Atropa* (1), *Datura* (4), *Hyoscyamus* (1), *Mandragora* (1), *Physochlaina* (2), *Scopolia* (3), *Withania* (1)

Ficine (fig. 76) is, says Manske (in *M.*, v.10, 1968), the first alkaloid known to yield a flavonoid compound when treated with alkali.
    Mor.   *Ficus pantoniana*

Gerrardamine ($C_8H_{15}OS_2N$): belongs here?
    Rhizophor.   *Cassipourea gerrardii*

Gerrardine ($C_{11}H_{19}O_2S_4N$; fig. 76) occurs with other sulfur-containing alkaloids in the *Rhizophoraceae* (which see for further discussion).
    Rhizophor.   *Cassipourea gerrardii*

Gerrardoline ($C_8H_{15}O_2S_2N$): belongs here?
    Rhizophor.   *Cassipourea gerrardii*

3-Hydroxy-stachydrine
    Capparid.   *Courbonia virgata* (frt)

dl-Hygrine (fig. 76)
    Crucif.   *Cochlearia arctica*
    Erythroxyl.   *Erythroxylum coca* (lvs), *truxillense* (lvs)
    Convolvul.   *Convolvulus hamadae* (rt)
    Solan.   *Nicandra physaloides* (rt), *Physalis* (4, rts)
    Orchid.   *Dendrobium chrysanthum, primulinum*

β-Hygrine
    Erythroxyl.   *Erythroxylum coca* (lvs), *truxillense* (lvs)
    Convolvul.   *Convolvulus hamadae*

Hygroline is the alcohol of *dl-hygrine*.
    Crucif.   *Cochlearia arctica* (− ?)
    Erythroxyl.   *Erythroxylum coca* (lvs, − ?), *truxillense* (lvs,− ?)
    Rhizophor.   *Carallia brachiata* (lvs, +), *Gynotroches axillaris* (bk, +)

Isoficine: see note under *ficine*.
    Mor.   *Ficus pantoniana*

β-Methyl-pyrroline
    Piper.   *Piper nigrum* (frt?)

N-Methyl-pyrrolidine
    Solan.   *Atropa, Nicotiana tabacum* (plt)

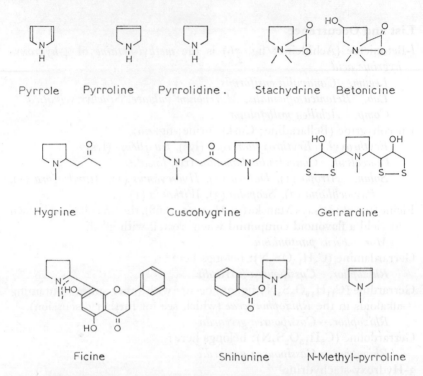

Fig. 76. Pyrrole, pyrroline, pyrrolidine, and derived alkaloids.

N-Methyl-pyrroline (fig. 76)

  Solan.   Atropa belladonna, Nicotiana tabacum

Pyrrole (fig. 76) has not, I think, been found free in higher plants.

Pyrrolidine (Tetrahydro-pyrrole; fig. 76)

  Umbell.   Daucus carota (lvs)

  Solan.   Nicotiana tabacum

Pyrroline (fig. 76)—has not, I think, been found free in higher plants.

Ryanodine

  Flacourti.   Ryania speciosa (st., rt)

Shihunine (fig. 76) has been described as a new type of alkaloid 'remotely related' to the *phthalide-isoquinolines.*

  Orchid.   Dendrobium lohohense

dl-Stachydrine (Leonucardine; fig. 76) is widely distributed. It is not always clear which of the stachydrines (*dl*- or *l*-) is present.

  Rut.   Citrus vulgaris (aurantium?) (lvs)

  Lab.   Betonica officinalis (and other spp.?); *Galeopsis grandiflora; Lagochilus hirtus, setulosus; Leonurus cardiaca; Stachys* (many spp.)

Comp.   Chrysanthemum cinerariaefolium, sinense (lvs, fl.)
Gram.   Oryza sativa (sd)
l-Stachydrine: see note under *dl-stachydrine*.
Capparid.   Capparis tomentosa (frt ?)
Legum.   Medicago sativa
Rut.   Citrus aurantium (lvs)
d-Turicine is a diastereoisomer of *betonicine*.
Lab.   Betonica officinalis, Stachys sylvatica

PYRROLIZIDINES

GENERAL

Leonard (in *M. & H.*, v.6, 1960) calls this family of alkaloids the ' *Senecio group*' from their frequent occurrence in *Senecio* of the *Compositae*. Many of them occur also in the *Boraginaceae* (p. 1751 and table 82), and in *Crotalaria* of the *Leguminosae*. There are records, too, from *Gramineae, Orchidaceae*; single species of *Rhizophoraceae* and *Santalaceae*; from two genera of the *Sapotaceae*; and possibly from the *Apocynaceae*. It seems better, in view of this wider distribution, to use the alternative name '*pyrrolizidine alkaloids*' for this rather large group.

There are, says Leonard, three main categories of *pyrrolizidine alkaloids*: (*a*) monoesters of a '*necine*' with a monocarboxylic '*necic acid*'; (*b*) diesters of a '*necine*' with two different monocarboxylic '*necic acids*'; (*c*) cyclic diesters of a '*necine*' with a dicarboxylic '*necic acid*'.

An interesting feature is that many of these alkaloids occur also as *N-oxides*. There is some evidence that these last are important in metabolism, predominating during the active vegetative stage and then decreasing.

Necines

These all have a *pyrrolizidine* nucleus with a —CH$_2$OH group at position 1 (fig. 77). Some of the necines seem to occur both free and as esters so we have included them in our list of alkaloids.

Necic acids

These are of bewildering variety and it is outside the scope of this book to discuss their spatial relationships in detail. We list them here but discuss them as *carboxylic acids* and *lactones,* though few of them seem to occur except in the *pyrrolizidine alkaloids.*

acetyl-senecic acid, β-acetyl-(−)-trachelanthic acid, angelic acid, carthamoidinecic acid, dicrotalic acid, echimidinic acid (macrotomic acid?), grantalic acid, grantianic acid, hastanecic acid, heliotrinic acid, hygrophyllinecic acid, integerrinecic acid, isatinecic acid, 'jacolic acid', jaconecic acid, jacozinecic acid, junceic acid, lasiocarpic acid, latifolic acid, mikanecic acid, monocrotalic acid, platynecic acid?, propionic acid, retronecic acid, riddellic acid, sarracinic acid, sceleranecic acid, senecic acid, senecifolic acid, seneciphyllic acid, squalinecic acid, trachelanthic acid, usaramoensinecic acid, viridifloric acid.

A recent treatment of this group is a book by Bull, Culvenor and Dick (1968). The authors point out that plants now known to contain these alkaloids, such as *Senecio jacobaea,* have been suspected of toxicity for at least 180 years.

They marvel at the curious distribution of *pyrrolizidines* and say:

> It is a remarkable coincidence that three completely unrelated groups of plant species in the families Compositae, Leguminosae and Boraginaceae should elaborate not only the unusual pyrrolizidine amino-alcohols but also the same highly unusual type of esterifying acid in association with the amino-alcohols. This situation suggests that precursors of the esterifying acids are part of the precursors of the pyrrolizidine ring, i.e. that the pyrrolizidine ring is itself formed from two relatively simple esters of which the acid portions are later elaborated into the known esterifying acids.

Their lists show how much our knowledge of these alkaloids has been extended since the review by Leonard.

From the chemotaxonomic point of view we may note:

(*a*) The few *pyrrolizidine alkaloids* of *Festuca, Lolium* and *Thelepogon* (*Gramineae*) seem only to occur in that family.

(*b*) The many *pyrrolizidine alkaloids* of the *Compositae* seem to be confined in that family to the *Eupatorieae* and *Senecioneae.* A few of them occur also in either the *Boraginaceae* or the *Leguminosae.*

(*c*) The many *pyrrolizidine alkaloids* of the *Leguminosae* seem to be confined in that family to 3 genera of the *Faboideae/Genisteae.* Each genus seems to have its own alkaloids and within the genus *Crotalaria* the distribution of the alkaloids seems to parallel more or less the classification.

(*d*) The many *pyrrolizidine alkaloids* of the large family *Boraginaceae* (100/2,000) distinguish it clearly from the other families of the **Tubiflorae.**

List and Occurrence

7β-Acetoxy-1-methoxymethyl-1,2-dehydro-pyrrolizidine
  Legum.   Crotalaria aridicola
Acetyl-indicine yields *retronecine* and β-*acetyl*-(−)-*trachelanthic acid*.
  Boragin.   Heliotropium indicum
Acetyl-monocrotaline (Sericine, Spectabiline)
  Legum.   Crotalaria sericea, spectabilis (plt, sd)
Amabiline yields *supinidine* and *viridifloric acid*.
  Boragin.   Cynoglossum amabile
Anacrotine yields *crotanecine* and *senecic acid*.
  Legum.   Crotalaria anagyroides, incana, laburnifolia
7-Angelyl-heliotridine (Rivularine)
  Boragin.   Heliotropium supinum
  Comp.   Senecio rivularis
7-Angelyl-heliotridine trachelanthate
  Boragin.   Heliotropium supinum
7-Angelyl-heliotridine viridiflorate
  Boragin.   Heliotropium supinum
7-Angelyl-retronecine
  Boragin.   Cynoglossum latifolium
Angularine yields *rosmarinecine* and *seneciphyllic acid*.
  Comp.   Senecio angulatus
Aquaticine ($C_{18}H_{25}O_5N$) is similar to *hieracifoline*.
  Comp.   Senecio aquaticus
Brasilinecine is possibly a mixture of *senecionine, seneciphylline*, and *jacobine*.
  Comp.   Senecio brasiliensis
Campestrine ($C_{13}H_{19}O_3N$)
  Comp.   Senecio campestris var. *maritimus*
Carategine yields ? and *viridifloric acid*.
  Boragin.   Lindelofia tschimganica; Rindera oblongifolia; Solenanthus circinatus, karateginus
Carthamoidine is said to give *retronecine* and *carthamoidinecic acid*, but it is possibly a mixture of *senecionine* and *seneciphylline*.
  Comp.   Senecio carthamoides
Cassipourine
  Rhizophor.   Cassipourea gummiflua var. *verticillata*
Chlorodeoxy-sceleratine
  Comp.   Senecio sceleratus
Crispatine yields *retronecine* and *crispatic acid* (one form of 3-*hydroxy-2,3,4-trimethyl-glutaric acid*).
  Legum.   Crotalaria crispata

Crosemperine
> Legum.   Crotalaria semperflorens

Cynaustine yields (+)-supinidine and viridifloric acid.
> Boragin.   Cynoglossum australe

Cynaustraline yields (+)-isoretronecanol and viridifloric acid.
> Boragin.   Cynoglossum australe

Decorticasine yields norloline and propionic acid.
> Legum.   Adenocarpus argyrophyllus, decorticans, grandiflorus, hispanicus

Dicrotaline (fig. 77) is a cyclic diester of retronecine and dicrotalic acid.
> Legum.   Crotalaria dura, globifera

'Douglasiine' is a mixture of senecionine, seneciphylline, retrorsine, and riddelline?
> Comp.   Senecio douglasii

Echimidine (fig. 77) is a diester of retronecine with angelic acid and echimidinic acid.
> Boragin.   Echium italicum, plantagineum (lycopsis)

Echinatine is a monoester of heliotridine and viridifloric acid.
> Boragin.   Cynoglossum amabile, officinale; Heliotropium supinum; Lindelofia tschimganica; Rindera austroechinata, baldschuanica, echinata, oblongifolia; Solenanthus karateginus
> Comp.   Eupatorium maculatum (rt)

Echiumine is a diester of retronecine, angelic acid, and trachelanthic acid.
> Boragin.   Amsinckia hispida, intermedia, lycopsoides; Echium plantagineum (lycopis)

'Eremophiline' is a mixture of senecionine, seneciphylline, and retrorsine?
> Comp.   Senecio eremophilus

1α-Ethoxycarbonyl-8β-pyrrolizidine
> Orchid.   Chysis bractescens

Europine is a monoester of heliotridine and lasiocarpic acid.
> Boragin.   Heliotropium europeum

Europine-N-oxide
> Boragin.   Heliotropium europeum

Festucine is isomeric with loline.
> Gram.   Festuca arundinacea (in a toxic var.)

Fuchsisenecionine
> Comp.   Senecio fuchsii, vulgaris

Fulvine yields retronecine and fulvinic acid (one form of 3-hydroxy-2,3,4-trimethyl-glutaric acid).
> Legum.   Crotalaria crispata, fulva, madurensis

Fulvine-N-oxide
> Legum.   Crotalaria fulva

Gerrardamine
  Rhizophor. Cassipourea gerrardii
Graminifoline ($C_{18}H_{23}O_5N$)
  Comp. Senecio graminifolius
Grantaline
  Legum. Crotalaria grantiana
Grantianine is a diester of *retronecine* and *grantianic acid.*
  Legum. Crotalaria grantiana
Hastacine yields *hastanecine* and *hastanecic acid.*
  Comp. Cacalia hastata
Hastanecine is isomeric with *platynecine.* It is the necine of *hastacine.*
  Does it occur free?
Heleurine is a monoester of *supinidine* and *heliotrinic acid.*
  Boragin. Heliotropium europeum
Heleurine-*N*-oxide
  Boragin. Heliotropium europeum
Heliosupine (Cynoglossophine) is a diester of *heliotridine* with *angelic acid* and *echimidinic acid.*
  Boragin. Cynoglossum officinale (plt), *Echium vulgare, Heliotropium supinum*
Heliosupine-*N*-oxide
  Boragin. Cynoglossum officinale (plt)
Heliotridine is a stereoisomer of *retronecine* (fig. 77).
  Boragin. Heliotropium europeum (free?)
Heliotridine-*N*-oxide
  Boragin. Heliotropium europeum (free?)
Heliotrine (Isoheliotrine) is a monoester of *heliotridine* and *heliotrinic acid.*
  Boragin. Heliotropium arguzioides, dasycarpum, eichwaldii, europeum, lasiocarpum
Heliotrine-*N*-oxide
  Boragin. Heliotropium europeum
Hieracifoline is a mixture of *senecionine* and *seneciphylline?*
  Comp. Erechtites hieracifolia
7α- and 7β-Hydroxy-1-methoxymethyl-1,2-dehydro-8α-pyrrolizidine
  Legum. Crotalaria aridicola, medicaginea (α- only?), *trifoliastrum*
7β-Hydroxy-1-methylene-pyrrolizidine
  Legum. Crotalaria goreënsis, maypurensis
7β-Hydroxy-1-methylene-8β-pyrrolizidine
  Legum. Crotalaria goreënsis, maypurensis
1-Hydroxymethyl-1β,2β-epoxy-pyrrolizidine
  Legum. Crotalaria grantiana, trifoliastrum
Hygrophylline
  Comp. Senecio hygrophyllus

1-Hydroxymethyl-7-hydroxy-pyrrolizidine
  Legum. Laburnum anagyroides
1-Hydroxymethyl-pyrrolizidine tiglate
  Sapot. Mimusops elengi
Incanine is a cyclic diester of *retronecine* and *2-hydroxy-3,5-dimethyl-hexane-2,4-dicarboxylic acid.*
  Boragin. Trichodesma incanum (sd)
Incanine-*N*-oxide
  Boragin. Trichodesma incanum (sd)
Indicine yields *retronecine* and (−)-*trachelanthic acid.*
  Boragin. Heliotropium amplexicaule, indicum
Indicinine
  Boragin. Heliotropium indicum
Integerrimine (Squalidine) is a cyclic diester of *retronecine* and *integer-rinecic acid.*
  Legum. Crotalaria breviflora, incana (sd), *mucronata, usaramoensis*
  Comp. Senecio erraticus var., *integerrimus, kleinia, magnificus, squalidus, viscosus*
Intermedine (Retronecine-(+)-trachelanthate)
  Boragin. Amsinckia hispida, intermedia, lycopsoides
Jacobine yields *retronecine* and *jaconecic acid.*
  Comp. Senecio brasiliensis, cineraria, jacobaea, paludosus
Jacoline yields *retronecine* and ?.
  Comp. Senecio jacobaea
Jaconine ($C_{20}H_{32}O_7NCl$): the first recorded example of a chlorine-containing alkaloid? It yields *retronecine* and ?.
  Comp. Senecio jacobaea
Jacozine yields *retronecine* and *jacozinecic acid.*
  Comp. Senecio jacobaea
Junceine is a cyclic diester of *retronecine* and *junceic acid.*
  Legum. Crotalaria juncea (sd), *rubiginosa* (*wightiana*)
Kumokirine: see also *kuramerine.*
  Orchid. Liparis kumokiri, kurameri
Laburnamine
  Legum. Laburnum anagyroides
Laburnine (fig. 77) is the optical antipode of *trachelanthamidine.* Leonard (1953) says, 'The most unusual feature of the alkaloid laburnine is that it belongs to the lupin alkaloid family by source and to the *senecio* alkaloid family due to its constitution as a derivative of pyrrolizidine....'
  Legum. Laburnum anagyroides (sd)
Laburnine angelate
  Sapot. Planchonella anteridifera, thyrsoidea

Laburnine benzoate
>Sapot. *Planchonella anteridifera, thyrsoidea*

Lanigerosine
>Comp. *Senecio paucicalyculatus, retrorsus*

Lasiocarpine is a diester of *heliotridine* with *angelic acid* and *lasiocarpic acid*.
>Boragin. *Heliotropium europeum* (plt, sd), *lasiocarpum* (plt)

Lasiocarpine-*N*-oxide
>Boragin. *Heliotropium europeum* (plt, sd)

Latifoline(2)- yields *retronecine, angelic acid,* and *latifolic acid*.
>Boragin. *Cynoglossum latifolium*

Lindelofamine is a monoester of *lindelofidine* and *trachelanthic acid*—the latter esterified with *angelic acid*?
>Boragin. *Lindelofia macrostyla, Paracaryum heliocarpum* (plt)

Lindelofidine (+-Isoretronecanol) is an isomer of *trachelanthamidine*. It is the necine of *lindelofamine, lindelofine, thesine, thesinine* (and *thesinicine*?).
>Santal. *Thesium minkwitzianum* (free?)

Lindelofine is a monoester of *lindelofidine* and *trachelanthic acid*.
>Boragin. *Lindelofia macrostyla, stylosa; Paracaryum heliocarpum* (plt)

Loline (fig. 77)
>Gram. *Lolium cuneatum* (sd)

Lolinidine: belongs here?
>Gram. *Lolium cuneatum* (sd)

Lolinine
>Gram. *Lolium cuneatum*

Lycopsamine (Retronecine-(−)-viridiflorate)
>Boragin. *Amsinckia hispida, intermedia, lycopsoides*

Macronecine is isomeric with *platynecine*. It is the necine of *macrophylline* (2).

Macrophylline (2) yields *macronecine* and *angelic acid*.
>Comp. *Senecio amphibolus, macrophyllus* (plt), *schvetzovii*

Macrotomine is a monoester of *trachelanthamidine* and *echimidinic* or *macrotomic acid*.
>Boragin. *Macrotomia echioides* (lvs, st.)

Madurensine yields *crotanecine* and *integerrinecic acid*.
>Legum. *Crotalaria agatiflora, madurensis*

Malaxin yields *glucose* and (+)-*trachelanthamidine*.
>Orchid. *Malaxis congesta*

1α-Methoxycarbonyl-8β-pyrrolizidine
>Orchid. *Chysis bractescens*

1-Methoxymethyl-1,2-dehydro-8α-pyrrolizidine
>Legum. *Crotalaria aridicola, medicaginea, trifoliastrum*

1-Methoxymethyl-1β,2β-epoxy-pyrrolizidine
> Legum.   Crotalaria trifoliastrum

1-Methylene-pyrrolizidine (Damarensine)
> Legum.   Crotalaria anagyroides, damarensis, rhodesiae, verrucosa

Mikanoidine is a mixture, including sarracine (Bull et al. 1968).
> Comp.   Senecio kaempferi, mikanoides

Monocrotaline is a cyclic diester of retronecine and monocrotalic acid.
> Legum.   Crotalaria (at least 9 species)

Monocrotaline-N-oxide
> Legum.   Crotalaria retusa (lf, sd)

N-Acetyl-loline
> Gram.   Lolium cuneatum

Neoplatyphylline yields platynecine and integerrinecic acid.
> Comp.   Senecio platyphyllus (rhombifolius)

Nervosine is closely related to kumokirine.
> Orchid.   Liparis nervosa

Nikanine ($C_{18}H_{27}O_5N$): belongs here?
> Boragin.   Trichodesma incanum (lf, st., sd)

Nikanine-N-oxide ($C_{18}H_{27}O_6N$): belongs here?
> Boragin.   Trichodesma incanum (lf, st., sd)

N-Methyl-loline
> Gram.   Lolium cuneatum?

Norloline
> Gram.   Lolium cuneatum

O-Acetyl-senkirkine
> Comp.   Senecio kirkii

Onetine yields otonecine and 'jacolic' acid.
> Comp.   Senecio othonnae

Otonecine (Othonecine, $C_9H_{15}O_3N$) is an unusual necine in that it has an N-methyl group. It is the necine of otosenine (othosenine), senkerkine, onetine, and retusamine.

Otosenine (Othosenine; Tomentosine) yields otonecine and jaconecic acid.
> Comp.   Senecio othonnae, tomentosus, and 2 other spp.

Paucicaline
> Comp.   Senecio paucicalyculatus

Planchonelline is the trans-β-methylthioacrylate ester of laburnine.
> Sapot.   Planchonella anteridifera, thyrsoidea

Platynecine (Mikanecine, fig. 77) is the necine of mikanoidine, platyphylline, and sarracine.

Platyphylline is a cyclic diester of platynecine and platynecic acid?
> Comp.   Petasites laevigatus (Nardosmia l.) Senecio platyphyllus (plt) and 4 or 5 other spp.

Platyphylline-*N*-oxide
> *Comp.* *Senecio platyphyllus*, etc.

'Pterophine' is a mixture of *senecionine* and *seneciphylline*?

Renarcine is said to be the necine of *senkirkine* (*renardine*).

Retronecine (fig. 77) is by far the commonest necine. It occurs in *dicrotaline, echimidine, echiumine, grantianine, integerrimine, jacobine, jacoline, jaconine, junceine, monocrotaline, retrorsine, riddelline, scleratine, senecifoline, senecionine, seneciphylline, spartioidine, squalidine, trichodesmine,* and *usaramoensine*.
> *Legum.* *Crotalaria retusa* (free?)

Retronecine-*N*-oxide (Isatinecine) is the necine of *retrorsine-N-oxide*.

Retrorsine (β-Longilobine) is a cyclic diester of *retronecine* and *isatinecic acid*.
> *Legum.* *Crotalaria spartioides, usaramoensis*
> *Comp.* *Erechtites quadridentata* (plt); *Senecio retrorsus* (lvs) and about 20 other spp.

Retrorsine-*N*-oxide (Isatidine)
> *Comp.* *Erechtites quadridentata, Senecio isatideus, retrorsus,* and other spp.

Retusamine
> *Legum.* *Crotalaria crassipes, mitchellii, novae-hollandiae, retusa* (sd)

Retusamine-*N*-oxide
> *Legum.* *Crotalaria retusa* (sd)

Retusine
> *Legum.* *Crotalaria retusa, spectabilis*

Riddelline is a cyclic diester of *retronecine* and *riddellic acid*.
> *Legum.* *Crotalaria juncea* (sd)
> *Comp.* *Senecio riddellii* and several other spp.

Rinderine (Hydroxy-supinine; Heliotridrine-(+)-trachelanthate)
> *Boragin.* *Rindera baldschuanica, Solenanthus turkestanicus*
> *Comp.* *Eupatorium serotinum* (lvs, st.)

Rosmarinecine (fig. 77) is the necine of *rosmarinine*. Does it occur (free?) in
> *Comp.* *Senecio adnatus* (*hygrophilus*)

Rosmarinine is a cyclic diester of *rosmarinecine* and *senecic acid*.
> *Comp.* *Senecio rosmarinifolius* and several other spp.

Rosmarinine-*N*-oxide
> *Comp.* *Senecio* (3 spp.)

Ruwenine ($C_{18}H_{27}O_6N$)
> *Comp.* *Senecio ruwenzoriensis* (plt)

Ruzorine ($C_{18}H_{27}O_8N$)
> *Comp.* *Senecio ruwenzoriensis* (plt)

Sarracine is a diester of *platynecine* with *angelic acid* and *sarracinic acid.*
>   *Comp.   Senecio mikanioides, rhombifolius (platyphyllus), sarracenicu* (plt)

Sarracine-*N*-oxide
>   *Comp.   Senecio sarracenicus* (plt)

Sceleratine is a cyclic diester of *retronecine* and *sceleranecic acid.*
>   *Comp.   Senecio sceleratus*

Senecifolidine ($C_{18}H_{25}O_7N$) is probably a mixture.

Senecifoline is probably a mixture.

Senecine
>   *Comp.   Senecio* (3)

Senecionine (Aureine) is a cyclic diester of *retronecine* and *senecic acid.*
>   *Legum.   Crotalaria anagyroides, juncea* (sd), *usaramoensis*
>   *Comp.   Brachyglottis repanda, Emilia sonchifolia, Erechtites* (2), *Petasites* (1), *Senecio* (about 30), *Tussilago farfara*

Senecionine-*N*-oxide
>   *Comp.   Erechtites quadridentata* (plt)

Seneciphylline (Jacodine; α-Longilobine) is a cyclic diester of *retronecine* and *seneciphyllic acid.*
>   *Legum.   Crotalaria juncea* (sd)
>   *Comp.   Erechtites* (2); *Senecio* (about 32)

Seneciphylline-*N*-oxide
>   *Comp.   Erechtites quadridentata* (plt), *Senecio platyphyllus*

Senkirkine (Renardine)
>   *Comp.   Brachyglottis repanda; Petasites laevigatus* (plt); *Senecio kirkii* (lf, bk), *kleinia renardii*

Silvasenecine ($C_{12}H_{21}O_4N$ or $C_{13}H_{21}O_3N$)
>   *Comp.   Senecio sylvaticus* (lf), *vulgaris*

Sincamidine
>   *Boragin.   Amsinckia intermedia*

Spartioidine is a cyclic diester of *retronecine* and an isomer of *seneciphyllic acid.*
>   *Comp.   Senecio spartioides*

Squalidine yields *retronecine* and *squalinecic acid.*
>   *Comp.   Senecio squalidus*

Strigosine
>   *Boragin.   Heliotropium strigosum*

Supinidine (fig. 77) is the necine of *heleurine* and *supinine.* It is said to occur (free?) in:
>   *Boragin.   Heliotropium supinum* (plt)

Supinine is a monoester of *supinidine* and *trachelanthic acid.*
>   *Chenopodi.   Anabasis aphylla* (occurrence not listed by Bull *et al.*)

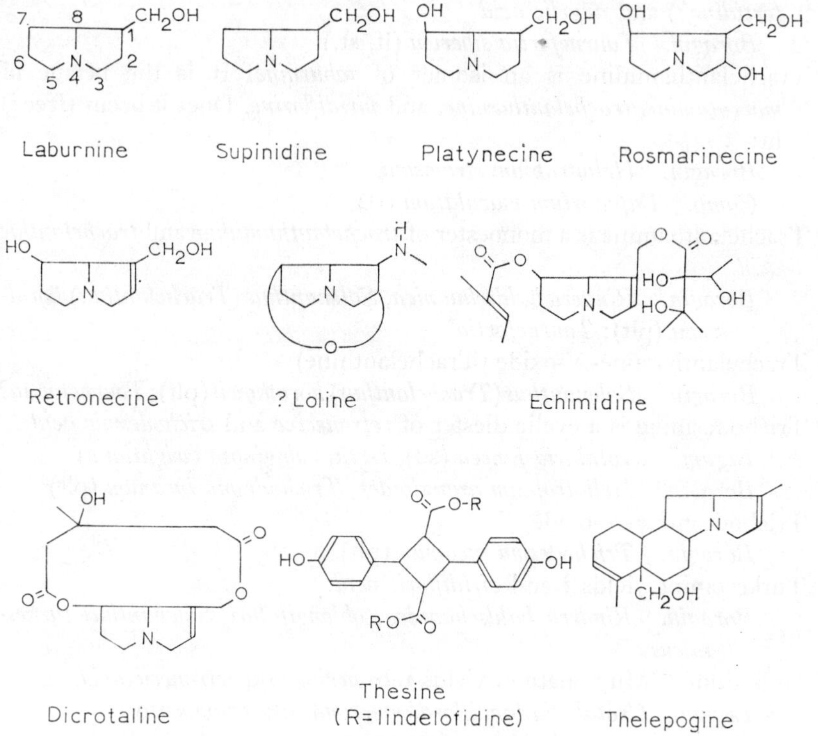

Laburnine   Supinidine   Platynecine   Rosmarinecine

Retronecine   ? Loline   Echimidine

Dicrotaline   Thesine   Thelepogine
                     (R=lindelofidine)

Fig. 77. Some necines and pyrrolizidines.

Boragin. Heliotropium europeum (plt), *supinum* (plt); *Tournefortia sarmentosa* (lf, st.); *Trichodesma zeylanicum*
Comp. Eupatorium serotinum (lf, st.) (occurrence not listed by Bull *et al.*)

Supinine-*N*-oxide
Boragin. Heliotropium; *Tournefortia*

Thelepogidine ($C_{18}H_{29}O_2N$): belongs here?
Gram. Thelepogon elegans

Thelepogine (fig. 77)
Gram. Thelepogon elegans

Thesine (fig. 77) is a very complicated alkaloid containing two *lindelofidine* groups.
Santal. Thesium minkwitzianum

Thesinicine ($C_{10}H_{11}O_2N$)
Santal. Thesium minkwitzianum

Tournefortidine (?Turneforcidine) is the necine of *tournefortine*?

Tournefortine ('Turneforcine, $C_{13}H_{21}O_3N$) yields *turneforcidine* (*tournefortidine*?) and *angelic acid*

>   Boragin.   *Tournefortia siberica* (lf, st.)

Trachelanthamidine is an isomer of *laburnine*. It is the necine of *macrotomine, trachelanthamine,* and *viridiflorine.* Does it occur (free?) in:

>   Boragin.   *Heliotropium strigosum*
>   Comp.   *Eupatorium maculatum* (rt)

Trachelanthamine is a monoester of *trachelanthamidine* and *trachelanthic acid.*

>   Boragin.   *Rindera baldschuanica, Solenanthus (Trachelanthus) korolkowii* (plt); *Tournefortia?*

Trachelanthamine-*N*-oxide (Trachelanthine)

>   Boragin.   *Solenanthus (Trachelanthus) korolkowii* (plt); *Tournefortia?*

Trichodesmine is a cyclic diester of *retronecine* and *trichodesmic acid.*

>   Legum.   *Crotalaria juncea* (sd), *recta, rubiginosa (wightiana)*
>   Boragin.   *Heliotropium arguzioides; Trichodesma incanum* (plt)

Trichodesmine-*N*-oxide

>   Boragin.   *Trichodesma incanum* (plt)

Turkestanine yields ? and *viridifloric acid.*

>   Boragin.   *Rindera baldschuanica, oblongifolia; Solenanthus turkestanicus*

Usaramine (?Mucronatine) yields *retronecine* and *retronecic acid.*

>   Legum.   *Crotalaria breviflora, mucronata, usaramoensis*

Usaramoensine is probably a mixture.

>   Legum.   *Crotalaria usaramoensis*

Viridiflorine yields *trachelanthamidine* and *viridifloric acid.*

>   Boragin.   *Cynoglossum viridiflorum* (plt); *Lindelofia olgae, pterocarpa, stylosa, tschimganica; Paracaryum himalayense*

QUINAZOLINES

GENERAL

This small group of alkaloids is based on the ring-system of *quinazoline* (1,3-*diaza-naphthalene*; fig. 79).

When Openshaw (in *M. & H.,* v.3, 1953) wrote of these substances only five alkaloids of established constitution were known to have the *quinazoline* ring system. Ten years later Amarego (1963) recognized four types of *quinazoline* alkaloids, represented by *arborine, peganine* (*vasicine*), *febrifugine,* and *rutaecarpine* respectively. Price (in Swain, 1963) would class *rutaecarpine* and its relatives as *indolo-quinazolines.* I have chosen to place them among the *indole* groups as *quinazolino-carbolines*.

Mothes (1966) gives the scheme shown in fig. 78 for the biosynthesis of *peganine* (*vasicine*). Johne and Gröger (1968) do not solve the problem of the unknown component of fig. 78, but Manske (in *M.*, v.10, 1968) says of the *Mackinlaya* alkaloids, 'since vasicine [peganine] is possibly derived biosynthetically from anthranilic acid and ornithine it is probable that these alkaloids are derived from anthranilic acid and lysine'.

Johne and Gröger say that *quinazoline alkaloids* occur in *Acanthaceae*, *Araliaceae*, *Leguminosae*, *Rutaceae*, *Saxifragaceae*, *Zygophyllaceae*, *Scrophulariaceae*, and *Palmae*. I have no records from the last.

List and Occurrence

Aegelinine (7-Hydroxy-1-phenyl-1,2-dihydro-4-quinazolone)
  Rut. Aegle marmelos (lvs)
Aniflorine (fig. 79)
  Acanth. Anisotes sessiliflorus
Anisessine
  Acanth. Anisotes sessiliflorus
Anisotine
  Acanth. Anisotes sessiliflorus
Arborine (Glycosine; 1-Methyl-2-benzyl-4(1H)-quinazolone)—a millipede is said to secrete two similar substances!
  Rut. Glycosmis arborea (I have been unable to disentangle
    G. arborea and *G. pentaphylla*. Are they distinct?)
Deoxy-aniflorine
  Acanth. Anisotes sessiliflorus
Deoxy-vasicinone
  Zygophyll. Peganum harmala (sd)
Dichroidine: belongs here?
  Saxifrag. Dichroa febrifuga
Febrifugine (β- and γ-Dichroines)
  Saxifrag. Dichroa febrifuga, Hydrangea sp.
Glycorine (1-Methyl-4-quinazolone; fig. 79)
  Rut. Glycosmis arborea
Glycosmicine
  Rut. Glycosmis arborea
Glycosmine (Glycosminine; 2-Benzyl-4-quinazolone; fig. 79)
  Rut. Glycosmis pentaphylla (*arborea*?)
6-Hydroxy-peganine (Vasicinol)
  Acanth. Adhatoda vasica

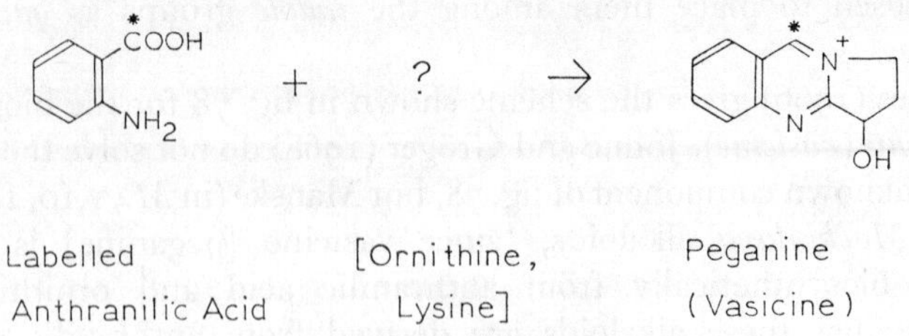
COOH
NH2
+
?
OH
Labelled
Anthranilic Acid
[Ornithine,
Lysine]
Peganine
(Vasicine)

Fig. 78. Biosynthesis of quinazolines.

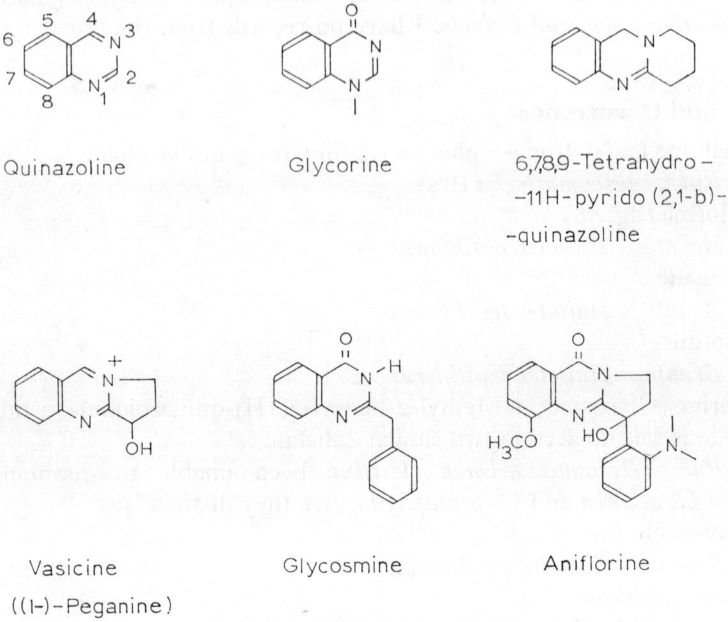
Quinazoline
Glycorine
6,7,8,9-Tetrahydro-
-11H-pyrido (2,1-b)-
-quinazoline
OH
H3CO
HO
Vasicine
((l-)-Peganine)
Glycosmine
Aniflorine

Fig. 79. Quinazoline and some quinazoline alkaloids.

Isofebrifugine (?α-Dichroine): a diastereoisomer of *febrifugine* ?
Saxifrag. *Dichroa febrifuga*

4-Keto-dihydro-quinazoline
Saxifrag. *Dichroa febrifuga* (lvs, rt)

Oxo-deoxy-peganine
Scrophulari. *Linaria transiliensis*

Oxo-peganine
Scrophulari. *Linaria* (?*vulgariformis*)

(+)-Peganine was found as late as 1962.
Legum. *Galega officinalis* (plt)

4-Quinazolone
  Saxifrag. Dichroa febrifuga
Sessiflorine
  Acanth. Anisotes sessiliflorus
6,7,8,9-Tetrahydro-11H-pyrido(2,1-b)-quinazoline (fig. 79)
  Arali. Mackinlaya macrosciadea, subulata
6,7,8,9-Tetrahydropyrido(2,1-b)-quinazoline-11-one
  Arali. Mackinlaya macrosciadea, subulata
l-Vasicine ((−)-Peganine; 3-Hydroxy-pegane; fig. 79). Manske (in *M.*,
  v.10, 1968) says: 'The synthesis of *dl*-vasicine under conditions which
  might occur in plant cells has been achieved by the condensation of
  o-amino-benzaldehyde with α-hydroxy-γ-aminobutyraldehyde followed by catalytic reduction...'
  Zygophyll. Peganum harmala (st., fl., sd)
  Acanth. Adhatoda vasica
  Scrophulari. Linaria (5 or 6 spp.)
Vasicinone may be formed by air-oxidation from *vasicine*, but it occurs
  as such in *Peganum*, at least.
  Zygophyll. Peganum harmala (sd)
  Acanth. Adhatoda vasica

QUINOLINE GROUPS

GENERAL

The members of this class may formally be thought of as derivatives of
quinoline (fig. 80). We may sub-divide the class as follows:

  I. Simple quinolines—almost all *quinolines* without other fused rings.
     About 30.
  II. Furoquinolines and related alkaloids, including some *near-
      furoquinolines*. About 50.
  III. Quinolyl-quinuclidines (Cinchona alkaloids, excluding the *indole*
       group (p. 218)). About 20?
  IV. Quinolyl-imidazole alkaloids. About 4.

Openshaw (in *M. & H.*, v.3, 1953), discussing 'quinoline alkaloids,
other than those of *Cinchona*', says:

  With one exception, the alkaloids discussed...are all derived from
  members of the Rutaceae, and they can be classified chemically into
  two groups. The members of one group are methoxylated derivatives
  of (2,3-b)-furoquinoline and closely related alkaloids...The second
  group comprises the numerous alkaloids of Angostura bark; apart

from some simpler bases, these are 2-substituted 4-methoxy-quinolines.

All the principal alkaloids of both groups possess as a common structural feature the 4-methoxyquinoline unit, in consequence of which they undergo a typical isomerization to N-methyl-4-quinolones on vigorous treatment with methyl iodide. This reaction...also provides a chemical relationship with the alkaloid of *Echinops* species (Compositae), which was shown to be N-Methyl-4-quinolone itself. The isomeric N-methyl-2-quinolone occurs in Angostura bark.

Actually, as we shall see, there are more occurrences outside the *Rutaceae* than Openshaw stated.

There is evidence that the *quinoline* part of *furoquinolines* such as *dictamnine* (fig. 80) and *skimmianine* is formed from *anthranilic acid* and *acetate*, the methyl groups coming from *methionine*.

I SIMPLE QUINOLINES

List and Occurrence

1-Acetoxymethyl-2-propyl-4-quinolone
  Rut. Boronia ternata (lvs)
2-Amyl-quinoline
  Rut. Galipea officinalis (bk)
2-Amyl-4-methoxy-quinoline (fig. 80)
  Rut. Galipea officinalis (bk)
Casimiroine (1-Methyl-4-methoxy-7,8-methylenedioxy-2-quinolone)
  Rut. Casimiroa edulis (bk, sd)
Casimiroitine (1-Methyl-4-O-ethyl-7,8-methylenedioxy-2-quinolone)
  Rut. Casimiroa edulis
Cuspareine
  Rut. Galipea officinalis (bk)
Cusparidine may be an artefact.
  Rut. Galipea officinalis (bk)?
Cusparine (fig. 80) seems to have an odd distribution. Its occurrence outside the *Rutaceae* should be carefully checked.
  Legum. Gastrolobium bilobum
  Euphorbi. Garcia nutans
  Rut. Cusparia angostura (Galipea?); *Galipea cusparia (febrifuga)* (bk), *dicatoma* (bk), *officinalis* (bk)
1,2-Dimethyl-4-quinolone
  Rut. Acronychia baueri (lvs), *Platydesma campanulata*

Dubamine
    Rut. *Haplophyllum dubium* (lvs., st., fl.)
Echinopseine: belongs here?
    Comp. *Echinops ritro* (sd)
Echinops-fluorescine: belongs here?
    Comp. *Echinops ritro* (sd)
Echinopsine (N-Methyl-4-quinolone; fig. 80)
    Comp. *Echinops ritro* (sd) and at least 14 other species.
β-Echinopsine: belongs here?
    Comp. *Echinops ritro* (sd)
Eduleine (N-Methyl-2-phenyl-7-methoxy-4-quinolone)
    Rut. *Casimiroa edulis* (bk); *Lunasia amara, quercifolia* (bk)
Eduline (N-Methyl-2-phenyl-6-methoxy-4-quinolone)
    Rut. *Casimiroa edulis* (sd)
Edulinine
    Rut. *Casimiroa edulis* (bk)
Edulitine (4,8-Dimethoxy-2-quinolone)
    Rut. *Casimiroa edulis*
Evocarpine
    Rut. *Evodia rutaecarpa* (frt)
Fagaramide (fig. 80) is a *near-quinoline.*
    Rut. *Fagara macrophylla* (rtbk), *xanthoxyloides* (rtbk)
Foliosidine
    Rut. *Haplophyllum foliosum* (aerial plts)
Galipine is very like *cusparine.*
    Rut. *Galipea officinalis* (bk)
Galipoidine: belongs here?
    Rut. *Galipea officinalis* (bk)
Galipoline: is very like *cusparine.*
    Rut. *Galipea officinalis* (bk)
Graveoline (N-Methyl-2-(3′,4′-methylenedioxyphenyl)-4-quinolone)
    Rut. *Ruta graveolens*
Graveolinine (2-(3′,4′-Methylenedioxyphenyl)-4-methoxy-quinoline)
    Rut. *Lunasia amara, Ruta graveolens*
Lunamarine (N-Methyl-2(3′,4′-methylenedioxyphenyl)-7-methoxy-4-quinolone)
    Rut. *Lunasia amara*
N-Methyl-2-phenyl-4-quinolone
    Rut. *Balfourodendron riedelianum*
N-Methyl-2-quinolone
    Rut. *Galipea officinalis* (bk)
2-Phenyl-4-methoxy-quinoline
    Rut. *Lunasia amara*

Quinaldine
>   *Rut.   Galipea officinalis* (bk)
Quinoline (fig. 80) is said to occur (free ?) in
>   *Rut.   Citrus aurantium, Galipea officinalis* (bk)
Rutamine (?Dimethyl-graveoline)
>   *Rut.   Ruta graveolens*

II FUROQUINOLINES AND RELATED ALKALOIDS

List and Occurrence

Acronidine is closely related to *choisyine*.
>   *Rut.   Acronychia baueri* (lvs, bk)
Acronycidine
>   *Rut.   Acronychia baueri* (lvs, bk), *Melicope fareana* (bk)
Choisyine
>   *Rut.   Choisya ternata*
Dictamnine (fig. 80)
>   *Rut.   Aegle* (1), *Balfourodendron* (1), *Boenninghausenia* (1), *Casimiroa* (1), *Dictamnus* (1), *Evodia* (2), *Flindersia* (4), *Glycosmis* (1), *Hortia* (1), *Orixa* (1), *Phebalium* (1), *Skimmia* (2), *Zanthoxylum* (2)
Dubinidine
>   *Rut.   Haplophyllum dubium* (lvs, st., fl.), *foliosum* (plt)
Dubinine
>   *Rut.   Haplophyllum dubium* (lvs, st., fl.)
Evodine
>   *Rut.   Evodia xanthoxyloides* (lvs)
Evolatine
>   *Rut.   Evodia alata* (lvs)
Evolitrine (7-Methoxy-dictamnine)
>   *Rut.   Cusparia macrocarpa* (lvs, st.); *Evodia belahe* (bk), *littoralis* (lvs, bk); *Orixa japonica* (rtbk); *Phebalium nudum* (bk); *Platydesma campanulata* (bk, rt)
Evoxine (Haploperine) is very like *evolatine*.
>   *Rut.   Choisya ternata, Evodia xanthoxyloides* (lvs), *Haplophyllum perforatum* (lvs, st., fl., sd)
'Evoxoidine' is an artefact
γ-Fagarine (Haplophine; 8-Methoxy-dictamnine)
>   *Rut.   Aegle* (1), *Casimiroa* (1), *Dictamnus* (1), *Fagara* (1), *Geijera* (1), *Glycosmis* (1), *Haplophyllum* (2), *Hortia* (1), *Phebalium* (1), *Ravenia* (1), *Ruta* (1), *Thamnosma* (1)

Flindersiamine (6,7-Methylenedioxy-8-methoxydictamnine)
  Rut. Balfourodendron riedelianum (bk), *Flindersia* (7), *Teclea sudanica* (lvs), *Vepris bilocularis* (bk)
Flindersine (fig. 80) is a *near-furoquinoline*, included here by Price (1963).
  Rut. Flindersia australis (wd)
Haplophyllidine
  Rut. Haplophyllum perforatum (sd)
Haplophylline: belongs here?
  Rut. Haplophyllum siewersii
Haplopine (7-Hydroxy-8-methoxy-dictamnine)
  Rut. Haplophyllum perforatum (sd)
Hydroxy-lunacridine is a *near-furoquinoline*.
  Rut. Lunasia amara
(−)-Hydroxy-lunacridine (Balfourolone)—note the odd distribution of alkaloids in *Lunasia* and *Balfourodendron*.
  Rut. Balfourodendron riedelianum (bk)
Hydroxy-lunacrine
  Rut. Lunasia amara
(+)-Hydroxy-lunacrine (Balfourodine)
  Rut. Balfourodendron riedelianum (bk)
Hydroxy-lunidine is a *near-furoquinoline*.
  Rut. Lunasia amara
Hydroxy-lunine is a *dihydro-furoquinoline*.
  Rut. Lunasia amara
Ifflaiamine is a *dihydro-furoquinoline*.
  Rut. Flindersia ifflaiana (wd)
Khaplofoline is a *near-furoquinoline*.
  Rut. Haplophyllum foliosum (rt, etc.)
Kokusagine (7,8-Methylenedioxy-dictamnine)
  Rut. Evodia xanthoxyloides (bk), *Lunasia amara* (lvs), *Orixa japonica* (bk, rt, frt)
Kokusaginine (6,7-Dimethoxy-dictamnine)
  Rut. Acronychia (1), *Balfourodendron* (1), *Evodia* (4), *Flindersia* (5), *Glycosmis* (1), *Orixa* (1), *Phebalium* (1), *Platydesma* (1), *Ruta* (1), *Vepris* (1)
Kokusaginoline: belongs here?
  Rut. Orixa japonica (rt)
Lunacridine (fig. 80) is a *near-furoquinoline*.
  Rut. Lunasia amara
(−)-Lunacrine (fig. 80) is the major *Lunasia* alkaloid.
  Rut. Lunasia amara (lvs, bk), *quercifolia* (bk)
Lunacrinol (Lunasia-II) is a *near-furoquinoline*.
  Rut. Lunasia amara (lvs)

(+)-Lunacrinol (Isobalfourodine)
> *Rut.*   *Balfourodendron riedelianum* (bk)

Lunasine is a *dihydro-furoquinoline*.
> *Rut.*   *Lunasia amara* (bk), *costulata* (bk), *quercifolia* (lvs, bk, -)

Lunidine is a *near-furoquinoline*.
> *Rut.*   *Lunasia amara* var. *repanda*

Lunine is a *dihydro-furoquinoline*.
> *Rut.*   *Lunasia amara, quercifolia* (bk)

Maculine (6,7-Methylenedioxy-dictamnine)
> *Rut.*   *Flindersia maculosa* (bk, wd) and 5 other species, *Vepris bilocularis* (bk)

Maculosidine (6,8-Dimethoxy-dictamnine)
> *Rut.*   *Balfourodendron riedelianum* (bk); *Eriostemon* (5); *Flindersia maculosa* (lvs), *pubescens* (lvs)

Maculosine
> *Rut.*   *Flindersia maculosa* (bk, wd)

Medicosmine: of uncertain structure?
> *Rut.*   *Medicosma cunninghamii* (bk)

6-Methoxy-dictamnine (Pteleine)
> *Rut.*   *Platydesma campanulata* (rt, bk), *Ptelea trifoliata* (rt, frt)

'Nor-γ-fagarine': an artefact?
> *Rut.*   *Hortia arborea* (bk)?

Nor-orixine is a *near-furoquinoline*.
> *Rut.*   *Orixa japonica* (rtbk)

O-Methyl-balfourodinium⁺ is a *dihydro-furoquinoline*.
> *Rut.*   *Balfourodendron riedelianum*

O-Methyl-luminium cation
> *Rut.*   *Lunasia quercifolia*

Orixine is a *near-furoquinoline*.
> *Rut.*   *Orixa japonica* (rt)

Pilokeanine is a *near-furoquinoline*.
> *Rut.*   *Platydesma campanulata* (rt, bk)

Platydesmine
> *Rut.*   *Geijera salicifolia, Platydesma campanulata* (rt, bk), *Skimmia japonica*

Platydesmine acetate
> *Rut.*   *Geijera salicifolia*

Ribalinine is a *pyran* derivative of *quinoline*.
> *Rut.*   *Balfourodendron riedelianum* (bk)

Robustine (8-Hydroxy-dictamnine)
> *Rut.*   *Haplophyllum robustum* (rt)

Skimmianine (Aegelenine; Chloroxylonine; β-Fagarine; Pentaphylline;

Rutacine; 7,8-Dimethoxy-dictamnine) might be called the 'protopine' of the *Rutaceae*!

    Rut. Acronychia (1), *Aegle* (1), *Balfourodendron* (1), *Boronia* (1), *Casimiroa* (1), *Chloroxylon* (1), *Choisya* (1), *Citrus* (2), *Dictamnus* (2), *Eriostemon* (3), *Fagara* (5), *Flindersia* (6), *Geijera* (1), *Glycosmis* (1), *Haplophyllum* (6), *Hortia* (1), *Lunasia* (1), *Melicope* (1), *Murraya* (1), *Orixa* (1), *Phebalium* (1), *Poncirus* (1), *Ptelea* (1), *Ruta* (1), *Skimmia* (3), *Vepris* (1), *Zanthoxylum* (4)

III QUINOLYL-QUINUCLIDINES (CINCHONA ALKALOIDS IN PART)

GENERAL

The alkaloids of *Cinchona* are mostly derivatives of *quinuclidine*. A few of them (*aricine, cinchonamine*, etc.) have also an *indole* moiety, and these are dealt with elsewhere. *Quinine* itself (fig. 80) and many other *Cinchona* alkaloids have also a *quinoline* moiety and these are considered here. Apparently the two groups are biogenetically related, and Hendrickson (1965) in discussing the *indole* group, has this to say: 'A number of other alkaloids are biogenetically derived from these by a few further transformations, as in the conversion of cinchonamine (or a close relative) to the quinine family skeleton via opening of the indole ring and reclosure of the aniline nitrogen on the side chain.'

Most of the *quinolyl-quinuclidine alkaloids* occur in the *Rubiaceae*, but they are also in the related *Loganiaceae*, and in the very distantly related *Annonaceae* and *Simaroubaceae*, where they must have arisen independently.

List and Occurrence

Chairamidine
    Rubi. Cinchona ledgeriana,* *Remijia purdieana*
Chairamine may not belong here.
    Rubi. Cinchona ledgeriana,* *Remijia purdieana*
Cinchamidine (Dihydro-cinchonidine; Hydro-cinchonidine)
    Rubi. Cinchona ledgeriana*
Cinchonicine
    Rubi. Cinchona ledgeriana*

---

* Many of the alkaloids assigned to *Cinchona ledgeriana* have been found in commercial cinchona-bark, not all of which is from this species.

Cinchonidine (Cinchovatine; α-Quinidine) is isomeric with *cinchonine*.
 Logani. *Strychnos pseudoquina* (bk, wd)
 Rubi. *Cinchona* (16), *Remijia* (2)
Cinchonine
 Rubi. *Cinchona* (22), *Remijia* (3)
Cinchotine (Cinchonifine; Dihydrocinchone; Hydrocinchonine; Pseudo-
 cinchonine)
 Rubi. *Cinchona ledgeriana,** succirubra; Remijia purdieana*
Conchairamidine
 Rubi. *Cinchona ledgeriana,** Remijia purdieana*
Conchairamine
 Rubi. *Cinchona ledgeriana,** Remijia purdieana*
Concusconine
 Rubi. *Cinchona ledgeriana,** Remijia purdieana*
Cupreine
 Logani. *Strychnos pseudoquina* (bk, wd) ?
 Rubi. *Cinchona ledgeriana;** Remijia pedunculata*
Cuscamidine: belongs here ?
 Rubi. *Cinchona pelletieriana*
Cuscamine: belongs here ?
 Rubi. *Cinchona pelletieriana, pubescens*
Cusconidine: belongs here ?
 Rubi. *Cinchona pelletieriana, pubescens*
Cusconine: belongs here ?
 Rubi. *Cinchona* (3)
Cusconinine: belongs here ?
 Occurrence ?
Dicinchonine (Dicinchonicine)
 Rubi. *Cinchona* (3), *Remijia pedunculata*
Diconquine (Diquinicine)
 Rubi. *Cinchona calisaya, ledgeriana**
Epiquinidine
 Rubi. *Cinchona ledgeriana**
Epiquinine
 Rubi. *Cinchona ledgeriana**
Hydroquinidine (Dihydroquinidine)
 Annon. *Enantia polycarpa*
 Rubi. *Cinchona ledgeriana**
Hydroquinine (Dihydroquinine)
 Rubi. *Cinchona ledgeriana*
Javanine: belongs here ?
 Rubi. *Cinchona* (3)

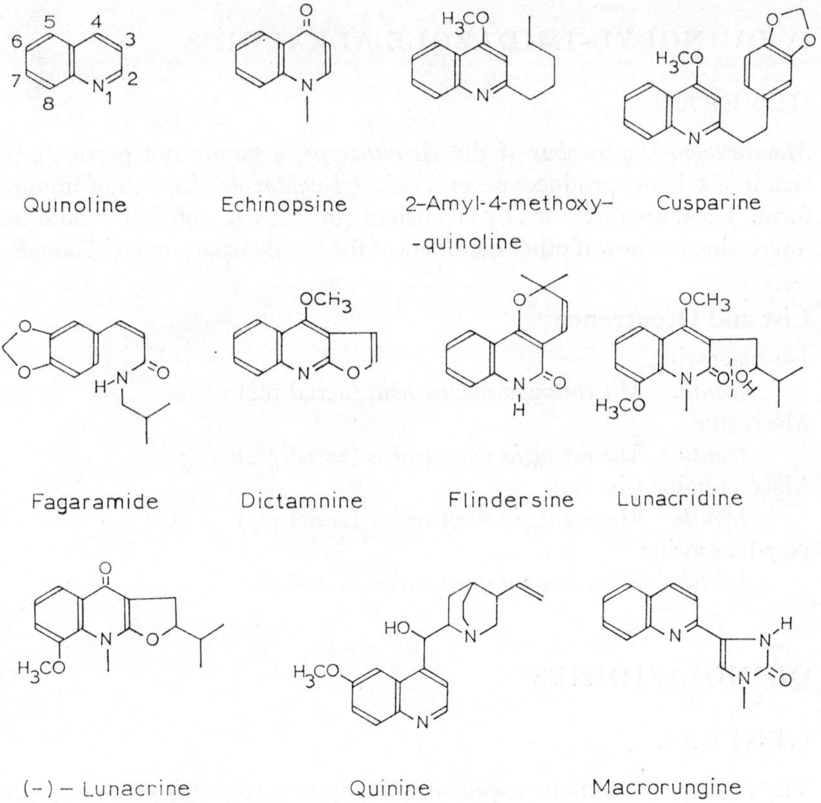

Quinoline   Echinopsine   2-Amyl-4-methoxy-   Cusparine
                            -quinoline

Fagaramide   Dictamnine   Flindersine   Lunacridine

(-) - Lunacrine   Quinine   Macrorungine

Fig. 80. Quinoline and some quinoline alkaloids.

Paricine: belongs here?
    Rubi.   Cinchona (3), *Remijia purdieana*
Quinidine (Conquinine): isomeric with *quinine*?
    Annon.   Enantia pilosa, polycarpa (bk)
    Logani.   Strychnos pseudoquina (bk, wd)
    Rubi.   Cinchona (15), *Coutarea latiflora, Remijia* (1 or 2)
Quinine (fig. 80)
    Annon.   Enantia polycarpa
    Simaroub.   Picrolemma pseudocoffea (st.)
    Logani.   Strychnos pseudoquina (bk, wd)
    Rubi.   Cinchona (19), *Coutarea latiflora, Ladenbergia*sp., *Remijia* (3)
h-Quinine (?Heteroquinine)
    Rubi.   Cinchona ledgeriana＊
Quinotoxine (Quinicine)
    Rubi.   Cinchona ledgeriana＊

＊ See note on p. 325.

IV QUINOLYL-IMIDAZOLE ALKALOIDS

GENERAL

Macrorungia longistrobus of the *Acanthaceae*, a family not particularly rich in alkaloids, produces several *quinolyl-imidazole alkaloids* of unique form. These are discussed by Openshaw (in *M.*, v.9, 1967). It would be interesting to know if other members of the family have similar alkaloids.

List and Occurrence
Iso-macrorine
   Acanth.   Macrorungia longistrobus (aerial pts)
Macrorine
   Acanth.   Macrorungia longistrobus (aerial pts)
Macrorungine (fig. 80)
   Acanth.   Macrorungia longistrobus (aerial pts)
Nor-macrorine
   Acanth.   Macrorungia longistrobus (aerial pts)

QUINOLIZIDINES

GENERAL

These alkaloids contain a *quinolizidine* system (fig. 80) or some near approach to or modification of it. Other names that have been applied to this nucleus are *norlupinane*, *octahydropyridocoline*, and *1-azabicyclo [4,4,O]-decane*.

They are overwhelmingly commonest in the *Leguminosae*, as the following list will show, but some are found, too, in the *Chenopodiaceae*; in *Ranunculaceae*, *Berberidaceae*, and *Nymphaeaceae* (of the **Ranunculales**); in *Monimiaceae* and *Lauraceae* (of the **Magnoliales**); in *Papaveraceae*; *Lythraceae*; in *Solanaceae* and *Scrophulariaceae* (of the **Tubiflorae**); and in *Compositae*.

Because many of them occur in the leguminous genus *Lupinus*, they are sometimes referred to as the 'lupin alkaloids' and are discussed as such by Leonard (in *M. & H.*, v.3, 1953; v.7, 1960) and by Bohlmann and Schumann (in *M.*, v.9, 1967). The term is a general one, however, and not accurate. Non-quinolizidine alkaloids may occur in *Lupinus*, and alkaloids that are typical of *Lupinus* may occur elsewhere.

The alkaloids of *Nuphar* (*Nymphaeaceae*), are *quinolizidine*, *bis-quinolizidine*, and *near-quinolizidine*. They have been discussed by Wróbel (in *M.*, v.9, 1967).

Unlike *nicotine*, which is formed in the root, the 'lupin alkaloids' seem to be synthesized in the upper parts of the plant. They increase during growth and then pass to fruits and seeds. They may protect against such animals as sheep, which are poisoned if they do feed on lupine. On the other hand *sparteine* is said to act as a feeding stimulus for aphids!

The skeletons of all (?) 'lupin alkaloids' are derived, probably, from *lysine* by way of *cadaverine*.

List and Occurrence

Allothio-binupharidine
  Nymphae.   Nuphar luteum
Aloperine is isomeric with *spartyrine*?
  Legum.   Sophora alopecuroides
  Scrophulari.   Leptorhabdos parviflora (plt)
Anagyrine (Monolupine; Rhombinine; Ulexine; fig. 81)
  Legum.   Ammodendron (1), *Anagyris* (1), *Baptisia* (3), *Cytisus* (3),
      Genista (incl. *Retama*) (6), *Lupinus* (5), *Sophora* (2), *Spartium*
      (1), *Thermopsis* (2), *Ulex* (2)
Angustifoline (Jamaicensine) is one of the C-14 'lupin-alkaloids';
  leontidine, leontamine, piptamine, and *piptanthine* are others.
  Legum.   Lupinus angustifolius, perennis var. *polyphyllus*; *Ormosia
      jamaicensis* (sd), *panamensis* (sd)
(−)-Aphyllidine (fig. 81)
  Chenopodi.   Anabasis aphylla
  Legum.   Argyrolobium megarhizum, Sophora microphylla
Aphylline (Dihydro-aphyllidine)
  Chenopodi.   Anabasis aphylla
Argyrolobine
  Legum.   Argyrolobium megarhizum
Baptifoline (*l*-13-Hydroxy-anagyrine)
  Legum.   Baptisia (2), *Sophora* (1)
(+)-Calpurnine (Oroboidine)
  Legum.   Calpurnia lasiogyne (*subdecandra*), *Virgilia capensis*
      (*oroboides*)
Calycotamine: belongs here?
  Legum.   Calycotome spinosa (sd)
Conolline: belongs here?
  Legum.   Ammodendron conollyi
Cryptopleurine (fig. 82) is said to be vesicant.
  Laur.   Cryptocarya pleurosperma (bk)
Cytisine (fig. 81) is widely distributed.
  Legum.   Anagyris (1), *Argyrolobium* (1), *Baptisia* (9), *Cladrastis* (1),

Coronilla (1), Cytisus (14), Euchresta (1), Genista (13), Gleditsia (1), Laburnum (3), Lotus (?), Piptanthus (1), Sophora (10), Spartium (1), Templetonia (1), Thermopsis (3), Ulex (2)

Comp. Senecio sp.

Cytisine-N-oxide
    Legum. Spartium junceum, Ulex nanus

Dasycarpine (fig. 82)
    Legum. Ormosia dasycarpa (sd)

Decaline
    Lythr. Decodon verticillatus

Decamine (Dihydro-vertine)
    Lythr. Decodon verticillatus

Decinine (Dihydro-lythrine)
    Lythr. Decodon verticillatus

Decodine
    Lythr. Decodon verticillatus

Dehydro-albine
    Legum. Lupinus albus (sd)

Dehydro-deoxy-nupharidine
    Nymphae. Nuphar japonicum (rt)

Δ^5-Dehydro-13-hydroxy-multiflorine
    Legum. Lupinus albus

Demethyl-decaline
    Lythr. Decodon verticillatus

Demethyl-vertaline
    Lythr. Decodon verticillatus

Deoxy-nupharidine
    Nymphae. Nuphar japonicum (rhiz.), variegatum (rhiz.)

Deoxy-nupharidine-N-oxide
    Occurrence?

Dilupine (?Amine oxide of C-methyl-lupanine)
    Legum. Lupinus barbiger

Diplospartyrine
    Occurrence?

(−)-Epibaptifoline (13-Epibaptifoline)
    Legum. Retama sphaerocarpa

13-Epihydroxy-lupanine (Jamaidine)
    Legum. Ormosia jamaicensis, panamensis

d-Epilupinine (d-Isolupinine; Tetralupine)
    Legum. Lupinus (3)

(+)-Epilupinine-N-oxide
    Legum. Lupinus (2)

13-Epimethoxy-lupanine
  Legum. Lupinus angustifolius
Heimine: belongs here?
  Lythr. Heimia salicifolia
Homothermopsine
  Legum. Lupinus lanceolatus, Thermopsis lanceolata
13α-Hydroxy-lupanine (Octalupine)
  Legum. Lupinus (7), *Ormosia panamensis* (sd)?, *Sarothamnus scoparius*
13α-Hydroxy-lupanine benzoate
  Legum. Lupinus angustifolius, polyphyllus
13α-Hydroxy-lupanine *cis-* and *trans-*cinnamates
  Legum. Lupinus angustifolius, polyphyllus
13α-Hydroxy-lupanine tiglic ester
  Legum. Lupinus angustifolius, polyphyllus
5-Hydroxy-matrine (Sophoranol)
  Legum. Sophora angustifolia (*flavescens*)
13-Hydroxy-multiflorine
  Legum. Lupinus albus
8-Hydroxy-spartalupine (8-Hydroxy-β-isosparteine?)
  Legum. Lupinus sericeus (plt)
13-Hydroxy-sparteine
  Legum. Baptisia spp.
Isoleontine (*l*-Allomatrine)
  Berberid. Leontice eversmanni (lvs, st.)
d-α-Isolupanine is a diastereoisomer of *d-lupanine*.
  Legum. Lupinus (3)
Isopiptanthine: an isomer of *piptanthine*?
  Legum. Piptanthus nanus (plt)
Isosophoramine
  Legum. Sophora pachycarpa
l-α-Isosparteine (Genisteine) is a stereoisomer of *sparteine*.
  Legum. Lupinus caudatus, Sarothamnus scoparius
l-β-Isosparteine (*l*-Pusilline; Spartalupine)
  Legum. Lupinus pusillus and 3 other spp.
Jamine
  Legum. Ormosia jamaicensis, panamensis
Leontalbine is closely related to *matrine*.
  Berberid. Leontice alberti
Leontamine: see note under *angustifoline*.
  Berberid. Leontice eversmanni
Leontidine: see note under *angustifoline*.
  Berberid. Leontice alberti (tuber), *eversmanni* (tuber)

Leontine
> Berberid. *Leontice eversmanni*

d-Lupanine (fig. 81)
> Legum. *Cytisus* (4), *Lupinus* (13), *Podalyria sericea*, *Sarothamnus scoparius*, *Virgilia capensis*

dl-Lupanine
> Legum. *Lupinus* (6); *Podalyria buxifolia*, *sericea*; *Virgilia capensis*
> Solan. *Solanum lycocarpum*

l-Lupanine (Hydro-rhombinine)
> Berberid. *Leontice eversmanni*
> Legum. *Baptisia versicolor*; *Lupinus* (3); *Podalyria buxifolia* (tops), *calyptrata* (tops)

Lupanoline
> Legum. *Lupinus sericeus*

Lupilaxine is isomeric with *hydroxy-lupanine*.
> Legum. *Lupinus laxus, sericeus*

Lupinine (fig. 81) is one of the simplest of the *quinolizidines*.
> Chenopodi. *Anabasis aphylla*
> Legum. *Lupinus* (4)

Lusitanine
> Legum. *Genista (Echinospartum) lusitanica*

Lyofoline (?Lyfoline): belongs here ?
> Lythr. *Heimia salicifolia*

Lythridine: belongs here ?
> Lythr. *Heimia myrtifolia, salicifolia* (see note under *Lythraceae*)

Lythrine (fig. 82)
> Lythr. *Heimia myrtifolia, salicifolia* (see note under *Lythraceae*)

Matrine (Lupanidine; Sophocarpidine; fig. 81) is said to exist in 4 forms.
> Legum. *Lupinus angustifolius*, *Sophora* (5) (α-matrine in *S. macrocarpa*)
> Comp. *Senecio* sp.

Monspessulanine is isomeric with *aphyllidine*.
> Legum. *Cytisus monspessulanus* (lvs, st.)

Multiflorine
> Legum. *Lupinus albus, multiflorus, varius*

Neothio-binupharidine: a stereoisomer of *thio-binupharidine*?
> Nymphae. *Nuphar luteum*

Nesodine
> Lythr. *Heimia salicifolia*

N-Methyl-albine is related to *multiflorine*.
> Legum. *Lupinus albus*

N-Methyl-cytisine (Caulophylline)
>   *Berberid.* *Caulophyllum thalictroides* (rhiz.), *Leontice alberti* (plt),
>   *eversmanni*
>   *Legum.* *Anagyris* (1), *Argyrolobium* (1), *Baptisia* (3), *Cytisus* (4),
>   *Genista* (4), *Ormosia* (1), *Sophora* (3), *Spartium* (1), *Thermopsis*
>   (3)
>   *Scrophulari.* *Pedicularis olgae?*
>   *Comp.* *Senecio* sp.

Nuphamine is a *near-quinolizidine.*
>   *Nymphae.* *Nuphar japonicum* (rhiz.)

Nupharamine (fig. 82) is a *near-quinolizidine.*
>   *Nymphae.* *Nuphar japonicum*

Nupharamine ethyl ether
>   *Nymphae.* *Nuphar japonicum*

Nupharamine methyl ether
>   *Nymphae.* *Nuphar japonicum*

Nupharidine (fig. 82)
>   *Nymphae.* *Nuphar japonicum* (rhiz.)

α- and β-Nupharidines: how do these differ?
>   *Nymphae.* *Nuphar luteum* (rhiz.)

Nupharine: what is this?

Nuphenine is a *near-quinolizidine.*
>   *Nymphae.* *Nuphar variegatum*

Nymphaeine: belongs here?
>   *Nymphae.* *Nymphaea alba* (rhiz.)

O-(2-Pyrrolylcarbonyl)-virgiline
>   *Legum.* *Calpurnia lasiogyne* (*subdecandra*)

Ormojanine
>   *Legum.* *Ormosia jamaicensis* (sd)

Ormojine: belongs here?
>   *Legum.* *Ormosia jamaicensis* (sd)

Ormosajine: belongs here?
>   *Legum.* *Ormosia jamaicensis* (sd)

Ormosine: belongs here?
>   *Legum.* *Ormosia coccinea* (sd), *dasycarpa* (sd)

Ormosinine
>   *Legum.* *Ormosia* (7)

17-Oxo-lupanine
>   *Legum.* *Lupinus angustifolius, polyphyllus*

d-Oxo-sparteine (?17-Oxo-sparteine)
>   *Legum.* *Genista monosperma*

Oxy-aphyllidine
>   *Chenopodi.* *Anabasis aphylla* (plt)

Oxy-aphylline
  Chenopodi. Anabasis aphylla (plt)
Oxymatrine (Ammothamnine; Matrine-*N*-oxide)
  Legum. Ammothamnus lehmanii (lvs, st.), *Sophora angustifolia* var.
  flavescens
Pachycarpidine: a di-*N*-oxide?
  Legum. Sophora pachycarpa
Panamine (fig. 82)
  Legum. Ormosia (6)
Pentalupine: belongs here?
  Legum. Lupinus palmeri
Piptamine (Ormosanine): see note under *angustifoline.*
  Legum. Piptanthus (2), *Ormosia* (7, sds)
Piptanthine: see note under *angustifoline.*
  Legum. Piptanthus (2)
Pseudo-binupharidine: what is this?
Retamine (fig. 81); according to Bohmann and Schumann (1967) it
  '...is present in virtually all species of *Genista* [including *Retama*]...
  In spring the green plants contain mostly (−)-sparteine, but in
  the fall, and particularly in older plants, retamine is the main
  [alkaloidal] constituent.'
  Legum. Genista spp.
Rhombifoline (*N*-(3-Butenyl)-cytisine)
  Legum. Sophora microphylla, Thermopsis rhombifolia
Sarothamnine: a bisparteine-type alkaloid?
  Legum. Laburnum vulgare, Sarothamnus scoparius
Sinicuichine: belongs here?
  Lythr. Heimia salicifolia
Sinine: belongs here?
  Lythr. Heimia salicifolia
Sophocarpine
  Legum. Ammothamnus lehmanni, Sophora (5)
Sophochrysine: is of uncertain structure?
  Legum. Sophora chrysophylla and 3 other spp.
Sophoramine is isomeric with *anagyrine*, and may be related to
  matrine.
  Legum. Sophora (2)
  Scrophulari. Leptorhabdos parviflora (plt)
Sophoridine
  Legum. Sophora alopecuroides (lvs)
  Scrophulari. Leptorhabdos parviflora (plt)
d-Sparteine (Pachycarpine; fig. 81)
  Monimi. Peumus boldus

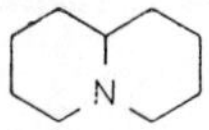
Quinolizidine

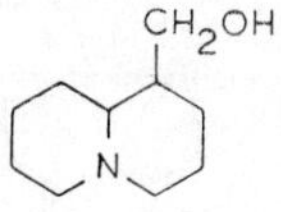

Lupinine

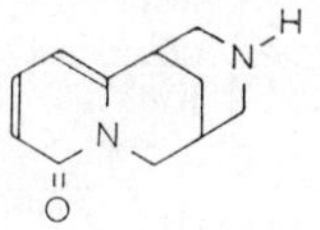
Cytisine

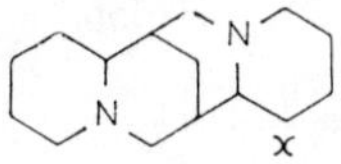
Sparteine
(Retamine has -OH at x)

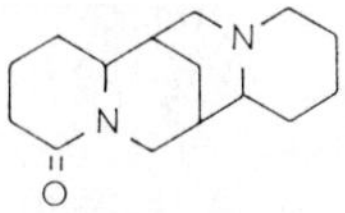
Lupanine

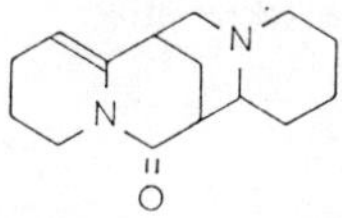
Aphyllidine

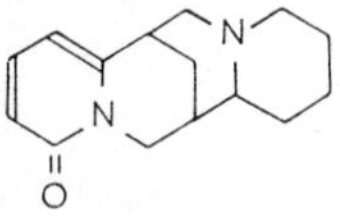
Anagyrine

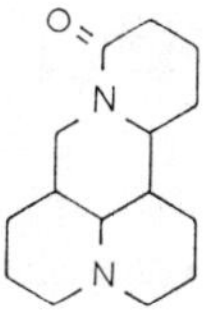
Matrine

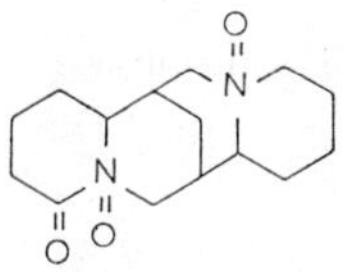
Trilupine

Fig. 81. Some quinolizidine alkaloids.

Ranuncul. *Aconitum* (*d*- ?)
Berberid. *Leontice eversmanni*
Papaver. *Chelidonium majus* (*d*- ?)
Legum. *Ammodendron* (1), *Ammothamnus* (1), *Anagyris* (1), *Baptisia* (4), *Cytisus* (1), *Genista* (incl. *Retama*) (3), *Hovea* (2), *Lupinus* (1), *Sophora pachycarpa* and 4 other spp., *Thermopsis* (1)
Scrophulari. *Leptorhabdos parviflora* (plt)

dl-Sparteine
Legum. *Adenocarpus hispanicus*, *Cytisus proliferus*

l-Sparteine (Lupinidine)
Papaver. *Chelidonium majus*
Legum. *Adenocarpus* (3), *Cytisus* (6), *Genista* (incl. *Retama*) (2), *Lupinus* (10), *Piptanthus* (1), *Sarothamnus* (2), *Spartium junceum*
Solan. *Solanum* (?)

Spartyrine: what is this ?

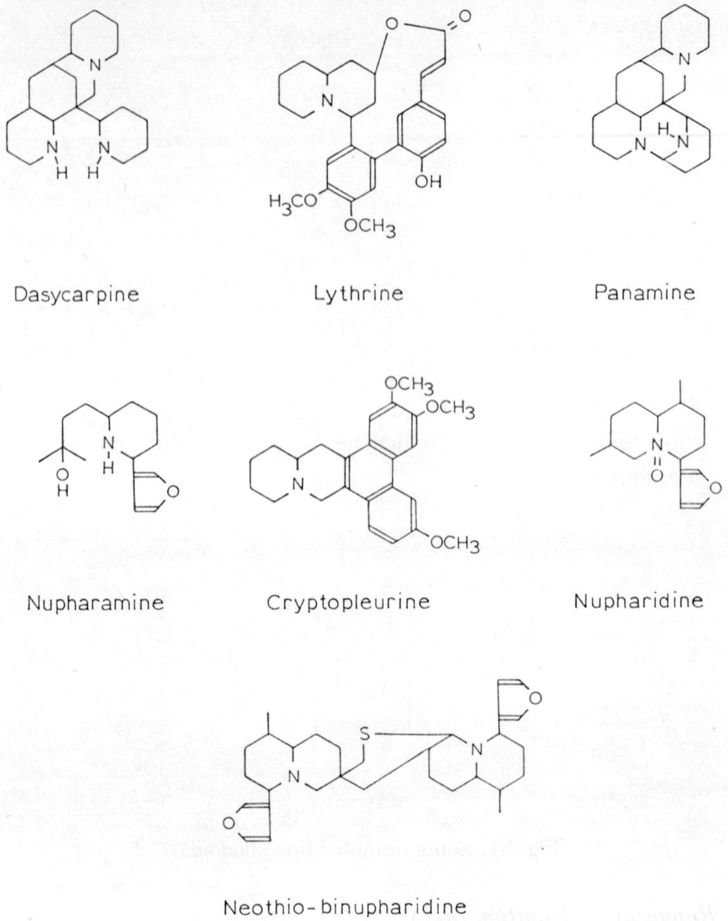

Dasycarpine   Lythrine   Panamine

Nupharamine   Cryptopleurine   Nupharidine

Neothio-binupharidine

Fig. 82. Some quinolizidine alkaloids.

Spathulatine (*l*-β-Isosparteine-hydrochloride hydrate; Nonalupine)
    Legum.   *Lupinus spathulatus* (sd) and 3 other spp.
Sweetine: belongs here?
    Legum.   *Sweetia panamensis*
Sweetinine resembles *piptamine*.
    Legum.   *Sweetia panamensis* (bk)
Tetrahydro-rhombifoline
    Legum.   *Lupinus angustifolius*
d-Thermopsine (Hexalupine) is a C-11-epimer of (−)-*anagyrine*.
    Legum.   *Baptisia* (several?), *Lupinus* (2)
l-Thermopsine
    Legum.   *Thermopsis* (2)

Thio-bideoxy-nupharidine
 Nymphae. Nuphar luteum
Thio-binupharidine is a dimer.
 Nymphae. Nuphar luteum
Trilupine (?d-Lupanine-*N,N'*-dioxide; fig. 81)
 Legum. Lupinus (2)
Vertaline is a diastereoisomer of *decaline*.
 Lythr. Decodon verticillatus
Verticillatine
 Lythr. Decodon verticillatus
Vertine (?Cryogenine)
 Lythr. Decodon verticillatus; Heimia myrtifolia, salicifolia (see
  note under *Lythraceae*)
Virgilidine is an isomer of lupinine.
 Legum. Virgilia capensis (plt)
Virgiline (13α-Hydroxy-aphylline)
 Legum. Virgilia capensis (plt)

THE STEROID ALKALOIDS

GENERAL

This is a large group—the following list has about 250 members—of restricted occurrence. Many of the *steroid alkaloids* are esters of acids, some of which are common and widely distributed, others less so. Among the acids which are known to occur in these alkaloids are:

Acetic, in many
Angelic, in *cevadine, escholerine, germinitrine*
d-(−)-α-Methyl-butyric, in many
(+)-α-Methyl-α,β-dihydroxy-butyric, in *germbudine, germitetrine, neo-germbudine, protoveratrine-B*
(+)-α-Methyl-α-hydroxy-butyric, in *deacetyl-neoprotoveratrine*
(+)-α-Oxy-α-methyl-butyric, in *germerine*?, *germitrine, protoveratrine-A*
Tiglic, in *germanitrine, germinitrine*
Vanillic, in *vanilloyl-veracevine, vanilloyl-zygadenine*
Veratric, in *veratridine, veratroyl-zygadenine*

A remarkable series of *steroid alkaloids* occur in the *Buxaceae*—see notes under that family. A few of them are common to the *Buxaceae* and *Apocynaceae*—families not at all closely related. A recent review of the *steroid alkaloids* of these two families is that of Černý and Šorm (in *M.*, v.9, 1967).

Another group occurs in the *Solanaceae* and these have been reviewed by Schreiber (in *M.*, v.10, 1968). The relatively recent discovery that *Solanum* alkaloids such as *solasodine* may serve as starting materials for the preparation of hormonal steroids has led to great interest in the genus, and alkaloids of perhaps 250 species (out of about 1,700!) are now known.

List and Occurrence

Amianthine: belongs here?
    Lili.   *Amianthus (Zigadenus) muscaetoxicum* (lvs, rt)
3-α-Amino-conan-5-ene
    Apocyn. *Holarrhena antidysenterica* (bk)
Angeloyl ester of cevinilic acid-δ-lactone.
    Lili. *Veratrum grandiflorum*
Angeloyl-zygadenine
    Lili. *Veratrum album* v. *stamineum*
Baleabuxidine
    Bux. *Buxus balearica*
Baleabuxine (*N*-3-Isobutyryl-cyclobuxine-F)
    Bux. *Buxus balearica*
Baleabuxoxazine-C
    Bux. *Buxus balearica* (lvs)
3β,20α-Bisdimethylamino-5α-pregnane (Pachysandra alkaloid-D)
    Bux. *Pachysandra terminalis*
Buxalphine: belongs here?
    Bux. *Buxus sempervirens* (lvs)
Buxamine-E
    Bux. *Buxus balearica* (lvs), *sempervirens*
Buxamine-G (Buxenine-G; Norbuxamine)
    Bux. *Buxus sempervirens*
Buxaminol-E
    Bux. *Buxus balearica* (lvs), *sempervirens*
Buxarine
    Bux. *Buxus sempervirens*
Buxdeltine: belongs here?
    Bux. *Buxus sempervirens* (lvs)
Buxenone
    Bux. *Buxus sempervirens*
Buxetine: belongs here?
    Bux. *Buxus sempervirens* (lvs)
Buxpsiine
    Bux. *Buxus sempervirens*

Buxtauine (Cyclobuxoxine; Cyclomicrobuxinine)

Bux.   Buxus microphylla v. *suffruticosa, sempervirens*

Buxus alkaloid-L

Bux.   Buxus microphylla v. *suffruticosa* f. *major*

Cevacine yields *veracevine* and *acetic acid.*

Lili.   Schoenocaulon officinale (sd)

Cevadine yields *veracevine* and *angelic acid.*

Lili.   Schoenocaulon officinale (sd), *Veratrum viride* (rhiz.)

'Cevagenine': an artefact arising in alkaline hydrolysis of *veratri-dine*?

Cevine (Sabadinine)

Lili.   Schoenocaulon officinale (sd)

Cevinilic acid-δ-lactone

Lili.   Schoenocaulon officinale (sd)

α-Chaconine yields *solanidine*, 2 × L-*rhamnose*, and D-*glucose.*

Solan.   Solanum chacoense

β- and γ-Chaconines: artefacts? See *Solanine*

Chonemorphine

Apocyn.   Chonemorpha macrophylla (rtbk), *penangensis* (rt)

Conamine

Apocyn.   Holarrhena antidysenterica (bk)

Conarrhimine

Apocyn.   Holarrhena antidysenterica (bk)

Conessidine

Apocyn.   Holarrhena antidysenterica (bk)

Conessimine

Apocyn.   Holarrhena floribunda (*africana*) (bk, rtbk), *anti-dysenterica* (bk)

Conessine

Apocyn.   Holarrhena (5–6), *Wrightia antidysenterica* (= *zeylanica*?)? Bisset (1958) says: 'neither this species nor any true *Wrightia* has yet been found definitely to contain alkaloids'.

Conimine

Apocyn.   Holarrhena antidysenterica (bk)

Conkurchine (Irehline)

Apocyn.   Holarrhena antidysenterica (bk)

'Conkurchinine' is an artefact.

Conkuressine

Apocyn.   Holarrhena antidysenterica (bk)

Conopharyngine is a glycoside of *holafebrine.*

Apocyn.   Conopharyngia pachysiphon (rt)

Cyclobuxamine-H

Bux.   Buxus sempervirens

Cyclobuxine-D (?Buxus alkaloid-A; Cyclobuxine of earlier work; fig. 83)
  Bux. *Buxus koreana, sempervirens* (lvs, principal alkaloid)
Cyclobuxomicreine
  Bux. *Buxus microphylla* v. *suffruticosa*
Cyclobuxophylline
  Bux. *Buxus microphylla* v. *suffruticosa* f. *major*
Cyclobuxophyllinine
  Bux. *Buxus koreana, microphylla* v. *suffruticosa* f. *major*
Cyclobuxosuffrine
  Bux. *Buxus microphylla* v. *suffruticosa* f. *major*
Cyclobuxoviridine
  Bux. *Buxus microphylla* v. *suffruticosa* f. *major*
Cyclobuxoxazine
  Bux. *Buxus microphylla* v. *suffruticosa*
Cyclobuxoxazine-A
  Bux. *Buxus rolfei* (lvs)
Cyclobuxoxazine-C
  Bux. *Buxus microphylla*
Cyclokoreanine-B
  Bux. *Buxus koreana*
Cyclomalayanine-B
  Bux. *Buxus malayana* (lvs)
Cyclomethoxazine-B
  Bux. *Buxus rolfei* (lvs)
Cyclomicrobuxeine
  Bux. *Buxus koreana, microphylla* v. *suffruticosa*
Cyclomicrobuxine (Buxpiine)
  Bux. *Buxus microphylla*
Cyclomicrophyllidine-A (Cyclomicrophylline-A-16-benzoate)
  Bux. *Buxus microphylla*
Cyclomicrophylline-A
  Bux. *Buxus microphylla* v. *suffruticosa*
Cyclomicrophylline-B (Cyclobaleabuxine)
  Bux. *Buxus balearica, malayana* (lvs), *microphylla*
Cyclomicrosine
  Bux. *Buxus microphylla* v. *suffruticosa*
Cyclomikuranine
  Bux. *Buxus microphylla* v. *suffruticosa* f. *major*
Cyclopamine (Alkaloid-V): belongs here?
  Lili. *Veratrum californicum* (rt)
Cycloprotobuxine-A
  Bux. *Buxus balearica* (lvs), *koreana, malayana*

Cycloprotobuxine-C
  Bux.   Buxus balearica (lvs), *koreana, sempervirens*
Cycloprotobuxine-D (Deoxy-cyclovirobuxine-D)
  Bux.   Buxus balearica (lvs), *sempervirens*
Cyclorolfeine
  Bux.   Buxus rolfei (lvs)
Cyclorolfoxazine
  Bux.   Buxus rolfei (lvs)
Cyclosuffrobuxine
  Bux.   Buxus koreana, microphylla v. *suffruticosa* f. *major*
Cyclosuffrobuxinine
  Bux.   Buxus microphylla v. *suffruticosa* f. *major*
Cyclovirobuxeine-A
  Bux.   Buxus malayana
Cyclovirobuxeine-B
  Bux.   Buxus sempervirens
Cyclobirovuxine-D (Bebuxine)
  Bux.   Buxus malayana, sempervirens
Deacetyl-germitetrine
  Lili.   Veratrum album
Deacetyl-neoprotoveratrine yields *protoverine, acetic acid, d-(−)-α-methyl-butyric acid,* and (+)-α-*methyl-α-hydroxy-butyric acid*
  Lili.   Veratrum album, viride (rhiz.)
Deacetyl-protoveratrine-A
  Lili.   Veratrum album
Deacetyl-protoveratrine-B
  Lili.   Veratrum album, viride
Dehydro-cevagenine
  Lili.   Schoenocaulon officinale (sd)
Demissidine (Solanidan-3β-ol) is the aglycone of *demissine.*
  Solan.   Solanum demissum and 6 or more other spp.
Demissine (Solanine-d) yields *demissidine* and *lycotetraose.*
  Solan.   Solanum demissum
Dictyodiamine (Epipachysamine-C)
  Bux.   Pachysandra terminalis
  Apocyn.   Dictyophleba lucida (rt)
Dictyolucidamine
  Apocyn.   Dictyophleba lucida (rt)
Dictyolucidine
  Apocyn.   Dictyophleba lucida (rt)
Dictyophlebine
  Apocyn.   Dictyophleba lucida (rt)

Dihydro-cyclomicrophyllidine-A
  Bux.   Buxus microphylla v. *suffruticosa*
Dihydro-cyclomicrophylline-A
  Bux.   Buxus microphylla
Dihydro-cyclomicrophylline-C (Cyclorolfeibuxine-C)
  Bux.   Buxus rolfei
Dihydro-cyclomicrophylline-F
  Bux.   Buxus microphylla
Dihydro-isoconessimine
  Apocyn.   Holarrhena antidysenterica (bk)
3α-Dimethylamino-5α-conanine
  Apocyn.   Holarrhena antidysenterica (bk)
20-Epi-*N*-methyl-paravallarine
  Apocyn.   Kibatalia gitingensis
Epipachysamine-A
  Occurrence?
Epipachysamine-B
  Bux.   Pachysandra terminalis
Epipachysamine-D yields *chonemorphine* and ? when hydrolysed.
  Bux.   Pachysandra terminalis
Epipachysamine-E yields *chonemorphine* and ? when hydrolysed.
  Bux.   Pachysandra terminalis
Epipachysamine-F
  Bux.   Pachysandra terminalis
Escholerine yields *protoverine,* 2 × *acetic acid, d-(−)-α-methyl-butyric acid* and *angelic acid.*
  Lili.   Veratrum eschscholtzii (rt)
Fritillarine (Verticinone): belongs here?
  Lili.   Fritillaria verticillata
Funtessine
  Apocyn.   Funtumia latifolia (bk)
Funtudiamine-A
  Apocyn.   Funtumia latifolia
Funtudiamine-B
  Apocyn.   Funtumia latifolia
Funtudienine
  Apocyn.   Funtumia latifolia (bk)
Funtuline
  Apocyn.   Funtumia latifolia (bk)
Funtumafrines-B and -C
  Apocyn.   Funtumia africana (lvs)
Funtumidine (3-α-Amino-allopregnan-20-ol)
  Apocyn.   Funtumia latifolia (lvs, st., rt)

Funtumine (3-α-Amino-allopregnan-20-one)
Apocyn. Funtumia latifolia (lvs, st., rt)
Funtuphyllamines-A, -B, and -C
Apocyn. Funtumia africana
Geralbidine
Lili. Veratrum album
Geralbine: differs from *geralbidine*?
Lili. Veratrum album (rt)
Germanitrine yields *germine, acetic acid, tiglic acid,* and *d-(−)-α-methyl-butyric acid.*
Lili. Veratrum fimbriatum (rt), *Zigadenus*?
Germbudine yields *germine, d-(−)-α-methyl-butyric acid,* and *α-methyl-α,β-dihydroxy-butyric acid.*
Lili. Veratrum viride (rt)
Germerine yields *germine, d-(−)-α-methyl-butyric acid,* and *(+)-α-oxy-α-methyl-butyric acid.* It may be an artefact.
Lili. Veratrum album (rhiz.), *nigrum, viride* (rt)
Germidine yields *germine, acetic acid,* and *d-(−)-α-methyl-butyric acid.*
Lili. Veratrum venenosus, viride (rt); *Zigadenus venenosus*
Germine (fig. 83) is the alkamine of many of the alkaloids of *Veratrum* and *Zigadenus.*
Lili. Veratrum album (rhiz.), *viride* (rt); *Zigadenus venenosus*
Germinitrine yields *germine, acetic acid, tiglic acid,* and *angelic acid.*
Lili. Veratrum fimbriatum (rt), *Zigadenus*?
Germitetrine (Germitetrine-B) yields *germine,* 2 × *acetic acid, d-(−)-α-methyl-butyric acid,* and *α-methyl-α,β-dihydroxy-butyric acid.*
Lili. Veratrum album (rhiz.)
Germitrine yields *germine, acetic acid, d-(−)-α-methyl-butyric acid,* and *(+)-α-oxy-α-methyl-butyric acid.*
Lili. Veratrum album, viride (rt)
Holadienine
Apocyn. Holarrhena floribunda (africana) (bk)
Holadysamine
Apocyn. Holarrhena antidysenterica (lvs)
Holadysine
Apocyn. Holarrhena antidysenterica (lvs)
Holafebrine (20-α-Amino-3β-hydroxy-5-pregnene) is the aglycone of *conopharyngine.*
Apocyn. Holarrhena febrifuga
Holafrine is the 2-methyl-$\Delta^{2,3}$-*pentenoic acid ester* of 12-β-hydroxy-conessimine.
Apocyn. Holarrhena floribunda (africana) (bk)

Holaline
  Apocyn.   Holarrhena floribunda (africana) (bk)
Holamine (3-α-Amino-Δ⁵-pregnan-20-one)
  Apocyn.   Holarrhena floribunda (africana) (lvs)
Holaphyllamine (3-β-Amino-Δ⁵-pregnan-20-one)
  Apocyn.   Holarrhena floribunda (africana) (lvs)
Holaphyllidine
  Apocyn.   Holarrhena floribunda (africana) (lvs)
Holaphylline (3-β-Methylamino-Δ⁵-pregnan-20-one)
  Apocyn.   Holarrhena floribunda (africana) (lvs)
Holarrheline
  Apocyn.   Holarrhena floribunda (africana) (bk)
Holarrhenine
  Apocyn.   Elytropus chilensis?; *Holarrhena antidysenterica* (bk),
    congolensis (bk, lvs), *floribunda* (*africana*)
Holarrhessimine
  Apocyn.   Holarrhena antidysenterica (bk)
Holarrhetine is the 2-*methyl-Δ²,³-pentenoic acid ester* of 12-β-*hydroxy-
  conessine.*
  Apocyn.   Holarrhena floribunda (africana)
Holarrhidine
  Apocyn.   Holarrhena antidysenterica (bk)
Holarrhimine (?Kurchicine; fig. 83)
  Apocyn.   Elytropus chilensis?; *Holarrhena antidysenterica* (bk),
    floribunda (*africana*) (bk)
Holarrhine
  Apocyn.   Holarrhena antidysenterica (bk)
Holonamine
  Apocyn.   Holarrhena antidysenterica (bk)
7α-Hydroxy-conessine
  Apocyn.   Holarrhena antidysenterica (bk)
7β-Hydroxy-conessine
  Apocyn.   Holarrhena antidysenterica (bk)
Imperialine (?Raddeanine; Sipeimine)
  Lili.   Fritillaria imperialis (bulb), *meleagris, raddeana* (bulb, as
    raddeanine)
Irehamine
  Apocyn.   Dictyophleba lucida, Funtumia elastica (lvs)
Irehdiamine-A
  Apocyn.   Funtumia elastica (lvs)
Irehdiamine-C
  Apocyn.   Funtumia elastica

Irehine (Buxomegine)
> *Bux.   Buxus sempervirens* (lvs)
> *Apocyn.   Funtumia elastica* (lvs)

Isoconessimine
> *Apocyn.   Holarrhena antidysenterica* (bk)

Isogermidine (?Neogermidine) yields *germine, acetic acid,* and *d*-(−)-α-
methyl-butyric acid.
> *Lili.   Veratrum viride* (rt); *Zigadenus paniculatus* (lvs, st., fl),
> *venenosus*

Isogermine: may be an artefact, but may also occur with *germine* ?

Isojervine: belongs here ?
> *Lili.   Veratrum viride*

Isorubijervine (fig. 83) is closely related to *solanidine*. It is the aglycone
of *isorubijervosine.*
> *Lili.   Veratrum eschscholtzii* (rt)

Isorubijervosine yields *isorubijervine* and D-*glucose*.
> *Lili.   Veratrum eschscholtzii* (rt)

Jervine (fig. 83)
> *Lili.   Amianthum* (*Zigadenus*) *muscaetoxicum* (lvs, rt), *Veratrum*
> (7 or 8)

Kibataline
> *Apocyn.   Kibatalia gitingensis*

Kurchaline
> *Apocyn.   Holarrhena antidysenterica* (lvs)

Kurchamine (Irehdiamine-B)
> *Apocyn.   Funtumia elastica* (lvs), *Holarrhena antidysenterica* (bk)

Kurchessine (Pachysandra alkaloid-E; Saracodinine)
> *Bux.   Pachysandra terminalis, Sarcococca pruniformis*
> *Apocyn.   Holarrhena antidysenterica* (bk)

α-Kurchessine
> *Apocyn.   Holarrhena antidysenterica* (bk)

Kurchiline
> *Apocyn.   Holarrhena antidysenterica* (lvs)

Kurchine
> *Apocyn.   Holarrhena antidysenterica* (bk)

Kurchiphyllamine (*N*-Demethyl-kurchiphylline)
> *Apocyn.   Holarrhena antidysenterica* (lvs)

Kurchiphylline is isomeric with *kurchiline.*
> *Apocyn.   Holarrhena antidysenterica* (lvs)

Kurcholessine
> *Apocyn.   Holarrhena antidysenterica*

Latifoline
> *Apocyn.   Funtumia latifolia* (bk)

Latifolinine
    Apocyn.   Funtumia latifolia (bk)
Leptines can be hydrolysed to acid components and glyco-alkaloids
    (*leptinines*). Further hydrolyses yield the alkamine *leptinidine*.
    Solan.   Solanum chacoense
Leptinidine—see above. Does it occur free?
Malarboreine
    Apocyn.   Malouetia arborea
Malarborine
    Apocyn.   Malouetia arborea
Malouetine
    Apocyn.   Malouetia bequaertiana (bk, rt)
Malouphyllamine
    Apocyn.   Malouetia bequaertiana (lvs)
Malouphylline
    Apocyn.   Malouetia bequaertiana (lvs)
Malouphyllinine
    Apocyn.   Malouetia bequaertiana
Methyl-holarrhimine-I
    Apocyn.   Holarrhena antidysenterica (bk)
Methyl-holarrhimine-II
    Apocyn.   Holarrhena antidysenterica (bk)
N-Acetyl-chonemorphine
    Apocyn.   Malouetia bequaertiana
Neo-germbudine yields *germine, d-(–)-α-methyl-butyric acid,* and α-
    methyl-α,β-dihydroxy-butyric acid.
    Lili.   Veratrum album, viride (rt)
Neo-germitrine yields *germine,* 2 × *acetic acid,* and *d-(–)-α-methyl-*
    butyric acid.
    Lili.   Veratrum album, eschscholtzii (rt), *fimbriatum* (rt), *viride* (rt);
        Zigadenus paniculatus (lvs, st., fl.), *venenosus*
Neo-sabadine (Sabine)
    Lili.   Schoenocaulon officinale (sd)
3-N-Methyl-holarrhimine
    Apocyn.   Holarrhena antidysenterica (bk)
20-N-Methyl-holarrhimine
    Apocyn.   Holarrhena antidysenterica (bk)
N,N,N',N'-Tetramethyl-holarrhimine
    Apocyn.   Holarrhena antidysenterica (bk)
Norconessine
    Apocyn.   Holarrhena antidysenterica (bk)
Norlatifoline
    Apocyn.   Funtumia latifolia (bk)

Pachysamines -A and -B
  Bux. Pachysandra terminalis
Pachysandrines -A, -B, -C, and -D
  Bux. Pachysandra terminalis
Pachysantermine-A
  Bux. Pachysandra terminalis
Pachystermine-A is a major alkaloid of
  Bux. Pachysandra terminalis
Pachystermine-B
  Bux. Pachysandra terminalis
Paravallaridine
  Apocyn. Paravallaris microphylla
Paravallarine
  Apocyn. Paravallaris microphylla (lvs)
Peiminine (?Verticilline)
  Lili. Fritillaria imperialis?, roylei, verticillata var. *thunbergii*
    (*'verticilline'*)
Peiminoside (*O*-β-D-Glucopyranosyl-(1 → 3)-peimine) yields *peimine*
  (?*verticine*) and D-*glucose*.
  Lili. Fritillaria thunbergii (bulb)
Protoveratridine yields germine and *d*-(−)-α-*methyl-butyric acid*.
  Lili. Veratrum album, viride (rt); *Zigadenus venenosus*
Protoveratrine: distinct from *protoveratines -A* and *-B* ?
  Lili. Veratrum album (rhiz.), *lobelianum* (lvs, st., rt)
Protoveratrine-A (Veratetrine) yields *protoverine*, 2 × *acetic acid*,
  d-(−)-α-*methyl-butyric acid*, and (+)-α-*oxy*-α-*methyl-butyric acid*.
  Lili. Veratrum album (lvs), *viride* (rt); *Zigadenus venenosus*
Protoveratrine-B (?Neo-protoveratrine) yields *protoverine*, 2 × *acetic
  acid, d*-(−)-α-*methyl-butyric acid*, and (+)-α-*methyl*-α,β-*dihydroxy-
  butyric acid*.
  Lili. Veratrum album (lvs), *viride* (rt); *Zigadenus venenosus*
Protoverine (fig. 83) is the alkamine of *deacetyl-protoveratrine-B?*,
  escholerine, and *protoveratrines -A* and *-B*. Does it occur free ?
Pseudojervine yields *isojervine* and D-*glucose*.
  Lili. Veratrum album (rhiz.) and subsp. *lobelianum, eschscholtzii,
    fimbriatum* (rt), *viride* (rt)
Rubijervine (Δ⁵-3β,χ-Dihydroxy-solanidene)
  Lili. Veratrum album (rhiz.), *eschscholtzii, nigrum, viride* (rt)
Rubiverine: belongs here ?
  Lili. Veratrum album (rt)
Sabadine (Acetyl ester of neosabadine; Sabatine)
  Lili. Schoenocaulon officinale (sd—'sabadilla')

Saracocine
> Bux.   Sarcococca pruniformis

Saracodine
> Bux.   Sarcococca pruniformis

Sarcococca alkaloid-A
> Bux.   Sarcococca pruniformis

Sarcococca alkaloid-B (?5,6-Dehydro-sarcococca alkaloid-A)
> Occurrence?

Soladulcidine (Megacarpidine; Solasodan-3β-ol) is the alkamine of the *soladulcines*.
> Solan.   Solanum dulcamara (lvs, frt), megacarpum (lvs, st.)

Soladulcines -α, -β, and -γ yield *soladulcidine* and ?
> Occurrence?

Solamargine
> Solan.   Solanum atropurpureum, douglasii (frt), gracile (frt), miniatum (frt), nigrum (frt)

α-Solamarine
> Solan.   Solanum dulcamara

β-Solamarine is said to be tumour-inhibiting.
> Solan.   Solanum dulcamara

γ₁-Solamarine is α-L-*rhamnopyranosyl*-($1 \to$ 2-β-D-*glucopyranosyltomatidenol*.
> Solan.   Solanum dulcamara

γ₂-Solamarine is isomeric with γ₁-*solamarine*.
> Solan.   Solanum dulcamara

δ-Solamarine (De-rhamnosyl-α-solamarine)
> Solan.   Solanum dulcamara

Solangustidine is the aglycone of *solangustine*.
> Solan.   Solanum pulverulentum (angustifolium) (lvs, st., fl.)

Solangustine yields *solangustidine*, D-*glucose*, and perhaps other sugars.
> Solan.   Solanum pulverulentum (lvs, st., fl.)

Solanidine (Solatubine; fig. 83) is the aglycone of the *chaconines*, and of *solanine*.
> Solan.   Capsicum annuum (plt)?; Lycopersicum esculentum (lvs); Physochlaina orientalis (rt); Scopolia carniolica, japonica; Solanum (more than 50 species)
> Lili.   Veratrum album subsp. lobelianum

Solanidine-t
> Solan.   Solanum tuberosum

Solanine (Solanine-t; Solatunine). According to Prelog and Jeger (in M., v.7, 1960) the original 'solanine' had at least 6 components— α-, β-, and γ-*solanines* and α-, β-, and γ-*chaconines*. Are all but α-*solanine* and α-*chaconine* artefacts?

α-Solanine yields *solanidine*, L-*rhamnose*, D-*glucose*, and D-*galactose*. The sugars are present as *solatriose (solanose)*.

> *Solan. Capsicum, Lycopersicum, Physochlaina, Solanum* (several spp.). Some records require confirmation.

Solanocapsidine

> *Solan. Solanum pseudocapsicum* (frt)

Solanocapsine

> *Solan. Solanum pseudocapsicum* (frt)

Solasodamine yields *solasodine* and L-*rhamnosido*-L-*rhamnosido*-D-*galactosido*-D-*glucose*.

> *Solan. Solanum sodomeum* (frt) and 3 other species

Solasodine (Solancarpidine; Solanidine-S) is the aglycone of *solasodamine, solasonine*, and *solamargine*.

> *Solan. Solanum* (10 or more species)

Solasonine (Solasonine-s; Solan(o)carpine; Purpurine) yields *solasodine*, and L-*rhamnosido*-D-*galactosido*-D-*glucose*.

> *Solan. Solanum atropurpureum*

Solauricidine is the aglycone of *solauricine*.

> *Solan. Solanum auriculatum*

Solauricine yields *solauricidine*, and L-*rhamnosido*-D-*galactosido*-D-*glucose*.

> *Solan. Solanum auriculatum*

Synaine: belongs here?

> *Lili. Veratrum album* (rt)

Terminaline

> *Bux. Pachysandra terminalis*

Tomatidine is the aglycone of *tomatine*.

> *Solan. Lycopersicum* (all (?) species)

Tomatine is said to be antibiotic. It yields *tomatidine, xylose, galactose*, and 2 × *glucose*.

> *Solan. Lycopersicum* spp.

Trimethyl-conkurchine

> *Apocyn. Holarrhena antidysenterica* (bk)

Vanilloyl-cevine yields *cevine* and *vanillic acid*.

> *Lili. Schoenocaulon officinale* (sd)

Vanilloyl-veracevine yields *veracevine* and *vanillic acid*.

> *Lili. Schoenocaulon officinale* (sd)

Vanilloyl-zygadenine yields *zygadenine* and *vanillic acid*.

> *Lili. Zigadenus (Zygadenus) paniculatus* (lvs, st., fl.), *venenosus*

Veracevine (γ-Cevine; Protocevine) is the alkamine of *vanilloyl-veracevine* and *veratridine*.

> *Lili. Schoenocaulon officinale* (sd)

Veragenine

> *Lili. Schoenocaulon officinale?, Veratrum* sp.

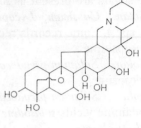

Protoverine ?

Germine

Cyclobuxine

Solanidine (R=CH3)
Isorubijervine (R=CH2OH)

Holarrhimine

Jervine

Fig. 83. Some steroid alkaloids.

Veragermine: belongs here?
    Lili.   *Schoenocaulon officinale* (sd)
Veralbidine: belongs here?
    Lili.   *Veratrum album* (rt)
Veralobine
    Lili.   *Veratrum album* subsp. *lobelianum*
Veramarine
    Lili.   *Veratrum album* subsp. *lobelianum*
Veratralbine: belongs here?
    Lili.   *Veratrum album, viride*

Veratramine is the alkamine of *veratrosine*.
    Lili.   *Veratrum* (6)
Veratridine yields *veracevine* and *veratric acid*.
    Lili.   *Schoenocaulon officinale* (sd); *Veratrum album, viride* (rt)
Veratrine: what is this?
    Sarraceni.   *Sarracenia flava* (rt)
Veratrobasine
    Lili.   *Veratrum album* (rt)
Veratrosine yields *veratramine* and D-*glucose*.
    Lili.   *Veratrum eschscholtzii, viride* (rt)
Veratroyl-zygadenine yields *zygadenine* and *veratric acid*.
    Lili.   *Veratrum* (4), *Zigadenus* (2)
Verine: belongs here?
    Lili.   *Veratrum album* (rt)
Verticine (?Peimine; ?Peimunine)
    Lili.   *Fritillaria verticillata*
Zygacine (Zygadenine-$O(3)$-acetate) yields *zygadenine* and *acetic acid*.
    Lili.   *Veratrum album* var. *grandiflorum*, var. *oxysepalum*; *Ziga-
        denus* (*Zygadenus*) *paniculatus* (lvs, st., fl.), *venenosus*
Zygadenilic acid-δ-lactone
    Lili.   *Veratrum album* var. *oxysepalum*
Zygadenine is the alkamine of *zygacine*.
    Lili.   *Zigadenus* (*Zygadenus*) (6 spp.)

THE TROPANE GROUP

GENERAL

The members of this relatively small group of alkaloids—my list includes just over 40—may be considered to be derivatives of *tropane* (fig. 84). Fodor (in *M.*, v.9, 1967) has reviewed our knowledge of them.

They are commonest in the *Solanaceae*, more than 20 occurring in that alkaloid-rich family. A member of the *Loranthaceae*, parasitic on *Duboisia* of the *Solanaceae*, is said to have one alkaloid of this group! A few are found in the *Convolvulaceae*, and at least one in a *Utricularia*, belonging to the *Lentibulariaceae*; both of these families are members of the same order, **Tubiflorae** (sensu *Syll.*12, 1964), as is the *Solanaceae*.

The next largest group of *tropane alkaloids* includes about a dozen in the *Erythroxylaceae* and one in the *Euphorbiaceae*, both families of the **Geraniales**. Single alkaloids of this series occur in the *Cruciferae*, the *Rhizophoraceae*, and the *Compositae*.

Are all these occurrences certain? If they are we must surely conclude that the ability to produce *tropane alkaloids* has evolved more than once in the dicotyledons.

The *tropane* ring-system may be taken as a *pyrrolidine* ring with a chain of 3 or 4 C-atoms attached at positions 1 and 5. The first part is derived from *ornithine* or *glutamic acid*, as shown by tracer experiments; the second from two molecules of *acetate*.

The tiglic acid portion of those alkaloids containing it is said to be derived from *isoleucine* by decarboxylation and oxidation. The tropic acid moiety of *hyoscyamine* and *hyoscine* (*scopolamine*) may come from *phenylalanine*.

List and Occurrence

3α-Acetoxy-tropane
> *Solan.* *Datura sanguinea*

Apoatropine
> *Solan.* *Atropa belladonna* (plt)

Atropine is the racemic form of (−)-*hyoscyamine*. It occurs only in small amounts.
> *Solan.* *Atropa* (3), *Datura* (6), *Duboisia* (1), *Hyoscyamus* (1), *Mandragora* (1), *Scopolia* (4), *Solandra* (1), *Solanum* (1)

Belladonnine
> *Solan.* *Atropa belladonna* (rt)

Benzoyl-ecgonine
> *Erythroxyl.* *Erythroxylum coca* (lvs), *truxillense* (lvs)

Benzoyl-tropine
> *Erythroxyl.* *Erythroxylum coca* (lvs), *truxillense* (lvs)

Brugine (Tropine-1,2-dithiolane-3-carboxylate)
> *Rhizophor.* *Bruguiera sexangula* (bk)

Butropine (fig. 84)
> *Solan.* *Duboisia leichhardtii* (lvs)

Cinnamyl-cocaine
> *Erythroxyl.* *Erythroxylum coca* (lvs), *monogynum* (lvs), *truxillense* (lvs)

Cinnamyl-ecgonine
> *Erythroxyl.* *Erythroxylum* sp.

(−)-Cocaine (Methyl-benzoyl-ecgonine; fig. 84)
> *Erythroxyl.* *Erythroxylum coca* (lvs), *lucidum* (lvs), *truxillense* (lvs)

'Cocamine' may be a mixture of α- and β-*truxillines*.

Cochlearine is an ester of *tropine* and *m-hydroxy-benzoic acid*.
> *Crucif.* *Cochlearia arctica* (*anglica*)

Convolvamine (Veratroyl-tropeine)
> *Convolvul. Convolvulus pseudo-cantabrica* (sd), *subhirsutus*

Convolvicine: belongs here?
> *Convolvul. Convolvulus pseudo-cantabrica* (sd), *subhirsutus*

Convolvidine is said to be a condensation product of 2 molecules of *convolvine*.
> *Convolvul. Convolvulus pseudo-cantabrica* (sd), *subhirsutus*

Convolvine (Veratroyl-nor-tropeine)
> *Convolvul. Convolvulus pseudo-cantabrica* (sd), *subhirsutus*

Dihydroxy-tropane
> *Erythroxyl. Erythroxylum coca* (lvs), *truxillense* (lvs)

7-Hydroxy-3,6-ditigloyloxy-tropane
> *Solan. Datura* (4)

(−)-6β-Hydroxy-hyoscyamine
> *Solan. Datura ferox*

(−)-Hyoscine (Atroscine; *l*-Scopolamine; Tropylscopeine; Tropylscopine; fig. 84)
> *Loranth. Loranthus* sp. (parasitic upon *Duboisia myoporoides!*)
> *Solan. Atropa belladonna*; *Datura* (11); *Duboisia leichhardtii, myoporoides* (sdlg); *Hyoscyamus* (3), *Mandragora vernalis*; *Physochlaina praealta* (lvs); *Scopolia* (2)
> *Lentibulari. Utricularia physalis*

(−)-Hyoscyamine is said to occur in *Amanita* (an agaric) and
> *Solan. Anthocercis* (3), *Atropa* (2), *Datura* (12), *Duboisia* (2), *Hyoscyamus* (4), *Mandragora* (5), *Physochlaina* (1), *Scopolia* (6), *Solandra* (1)
> *Comp. Lactuca virosa* (lvs)

Isoporoidine (*d*-α-Methylbutyryl-nortropeine)
> *Solan. Duboisia myoporoides* (lvs)

Littorine
> *Solan. Anthocercis littorea* (major alkaloid), *Datura sanguinea* (rt)

Mandragorine: belongs here?
> *Solan. Brunfelsia hopeana, Mandragora* spp.

Meteloidine yields *teloidine* and *tiglic acid*.
> *Erythroxyl. Erythroxylum australe* (lvs)
> *Solan. Anthocercis littorea, Datura meteloides* (plt) and 3 other species.

Methyl-cocaine
> *Erythroxyl. Erythroxylum coca* (lvs), *truxillense* (lvs)

Methyl-ecgonidine
> *Erythroxyl. Erythroxylum coca* (lvs), *truxillense* (lvs)

Noratropine
> *Solan. Solandra laevis*

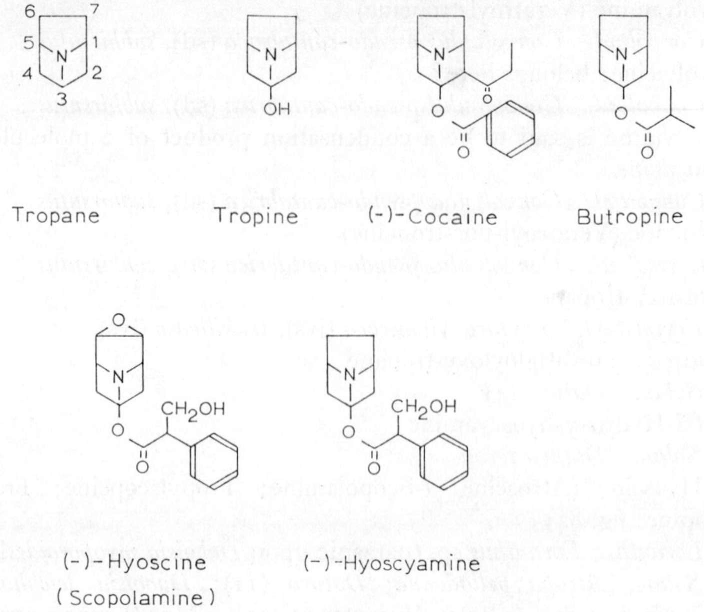

Tropane   Tropine   (-)-Cocaine   Butropine

(-)-Hyoscine   (-)-Hyoscyamine
(Scopolamine)

Fig. 84. Tropane and some tropane alkaloids.

Norhyoscyamine (Pseudo-hyoscyamine; Solandrine; Tropyl-tropeine)
    Solan. *Datura* (2), *Duboisia* (2), *Mandragora* (2), *Scopolia* (2), *Solandra* (2)

Oscine ($3\alpha,6\alpha$-Oxido-7β-hydroxy-tropane)
    Occurrence?

Phyllalbine can be hydrolysed to *tropine* and *vanillic acid.*
    Euphorbi. *Phyllanthus discoides* (rt)

Poroidine (Isovaleryl-nor-tropeine)
    Solan. *Duboisia myoporoides* (lvs)

Pseudotropine
    Solan. *Datura* (2), *Scopolia carniolica*, *Withania somnifera* (rt)

Tigloidine (?($\pm$)-$3\alpha,6\beta$-Ditigloyloxy-7β-hydroxy-tropane; Tiglyl-pseudotropeine)
    Solan. *Datura ferox* (rt), *innoxia* (rt); *Duboisia* (2)

($-$)-3α-Tigloyloxy-6β-acetoxy-tropane
    Solan. *Datura sanguinea*

3α-Tigloyloxy-tropane
    Solan. *Datura ferox* (rt), *Scopolia carniolica*, *Withania somnifera* (rt)

6β-Tigloyloxy-3α-tropanol
    Solan. *Datura cornigera*

Tropacocaine (Benzoyl-pseudotropeine)
    Erythroxyl.   Erythroxylum coca (lvs), *truxillense* (lvs)
Tropine (fig. 84)
    Solan.   Atropa belladonna, Datura (2), *Withania somnifera* (rt)
α-Truxilline (α-Truxillyl-*l*-ecgonine-methyl ether)
    Erythroxyl.   Erythroxylum coca (lvs), *truxillense* (lvs)
β-Truxilline (β-Truxillyl-*l*-ecgonine-methyl-ether)
    Erythroxyl.   Erythroxylum coca (lvs), *truxillense* (lvs)
'Valeroidine' is probably *N-formyl-nor-valeroidine*.
    Solan.   Duboisia myoporoides (lvs)
Valtropine
    Solan.   Duboisia leichhardtii (lvs)

TROPOLONES (Colchicine and Related Alkaloids)

GENERAL

Colchicine has been known for a long time. Its medicinal properties and its ability to interfere with mitosis have made it the subject of intensive study. More recently several related alkaloids have been found.

The chemistry and occurrence of these *tropolones* have been reviewed by Wildman (in *M. & H.*, v.6, 1960) and by Wildman and Pursey (in *M.*, v.11, 1968).

They are confined, so far as we know, to a few genera of the *Liliaceae* (which see for further discussion).

Should the alkaloids of *Kreysigia* be placed here? They are really *isoquinolines* (as is *androcymbine*). Some of them have been called *homo-aporphines* and some *homo-morphines*.

List and Occurrence

Androcymbine (fig. 85) occurs with *melanthioidine* and *colchicine*. Battersby *et al.* (1966) suggest that it arises from a *phenylethyl-isoquinoline* ancestor (and *melanthioidine* is a dimer of such a compound).
    Lili.   Androcymbium melanthioides var. *stricta* (corm)
Bechuanine: belongs here?
    Lili.   Iphigenia bechuanica (all pts?), *indica* (sd), *pallida* (sd)
Bulbocodine: belongs here?
    Lili.   Bulbocodium (*Colchicum*) *vernum* (lvs, corm)
Colchamine (Demecolcine; *N*-Methyl-deacetyl-colchicine)
    Lili.   Colchicum spp., *Gloriosa* spp. (tubers), *Merendera* spp.

Colchiceine
>   *Lili.* *Colchicum autumnale* (fl., corm), *kesselringii, luteum* (corm);
>   *Merendera robusta*

Colchicerine
>   *Lili.* *Colchicum speciosum* (corm)

Colchicine (fig. 85) has been reported from many liliaceous plants. Wildman (1960) says that careful re-examination of some of these leads to the conclusion that *colchicine* and/or *related alkaloids* are:

Present in:
>   *Lili.* *Androcymbium* (1), *Colchicum* (23), *Gloriosa* (4), *Littonia* (1), *Merendera* (8). We can now add *Camptorrhiza strumosa, Dipidax triquetra, Iphigenia* (3), *Kreysigia multiflora*

Absent from:
>   *Lili.* *Anthericum, Asphodelus, Chamaelirium, Chlorogalum, Fritillaria, Hemerocallis, Lloydia, Muscari, Narthecium, Ornithogalum* (3), *Tofieldia* (2), *Tulipa, Veratrum* (3), *Zigadenus*
>   *Irid.* *Crocus sativus.* The reported occurrence seems to be due to a translator's error in recording 'Herbstzeitlose' as *Crocus* instead of Autumn Crocus (*Colchicum*)!

Colchioside is 3-demethyl-colchicine-3-glucoside.
>   *Lili.* *Colchicum autumnale* (sd)

Cornigerine
>   *Lili.* *Camptorrhiza strumosa* (corm, sd); *Colchicum cornigerum* (corm only. *Colchicine* is said to be absent); *Dipidax triquetra* (*rosea*)?; *Iphigenia* (3)

2-Demethyl-colchicine: does this occur naturally?

3-Demethyl-colchicine
>   *Lili.* *Androcymbium melanthioides, Gloriosa* (3, tubers)

3-Demethyl-demecolcine
>   *Lili.* *Colchicum cornigerum*

(−)-Floramultine is a *homo-aporphine.*
>   *Lili.* *Kreysigia multiflora*

(+)-Floramultinine: resembles *floramultine*?
>   *Lili.* *Kreysigia multiflora*

Gloriosine is said, when hydrolysed with acid, to yield *colchiceine.*
>   *Lili.* *Gloriosa superba* (tuber)

Kesselringine: belongs here?
>   *Lili.* *Colchicum kesselringii* (aerial pts)

(+)-Kreysigine is a *homo-aporphine.*
>   *Lili.* *Kreysigia multiflora*

(+)-Kreysiginine is a *homo-morphine* (compare *androcymbine*).
>   *Lili.* *Kreysigia multiflora*

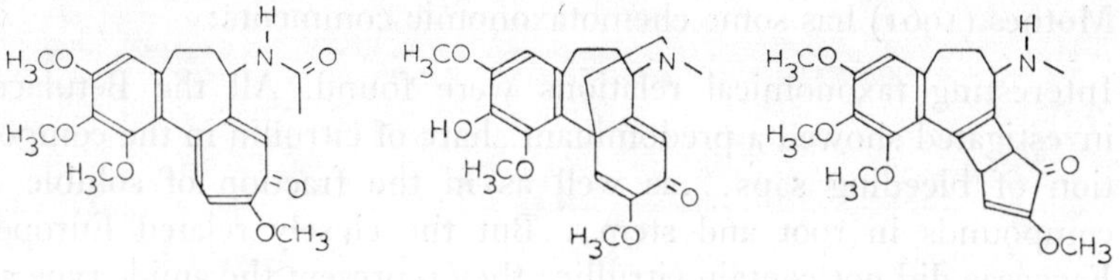

Colchicine   Androcymbine   Lumidemecolcine

Fig. 85. Cochicine and some related alkaloids.

Kreysiginone
    Lili.   Kreysigia multiflora
Lumicolchicines are, in general, produced by the action of sunlight on
    colchicine, etc.
γ-Lumicolchicine is said to occur naturally in
    Lili.   Colchicum spp., *Merendera* spp.
Lumidemecolcine (fig. 85) is said to occur naturally in
    Lili.   Colchicum autumnale
N-Formyl-N-deacetyl-colchicine
    Lili.   Androcymbium melanthioides, Gloriosa (3), *Kreysigia multiflora*
N-Methyl-demecolcine
    Lili.   Colchicum cornigerum
O-Demethyl-N-methyldeacetyl-colchicine
    Lili.   Colchicum sp. (sd)
Speciosine: belongs here?
    Lili.   Colchicum speciosum (corm)
Strumosine: belongs here?
    Lili.   Camptorrhiza strumosa (corm, sd)
Umtaline: belongs here?
    Lili.   Camptorrhiza strumosa (corm, sd)

AMIDES

GENERAL

As treated here this is a relatively small group of compounds. We have
placed the *amides* of some of the *amino-acids* with the *amino-acids*; the
purine bases have been placed with the *alkaloids*; and at least one *amide*
(*anacycline*) is with the *acetylenic compounds*.

    Reinbothe and Mothes (1962) have reviewed our knowledge of *urea*,
ureides, and *guanidines*.

Mothes (1961) has some chemotaxonomic comments:

Interesting taxonomical relations were found. All the Betulaceae investigated showed a predominant share of citrullin in the composition of bleeding saps...as well as in the fraction of soluble N-compounds in root and stem...But the closely related European Fagaceae did not contain citrullin; they represent the amide type and possess glutamine and asparagine (sometimes also alanine) in bleeding sap and stem. Furthermore, it is remarkable that the genera of the Juglandaceae examined—that is, *Juglans*, *Carya*, and *Pterocarya*—show the Betulaceae type of metabolism.

Is it chance that the *Aceraceae*, *Sapindaceae*, and *Hippocastanaceae* (families 3, 5, and 6 of the **Sapindales** of Scholz in *Syll*.12, 1964) are reported to have derivatives of *urea*? Or that several genera of the *Compositae.Asteroideae* have insecticidal amides of unsaturated acids?

List and Occurrence

Acetamide ($CH_3.CO.NH_2$) is said to occur in *Gnetum* and:
  Chenopodi. *Beta vulgaris* (steam distillation)
  Calycanth. *Chimonanthus fragrans* (fl.)
  Punic. *Punica*? (see note under 'Saponin Test B (NH_3)')
Affinin (*N*-Isobutyl-deca-2,6,8-trienoamide) is said to be insecticidal.
  Comp. *Erigeron affinis* (rt), *Heliopsis longipes* (rt)
Allantoic acid (Hidantoic acid; fig. 86) arises enzymatically from
  allantoin. It occurs in fungi and in
  Betul. *Corylus avellana* (lvs)
  Laur. *Persea*
  Platan. *Platanus* (lvs)
  Legum. *Glycine max* (sdlgs, especially when etiolated), *Lupinus alba* (sdlg), *Melilotus officinalis* (sdlg), *Phaseolus vulgaris* (young frt), *Trifolium pratense* (sdlg), *Wisteria sinensis*
  Gerani. *Pelargonium zonale*
  Acer. *Acer pseudoplatanus* (sap), *Negundo aceroides* (lvs)
  Sapind. *Alectryon*
  Hippocastan. *Aesculus hippocastanum*
  Polemoni. *Cobaea*
Allantoin (Cordianin; 5-Ureido-hydantoin; fig. 86): occurs as the *dl*-form in most cases?
  Caryophyll. *Agrostemma githago* (sdlg)
  Chenopodi. *Arthrophytum leptocladum*
  Aristolochi. *Aristolochia cymbifera* (rt), *indica* (rt)
  Platan. *Platanus* (*d*- form?)

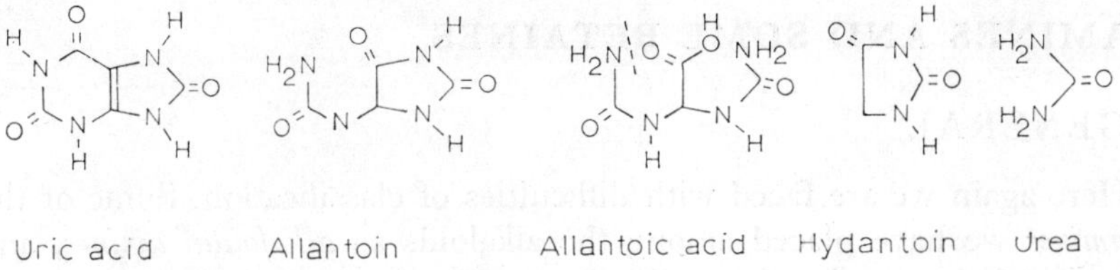

Uric acid   Allantoin   Allantoic acid   Hydantoin   Urea

Fig. 86. Uric acid and some amides.

Legum. *Lupinus albus* (sdlg), *Melilotus officinalis* (sdlg), *Phaseolus multiflorus* (rt), *Trifolium pratense* (sdlg)

Acer. *Acer* (8 spp.), *Negundo aceroides* (frt)

Hippocastan. *Aesculus flava, hippocastanum* (bk)

Boragin. *Anchusa officinalis* (lvs), *Cordia* (2), *Ehretia thyrsifolia* (bk), *Rhabdia lycioides* (rt), *Symphytum officinale* (rt)

Lab. *Stachys silvatica* (lvs)

Solan. *Datura metel, Nicotiana tabacum*

Acanth. *Blepharis edulis* (sd, to 2·1%)

Fagaramide has been treated as a *near-quinoline alkaloid.*

Herculin (*N*-Isobutyl-dodeca-2,8-dienoic acid amide) is said to occur in

Rut. *Zanthoxylum clava-herculis* (bk) (It is *neo-herculin* rather than *herculin*?)

Hydantoin (fig. 86)

Chenopodi. *Beta*

5-Hydroxy-hydantoin

Occurrence?

Neo-herculin (*N*-Isobutyl-dodeca-2,6,8,10-tetraenoic acid amide;? Echinacein) is insecticidal.

Rut. *Zanthoxylum clava-herculis* (bk)

Comp. *Echinacea angustifolia* (rt, 'echinacein')

'Pellitorine' is, says Hegnauer (1964), a mixture of *isobutylamides* of unsaturated C_{10}, C_{12}, and C_{14} acids.

Comp. *Anacyclus pyrethrum* (rt)

Scabrin (*N*-Isobutyl-octadeca-pentenoic acid amide) is said to be more toxic to house-flies than *pyrethrum.*

Comp. *Heliopsis gracilis* (rtbk), *parvifolia* (rtbk), *scabra* (rtbk)

Spilanthol (*N*-Isobutyl-deca-4,6-dienoic acid amide)

Comp. *Spilanthes acmella, oleracea* (flg pts)

Urea (fig. 86) is said to occur in large amounts in some fungi: in small amounts in many higher plants. Mothes (1961), however, says: 'But urea is remarkably rare, and it is often only a product of the analysis of plant material. It may be derived from labile ureide-like allantoic acid.'

AMINES AND SOME BETAINES

GENERAL

Here again we are faced with difficulties of classification. Some of the *amines* we have placed among the alkaloids as *alkaloidal amines*, and some of the *betaines* have also been treated as *alkaloids* (*pyrrolidine*, *pyridine*, and *indole*).

Our distribution lists are very uneven. Many plants have never been investigated for their amines. Others—often rank or ill-smelling—have received much attention. Although many of our records do not specify the parts examined they often refer to flower material. Many fly-pollinated flowers have an unpleasant odour (to the human nose, at least) and *amines* are usually implicated. Thus Klein and Steiner (1928) say: 'Unter den Rosaceen, besonders in den subfamilien der Prunoideae und Pomoideae tritt eine Gruppe von Arten hervor, die sich durch z. T. sehr erheblichen Amingehalt auszeichnet. Da fast alle diese Formen (*Sorbus*, *Pirus*, *Crataegus*) auch in der Literatur als ausgesprochene Käfer order Fliegenblumen bezeichnet werden, sind biologische Zusammenhänge wohl ausser aller Frage.'

We are indebted to Stein von Kamienski (1958) for an extensive piece of work in this field.

The rapid production at anthesis of *amines* in such ill-smelling inflorescences as those of some aroids is quite remarkable. We have discussed this elsewhere (p. 44).

It is interesting that the *amines* of flowers are attractive to some insects, because, on the other hand, *amides* resulting from the union of an *amine* and an *acid* may be among the most effective insecticidal substances known. We may note as an example *scabrin* which is said to be more toxic to house-flies than *pyrethrum*.

It is tempting to suppose that *amines* arise in plants by the decarboxylation of the corresponding *amino-acids*. McKee (1962) discusses some negative results obtained by workers in this field, and says: 'The chemically attractive theory of amine formation by decarboxylation of amino-acids has thus received very little experimental support in higher plants.'

List and Occurrence

Acetylcholine appears to be widely distributed in higher plants.

    Mor.   *Artocarpus champeden* (little), *integra*
    Urtic.   *Laportea gigas*; *Urtica dioica*, *urens*
    Loranth.   *Viscum album*

Crucif. *Capsella bursa-pastoris*
Ros. *Crataegus*
Solan. *Solanum*
Scrophulari. *Digitalis* (2)

Agmatine $\left(\begin{matrix} H_2N \\ HN \end{matrix} \geqslant C\text{-}NH(CH_2)_4NH_2\right)$

Legum. *Pisum sativum*
Euphorbi. *Ricinus communis*
Comp. *Ambrosia artemisiifolia* (pollen)
Arac. *Amorphophallus konjac* (*Hydrosme rivieri*) (infl.), *Arum italicum* (infl.), *Sauromatum guttatum* (infl.)

Ammonia is widespread in the plant kingdom. I give only a few records.

Solan. *Nicotiana*
Arac. *Amorphophallus konjac* (*Hydrosme rivieri*) (infl.); *Arum dioscoridis* (infl.), *italicum* (infl.); *Dracunculus vulgaris* (infl.); *Sauromatum guttatum* (infl.)

Betaine (Glycocoll-betaine; Lycine; Oxyneurine;
$(CH_3)_3\overset{+}{N}.CH_2.COO^-$)

Chenopodi. *Atriplex canescens* (lvs, $>5\%$ dry wt), *Beta vulgaris* (young lvs, $>5\%$)
Solan. *Lycium barbarum* (lvs, st.; 'lycine', $>3\%$), *Scopolia*
Lab. *Orthosiphon*
Comp. *Parthenium argentatum* (plt)

Cadaverine (1,5-Diamino-pentane; Pentamethylene diamine;
$NH_2(CH_2)_5NH_2$)

Legum. *Glycine max*, *Pisum sativum*
Solan. *Solanum tuberosum*
Arac. *Arum italicum* (infl.), *Sauromatum guttatum* (infl.)

Choline (Amanitin; Bilineurin; Combretine; Neurin; Sinkalin;
$[(CH_3)_3\overset{+}{N}.CH_2CH_2OH]OH^-$) may be universal in plants. I have the following records:

Mor. *Humulus*
Monimi. *Doryphora*
Ranuncul. *Caltha*
Crucif. from *sinapin*?
Legum. *Glycine max* (sd), *Phaseolus*, *Trigonella*, *Vicia sativa* (sd)
Gerani. *Erodium*
Combret. *Combretum micranthum* (lvs)
Ole. *Olea*
Solan. *Atropa*, *Scopolia*, *Withania somnifera* (rt)
Lab. *Orthosiphon*

Scrophulari. *Digitalis* (2)
Valerian. *Valeriana officinalis*
Lili. *Convallaria*
Citrosamine (Glucosamido-glucuronido-inositol)
    Rut. *Citrus* (lvs of 'Dancy' tangerine)
p-Coumaroyl-agmatine
    Gram. *Hordeum vulgare* (young shoots)
Creatinine has been recorded from wheat, rye, clover, lucerne, potato, etc.
Diethylamine (($CH_3CH_2)_2NH$)
    Arac. *Arum italicum* (infl.), *Sauromatum guttatum* (infl.)
Dimethylamine (($CH_3)_2NH$) occurs in fungi and
    Capparid. *Courbonia virgata* (frt)
    Ros. *Crataegus*
    Umbell. *Heracleum sphondylium* (fl.)
    Arac. *Arum dioscoridis* (infl.) ?, *italicum* (infl.); *Dracunculus vulgaris* (infl.); *Sauromatum guttatum* (infl.)
bis-1,4-Dimethylamino-butane (?Tetramethylputrescine)
    Solan. *Hyoscyamus muticus*
Dimethylamino-ethanol (($CH_3)_2N.CH_2CH_2OH$) occurs only (?) esterified in the alkaloids *cassain, cassaidin*, etc.
Ergothioneine is a *betaine.*
    Euphorbi. *Hevea brasiliensis* (latex), *benthamiana* (latex), *spruceana* (latex)
Ethanolamine (2-Amino-ethanol; Colamine; $NH_2.CH_2CH_2OH$) may be obtained by hydrolysis of *cephalins* from all plants? It *may* occur (free?) in
    Ros. *Crataegus*
    Legum. *Pisum sativum*
    Arac. *Amorphophallus konjac* (*Hydrosme rivieri*) (infl.), *Sauromatum guttatum* (infl.)
Ethylamine ($CH_3CH_2NH_2$)
    Ros. *Crataegus oxyacantha*
    Gerani. *Erodium*
    Cucurbit. *Bryonia dioica* (fl.)
    Caprifoli. *Sambucus nigra*
    Arac. *Amorphophallus konjac* (*Hydrosme rivieri*) (infl.); *Arum italicum* (infl.), *maculatum* (infl.); *Dracunculus vulgaris* (infl.); *Sauromatum guttatum* (infl.)
Galegine (($CH_3)_2C$=$CH_2NH.C$(=$NH)NH_2$) is a derivative of *guanidine.*
    Legum. *Galega officinalis* (lvs, sd)
    The. *Camellia* (*Thea*)

Guanidine ($HN={=}C(NH_2)_2$) is said to occur in algae, fungi, and higher plants. *Guanidine* derivatives have been recorded from many families (Reuter, 1957–8) among the 'soluble nitrogenous substances'.

    Chenopodi. *Beta*

    Legum. *Galega officinalis, Glycine max* (sd), *Vicia sativa*

    Gram. *Zea*

Hercynine (Histidine-betaine)

    Euphorbi. *Hevea brasiliensis* (latex)

1,6-Hexanediamine

    Arac. *Arum italicum* (infl.), *Sauromatum guttatum* (infl.)

Histamine (fig. 19) is said to be associated with the burning or stinging sensation caused by many irritant plants. Werle and Raub (1948) have studied its distribution, and Werle and Zabel (1948) have investigated the distribution of *histaminase*. I have records of presence or absence of *histamine* from fungi and

    Urtic. *Laportea gigas*; *Urera* sp. (lvs); *Urtica dioica, urens*

    Loranth. *Viscum*

    Chenopodi. *Beta vulgaris* var. *rapa* (lvs), *trigyna* (lvs); *Chenopodium bonus-henricus* (lvs, fl.); *Salsola kali* (lvs); *Spinacia oleracea* (fl.)

    Ranuncul. *Delphinium* sp. (fl.)

    Piper. *not* in *Piper nigrum*

    Sarraceni. *Sarracenia* (lvs)

    Nepenth. *Nepenthes* (lvs)

    Droser. *Drosera* (lvs)

    Papaver. *Chelidonium majus* (lvs); *not* in *Corydalis glauca*

    Crassul. *not* in one

    Saxifrag. *not* in one

    Legum. *Mimosa* sp. (lvs); *Trifolium pratense* (lvs), *repens* (lvs)— but *not* in *Genista, Tamarindus*

    Gerani. *Erodium* (1)—but *not* in *Pelargonium* (1)?

    Rut. *Citrus* (1)—but *not* in *Ruta* (1)

    Aquifoli. *not* in one

    Sterculi. *not* in *Theobroma cacao*

    Cucurbit. *Cucumis* sp.

    Arali. *not* in one

    Primul. *Cyclamen* (1, lvs, fl., corm, rt)—but *not* in *Primula* (1)

    Lab. *Lamium album* (lvs), *Salvia*

    Solan. *Lycopersicum esculentum* (sap)

    Orobanch. *not* in *Orobanche* (1)

    Lentibulari. *Pinguicula* (1) (lvs)

    Plantagin. *Plantago lanceolata* (lvs)

    Comp. *Silybum marianum*

    Arac. *Amorphophallus konjac* (*Hydrosme rivieri*) (infl.)

4-Hydroxy-galegine
> Legum.   Galega officinalis (sd)

Isoamylamine ($(CH_3)_2CH.CH_2.CH_2.NH_2$) is very widely distributed (McKee, 1962; Stein von Kamienski, 1957–8). I have records of it from fungi and

> Polygon.   Polygonum cuspidatum (fl.)
> Berberid.   Mahonia aquifolium—but not in Berberis (1)
> Nymphae.   Nuphar luteum (fl.)
> Saxifrag.   Chrysosplenium, Hydrangea quercifolia (fl. ?), Ribes
> Ros.   Amelanchier rotundifolia (fl.); Aruncus sylvester (fl.); Chaenomeles (fl., 2); Cotoneaster (2); Crataegomespilus; Crataegus (12); Filipendula (2), Prunus (fl., 5 or 6); Pyracantha coccinea; Pyrus communis (piraster); Sanguisorba; Sorbaria (1, fl.); Sorbus aria, domestica?, × latifolia; Spiraea (2)
> Euphorbi.   Mercurialis (plt, 2)
> Rut.   Phellodendron amurense (fl.)
> Acer.   Acer pseudoplatanus
> Staphyle.   Staphylea colchica (fl.)
> Cucurbit.   Bryonia dioica (fl.)
> Onagr.   Oenothera lamarckiana (fl.)
> Corn.   Cornus sanguinea
> Umbell.   Anthriscus (fl.); Chaerophyllum (fl.), Heracleum; Peucedanum; Pimpinella
> Asclepiad.   Vincetoxicum officinale (fl.)
> Rubi.   Galium (fl. of 2 or 3 spp.)
> Solan.   Atropa belladonna (fl.); Nicotiana (lvs and/or fl. of 5)
> Caprifoli.   Sambucus nigra, Viburnum (fl. of 4)
> Arac.   Amorphopallus konjac (Hydrosme rivieri) (infl.), Arum dioscoridis (infl.)?, Dracunculus vulgaris (infl.), Sauromatum guttatum (infl.)

Isobutylamine ($(CH_3)_2CH.CH_2NH_2$) occurs free (?) and as amides such as fagaramide, spilanthol, etc.

> Nymphae.   Nuphar luteum (fl.)
> Berberid.   Berberis vulgaris, Mahonia aquifolium
> Ros.   Crataegus (6 spp., says McKee, 1962), Filipendula ulmaria (fl.), Pyrus communis, Rosa sp., Sorbus aucuparia (fl.)
> Umbell.   Conium maculatum
> Asclepiad.   Vincetoxicum officinale (fl.)
> Caprifoli.   Sambucus nigra (sap); Viburnum lantana, prunifolia
> Arac.   Amorphophallus konjac (Hydrosme rivieri) (infl.); Arum italicum (infl.), maculatum (infl.), nigrum, nickelii; Sauromatum guttatum

Isopropylvinyl-putrescine ($(CH_3)_2CH.CH=CH.NH(CH_2)_4NH_2$)
> Legum.   Eremosparton flaccidum (lvs, st.), Sphaerophysa

Methylamine (Mercurialin; CH_3NH_2) is said to occur in seaweeds and in

Chenopodi. Beta

Ranuncul. *Delphinium consolida* (fl.), *Thalictrum flavum* (fl.)

Nymphae. *Nuphar luteum* (fl.)

Saxifrag. *Philadelphus lemoinei* (fl.)

Euphorbi. *Mercurialis annua* (lvs), *perennis* (lvs)

Staphyle. *Staphylea colchica* (fl.)

Umbell. *Chaerophyllum aromaticum* (fl.), *Conium maculatum* (fl.), *Heracleum sphondylium* (fl.), *Leptotaenia dissecta* (rt)

Asclepiad. *Stapelia?*

Lab. *Mentha*

Solan. *Atropa belladonna* (lvs, fl.), *Nicotiana* (fls of 5)

Caprifoli. *Sambucus nigra* (fl.), *Viburnum opulus* (fl.)

Lili. *Lilium candidum* (fl.), *martagon* (fl.); *Veratrum nigrum* (fl.)

Irid. *Iris germanica* (fl.)

Arac. *Acorus?*; *Amorphophallus konjac* (*Hydrosme rivieri*) (infl.); *Arum dioscoridis* (infl.), *italicum* (infl.), *maculatum* (fl.); *Dracunculus vulgaris* (infl.); *Sauromatum guttatum* (infl.)

Methylamino-ethanol ($CH_3NHCH_2CH_2OH$) occurs free (?) in fungi and as esters in *Erythrophleum* alkaloids.

N-Acetyl-histamine

Chenopodi. *Spinacia oleracea*

N-Carbamyl-putrescine ($NH_2CO.NH(CH_2)_4NH_2$) may be an intermediate in the formation of *putrescine* from *agmatine* by

Gram. *Hordeum vulgare*

N,N-Dimethyl-histamine

Chenopodi. *Spinacia oleracea*

β-Phenylethylamine has been treated also as an alkaloid. Here it occurs in flowers of:

Saxifrag. *Philadelphus delavayi*

Ros. *Crataegus* (ca. 8), *Pyrus communis*, *Sorbus aucuparia*, *Spiraea sorbifolia*

Corn. *Cornus* (2)

Asclepiad. *Vincetoxicum officinale*

1,2-Propanediamine

Arac. *Arum italicum* (infl.), *Sauromatum guttatum* (infl.)

Propionyl-choline

Loranth. *Viscum album*

Propylamine ($CH_3CH_2CH_2NH_2$) occurs in ergot and

Chenopodi. *Camphorosma monspeliacum*

Putrescine (1,4-Diamino-butane; $NH_2(CH_2)_4NH_2$) may be formed from *agmatine* by barley. It occurs in fungi and

Legum. *Pisum sativum*

Gerani.   *Erodium*
Rut.   Citrus grandis (and other spp. ?)
Solan.   Atropa belladonna, Datura stramonium
Arac.   Arum italicum (infl.), *Sauromatum guttatum*

Sinapin is the *sinapic acid* ester of *choline*. It occurs in the glycoside *sinalbin*.

Crucif.   Draba nemorosa (free ?)

Tetramethyl-ammonium hydroxide ('Tetramine; $(CH_3)_4N.OH$) occurs in sea-anemone and

Capparid.   Courbonia pseudopetalosa, virgata (rt)

Trimethylamine $((CH_3)_3N)$: secondary in many cases? It has been reported from red and brown algae and from many higher plants.

Fag.   Fagus
Chenopodi.   Beta vulgaris, Chenopodium vulvaria (lvs), *Rhagodia hastata*
Ranuncul.   Clematis—not in *Thalictrum*
Aristolochi.   Aristolochia gigas, grandiflora (fl.) ?
Capparid.   Courbonia virgata
Crassul.   Cotyledon umbilicus (plt)
Saxifrag.   Chrysosplenium
Ros.   Crataegus (fls of 9 spp.); *Prunus padus, serotina* (fl.); *Pyrus communis* (fl.); *Sorbaria* (1, fl.); *Sorbus aucuparia* (fl.), *latifolia; Spiraea sorbifolia* (fl.)
Euphorbi.   Mercurialis perennis (plt)
Malv.   Gossypium (fl.)
Corn.   Cornus sanguinea (fl.)
Umbell.   Chaeophyllum cicutaria, Heracleum sphondylium (fl.)
Menyanth.   Menyanthes?
Solan.   Nicotiana
Caprifoli.   Viburnum lantanum
Comp.   Arnica montana, Taraxacum officinale (fl.)
Lili.   Hyacinthus orientalis
Arac.   Acorus calamus (rhiz.), *Amorphophallus konjac* (*Hydrosme rivieri*) (infl.), *Dracunculus vulgaris* (infl.), *Sauromatum guttatum* (infl.), *Spathiphyllum heliconiaefolium*

AMINO-ACIDS, PEPTIDES, AND PROTEINS
(including Enzymes)

GENERAL

We have here the same kind of problem which faces us when we consider *carbohydrates*, *terpenoids*, and any other chemical units which may occur singly or linked in chains of from two to a few to many units.

The *amino-acids* are very numerous and often occur singly in the plant. They may also be found linked together as *peptides*, two to many units being involved. Finally, chains of very many units are known as *proteins* and *enzymes*. But where is the boundary between a big *peptide* and a small *protein*? Elmore, in his *Peptides and Proteins* (1968), sees no boundary between them. He asks, is *adrenocorticotrophic hormone* (with 39 amino-acid residues) to be called a large peptide or a small protein? And is there any real distinction to be drawn, except in function, between an 'ordinary' *protein* and an *enzyme*?

We shall divide our discussion here, ignoring these difficulties more or less, into three major sections dealing with:

I. Amino-acids.
II. Peptides.
III. Proteins (including enzymes).

I AMINO-ACIDS

GENERAL

There is no clear distinction between some *amino-acids*, such as *histidine*, and some *alkaloids*; nor can we always place *amides* logically—some substances, such as *glutamine* and *asparagine*, are *amides* of *amino-acids*!

About 20 *amino-acids* occur in *proteins*, and these have been called the 'magic twenty'. Actually we are by no means certain that all of these occur in all proteins. Davies *et al.* (1964) include *hydroxyproline* and *cystine* in their list, making a total of 22. They say, however: 'Current theories of coding can account for twenty amino-acids; hence it is necessary to assume that hydroxyproline is alternative to proline as one of the "magic twenty" and that cysteine but not cystine is coded.'

Fowden (1962) points out that further *amino-acids* may occur in individual *proteins*, such as *enzymes*. He mentions α-*amino-adipic acid*, for example, as being present to the extent of 0·06% of the dry weight of the water-soluble *proteins* of *Zea mays*, and *sarcosine* as occurring in a peanut *protein*.

Most, if not all, of the 'magic twenty' occur free as well as in the bound form. In addition many other *amino-acids* have been found in the free state, sometimes in rather large amount. Fowden (1962) has a dramatic graph to show how the adoption of chromatography as a tool has resulted in a tremendous increase in the number of non-protein *amino-acids* known. It would seem that *our* list is incomplete, but we have placed a few *amino-acids* elsewhere. Fowden points out that:

> Unlike animals, plants must synthesize all the amino-acids necessary for the formation of protein. In addition, however, they synthesize at least sixty amino-acids which, so far as is known, are not incorporated into protein. Some of these amino-acids are found in only a very few species, and many have unusual structural features not found in other natural products...the degree of uncertainty that is at present associated with the function of these compounds resembles that surrounding other types of plant products, including the alkaloids, floral pigments, essential oils, and polyphenols.

Writing in 1965, Dunnill and Fowden estimated that at least 100 non-protein *amino-acids* were known at that time from plants, occurring either free or as *γ-glutamyl peptides.*

The chemotaxonomy of *amino-acids* is discussed elsewhere in this book. We may note:

(*a*) The work of Bell (1962, 1963, 1964), Bell and Tirimanna (1963), and Bell and O'Donovan (1966) on the *amino-acids* of *Lathyrus* and *Vicia* (both *Leguminosae*).

(*b*) That of Montant (1957) on the free *amino-acids* of *Euphorbia*.

(*c*) The distribution of *djenkolic acid* and *N-acetyl-djenkolic acid* in the subfamily *Mimosoideae* of the *Leguminosae*.

(*d*) The occurrence of δ-*acetyl-ornithine* in the *Papaveraceae*.

(*e*) The amino-acids of the *Cucurbitaceae*.

(*f*) The cyclopropyl amino-acids of the *Sapindaceae–Hippocastanaceae* group.

It is tempting to discuss the biosynthesis of amino-acids in higher plants, but the temptation must be resisted. The interested reader is referred to such reviews as those of Fowden (in *Plant Biochemistry*, edited by Bonner and Varner, 1965; and *Ann. Rev. Plant Physiol.* 1967).

We may note, however, that a relationship between α-*amino-acids* and *cyanogenic glycosides*:

$$\begin{array}{c} R \\ \diagdown \\ \diagup \\ R' \end{array} CH.CH(NH_2).COOH \rightarrow \begin{array}{c} R \diagdown \diagup O.Glucose \\ C.CN \\ \diagup \diagdown \\ R' \end{array}$$

has been established for *linamarin, lotaustralin, prunasin,* and *dhurrin.*

It is interesting that free labelled *HCN* may be incorporated into *asparagine* by *Vicia* (some species), *Lathyrus odoratus*, *Ecballium elaterium*, and *Cucumis sativus*; but into *γ-glutamyl-β-cyano-alanine* by some other *Vicia* species (including *sativa*, *monantha* and *ferruginea*). Free *β-cyano-alanine*, which is neurolathyritic, occurs in *V. sativa*.

List and Occurrence

δ-Acetyl-ornithine (H₃CO.NH.CH₂.CH₂.CH₂.CH(NH₂).COOH)

δ-Acetyl-ornithine ($H_3CO.NH.CH_2.CH_2.CH_2.CH(NH_2).COOH$)

> *Papaver.* General? Tyler (1960) says: 'Its usefulness a sa chemo-taxonomic indicator would appear to rank with protopine [an alkaloid]. Both compounds distinguish the Papaveraceae and Fumariaceae [we treat these as sub-families of the *Papaveraceae*] from other families but not necessarily from each other.' Unfortunately for this statement δ-*acetyl-ornithine* does occur elsewhere:
> *Legum.* *Onobrychis viciifolia* and other members of the family
> *Gram.* some members of the *Festuceae* (Fowden, 1958)

l-Alanine (α-Amino-propionic acid; CH₃.CH(NH₂).COOH) is one of the 'protein' amino-acids. Many derivatives occur as 'non-protein' amino-acids.

β-Alanine (β-Amino-propionic acid) seems to be widely distributed.
> *Crassul.* *Kalanchoë*
> *Legum.* in root nodules, etc.
> *Irid.* *Iris*
> *Gram.* *Agropyrum, Lolium*

Albiziine (3-Ureido-alanine)
> *Legum.* *Mimosoideae*

α-Amino-γ-acetylamino-butyric acid (γ-Acetyl-diamino-butyric acid)
> *Euphorbi.* *Euphorbia pulcherrima* (latex)

l-α-Amino-adipic acid (HOOC.CH₂.CH₂.CH₂.CH(NH₂).COOH) is widely distributed in the free state (Fowden, 1962). Is it involved in the synthesis of *lysine*?
> *Legum.* *Pisum* (sd)
> *Gram.* probably present in small amounts in: *Avena, Brachypodium, Bromus, Dactylis, Festuca, Hordeum, Lolium, Poa, Zea*

l-α-Amino-butyric acid (CH₃.CH₂.CH(NH₂).COOH)
> *Solan.* *Solanum tuberosum* (lvs, but not tubers)
> *Gram.* *Zea mays* (lvs, free (?) and combined)

γ-Amino-butyric acid—writing in 1962, Fowden says that it: '...seems to be distributed universally—a plant that did not contain it would be considered odd'. It is probably produced by decarboxylation of glutamate. I have records of it from: *Betul., Ulm., Chenopodi.,*

Calycanth., *Piper.*, *Legum.*, *Euphorbi.*, *Hippocastan.*, *Solan.*, *Lili.* (general ?), *Gram.*, etc.

1-Amino-cyclopropane-1-carboxylic acid
    Ros.   *Malus* (apple), *Pyrus* (pear) (unripe frt)
    Eric.   *Vaccinium vitis-idaea*

2-Amino-4-hydroxyhept-6-ynoic acid
    Sapind.   *Euphoria longana* (sd)

2-Amino-6-hydroxy-4-methylhex-4-enoic acid
    Hippocastan.   *Aesculus californica* (sd)

2-Amino-4-hydroxymethylhex-5-ynoic acid
    Sapind.   *Euphoria longana* (sd)

β-Amino-isobutyric acid ($H_2N.CH_2.CH(CH_3).COOH$): arises by breakdown of *thymine*?
    Irid.   *Iris tingitana*

2-Amino-4-methylhex-4-enoic acid and its γ-glutamyl peptide
    Hippocastan.   *Aesculus californica* (sd)

2-Amino-4-methylhex-5-ynoic acid (fig. 87)
    Sapind.   *Euphoria longana* (sd)

α-Amino-γ-oxalylamino-butyric acid occurs in equilibrium with α-*oxalylamino-β-amino-butyric acid* (Bell and O'Donovan, 1966) in
    Legum.   *Lathyrus* spp.

α-Amino-β-oxalylamino-propionic acid is a neurotoxin. It occurs in equilibrium with α-*oxalylamino-β-amino-propionic acid* (Bell and O'Donovan, 1966) in
    Legum.   *Lathyrus* spp.

α-Amino-pimelic acid ($HOOC.(CH_2)_4.CH(NH_2).COOH$) occurs in a fern and in
    Legum.   *Ceratonia siliqua* (sd)

α-Amino-β-(pyrazolyl-*N*)-propionic acid (β-Pyrazol-1-yl-alanine) is formed from *pyrazole* and *serine* in cucumber seedlings.
    Cucurbit.   see discussion under family

l-Arginine (α-amino-δ-guanidino-valeric acid; $H_2N.C(=NH).NH.$ $(CH_2)_3.CH(NH_2).COOH$) is a 'protein' amino-acid which, according to Mothes (1961) is also 'a frequent form of nitrogen-storage in underground organs and stems'. I have records of it combined and/or free from algae, gymnosperms, at least 25 families of dicotyledons, and 5 families of monocotyledons.

Asparagine ($H_2N.CO.CH_2.CH(NH_2).COOH$) is the amide of *aspartine* (an *amino-acid*). It was crystallized from juice of *Asparagus* in 1806! It is a constituent of proteins and therefore universally (?) distributed. I have records of it from 22 families of dicotyledons and 6 families of monocotyledons. Several derivatives of *asparagine* are known to occur.

l-Aspartic acid (α-Amino-succinic acid; $HOOC.CH_2.CH(NH_2).COOH$) is one of the 'magic twenty' protein amino-acids. It may also occur free in

> Bromeli. *Aechmea purpurea rosea, Ananas comosus, Billbergia nutans* (An important storage material in all—Reuter, 1957–8)
> Arac. It is the chief soluble nitrogenous substance in some.

Azetidine-2-carboxylic acid (Homoserine lactone; fig. 87) is an *imino-acid* found by Fowden and Steward (1957) in many related monocotyledons, and often in considerable amount. It '...may contain as much as 50% of the total nitrogen present in the rhizome of Solomon's seal (*Polygonatum multiflorum*)'. Writing in 1962 Fowden says: 'azetidine-2-carboxylic acid occurs in a high proportion of liliaceous species [including our Agavaceae] but has not been detected in members of other plant families except in a few species of Amaryllidaceae [species which *we* include in Liliaceae]...'.

> Lili. *Bowiea volubilis* (st.), *Camassia* sp. (sd), *Convallaria majalis* (lvs, sd), *Danae racemosa* (sd), *Fritillaria imperialis* (sd), *Gasteria verrucosa* (lvs), *Hosta glauca* (sd), *Liriope muscari* (lvs, sd), *Littonia modesta* (sd), *Maianthemum canadense* (lvs, sd), *Milla biflora* (sd), *Polygonatum* sp. (lvs), *Rohdea japonica* (lvs), *Ruscus aculeatus* ('lvs'), *Scilla hohenackeri* (sd), *Smilacina racemosa* (sd)
> Agav. *Dracaena deremensis* (lvs), *fragrans* (lvs), *godseffiana* (lvs), *sanderiana* (lvs)
> Amaryllid. ?

Canaline (α-Amino-γ-*O*-hydroxylamino-butyric acid; $H_2N.O.CH_2.CH_2.CH(NH_2).COOH$) is formed enzymatically from *canavanine*. Does it occur free in any amount?

Canavanine (α-Amino-γ-hydroxyguanidino-butyric acid; $H_2N.C(=NH).NH.O.CH_2.CH_2.CH(NH_2).COOH$) is known only from the *Leguminosae* and in that great family only from the *Faboideae*.

cis-α-(Carboxycyclopropyl)-glycine

> Hippocastan. *Aesculus parviflora* (sd)

trans-α-(Carboxycyclopropyl)-glycine

> Sapind. *Blighia sapida* (sd)

m-Carboxyphenyl-*l*-alanine (fig. 87) seems to be rather widely distributed.

> Crucif. *Lunaria*
> Resed. *Reseda*
> Cucurbit. many (p. 1256)
> Irid. *Iris tingitana*

l-(+)-Citrulline (α-Amino-δ-carbamido-valeric acid; $H_2N.CO.NH(CH_2)_3.CH(NH_2).COOH$) is discussed by Dunnill and Fowden (1965) who say that as an intermediate in the *glutamic acid → arginine* pathway it is probably present in all plants but often in very small amount. The 3 acids *arginine, citrulline,* and *ornithine* have been called the 'ornithine family'. They seem to be interconvertible in the plant. I have records of *citrulline* from

Jugland. *Carya, Juglans, Pterocarya*
Betul. *Alnus, Betula, Carpinus, Corylus, Ostrya*
Fag. *Nothofagus*
Caryophyll. *Agrostemma*
Annon. *Annona*
Calycanth. *Calycanthus*
Laur. *Persea*
Crucif. *Brassica*
Vitac. *Vitis* (sap)
Cucurbit. *Citrullus lanatus* (where it was first found), and many others, in relatively large amount (p. 1256)
Eben. *Diospyros*
Lili. *Galtonia*
Irid. *Freesia*

Cucurbitin (3-Amino-pyrrolidine-3-carboxylic acid; fig. 87)
Cucurbit. *Cucurbita moschata*

Cyclo-alliin (fig. 87) contains *sulfur.*
Lili. *Allium* spp.

Cystathionine is known in combination as *selenocystathionine.* Does it occur free in higher plants?

Cysteine (HS.CH$_2$.CH(NH$_2$).COOH) is a 'protein' amino-acid, but may be lacking in protein-hydrolysates, presumably because it is easily oxidized to *cystine.*

Δ^{4,5}-Dehydro-pipecolic acid (Baikiain; fig. 87)
Legum. *Acacia* spp., *Baikiaea plurijuga* (wd)
Palmae. *Phoenix dactylifera* (frt)

Deamino-canavanine may be secondary.
Legum. *Canavalia ensiformis*

α,γ-Diamino-butyric acid
Legum. *Lathyrus* spp. (sds)
Lili. *Polygonatum multiflorum* (rhiz.)

α,β-Diamino-propionic acid (H$_2$N.CH$_2$.CH(NH$_2$).COOH)
Legum. *Mimosoideae*

Dihydro-alliin (H$_3$C.CH$_2$.CH$_2$.SO.CH$_2$.CH(NH$_2$).COOH)
Lili. *Allium* spp.

2,4-Dihydroxy-6-methyl-phenylalanine
Caryophyll. *Agrostemma githago* (sd)

l-3,4-Dihydroxy-phenylalanine (DOPA) is probably formed by oxidation of *phenylalanine* and/or *tyrosine.* See also *melanins.*

Legum. *Cytisus*; *Mucuna capitata, pruriens*; *Stizolobium* (*Mucuna*) *deeringianum* (sd); *Vicia faba* (sd, sdlg)

Euphorbi. *Euphorbia lathyris* (Liss, 1961), but *not* in 19 other spp. (Montant, 1957)

Djenkolic acid (fig. 87)

Legum. *Albizia lophantha*; *Pithecolobium bigeminum, dulce, lobatum* ('Jèngkol'), *multiflorum*. See discussion under *Leguminosae*.

l-Glutamic acid (α-Amino-glutaric acid;

$HOOC.CH_2.CH_2.CH(NH_2).COOH$) is a 'protein' amino-acid and therefore universally distributed. It may also be free and occur as one of the main nitrogen-storage acids in several families. Several derivatives also occur. I have the following records:

Myric.; *Salic.* (*Salix, Populus*); *Betul.* (*Alnus, Betula, Carpinus, Corylus*); *Fag.* (*Castanea, Fagus, Quercus*); *Ulm.* (*Ulmus,* much); *Cact.* (in all tested: one of main N-storage materials); *Ranuncul.* (several); *Berberid.* (*Mahonia*); *Nymphae.* (*Nuphar, Nymphaea*); *Calycanth.*; *Papaver.* (*Papaveroideae,* several); *Saxifrag.* (*Philadelphus, Ribes*); *Ros.* (Many); *Legum.* (*Faboideae,* several); *Euphorbi.* (*Ricinus*); *Rut.* (*Phellodendron*); *Simaroub.* (*Ailanthus*); *Anacardi.* (*Rhus*); *Hippocastan.* (*Aesculus*); *Rhamn.* (*Rhamnus*); *Corn.* (*Cornus*); *Primul.* (*Cyclamen*); *Ole.* (*Forsythia, Fraxinus, Syringa*); *Gentian.* (*Gentiana*); *Solan.* (*Solanum*); *Bignoni.* (*Catalpa*); *Gesneri.* (*Achimenes*); *Caprifoli.* (*Symphoricarpos, Viburnum*); *Valerian.* (*Valeriana*); *Lili.* (one of the main N-storage materials); *Amaryllid.* (*Bravoa, Narcissus*); *Dioscore.* (*Dioscorea*); *Irid.* (*Tigridia*); *Bromeli.* (in all tested: one of the main N-storage materials); *Arac.* (in all storage organs?); *Zingiber.* (*Alpinia*); *Marant.* (*Maranta*)

l-Glutamine ($H_2N.CO.CH_2.CH_2.CH(NH_2).COOH$) is the *amide* of *glutamic acid* (above). It is a 'protein' amino-acid, but also occurs free:

Cact. in all examined?

Ranuncul. several

Arac. in several, as a N-storage material

Glycine (α-Amino-acetic acid; $H_2N.CH_2.COOH$) is the simplest of the 'protein' amino-acids, and one of the first to be discovered. It seems not to occur in quantity in the free state.

l-Histidine (β-Imidazole-α-amino-propionic acid; fig. 87) is a 'protein' amino-acid. I have only a few records of it in the free state:

Legum. *Lupinus albus, luteus*

Comp. *Helianthus annuus, Scorzonera hispanica*

Lili. *not* found by Fowden and Steward (1957)

Gram. *Secale cornutum*

l-Homoarginine (α-Amino-ϵ-guanidino-caproic acid) is obviously closely related to *γ-hydroxy-homoarginine* and *lathyrine*.

  Legum. Lathyrus (sds of at least 36 spp., Bell, 1962)

l-Homoserine (γ-Hydroxy-α-amino-butyric acid) is, says Fowden (1962), an obligatory intermediate for the production of *methionine* and *threonine* from *aspartic acid*. See also *azetidine-2-carboxylic acid*.

  Legum. Pisum sativum (sdlg)

γ-Hydroxy-arginine occurs in marine animals and in

  Legum. Vicia (in all (17) examined; Bell and Tirimanna, 1963)

l-β-Hydroxy-glutamic acid ($HOOC.CH_2.CH(OH).CH(NH_2).COOH$)

  Legum. Stizolobium niveum (in a *globulin*)
  Cucurbit. Cucurbita pepo (sd)

γ-Hydroxy-glutamic acid ($HOOC.CH(OH).CH_2.CH(NH_2).COOH$)

  Polemoni. Phlox decussata (free and in protein?)
  Scrophulari. Linaria vulgaris (free)
  Lili. in at least 2 genera

γ-Hydroxy-homoarginine: a link between *l-homoarginine* and *lathyrine*?

  Legum. Lathyrus (4 spp. of Bell's 'group 3')

4-Hydroxy-hygric acid (4-Hydroxy-*N*-methyl-pyrrolidine-2-carboxylic acid) is related to *betonicine* and *turicine*.

  Euphorbi. Croton gubouga (bk)

δ-Hydroxy-lysine ($H_2N.CH_2.CH(OH).CH_2.CH_2.CH(NH_2).COOH$) does not occur in higher plants?

γ-Hydroxy-γ-methyl-glutamic acid occurs in large amount in a fern and, say Fowden and Steward (1957), in

  Lili. Calochortus sp. (sd, trace); Erythronium sp. (lvs, trace); Lilium longiflorum (lvs, trace); Littonia modesta (sd, trace); Puschkinia sp. (lvs, trace); Tulipa acuminata (lvs, trace), biflora (lvs, trace), clusiana (lvs, trace), fosteriana (lvs, trace), gesneriana (lvs, trace), linifolia (lvs, trace), praestans (lvs, trace), stellata (lvs, trace), sylvestris (lvs, trace), tarda (lvs, trace)

4-Hydroxy-pipecolic acid (4-Hydroxy-piperidine-2-carboxylic acid)

  Legum. Acacia, Albizia, Baikiaea
  Mus. Strelitzia reginae

5-Hydroxy-pipecolic acid has been found in ferns and in

  Legum. Acacia, Baikiaea, Saraca?
  Palmae. Phoenix, Rhapis

l-Hydroxy-proline occurs in 2 forms (free, or combined?).

  Salic. Populus (1 form, pollen)
  Betul. Betula, Corylus (1 form, pollen?)
  Santal. Santalum album (lvs, 2 forms)
  Gerani. Erodium
  Agav. Dracaena (free)

Hypoglycin-A (β-(Methylenecyclopropyl) alanine; fig. 87)

    Sapind. Blighia sapida (unripe aril, sd)

Hypoglycin-B is a *glutamyl-peptide* of *hypoglycin-A*.

    Sapind. Blighia sapida

Isoleucine (β-Methyl-α-amino-valeric acid;

    $H_3C.CH_2.CH(CH_3).CH(NH_2).COOH$) is a 'protein' amino-acid which also occurs free in

    Fag. Fagus sylvatica (trace in bleeding sap)

    Legum. Glycine, Lupinus, Vicia

    Hippocastan. Aesculus hippocastanum (a little in bleeding sap)

Lathyrine (β-(2-Aminopyrimidin-4-yl) alanine; ?Tingitanine; fig. 87) is nearly related to *l-homoarginine*.

    Legum. Lathyrus (at least 12 spp.)

    Irid. Iris tingitanus?

l-Leucine (?Chenopodin; β-Isopropyl-α-amino-propionic acid; $(H_3C)_2CH.CH_2.CH(NH_2).COOH$) was one of the first 'protein' amino-acids to be isolated. It is one of the more abundant acids of plant proteins. It, and *isoleucine* may be important in the production of *hemiterpenes*.

    Chenopodi. Chenopodium album (sap, 'chenopodin')

    Legum. Lupinus, Pisum (etiolated sdlg), *Vicia*

    Hippocastan. Aesculus hippocastanum (trace in sap)

    Solan. Solanum tuberosum (tuber)

    Lili. present in all of the many species examined (Fowden and Steward, 1957)

l-Lysine (α-ϵ-Diamino-caproic acid) is a 'protein' amino-acid, occurring to the extent of 1–6% in plant proteins. Vogel (1959) says that 2 biosynthetic pathways of *lysine* formation are known—via α-*amino-adipic acid* and via α-ϵ-*diamino-pimelic acid*. All of the few higher plants that he studied used the latter path.

    Legum. Lupinus, Pisum, Robinia, Vicia

    Lili. in some, at least

exo(cis)--3, 4 Methanoproline

    Hippocastan. Aesculus parviflora (sd)

l-Methionine ($H_3C.S.CH_2.CH(NH_2).COOH$) is a constituent of most *proteins* and *enzymes*. Karrer (1958) says that it seldom occurs in the free state. It may arise from *aspartic acid* via *homoserine*. It is important in methylation.

    Lili. not found by Fowden and Steward (1957)

    Gram. 'Phyllostachys edulis' (whatever that is, shoots) and in some other grasses (sds)

α-Methylene-cyclopropyl-glycine (fig. 87) is a most unusual amino-acid. The next higher member of the series, *hypoglycin-A*, also occurs in the *Sapindaceae*. See discussion under that family.

Sapind.   *Litchi chinensis* (sd)

γ-Methylene-glutamic acid (fig. 87)

Legum.   *Arachis hypogaea* (sdlg)

Lili.   *Calochortus* sp. (sd); *Erythronium* sp. (lvs, sd); *Fritillaria meleagris* (lvs, much); *Haworthia coarctata* (lvs); *Lilium longiflorum* (lvs, much); *Notholirion (Lilium) thomsonianum* (lvs); *Tulipa acuminata* (lvs), *biflora* (lvs), *clusiana* (lvs), *fosteriana* (lvs), *gesneriana* (lvs, sd), *greigii* (lvs), *kaufmanniana* (lvs), *linifolia* (lvs), *montana* (lvs), *praestans* (lvs), *pulchella* (lvs), *stellata* (lvs, much), *sylvestris* (lvs), *tarda* (lvs)

γ-Methylene-glutamine

Legum.   *Arachis hypogaea* (sdlg and plt—over 95% of total N in exuding sap is in this amide, says Fowden, 1962), *Saraca indica* (sd)

Lili.   *Erythronium* sp. (lvs, much; sd); *Tulipa acuminata* (lvs, much), *biflora* (lvs), *clusiana* (lvs), *fosteriana* (lvs, much; sd), *gesneriana* (lvs, much), *greigii* (lvs, much), *kaufmanniana* (lvs, much), *linifolia* (lvs), *montana* (lvs), *praestans* (lvs, much), *pulchella* (lvs, much), *stellata* (lvs), *sylvestris* (lvs), *tarda* (lvs, much)

γ-Methyl-glutamic acid

Legum.   *Glycine*?; *Lathyrus aphaca, maritimus*

Polygal.   *Polygala vulgaris*

Lili.   *Calochortus* sp. (sd, much); *Erythronium* sp. (sd); *Lilium longiflorum* (lvs, much); *Notholirion macrophyllum* (lvs), *thomsonianum* (lvs); *Puschkinia* sp. (lvs); *Tulipa biflora* (lvs), *clusiana* (lvs), *fosteriana* (lvs), *gesneriana* (lvs), *greigii* (lvs), *kaufmanniana* (lvs), *linifolia* (lvs), *montana* (lvs), *praestans* (lvs), *pulchella* (lvs), *stellata* (lvs), *sylvestris* (lvs)

5-Methyl-pipecolic acid

Solan.   *Lycopersicum pimpinellifolium*. Prelog and Jeger (1960) say: 'The occurrence of 5-methyl pipecolic acid in the leaves of the tomatine-containing primitive *Lycopersicum pimpinellifolium* Mill. is of unusual interest in that it embraces in its structure that of ring F of the *Solanum* alkaloids.'

Mimosine is treated as a *pyridine alkaloid*.

N-Acetyl-*l*-djenkolic acid

Legum.   *Mimosoideae* (sds)

N^4-Ethyl-asparagine ($HN(C_2H_5).CO.CH_2.CH(NH_2).COOH$)

Cucurbit.   *Ecballium elaterium* and others. Fowden (1962) says it is not known from other families and that it may be regarded as an alternative to *asparagine* as a form of N-storage.

N^4-Hydroxyethyl-asparagine
>   Cucurbit.   *Bryonia dioica*

N^4-Methyl-asparagine
>   Cucurbit.   *Corallocarpus epigaeus* (Fowden and Dunnill, 1965)

l-*N*-Methyl-tyrosine (Andirine; Geoffroyin; Ratanhin; Surinamin; fig. 87)
>   Legum.   *Andira inermis, Ferreirea (Andira) spectabilis, Geoffraea surinamensis*
>   Krameri.   *Krameria triandra*

l-Norleucine (α-Amino-caproic acid)
>   Euphorbi.   *Ricinus communis* (a doubtful record)

O-Acetyl-homoserine
>   Legum.   *Pisum sativum*

Orcyl-alanine
>   Caryophyll.   *Agrostemma githago* (sd). It appears to be used in germination. It is formed from *acetate* and *serine*, through *orsellinic acid* (Hadwiger *et al.* 1965)

α-Oxalylamino-γ-amino-butyric acid occurs in equilibrium with α-*amino-γ-oxalylamino-butyric acid* (Bell and O'Donovan, 1966) in
>   Legum.   *Lathyrus* spp.

α-Oxalylamino-β-amino-propionic acid occurs in equilibrium with α-*amino-β-oxalylamino-propionic acid* (Bell and O'Donovan, 1966) in
>   Legum.   *Lathyrus* spp.

l-Ornithine (α,δ-Diamino-valeric acid; $H_2N.CH_2.CH_2.CH_2.CH(NH_2).COOH$) has been reported to occur in red algae, ferns, and a few higher plants.
>   Betul.   *Alnus glutinosa* (rt)
>   Celastr.   *Catha edulis* (lvs)

l-Phenyl-alanine (β-Phenyl-α-amino-propionic acid) is a 'protein' amino-acid, amounting to from 3 to 5% or more in plant proteins. Its metabolism has been much studied. It has been reported to occur free in
>   Legum.   *Lupinus, Phaseolus, Vicia*
>   Lili.   less general than some other amino-acids (Fowden and Steward, 1957)

l-Pipecolic acid (Pipecolinic acid; Piperidine-2-carboxylic acid) seems to be rather common in the free state. Fowden (1962) says: 'The legumes *Baikiaea plurijuga*...and several species of *Acacia*, contain mixtures of pipecolic acid, 5-hydroxy- and 4-hydroxy-pipecolic acids, and baikiain ($\Delta^{4,5}$-dehydro-pipecolic acid). Interconversion of these amino acids may depend on...enzymes.'
>   Legum.   *Acacia* spp., *Baikiaea plurijuga, Phaseolus vulgaris* (from lysine), *Saraca indica* (sd), *Trifolium repens* (lvs)

Solan. *Lycopersicum esculentum* (in plts deficient in Fe and Mn; Possingham, 1956)

Lili. *Chionodoxa luciliae* (lvs), *Convallaria majalis* (sd), *Fritillaria imperialis* (sd), *Haworthia coarctata* (lvs), *Hosta lancifolia* (lvs), *Hyacinthus orientalis* (lvs), *Maianthemum canadense* (lvs), *Muscari armeniacum* (lvs), *Smilacina racemosa* (lvs)

l-Proline (Pyrrolidine-α-carboxylic acid; fig. 87) is a 'protein' amino-acid. In plant proteins it amounts to from 3 to 5, or more rarely to 9%. Davies *et al.* (1964) say that tracer experiments support the view that it may arise from an α-*amino-acid* such as *glutamic acid*. It seems to be widely spread also in the free state.

Betul. *Betula* (pollen), *Corylus* (pollen)

Legum. it may be the chief soluble nitrogenous substance in members of the *Faboideae*.

Rut. *Citrus* spp. (lvs, much)

Gram. *Phyllostachys* (shoot), *Zea* (pollen)

Lili. 'less general' than some other amino-acids

Sarcosine (*N*-Methyl-glycine; $H_3C.NH.CH_2.COOH$)

Legum. *Arachis hypogaea* (in protein)

Seleno-cystathionine: see also *Selenium* and *Selenium compounds*

Legum. *Astragalus pectinatus* is said to have a compound of 2 × *selenocystathionine* and 1 × *cystathionine*

Se-Methyl-selenocysteine

Legum. *Astragalus*

l-Serine (β-Hydroxy-α-amino-propionic acid; $CH_2OH.CH(NH_2).COOH$) is a 'protein' amino-acid. It occurs in large amount in proteins of seaweeds, but in small amount in those of higher plants. It may arise from *glycine* and *formate*. It seems to occur free in many plants:

Betul. *Alnus, Carpinus, Corylus* (little in all)

Cact. *Opuntia ficus-indica* (little?)

Simaroub. *Ailanthus* (little)

Lili. general

Irid. *Gladiolus*

Bromeli. *Ananas, Billbergia*

Arac. *Zantedeschia aethiopica* (rt, tuber)

S-Methyl-*l*-cysteine

Legum. *Astragalus bisulcatus, Phaseolus vulgaris*

S-Methyl-cysteine-sulfoxide ($H_3C.SO.CH_2.CH(NH_2).COOH$)

Crucif. Cabbage (lvs), turnip (lvs)

Lili. *Allium* spp.

S-Methyl-methionine ($(CH_3)_2\overset{+}{S}.CH_2.CH_2.CH(NH_2).COOH$) may, says Kjaer (1958), 'be identical with the so-called vitamin U of cabbage

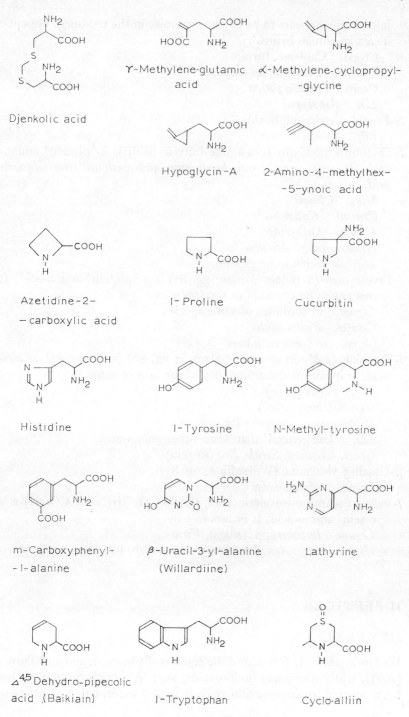

Fig. 87. Some amino-acids.

juice which appears to be of some promise in the treatment of peptic ulcers in human beings'.

Crucif. Cabbage, turnip
Umbell. Petroselinum crispum
Comp. Lactuca sativa
Lili. Asparagus

S-Propyl-cystein-sulphoxide

Lili. Allium

l-Threonine (β-Hydroxy-α-amino-butyric acid) is a 'protein' amino-acid. It may arise from *homoserine* and perhaps from *aspartic acid.*

Ulm. Ulmus?
Crassul. Kalanchoë
Legum. Lathyrus?
Hippocastan. Aesculus
Lili. it seems to be general.

l-Tryptophan (β-Indole-alanine; fig. 87) is a 'protein' amino-acid. It seems not to be common in the free state.

Legum. in seedlings of some species
Celastr. Catha edulis
Gram. in some members

l-Tyrosine (*p*-Hydroxy-phenyl-alanine; fig. 87) is a 'protein' amino-acid. It is said to constitute 10% of the *zein* of maize.

Fag. Fagus (trace)
Ulm. Ulmus (trace)
Hippocastan. Aesculus (tr.)
Lili. 'less general' than some other amino-acids
Gram. Lolium, Secale, Zea (in zein)

β-Uracil-3-yl-alanine (Willardiine; fig. 87)

Legum. Mimosoideae

l-Valine (α-Amino-isovaleric acid; $(CH_3)_2CH.CH(NH_2).COOH$) is a 'protein' amino-acid. It occurs free in

Legum. Lupinus spp. (sdlgs), *Vicia*
Hippocastan. Aesculus hippocastanum (sap, little)

II PEPTIDES

GENERAL

We know relatively little about the *peptides* of plants. Alston and Turner (1963), while discussing amino-acids, say: 'Although most work has been devoted to single amino acids it is now evident that a variety of peptides may exist, and these may prove, eventually, of considerable taxonomic importance.'

The *peptides* consist of *amino-acids*, linked by so-called *peptide linkages* (—CO.NH—). The simplest of them, of which many are known, have but two amino-acids linked together. In these *dipeptides* the same acid may be repeated, as in *glycyl-glycine*, or two different ones may be involved, as in *γ-L-glutamyl-β-alanine*. Compare these with the *disaccharides*. Somewhat more complicated are the *tripeptides* such as *glutathione* and the fungal *tetrapeptide—malformin—*of *Aspergillus niger*. I do not know of *tetra-* and *pentapeptides* from higher plants, but they are said to occur in marine algae.

Some peptides are antibiotic, an example being *gramicidin-S* which is a *cyclic decapeptide*:

$$\text{Val} \rightarrow \text{Orn} \rightarrow \text{Leu} \rightarrow \text{D-Phe} \rightarrow \text{Pro}$$
$$\uparrow \qquad\qquad\qquad\qquad\qquad \downarrow$$
$$\text{Pro} \leftarrow \text{D-Phe} \leftarrow \text{Leu} \leftarrow \text{Orn} \leftarrow \text{Val}$$

The corresponding *pentapeptide* is said to be inactive.

Some *polypeptides* are inhibitors of enzymes.

The *alkaloidal peptides* have been discussed as *alkaloids* (p. 146).

Our list of peptides is probably far from complete. The little book *Aminosauren—Peptide—Proteine* by Jakubke and Jeschkeit (1969), in which a survey of the most important naturally occurring peptides is given, is of little help to us. The peptides occurring in species of *Allium* are mostly sulfur-containing. The distribution of sulfur compounds in *Allium* has been much studied and may eventually prove to be of great taxonomic interest (see Saghir and Mann, 1964; Saghir, Mann, Ownbey and Berg, 1966; and also under odoriferous constituents, p. 49 of this book).

List and Occurrence

γ-L-Glutamyl-β-alanine
    Crucif. Lunaria annua
    Irid. Iris sp. (lvs), *tingitana* 'Wedgwood' (bulb)
γ-L-Glutamyl-*S*-allyl-L-cysteine
    Lili. Allium sativum
γ-L-Glutamyl-γ-aminobutyric acid
    Crucif. Lunaria annua (sd)
γ-L-Glutamyl-β-aminoisobutyric acid
    Irid. Iris tingitana 'Wedgwood' (bulb)
γ-L-Glutamyl-*S*(2-carboxy-1-propyl)-cysteinyl-glycine
    Lili. Allium cepa

γ-L-Glutamyl-β-cyano-L-alanine is a toxin.
>   Legum.   *Vicia sativa*
γ-L-Glutamyl-L-cysteinyl-β-alanine (Homoglutathione)
>   Legum.   *Phaseolus aureus* (sd)
γ-L-Glutamyl-L-isoleucine
>   Lili.   *Allium cepa*
γ-L-Glutamyl-L-leucine
>   Legum.   *Phaseolus* sp.
>   Lili.   *Allium cepa*
γ-L-Glutamyl-L-methionine
>   Legum.   *Phaseolus vulgaris* (sd)
>   Lili.   *Allium cepa*
γ-L-Glutamyl-S-methyl-L-cysteine
>   Legum.   *Phaseolus limensis* (sd), *vulgaris* (sd); *Vigna sinensis* (sd)
>   Lili.   *Allium cepa*
γ-L-Glutamyl-L-phenylalanine
>   Legum.   *Glycine max* (frt, or sd ?)
>   Lili.   *Allium cepa*
γ-L-Glutamyl-S(prop-1-enyl)-L-cysteine
>   Lili.   *Allium schoenoprasum* (sd)
γ-L-Glutamyl-S(prop-1-enyl)-L-cysteine sulfoxide
>   Lili.   *Allium cepa*
γ-L-Glutamyl-β-pyrazol-1-yl-L-alanine is said by Dunnill and Fowden
>   (1965) to occur always with
>   *α-amino-β(pyrazolyl-N)-propionic acid (β-pyrazol-1-yl-alanine)*
>   Cucurbit.   *Cucumis sativa* (sd)
γ-L-Glutamyl-L-tyrosine
>   Legum.   *Glycine max* (sd)
γ-L-Glutamyl-L-valine
>   Lili.   *Allium cepa*

Glutathione is a tripeptide of *glutamic acid, cysteine,* and *glycine.* It is
very widely distributed. It is said to be the prosthetic group of at
least one enzyme.

III PROTEINS (INCLUDING ENZYMES)

If any one group of compounds can be singled out as 'the stuff of life'
it is the great group of *proteins.* The unconjugated proteins consist of
chains of *amino-acids,* the links being of *peptide* nature, forming often
molecules of very high molecular weight. In other words they are
polypeptides of large size.

All living things have *proteins*, and the viruses, if they can be considered to be living things, are little if anything else.

About twenty *amino-acids*, as we have seen, occur in virtually all *proteins*, and *proteins* in general are so similar that it is almost certain that all living things are related.

Smith (1968), in a lecture delivered in 1967, says that the amino-acid sequences of *cytochrome-c* from 25 species of plants and animals have been determined; that all are of 'mammalian type'; and that: 'This indicates in molecular terms that all aerobic life including lower and higher plants and animals must have evolved from common ancestors.'

Crick earlier (1958) pointed out that the 'same' *protein* molecules (e.g. *haemoglobin* from man and the horse) are very much alike and that this 'family likeness' is the rule rather than the exception. He quotes Sanger and his co-workers as having found that the *insulins* of five species studied differ slightly, except that those of the pig and a whale are alike.

He goes on to say: 'Biologists should realize that before long we shall have a subject which might be called 'protein taxonomy'—the study of the amino-acid sequences of the proteins of an organism and the comparison of them between species. It can be argued that these sequences are the most delicate expression possible of the phenotype of an organism and that vast amounts of evolutionary information may be hidden away within them.'

We may remark here that while waiting for this information to be retrieved we may proceed with other aspects of chemotaxonomy. There is, perhaps, a parallel to be drawn from 'numerical taxonomy'. Eventually it may supersede the traditional approach to the subject but we cannot mark time until that happens!

That 'protein taxonomy' is on the way may be inferred from further statements of Smith (loc. cit.). He says that the numbers of variant residues in the *cytochromes* studied so far increase with distances of biological relationship. He gives the following numbers: man 0, chimpanzee 0, rabbit 9, horse 12, rattlesnake 14, moth 31, wheat 35, *Neurospora* 43, yeast 44.

The amino-terminal sequences of some of the *cytochromes* are interesting. Smith includes the following:

	-9	-8	-7	-6	-5	-4	-3	-2	-1	1
Wheat	Acetyl,	Ala,	Ser,	Phe,	Ser,	Glu,	Ala,	Pro,	Pro,	Gly-
Yeast					Thr,	Glu,	Phe,	Lys,	Ala,	Gly-
Moth					Gly,	Val,	Pro,	Ala,		Gly-
Vertebrates									Acetyl,	Gly-

He goes on to stress the great similarities in the rest of the chain in each of the *cytochromes* studied and says that 35 constant residues are present:

$$1$$
— — — — — — — — — — Gly — — — — — —

$$10$$
Gly — — — Phe — — — CyS — — CyS, His,

$$20$$ $$30$$
— — — — — — — — — — Lys — Gly, Pro —

$$40$$
Leu — Gly — — — Arg — — Gly — — —

$$50$$
Gly — — Tyr — — Ala, Asn — — — — — — —

$$60$$ $$70$$
Trp — — — — — — — — Tyr, Leu — Asn,

$$80$$
Pro, Lys, Lys, Tyr, Ile, Pro, Gly, Thr, Lys, Met

$$90$$
— Phe — Gly — — Lys — — — Arg — —

$$100$$ $$104$$
— — — — — — — — — — — — — —

Only one higher plant (wheat) was included in the work mentioned above. More recently Boulter, Laycock, Ramshaw and Thompson (1970) have determined the amino-acid sequences of *cytochromes-c* from mung bean and sunflower, and have compared them with that from wheat-germ. They say: 'If the present potential of the method continues to be realized it is hoped to establish the major branches of a phylogenetic tree for the plant kingdom in the future.'

This may remind us a little of the early claims for *serology*, a branch of our subject which we may consider briefly here.

Serology

I have already written on the history of this field (in Swain, 1963, pp. 64–8), but a note or two is in order here. Near the end of the last century it was noted that extracts of some plants can haemolyse red corpuscles of the blood, and that when an animal has been immunized with an active extract it may develop antibodies able to inhibit normal haemolysis. Ehrlich, as early as 1891, was able to immunize animals to the toxalbumins *abrin* and *ricin*.

The 'precipitin' reaction was one of the earliest tests to be employed. Proteins are not the only antigens responsible for the production in the animal of precipitins, but they are most often employed.

Mez and others of the 'Königsberg school' adopted and modified procedures based on the precipitin reaction and their results were summarized by Mez and Ziegenspeck (1926) in the famous 'tree' which purported to show relationships within the plant kingdom. Their work was opposed by the 'Berlin school' of Gilg and Schurhoff (1927, for example), and others. Chester (1937) reviewed the controversy that raged between the two schools. He concluded that the attacks of the 'Berlin school' were intemperate and not wholly unprejudiced, and that they set back acceptance by taxonomists of serological results. They also set back interest in chemotaxonomy in general.

Careful work with the precipitin reaction, and with other methods for comparing the proteins of different taxa, have led to an acceptance by most taxonomists of this approach to taxonomy. We have mentioned elsewhere some specific cases, but a few examples may be noted here.

An early group of examples stems from the workers at Rutgers. Boyden (1954) introduces papers by Johnson (1954) on *Magnoliaceae*, Baum (1954) on *Cucurbitaceae* and Hammond (1955) on *Ranunculaceae* and on *Solanaceae*.

Within the genus we may note the work of Gell, Hawkes, and Wright (1960) on *Solanum*. They say: 'The results show in their main outline a remarkably close agreement with those obtained from the classical taxonomic methods, and with the general conclusions arrived at from cytological and genetical studies.'

A more recent example may be drawn from Fairbrothers (1966). The first part of his paper should be required reading for those critical of serology. The second part deals with a study of seed-proteins of *Cornus*, *Davidia*, *Garrya* and *Nyssa*, genera which have proven difficult to place by traditional taxonomic methods.

Cornus canadensis and *C. suecica*, as might be expected, proved to be serologically very similar. Of the four species of *Nyssa* studied *N. biflora* and *N. sylvatica* were serologically closely related, again in line with recent taxonomic thinking. *N. aquatica* and *N. ogeche* are distinct. Four species of *Garrya* had only slight serological relationship with *Cornus* and *Nyssa*. *Davidia involucrata* resembles *Nyssa*.

A still more recent paper is one by Vaughan (1968) which outlines in simple terms for those not familiar with serology the precipitin reaction; gel diffusion methods, illustrated by work on *Brassica* spp.; and also other methods of protein analysis.

Boulter, Thurman and Turner (1966) have discussed the use of *disc electrophoresis* of proteins in plant systematics. They say: 'it is as easy to become familiar with the techniques for the acquisition of protein-band data as it is to perform paper chromatography for spot data'. They consider that the level at which disc electrophoresis may be valuable varies with the material. They give some data derived from studies of *Leguminosae* at the tribal level.

Vaughan and Waite (1967) have used electrophoretic methods on seed-proteins of *Brassica* and *Sinapis*.

Classification of Proteins

No completely satisfactory or generally accepted classification of proteins has been produced. Here are two:

I. Simple proteins
    a. Albumins, *b*. Globulins, *c*. Prolamins, *d*. Glutelins, *e*. Histones, *f*. Protamins
II. Conjugated proteins
    a. Metalloproteins, *b*. Haemoproteins, *c*. Flavoproteins, *d*. Nucleo-proteins, *e*. Nucleotide proteins, *f*. Thiamine proteins, *g*. Lipoproteins
III. Derived proteins
    1. Primary: *a*. Proteans, *b*. Metaproteins, *c*. Coagulated proteins
    2. Secondary: *a*. Proteoses, *b*. Peptones, *c*. Peptides

and:

Albumins: soluble in water and dilute salt solutions.

Globulins: sparingly soluble in water. Soluble in dilute salt solutions.

Prolamins: insoluble in water. Soluble in 50–90% aqueous alcohol.

Glutelins: insoluble in the above, but soluble in dilute acids and bases.

Scleroproteins (Albuminoids—an unsuitable name): insoluble in most solvents. Do these occur in plants?

Protamines: strongly basic; high in *arginine*.

Histones: strongly basic.

Nucleoproteins: complexes of protamins, histones, etc., with nucleic acids.

Lipoproteins: proteins linked to lipids.

Glycoproteins (Mucoproteins): proteins linked to carbohydrates.

Chromoproteins (Metalloproteins): proteins which absorb light in the visible portion of the spectrum.

Enzymes

One gets the impression that these are infinite in number! Certainly, hundreds of enzymes have been named (see below), but there is probably some synonymy. It seems to be pretty generally agreed that all enzymes are proteins, but not all proteins are enzymes! The first enzyme was crystallized in 1926. By 1964 about 100 had been crystallized. They are all proteins, though some may have a non-protein *prosthetic group* which may be coloured. The molecular weights of these pure enzymes range from about 9,000 to more than 1,000,000.

Each enzyme is said to have an *active centre* consisting of a *catalytic site* and a (nearby?) *binding site* which is responsible for the complexing with the *substrate* which is known to occur. The *active centre* is supposed to give the enzyme its specificity. The many other amino-acids are in a sense redundant, but they contribute to the overall 'shape' or spatial relations of the enzyme, and it has been suggested that they may be important in 'absorbing' mutations.

One remarkable feature of some enzymes is that they contain metals, as we shall see in our section on the elements. *Copper* occurs in many, *iron* in some, *manganese* in others, and *molybdenum* in the metalloflavin enzymes. Some elements which are not actually constituents may *activate* enzymes. These include *chromium, cobalt, magnesium,* and perhaps *sodium, selenium* and *vanadium*.

This book deals largely with the substances synthesized by higher plants and—the essence of chemotaxonomy—with the restriction in distribution of them. Presumably the enzymes involved are also restricted in their distribution, but this is not necessarily so. The appropriate enzyme may be present but the substrate not, or an activator or co-enzyme may be absent. In other cases both enzyme and substrate may be present and function to produce a given substance, but it may be transformed so rapidly by other enzymes that it is only rather rarely under normal conditions allowed to accumulate in quantities detectable by ordinary methods. This may be true of *sedoheptulose*, for example.

In spite of these difficulties we might yet hope to construct at least a partial 'enzyme taxonomy' of plants. This, however, would be a colossal task. For the present I have noted a few cases of apparent restrictions in enzyme distribution. No doubt there are many others in the vast literature of enzymology.

Alliinase is said to hydrolyse *S-allyl-cysteine sulfoxide* to *allicin, pyruvic acid*, and *ammonia*. Is it restricted to *Allium*?

Aucubinase is said to be specific for *aucubin* and to occur in *Aucuba* and *Plantago*. The *aucubin-type glycosides* have a restricted distribution. Is there a specific enzyme for each glycoside?

Elaterase is said to hydrolyse the bitter glycosides of the *Cucurbitaceae* to *cucurbitacins* and *glucose*. Lavie *et al.* (1964) say that it is present in *Cucumis* and *Lagenaria*, but absent from *Citrullus* and *Cucurbita* (which *do*, however, have *cucurbitacins*). Enslin and Rehm (1958) say that *elaterase* hydrolyses other glucosides, too.

Emulsin. A commercial preparation, not a single pure enzyme, is regularly used by me in carrying out *HCN (Test A)*. See p. 58.

Histaminase. Werle and Zabel (1948) have tried to determine the distribution of this enzyme in higher plants. They found it to be restrictɘd to relatively few of the plants they studied:

Absent from

Gymnospermae *Cycas* (1), *Ginkgo* (1), *Taxus* (1), *Abies* (1), *Picea* (2), *Larix* (1), *Pinus* (1).

Monocotyledonae *Allium* (1), *Clivia* (1), *Agave* (1), *Ananas* (1), *Triticum* (1), *Musa* (1), *Zingiber* (1).

Dicotyledonae *Ficus* (1), *Laportea* (1), *Viscum* (1), *Piper* (1), *Euphorbia* (1), *Mercurialis* (1), *Spinacia* (1), *Chenopodium* (1), *Mesembryanthe-mum* (1), *Opuntia* (1), *Helleborus* (1), *Cinnamomum* (1), *Nepenthes* (1), *Papaver* (1), *Bocconia* (1), *Corydalis* (1), *Brassica* spp., *Tilia* (1), *Geranium* (1), *Pilocarpus* (1), *Sedum* (1), *Sempervivum* (1), *Lupinus* (1), *Trifolium* (2, but seed only of 1), *Ornithopus* (1), *Medicago* (1), *Daucus* (1), *Apium* (1), *Primula* (1), *Cyclamen* (1), *Hoya* (1), *Solanum* (1), *Datura* (1), *Sambucus* (1), *Cichorium* (1), *Tussilago* (1).

Present in

Dicotyledonae *Paeonia* (1), *Laurus* (1), *Fragaria* (1), *Rubus* (1), *Cydonia* (1), *Eriobotrya* (1), *Trifolium* (1, except seed), *Hedera* (1), *Aegopodium* (1), *Jasminum* (1), *Salvia* (1), *Lavandula* (2), *Rosmarinus* (1), *Thymus* (1), *Taraxacum* (1), *Artemisia* (1).

Is this enzyme really *absent* from Gymnosperms and Monocotyledons ? And in the **Tubiflorae** is it *absent* from *Solanaceae* (2/2, above) but *present* in *Labiatae* (4/5, above) ? We need to know more.

The same authors found much the same distribution of *diamine oxidase*—absence from gymnosperms and monocotyledons, presence in many dicotyledons.

Myrosinase (Myrosin)   see also *sinigrinase*

Kjaer (1960) credits Guignard as having first demonstrated the accumulation of 'myrosin' in idioblasts. He believes it to be a single enzyme, not two as has been suggested. Farnsworth (1966) says: 'Myrosinase (myrosin), the specific enzyme catalysing the hydrolysis of all isothiocyanate glycosides has been found in all plants containing this substrate. However, it accumulates in particular cells (idioblasts) which do not contain the glycosides.'

Vaughan, Gordon and Robinson (1968) report a method for identification of *myrosinase*.

Sinigrinase A few species of *Aspergillus* are said to have an enzyme, distinct from *myrosinase* (above), which can split *sinigrin* to give the same end-products as are given by the action of *myrosinase*.

We shall have more to say about the *Umbelliferae* when discussing the **Umbellales**, but it may be noted here that a recent paper by Crowden, Harborne and Heywood (1969) stresses the usefulness in the chemotaxonomy of that great family of protein and enzyme patterns.

Classification of Enzymes

Volume 13 (1964) of *Comprehensive Biochemistry* (edited by Florkin and Stotz) contains a report of the commission on enzymes of the International Union of Biochemists. This recognizes about 650 enzymes in six main groups:

1. Oxidoreductases. About 130 in 13 sub-groups
2. Transferases. Over 170 in 8 sub-groups
3. Hydrolases. About 180 in 9 sub-groups
4. Lyases. Nearly 90 in 5 sub-groups
5. Isomerases. Nearly 40 in 4 sub-groups
6. Ligases (Synthetases). Over 40 in 4 sub-groups

AMINO-SUGARS

GENERAL

Sharon (in Balazs and Jeanloz, 1965) has given us a review of the distribution of *amino-sugars* in nature. He says that more than 20 have been identified, mostly from micro-organisms. So few are known from higher plants that they are not, as yet, of any use in chemotaxonomy, but they *are* of use in the taxonomy of lower plants. It is, of course, possible that further research may show them to be of much wider distribution in flowering plants, and they may then become of chemotaxonomic importance.

Sharon accepts only some of the records as trustworthy. We have followed him substantially in the following list.

List and Occurrence

Chitin has been called *acetamido-cellulose* and *fungal-cellulose*. Foster and Webber (1960) say that it is chiefly, if not entirely, a chain of *N-acetyl*-D-*glucosamine* residues linked $1 \to 4$. It is widely distributed in the fungi, and occurs in some algae, but it has not been reported with certainty from any higher plant.

Galactosamine (Chondrosamine; 2-Amino-2-deoxy-D-galactose, fig. 88)
    Comp.   *Dahlia* (tubers, as UDP-derivatives)

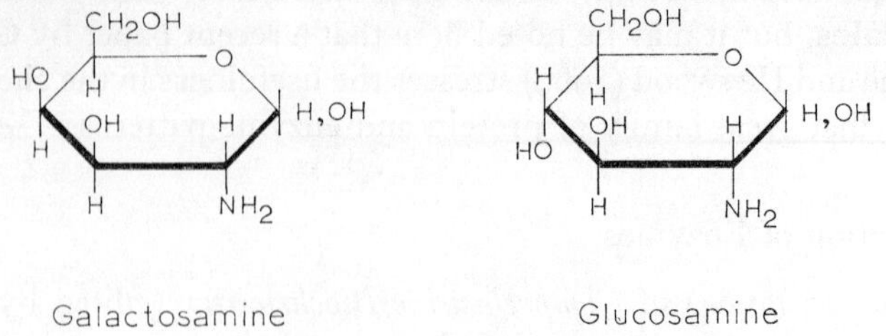

Fig. 88. Amino-sugars.

Glucosamine (Chitosamine; 2-Amino-2-deoxy-D-glucose; fig. 88)
>   Legum.   *Glycine max* (sd, hydrolysates of *haemaglutenin*), *Phaseolus aureus* (sdlg, as *UDP-N-acetyl-glucosamine*)
>   Comp.   *Dahlia* (tubers, hydrolysates of *nucleotides*)

Hexosamines, not fully characterized, have been reported recently from haricot (pt ?) and potato (lvs).

BETALAINS (BETACYANINS AND BETAXANTHINS)

GENERAL

It was recognized long ago that some plant pigments which behave superficially like *anthocyanins* are, in fact, quite distinct from them. It was shown that they contain nitrogen, and because of this they were for many years known as 'nitrogenous anthocyanins'. Only in the last few years has it been shown that they are not chemically like the *anthocyanins* at all. Furthermore, the two groups are said to be mutually exclusive—plants possess 'ordinary' *anthocyanins* or they have these other pigments.

It is now clear that the *betacyanins* (as the 'nitrogenous anthocyanins' are now called, after the pigment of *Beta*) and a second group of non-red pigments which occur with them, the *betaxanthins*, are structurally related. It has been proposed to use the name *betalains* for the two groups. We have adopted this proposal here.

We do not need to go deeply into the history of the subject; there are reviews in plenty. A recent treatment by Mabry (1966) may be used as a basis, and the interested reader is referred also to an even more recent paper by Wohlpart and Mabry (1968).

The chemistry of these substances may be seen in fig. 89, which shows *betanidin* (a *betacyanin*) and *indicaxanthin* (a *betaxanthin*). The latter may be transformed into the former, says Mabry (1966), by allowing it to react with 5,6-dihydroxy-2,3-dihydroindole-2-carboxylic acid. Mabry includes a tentative scheme for the biogenesis of these pigments (fig. 89).

Chemotaxonomically these pigments are of the greatest interest. They seem to be restricted to the **Centrospermae** and closely related families. See that order for further discussion.

Piattelli and Minale (1964) say that at least 44 different *betacyanins* occur in plants, all (?) yielding *betanidin* (fig. 89) or *isobetanidin*.

The name *flavocyanin* has been used for the 'yellow nitrogenous anthocyanins'. Our modern knowledge of these substances dates only from about 1965 (Piattelli, Minale and Prota; Piattelli, Minale and Nicolaus). Relatively few of these substances have as yet been fully characterized. No doubt many remain to be discovered.

a BETACYANINS

List and Occurrence

Amarantin (*O*-(β-D-Glucopyranosyluronic acid)-5-*O*-β-D-glucopyrano-side of betanidin)
    Amaranth. in 5/12
    Chenopodi. 4/5
Basellains-r and -v
    Basell. Basella
Betanidin (fig. 89) is the aglycone of many *betacyanins*. It occurs free in
    Cact. Cleistocactus parviflorus (5% of pigment of fl.), *Opuntia* (2),
      Pilosocereus (1)
Betanidin-6-*O*-β-D-glucopyranoside (Gomphrenin-I)
    Amaranth. Gomphrena globosa (infl.)
Betanin (Phytolaccanin; Betanidin-5-*O*-β-D-glucopyranoside; fig. 89)
    Aizo. 1/1
    Amaranth. 4/7
    Cact. Aporocactus (1), *Borzicactus* (1), *Cereus* (2), *Cleistocactus* (2),
      Eriocereus (1), *Haageocereus* (1), *Mammillaria* (4), *Nopalea* (1),
      Opuntia (7), *Pereskia* (1), *Phyllocactus, Pilosocereus* (3), *Soehrensia*
      (1), *Stenocereus* (1)
    Chenopodi. 4/5 (including *Beta*)
    Nyctagin. 1/1
    Phytolacc. 2/2 (incl. *Phytolacca*)
    Portulac. 1/2
Bougainvilleins-I to -XVI
    Nyctagin. Bougainvillea

Celosianin is a *p-coumaroyl-feruloyl-amarantin.*
>   *Amaranth.*   2/2 (incl. *Celosia cristata* var.)
>   *Chenopodi.*   1/1

Gomphrenins-I to -VIII have not all been fully worked out.
>   *Amaranth.   Gomphrena globosa* (infl.)

Gomphrenin-I: see *betanidin-6-O-β-D-glucopyranoside.*

Gomphrenin-II: see *isobetanidin 6-O-β-D-glucopyranoside.*

Gomphrenin-III is a *cis-p-coumaroyl* derivative of *betanidin-* or *iso-betanidin-glucoside.*

Gomphrenin-V is a *trans-feruloyl ester* of a *betanidin-glucoside.*

Gomphrenin-VI is a diastereoisomer of V.

Gomphrenin-VII is said to yield *trans-ferulic acid* and a mixture of *gomphrenin-I* and *-II.*

Gomphrenin-VIII is said to yield *trans-p-coumaric acid* and a mixture of *gomphrenin-I* and *-II.*

Iresinin-I is said to be *betanidin-5-O[2-O-(β-D-glucopyranosyluronic acid)-6-O-(3-hydroxy-3-methyl-glutaryl)-β-D-glucopyranoside]*!
>   *Amaranth.   Iresine herbstii* (lvs) and another sp.

Iresinin-III is, say Minale *et al.* (1966), 'the first acylated betacyanin in which the acid is directly linked to the aglycone'.
>   *Amaranth.   Iresine herbstii* (lvs)

Iresinin-IV: of unknown structure (1966).
>   *Amaranth.   Iresine herbstii* (lvs)

Isoamarantin is the *O-(β-D-glucopyranosyluronic acid)-5-O-β-D-gluco-pyranoside* of *isobetanidin.*
>   *Amaranth.*   4/10
>   *Chenopodi.*   3/4

Isobetanidin is the aglycone of *betacyanins-B* and *-D.*
>   *Cact.   Opuntia* (1, free), *Phyllocactus* (as glycosides)

Isobetanidin-6-O-β-D-glucopyranoside (Gomphrenin-II)
>   *Amaranth.   Gomphrena globosa* (infl.)

Isobetanin (5-O-β-D-glucopyranosyl-isobetanidin)
>   *Aizo.*   1/3
>   *Amaranth.*   2/3
>   *Cact.   Borzicactus* (1, tr.), *Cereus* (2), *Cleistocactus* (1), *Eriocereus* (1), *Haageocereus* (1), *Mammillaria* (4), *Nopalea* (1), *Opuntia* (6), *Pereskia* (1), *Phyllocactus, Pilosocereus* (tr. in 3), *Soehrensia* (1), *Stenocereus* (1)
>   *Chenopodi.*   4/4 (incl. *Beta*)
>   *Nyctagin.*   1/1
>   *Phytolacc.*   2/2
>   *Portulac.*   1/2

Isocelosianin is a *p-coumaroyl-feruloyl-isoamarantin.*
> Amaranth. Celosia cristata var.
> Chenopodi. Spinacia

Isoiresinin-I was called iresinin-II. It is said to be *isobetanidin-5-O* [*2-O-(β-D-glucopyranosyl-uronic acid)-6-O-(3-hydroxy-3-methylglu-taryl)-β-D-glucopyranoside*]
> Amaranth. Iresine herbstii (lvs)

Isophyllocactin is an isomer of *phyllocactin.*
> Cact. Borzicactus (1), Cereus (2), Cleistocactus (2), Eriocereus (1), Haageocereus (1), Mammillaria (4), Opuntia (2), Phyllocactus (1), Pilosocereus (tr. in 3), Soehrensia (1), Stenocereus (tr. in 1)
> Chenopodi. Kochia

Isoprebetanin
> Chenopodi. Beta
> Phytolacc. Phytolacca

Mesembryanthemins-I to -III
> Aizo. Mesembryanthemum
> Portulac. Portulaca (has II and III)

Monvillein-1/34
> Cact. Monvillea spegazzinii

Oleracin-I and -II
> Portulac. Portulaca oleracea (st.)

Parodin
> Cact. Parodia stuemeri v. tilcarensis

Phyllocactin has an acyl group attached to the sugar.
> Cact. Aporocactus (1), Borzicactus (1), Cereus (2), Cleistocactus (2), Eriocereus (1), Haageocereus (1), Mammillaria (4), Nopalea (1), Opuntia (4), Pereskia (tr. in 1), Phyllocactus (1), Pilosocereus (3), Soehrensia (1), Stenocereus (1)
> Chenopodi. Kochia, Spinacia

Prebetanin
> Chenopodi. Beta
> Phytolacc. Phytolacca?

Rivinianin
> Phytolacc. Rivina humilis

b BETAXANTHINS

List and Occurrence

Indicaxanthin (fig. 89)
> Cact. Opuntia ficus-indica

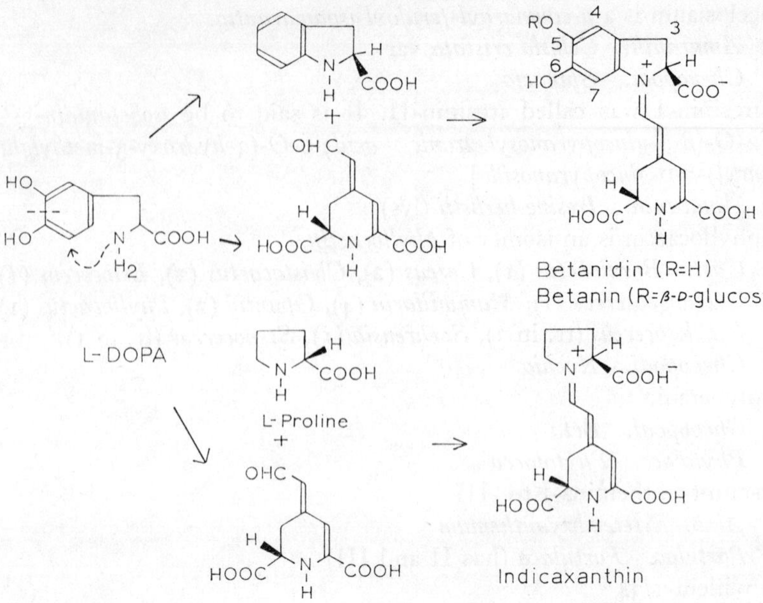

Fig. 89. Betalains. Possible biogenesis of betanidin and indicaxanthin.

Miraxanthins-I to -VI
    Nyctagin.   *Mirabilis jalapa*
Vulgaxanthins-I and -II
    Chenopodi.   *Beta vulgaris*

CARBOHYDRATES
I MONOSACCHARIDES

GENERAL

It is usual to speak of a 5-carbon sugar as a *pentose*, of a 6-carbon sugar as a *hexose*, and so on. Logically then, we should start with a *monose*, proceed to a *biose*, and so on. Staněk, Černý, Kocourek and Pacák (1963), in their large work *The Monosaccharides*, however, start only with *trioses*. We shall differ from them in this point.

Our arrangement, which includes about 60 monosaccharides, is as follows:

1. Monose
2. Biose
3. Trioses: 2 only

4. Tetroses: do not occur in angiosperms?
5. Pentoses: 6 occur
6. Hexoses: 9 occur
7. Heptoses: 3 are known from angiosperms
8. Octoses: 1 is known
9. Nonoses: 1 is known
10. Deoxy-sugars
    a. Deoxy-pentoses: 1 is known
    b. Deoxy-hexoses: 10 are known
    c. 2,6-Dideoxy-hexoses: 4 are known
11. Monomethyl ethers of monosaccharides (most of which are also deoxy-sugars): 16 are known
12. Dimethyl ethers of monosaccharides: 2 are known
13. Acetyl-hexoses: 2 are known
14. Branched-chain monosaccharides: 2 are known

List and Occurrence

1. Monose: only one is possible
Formaldehyde (fig. 90) is reported, secondarily (?), from essential oils. Does it occur free in higher plants?
2. Biose: only one is possible.
Glycollic aldehyde (Biose; Glycolose; fig. 90)
    Caprifoli.   Sambucus nigra (lvs)
3. Trioses: 2 are possible.
Dihydroxy-acetone (fig. 90) is a *ketose*. It is reported from lower plants, and perhaps is a universal intermediate in carbohydrate metabolism.
D-Glyceric aldehyde (fig. 90) is an *aldose*. Is it universally present in higher plants?
4. Tetroses: 4 are possible, but I have no records of them from angiosperms.
5. Pentoses: several of these are known to occur in higher plants. They are discussed below.
D-Arabinose (Aloinose; fig. 90) occurs in *barbaloin* and *euatromonoside?*
L-Arabinose (Pectinose; fig. 90) occurs in conifers (free?). In angiosperms it is widespread as *araban*, and occurs free (?) in:
    Legum.   Prosopis juliflora (exudate)
    Lili.   Aloë?
L-Lyxose occurs in *yeast ribonucleic acid.*
    Myrt.   Eucalyptus (D- or L- ?)
D-Ribose (Carnose; fig. 90) occurs in *nucleic acids*, in *crotonoside*, in *coenzymes*, and in *vitamins B_2* and *B_{12}.*

D-Ribulose (D-Adonose; D-Arabulose; D-Erythro-pentulose; fig. 90) is an intermediate in photosynthesis?

D-Xylose (Wood Sugar; fig. 90) is very widely spread in plants. It is rarely free in higher plants but occurs as *xylans*, and as a constituent of *primeverose, saponins, cardiac glycosides*, etc.

6. Hexoses. Theoretically a fairly large number of *hexoses* can be formed and most (all?) of them are known to the chemist. Several occur widely in plants, some are more restricted in their occurrence, and some are not known at all from natural sources. It is not clear why Nature has been so selective.

D-Fructose (Fruit Sugar; Levulose; fig. 90) is very widely spread, both free and in *di-(sucrose), oligo-(raffinose)*, and *polysaccharides (inulin and other fructosans)*. It is particularly important in the furanose form.

D-Galactose seems rarely to occur in the free state. It is a constituent of *di-(lactose), oligo-(raffinose, stachyose*, etc.) and *polysaccharides (galactans)*.

L-Galactose seems to be much less common than D-*galactose*. It is said to occur in agar and in

    Lin. Linum usitatissimum (mucilage)
    Gram. Zea mays

D-Glucose (D-Glycose; Dextrose; Grape Sugar; fig. 90) is possibly universal in plants. As a constituent of *di-(sucrose), oligo-(raffinose, stachyose*, etc.), and *polysaccharides (starch, cellulose)* it is one of the most abundant of organic substances in Nature. Add to this its very frequent occurrence in α- and β-*glycosides*.

L-Glucose is apparently very uncommon. It is said to occur in *capsularin* and (free?) in

    Comp. Grindelia robusta (lvs, fl.)

D-Mannose (Carubinose; Seminose) is widely spread in *mannans, hemicelluloses*, etc. It is said to occur in bacteria and yeasts. In higher plants it occurs (free?) in

    Corynocarp. Corynocarpus laevigata (sd)
    Arac. Amorphophallus konjak (st.)

D-Psicose (D-Allulose; Pseudo-fructose; D-Ribo-hexulose) is said to occur in molasses and in

    Saxifrag. Itea spp. ('occurs...as a major component of the leaves, stems, and flowers'—Hough and Stacey, 1963)

L-Sorbose (Sorbin; Sorbinose)

    Ros. Sorbus aucuparis (frt, but secondarily?)
    Passiflor. Passiflora edulis (frt, in *pectin*)

D-Tagatose (D-Lyxo-hexulose)

    Sterculi. Sterculia setigera (in gum)

7. Heptoses were thought until recently to be very rare in plants. It is now known that one is very common and that at least 3 others occur. I have records of

L-Gala-D-mannoheptose from bacteria, but not, I think, from higher plants.

D-Manno-heptulose (D-Manno-D-tagatoheptose; D-Manno-ketoheptose)
    Laur.   *Persea gratissima* (lvs, frt)
    Primul.   *Primula elatior* (rt) ?

Sedoheptulose (Sedoheptose; D-Altro-heptulose; D-Altro-D-fructo-heptose; Volemose; Volemulose; fig. 90) is a very interesting, many-named sugar. It was first found in *Sedum* (hence its common name) and then in other members of the *Crassulaceae*. We looked for it and found it in *Penthorum*. It may be an intermediate in photosynthesis, but it *accumulates* only in a limited number of plants, which may have something unusual in their metabolism.
    Betul.   *Alnus* (1), *Betula* (5)
    Crassul.   general ?
    Saxifrag.   in several, including *Penthorum*, but *absent* from some
    Legum.   *Gleditsia* (1), *Robinia* (1)
    Oxalid.   *Oxalis* (1)
    Gerani.   *Geranium* (1)
    Malv.   *Hibiscus* (1), *Sida* (1)
    Melastomat.   *Rhexia* (2)
    Primul.   *Primula* (1)
    Ole.   *Chionanthus* (1), *Fraxinus* (1), *Ligustrum* (1)
    Gentian.   *Sabbatia* (1)
    Lab.   *Coleus* (1), *Teucrium montanum* (lvs)
    Scrophulari.   *Verbascum* (1)
    Comp.   *Liatris* (1), but *absent* from many

D-Talo-heptulose
    Laur.   *Persea gratissima*

8. Octoses are apparently very rare indeed.

D-Glycero-D-manno-octulose (fig. 90)
    Laur.   *Persea gratissima*

9. Nonoses: a recent report says that a *nonose* has been found.

D-Erythro-L-gluco-nonulose
    Laur.   *Persea gratissima*

10. Deoxy-sugars

a. Deoxy-pentoses are very rare. I have a record of one only.

2-Deoxy-D-ribose (2-Deoxy-D-erythro-pentose; Thyminose; fig. 91) is a constituent of the universally (?) distributed *deoxyribonucleosides*.

b. Deoxy-hexoses: several of these are known. Most of them are 6-*deoxy-hexoses* (*methyl-pentoses*), but at least two 2-*deoxy-hexoses* occur also in higher plants. The *deoxy-hexoses* occur principally in *cardiac glycosides*.

D-Antiarose (6-Deoxy-D-gulose; D-Gulomethylose; fig. 90) occurs in several *cardiac glycosides* (α-*antiarin*, etc.).

    Convolvul. *Ipomoea parasitica* (in a *glycolipid*)

6-Deoxy-D-allose (D-Allomethylose) is a constituent of several *cardiac glycosides*.

6-Deoxy-D-altrose (D-Altromethylose) has been found in at least 2 *cardiac glycosides*.

2-Deoxy-D-arabino-hexose occurs in *perofskoside*.

2-Deoxy-D-xylo-hexose occurs in *kabuloside*.

Epifucose (6-Deoxy-L-talose; L-Talomethylose) is a constituent of several *cardiac glycosides*.

D-Fucose (6-Deoxy-D-galactose; D-Galactomethylose; D-Rhodeose; fig. 90) occurs in a number of *cardiac glycosides*, and in

    Caryophyll. *Gypsophila* (in *saponins*)

    Convolvul. in *convolvulin, jalapin*, and β-*turpethein*

L-Fucose (6-Deoxy-L-galactose; L-Galactomethylose; L-Rhodeose) occurs in algae and

    Meli. *Melia azedarach* (in gum)

D-Quinovose (6-Deoxy-D-glucose; D-Glucomethylose; D-Isorhamnose; D-Epirhamnose; Isorhodeose; fig. 90)

    Rubi. *Cinchona* spp. (in α- and β-*chinovin*)

    Convolvul. in *purgic acid*

    Scrophulari. *Digitalis* (in a *cardiac glycoside*)

L-Rhamnose (6-Deoxy-L-mannose; L-Mannomethylose; Lokaose; Isodulcite; fig. 90) occurs in many *glycosides*, including about a dozen *cardiac glycosides*.

    Anacardi. *Rhus toxicodendron* (free ?)

    Rhamn. *Rhamnus* spp. (in the pigment, 'lakao', of bk)

    Datisc. *Datisca cannabina* (free ?)

c. 2,6-Dideoxy-hexoses are infrequent in higher plants. It is interesting that while the *dideoxy-hexoses* of higher plants seem to be 2,6-, the corresponding sugars of bacteria (*abequose, tyvelose*, etc.) seem to be 3,6-.

D-Boivinose (2,6-Dideoxy-D-xylohexose; 2-Deoxy-xylo-hexamethylose; fig. 90) occurs in a few *cardiac glycosides* (*corchoroside, stroboside*, etc.).

D-Canarose (prob. 2,6-Dideoxy-D-arabino-hexose) is said to occur in

    Scrophulari. *Digitalis canariensis*

2,6-Dideoxy-L-lyxo-hexose is known only (?) from

    Asclepiad. *Pentopetia androsaemifolia* (in a *cardiac glycoside*)

D-Digitoxose (2,6-Dideoxy-D-ribo-hexose) is a very common sugar in *cardiac glycosides*.

11. Monomethyl ethers of monosaccharides

Many of these are known. Most, but not all of them, are of *deoxy-* or of *dideoxy-* sugars. All but one are 3-*O-methyl* derivatives. Almost all are known only from *cardiac glycosides*. What is the significance of these facts?

L-Acofriose (6-Deoxy-3-*O*-methyl-L-mannose; 3-*O*-Methyl-L-rhamnose; fig. 91): occurs in a *hemicellulose* of *Picea*? In angiosperms it is in *acofriosides* and other *cardiac glycosides* of:

Apocyn.   Acokanthera friesiorum

L-Acovenose (6-Deoxy-3-*O*-methyl-L-talose) occurs in *cardiac glycosides*.

Apocyn.   Acokanthera venenata

Corchsularose is a 2-deoxy-3-*O*-methyl-pentose.

Tili.   Corchorus spp. (in *corchsularin*)

D-Cymarose (2,6-Dideoxy-3-*O*-methyl-D-ribo-hexose; 2,6-Dideoxy-3-*O*-methyl-D-allose; Digitoxose-3-methyl ether; fig. 91) is a constituent of *cymarin* and other glycosides from the *Apocynaceae* and *Asclepiadaceae*.

L-Cymarose (2,6-Dideoxy-3-*O*-methyl-L-ribo-hexose)

Apocyn.   Beaumontia (in *glycosides*)

6-Deoxy-3-*O*-methyl-D-altrose occurs in *cardiac glycosides*.

6-Deoxy-2-*O*-methyl-D-galactose (2-*O*-Methyl-D-fucose)

Mor.   Streblus asper (in a *cardiac glycoside*)

D-Diginose (2,6-Dideoxy-3-*O*-methyl-D-lyxo-hexose) seems to occur in *glycosides* of *Apocynaceae*, *Asclepiadaceae*, and *Scrophulariaceae*.

L-Diginose (2,6-Dideoxy-3-*O*-methyl-L-lyxo-hexose) occurs in a few *cardiac glycosides*.

D-Digitalose (6-Deoxy-3-*O*-methyl-D-galactose; 3-*O*-Methyl-D-fucose; fig. 91) occurs in *cardiac glycosides* of *Apocynaceae* and *Scrophulariaceae*.

D-Oleandrose (2,6-Dideoxy-3-*O*-methyl-L-arabino-hexose; 2-Deoxy-L-thevetose; 2-Deoxy-L-rhamnose-3-methyl ether) can be obtained from *oleandrin* and other *cardiac glycosides*.

3-*O*-Methyl-D-galactose

Ulm.   Ulmus fulva (bk, in a polysaccharide), *glabra* (mucilage)

3-*O*-Methyl-D-glucose

Mor.   Streblus asper (Reichstein and Weiss (1962) say: 'Only by paper-chromatographic analysis has 3-*O*-methyl-glucose been recognized in a non-cardiac glycoside accompanying the cardiac glycosides').

D-Sarmentose (2,6-Dideoxy-3-*O*-methyl-D-xylo-hexose; fig. 91) occurs in cardiac glycosides of *Apocynaceae* (*sarmentocymarin*, etc.) and *Asclepiadaceae*.

D-Thevetose (6-Deoxy-3-*O*-methyl-D-glucose) is a constituent of some cardiac glycosides of the *Apocynaceae*.

L-Thevetose (6-Deoxy-3-O-methyl-L-glucose; Cerberose) occurs in *cardiac glycosides* of

 Apocyn.   *Cerbera, Tanghinia, Thevetia*

12. Dimethyl ethers of monosaccharides are known from *Streblus*. An *acetyl-dimethyl-hexose* is known from *Mansonia*.

6-Deoxy-2,3-di-O-methyl-D-galactose (2,3-Di-O-methyl-D-fucose)

 Mor.   *Streblus asper* (in a *cardiac glycoside*)

2,3-Di-O-methyl-D-glucose

 Mor.   *Streblus asper* (in a *cardiac glycoside*)

13. Acetyl-hexoses: known only from *cardiac glycosides*?

Acetyl-dimethyl-hexose, whose exact constitution is unknown to me, is said to occur in

 Sterculi.   *Mansonia altissima* (bk, in *mansonin*, a *cardiac glycoside*)

Acetyl-thevetose is said to occur in *cardiac glycosides* of *Apocyn*.

14. Branched-chain monosaccharides are very uncommon in higher plants.

D-Apiose (3-C-(Hydroxymethyl)-D-glycero-aldotetrose; fig. 91) was first isolated from apiin, a *flavone glycoside*. It was thought to be rare, is now known to be widely distributed, and is considered by Beck and Kandler (1965) to occur sometimes as a cell-wall component. Van Beusekom (1967) reports that it may be obtained from the cell-walls (?) of many aquatic monocotyledons

 Hydrocharit.   *Thalassia hemprichii*

 Potamogeton.   *Phyllospadix* sp., *Posidonia oceanica, Potamogeton pectinatus, Ruppia spiralis, Zostera nana* (and another sp. ?)

 Zannichelli.   *Cymodocea nodosa*

 Lemn.   *Lemna* spp.

Hamamelose (2-C-(Hydroxymethyl)-D-ribose; fig. 91) was known until recently only from *hamameli-tannin*. It does *not* occur in mosses, ferns, and gymnosperms? Scherpenberg, Gröbner and Kandler (1965) now say that it occurs free in

 Salic.   *Salix* spp.

 Betul.   *Alnus, Betula* spp., *Carpinus, Corylus, Ostrya*

 Fag.   *Castanea, Fagus, Nothofagus*

 Cercidiphyll.   *Cercidiphyllum*

 Hamamelid.   *Corylopsis* spp., *Hamamelis* spp., *Liquidambar*

 Saxifrag.   *Hydrangea, Philadelphus, Ribes* spp.

 Tili.   *Tilia*

 Primul.   *Primula* (21 spp.)

 Buddlej.   *Buddleja*

 Caprifoli.   *Lonicera*

They *failed* to find it in: *Jugland.* (*Juglans*); *Ulm.* (*Ulmus*); *Mor.* (*Morus, Humulus*); *Urtic.* (*Urtica*); *Magnoli.* (*Liriodendron, Magnolia*);

Calycanth. (*Calycanthus*); *Platan.* (*Platanus*); *Ros.* (*Crataegus, Malus, Prunus, Sorbus*); *Acer.* (*Acer*); *Hippocastan.* (*Aesculus*); *Corn.* (*Cornus*); *Arali.* (*Aralia*); *Umbell.* (*Apium*); *Ole.* (*Fraxinus*); *Logani.* (*Strychnos*); *Apocyn.* (*Strophanthus*)

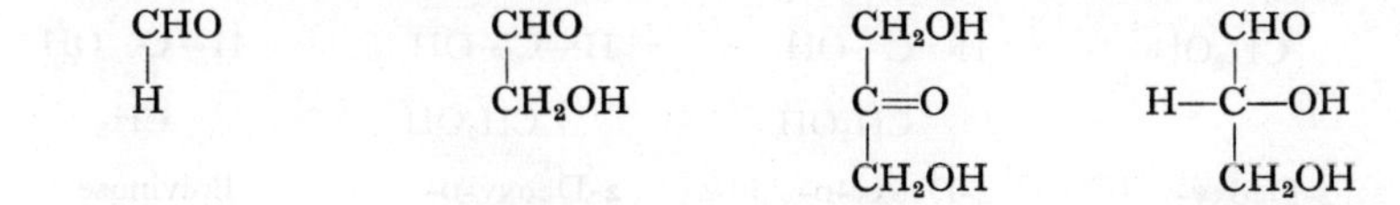

Formaldehyde (Monose) — Glycollic aldehyde (Biose) — Dihydroxy-acetone — Glyceric aldehyde (Trioses)

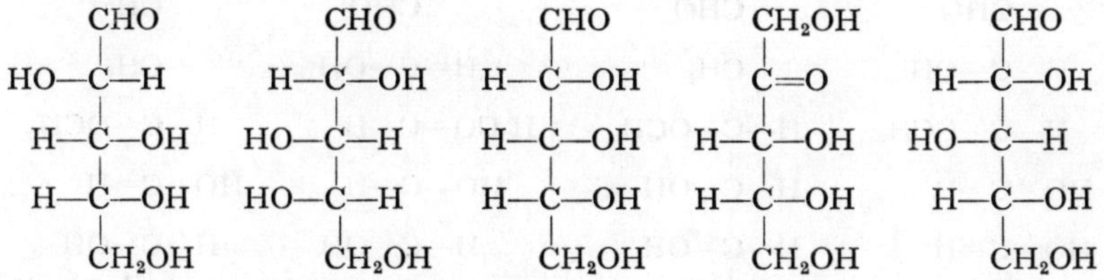

D-Arabinose — L-Arabinose — D-Ribose — D-Ribulose — D-Xylose (Pentoses)

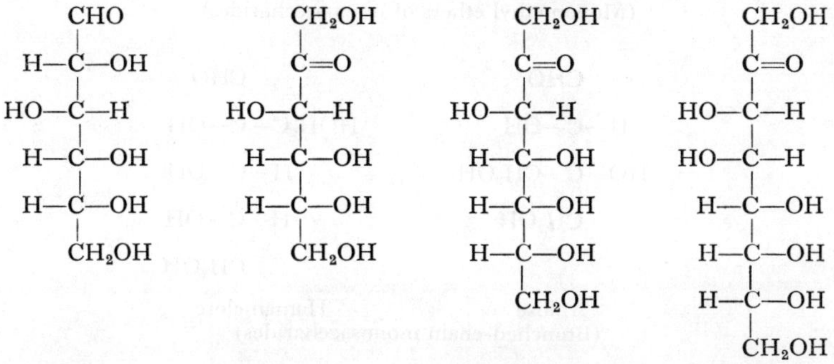

D-Glucose — D-Fructose (Hexoses) — Sedoheptulose (Heptose) — D-Glycero-D-manno-octulose (Octose)

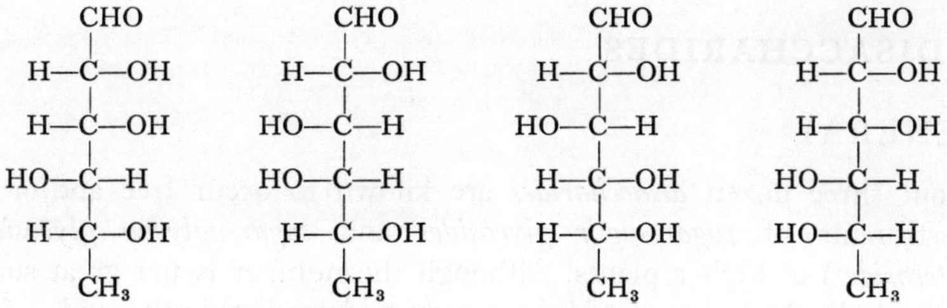

D-Antiarose — D-Fucose — D-Quinovose — L-Rhamnose
(6-Deoxy-Hexoses or Methyl pentoses)

Fig. 90. Some monosaccharides.

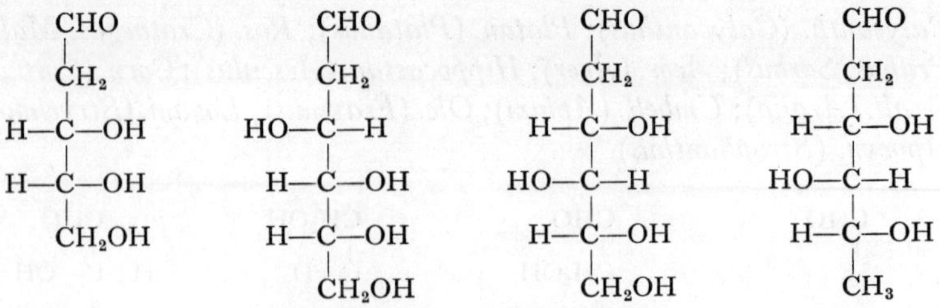

CHO
|
CH₂
|
H—C—OH
|
H—C—OH
|
CH₂OH

2-Deoxy-
D-ribose

CHO
|
CH₂
|
HO—C—H
|
H—C—OH
|
H—C—OH
|
CH₂OH

2-Deoxy-D-
arabino-hexose
(2-Deoxy-monosaccharides)

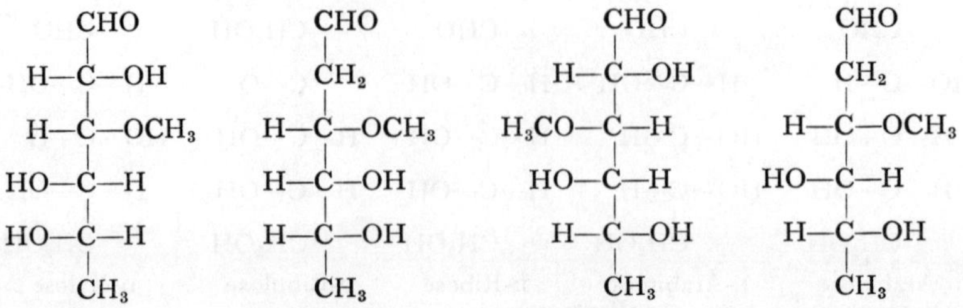

CHO
|
CH₂
|
H—C—OH
|
HO—C—H
|
H—C—OH
|
CH₂OH

2-Deoxy-D-
xylo-hexose

CHO
|
CH₂
|
H—C—OH
|
HO—C—H
|
H—C—OH
|
CH₃

Boivinose
(a 2,6-Dideoxy-hexose)

CHO
|
H—C—OH
|
H—C—OCH₃
|
HO—C—H
|
HO—C—H
|
CH₃

L- Acofriose

CHO
|
CH₂
|
H—C—OCH₃
|
H—C—OH
|
H—C—OH
|
CH₃

D-Cymarose
(Monomethyl ethers of monosaccharides)

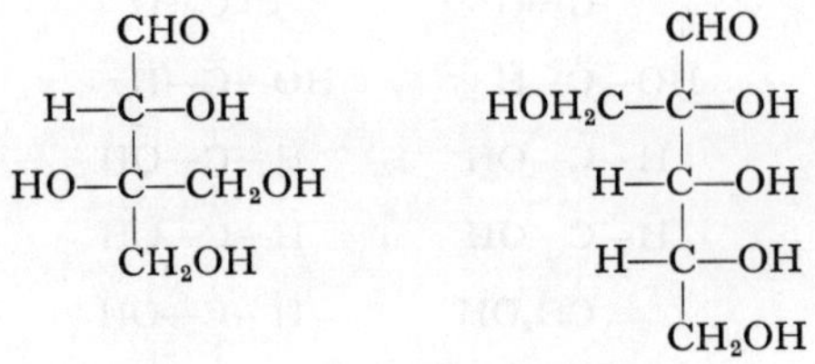

CHO
|
H—C—OH
|
H₃CO—C—H
|
HO—C—H
|
H—C—OH
|
CH₃

D-Digitalose

CHO
|
CH₂
|
H—C—OCH₃
|
HO—C—H
|
H—C—OH
|
CH₃

D-Sarmentose

CHO
|
H—C—OH
|
HO—C—CH₂OH
|
CH₂OH

Apiose

CHO
|
HOH₂C—C—OH
|
H—C—OH
|
H—C—OH
|
CH₂OH

Hamamelose
(Branched-chain monosaccharides)

Fig. 91. Some monosaccharides.

II DISACCHARIDES

GENERAL

About three dozen *disaccharides* are known to occur free and/or as constituents of *sugar-sugar glycosides* and *sugar-aglycan glycosides* (*heterosides*) of higher plants. Although the number is not great some of the individual *disaccharides* are very widely distributed and a few occur in very large amounts. We shall list them alphabetically under trivial names (where such are used).

Staněk, Černý and Pacák include the *disaccharides* in their recent monograph *The Oligosaccharides* (1965), but we have thought it better to handle them separately.

List and Occurrence

Acetyl-digilanidobiose occurs in some *digitalis-glycosides*.

Alliuminoside is a non-reducing *disaccharide*, known only (?) from
  Lili. Allium sewertzowi (bulb)

2-Apiosyl-glucose occurs in *apiin* and *lutean*.

6-Apiosyl-glucose occurs in *furcatin*.

Cellobiose (Cellose; 4-(β-D-Glucosido)-D-glucose) does not occur free, says Karrer (1958), but it *has* been reported from Scots pine. It occurs as a moiety of some *glycosides*. It can be prepared from *cellulose*.
  Scrophulari. Digitalis (in *gitostin*?)
  Haemodor. Haemodorum corymbosum (in *hemocorin*)

Ceratose: a *fructisido-glucose*? It is reported so far only from
  Legum. Ceratonia siliqua (frt)

Condurangobiose (Glucosyl-thevetose) occurs only (?) in *marsdenin* (?*condurangin*).

2-Deoxy-cellobiose has been found only (?) in
  Crucif. Erysimum canescens (in a *cardiac glycoside*)

Digilanidobiose (4-*O*-β-D-Glucopyranosyl-D-digitoxose) occurs in *cardiac glycosides* of
  Crucif. Erysimum perofskianum
  Asclepiad. Strophanthus kombe
  Scrophulari. Digitalis lanata, purpurea; Isoplexis isabelliana?

Epimelibiose (6-*O*-α-D-Galactopyranosyl-D-mannose) does not occur free ? It is formed by acid hydrolysis of *guaran*, from some *gluco-* and *galacto-mannans*.

Fructosyl-fructose, of unknown structure, is known only (?) from
  Comp. Helianthus tuberosus (plt, free ?)

Gentiobiose (6-(β-D-glucosido)-D-glucose; Amygdalinbiose) is a constituent of some *cardiac* and other *glycosides* (such as *amygdalin*). It also occurs free.
  Combret. Terminalia spp. (frts, free ?)
  Gentian. Gentiana lutea (rt, free)
  Gram. Poa trivialis (free ?)

Isomaltose
  Gram. Oryza sativa (frt, only in old samples)
  Typh. Typha latifolia (pollen)

Kojibiose (2-*O*-α-D-Glucopyranosyl-D-glucose), whose isomer is *sophorose*, is said to occur in

    Typh.   *Typha latifolia* (pollen)

Lactose (Lactobiose; Milk sugar; 4-(β-D-Galactosido)-D-glucose) was, at one time, said not to occur in plants. We know today that it is rather widely distributed. I have the following records:

    Legum.   *Ceratonia siliqua* (frt ?)

    Sapind.   *Sapindus saponaria* (in *saponin*)

    Sapot.   *Achras sapota* (frt), *Mimusops roxburghiana* (frt), *Pouteria campechiana* (frt). Reithel and Venkataraman (1956) found only very small amounts in these sugar-rich fruits.

    Ole.   *Forsythia suspensa* (pollen of long-shafted fl.)

    Rubi.   *Oldenlandia biflora*

    Verben.   *Lippia nodiflora* (plt)

Leucrose (5-*O*-α-D-Glucopyranosylo-D-fructose) is formed by *Leuconostoc*. In higher plants it is reported from

    Typh.   *Typha latifolia* (pollen)

Maltose (Maltobiose; Malt sugar; 4-(α-D-Glucopyranosylo)-D-glucose) can be obtained from starch. It seems only rarely to occur free in any quantity, but is very widely distributed.

    Ranuncul.   *Aconitum napellus* (st., tuber)

    Crassul.   *Bryophyllum calycinum, Umbilicus pendulinus*

    Ros.   *Malus*

    Legum.   *Ceratonia* (1), *Glycine* (1), *Lathyrus* (2), *Phaseolus* (1), *Trifolium* (2)

    Tropaeol.   *Tropaeolum majus*

    Euphorbi.   *Mercurialis perennis* (rhiz., rt)

    Cucurbit.   *Schizopepon fargesii* (tuber)

    Arali.   *Panax schinseng*

    Umbell.   *Daucus carota*

    Sapot.   *Bassia latifolia* (fl.)

    Verben.   *Lippia nodiflora* (plt)

    Acanth.   *Hygrophila spinosa* (rt)

    Comp.   *Chrysactinia mexicana*

    Gram.   *Oryza sativa* (frt, old sample only)

    Typh.   *Typha latifolia*

    Mus.   *Musa*

Melibiose (Eucalyn; *O*-α-D-Galactopyranosyl-(1 → 6)-D-glucose) occurs free (?) in leaves of Scots pine. In angiosperms it occurs free or combined in

    Betul.   *Betula papyrifera* (sap, in Spring); *Corylus avellana* (sd, trace), *colurna* (sd, trace)

    Ranuncul.   *Aconitum napellus* (st., tuber; free)

Malv. *Malva* (secretion from stem-wounds)
Sterculi. *Theobroma cacao* (sd)
Myrt. *Eucalyptus*
Ole. *Fraxinus*
Lab. *Teucrium canadense* (rhiz., after hyd.)

Neohesperidose (Sophorabiose; 2-*O*-α-L-Rhamnopyranosyl-D-glucopyranose) is the sugar moiety of *neohesperidin* and *naringin*.

Nigerose (Sakébiose; 3-*O*-α-D-Glucopyranosyl-D-glucose; fig. 92) is an unusual *disaccharide* with a 1 → 3 linkage. It has been found in beer and in:

Typh. *Typha latifolia* (pollen)

2-*O*-α-L-Rhamnopyranosyl-D-galactose is known only (?) as part of *solatriose*.

Planteobiose (Melibiulose; 6-(α-D-Galactopyranosyl)-D-fructose) can be obtained from *planteose* by mild acid hydrolysis.

Ole. *Fraxinus ornus* (free, and by hydrolysis of its manna)
Lab. *Teucrium canadense* (rhiz., after hydrolysis)

Primverose (Primeverose; 6-*O*-β-D-Xylopyranosyl-D-glucose; fig. 92) is a constituent of many *glycosides*, including *primverin*, *primulaverin*, *gentiacaulin*, *monotropitoside*, *rhamnicoside*, α- and β-*sorinins*, *ruberythric acid*, *fabiatrin*, *morindin*, *caesioside*, and *galiosin*. Does it occur free as well?

Legum. *Ceratonia siliqua* (frt, free?)
Primul. *Primula* (free?)

Robinobiose (Robinose; 6-*O*-α-L-Rhamnopyranosyl-D-galactose) is the sugar moiety of *robinin*.

Rutinose (Lusitanicose; 6-*O*-α-L-Rhamnopyranosyl-D-glucose) is a constituent of *rutin*, *lusitanicoside*, *datiscin*, *nicotiflorin*, and many *anthocyanins*.

Sambubiose is said by Harborne (1963) to be a β-(1 → 2)-*xylosylglucose*, occurring in *anthocyanins* of *Begonia*, *Sambucus*, *Streptocarpus*, and *Ilex*; yet Karrer (1958), Dean (1963), and Staněk *et al.* (1965) do not even mention it!

Scillabiose (4-*O*- ?-D-Glucopyranosyl-L-rhamnose) can be obtained from *scillaren-A* and *glucoscilliphaeoside*.

Sogdianose is said to be a *fructose-fructose disaccharide*.

Lili. *Eremurus sogdianus* (rt)

Solabiose (3-*O*-β-D-Glucopyranosyl-D-galactose) can be obtained from *solatriose*. Does it occur naturally?

Sophorose (2-*O*-β-D-Glucopyranosyl-D-glucose) is an isomer of *kojibiose*. It is a constituent of *kaempferol-3-sophoroside*, *stevioside*, and of some anthocyanins (Harborne, 1963)

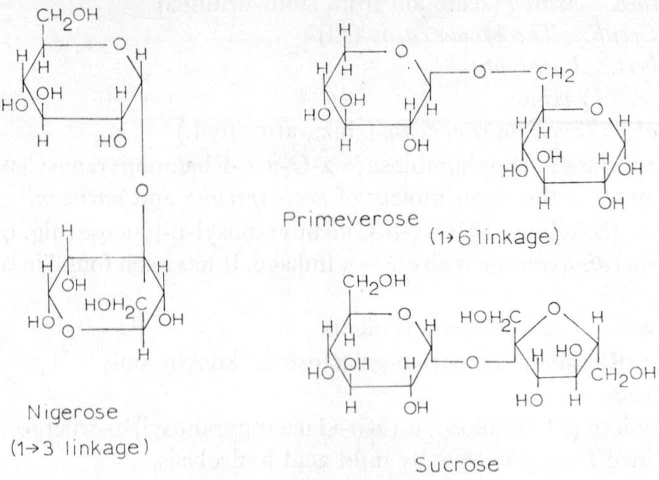

Fig. 92. Some disaccharides.

Strophanthobiose (Periplobiose; 4-*O*-β-D-Glucopyranosyl-D-cymarose) occurs in some *cardiac glycosides*, such as *periplocin* and *strophanthin-K*.

Sucrose (Saccharose; Cane and Beet Sugar; α-D-Glucopyranosyl-β-D-fructofuranoside; fig. 92) is probably universally present in the free state in higher plants. I have no very recent figures, but as long ago as 1947 nearly 9,000,000 tons of beet sugar and more than 25,000,000 tons of cane sugar were produced annually.

It is, of course, dangerous to say that a substance is universally present, but without really trying I have collected records of the occurrence of *sucrose* in 33 families of flowering plants. I know of no case where it is said to be *absent*. In addition to its occurrence in the free state we must add its presence as the nucleus of the *raffinose* group of sugars, and as a constituent of *erlose* and *sessilifolan*.

Swietenose (6-*O*-α-D-Galactopyranosyl-D-galactose)

    Ole.   *Schrebera swietenoides* (mokha, gum, free?)

Trehalose (Mycose; α-D-Glucopyranosyl-α-D-glucopyranoside) has been reported from fungi, algae, lichens, a *Selaginella* (a good source), a fern, and

    Fag.   *Fagus sylvatica* (cambial sap, under conditions practically precluding secondary action—Oesch and Meier, 1967)

    Ole.   *Fraxinus ornus* (manna from lvs after insect bites? Perhaps secondary)

    Cyper.   *Carex brunescens* (exudate after frost? perhaps secondary)

Turanose (3-α-D-Glucopyranosyl-D-fructose) has been obtained by partial hydrolysis of *melezitose*. It is also reported from
  Typh.   *Typha latifolia* (pollen)
Vicianose (6-*O*-α-L-Arabinopyranosyl-D-glucose) occurs in *gein, vicianin,* and *violutin.*

III OLIGOSACCHARIDES

GENERAL

We have dealt above with *monosaccharides* and *disaccharides*, the latter consisting of 2 linked *monosaccharides*. We deal here with sugars having 3 or more, but still few, *monosaccharide* units linked together. There is no sharp limit between the 'longer' *oligosaccharides* and the 'shorter' *polysaccharides*. Staněk *et al.*, in their monograph *The Oligosaccharides* (1965), include all sugars with from 2 (our *disaccharides*) to 10 units.
    We distinguish for convenience:

1. Trisaccharides: more than two dozen are known
2. Tetrasaccharides: about a dozen are known
3. Other oligosaccharides, with from 5 to 10 or more units. We list 9.
4. Oligosaccharides containing uronic acids: more than two dozen are known.

These distinctions separate related substances in many cases. Thus we may recognize several series of oligosaccharides ranging from 2 to 10 or so units. I have found it so difficult to assign all the carbohydrates listed to their respective series that I have abandoned the attempt as a means of classification. We may note the *raffinose* series, however, as one example.
    The raffinose series and its occurrence in the **Tubiflorae** (*sensu* Melchior in *Syll.*12, 1964). Figures in parentheses after family names indicate numbers of genera known to have the sugars:
Fruct.-gluc.-(galact.)$_0$ 'Sucrose'
    Probably in all 26 families
Fruct.-gluc.-(galact.)$_1$ 'Raffinose'
    Boragin. (2), *Lab.* (many), *Solan.* (3), *Scrophulari.* (5)
Fruct.-gluc.-(galact.)$_2$ 'Stachyose'
    Boragin. (2), *Verben.* (1), *Lab.* (many), *Solan.* (1), *Scrophulari.* (many), *Bignoni.* (1)
Fruct.-gluc.-(galact.)$_3$ 'Verbascose'
    Lab. (many), *Scrophulari.* (1)

Fruct.-gluc.-(galact.)$_4$ 'Ajugose'
Lab. (2), Scrophulari. (1)
Fruct.-gluc.-(galact.)$_5$ Penta-D-galactosylsucrose
Lab. (1), Scrophulari. (1)
Fruct.-gluc.-(galact.)$_6$ Hexa-D-galactosylsucrose
Scrophulari. (1)
Fruct.-gluc.-(galact.)$_7$ Hepta-D-galactosylsucrose
Scrophulari. (1)
Fruct.-gluc.-(galact.)$_{8-10}$? 'Lactosin'
Lab. (3)
See **Tubiflorae** for further discussion.

List and Occurrence

1. Trisaccharides are quite numerous. Some occur free; others are known to be constituents of *glycosides*, or to arise secondarily by partial hydrolysis of *glycosides*. The rational names become so fearsome with larger numbers of sugar units that we shall give few of them.
4-β-Cellobiosyl-D-fucose occurs in *digifucocellobioside*.
Chacotriose (L-Rhamnose-D-glucose-L-rhamnose)
    Solan. Solanum chacoense, etc. (in *chaconin*, a *cardiac glycoside*)
Erlose (Glucosucrose; α-Maltosyl-β-D-fructofuranoside) occurs in honey and
    Arali. Panax schinseng
α-D-Galactosyl-3-α-D-glucopyranosyl-2-β-D-fructofuranoside (?) occurs, say MacLeod and McCorquodale (1958), in
    Gram. Festuca (4), *Lolium* (3)
Gentianose (6^G-β-Glucosylsucrose) has been found, I think, only in *Gentiana* (rts). Has it been searched for in other genera?
    Gentian. Gentiana asclepiadea, cruciata, lutea, punctata, purpurea
Glucorhamnotriose (L-Rhamnose-L-rhamnose-D-glucose) occurs in *solamargine*, a *steroidal glycoalkaloid*.
Impatiose (?Fructosyl-sucrose)
    Balsamin. Impatiens holstii (nectar, when monosaccharides are injected into the phloem)
Isokestose (1^F-β-Fructosyl-sucrose) may be obtained from *inulin*, and may be an intermediate in its formation.
    Salic. Populus grandidentata (spwd), *tremuloides* (spwd)
    Arali. Panax schinseng (rt)
    Camp. Campanula rapunculus
    Comp. Helianthus tuberosus (tuber)
    Lili. Allium cepa, porrum

Gram. *Arrhenatherum elatius, Lolium multiflorum,* barley and rice straws

Kestose (6^F-β-Fructosyl-sucrose) has been obtained from *inulin* and:

Betul. *Betula papyrifera* (sap)

Gram. *Arrhenatherum elatius*; *Lolium multiflorum, perenne* (where it is the main *trisaccharide*); barley, rice, and oat straws

Labiose   yields $2 \times$ *fructose* and $1 \times$ *galactose*.

Lab. *Eremostachys labiosa* (tuber)

Lycotriose-I (D-Glucose-D-glucose-D-galactose) has been obtained by splitting *xylose* from *lycotetraose*.

Lycotriose-II (D-Xylose-D-glucose-D-galactose) has been obtained from *tomatine* and *demissine*.

Manninotriose (Galactose-galactose-glucose) has been obtained from *stachyose* and

Betul. *Betula papyrifera* (sap, free?); *Corylus avellana* (sd, free?, trace), *colurna* (sd, free?, trace)

Sterculi. *Theobroma cacao* (sd, free?)

Ole. *Fraxinus* (manna)

Mannotriose (O-β-D-Mannopyranosyl-($1 \rightarrow 4$)-O-β-D-mannopyranosyl-($1 \rightarrow 4$)-D-mannose) has been obtained from gymnosperms, *guaran* and

Legum. *Medicago sativa* (*galactomannans*)

Acer. *Acer rubrum* (*glucomannans*)

Palmae. *Borassus flabellifer* (*galactomannan*)

Melezitose (3^F-Glucosyl-sucrose) occurs in various *mannas*

Salic. *Populus nigra* (lvs, honeydew)

Legum. *Alhagi camelorum, maurorum* (mannas); *Laburnum*

Tili. *Tilia* sp. (lvs, honeydew)

Ole. *Fraxinus ornus* (lvs, free? in manna after insect bites)

Neokestose (6^G-β-Fructosyl-sucrose)

Acer. *Acer saccharum*

Lili. *Allium cepa, porrum*

Gram. *Arrhenatherum elatius, Lolium multiflorum*

Mus. *Musa chinensis*?

Odorotriose (4-O-β-Gentiobiosyl-D-diginose) occurs in *odoroside-K*, etc.

Planteose (6^F-α-Galactosyl-sucrose) yields *glucose* and *planteobiose*. It can be obtained from *lychnose*.

Sterculi. *Theobroma cacao* (sd, free?)

Ole. *Fraxinus ornus* (manna, free?)

Lab. many

Solan. *Nicotiana tabacum* (sd)

Pedali. *Sesamum indicum* (sd)

Plantagin. *Plantago major* (sd), *ovata* (sd), *psyllium*

Polygon(a)tin yields 3 × *fructose*?
> *Lili.* *Polygonatum sewertzowi* (rt)

Raffinose (Gossypose; Melitose; Melitriose; 6^G-α-Galactosyl-sucrose) was once thought to be a rare sugar. French (1954) says: 'next to sucrose itself, raffinose is probably the most abundant oligosaccharide of the plant world'. I have records of it in lower plants, gymnosperms, and in

> *Jugland.* (*Juglans*); *Salic.* (*Populus*); *Betul.* (*Corylus*); *Fag.* (*Castanea*); *Caryophyll.* (*Lychnis, Saponaria, Silene*); *Chenopodi.* (*Beta*); *Amaranth.* (*Amaranthus*); *Ranuncul.* (*Actaea, Aquilegia*); *Papaver.* (*Papaver*); *Crucif.* (many); *Resed.* (*Reseda*); *Saxifrag.* (*Saxifraga*); *Ros.* (*Malus, Potentilla*); *Legum.* (*Anthyllis, Arachis; Lotus, Phaseolus*); *Lin.* (*Linum*); *Hippocastan.* (*Aesculus*); *Tili.* (*Corchorus*); *Malv.* (*Abutilon, Gossypium*); *Bombac.* (*Adansonia*); *Sterculi.* (*Theobroma*); *Cucurbit.* (*Cucumis*); *Myrt.* (*Eucalyptus*); *Onagr.* (*Oenothera*); *Umbell.* (*Angelica, Bupleurum, Daucus, Eryngium, Ferula*); *Boragin.* (*Cynoglossum, Lithospermum*); *Lab.* (many); *Solan.* (*Atropa, Lycopersicum, Solanum*); *Scrophulari.* (*Antirrhinum, Digitalis, Linaria, Scrophularia, Verbascum*); *Comp.* (*Helianthus, Lapsana*); *Butom.* (*Butomus*); *Lili.* (*Allium*); *Gram.* (*Avena, Festuca, Hordeum, Triticum*); *Cann.* (*Canna*)

Rhamninose (Galactose-rhamnose-rhamnose) occurs in *xanthorhamnin*. 4^2-α-L-Rhamnosylgentiobiose
> *Umbell.* *Centella asiatica* (in *asiaticoside*)

Scillatriose (L-Rhamnose-glucose-glucose) occurs in *glucoscillaren-A*.

Secalose (Graminin; Levosine; Synanthrose) yields only *fructose*. It *may* be a *tetra*- rather than a *trisaccharide*.
> *Gram.* *Secale cereale* (plt)

Solatriose (Solanose; Glucose-galactose-L-rhamnose) occurs in *solanin* and *solasonine* (*steroidal glycoalkaloids*).

Strophanthotriose (4-*O*-β-Gentiobiosyl-D-cymarose) occurs in *echujin* and *strophanthin-K* (*cardiac glycosides*).

Umbelliferose (Isoraffinose; 2^G-α-Galactosyl-sucrose)
> *Legum.* occurrence?
> *Umbell.* *Angelica archangelica* var. (rt)

2. Tetrasaccharides are less numerous than the *trisaccharides*.

Bifurcose is a branched *tetrasaccharide*.
> *Gram.* Oat, barley, rye, and wheat straws

Isolychnose (Galactose-(1 → 6)-glucose-(1 → 2)-fructose-(3 → 1)-galactose) differs only in linkage from *lychnose*.
> *Caryophyll.* *Cucubalus baccifer* (rt), *Dianthus caryophyllus* (rt), *Lychnis dioica* (rt)

Lychnose (Galactose-(1 → 6)-glucose-(1 → 2)-fructose-(1 → 1)-galactose)

    Caryophyll. *Cucubalus baccifer* (rt), *Dianthus caryophyllus* (rt), *Lychnis dioica* (rt), *Silene inflata* (rt)

    Pedali. ?*Sesamum indicum* (sd)

Lycotetraose (Xylose-(1 → 3)[glucose-(1 → 2)]-glucose-(1 → 4)-galactose) is a branched-chain *tetrasaccharide* occurring in *tomatine* and *demissine*.

Maltotetraose (Glucose-(1 → 4)-glucose-(1 → 4)-glucose-(1 → 4)-glucose; Amylotetraose) occurs in malt extracts and in

    Sapot. *Achras sapota*

    Gram. *Oryza sativa* (in an old sample only)

Neobifurcose is a branched-chain *tetrasaccharide*.

    Gram. Oat straw

Planteotetraose (6^{Gal}-α-Galactosyl-planteose) may occur in

    Ole. *Fraxinus ornus* (manna)

    Pedali. *Sesamum indicum* (sd)

Scorodose is said to yield 4 × *fructose*.

    Lili. *Allium bakeri* (bulb), *nipponicum* (bulb, much); but *not* in *A. fistulosum* (st.), *cepa* (bulb), *odorum* (lvs, sd)

Sesamose (6^F-α-Galactosylraffinose) is thought to occur in:

    Pedali. *Sesamum indicum* (sd)

Stachyose (Cicerose; Lupeose; Manneotetrose; 6^G-Galactobiosyl-sucrose) is in the *raffinose* series. It is the commonest of the *tetrasaccharides*. I have records of it from

    Jugland. (*Juglans*); *Salic.* (*Populus*); *Betul.* (*Betula*, *Corylus*); *Fag.* (*Castanea*); *Mor.* (*Morus*); *Caryophyll.* (*Cucubalus*, *Lychnis*, *Silene*); *Crucif.* (many); *Ranuncul.* (*Actaea*); *Ros.* (*Malus*, *Prunus*, *Pyrus*); *Legum.* (many); *Hippocastan.* (*Aesculus*); *Sterculi.* (*Theobroma*); *Cucurbit.* (*Cucumis*, *Cucurbita*); *Hippurid.* (*Hippuris*); *Ole.* (*Fraxinus*, *Jasminum*); *Boragin.* (*Cynoglossum*, *Lithospermum*); *Verben.* (*Verbena*); *Lab.* (many); *Solan.* (*Atropa*); *Scrophulari.* (many); *Bignoni.* (*Catalpa*); *Plantagin.* (*Plantago*); *Butom.* (*Butomus*); *Lili.* (*Allium*); *Gram.* (*Sorghum*); *Cann.* (*Canna*)

Verbascotetraose (Galactose-galactose-galactose-glucose) can be obtained from *verbascose* by elimination of *fructose*. It occurs in

    Betul. *Betula papyrifera* (sap)

    Sterculi. *Theobroma cacao* (sd)

Xylotetraose (Xylose-xylose-xylose-xylose) occurs in, or can be prepared from corn hull *hemicellulose*, *xylans*, and *glucuronoxylan*.

    Betul. *Betula papyrifera* (free ?)

3. Other Oligosaccharides

Sugars having 5 or more units do not, I think, occur in *glycosides*. They may be steps on the way to *polysaccharides*, or they may represent stages in the breaking down of such complex carbohydrates. Some of them belong to well-recognized series (p. 407). There is, as we have said, no sharp line between *oligo-* and *polysaccharides*. This is emphasized by Bacon (1960) in reviewing the 'oligofructosides' of *Helianthus tuberosus*. He says that there is, in that plant, an unbroken series from the disaccharide *sucrose* to the polyfructoside *inulin*!

Ajugose (Fructose-glucose-(galactose)$_4$) belongs to the *raffinose* series.
    Legum.   Vicia sativa (sd)
    Lab.   Ajuga nipponensis (rt), *Salvia pratensis* (rt)
    Scrophulari.   Verbascum thapsus (rt), *thapsiforme* (rt)
Asphodeloside (Asphodelin) is said to yield $5 \times fructose$ and $1 \times glucose$.
    Primul.   Cyclamen spp. (corms have 'fructosan' that seems to be asphodeloside—Lys (1954))
    Lili.   Asphodelus microcarpus (tuber)
    Amaryllid.   Lycoris squamigera (lycoriside-B is *asphodeloside?*)
    Irid.   Iris?
Hepta-D-galactosylsucrose
    Scrophulari.   Verbascum thapsus (rt)
Hexa-D-galactosylsucrose
    Scrophulari.   Verbascum thapsiforme (rt), *thapsus* (rt)
Lactosin may be a member of the *raffinose* series in the 8–10 unit range.
    Caryophyll.   Melandrium album (rt), *Silene vulgaris* (rt)
    Lab.   Ajuga decumbens (rhiz.), *Comanthosphace sublanceolata* (rhiz.), *Lycopus lucidus* (rhiz.)
Lycopose (?(Galactose)$_5$-fructoside)
    Lab.   Lycopus lucidus
Penta-D-galactosylsucrose is a member of the *raffinose* series.
    Lab.   Salvia pratensis (rt)
    Scrophulari.   Verbascum thapsiforme (rt), *thapsus* (rt)
Sessilifolan is said to yield $5 \times fructose$ and $2 \times glucose$.
    Campanul.   Lobelia sessilifolia (plt)
Verbascose (Tri-D-galactosyl-sucrose) is a widely distributed member of the *raffinose* series.
    Legum.   Glycine max, Lens esculenta (sd), *Medicago sativa* (sd), *Vicia sativa* (sd)
    Sterculi.   Theobroma cacao (sd)
    Cucurbit.   Cucurbita pepo (st.)

Lab. many
Scrophulari.   *Verbascum thapsiforme* (rt), *thapsus* (rt)
Plantagin.   *Plantago maritima* (rt), *rugelii* (rt)

4. Oligosaccharides containing uronic acids

Many plant *gums*, *mucilages*, and *hemicelluloses* yield on partial hydrolysis *aldobiouronic* acids and other substances which on further hydrolysis yield one or more sugar units and/or *uronic acid* units.

The substances listed below, then, are not strictly *oligosaccharides*, but it is convenient to treat them here. It is highly probable that information of chemotaxonomic importance will become available as more systematic studies of these difficult substances are carried out, though present information suggests that some of them—such as 2-α-*galacturonosyl-L-rhamnose* and 6-β-*glucuronosyl-galactose*—are widely distributed.

I do not know if any of these substances occur in the free state.

Galactosylgalacturonosyl-L-rhamnose
    Malv. *Hibiscus esculentus* (mucilage)
Galacturonosyl-L-arabinose
    Plantagin.   *Plantago fastigiata* (sd-mucilage), *psyllium* (sd-mucilage)
Galacturonosyl-L-arabinosylxylose
    Plantagin.   *Plantago psyllium* (sd-mucilage)
Galacturonosyl-fucose
    Legum. *Medicago sativa*
3-Galacturonosyl-galactose
    Anacardi. *Odina wodier* (gum)
4-Galacturonosyl-galactose
    Cochlosperm. *Cochlospermum gossypium* (gum)
    Sterculi. *Sterculia setigera* (gum)
2 (or 3)-Galacturonosyl-galacturonic acid
    Sterculi. *Sterculia setigera* (gum)
4-α-Galacturonosyl-galacturonic acid can be obtained from various
    pectins.
(Galacturonosyl)$_2$-L-rhamnose
    Malv. *Hibiscus manihot* (rt-mucilage)
[(Galacturonosyl)$_2$-L-rhamnose]$_2$
    Malv. *Hibiscus manihot* (rt-mucilage)
2-α-Galacturonosyl-L-rhamnose seems to be obtainable from a wide variety of plants:
    Ulm. *Ulmus fulva* (mucilage)
    Legum. *Medicago sativa* (pectin)

Lin. Linum usitatissimum (sd-mucilage)
Meli. Khaya grandifolia (gum), senegalensis (gum)
Vit. Vitis vinifera (grape-juice)
Malv. Hibiscus esculentus (mucilage)
Sterculi. Sterculia setigera (gum)
Cochlosperm. Cochlospermum gossypium (gum)
Lab. Salvia aegyptica (mucilage)
Plantagin. Plantago sp. (sd-mucilage)
2^2-α-Galacturonosyl-4-L-rhamnosyl-galactose
  Meli. Khaya grandifolia (gum)
  Malv. Hibiscus esculentus (mucilage)
2^2-α-Galacturonosyl-L-rhamnosyl-galactose: distinct   from   the
preceding?
  Lin. Linum usitatissimum (sd-mucilage)
3-α-Glucuronosyl-galactose
  Rut. Feronia elephantum (gum)
4-α-Glucuronosyl-galactose
  Legum. Acacia karoo (gum)
  Meli. Melia azadarach (gum)
6-β-Glucuronosyl-galactose is, says Bailey (1965), probably the com-
monest *aldobiouronic acid* occurring as a structural unit in *gums*.
  Ros. Prunus amygdalus, domestica, persica (in gums)
  Legum. Acacia (gums of at least 6 spp.), Virgilia oroboides
  Rut. Afraegle paniculata
  Combret. Anogeissus latifolia, schimperi (gums)
  Umbell. Ferula asafoetida (gum)
  Gram. Triticum (wheat straw)
2-β-Glucuronosyl-glucuronic acid
  Legum. Glycyrrhiza glabra (rt, from glycyrrhinic acid)
2-β-Glucuronosyl-mannose
  Prote. Hakea acicularis (gum)
  Ros. Prunus cerasus, insititia (gums)
  Legum. Albizia zygia, Virgilia oroboides (gums)
  Combret. Anogeissus latifolia, schimperi (gums)
  Lili. Asparagus filicinus?
2-α-Glucuronosyl-L-rhamnose
  Sterculi. Brachychiton diversifolium (gum)
2-α-Glucuronosyl-xylose
  Gram. Corn-hulls, oat-hulls, wheat-straw, etc.
3-α-Glucuronosyl-xylose
  Ros. Pyrus communis (hemicellulose)
  Comp. Helianthus annuus (infl., hemicellulose)
  Gram. Wheat-straw

3-α-4-*O*-Methyl-glucuronosyl-L-arabinose
  Anacardi.   Spondias cytherea (gum)
4-α-4-*O*-Methyl-glucuronosyl-L-arabinose
  Ros.   Prunus spp. (gums)
  Rut.   Citrus spp. (gums)
4-α-4-*O*-Methyl-glucuronosyl-galactose
  Legum.   Albizia zygia, Prosopis juliflora (gums)
  Rut.   Citrus sp. (gum)
  Burser.   Commiphora myrrha (gum)
  Meli.   Khaya grandifolia, senegalensis (gums)
6-β-4-*O*-Methyl-glucuronosyl-galactose
  Legum.   Prosopis juliflora (gum)
  Burser.   Boswellia carteri, Commiphora myrrha (gums)
  Anacardi.   Spondias cytherea (gum)
  Umbell.   Ferula asafoetida (gum)
2-α-4-*O*-Methyl-glucuronosyl-xylose may be regarded, says Bailey
  (1965), as a structural unit of plant-fibre *hemicelluloses*. A series with
  from 1 to 5 *xylose* units has been recognized.

IV POLYSACCHARIDES

GENERAL

We have seen, in discussing the *oligosaccharides*, that there is no sharp
distinction between them and the *polysaccharides*. Carbohydrates
having more than 10 sugar units may be classed arbitrarily as *poly-saccharides*.

These last are difficult substances to handle. They occur mixed, or
even more or less combined, with other complex entities (or mixtures!)
such as *lignins*. Isolation without change is often virtually impossible.
It is not surprising, therefore, that few *polysaccharides* are completely
known. Nor is it surprising that they can be used only in a limited way
in chemotaxonomy. The following notes are intended more to show our
ignorance than our knowledge.

List and Occurrence

Amylopectins are very like *glycogens*. They constitute the main fraction
  (75–85%) of most *starches*. They have high molecular weights (about
  10×10^6) and consist usually of chains of 20 to 25 α-D-*glucose* units
  linked ($1 \rightarrow 4$), connected in turn by ($1 \rightarrow 6$) linkages. Shorter chain
  amylopectins are present in some starches.

Amyloses are minor components of most *starches*. It is believed that they are absent from waxy cereal starches and that they may be the major components of some corn and pea starches. They consist essentially of chains of several thousand α-D-*glucose* units linked ($1 \rightarrow 4$).

Arabans are *polysaccharides* composed chiefly or entirely of L-*arabinose* units. Comparatively little is known about them. They occur in small amounts in some *cellulose* preparations and in some *gums* such as *gum tragacanth*. The *arabans* of peanut, apple, citrus fruits, and beet have been studied, and prove to be very similar in nature. They are associated with, or are a part of, *pectins*.

Arabinogalactans seem to be mixed *polysaccharides* yielding *arabinose*, *galactose*, and in some cases *rhamnose*?

> *Acer.* *Acer saccharum* (sap, is said to have a carbohydrate yielding *galactose*, *arabinose* and *rhamnose* in the proportions 50:45:5).

Asparagosin is, like many 'polyfructosans', derived from a monocotyledon. It may have as few as 9 units and would then qualify as an *oligosaccharide*.

> *Lili.* *Asparagus officinalis* (rt)

Cellulose(s): it is still not certain that there is more than one true *cellulose*. As a major constituent of cell-walls *cellulose* is universal in higher plants. Chemotaxonomically the proportion of *cellulose* to other constituents of the wall might be a useful character.

Dextran(s): although Neely (1960) seems to use *dextran* in the singular he says: 'The term dextran has been used for a class of D-glucose polysaccharides produced by bacteria growing on a sucrose substrate. In this article, "dextran" will refer to those polysaccharides containing a backbone of D-glucose units linked predominantly α-D-($1 \rightarrow 6$).' I do not think that *dextrans* occur in higher plants, but *dextrins* do.

Dextrins are composed of D-*glucose* units. Several types are recognized— α-*dextrins*, β-*dextrins*, γ-*dextrins*, φ-*dextrins*, etc. They may be derived from *amylopectins*, *glycogen*, *starch*, etc. Are they also formed in the building-up of such complex substances?

> *Schardinger-dextrins*, which have 6 to 8 units in a ring, seem always to be secondary. I know of no work suggesting the use of *dextrins* in chemotaxonomy.

Elymoside is a 'fructosan'.

> *Gram.* *Elymus arenarius* (other species, too, are said to have *fructosans*)

Eremuran is said to be a *glucomannan*.

> *Lili.* *Eremurus regelii* (rt)

Fructosans (?Levulins, Levulosans) are, in theory, carbohydrates with from 3 (*secalose*) to many (*inulin*) *fructose* units. The lower members may indeed be true *fructosans*, the higher are said by Bacon (1960) to have *glucose* present as well: 'I think we must now accept that all the plant fructosans contain at least one glucose residue per molecule, and that this forms a non-reducing (sucrose) end-group. From now on we require to be convinced that there are exceptions to the rule.' Bacon distinguishes 3 types of fructosans; those resembling *inulin*, with (2 → 1) links; those resembling the bacterial *levans*, with (2 → 6) links; and those, such as the fructosans of *Iris*, with both.

Individual fructosans (bracketed numbers indicate the number of *fructose* units) include: *inulin* (many), *scorodose* (4), *secalose* (3), *sinistrin* (? *scillin*, 30 to 33 ?), *irisin* (?), *tuberoholoside* (?), *asphodeloside* (5 + 1 *glucose*?), *lycoroside* (?), *asparagosin* (9), *triticin* (14 to 15), *elymoside* (?), *hordeoside* (?), *phlein* (15 to 16), *graminin* (5 to 6), *synanthrose* (?), and *levosine* (?). Are these all actual entities? It will be noted that some of these are *oligosaccharides*, that most are derived from monocotyledons, a high proportion from the *Gramineae*.

Galactans are supposedly composed of *galactose* units. They are said to occur in the woods of conifers and of dicotyledonous trees, in seeds, and in *pectins*, but most of these substances contain also units other than *galactose*. Aspinall (1959) says: 'the only true galactans known in land plants, namely those from *Lupinus albus* pectin and from *Strychnos nux-vomica* seeds...contain essentially linear chains of (1 → 4)-linked β-D-galactopyranose residues.'

Galactoglucomannans occur generally, thinks Timell (1964), in woods of conifers. They yield D-*galactose*, D-*glucose*, and D-*mannose*. Do they occur, too, in the woods of angiosperms?

Galactomannans are said to be chains of β-D-*mannose* units linked (1 → 4), with (1 → 6) linked α-D-*galactose* units as side appendages. They have been reported from

    Legum. *Caesalpinia spinosa* (sd), *Ceratonia siliqua* (sd), *Cyamopsis psoraloides* (sd), *Gleditsia triacanthos* (sd), *Medicago sativa* (sd), *Trifolium* sp. (sd), *Trigonella foenum-graecum* (sd)
    Irid. *Iris* sp. (sd)

Glucomannans are often included among the *hemicelluloses*. They occur in woods of conifers, and in small amounts (3 to 5%) in hardwoods. Timell (1964) is responsible for the analyses of most of the following. He finds them much alike with a *mannose:glucose* ratio of about 1:2, except in *Betula* where the ratio is nearer 1:1. They seem to be linear with from 26 to 70 units.

    Salic. *Populus tremuloides*
    Betul. *Alnus rubra*, *Betula* (2)
    Fag. *Fagus* (2)
    Acer. *Acer* (2)
    Lili. *Eremurus* ? (*eremuran*)

Glycogens are characteristic polysaccharides of fungi and of animals. They do not, I think, occur in higher plants.

Graminin is one of the '*fructosans*'. It may have only 5 to 6 units and might therefore be classed as an *oligosaccharide*.

    Gram. Secale cereale

Hemicelluloses, as the name implies, resemble true *cellulose*, and are associated with it in the cell wall. They have been discussed by Aspinall (1959) and by Timell (1964). Several other groups of sub-stances—*glucomannans, xylans, mannans, galactans, arabinogalactans,* and *O-acetyl-(4-O-methylglucurono) xylans*—have been called *hemicelluloses*.

Hordeoside is a 'fructosan'.

    Gram. Hordeum bulbosum

Inulin is considered to be a '*fructosan*', but like most such substances it probably has *glucose*, too, in its molecule. It is thought to have a chain of about 30 D-*fructose* units, but where is the *glucose*?

It is difficult to record the distribution of *inulin*, for many reports are old ones and untrustworthy. If distribution of *inulin* is to be used with confidence in chemotaxonomy a careful modern survey must be made.

    Chenopodi. Beta
    Aristolochi. Aristolochia
    Marcgravi. Marcgravia (2 or 3)
    Droser. Drosophyllum
    Euphorbi. Aleurites
    Viol. Ionidium (4)
    Myrt. Eucalyptus
    Punic. Punica
    Eric. Calluna
    Menyanth. Menyanthes
    Rubi. Cinchona
    Boragin. Cynoglossum
    Solan. Solanum
    Dipsac. Cephalaria
    Campanul. many, if not all
    Goodeni. Goodenia, Scaevola, Selliera, Velleia
    Stylidi. Donatia, Stylidium (2 or 3)
    Comp. many, perhaps all, but Colin (1935(6)) says that while perennial species of *Helianthus* make *inulin*, annual ones do not. This should be checked.
    Lili. Allium, Hyacinthus
    Agav. Yucca filamentosa (lvs)
    Amaryllid. Galanthus, Leucojum, Narcissus

Irisin is said to be a 'fructosan'.

    Irid. *Iris pseudacorus* (rt, or rhiz.)

Levans (Levulosans) are *'fructosans'* produced by bacterial actions; not known from higher plants?

Lycoroside-A is said to be a *'fructosan'*.

    Amaryllid. *Lycoris squamigera*

Mannans are chains of $(1 \to 4)$ linked β-D-*mannose* (with some β-D-*glucose*?). They occur more abundantly in woods of conifers than in those of dicotyledons. In the latter they constitute only about 1% of the dry weight of the wood.

    Palmae. *Phytelephas* (sd—the reserve material, known as 'vegetable ivory', is said to yield 95% or more of D-*mannose*)

    Orchid. 'Salep', from some orchids, is said to contain *mannans.*

O-Acetyl-(4-O-methylglucurono)xylans are included among the *hemicelluloses.* Timell (1964) says: 'It is now abundantly clear that the wood of these trees [woody angiosperms] contain, as a preponderant hemicellulose, an O-acetyl-(4-O-methylglucurono)xylan, the structural details and molecular proportions of which vary only little, or not at all, from one species to another.'

If this is true they will be of little use in chemotaxonomy. Timell gives a list (below) which shows them to be widely distributed.

    Salic. *Populus tremuloides*
    Betul. *Alnus rubra*; *Betula lutea, papyrifera, populifolia, verrucosa*
    Fag. *Fagus sylvatica, grandifolia*; *Quercus alba, robur*
    Ulm. *Ulmus americana, davidiana*
    Ros. *Malus pumila, Prunus avium*
    Legum. *Prosopis juliflora, Robinia pseudacacia*
    Rut. *Citrus limonia*
    Acer. *Acer saccharum*
    Myrt. *Eucalyptus regnans*
    Eric. *Arbutus menziesii*

Phlein is yet another *'fructosan'*. It is thought to be a ring of 15 to 16 D-*fructose* units linked $(2 \to 6)$.

    Gram. *Phleum pratense* (rt)

Poan is a *'fructosan'* similar to the *levans.*

    Gram. *Poa trivialis*

Secalin is a *'fructosan'*.

    Gram. *Secale cereale* (st.)

Sinistrin (?Scillin) is a *'fructosan'* with from 30 to 33 D-*fructose* units.

    Lili. *Urginea scilla* (*maritima*)
    Agav. *Yucca filamentosa* (lvs)?

Starch (or should it be Starches?)

    Whole books have been written about this abundant polysaccharide.

Many higher (and lower) plants lay down in their cells as reserve foodstuffs 'starch-grains' which are visible under the microscope. These are often of such characteristic size and appearance that the expert can identify the source of the grains. Many years ago Reichert (1913, 1919) made a remarkable study of starch. His claims may have been exaggerated, but there is no doubt that the visible, physical, and chemical properties of starch-grains (which are more than just a single polysaccharide) may be used to advantage in chemotaxonomy. We cannot forbear to quote briefly from Reichert:

> One may lay down the dictum *that each and every form of proto-plasm existent in any organism is stereochemically peculiarly modified in specific relationship to that organism, and that, as a corollary, the products of synthesis will be modified in conformity with the molecular peculiarities of the protoplasm giving rise to them.* It follows, there-fore, that if the plastids of any given plant be of different stereo-chemical structure from those of others, *the starch produced will show corresponding stereochemic variations, and hence be absolutely diagnostic in relation to the plant.* Abundant evidence will be found in the pages which follow in justification of this statement. Moreover, if such differences are diagnostic, it is evident that they constitute *a strictly scientific basis for the classification of plants.*

Triticin is a '*fructosan*' with 14 to 15 *fructose* units.
    Gram.   *Agropyron repens*
Tuberoholoside is yet another '*fructosan*'.
    Lili.   *Allium sativum* (plt), *vineale*; but *not* in *A. ascalonicum, cepa*
    Agav.   *Polianthes tuberosa*
Xylans are included among the *hemicelluloses* by some writers. Whistler (1950) says that two kinds, one with and one without a *glucuronic acid* unit seem to occur. They are said to be the most abundant of *pento-sans*, being found in practically all land-plants.

    Aspinall (1959) says that all *xylans* have chains of $(1 \to 4)$ linked β-D-*xylopyranose* units and that they differ from each other in the arrangement of L-*arabinose*, D-*glucuronic acid*, and *glucuronic acid*-4-*methyl ether*, which are attached as side-chains. *Xylans* of grasses yield L-*arabinose* units: those of dicotyledonous wood yield *O*-(4-*O*-methyl-α-D-*glucosyluronic acid*)-$(1 \to 2)$-D-*xylose*.

CARBOXYLIC ACIDS

GENERAL

As in so many other cases we are faced with problems of nomenclature and of classification. Botanists have often used the term 'vegetable acids' for at least the aliphatic carboxylic acids of plants. A more general term, 'organic acids', is also to be found, and a recent treatment by Whiting (1964) bears this title. Whiting distinguishes:

1. Aliphatic Acids
    (a) Fatty Acids
    (b) Other
2. Alicyclic Acids, with 1 or more non-benzenoid C-rings.
3. Aromatic Acids, with a benzene ring.
4. Heterocyclic Acids, with rings containing C and O, N, or S.
5. Amino-acids.

We have dealt with some of Whiting's groups elsewhere. Our present grouping is as follows:

I. Aliphatic Monocarboxylic Acids—about 35
    1. Normal Saturated Acids of the Fatty Acid Series
    2. Branched Chain Saturated Acids
    3. Unsaturated Acids
II. Aliphatic Dicarboxylic Acids—about 43
    1. Oxalic Acid Series
    2. Other Acids
III. Aliphatic Tricarboxylic Acids—about 5
IV. Aromatic Carboxylic Acids (including most of the Phenolic Acids, but excluding those of the *Anacardiaceae*)—about 56

We have excluded the obviously *terpenoid acids* and the *amino-acids*.

I MONOCARBOXYLIC ALIPHATIC ACIDS

GENERAL

The acids of this series have the general formula $CH_3.(CH_2)_n.COOH$, or, if we include *formic acid*, $C_nH_{2n}O_2$. The higher members with even C-numbers have been dealt with in our section on *fats* and *fatty acids*; the lower members, and those with odd C-numbers, may be considered briefly here. Some of the acids listed seem rarely to occur free. They are found instead as *esters*.

I.1 Normal saturated acids

List and Occurrence

Formic acid (H.COOH): in most cases produced secondarily? It has been detected (free?) in many fruits. I have the following additional records

> *Urtic. Urtica* (2)—but *formic acid* is not the only stinging agent?
> *Euphorbi. Ricinus communis* (sdlg)
> *Cist. Cistus labdanum*
> *Comp. Arnica* (rt), *Artemisia transiliensis* (oil)
> *Gram. Triticum* (frt)

Acetic acid (CH_3.COOH) is very widely spread both free and in various combinations.

Propionic acid (CH_3.CH_2.COOH) is, like *acetic acid*, very widely spread, usually as esters; also as *amino-acids*.

n-Butyric acid: see *n-tetranoic acid* under fats.

n-Valeric acid (CH_3.$(CH_2)_3$.COOH) is not very common. It is said to be the sex-attractant of adult females of the sugar-beet wireworm. Many reported occurrences in plants have been of branched-chain forms. Are the following records reliable?

> *Euphorbi. Croton* spp. (ess. oil)
> *Rut. Boronia anemonifolia* (ess. oil, as ethyl ester)
> *Caprifoli. Viburnum?*
> *Comp. Atractylis gummifera*
> *Bromeli. Ananas sativa* (frt, as methyl ester)
> *Gram. Andropogon?*

n-Heptanoic acid (Oenanthic acid; CH_3.$(CH_2)_5$.COOH)

> *Legum. Acacia dealbata* (fl.-oil)
> *Viol. Viola* (lvs, oil)?
> *Comp. Arnica?*
> *Arac. Acorus calamus*

n-Nonanoic acid (*n*-Nonylic acid; Pelargonic acid; CH_3.$(CH_2)_7$.COOH) is present usually as esters. It occurs in conifers and in

> *Laur. Litsea cubeba* (st.-oil)
> *Gerani. Pelargonium roseum* (ess. oil)
> *Rut. Eremocitrus glauca* (ess. oil)
> *Anacardi. Rhus succedanea* ('wax')
> *Lythr. Cuphea llavea* (sd-oil, less than 1%)
> *Lab. Lavandula* (ess. oil)
> *Comp. Artemisia arborescens* (ess. oil)
> *Irid. Iris* (oil)

n-Undecanoic (*n*-Undecylic acid; $CH_3.(CH_2)_9.COOH$) is said to occur in conifers and

    Lab.   *Thymus serpyllum* (ess. oil)
    Comp.   *Artemisia frigida* (ess. oil, tr.)
    Irid.   *Iris germanica* (rt)
    Palmae.   *Cocos nucifera* (oil)

n-Tridecanoic acid (*n*-Tridecylic acid; $CH_3.(CH_2)_{11}.COOH$)

    Irid.   *Iris germanica* (rt-oil)
    Palmae.   *Cocos nucifera* (oil)

n-Pentadecanoic acid (*n*-Pentadecylic acid; $CH_3.(CH_2)_{13}.COOH$)

    Rut.   *Zanthoxylum carolinianum* (bk)
    Comp.   *Calendula officinalis* (fl.)

n-Heptadecanoic acid (Daturinic acid; Margaric acid; $CH_3.(CH_2)_{15}.COOH$) is of doubtful occurrence.

    Guttif.   *Symphonia* spp. (Hébert, 1913)

I.2 Branched-chain saturated acids

GENERAL

Only a few of these seem to occur in higher plants. Some are *necic acids* of *pyrrolizidine alkaloids*.

List and Occurrence

Echimidinic acid ($CH_3.CHOH.C(OH)(C.OH(CH_3)_2).COOH$; ?Macrotomic acid) is a *necic acid*.

Heliotrinic acid ($CH_3.CH(OCH_3).C(OH)(CH.(CH_3)_2).COOH$) is the *necic acid* of *heleurine* and *heliotrine*.

Isobutyric acid (Dimethyl-acetic acid; 2-Methylpropionic acid; $CH_3.CH(CH_3).COOH$) is secreted with α(2)-*methyl-butyric acid* by a caterpillar fed on *Daucus*, *Foeniculum*, and *Pastinaca* (which are not known to have these acids, though other umbellifers do). It occurs (chiefly as esters) in conifers and in

    Ros.   *Prunus*?
    Legum.   *Ceratonia siliqua* (frt)
    Euphorbi.   *Croton tiglium* (oil)
    Myrt.   *Eucalyptus* (ess. oil)
    Umbell.   *Peucedanum ostruthium*, *Seseli tortuosum* (ess. oil, free)— and see above
    Lab.   *Lavandula vera* (oil)
    Comp.   *Anthemis nobilis* (oil), *Arnica montana* (rt, free), *Artemisia transiliensis* (oil), *Euryops floribundus* (st., free and bound)

Iso-caproic acid (Isobutyl-acetic acid; 4-Methyl-valeric acid; $CH_3.CH(CH_3).CH_2.CH_2.COOH$)

    Bromeli. *Ananas sativa* (frt, as methyl ester)

Isovaleric acid (Baldrianic acid; Isopropyl-acetic acid; $\beta(3)$-Methyl-butyric acid; Viburnum acid; $CH_3.CH(CH_3).CH_2.COOH$) is said to occur in depot-fats of porpoise and dolphin; in conifers; and (free, and/or as esters) in

    Mor. *Humulus lupulus* (hop-oil)

    Ros. *Malus, Prunus persica*

    Gerani. *Pelargonium* sp. (ess. oil)

    Euphorbi. *Croton tiglium* (oil, as glyceride?)

    Rut. *Ruta* spp.

    Sterculi. *Theobroma cacao* (oil)

    Myrt. *Eucalyptus* (oil), *Melaleuca leucadendron* (oil)

    Umbell. *Angelica, Levisticum officinale* (oil)

    Asclepiad. *Calotropis* (resin)

    Verben. *Lippia citriodora* (ess. oil)

    Lab. *Mentha piperita* (ess. oil), *Rosmarinus officinalis* (oil)

    Caprifoli. *Viburnum opulus* (bk, frt)

    Valerian. *Valeriana officinalis* (rt)

    Comp. *Achillea millefolium, Artemisia absinthium* (oil)

    Mus. *Musa sapientum* (frt)

Lasiocarpic acid ($?CH_3.CH(OCH_3).C(OH)(C(OH)(CH_3)_2).COOH$) is one of the two *necic acids* of *lasiocarpine.*

α-(2)-Methyl-butyric acid (Methyl-ethyl-acetic acid; $CH_3.CH_2.CH(CH_3).COOH$) is, as the *d*-(−)-form, a constituent of at least 14 *steroid alkaloids.*

    Magnoli. *Michelia champaca* (fl., free and as ester), *longifolia* (fl., free and as ester)

    Umbell. *Angelica archangelica* (rt, frt; oils), *Heracleum* sp. (frt, as ester), *Seseli bocconi* (ess. oil)

    Convolvul. *Ipomoea* spp. (secondary?)

    Lab. *Lavandula* (oil, *d*-)

(+)-α-Methyl-α,β-dihydroxy-butyric acid is a constituent of at least 4 *steroid alkaloids.*

(+)-α-Methyl-α-hydroxy-butyric acid: a constituent of at least 4 *steroid alkaloids?*

α-Methyl-β-hydroxy-butyric acid (?Nilic acid; $CH_3.CH(OH).CH(CH_3).COOH$)

    Convolvul. *Pharbitis nil* (in *pharbitin*)

β-Methyl-α-hydroxy-butyric acid

    Valerian. *Valeriana officinalis* (rt, as ester with *isovaleric acid*)

$\beta(3)$-Methyl-valeric acid (Methyl-ethyl-propionic acid;
$\quad$ $CH_3.CH_2.CH(CH_3).CH_2.COOH)$
$\qquad$ *Solan.* *Nicotiana tabacum* (lvs)
Trachelanthic acid $(CH_3.CH(OH).C(OH)(CH.(CH_3)_2).COOH)$ is the
necic acid of *trachelanthamine.*
Viridifloric acid is a diastereoisomer of *trachelanthic acid.* It is the
necic acid of *viridiflorine.*

I.3 Unsaturated monocarboxylic acids

List and Occurrence

cis-n-But-2-enoic acid (Isocrotonic acid)
$\qquad$ *Crucif.* *Brassica oleracea* var. (Kohlrabi)
trans-n-But-2-enoic acid (Crotonic acid; $CH_3.CH{=}CH.COOH)$
occurs in bacteria and in
$\qquad$ *Euphorbi.* *Croton tiglium* (sd-oil, doubtful)
$\qquad$ *Solan.* *Nicotiana* (ess. oil of fermented lvs)
n-Hex-2-enoic acid
$\qquad$ *Lab.* *Mentha piperita* (ess. oil, as ester)
2-Methyl-but-2(*cis*)-enoic acid (Angelic acid;
$\quad$ $CH_3.CH{=}C(CH_3).COOH)$ occurs in some *steroid ester-alkaloids*
(*cevadine, escholerine, germinitrine*) and in
$\qquad$ *Euphorbi.* *Croton campestris, humilis*
$\qquad$ *Umbell.* *Angelica archangelica* (rt), *Ferula sumbul* (rt), *Lomatium*
$\qquad\quad$ (*Cynomarathrum*) *nuttallii*
$\qquad$ *Comp.* *Anthemis nobilis* (as esters), *Euryops floribundus* (st., resin;
$\qquad\quad$ free and combined)
2-Methyl-but-2(*trans*)-enoic acid (α-Methyl-crotonic acid; Tiglic acid)
occurs in some *steroid ester-alkaloids* (*germanitrine, germinitrine*).
$\qquad$ *Illici.* *Illicium* (oil)
$\qquad$ *Gerani.* *Pelargonium* spp. (as *geranyl ester*)
$\qquad$ *Euphorbi.* *Croton tiglium* (sd)
$\qquad$ *Umbell.* *Ferula sumbul* (rt)
$\qquad$ *Lab.* *Lavandula* (oil)
$\qquad$ *Comp.* *Anthemis nobilis* (oil, as ester), *Euryops floribundus* (st.,
$\qquad\quad$ bound)
3-Methyl-but-2-enoic acid (Dimethyl-acrylic acid; Senecioic acid) is
said to be important in the biosynthesis of *terpenes.*
$\qquad$ *Euphorbi.* *Omphalea diandra* (frt-oil)
$\qquad$ *Umbell.* *Peucedanum ostruthium* (rt, as ester)
$\qquad$ *Comp.* *Senecio kaempferi* (rhiz.), *mikanoides*

4-Methyl-pent-2-enoic acid (3-Isopropyl-acrylic acid;
  $CH_3.CH(CH_3).CH=CH.COOH$)
  Mor.   Humulus lupulus
4-Methyl-pent-3-enoic acid
  Asclepiad.   Calotropis procera (latex, as *ester* with α-*lactucerol*)
2-Methyl-prop-2-enoic acid (2-Methyl-acrylic acid)
  Comp.   Anthemis nobilis (oil)
Prop-2-enoic acid (Acrylic acid; $CH_2=CH.COOH$) may not occur free.
  See *petasolesters* and *petasitolides*.
  Sarraceni.   Sarracenia purpurea (lvs, rt)
  Bromeli.   Ananas?
Sarracenic acid (probably $CH_3.C(OH)(CH=CH_2).COOH$) is the
  necic acid of *sarracine*.

II ALIPHATIC DICARBOXYLIC ACIDS

GENERAL

As in the case of the *monocarboxylic acids* (above) we may distinguish a
series of normal acids which we may call the *oxalic acid series* (1).These have
the general formula $HOOC.(CH_2)_n.COOH$ ($n = 0$ for *oxalic acid* itself).
We have lumped other *dicarboxylic acids* together (2).

II.1 Oxalic acid series

List and Occurrence

Oxalic acid ($HOOC.COOH$) occurs very frequently as calcium salts:
  see *raphides* and *calcium oxalate*. I have a few specific records of the
  free (?) acid:
    Polygon.   Rumex acetosa
    Chenopodi.   Beta vulgaris (lvs), *Halogeton glomeratus*, *Spinacia
      oleracea* (lvs)
    Oxalid.   Oxalis acetosella
Malonic acid ($HOOC.CH_2.COOH$)
    Crucif.   Bunias orientalis
    Legum.   Bentley (1952) recorded it in at least 18 legumes including:
      *Anthyllis, Astragalus, Colutea, Lotus, Lupinus, Medicago, Meli-
      lotus, Ononis, Phaseolus coccineus, Sophora, Thermopsis, Trifolium,
      Trigonella.* He did *not* find it in: *Cassia, Cercis, Gleditsia, Hedy-
      sarum, Lathyrus, Mimosa, Onobrychis, Piptanthus*
    Umbell.   Anthriscus, Apium

Comp. Helianthus annuus (little)
Stemon. Stemona tuberosa (rt)
Gram. Avena sativa (plt), *Hordeum sativum* (plt), *Triticum sativum* (plt)

Succinic acid ($HOOC.(CH_2)_2.COOH$) is probably of general occurrence. It is said to have been found in about 30 families of higher plants, but I have only the following records:

Crassul. Sedum
Ros. Pyrus
Legum. Phaseolus coccineus
Gerani. Erodium
Vit. Vitis
Malv. Gossypium
Solan. Atropa belladonna
Comp. Artemisia, Helianthus annuus
Gram. Saccharum

Glutaric acid ($HOOC.(CH_2)_3.COOH$)
Chenopodi. Beta

Adipic acid ($HOOC.(CH_2)_4.COOH$)
Chenopodi. Beta

Pimelic acid ($HOOC.(CH_2)_5.COOH$): has not been recorded from higher plants?

Suberic acid ($HOOC.(CH_2)_6.COOH$) has been obtained from cork.

Azelaic acid ($HOOC.(CH_2)_7.COOH$)
Comp. Chrysanthemum cinerariaefolium (fl., tr.)

Sebacic acid ($HOOC.(CH_2)_8.COOH$) has been obtained from:
Convolvul. Ipomoea jalapa (resin?)

Tetradecamethylene-dicarboxylic acid (Thapsia-acid; $HOOC.(CH_2)_{14}.COOH$)
Umbell. Thapsia garganica (rt, resin)
Scrophulari. Verbascum thapsus (fl.)

Heptadecamethylene-dicarboxylic acid ($HOOC.(CH_2)_{17}.COOH$)
Anacardi. Rhus succedanea ('wax'? Not confirmed)

Octadecamethylene-dicarboxylic acid ($HOOC.(CH_2)_{18}.COOH$)
Anacardi. Rhus succedanea (sd, 'wax'), *vernicifera* (latex, 'wax')

Nonadecamethylene-dicarboxylic acid ($HOOC.(CH_2)_{19}.COOH$)
Anacardi. Rhus succedanea (sd, 'wax')

Eicosamethylene-dicarboxylic-acid (?Phellogenic acid; $HOOC.(CH_2)_{20}.COOH$) has been obtained from cork.
Anacardi. Rhus succedanea (sd, 'wax'), *trichocarpa* (sd, 'wax'), *vernicifera* (frt)

Heneicosamethylene-dicarboxylic acid ($HOOC.(CH_2)_{21}.COOH$)
Anacardi. Rhus silvestris (frt), *toxicodendron* (frt)

II.2 Other Dicarboxylic Acids

List and Occurrence

Citramalic acid (α-Methyl-malic acid)
> *Ros.*   *Malus* (apple-peel)

Dicrotalic acid (β-Hydroxy-β-methyl-glutaric acid;
$HOOC.CH_2.C(OH)(CH_3).CH_2.COOH$)
> *Legum.*   occurs in *dicrotaline*.
> *Lin.*   *Linum usitatissimum* (sd, as a glycoside)

Dihydroxy-maleic acid
> *Papaver.*   *Glaucium luteum* (plt)

β-Ethyl-malic acid ($HOOC.CH(OH).CH(C_2H_5).COOH$)
> *Euphorbi.*   *Euphorbia biglandulosa* (latex)

Fumaric acid (*trans*-$HOOC.CH{=}CH.COOH$) is probably of general
occurrence. It has been recorded from fungi, conifers, and:
> *Papaver.*   *Corydalis, Dicentra, Fumaria officinalis, Glaucium luteum*
> *Crucif.*   *Capsella bursa-pastoris*
> *Legum.*   *Phaseolus coccineus* (lvs)
> *Euphorbi.*   *Ricinus communis* (sdlg)
> *Acer.*   *Acer*
> *Umbell.*   *Angelica* (rt), *Myrrhis odorata*
> *Rubi.*   *Oldenlandia*
> *Comp.*   *Arnica* (rt), *Carduus marianus* (lvs), *Helianthus annuus* (lvs),
> *Senecio, Silybum*

3-Hydroxy-2,3,4-trimethyl-glutaric acid is a *necic acid* which occurs in
two forms—*crispatic acid* (in *crispatine*) and *fulvinic acid* (in *fulvine*
and *fulvine-N-oxide*).

Integerrinecic acid
($HOOC.C({=}CH.CH_3).CH_2.CH(CH_3).C(OH)(CH_3).COOH$)
appears to be terpenoid. It is the *necic acid* of *integerrimine*.

Isatinecic acid
($HOOC.C({=}CH.CH_3).CH_2.CH(CH_3).C(OH)(CH_2OH).COOH$)
is the *necic acid* of *retrorsine* and *retrorsine-N-oxide*.

Jaconecic acid is the *necic acid* of *jacobine, jacosine,* and *tomentosine*.

α-Ketoadipic acid
> *Legum.*   *Pisum sativum* (sdlg)

α-Ketoglutaric acid ($HOOC.CH_2.CH_2.CO.COOH$) has been found in
ferns and in
> *Crassul.*   *Kalanchoë daigremontiana* (lvs)
> *Legum.*   *Arachis* (sdlg), *Medicago, Pisum, Trifolium*
> *Euphorbi.*   *Ricinus communis* (sdlg)
> *Umbell.*   *Daucus carota*

    Lab.   *Mentha piperita*
    Solan.   *Solanum tuberosum*
    Lili.   *Tulipa gesneriana* (bulb)
d-(+)-Malic acid ($HOOC.CH(OH).CH_2.COOH$)
    Malv.   *Hibiscus sabdariffa* (lvs, st., frt)
l-(−)-Malic acid is frequent in fruits, but also occurs widely in other organs.
    Polygon.   *Rumex* (st.)
    Chenopodi.   *Beta*
    Crassul.   *Bryophyllum, Sedum, Sempervivum*
    Saxifrag.   *Ribes* spp. (frt)
    Ros.   *Prunus* spp., *Rubus* spp., *Sorbus aucuparia* (frts)
    Legum.   in at least 27 species (Bentley, 1952)
    Euphorbi.   *Ricinus communis* (sdlg)
    Anacardi.   *Rhus coriaria*
    Acer.   *Acer saccharum*
    Vit.   *Vitis vinifera* (frt)
    Elaeagn.   *Hippophaë rhamnoides* (frt)
    Eric.   *Vaccinium myrtillus* (frt)
    Ole.   *Fraxinus* (lvs)
    Solan.   *Capsicum, Lycopersicum* (frt), *Nicotiana tabacum* (lvs), *Solanum tuberosum*
    Caprifoli.   *Sambucus nigra* (frt)
    Comp.   *Helianthus annuus*
    Bromeli.   *Ananas sativus* (frt)
    Mus.   *Musa sapientum* (frt)
Mesaconic acid (Methyl-fumaric acid; $HOOC.CH=CH(CH_3).COOH$)
    Crucif.   *Brassica oleracea* (lvs)
Mesoxalic acid (Dihydroxy-malonic acid;
  $HOOC.C(OH)(OH).COOH$)
    Chenopodi.   *Beta vulgaris* var. *rapa*
    Legum.   *Medicago sativa*
γ-Methylene-α-ketoglutaric acid ($HOOC.C(=CH_2).CH_2.CO.COOH$)
    Legum.   *Arachis hypogaea* (sdlg)
    Lili.   *Tulipa gesneriana* (lvs)
Mikanecic acid.
  (?$HOOC.C(=CH.CH_3).CH=C(CH_3).C(=CH_2).COOH$) is a *necic acid.*
Mucic acid ($HOOC.(CHOH)_4.COOH$) is said to occur in algae and in
    Ros.   *Prunus armeniaca* (frt)?, *persica* (frt); *Rubus fructicosus* (frt)?
    Elaeocarp.   *Elaeocarpus serratus* (frt)
Oxalacetic acid ($HOOC.CH_2.CO.COOH$)
    Legum.   *Pisum, Trifolium pratense, Vicia faba*

Umbell. *Daucus carota*
Lili. *Tulipa gesneriana* (bulb)
Gram. *Avena sativa, Phleum pratense*
Pedicellic acid (2-Methyl-3-tridecyl-succinic acid)
Gesneri. *Didymocarpus pedicellata* (lvs)
Platynecic acid is a *necic acid* reported from *platyphylline*. It may be *senecic acid*.
Retronecic acid
$(HOOC.C(=CH.CH_3).CH_2.CH(CH_3).C(OH)(CH_2OH).COOH)$
is a *necic acid*.
Riddellic acid
$(HOOC.C(=CH.CH_3).CH=C(CH_3).C(OH)(CH_2OH).COOH)$
is the *necic acid* of *riddelline*.
d-Saccharic acid $(HOOC.(CHOH)_4.COOH)$
Mor. *Ficus elastica* (latex, as Mg-salt)
Senecic acid (?Platynecic acid;
$HOOC.C(=CH.CH_3).CH_2.CH(CH_3)C(OH)(CH_3).COOH)$ is the *necic acid* of *rosmarinine, senecionine,* and (?) *senkirkine* and *platyphylline*.
Seneciphyllic acid (α-Longinecic acid;
$?HOOC.C(=CH.CH_3).CH=C(CH_3).C(OH)(CH_3).COOH)$ is the *necic acid* of *seneciphylline*.
d-(+)-Tartaric acid $(HOOC.(CHOH)_2.COOH)$ occurs in part as Ca and K salts.
Chenopodi. *Beta*
Saxifrag. *Ribes* spp.
Ros. *Cydonia vulgaris; Eriobotrya japonica; Prunus armeniaca, mahaleb; Sorbus aucuparia*
Legum. *Tamarindus indica* (frt)
Acer. *Acer saccharum*
Comp. *Tanacetum vulgare, Taraxacum officinale, Tussilago farfara* (plt)
l-(−)-Tartaric acid
Legum. *Bauhinia reticulata* (lvs, frt)
dl-Tartaric acid
Vit. *Vitis vinifera*

III ALIPHATIC TRICARBOXYLIC ACIDS

GENERAL

These are few in number but may be important in metabolism (see note under *isocitric acid*).

List and Occurrence

Aconitic acid (1,2,3-Propene-tricarboxylic acid;

   HOOC.CH$_2$.C(COOH)=CH.COOH) is reported from *Equisetum* and from

   Chenopodi. *Beta*
   Ranuncul. *Aconitum, Adonis, Delphinium*
   Gerani. *Pelargonium peltatum* (lvs)
   Rhamn. *Helinus ovatus* (lvs, 1·9%)
   Comp. *Achillea millefolium* (not confirmed)
   Agav. *Sansevieria*
   Gram. many

Citric acid (HOOC.CH$_2$.C(OH)(COOH).CH$_2$.COOH) is probably of universal or nearly universal distribution. It has been found in seaweeds, in ferns, and in the fruits of many plants. My records include the following:

   Fag. *Fagus sylvatica* (bk)
   Chenopodi. *Beta* (rt), *Spinacia* (lvs)
   Papaver. *Chelidonium majus* (lvs)
   Crassul. *Bryophyllum, Sedum*
   Ros. *Malus* (bk)
   Rut. *Citrus*
   Malv. *Hibiscus sabdariffa* (lvs, fl.; much)
   Umbell. *Angelica* (rt)
   Rubi. *Cephaëlis* (rt)
   Solan. *Nicotiana tabacum* (lvs)
   Scrophulari. *Digitalis purpurea* (lvs)
   Plantagin. *Plantago* (lvs)
   Comp. *Kleinia* spp., *Tanacetum vulgare* (lvs)
   Bromeli. *Ananas sativus* (frt, as dimethyl ester)

Hydroxy-citric acid (HOOC.CH$_2$.C(OH)(COOH).CH(OH).COOH)

   Chenopodi. *Beta*

Isocitric acid (HOOC.CH$_2$.CH(COOH).CH(OH).COOH) has been studied by Soderstrom (1962). He says it 'is probably present in traces in the tissues of most higher plants where it acts as a non-accumulating intermediate acid in the normal respiratory pathway... a block in the isocitric acid system apparently has become established genetically in widely unrelated plants. For example it seems to be characteristic of the whole family Crassulaceae, but only in some genera of the Piperaceae and Liliaceae.'

My records show the following:

Present in:
   Piper. *Peperomia*

    Crassul. in almost all (see above)
    Ros. Rubus caesius (*d*-, *dl*-, and *l*-), *fruticosus* (frt)
    Lecythid. Couroupita guianensis (frt, little)
    Solan. Solanum tuberosum (trace)
    Scrophulari. Digitalis purpurea
    Lili. Aloë, Gasteria
Absent from: *Cact.* (*Opuntia, Zygocactus*); *Piper.* (*Piper*); *Euphorbi.*
    (*Euphorbia*); *Begoni.* (*Begonia*); *Asclepiad.* (*Huernia*); *Comp.*
    (*Senecio*); *Agav.* (*Agave, Sansevieria*)
Phorbic acid
    ($CH_2(COOH).CH_2.C(OH)(COOH).CH_2.CH(OH).COOH$) is un-
    stable, forming a *dilactone* (*dilactophorbic acid*).
    Euphorbi. Euphorbia spp.
Tricarballylic acid ($HOOC.CH_2.CH(COOH).CH_2.COOH$)
    Chenopodi. Beta (as amide or imide?)
    Acer. Acer saccharum
    Gram. Hordeum sativum, Zea mays

IV AROMATIC CARBOXYLIC ACIDS (including most phenolic acids, but excluding those of the *Anacardiaceae*, etc.)

GENERAL

Again we face dilemmas. Many of the acids listed here occur principally (or only?) as *esters* and/or *glycosides*. Should these be included at this point or should we deal with them in separate sections? We have followed the latter course. A second decision which we have had to make is whether or not to use trivial names—*caffeic acid* for 3,4-*dihydroxycinnamic acid*, for example. We have decided in favour of trivial names in most cases because they are so commonly employed in the chemotaxonomic literature.

The treatment here is necessarily very uneven. It is quite impossible to deal with all the recent work on 'phenolics'. We have, however, taken into consideration the extensive papers by Bate-Smith (1958, 1962, 1968); a review edited by Ollis (1960); papers by Ibrahim and Towers (1960), and by Ibrahim, Towers and Gibbs (1962); and many other contributions to the subject, some of which are cited in the following pages.

Almost all the acids discussed in this section are *monocarboxylic*, but a very few *di-* and *tricarboxylic* acids are included.

The *Anacardiaceae* and a few other plants have some remarkable phenolics (including some acids) which are dealt with elsewhere.

List and Occurrence

Benzoic acid (fig. 93) occurs free and/or as *esters* and/or *glycosides* in
many plants. I have the following records:

    Annon. *Cananga odorata*
    Laur. *Aniba firmula, Cinnamomum*
    Legum. *Myroxylon*
    Myrt. *Eugenia*
    Eric. *Gaultheria, Vaccinium vitis-idaea*
    Globulari. *Globularia*
    Xanthorrhoe. *Xanthorrhoea*

Caffeic acid (3,4-Dihydroxy-cinnamic acid) occurs free or combined.
Bate-Smith and Swain (1965) say: 'The commonest phenolic compound found in the angiosperms is caffeic acid...which was found
to be present in over half of the monocotyledons and over two-thirds of the dicotyledons examined in our laboratory.' See under
individual families and orders for distribution.

Chavicinic acid is an isomer of *piperic acid*. It is part of the alkaloid
chavicine.

trans-Cinnamic acid (fig. 93) occurs free (?) and as esters in resins and
balsams. Records are often unclear. I have:

    Salic. *Populus*
    Mor. *Antiaris*
    Laur. *Cinnamomum* (2)
    Hamamelid. *Liquidambar*
    Legum. ?
    Rut. *Zanthoxylum*
    Myrt. *Eucalyptus, Melaleuca*
    Eric. *Enkianthus*
    Lab. *Scutellaria*
    Globulari. *Globularia*
    Comp. *Parthenium*
    Lili. *Aloë, Lilium*
    Xanthorrhoe. *Xanthorrhoea*
    Zingiber. *Alpinia, Kaempferia*

cis-Cinnamic acid
    Erythroxyl. *Erythroxylon coca* (lvs)

o-Coumaric acid (*trans-o*(2)-Hydroxy-cinnamic acid) seems to be rare.
I have the following records (free or combined):

    Casuarin. *Casuarina*
    Betul. *Betula*
    Ros. *Prunus*
    Legum. *Melilotus* (free, as *ester*, and as *glycoside*)

Gram.   *Hierochloë odorata*
Orchid.   *Angraecum fragrans* (as ester)
It is said to be *absent* from: Salic. (*Populus*); Polygon. (*Polygonum*);
Ros. (*Malus, Pyrus*); Eric. (*Gaultheria*); Primul. (*Primula*); Apocyn.
(*Vinca*); Lili. (*Gloriosa*)

p-Coumaric acid (trans-*p*(4)-Hydroxy-cinnamic acid; fig. 93) is one of
the acids recorded in leaf-hydrolysates of many plants by Bate-Smith.
It seems to be almost as common in the *hydrolysates* as *caffeic acid*.
See individual families and orders for discussions.

Coumarinic acid (*cis-o*(2)-Hydroxy-cinnamic acid) cyclizes to *coumarin*, so
it is not known in the free state.

Dehydro-digallic acid
Fag.   *Castanea sativa* (lvs, etc.)

Dihydro-caffeic acid (3,4-Dihydroxy-dihydrocinnamic acid) is said to
occur in *Lycopodium* and
Chenopodi.   *Beta* (old lvs)
Vit.   *Ampelopsis hederacea* (old lvs)

Eudesmic acid (3,4,5-Trimethoxy-benzoic acid)
Ros.   *Prunus serotina*
Myrt.   *Eucalyptus aggregata* (ess. oil)
Apocyn.   *Rauwolfia vomitoria* (as *alkaloid ester*)

Ferulic acid (4-Hydroxy-3-methoxy-cinnamic acid; fig. 93) is said
to be used by *Elodea* in the synthesis of *lignin* (Siegel, 1954).
It seems only rarely to occur free. It is one of the acids recorded by
Bate-Smith (1962, 1968) in leaf-hydrolysates, in which, although
somewhat less common than *caffeic* and *p-coumaric acids*, it is
still very widely distributed. See families and orders for further
discussion.

Gallic acid (3,4,5-Trihydroxy-benzoic acid; fig. 93) is said to arise in
at least 2 ways. It occurs free and as *glycosides* in a vast number of
plants, but is by no means universal. Within the *Saxifragaceae* (*s.l.*),
for example, it is said to occur in *Astilbe, Bergenia* and *Rodgersia*; but
not in *Deutzia, Escallonia, Heuchera, Philadelphus* and *Ribes*.

Gentisic acid (2,5-Dihydroxy-benzoic acid; Hydroquinone-carboxylic
acid; fig. 93) is said to occur only (?) in combination. Griffiths (1958)
reported it to be present in 73 out of 80 families studied. In 1958 and
1959 he found it to be *absent* from or present in low amount in
monocotyledons and in many of Hutchinson's 'Herbaceae'. I have
records of it from at least 75 families of dicotyledons and 7 families of
monocotyledons.

See families and orders for further discussions.

Hemipinic acid (2,3-Dimethoxy-phthalic acid; fig. 93)
Papaver.   *Papaver somniferum*

Homogentisic acid
>   *Legum.   Lupinus albus* (sdlg)

p-(4)-Hydroxy-benzoic acid (Catalp(in)ic acid; fig. 93) is one of the acids recorded in leaf-hydrolysates. Does it occur free at all frequently? I have records of it (combined?) from at least 77 families of dicotyledons and a few families of monocotyledons. See families and orders for further discussions.

2-Hydroxy-4-methoxy-benzoic acid seems to be of limited distribution. It is said to occur in
>   *Primul.   Primula veris* (after hyd.)
>   *Lili.   Gloriosa*

It was *not* found in: *Salic. (Populus); Betul. (Betula); Polygon. (Polygonum); Ros. (Malus, Pyrus); Eric. (Gaultheria); Apocyn. (Vinca)*

2-Hydroxy-5-methoxy-benzoic acid seems also to be rare.
>   *Primul.   Primula veris* (after hyd.)

It was *not* found in: *Salic. (Populus); Betul. (Betula); Polygon. (Polygonum); Ros. (Malus, Pyrus); Eric. (Gaultheria); Apocyn. (Vinca); Lili. (Gloriosa)*

3-Hydroxy-5-methoxy-benzoic acid has not, I think, been found in higher plants. It was *not* detected in: *Salic. (Populus); Betul. (Betula); Polygon. (Polygonum); Ros. (Malus, Pyrus); Eric. (Gaultheria); Primul. (Primula); Apocyn. (Vinca); Lili. (Gloriosa)*

2-Hydroxy-6-methoxy-benzoic acid seems to be rare.
>   *Lili.   Colchicum autumnale, speciosum* (bulb); *Gloriosa superba*
>   (bulb): but *not* found by Ibrahim and Towers.

It was *not* found in: *Salic. (Populus); Betul. (Betula); Polygon. (Polygonum); Ros. (Malus, Pyrus); Eric. (Gaultheria); Primul. (Primula); Apocyn. (Vinca)*

2-Hydroxy-6-methyl-benzoic acid (6-Methyl-salicylic acid) has been obtained from *Penicillium* and:
>   *Hydrophyll.   Eriodictyon angustifolium*

o-(2)-Hydroxy-phenylacetic acid has been found in fungi and:
>   *Saxifrag.   Astilbe*

Billek and Kindl (1962) say: 'Die Gattung *Astilbe*...unterscheidet sich von den anderen Gattungen der *Saxifragaceae* durch das Auftreten der 2-Hydroxy-phenyl-essigsäure.'

p-(4)-Hydroxy-phenylacetic acid
>   *Saxifrag.   Astilbe, Bergenia, Deutzia, Escallonia, Heuchera, Hydrangea, Philadelphus, Ribes, Rodgersia*
>   *Comp.   Taraxacum officinale* (rt)

Isochavic(in)ic acid is a stereoisomer of *piperic acid.*
>   *Piper.   Piper nigrum* (frt)

Isoferulic acid (Hesperet(in)ic acid; 3-Hydroxy-4-methoxy-cinnamic acid)

> *Ranuncul. Cimicifuga racemosa* (rhiz.)
> *Bignoni. Catalpa ovata* (stbk, rtbk)

Isovanillic acid (3-Hydroxy-4-methoxy-benzoic acid)

> *Saxifrag. Hydrangea* (in 1 sp. only?)

Mandelic acid (Phenyl-glycollic acid) occurs as its *nitrile* in some *cyanogenic glycosides.*

Melilotic acid (*o*(2)-Hydroxy-dihydrocinnamic acid; Dihydro-*o*-coumaric acid) occurs free, as *esters,* and as *glycoside(s)*. Siegel (1954) says it may be used as a precursor of *lignin* by *Elodea.* It seems to be rather rare:

> *Legum. Melilotus caspicus (glycoside), officinalis (ester)*
> *Solan. Nicotiana tabacum* (free?)
> *Gram. Hierochloë odorata*
> *Orchid. Angraecum fragrans* (free and as *ester*)

It was *not* found in: *Salic. (Populus)*; *Betul. (Betula)*; *Polygon. (Polygonum)*; *Ros. (Malus, Pyrus)*; *Eric. (Gaultheria)*; *Primul. (Primula)*; *Apocyn. (Vinca)*; *Lili. (Gloriosa)*

Metahemipinic acid (3,4-Dimethoxy-phthalic acid)

> *Papaver. Papaver somniferum*

o-(2)-Methoxy-benzoic acid

> *Lili. Hyacinthus* (as *ester?*)

p-(4)-Methoxy-benzoic acid (Anisic acid; Umbellinic acid) occurs in fungi. It is found (secondarily by oxidation?) in essential oils.

> *Rut. Ruta montana* (oil)
> *Cist. Cistus ladaniferus* (gum)
> *Comp. Euryops floribundus* (st., free and combined).

p-(4)-Methoxy-cinnamic acid occurs chiefly (always?) as *esters.*

> *Eric. Leucothoë grayana* (lvs)
> *Scrophulari. Veronicastrum virginicum* (rhiz., *ester*)
> *Lili. Aloë* (as *ethyl ester?*)
> *Gram. Andropogon odoratus* (plt; ess. oil)
> *Zingiber. Curcuma aromatica* (rtsk; *ester?*), *Hedychium spicatum* (rhiz., *ethyl ester*), *Kaempferia galanga* (rt, *ethyl ester*)

3,4-Methylenedioxy-cinnamic acid

> Occurrence? It 'should' occur in *Piper*! The *amide* is *fagaramide.*

Phenyl-acetic acid

> *Ros. Rosa centifolia*
> *Rut. Citrus* (fl., ess. oil)
> *Solan. Nicotiana tabacum* (lvs)

β-Phenyl-propionic acid (Dihydro-cinnamic acid)

> *Legum. Cassia* (as *ester*)

Phloretic acid (*p*-(4)-Hydroxy-dihydrocinnamic acid)
> *Ros.* *Malus* (chief phenolic acid of apple lvs ?), *Pyrus*
> *Primul.* *Primula veris* (lvs, hyd.)
> *Lili.* *Gloriosa*
> *Gram.* *Triticum*
> It was *not* found in: *Salic.* (*Populus*); *Betul.* (*Betula*); *Polygon.* (*Polygonum*); *Eric.* (*Gaultheria*); *Primul.* (*Primula,* other than *veris*); *Apocyn.* (*Vinca*)

Phthalic acid (fig. 93)
> *Papaver.* *Papaver somniferum*

Piperettic acid (7-(3,4-Methylenedioxyphenyl)-hepta-2,4,6-trienoic acid) is part of the alkaloid *piperettine.*

Piperic acid (5-(3,4-Methylenedioxyphenyl)-penta-2,4-dienoic acid) is part of the alkaloid *piperine.*

Piperonylic acid (3,4-Methylenedioxy-benzoic acid)
> *Laur.* *Cinnamomum kanahirai* (ess. oil), *Ocotea pretiosa*
> *Piper.* *Piper longum* (frt)
> *Rut.* *Melicope simplex* (bk)

Piscidic acid (fig. 93) has a queer distribution.
> *Cact.* *Opuntia ficus-indica*
> *Legum.* *Piscidia erythrina* (rtbk)
> *Agav.* *Agave americana*
> *Amaryllid.* *Narcissus poeticus* (bulb)

Protocatechuic acid (3,4-Dihydroxy-benzoic acid; fig. 93) is said to occur free and as *esters.* It seems to be quite widely distributed.
> *Casuarin.* *Casuarina*
> *Salic.* *Populus*
> *Betul.* *Alnus, Betula*
> *Polygon.* *Polygonum*
> *Illici.* *Illicium religiosum* (frt, free)
> *Saxifrag.* *Astilbe, Bergenia, Deutzia, Escallonia, Heuchera, Hydrangea, Philadelphus, Ribes, Rodgersia*
> *Ros.* *Malus, Prunus lusitanica* (lvs), *Pyrus calleryana* (lvs)
> *Legum.* *Pisum*
> *Euphorbi.* *Phyllanthus*
> *Vit.* *Vitis*
> *Malv.* *Althaea, Hibiscus sabdariffa* (fl., free), *Thespesia lampas* (fl., free)
> *Myrt.* *Eucalyptus*
> *Arali.* *Aralia*
> *Eric.* *Gaultheria*
> *Primul.* *Primula*
> *Apocyn.* *Vinca*

Verben. *Vitex negundo* (lvs)
Globulari. *Globularia*
Lili. *Allium, Gloriosa*

o-Pyrocatechuic acid (2,3-Dihydroxy-benzoic acid) seems to be rare.
Salic. *Populus balsamifera* (buds)
Eric. *Arctostaphylos, Erica, Gaultheria, Pentapterygium, Rhododendron*

α-Resorcylic acid (3,5-Dihydroxy-benzoic acid): rare?
Primul. *Primula veris* (lvs, hyd.)
It was *not* found in: *Salic.* (*Populus*); *Betul.* (*Betula*); *Polygon.* (*Polygonum*); *Ros.* (*Malus, Pyrus*); *Eric* (*Gaultheria*); *Apocyn.* (*Vinca*); *Lili.* (*Gloriosa*)

β-Resorcylic acid (2,4-Dihydroxy-benzoic acid): rare?
Lili. *Gloriosa superba* (lvs, hyd.)
It was *not* found in: *Salic.* (*Populus*); *Betul.* (*Betula*); *Polygon.* (*Polygonum*); *Ros.* (*Malus, Pyrus*); *Eric.* (*Gaultheria*); *Primul.* (*Primula*); *Apocyn.* (*Vinca*)

γ-Resorcylic acid (2,6-Dihydroxy-benzoic acid): not yet found in higher plants?
It was *not* found in: *Salic.* (*Populus*); *Betul.* (*Betula*); *Polygon.* (*Polygonum*); *Ros.* (*Malus, Pyrus*); *Eric.* (*Gaultheria*); *Primul.* (*Primula*); *Apocyn.* (*Vinca*); *Lili.* (*Gloriosa*)

Salicylic acid (*o*-(2)-Hydroxy-benzoic acid; fig. 93) occurs most often as *methyl salicylate* (which see for distribution). The following records may include some occurrences as esters.
Salic. *Populus, salix*
Betul. *Betula* (some spp. have *methyl s.*)
Ros. *Spiraea*
Euphorbi. *Ophthalmoblapton macrophyllum* (free?)
Polygal. *Polygala senega* (rt)
Viol. *Viola* spp.
Eric. *Arctostaphylos, Gaultheria procumbens* (free?, and as *methyl salicylate*)
Primul. *Primula*
Lili. occurrence?

Sinapic acid (4-Hydroxy-3,5-dimethoxy-cinnamic acid; fig. 93) is one of the *phenolic acids* recorded by Bate-Smith (1954, 1962, 1968) in leaf-hydrolysates. It is somewhat less common than *ferulic acid*, but is still widely spread. See families and orders for further discussions.

Syringic acid (4-Hydroxy-3,5-dimethoxy-benzoic acid; fig. 93) seems rarely to occur free. I have the following records (free and/or combined):
Salic. *Populus*

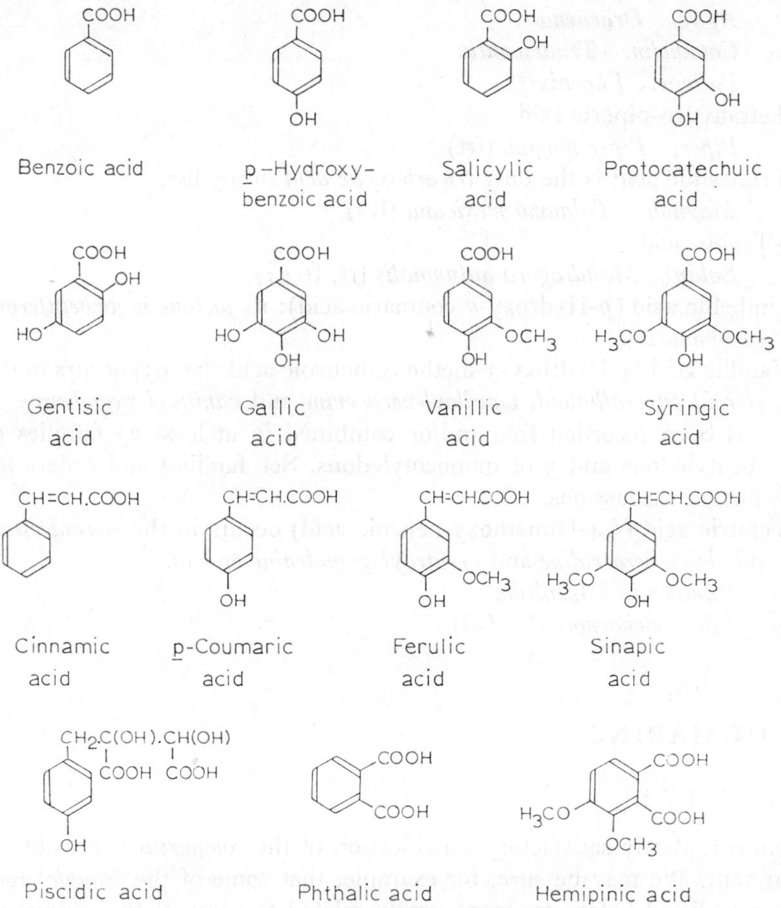

COOH

COOH

OH

COOH
OH

COOH
OH
OH

Benzoic acid

p–Hydroxy-benzoic acid

Salicylic acid

Protocatechuic acid

COOH
OH
HO

COOH
HO OH
OH

COOH
OCH$_3$
OH

COOH
H$_3$CO OCH$_3$
OH

Gentisic acid

Gallic acid

Vanillic acid

Syringic acid

CH=CH.COOH

CH=CH.COOH
OH

CH=CH.COOH
OCH$_3$
OH

CH=CH.COOH
H$_3$CO OCH$_3$
OH

Cinnamic acid

p-Coumaric acid

Ferulic acid

Sinapic acid

CH$_2$C(OH).CH(OH)
COOH COOH

OH

COOH
COOH

COOH
H$_3$CO COOH
OCH$_3$

Piscidic acid

Phthalic acid

Hemipinic acid

Fig. 93. Some aromatic carboxylic acids.

Betul. *Betula*
Saxifrag. in some genera: *absent* from others
Ros. *Malus, Pyrus*
Legum. *Acacia, Robinia pseudacacia* (bk, combined)
Euphorbi. *Phyllanthus*
Rhamn. *Rhamnus*
Eric. *Erica, Gaultheria*
Primul. *Primula*
Apocyn. *Vinca* (but *not* found by Ibrahim and Towers (1960))
Lab. *Mentha, Salvia*
Lili. *Gloriosa* (but Ibrahim and Towers (1960) did not find it),
  Tulipa

Agav. Dracaena
Commelin. Tradescantia
Palmae. Phoenix
Tetrahydro-piperic acid
    Piper. Piper longum (frt)
Trimesinic acid is the only *tricarboxylic acid* in my list.
    Magnoli. Talauma mexicana (lvs)
l-Tropic acid
    Solan. Mandragora autumnalis (rt, free ?)
Umbellic acid (*p*-Hydroxy-*o*-coumaric acid): its *lactone* is *umbelliferone* (a *coumarin*).
Vanillic acid (4-Hydroxy-3-methoxy-benzoic acid; fig. 93) occurs in the *steroid ester-alkaloids vanilloyl-veracevine* and *vanilloyl-zygadenine*. It has been recorded free and/or combined in at least 23 families of dicotyledons and 5 of monocotyledons. See families and orders for further discussions.
Veratric acid (3,4-Dimethoxy-benzoic acid) occurs in the *steroid ester-alkaloids veratridine* and *veratroyl-zygadenine* and in
    Ranuncul. Aconitum
    Lili. Schoenocaulon (sd)

COUMARINS

GENERAL

No completely satisfactory classification of the *coumarins* is possible at present. We may be sure, for example, that some of the 'simple' *coumarins* listed below are more nearly related to some of the coumarins with extra rings that are placed in other sections than they are to other members of the 'simple' group. For convenience we recognize here the following groups:

    I. 'Simple' Coumarins, of which we list nearly 70.
    II. 3,4-Furocoumarins: *glaupalol* only.
    III. 6,7-Furocoumarins (Psoralens): more than 30.
    IV. 7,8-Furocoumarins (Isopsoralens): more than 20.
    V. Chromano-coumarins: I have records of 12 or so.
    VI. Coumarono-coumarins seem to be rare.
    VII. 3,4-Benzocoumarins, including *ellagic acid* and its derivatives. Less than a dozen known.
    VIII. Iso-coumarins are few (6) in number.

That *coumarins* may be useful in chemotaxonomy will be clear from the following lists. In fact they have been used already by others. Thus Price (in Swain, 1963) says:

Further support for the view that the Rutaceae is a distinct and homogeneous group is provided by its essential oils and coumarins... Within the Rutaceae coumarins are distributed throughout the four subfamilies Aurantioideae, Rutoideae, Toddalioideae and Flindersioideae... On the other hand, though it is negative evidence, there is not one report of the isolation of a coumarin from the Meliaceae,[1] Burseraceae, Simarubaceae, Zygophyllaceae or Cneoraceae.

Fujita (1965) is said to have used *coumarins* in elucidating the taxonomy of *Angelica*. Unfortunately his work is in Japanese and has not been available to me.

We have not ourselves worked directly upon *coumarins* but have made some observations on their probable presence or absence by looking for bright fluorescence when performing the Juglone Test (p. 70).

Apparently *coumarins* are almost unknown in the animal kingdom. Dean (1952) says that Lederer has demonstrated the presence of 3,4-*benzocoumarins* in the scent gland of the beaver. In the plant kingdom, on the other hand, they are widely but by no means universally distributed.

The means by which *coumarins* arise have been discussed by several authors. Brown (1963) says that *Streptomyces* uses a different route from that 'chosen' by higher plants: 'At the moment we can most reasonably conclude that higher plants have evolved pathways for the synthesis of cis-2-glucosyloxycinnamic acids (and possibly free coumarins) by *ortho* hydroxylation of cinnamic acids, while *Streptomyces* has independently developed a route to a free coumarin by oxidative cyclization directly from tyrosine.'

According to Brown, Towers and Chen (1964) the route to *umbelliferone* in *Hydrangea macrophylla* is that shown in fig. 94.

Hendrickson (1965) says: 'The phenylpropane $[C_6C_3]$ skeleton is also probably the basis of most of the nearly one hundred known natural coumarins [our list is longer], which are apparently produced by oxidative cyclization of a cinnamic acid. The coumarins display an impressive selection of variants derived from alkylation as compounds [such as *scopoletin*, *xanthoxyletin*, *bergamotin*, *braylin*] will testify. The methyl and isopentenyl substituents are always found at aromatic sites consonant with the mechanism of enol alkylation.'

---

[1] One of my students, Mrs Sally Liau, tells me that some of the *Meliaceae* fluoresce strongly in 'Juglone Test C'. She finds spots on chromatograms that coincide with those for *scopoletin* and *umbelliferone*. See also p. 1675.

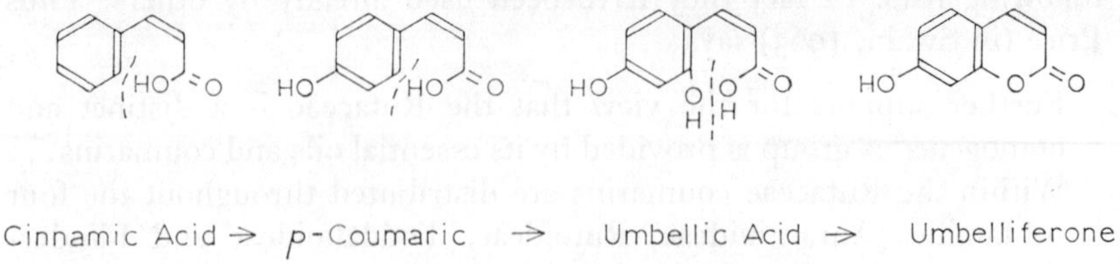

Cinnamic Acid → ρ-Coumaric → Umbellic Acid → Umbelliferone

Fig. 94. Synthesis of *umbelliferone* in *Hydrangea* (after Brown, Towers, and Chen).

I 'SIMPLE' COUMARINS

GENERAL

The *'simple' coumarins* included here are widely distributed but there are some curious restrictions, of which we may mention an example or two.

(*a*) The great family *Umbelliferae* (*Apiaceae*) is rich in these compounds. At least 13 occur and one or more of them has been found in at least 16 genera. The family, *Araliaceae*, on the other hand—which Cronquist (1968) says is generally admitted to be intimately related to the *Umbelliferae*, and which Thorne (1968) actually fuses with the *Umbelliferae* (as *Araliaceae*)—seems not to have a single 'simple' coumarin!

(*b*) The genus *Angelica*, of the *Umbelliferae*, has different simple coumarin combinations in different species:

A. *archangelica*   *archicin, osthol, osthenol, umbelliprenin*
A. *japonica* and *ursina*   *osthol*
A. *pubescens*   *angelicol, angelol*
A. *schishiudo*   *angelicone*
A. *ubatakensis*   *calcicolin*

List and Occurrence

Aculeatin is probably the epoxide corresponding to *toddalolactone* (*aculeatinhydrate*?).
    Rut.   Toddalia aculeata (rtbk)
Aesculetin (Cichorigenin; 6,7-Dihydroxy-coumarin; Esculetin; fig. 95) occurs more commonly as its glycoside *aesculin*.
    Euphorbi.   Euphorbia lathyris (sd.). Paris says *daphnetin* (rather than *aesculetin*?) is present.

Hippocastan. *Aesculus turbinata*
Ole. *Fraxinus*
Caprifoli. *Symphoricarpos occidentalis*
Aesculin (Aesculetin-6-β-glucoside; Bicolorin; Crataegin; Polychrom; Schillerstoff) occurs widely.
Ros. *Crataegus* (doubtful, says Paris)
Pittospor. *Bursaria spinosa* (lvs, 4–5% of dry wt)
Euphorbi. *Euphorbia lathyris* (but see *daphnetin*)
Hippocastan. *Aesculus* (2)
Ole. *Fraxinus ornus*
Logani. *Gelsemium*? (prob. not—see *scopolin*)
Caprifoli. *Symphoricarpos occidentalis* (st.)
Solan. *Brunfelsia hopeana* (and other spp. ?)
Ammoresinol (4,7-Dihydroxy-3-farnesyl-coumarin)
Umbell. *Dorema ammoniacum* (resin)
Angelical (fig. 95)
Umbell. *Angelica pubescens*
Angelicone
Umbell. *Angelica schishiudo*
Angelol
Umbell. *Angelica pubescens* (rt)
Archicin ($C_{15}H_{18}O_4$): belongs here?
Umbell. *Angelica archangelica* (rt)
Auraptene (1) is 7-*geranyloxy-coumarin*.
Rut. *Aegle marmelos* (rt), *Citrus* (orange and grapefruit peel-oil)
Auraptenol
Rut. *Citrus aurantium* subsp. *amara* (frt-oil?)
Ayapin (6,7-Methylenedioxy-coumarin)
Comp. *Eupatorium ayapana*
Orchid. *Dendrobium thyrsiflorum* (lvs, after hyd.)
Brayleyanin: of doubtful structure? See also *braylin.*
Rut. *Flindersia brayleyana*
Calcicolin
Umbell. *Angelica ubatakensis*
Cichoriin (Aesculetin-7-β-glucoside) is isomeric with *aesculin.*
Ole. *Fraxinus ornus* (lvs)
Comp. *Cichorium intybus* (fl.)
Cnidicin: belongs here?
Umbell. *Cnidium dubium* (sd)
Collinin (7-Geranoxy-8-methoxy-coumarin)
Rut. *Flindersia collina* (bk)

Coumarin (fig. 95) is apparently very widely distributed, though some of the reported occurrences may be of closely related substances. It is said to occur in ferns and in

Mor. *Ficus radicans*
Caryophyll. *Herniaria*
Magnoli. *Talauma*
Berberid. *Achlys*
Ceratophyll. *Ceratophyllum* (2?)
Cunoni. *Ceratopetalum* (1, bk)
Ros. *Prunus* (3)
Legum. *Dipteryx* (*Coumarouna*) and others
Rut. *Ruta*
Vit. *Vitis*
Umbell. *Laserpitium, Levisticum, Pastinaca, Petroselinum*
Sapot. *Chrysophyllum*
Apocyn. *Alyxia, Macrosiphonia*
Asclepiad. *Hemidesmus*
Acanth. *Peristrophe, Rhinacanthus*
Scrophulari. *Verbascum*
Lab. *Lavandula, Melittis*
Bignoni. *Stenolobium, Tabebuia*
Rubi. many
Comp. many
Palmae. *Phoenix*
Gram. several
Orchid. several

Daphnetin (7,8-Dihydroxy-coumarin) is the aglycone of *daphnin*.
Euphorbi. *Euphorbia lathyris* (sd)
Thymelae. mostly (always?) as the glycoside *daphnin*.

Daphnetin-glucoside is not identical with *daphnin* (Rindl, 1934).
Thymelae. *Arthrosolen* (*Gnidia*)

Daphnin (Daphnetin-7-glucoside): according to Dean (1952) newly opened leaf-buds of *Daphne odora* may have 27% (dry wt.) of *daphnin*!
Thymelae. *Arthrosolen*?, *Daphne* (6)

Dehydro-geijerin
Rut. *Geijera parviflora* (lvs)

7-Demethyl-2′,3′-dihydro-suberosine
Rut. *Evodia belahe* (bk)

7-Demethyl-suberosine
Rut. *Chloroxylon swietenia* (htwd)

Dichrin-B: belongs here?
Saxifrag. *Dichroa febrifuga* (rt)

Dicoumarol is said to be formed by bacterial action in improperly cured sweet-clover (*Melilotus*) hay. Does it ever occur normally in higher plants?

Dihydro-coumarin (Hydro-coumarin; Melilotic anhydride; Melilotol; Melilotin. (2); fig. 95)

 Legum. *Melilotus*

6,7-Dimethoxy-coumarin (Aesculetin-dimethyl ether; Scoparin (2); Scoparone)

 Rut. *Fagara*

 Comp. *Artemisia* (3)

 Orchid. *Dendrobium thyrsiflorum* (lvs, hyd.)

5,7-Dimethoxy-8-(3-methyl-2-oxobutyl)-coumarin

 Rut. *Severinia buxifolia* (lvs)

8-(Dimethylallyl)-7-hydroxy-6-methoxy-coumarin

 Meli. *Cedrelopsis grevei*

Fabiatrin (Scopoletin-7-primeveroside)

 Solan. *Fabiana imbricata* (lvs, st.)

Ferruol-A

 Gutt. *Mesua ferrea* (bk)

Fraxetin (6-Methoxy-7,8-dihydroxy-coumarin) is the aglycone of *fraxin.* It occurs (free?) in

 Hippocastan. *Aesculus*

 Ole. *Fraxinus*

Fraxidin (6,7-Dimethoxy-8-hydroxy-coumarin)

 Ole. *Fraxinus* (as glucoside)

Fraxin (Fraxetin-8-glucoside; Paviin)

 Hippocastan. *Aesculus pavia, turbinata*

 Ole. *Fraxinus* (bk of several spp.)

 Caprifoli. *Diervilla* (all spp.?)

Fraxinol (5,7-Dimethoxy-6-hydroxy-coumarin)

 Ole. *Fraxinus* spp. (as glucoside)

Geijerin

 Rut. *Geijera salicifolia* (bk)

Geijparvarin

 Rut. *Geijera parviflora* (lvs)

Herniarin (Ayapanin; 7-Methoxy-coumarin)

 Caryophyll. *Herniaria glabra, hirsuta*

 Ros. *Prunus* (Bate-Smith (1961) found it in the lvs of only 5 of more than 40 spp. tested)

 Rut. *Ruta montana*

 Lab. *Lavandula* (?'oil of lavender')

 Comp. *Artemisia dracunculus?, Eupatorium ayapana, Matricaria chamomilla*

7-Hydroxy-8-methoxy-coumarin
>*Saxifrag.* *Astilbe, Deutzia, Philadelphus*; but not in *Bergenia,*
>*Escallonia, Heuchera, Ribes, Rodgersia*

Iso-fraxidin (6,8-Dimethoxy-7-hydroxy-coumarin; Calycanthogenol)
>*Calycanth.* *Calycanthus occidentalis* (st.)
>*Ole.* *Fraxinus*?

Iso-shehkangenin (fig. 95) is very like an *isoflavone*. It is the aglycone of
isoshehkanin. Does it occur free?

Iso-shehkanin (Iso-shehkangenin-7-glucoside)
>*Irid.* *Iris wattii*

Limettin (Citropten; 5,7-Dimethoxy-coumarin)
>*Rut.* *Citrus limetta* (frt) and some other spp.

Mahaleboside: a glycoside of 5-*hydroxy-coumarin*?
>*Ros.* *Prunus mahaleb* (bk)

Marmin
>*Rut.* *Aegle marmelos* (bk, rt)

Meranzin (Auraptene (2); 7-Methoxy-8-epoxyisopentenyl-coumarin)
>*Rut.* *Citrus* (*bigaradia*?) (frt)

7-Methoxy-8-(2-formyl-2-methylpropyl)-coumarin
>*Rut.* *Citrus* (grapefruit peel-oil)

7-Methoxy-5-geranoxy-coumarin
>*Rut.* *Citrus aurantium* (oil), *Luvunga scandens* (oil)

8-Methoxy-4-methyl-coumarin
>*Meli.* *Ekebergia senegalensis*

Mexoticin (8-(2′,3′-Dihydroxy-isopentenyl)-5,7-dimethoxy-coumarin)
>*Rut.* *Murraya exotica* (bk)

Micromelin
>*Rut.* *Micromelum minutum*

Neohydrangin: an *umbelliferone-diglucoside*?
>*Saxifrag.* *Hydrangea paniculata* (bk)

Obliquetin (fig. 95)
>*Meli.* *Ptaeroxylon obliquum* (htwd)

Obliquetol is *demethyl-obliquetin.*
>*Meli.* *Ptaeroxylon obliquum* (htwd)

Osthenol (7-Hydroxy-8-isopentenyl-coumarin)
>*Umbell.* *Angelica archangelica*

Osthol (7-Methoxy-8-isopentenyl-coumarin; fig. 95)
>*Rut.* *Flindersia* (3)
>*Umbell.* *Angelica* (3), *Peucedanum osthruthium, Prangos, Seseli*
>*sibiricum* (rt)

Ostruthin (6-Geranyl-7-hydroxy-coumarin)
>*Umbell.* *Peucedanum ostruthium*

Prenyletin (7-O-(3,3-Dimethylallyl)-aesculetin)
 Meli. Ptaeroxylon obliquum (htwd)
Prenyletin-6-O-methyl ether
 Meli. Ptaeroxylon obliquum (htwd)
Scopoletin (Chrysatropic acid; Gelsemic acid; 6-Methyl-aesculetin;
 fig. 95) is very widely distributed both free (?) and as the glycosides
 fabiatrin and *scopolin*.
 Ros. Prunus serotina (bk)
 Legum. Baptisia lecontei (lvs)
 Zygophyll. Zygophyllum fabago?
 Rut. Casimiroa edulis (bk), *Skimmia laureola* (bk)
 Apocyn. Nerium odorum (lvs?)
 Logani. Gelsemium sempervirens (rt)
 Eben. Diospyros maritima (bk)
 Convolvul. Convolvulus, Ipomoea
 Solan. Atropa, Fabiana, Mandragora, Nicotiana, Scopolia
 Caprifoli. Weigela floribunda (after hyd.?), *florida* (after hyd.?)
 Dispac. Succisa pratensis? (after hyd.)
 Gram. Avena sativa, whose roots are said to excrete it (Eberhardt,
 1954)
 Orchid. Dendrobium thyrsiflorum (lvs, hyd.)
Scopolin (Scopoletin-7-glucoside)
 Legum. Baptisia lecontei (lvs)
 Rut. Murraya exotica (fl.)
 Apocyn. Nerium odorum
 Logani. Gelsemium sempervirens
 Convolvul. Convolvulus, Ipomoea
 Solan. Atropa, Mandragora, Scopolia
 Comp. Artemisia
Skimmin (Umbelliferone-7-glucoside)
 Saxifrag. Hydrangea (bk of 4 spp.), *Jamesia americana* (bk)
 Rut. Skimmia japonica (bk), *laureola* (bk)
 Umbell. Ferula sumbul (and other spp.?)
 Comp. Hieracium pilosella (lvs)
Suberosin (6-(γ,γ-Dimethylallyl)-7-methoxy-coumarin; fig. 95)
 Rut. Zanthoxylum flavum (htwd), *suberosum* (bk)
Toddalo-lactone (Aculeatin-hydrate?; 5,7-Dimethoxy-6(2,3-dihydroxy-
 isopentenyl)-coumarin)
 Rut. Toddalia aculeata
6,7,8-Trimethoxy-coumarin (Dimethyl-fraxetin)
 Rut. Fagara ailanthoides (wd)
4,5,7-Trimethoxy-3-(3,4-methylenedioxyphenyl)-coumarin
 Legum. Derris robusta

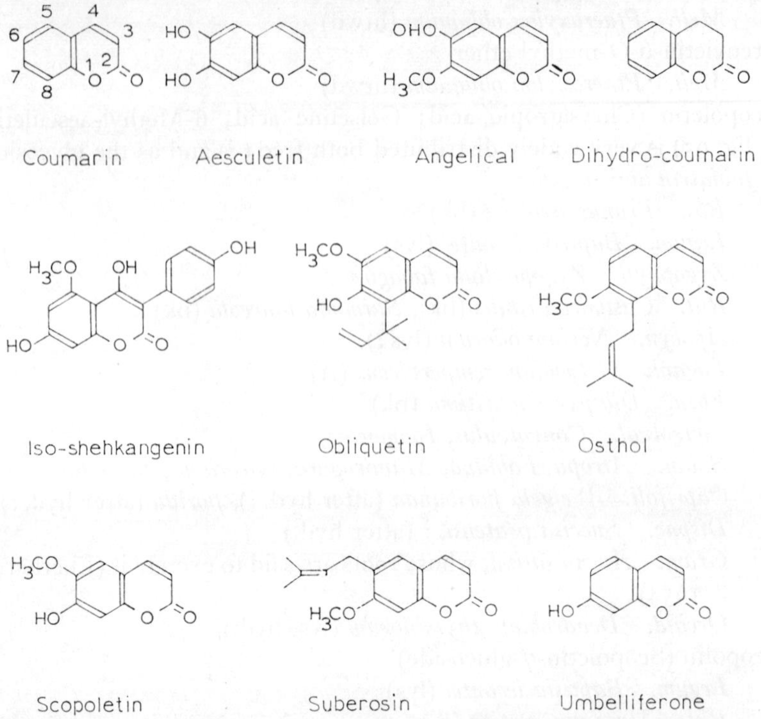

Coumarin   Aesculetin   Angelical   Dihydro-coumarin

Iso-shehkangenin   Obliquetin   Osthol

Scopoletin   Suberosin   Umbelliferone

Fig. 95. Some 'simple' coumarins.

Umbelliferone (Dichrin-A; Hydrangin; 7-Hydroxy-coumarin; Skim-metin; fig. 95) is the lactone of *umbellic acid*, and the aglycone of *neohydrangin* and *skimmin*. It seems to be widely distributed.

>Saxifrag. *Deutzia, Dichroa, Escallonia, Heuchera, Hydrangea, Philadelphus, Ribes, Rodgersia*; but *not* in *Astilbe, Bergenia*.
>Rut. *Aegle, Citrus, Skimmia*
>Thymelae. *Daphne*
>Umbell. *Apium, Daucus, Ferula, Heracleum, Laretia, Levisticum, Peucedanum, Pimpinella*
>Solan. *Atropa*
>Comp. *Hieracium, Matricaria, Pilosella* (Bate-Smith *et al.* 1968 have used distribution of *umbelliferone* in studying the taxonomy of the *Hieracium–Pilosella* complex).

Umbelliprenin (7-Farnesyloxy-coumarin)
>Umbell. *Angelica archangelica, Peucedanum palustre* (frt)

Vellein (Osthenol-7-β-glucoside?)
>Goodeni. *Velleia discophora*

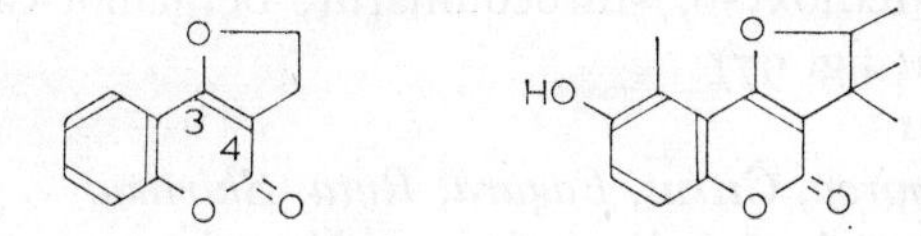

3,4−Furocoumarin   Glaupalol

Fig. 96. 3,4-Furocoumarins.

II 3,4-FUROCOUMARINS

GENERAL

I know of but one substance (*glaupalol*) that should be placed here. It occurs in an unusual member (*Glaucidium*) of the *Ranunculaceae*, a family not rich in *coumarins*.

Note the relationship to the *coumarono-coumarins* (fig. 100).

List and Occurrence

Glaupalol (fig. 96)
    Ranuncul.   *Glaucidium palmatum* (rhiz.)

III 6,7-FUROCOUMARINS (PSORALENS)

GENERAL

These substances may be considered to be derivatives of 6,7-*furocoumarin* (*psoralen*) (fig. 97). At least one of the naturally occurring *furocoumarins* (*erosnin*) is a *coumarono-coumarin*; another (*pachyrhizin*) is obviously 'almost' a *coumarono-coumarin*.

Again, the *Umbelliferae* abound in these compounds (at least 13 genera have yielded more than 20 6,7-*furocoumarins*). The closely related family *Araliaceae* has yielded none!

Again, the *Rutaceae* are prodigal in their production of *coumarins*, yielding at least 15 6,7-*furocoumarins* from 15 genera.

List and Occurrence

Allo-imperatorin: belongs here?
    Rut.   *Aegle marmelos* (frt)

15

Bergaptene (5-Methoxy-6,7-furocoumarin; Bergamot camphor; Hera-clin; Majudin; fig. 97)
    Mor. Ficus
    Rut. *Casimiroa, Citrus, Fagara, Ruta, Skimmia*
    Umbell. *Ammi, Angelica, Apium, Heracleum, Levisticum, Ligus-ticum, Pastinaca, Petroselinum, Pimpinella, Seseli*
Bergaptin (5-Geranyloxy-6,7-furocoumarin; Bergamottin)
    Rut. *Citrus bergamia* (oil)
Bergaptol (5-Hydroxy-6,7-furocoumarin)
    Rut. *Citrus bergamia*
Byak-angelicin (5-Methoxy-8-(2,3-dihydroxy-isopentenyloxy)-6,7-furo-coumarin)
    Umbell. *Angelica* (2), *Heracleum*
Byak-angelicol (5-Methoxy-8-(2,3-Epoxyisopentenyloxy)-6,7-furocou-marin) may be identical with *ferulin* of *Ferula alliacea.*
    Umbell. *Angelica dahurica* ('byakusi')
Chalepensin
    Rut. *Ruta chalepensis*
Chalepin
    Rut. *Ruta chalepensis*
5-[(3,6-Dimethyl-6-formyl-2-heptenyl)oxy]-psoralen
    Rut. *Citrus* (grapefruit peel-oil)
6,7-Furocoumarin (Ficusin; Psoralen; fig. 97) seems to be rather widely distributed:
    Mor. Ficus
    Legum. *Coronilla* (in many, but not all spp.), *Psoralea corylifolia* (sd)
    Rut. *Phebalium, Zanthoxylum*
    Umbell. *Angelica keiskei*
Halfordin: may be a 7,8- rather than a 6,7-*furocoumarin*?
    Rut. *Halfordia kendack* (bk), *scleroxyla* (bk)
Heliettin
    Rut. *Helietta longifoliata* (bk)
Imperatorin (8-Isopentenyloxy-6,7-furocoumarin; Ammidin; Marmel-osin; fig. 97)
    Rut. *Aegle marmelos* (frt), *Ruta chalepensis*
    Umbell. *Ammi, Angelica, Pastinaca, Peucedanum* (*Imperatoria*), *Prangos*
Iso-imperatorin (5-Isopentenyloxy-6,7-furocoumarin)
    Umbell. *Pastinaca, Peucedanum* (*Imperatoria*) spp.
Iso-oxypeucedanin
    Umbell. *Peucedanum*

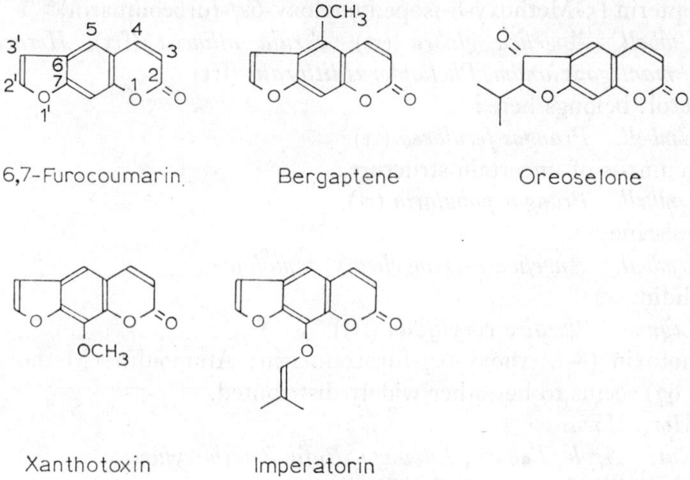

6,7-Furocoumarin   Bergaptene   Oreoselone

Xanthotoxin   Imperatorin

Fig. 97. Some 6,7-furocoumarins.

Iso-pimpinellin (5,8-Dimethoxy-6,7-furocoumarin)
> *Rut. Casimiroa, Citrus, Fagara, Flindersia, Luvunga, Skimmia, Thamnosma*
> *Umbell. Angelica, Ferula, Heracleum, Pimpinella, Seseli*

Iso-psoralidin: belongs here?
> *Legum. Psoralea* (what sp.?)

Marmesin is the optical isomer of *nodakenetin*?
> *Rut. Aegle marmelos, Evodia belahe* (bk)
> *Umbell. Ammi*

5-Methoxy-8-hydroxy-6,7-furocoumarin
> *Umbell. Angelica japonica*

Nodakenetin is the aglycone of *nodakenin*.

Nodakenin (2′,3′-Dihydro-2′-(1-glucosoxy-isopropyl)-6,7-furocoumarin)
> *Umbell. Peucedanum decursivuu*

Oreoselone (fig. 97)
> *Umbell. Peucedanum oreoselinum*

Ostruthol
> *Umbell. Peucedanum officinale, ostruthium*

(+)-Oxypeucedanin (5-Epoxy-isopentenyloxy-6,7-furocoumarin; Hydroxy-peucedanin)
> *Umbell. Angelica sylvestris; Peucedanum officinale, ostruthium, palustre* (frt); *Prangos*

Peucedanin (2′-Isopropyl-3′-methoxy-6,7-furocoumarin)
> *Umbell. Peucedanum officinale* (rhiz.)

Phellopterin (5-Methoxy-8-isopentenyloxy-6,7-furocoumarin)
    Umbell. Angelica glabra (rt), *Ferula alliacea* (frt), *Heracleum mantegazzianum, Phellopterus littoralis* (frt)
Pranferol: belongs here ?
    Umbell. Prangos ferulacea (rt)
Prangenin: is of uncertain structure ?
    Umbell. Prangos pabularia (rt)
Prangolarine
    Umbell. Angelica archangelica v. *himalaica*
Psoralidin
    Legum. Psoralea corylifolia (frt)
Xanthotoxin (8-Methoxy-6,7-furocoumarin; Ammoidin; Methoxalin; fig. 97) seems to be rather widely distributed.
    Mor. Ficus
    Rut. Aegle, Fagara, Luvunga, Ruta, Zanthoxylum
    Umbell. Ammi, Angelica, Pastinaca
Xanthotoxol (8-Hydroxy-6,7-furocoumarin)
    Umbell. Angelica
Xanthoxyletin (Xanthoxylin-N; Xanthoxyloin)
    Rut. Halfordia, Melicope, Zanthoxylum

IV 7,8-FUROCOUMARINS (ISOPSORALENS)

GENERAL

These coumarins resemble the 6,7-*furocoumarins* closely in structure and in distribution.

The *Umbelliferae* are very rich in these substances, at least 16 of the 21 compounds listed here occurring in the 7 genera investigated. In contrast, not one 7,8-*furocoumarin* is recorded from the *Araliaceae*.

List and Occurrence

Archangelicin
    Umbell. Angelica archangelica
Archangelin (fig. 98)
    Umbell. Angelica archangelica v. *himalaica*
Athamantin (2′,3′-Dihydro-2′-(1-hydroxyisopropyl)-3′-hydroxydiiso-valeryl-7,8-furocoumarin ?)
    Umbell. Peucedanum (Athamanta) oreoselinum (rt)
Columbianadin (fig. 98)
    Umbell. Lomatium columbianum, Peucedanum palustre (frt)

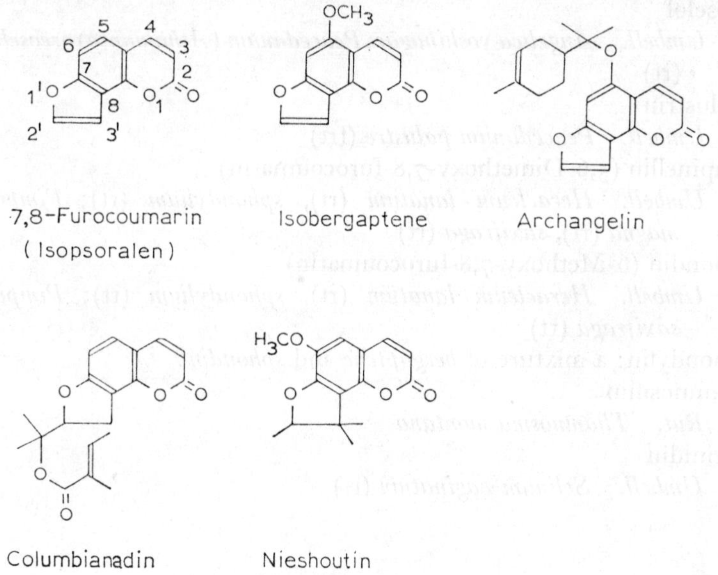

7,8-Furocoumarin   Isobergaptene   Archangelin
(Isopsoralen)

Columbianadin   Nieshoutin

Fig. 98. Some 7,8-furocoumarins.

Columbianadin oxide
Umbell.   Peucedanum palustre (frt)
Columbianetin (Dihydro-orselol)
Umbell.   Leptotaenia (Ferula) multifida, Lomatium columbianum
Columbianin is the D-glucoside of columbianetin.
Umbell.   Lomatium columbianum
Edultin
Umbell.   Angelica edulis
7,8-Furocoumarin (Angelicin; Isopsoralen; fig. 98)
Legum.   Psoralea corylifolia (frt)
Umbell.   Angelica archangelica and another sp.
Isobergaptene (5-Methoxy-7,8-furocoumarin, fig. 98)
Umbell.   Heracleum (2 or 3), Pimpinella (2)
Isohalfordin may be a 7,8-furocoumarin or a 5,6-furocoumarin.
Rut.   Halfordia scleroxyla
Isopeulustrin
Umbell.   Peucedanum palustre (frt)
Nieshoutin (Cyclo-obliquetin; fig. 98) is obviously related to obliquetin,
a 'simple' coumarin.
Meli.   Ptaeroxylon obliquum ('nieshout', htwd)
Nieshoutol: belongs here?
Meli.   Ptaeroxylon obliquum (htwd)

Oroselol
> *Umbell.   Angelica yoshinagae; Peucedanum (Athamanta) oreoselinum*
> (rt)

Peulustrin
> *Umbell.   Peucedanum palustre* (frt)

Pimpinellin (5,6-Dimethoxy-7,8-furocoumarin)
> *Umbell.   Heracleum lanatum* (rt), *sphondylium* (rt); *Pimpinella magna* (rt), *saxifraga* (rt)

Sphondin (6-Methoxy-7,8-furocoumarin)
> *Umbell.   Heracleum lanatum* (rt), *sphondylium* (rt); *Pimpinella saxifraga* (rt)

Sphondylin: a mixture of *bergaptene* and *sphondin*?

Thamnosmin
> *Rut.   Thamnosma montana*

Vaginidin
> *Umbell.   Selinum vaginatum* (rt)

V CHROMANO–COUMARINS

GENERAL

A few coumarins have a 6-membered heterocyclic ring, rather than the 5-membered ring of the *furo-coumarins*, fused to the benzene ring. These coumarins may be called *chromano-coumarins*. The ring may be variously placed: 5,6- in *alloxanthoxyletin*, for example; 6,7- in *xanthyletin*; and 7,8- in *braylin*. We have not made separate groups of these.

Yet again, the *Umbelliferae* are rich in these compounds, 8 occurring in 5 genera. Again, there are no reports from the *Araliaceae*.

List and Occurrence

Allo-xanthoxyletin (fig. 99)
> *Rut.   Zanthoxylum (Xanthoxylum) americanum* (bk)

Braylin (fig. 99)
> *Rut.   Flindersia brayleyana* (bk)

Calophyllic acid is a near chromano-coumarin.
> *Guttif.   Calophyllum inophyllum* (frt)

Calophyllolide: belongs here?
> *Guttif.   Calophyllum inophyllum* (frt)

Dihydro-samidin
> *Umbell.   Ammi visnaga* (sd)

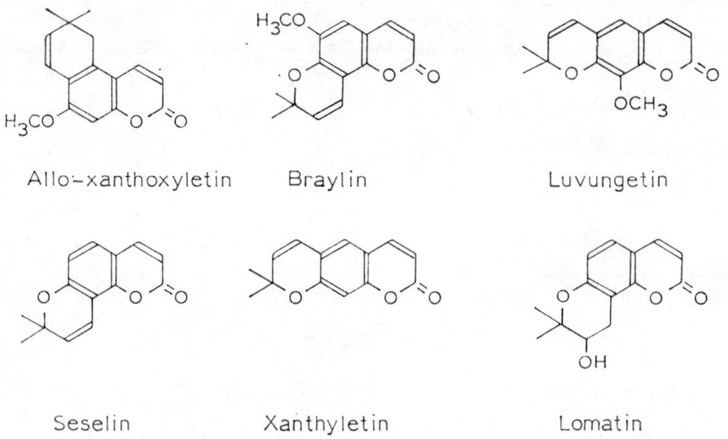

Allo-xanthoxyletin   Braylin   Luvungetin

Seselin   Xanthyletin   Lomatin

Fig. 99. Some chromano-coumarins.

Khel-lactone is closely related to *braylin*.
   Umbell.   *Angelica cartilagino-marginata, shikokiana*
Lomatin (Jatamansinol; fig. 99)
   Umbell.   *Lomatium nuttallii, Selinum vaginatum* (rt)
   Valerian.   *Nardostachys jatamansi*
Luvungetin (fig. 99)
   Rut.   *Luvunga scandens* (frt)
Samidin
   Umbell.   *Ammi visnaga* (frt)
Selinidin (Jatamansin) is the *tiglyl ester* of *lomatin*. Erroneously reported
  as present in *Nardostachys*.
   Umbell.   *Selinum vaginatum* (rt)
Seselin (fig. 99)
   Rut.   *Flindersia bennettiana* (lvs, bk, wd); *Skimmia japonica* (lvs),
    repens (lvs)
   Umbell.   *Seseli indicum* (frt)
Suksdorfin
   Umbell.   *Lomatium suksdorfii*
Visnadin (Provismine)
   Umbell.   *Ammi visnaga*
Xanthyletin (fig. 99)
   Rut.   *Chloroxylon, Citrus, Luvunga, Zanthoxylum (Xanthoxylum)*

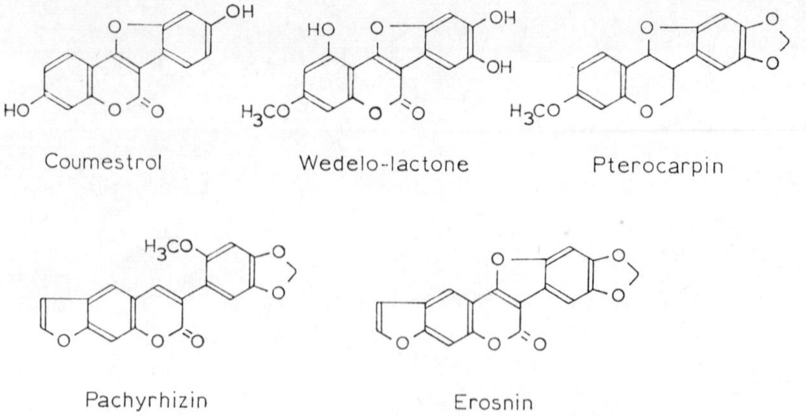

Coumestrol   Wedelo-lactone   Pterocarpin

Pachyrhizin   Erosnin

Fig. 100. Coumarono-coumarins and related substances.

VI COUMARONO-COUMARINS

GENERAL

Only a few substances belonging to this group are known. They are obviously related to the *isoflavanone* derivatives (*coumarano-chromans*) such as *pterocarpin* (fig. 100) and *homopterocarpin*.

Pachyrhizin (fig. 100) is placed here, though it is really a 6,7-*furo-coumarin*, because it is closely related to *erosnin* (fig. 100), with which it occurs. *Erosnin* is both a 6,7-*furocoumarin* and a *coumarono-coumarin*. How difficult it is to classify these substances! I could do better if I knew their biogenetic histories!

One could also regard the *coumarono-coumarins* as derivatives of 3,4-*furocoumarin*, the sole representative of which—*glaupalol* (fig. 96)—is listed in an earlier section.

List and Occurrence

Coumestrol (fig. 100) is the oestrogenic principle of ladino clover.
> Legum. *Medicago hispida* (plt), *sativa* (plt); *Trifolium fragiferum* (plt), *pratense* (plt), *repens* (plt), *subterraneum* (plt)

Erosnin (fig. 100) is, as we have seen, also a 6,7-*furocoumarin*.
> Legum. *Pachyrhizus erosus* (sd)

Pachyrhizin (fig. 100) is almost a *coumarono-coumarin*.
> Legum. *Pachyrhizus erosus* (sd)

Wedelo-lactone (fig. 100)
> Comp. *Eclipta alba* (lvs), *Wedelia calendulacea* (lvs)

VII 3,4-BENZOCOUMARINS

GENERAL

Dean (1952) says: 'The few coumarins which have been found outside the plant world are those 3:4 benzocoumarins which Lederer has shown to be constituents of the scent-glands of the beaver.'

The 3,4-*benzocoumarins* known to occur in higher plants are few in number. One of them—*ellagic acid*—is, however, of very wide distribution. The others are known only from one or a few sources. It is surely significant that the order **Myrtales** is rich in these substances, at least 9 families having *ellagic acid* and at least 4 having other 3,4-*benzocoumarins* (table 49).

List and Occurrence

Ellagic acid (Alizarin yellow; Benzoar acid; fig. 101) is very widely
   distributed (Bate-Smith, 1956; Hegnauer, 1964–1966). In the
   Myrtales it is in almost all families (table 49). Bate-Smith (1968) says
   it is *absent* from monocotyledons.
Ellagic acid-3,3'-dimethyl ether
   Fag.   Nothofagus fusca (htwd)
   Euphorbi.   Euphorbia formosanum (rt)
   Myrt.   Leptospermum scoparium (bk, lvs, wd)
   Sonnerati.   Sonneratia apetala (wd, etc.)
   Combret.   Terminalia paniculata (htwd)
Ellagic acid-3,3'-dimethyl ether-4-glucoside
   Combret.   Terminalia paniculata (wd, etc.)
Ellagic acid-4-β-gentiobioside (Armritoside) has been found by Seshadri
   and Vasishta (1965) in
   Myrt.   Psidium guava
Ellagic acid-3-methyl ether
   Myrt.   Leptospermum scoparium (bk, lvs, wd)
Ellagic acid-3,3',4-trimethyl ether
   Myrt.   Eugenia maire (bk, wd), *Leptospermum scoparium* (bk, lvs, wd)
   Sonnerati.   Sonneratia apetala (wd)
Flavellagic acid-3,3',4-trimethyl ether (fig. 101)
   Combret.   Terminalia paniculata (htwd)
Luteic acid (fig. 101)
   Ros.   Alchemilla vulgaris?
   Combret.   Terminalia chebula (frt)
Luteic acid-diglucoside
   Lythr.   Lagerstroemia subcostata (lvs)

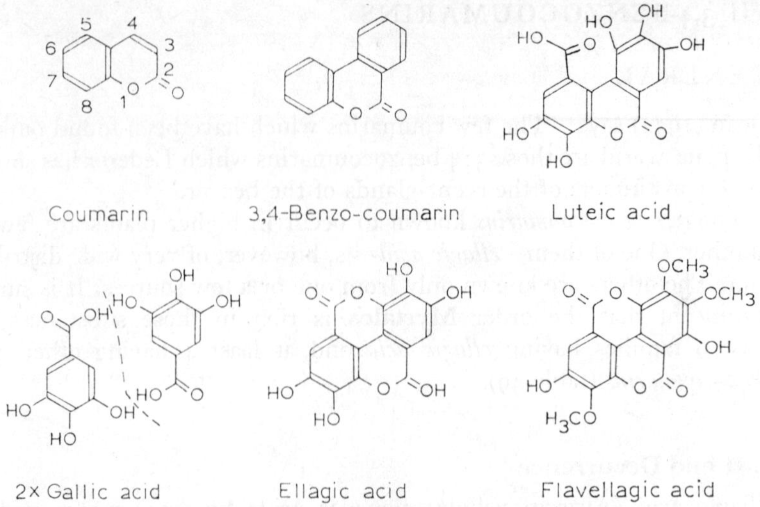

Coumarin   3,4-Benzo-coumarin   Luteic acid

2× Gallic acid   Ellagic acid   Flavellagic acid

Fig. 101. 3,4-Benzocoumarins and related substances.

VIII ISO-COUMARINS

GENERAL

This small group of plant constituents contains derivatives of *iso-coumarin* (fig. 102). They are also *α-pyrones* and illustrate once more the difficulties of classification. At least one *isocoumarin* is an *acetylene compound*!

Their distribution is quite different from that of the true *coumarins*, suggesting that they are not closely related to them.

List and Occurrence

Bergenin (Bergenit; Corylopsin; fig. 102) has been known for nearly 90 years. I have 3 different formulae for it, the one shown being that of Haynes (1963). The third ring is really a sugar ring and Haynes says that *bergenin* has been synthesized from *tetra-O-acetyl-α-D-gluco-pyranosyl bromide* and *4-O-methyl-gallic acid*.

It seems to be of wide distribution.

Dipterocarp. Shorea leprosula, robusta

Saxifrag. Astilbe, Bergenia, Peltoboykinia, Rodgersia

Hamamelid. Corylopsis (all spp.?), *Fortunearia sinensis, Liquid-ambar styraciflua*

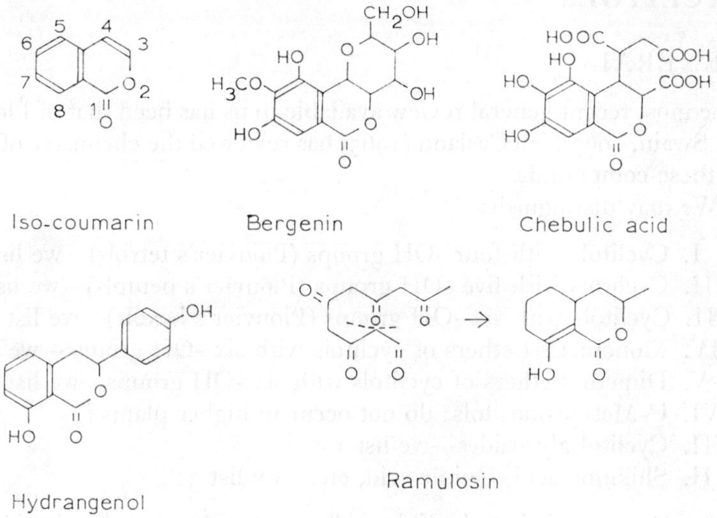

Iso-coumarin   Bergenin   Chebulic acid

Hydrangenol   Ramulosin

Fig. 102. Isocoumarins.

Connar.   Connarus
Legum.   Occurrence?
Lin.   Humiria balsamifera
Euphorbi.   Mallotus japonicus
Myrsin.   Ardisia hortorum, japonica
Convolvul.   Cuscuta reflexa
Blepharin is possibly a *dihydro-furo-isocoumarin.*
    Acanth.   Blepharis edulis (sd)
Chebulic acid (fig. 102): does not occur free?
    Combret.   Terminalia chebula (tannin)
Hydrangenol (fig. 102)
    Saxifrag.   Hydrangea macrophylla (acid hydrolysates of fl., rt, and
    lvs yield *hydrangenol,* say Ibrahim and Towers (1960). They
    concluded (in 1962) that it arises from 3 × acetate and a C_6C_3
    compound).
Hydrangenol-3-glucoside (8-glucoside, following our numbering)
    Saxifrag.   Hydrangea macrophylla (fl.)
Isocoumarin (fig. 102): does not occur as such?
Phyllodulcin
    Saxifrag.   Hydrangea macrophylla
Ramulosin (fig. 102) is acetate-derived, according to Mentzer (in Swain,
    1966).
    Cucurbit.   Pestalozzia (Gymnostemma ?) ramulosa

CYCLITOLS

GENERAL

The most recent general review available to us has been that of Plouvier (in Swain, 1963). McCasland (1965) has reviewed the chemistry of some of these compounds.

We may distinguish:

    I. Cyclitols with four -OH groups (Plouvier's tetrols)—we list 4.
    II. Cyclitols with five -OH groups (Plouvier's pentols)—we list 3.
  III. Cyclitols with six -OH groups (Plouvier's hexols)—we list 5.
  IV. Monomethyl ethers of cyclitols with six -OH groups—we list 7.
    V. Dimethyl ethers of cyclitols with six -OH groups—we list 2.
  VI. C-Methyl-inositols: do not occur in higher plants?
 VII. Cyclitol glycosides—we list 1.
VIII. Shikimic acid, Quinic acid, etc.—we list 3.

Depsides of *shikimic* and *quinic acids* are considered under *depsides*.

I CYCLITOLS WITH 4 -OH GROUPS

List and Occurrence

Betitol: the structure of which is unknown?
    Chenopodi. *Beta* (molasses in preparation of beet-sugar)
Conduritol (Conduritol-A; fig. 103)
    Asclepiad. *Marsdenia cundurango* (bk)
Dihydro-conduritol
    Asclepiad. *Marsdenia cundurango* (bk, trace)
l-Leucanthemitol (fig. 103)
    Fag. *Quercus* (2)
    Comp. *Chrysanthemum*; but *absent* from related genera?

II CYCLITOLS WITH 5 -OH GROUPS

List and Occurrence

d-Quercitol (Proto-quercitol; fig. 103) seems to be rather widely spread in higher plants. It has been recorded from
    Fag. *Quercus** (lvs of all examined, Plouvier); but *absent* from *Castanea, Fagus*.

Loranth. Viscum album (*growing on Quercus?)

Magnoli. Talauma mexicana (lvs)

Menisperm. Cissampelos, Cocculus, Cyclea, Legnephora, Tiliacora, Triclisia; but absent from Menispermum.

Legum. Pterocarpus lucens (lvs, st.)

Myrt. Eugenia jambolana

Myrsin. Embelia ribes, robusta; Myrsine africana, semiserrata

Sapot. Achras sapota (lvs, sd); Butyrospermum parkii; Mimusops caffra (lvs), elengi (lvs, sd)

Logani. Strychnos toxifera

Palmae. Chamaerops humilis (lvs, rt), but absent from some spp., and from Corypha, Erythea, Livistona, Phoenix, Rhapis, Trachycarpus, Washingtonia.

l-Quercitol is apparently very rare:

Fag. Quercus cerris (lvs), robur (lvs, bk)

Myrt. Eucalyptus populnea; but absent from some other members of the family.

l-Viburnitol (fig. 103) has been wrongly called l-quercitol (see above). It is interesting to find here so many records of absence.

Fag. Quercus cerris (lvs), robur (lvs, bk)

Menisperm. Menispermum canadense (lvs, st.), Stephania hernandifolia

Asclepiad. Gymnema sylvestre?; but absent from Asclepias, Periploca, Tylophora, Vincetoxicum

Caprifoli. Viburnum tinus (lvs, frt)

Comp. Achillea, Chrysanthemum (some spp.), Tanacetum; but absent from: Arctium, Bellis, Eupatorium, Helichrysum, Matricaria, Serratula, Solidago

It is said to be absent also from: Ranuncul. (Clematis, Ranunculus); Berberid. (Berberis, Mahonia); Lardizabal. (Akebia, Decaisnea, Holboellia, Lardizabala); Paeoni. (Paeonia).

III CYCLITOLS WITH 6 -OH GROUPS

List and Occurrence

d-Inositol (fig. 103) is known, according to Plouvier (in Swain, 1963), only from the wood of a conifer. He says, however, that 'it exists perhaps (in traces) in numerous pinitol-containing plants'.

dl-Inositol

Loranth. Viscum album (frt)

Menisperm. Triclisia gilletii (st.)

l-Inositol

> *Euphorbi.*   *Euphorbia pilulifera*
>
> *Comp.*   *Anthemis, Centaurea, Chrysanthemum, Erigeron, Eupatorium, Helichrysum, Inula, Pulicaria, Serratula, Sonchus, Vernonia*; but *absent* from: *Ageratum, Arctium, Baccharis, Bellis, Calendula, Coreopsis, Gaillardia, Galinsoga, Gazania, Grindelia, Helianthus, Polymnia, Senecio, Solidago, Tagetes, Tussilago.*

Myo-inositol (Meso-inositol; fig. 103) is very widely spread in Nature, mostly in the bound form. It is said to be formed from D-*glucose* by *cyclase.* We have come across records of it (free?) in bacteria, in conifers, and in

> *Jugland.*   *Juglans*
>
> *Betul.*   *Alnus*
>
> *Fag.*   *Quercus cerris* (lvs), *robur* (lvs, bk)
>
> *Loranth.*   *Viscum*
>
> *Legum.*   *Phaseolus*
>
> *Anacardi.*   *Cotinus, Rhus*
>
> *Caprifoli.*   *Viburnum tinus*
>
> *Gram.*   *Zea*

Scyllitol (Scyllo-inositol; fig. 103) appears to be rather widely distributed. It has been found in fishes, in red algae, and in

> *Fag.*   *Quercus cerris* (lvs), *robur* (lvs, bk, frt), *suber* (frt)
>
> *Calycanth.*   *Calycanthus, Chimonanthus*
>
> *Rhamn.*   *Helinus ovatus* (lvs)
>
> *Tili.*   *Tilia tomentosa* (lvs)
>
> *Corn.*   *Cornus florida* (fl., etc.)
>
> *Comp.*   *Vernonia altissima* (lvs)
>
> *Palmae.*   *Cocos nucifera* (lvs), *plumosa* (lvs)

IV MONOMETHYL ETHERS OF CYCLITOLS WITH 6 -OH GROUPS

List and Occurrence

d-Bornesitol (1-*O*-Methyl-myo-inositol; fig. 103)

> *Apocyn.*   *Amsonia, Dyera, Urceola* (2), *Vinca*
>
> *Rubi.*   *Sarcocephalus diderrichii* (bk, wd)

l-Bornesitol may be interestingly restricted within the families in which it is known to occur. We have an unusually long list of reported absences.

> *Prote.*   *Banksia, Macadamia, Stenocarpus*
>
> *Legum.*   *Lathyrus* (in 10 spp.)

Rhamn. *Berchemia racemosa* (lvs), *Rhamnus* (many); but *absent* from: *Ceanothus, Colletia, Hovenia, Paliurus, Phylica, Ziziphus*

Apocyn. *Apocynum androsaemifolium* (lvs), *cannabinum* (lvs)

Boragin. *Alkanna, Anchusa, Borago* (in some spp.), *Cerinthe, Cynoglossum, Echium, Lindelofia, Lithospermum, Lycopsis, Myosotis, Omphalodes, Onosma, Pulmonaria, Solenanthus, Symphytum*; but *absent* from: *Caccinia, Ehretia, Heliotropium, Tournefortia.*

It is said to be *absent* from: *Celastr.* (*Celastrus, Elaeodendron, Euonymus*); *Vit.* (*Ampelopsis, Parthenocissus, Vitis*); *Polemoni.* (*Cobaea, Phlox*); *Convolvul.* (*Convolvulus, Ipomoea*); *Hydrophyll.* (*Hydrophyllum*); *Verben.* (*Clerodendron, Verbena, Vitex*); *Lab.* (*Ballota, Coleus, Glechoma, Lamium, Lavandula, Salvia, Scutellaria, Teucrium*); *Solan.* (*Datura, Lycium, Petunia, Solanum*); *Scrophulari.* (*Digitalis, Linaria, Paulownia, Penstemon, Scrophularia, Verbascum, Veronica*); *Bignoni.* (*Bignonia, Campsis*).

d-Ononitol (4-*O*-methyl-myo-inositol; fig. 103) seems to be of very restricted distribution.

Legum. *Dolichos, Leucaena, Medicago, Ononis* (2, but *absent* from several), *Vigna*

Flacourti. *Kiggelaria africana* (lvs)

d-Pinitol (3-*O*-Methyl-*d*-inositol) has been much studied by Plouvier. He says that it occurs in every pinaceous plant examined. Most of the following records come from Plouvier's papers (1949, 1950, 1952, 1953, 1955, 1957). It is noteworthy that no records refer to monocotyledons. Has *d-pinitol* been looked for in that group?

Olac. *Ximenia* (1)

Loranth. *Viscum* (1)

Phytolacc. *Phytolacca*

Nyctagin. *Bougainvillea, Mirabilis, Oxybaphus*

Aizo. *Tetragonia*; but *absent* from *Mesembryanthemum*

Caryophyll. general in the family

Magnoli. *Magnolia* (in all spp.?); but *absent* from *Liriodendron*

Aristolochi. *Aristolochia*; but *absent* from *Asarum*

Legum. widely spread, *except* in *Dalbergieae, Phaseoleae*, and *Vicieae*

Zygophyll. *Zygophyllum*; but *absent* from *Peganum*

Euphorbi. *Euphorbia* (some spp.); but *absent* from *Acalypha, Andrachne, Mercurialis, Ricinus, Securinega*

Cist. *Halimium, Helianthemum*; but *absent* from *Cistus, Fumana*

Apocyn. *Landolphia*; but *absent* from *Amsonia, Apocynum, Nerium, Vinca*

It is said to be *absent* from: *Jugland.* (*Carya, Juglans, Pterocarya*); *Fag.* (*Castanea, Fagus, Quercus*); *Mor.* (*Broussonetia, Cannabis, Ficus,*

Humulus, Maclura, Morus); *Urtic.* (*Boehmeria, Parietaria, Urtica*); *Mollugin.* (*Mollugo*); *Portulac.* (*Portulaca*); *Basell.* (*Basella, Bous-singaultia*); *Chenopodi.* (*Atriplex, Beta, Chenopodium, Kochia, Salsola, Spinacia*); *Amaranth.* (*Achyranthes, Alternaria, Amaran-thus, Celosia, Iresine*); *Schisandr.* (*Schisandra*); *Calycanth.* (*Caly-canthus, Chimonanthus*); *Laur.* (*Laurus, Persea, Sassafras, Umbel-lularia*); *Euptele.* (*Euptelea*); *Cercidiphyll.* (*Cercidiphyllum*); *Ranun-cul.* (*Aconitum, Aquilegia, Clematis, Delphinium, Ranunculus, Thalictrum*); *Berberid.* (*Berberis, Mahonia*); *Lardizabal.* (*Akebia, Decaisnea, Holboellia*); *Platan.* (*Platanus*); *Hamamelid* (8, Plouvier); *Saxifrag.* (22, Plouvier); *Ros.* (73, Plouvier); *Connar.* (*Cnestis, Rourea*); *Paeoni.* (*Paeonia*); *Actinidi.* (*Actinidia*); *The.* (*Camellia, Visnea*); *Guttif.* (*Hypericum*); *Oxalid.* (*Oxalis*); *Gerani.* (*Erodium, Geranium, Pelargonium*); *Tropaeol.* (*Tropaeolum*); *Lin.* (*Linum*); *Flacourti.* (*Flacourtia, Hydnocarpus, Kiggelaria, Poliothyrsis*); *Viol.* (*Hymenanthera, Viola*); *Stachyur.* (*Stachyurus*); *Passiflor.* (*Passi-flora*); *Bix.* (*Bixa*); *Tamaric.* (*Myricaria, Tamarix*); *Loas.* (*Blumen-bachia*); *Datisc.* (*Datisca*); *Begoni.* (*Begonia*)

l-Pinitol

Comp.   Artemisia dracunculus; but *absent* from several genera

l-Quebrachitol (2-*O*-Methyl-*l*-inositol; fig. 103) occurs, says Plouvier (in Swain, 1963), in 11 families of dicotyledons. We have records from 12. As in the case of *d-pinitol* no records come from mono-cotyledons.

Ulm.   in some (see under family)

Mor.   Cannabis, Humulus; but *absent* from many

Prote.   Grevillea, Hakea; but *absent* from *Banksia*

Loranth.   Viscum

Euphorbi.   Acalypha, Hevea; but *absent* from many

Anacardi.   Schinopsis

Acer.   Acer, Negundo; but *absent* from *Dipteronia*

Sapind.   in many; perhaps general

Hippocastan.   Aesculus

Elaeagn.   in all?

Apocyn.   Aspidosperma, Conopharyngia, Haplophyton; but *absent* from many

Comp.   Artemisia (all spp.?); but *absent* from other genera of *Anthemideae*?

It is said to be *absent* from: *Rut.*; *Simaroub.*; *Meli.*; *Rhamn.*; *Vit.*; *Thymelae.* (*Daphne*); *Lythr.* (*Cuphea, Lythrum*); *Trap.* (*Trapa*); *Myrt.* (*Callistemon, Eucalyptus, Eugenia*); *Punic.* (*Punica*); *Onagr.* (*Epilobium, Fuchsia, Gaura, Lopezia*); *Alangi.* (*Alangium*); *Davidi.* (*Davidia*); *Nyss.* (*Nyssa*).

Sequoyitol (Sequoitol; 5-O-Methyl-myo-inositol) is restricted, said Plouvier (1960), to gymnosperms, and is there widely distributed. We cannot be sure that it is *absent* from all angiosperms, but the list of plants in which it has *not* been found is impressive. Actually I have a record (Scholda, Billek and Hoffmann-Ostenhoff, 1963) that it *has* been found in *Trifolium incarnatum* (*Legum.*). It is said to be *absent* from: *Casuarin.* (*Casuarina*); *Myric.* (*Myrica*); *Jugland.* (*Juglans*); *Betul.* (*Alnus, Carpinus*); *Fag.* (*Castanea, Fagus*); *Ulm.* (*Ulmus, Zelkova*); *Mor.* (*Ficus, Morus*); *Magnoli.* (*Magnolia*); *Piper.* (*Peperomia*); *Legum.* (*Phaseolus, Vicia*); *Euphorbi.* (*Euphorbia, Mallotus*); *Hippocastan.* (*Aesculus*); *Staphyle.* (*Staphylea*); *Thymelae.* (*Daphne*); *Cist.* (*Cistus*); *Apocyn.* (*Amsonia, Nerium, Vinca*); *Comp.* (*Chrysanthemum*).

V DIMETHYL ETHERS OF CYCLITOLS WITH 6 -OH GROUPS

List and Occurrence

Dambonitol (1,3-Di-O-methyl-myo-inositol; fig. 103)
    Mor.   *Castilloa*; but *absent* from *Ficus*
    Apocyn.   *Dyera, Nerium, Trachelospermum, Vinca*
Liriodendritol (1,4-Di-O-methyl-myo-inositol; fig. 103)
    Magnoli.   *Liriodendron*

VI C-METHYL-INOSITOLS

Do these not occur in higher plants? Two (*l-laminitol* and *mytilitol*) occur in algae.

VII CYCLITOL GLYCOSIDES

List and Occurrence

Galactinol (O-α-D-Galactopyranosyl-(1 → 1)-D-myo-inositol) was said to occur only in beet, but a recent paper by Senser and Kandler (1967) greatly extends our knowledge of its distribution. They found *galactinol* in all plants with *raffinose* and *stachyose* which they investigated. Tanner and Kandler (1966) described an enzyme '*galactinol: raffinose-6-galactosyl-transferase*' 'which transfers galactose specifically and with high yield from galactinol to raffinose giving rise to stachyose and *myo*-inositol'.

Chenopodi. Beta

Onagr. Oenothera pumila (lvs, st.)

Eric. Andromeda japonica (lvs, st.)

Lab. Lamium maculatum (lvs, rt, etc.), *Lycopus europaeus* (lvs, rt), *Marrubium vulgare* (lvs, rt), *Origanum vulgare* (lvs, rt), *Prunella grandiflora* (lvs, rt, etc.)

Buddlej. Buddleja davidii (lvs)

Bignoni. Catalpa bignonioides (lvs)

VIII SHIKIMIC ACID AND QUINIC ACID, etc.

GENERAL

Although *shikimic* and *quinic acids* are not strictly *cyclitols*, they may be considered here for convenience. They may occur as *depsides* (qq.v.).

List and Occurrence

Dihydroshikimic acid

Combret. Terminalia chebula (myrobalans—little)

Quinic acid (fig. 103) seems to be widely spread in Nature. It has been reported from conifers and from:

Illici. Illicium

Ranuncul. Aconitum

Hamamelid. Many

Ros. Malus, Prunus, Rosa

Lin. Linum

Anacardi. Pistacia (in 3 out of 4 spp. tested); but *absent* from *Cotinus* (1), *Lithraea* (1), *Pistacia* (1), *Poupartia* (1), *Rhus* (1), *Schinus* (2).

Myrt. Eucalyptus

Combret. Terminalia

Umbell. Angelica

Eric. Arctostaphylos, Vaccinium

Gram. ?

Shikimic acid (fig. 103) has been reviewed by Bohm (1965). He says that it was first isolated 80 years ago from 'shikimi-noki' (*Illicium*), hence the name. It is well known, now, that *shikimic acid* and related substances are important in biosynthesis. Bohm says, for example (italics mine): 'In nature there are two sequences of reactions by which aromatic compounds are formed. In one a poly β-compound formed from *acetate* cyclizes to form an aromatic ring which usually retains several hydroxyl groups. This is the so-called "*acetate pathway*". The second method for forming aromatic compounds involves *shikimate* and some of its derivatives and derives its carbon from *glucose* metabolism.' Within the plant *shikimic acid* may occur in any part. It has been found, according to Bohm's list, in a liverwort, but *not* in a moss; in about a dozen ferns; in *Isoetes*, but *not* in *Equisetum*, *Lycopodium*, and *Selaginella*; in many but not all gymnosperms; in 11 out of 26 monocotyledons examined; in many dicotyledons, but with interesting exceptions.

Myric.   *Myrica rubra*
Jugland.   *Petrophiloides strobilacea*
Salic.   *Salix babylonica*
Betul.   *Carpinus tschonoskii*
Fag.   *Corylus* (1), *Cyclobalanopsis* (2 out of 3), *Kuromatea* (1),   *Quercus* (2), *Shiia* (2)
Magnoli.   *Liriodendron*, *Magnolia* (5), *Michelia* (1)
Schisandr.   *Kadsura japonica*
Illici.   *Illicium anisatum, religiosum*
Laur.   *Cinnamomum camphora*
Euptele.   *Euptelea polyandra*
Cercidiphyll.   *Cercidiphyllum japonicum*
Ranuncul.   *Thalictrum* (1)
Lardizabal.   *Akebia trifoliata*
Berberid.   *Mahonia fortunei*
Saurur.   *Houttuynia cordata*
Chloranth.   *Sarcandra glabra*
The.   *Cleyera ochnacea, Ternstroemia japonica*; but *absent* from *Thea*
Gutt.   *Hypericum* (some), *Mammea* (1); but *absent* from *Calophyllum* (1), *Clusia* (1), *Mesua* (1)
Papaver.   *Macleaya cordata*
Saxifrag.   *Ribes grossularia, Saxifraga stolonifera*
Platan.   *Platanus occidentalis*
Hamamelid.   *Distylium* (1), *Liquidambar* (1); but *absent* from *Corylopsis* (6), *Fothergilla* (1), *Hamamelis* (4), *Parrotia* (1), *Parrotiopsis* (1), *Sycopsis* (1)
Ros.   *Aruncus* (1), *Cydonia* (1), *Eriobotrya* (1), *Malus* (1), *Pyrus* (1), *Rubus* (1 of 2); but *absent* from *Prunus* (1)
Legum.   *Caesalpinia* (2), *Lespedeza* (1), *Vicia* (1)
Gerani.   *Geranium thunbergii*
Anacardi.   *Lithraea* (1), *Pistacia* (4), *Schinus* (2); but *absent* from *Poupartia* (1)

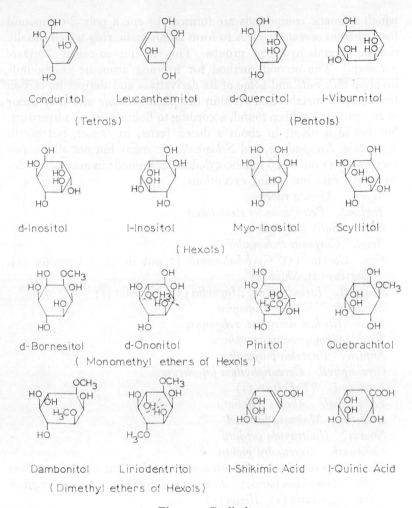

Fig. 103. Cyclitols.

Acer.   *Acer distylum*
Sapind.   *Sapindus mukurossi*
Hippocastan.   *Aesculus turbinata*
Celastr.   *Euonymus japonicus*
Vit.   *Vitis* sp.; but *absent* from *Cayratia japonica*
Elaeagn.   *Elaeagnus pungens* var.
Cucurbit.   *Lagenaria* (1); but *absent* from *Trichosanthes* (1)
Myrt.   *Eucalyptus* (5)
Combret.   *Anogeissus* (1), *Terminalia* (1)
Corn.   *Aucuba japonica*

Arali. Hedera tobleii
Eric. Pieris japonica
Ole. Ligustrum (1), *Syringa* (1); but *absent* from *Osmanthus* (1)
Rubi. Gardenia (1), *Rubia* (1)
Polemoni. Phlox paniculata
Verben. Vitex cannabifolia
Solan. Solanum lycopersicum var.; but *absent* from *Nicotiana tabacum*
Caprifoli. Viburnum (2), *Weigela* (1)
Valerian. Patrinia villosa
Comp. Dahlia (1), *Helianthus* (1); but *absent* from *Chrysanthemum* (1)
Gram. Lolium
It is said to be *absent* from: *Clethr. (Clethra); Eben. (Diospyros); Styrac. (Halesia), Symploc. (Bobua); Gentian. (Gentiana); Apocyn. (Nerium); Convolvul. (Ipomoea); Boragin. (Ehretia); Lab. (Perilla); Bignoni. (Paulownia); Gesneri (Conandron); Plantagin. (Plantago).*

DEPSIDES AND DEPSIDONES

GENERAL

Karrer (1958) defines *depsides* as ester-like derivatives of 2 or more *phenolic acids*, and *depsidones* as *depsides* with one —O— linkage making a third ring.

The former are characteristic constituents of lichens, and have been found, too, in a few fungi. Several are known from higher plants, and these are listed and discussed below. They are mostly derivatives of *quinic* and *shikimic acids.*

The latter also occur in lichens and in fungi, but I have no records of them from higher plants.

It is obvious that not much use can be made chemotaxonomically of the scattered records for *depsides* in higher plants. Perhaps further careful work will yield results of importance.

List and Occurrence

p-Coumaroyl-quinic acid
    Ros. Malus
    Myrt. Eucalyptus
p-Coumaroyl-shikimic acid
    Solan. Solanum tuberosum (tuber)?

Cynarine, an 'active principle', is said to be a 1,4-*dicaffeic ester* of *quinic acid*.

> Comp. *Cynara scolymus*

3,5-Dicaffeoyl-D-quinic acid is said to be a constituent of 'isochlorogenic acid'. If it is it probably occurs in

> Ros. *Prunus*
> Eric. *Vaccinium*
> Rubi. *Coffea*
> Comp. *Chrysanthemum coronarium* (lvs), *Helianthus annuus* (lvs)

4,5-Dicaffeoyl-D-quinic acid is also a constituent of 'isochlorogenic acid' and has the same distribution.

m-Galloyl-gallic acid (*m*-Digallic acid)

> The. *Thea*?

'Isochlorogenic acid' is, say Zane and Wender (1966), a mixture of 3 or more *depsides*, including 3,5-*dicaffeoyl*-D-*quinic acid* and 4,5-*dicaffeoyl*-D-*quinic acid* (above).

3-*O*-Caffeoyl-quinic acid (Chlorogenic acid; fig. 104) has long been known to be a constituent of higher plants. Gorter (1909) published a test for 'chlorogenic acid' and a long list of plants supposed to contain it. Unfortunately the test seems not to be specific, being given also by *caffeic acid*. I am not sure how many of the records are reliable.

> Eucommi. *Eucommia*
> Ranuncul. *Aconitum, Clematis*
> Ros. *Malus, Spiraea*
> Aquifoli. *Ilex*
> Corn. *Aucuba*
> Arali. *Aralia*
> Umbell. general?
> Logani. *Strychnos*
> Apocyn. *Kopsia*
> Rubi. *Coffea*
> Convolvul. *Ipomoea*
> Boragin. *Symphytum*
> Solan. *Solanum*
> Caprifoli. *Sambucus, Viburnum*
> Comp. *Chrysanthemum* (and many others?)

5-*O*-Caffeoyl-D-quinic acid (Neochlorogenic acid)

> Ros. *Prunus persica*
> Solan. *Lycopersicum esculentum* (lvs, st., rt)
> Comp. *Helianthus annuus* (lvs)

3-*O*-Caffeoyl-shikimic acid (Dactylic acid)

> Solan. *Solanum tuberosum* (tuber) *may* have this *depside*.
> Palmae. *Phoenix dactylifera* (frt)

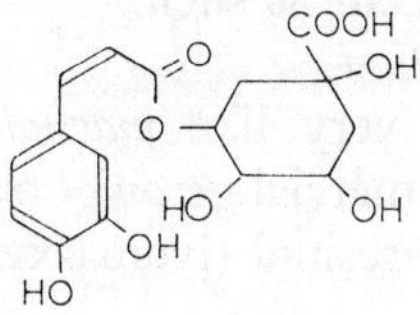

3-O-Caffeoyl-quinic acid
(Chlorogenic acid)

Fig. 104. A depside.

3-*O*-Feruloyl-D-quinic acid is said to occur in
> *Rubi.   Coffea*
> *Solan.   Lycopersicum esculentum*
> *Comp.   Helianthus annuus* (lvs)

α,ω-DIPHENYL-ALKANES

GENERAL

Two phenyl groups may be linked by a common bond ($n=0$), by a chain having one C-atom ($n = 1$), by a chain of 2 C-atoms ($n = 2$), and so on.

Thus we have:

I. *Diphenyl compounds* (n=0; fig. 105)—considered below.

II. *Diphenyl-methane derivatives* ($n=1$; fig. 105). Here belong the *benzophenones*, which are considered under *ketones*; and the *kosins*, which are discussed below.

III. *α,ω-Diphenyl-ethane derivatives* ($n=2$; fig. 105). Here belong the *stilbenes*, which are discussed below.

IV. *α,ω-Diphenyl-propane derivatives* ($n=3$). Here we might include the *chalcones*, which are dealt with as *flavonoids*.

I DIPHENYL COMPOUNDS

List and Occurrence

Aucuparin (4-Hydroxy-3,5-dimethoxy-diphenyl; fig. 105)
> *Ros.   Sorbus decora* (wd)

Cannabidiol (fig. 105) is a *phenol*.
> *Mor.   Cannabis sativa*

Cannabinol: does not occur as such?

> Mor.   Cannabis sativa

Dehydro-di-eugenol is very like *magnolol*. It has been found (but secondarily ?) in commercial *geraniol* from Java-citronellol.

(+)-Dimethoxy-isolariciresinol (lyonia-xyloside) has been treated as a *lignan*.

Diphenyl (Phenyl-benzene; fig. 105) does not, I think, occur free in Nature.

Hexahydroxy-diphenic acid may be obtained from *ellagitannins*. It is usually isolated as its stable lactone *ellagic acid* (which has been treated as a 3,4-*benzocoumarin*)

Magnolol (fig. 105)

> *Magnoli.   Magnolia obovata* (bk), *officinalis* (bk)

2'-Methoxy-aucuparin

> *Ros.   Sorbus decora* (wd)

$\Delta^{1(6)}$-3,4-*trans*-Tetrahydro-cannabinol (Δ^8-Tetrahydro-cannabinol) is an active component of hashish.

> Mor.   Cannabis sativa

II DIPHENYL-METHANE DERIVATIVES

List and Occurrence

α- and β-Kosin (fig. 105)

> *Ros.   Hagenia abyssinica* ('Koso', fl.)

Protokosin (fig. 105)

> *Ros.   Hagenia abyssinica* (fl.)

III STILBENES AND STILBENE GLYCOSIDES

GENERAL

Most of the *stilbenes* occur in woods. They are fungicidal and may well be protective. They are commonest in woods of gymnosperms (examples being *pinosylvin, pinosylvin-methyl ether, pinosylvin-dimethyl ether, 4-hydroxy-stilbene*). The only *stilbenes* of which I have records from gymnosperms *and* angiosperms are *piceatannol* and *resveratrol*. Some of the *stilbenes* occur as glycosides.

Hillis (1966) has found *stilbenes* in many species of *Eucalyptus*—which see for further discussion.

Madhav, Seshadri and Subramanian (1967) say: 'The polyphenol isolated from *Shorea talura* and *S. robusta* belonging to the family

Dipterocarpaceae has now been identified as hopeaphenol originally found in *Hopea odorata* and *Balanocarpus heimii*. Therefore, its occurrence should be considered characteristic of this family.'

We may object that since Gilg (in EP2, 1925) places *Shorea, Hopea*, and *Balanocarpus* in the same tribe (*Shoreeae*), this evidence indicates only the near relationship of the three genera. We need to have records of *hopeaphenol* from the other five tribes before we can say that it is 'characteristic of this family'.

List and Occurrence

Chlorophorin (2-Homogeranyl-2',3',3,5-tetrahydroxy-stilbene)
  Mor.   *Chlorophora excelsa* (wd)
3',5'-Dihydroxy-resveratrol (3,5,3',4',5'-Pentahydroxy-stilbene)
  Legum.   *Vouacapoua macropetala* (htwd)
Hopeaphenol (fig. 106) is a complex of 4 *stilbene* units, say Madhav, Seshadri and Subramanian (1967).
  Dipterocarp.   *Balanocarpus heimii*; *Hopea odorata*; *Shorea robusta* (bk, htwd), *talura* (bk, htwd)
Hydrangeic acid (Hydrangea-acid; Isohydrangenol; fig. 106)
  Saxifrag.   *Hydrangea macrophylla* var. (fl.) (see also *hydrangenol*, an *isocoumarin*)
2'-Hydroxy-resveratrol (2',4',3,5-Tetrahydroxy-stilbene)
  Mor.   *Artocarpus lakoocha, Maclura pomifera* (*aurantiaca*) (htwd)
  Lili.   *Veratrum grandiflorum* (rt)
3'-Hydroxy-resveratrol (3',4',3,5-Tetrahydroxy-stilbene) has been found in *Picea abies*, but it is *not* identical with *piceatannol*?
  Legum.   *Laburnum*; *Vouacapoua americana* (htwd), *macropetala* (htwd)
3'-Hydroxy-resveratrol-3-glucoside (Astringin?; Piceid; Polydatin?; Polydatoside?; fig. 106)
  Polygon.   *Polygonum cuspidatum*
  Myrt.   *Eucalyptus*
Phyllodulcic acid (fig. 106)
  Saxifrag.   *Hydrangea* (lvs of 1 sp.) (see also *phyllodulcin*, an *isocoumarin*)
Pterostilbene (4'-Hydroxy-3,5-dimethoxy-stilbene; fig. 106)
  Legum.   *Pterocarpus santalinus* (htwd) and 4 other spp. Four of the five spp. also have the related *isoflavanones*.
Resveratrol (4',3,5-Trihydroxy-stilbene; fig. 106) is said to occur in 3 spp. of *Picea* and in
  Myrt.   *Eucalyptus wandoo* (htwd) and many other spp. (free)?
  Lili.   *Veratrum grandiflorum* (rt)

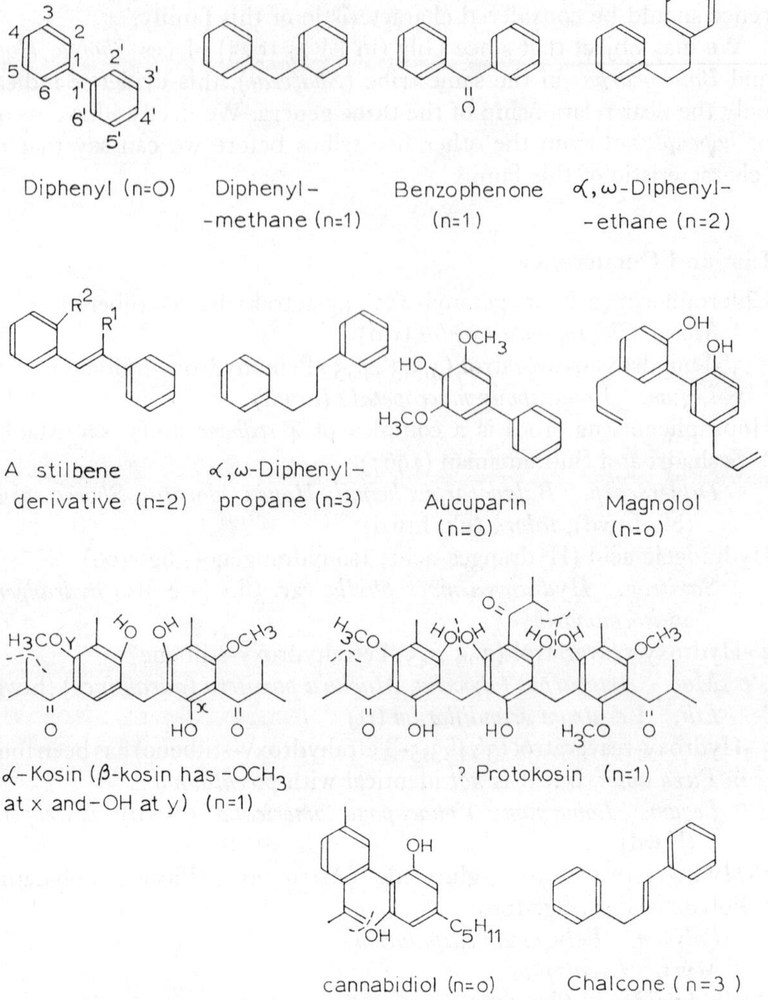

Fig. 105. Diphenyl, diphenyl-methane and some related diphenyls.

Resveratrol-3-β-D-glucoside
    Myrt.   Eucalyptus wandoo (htwd)
Rhapontigenin (Pontigenin; 3′,3,5-Trihydroxy-4′-methoxy-stilbene) is
    reported (free ?) from
        Polygon.   Polygonum (1), *Rheum* (3)
        Myrt.   Eucalyptus

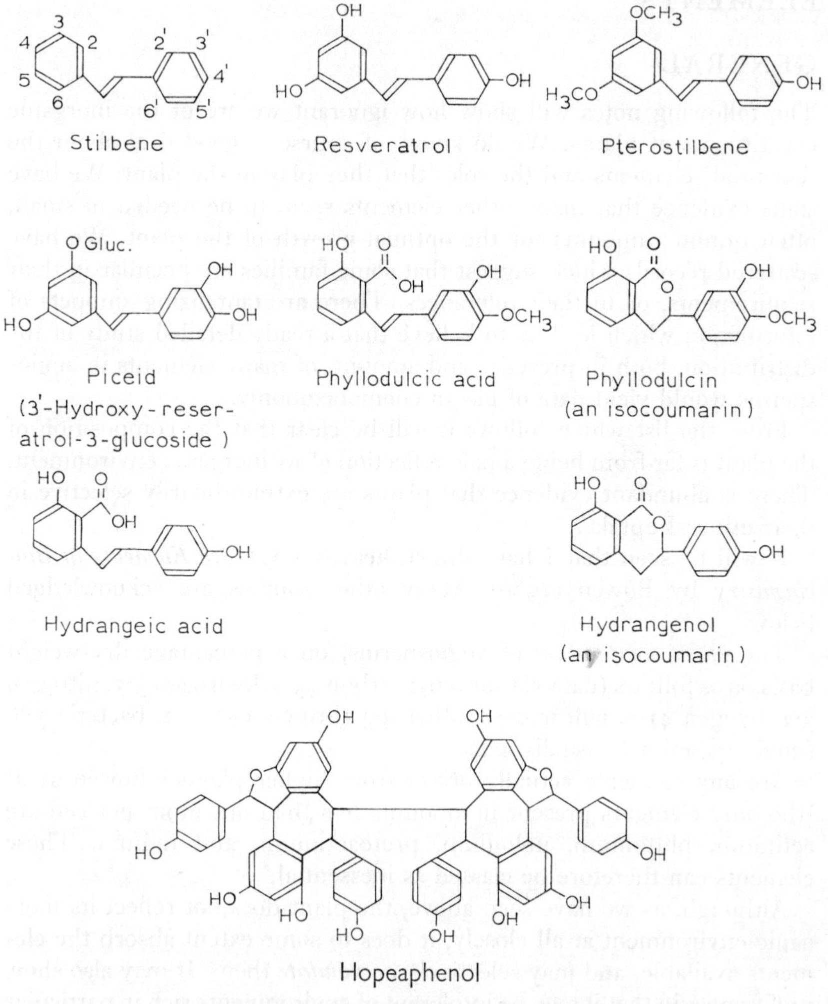

Fig. 106. Stilbene and some related substances.

Rhapontigenin-5-glucoside (Rhapontin; Rhaponticin; Ponticin)
    Polygon. *Polygonum multiflorum* (rhiz., rt); *Rheum emodi* (rt), *rhaponticum* (rt)
    Myrt. *Eucalyptus* sp. (lvs)
Stilbene (fig. 106): does not occur as such?
3,4',5-Trimethoxy-*trans*-stilbene
    Myristic. *Virola cuspidata* (bk)

ELEMENTS

GENERAL

The following notes will show how ignorant we are of the inorganic constituents of plants. We do know, of course, a good deal about the 'essential' elements and the roles that they play in the plant. We have some evidence that many other elements seem to be needed in small, often minute, amounts for the optimal growth of the plant. We have scattered records which suggest that some families are peculiar in their requirements, or in their tolerances. There are tantalizing snippets of information which lead us to believe that a really detailed study of the distribution, both in presence and amount, of many elements in angiosperms would yield data of use in chemotaxonomy.

From the list which follows it will be clear that the composition of the plant is far from being a pale reflection of its inorganic environment. There is abundant evidence that plants are extraordinarily selective in their mineral uptake.

It will be seen that I have drawn heavily on *Trace Elements in Biochemistry* by Bowen (1966). Many other sources are acknowledged below.

The *mean composition* of angiosperms, on a percentage dry-weight basis, is as follows (data via Bowen): carbon 45·4, hydrogen 5·5, nitrogen 3·3, oxygen 41·0, sulfur 0·44, other 4·4 (brown algae 22, bacteria 5·8, fungi 5·7, animals usually 4·4).

Are any elements actually *absent* from higher plants? Bowen says: 'the only elements present in amounts less than one atom per cell are actinium, plutonium, polonium, protoactinium, and radium. These elements can therefore be classed as inessential.'

Although, as we have seen above, the plant does not reflect its inorganic environment at all closely, it does to some extent absorb the elements available, and may selectively *accumulate* them. It may also show preferences in that it may be intolerant of environments rich in particular elements, or may occur only or chiefly in situations where certain ones are in large amount. Man has recognized these facts and has made use of them in prospecting for inorganic materials of commercial importance.

Cannon (1960) has discussed this. We learn that the use of plants in prospecting goes back at least to 1828; and that it has prospered particularly in the USSR. Tkalich (1938) used *indicator* plants and also plant analysis. Palmquist and Brudin are said to have discovered *vanadium*-bearing shale in Sweden, and *tungsten* in Cornwall, by spectrographic analysis of plant ash. Prospecting has been assisted in at least 3 ways: by noting *distribution of indicator plants*, by observing the *appearance* of plants (unusual physiological and morphological changes), and by actual *analysis of plants*.

The chemotaxonomic usefulness of the elements is hinted at in the following list, though many of the records are of dubious value. We may wonder if *Carya* of the *Juglandaceae*, for example, is *really* an accumulator of *cerium, dysprosium, erbium, europium, gadolinium, holmium, lanthanum, lutecium, neodymium, praseodymium, samarium, terbium, thulium, ytterbium,* and *yttrium*!

(Robinson, Bastron, and Murata, 1958, say:

Hickory trees concentrate the rare-earth elements in their leaves [actually leaflets of *Carya glabra* and *C. ovalis* were used] to a phenomenal degree and may contain as much as 2,300 ppm of total rare earths based on the dry weight of the leaves...The similarity in the proportions of the rare-earth elements in the leaves and in the exchange complex of the soil...indicates that the trees do not fractionate the rare earths appreciably.)

List and Occurrence

Actinium (Ac) is radioactive. It usually occurs, says Bowen (1966), in amounts of less than 1 atom per cell! 6·1-hour ^{228}Ac has been found in plants from *thorium*-rich soils.

Alabamine (Ab) is not mentioned by Bowen (1966) as occurring in plants.

Aluminium (Al) is, says Hutchinson (1943): 'the 3rd most abundant element of the accessible parts of the lithosphere, following oxygen and silicon...'.

He concludes that about 0·002% Al (fresh weight) would be about the average for plants. This might correspond to 0·005–0·02% of dry weight. Bowen (1966) gives a figure of 550 ppm as average for woody angiosperms.

Al is only available to plants in acid soils. It is moderately toxic to most plants. Among the most assiduous workers in this field we may rate Chenery (1946, 1948), Hutchinson (1943), and Webb (1954). Their work shows that while all plants contain Al, only a minority *accumulate* it. Many accumulators have *blue fruits*, but not all blue-fruited plants are accumulators. *Delarbrea* (*Araliaceae*) has bright blue fruits but does not accumulate Al (Webb, 1954). Chenery (1946) says that no *blue-flowered* accumulators are known.

Many have acid cell-saps. Chenery (1946) says that values of pH 4·3–5·5 had been recorded, but that he had found acidities as high as pH 3·6. In acid cell-saps *delphinidin* may be red; but *delphinidin-aluminium* lakes are blue.

In 1948 he says that many aluminium-accumulators have been used in dyeing as mordants, and that they often dry yellow-green.

There is some evidence that Al is required by *Symplocos* spp. Hutchinson (1943) says that there is antagonism between *copper* and *aluminium*.

Are there plants which absorb *less* Al than the average? Moomaw *et al.* (1959) seem to think that there are, and propose the term '*aluminum-excluders*' for such. They say: 'The widespread and remarkably adaptable ohia lehua (*Metrosideros collina* subsp. *polymorpha*) was very low [in Al], as was the closely related Macadamia nut (a member of the Proteaceae).[1] These two plants and pangola grass [*Digitaria decumbens*] show such low levels [70, 60, and 64 ppm respectively] that a metabolic device for excluding aluminum seems probable.'

Among *aluminium-accumulators* we may include: *Jugland.* some; *Prote.* many; *Olac.* some; *Monimi.* some; *Laur.* some; *The.* some; *Saxifrag.–Hydrangioideae Hydrangea* (some spp.), *Escallonioideae* some, *Phyllonomoideae* all?; *Cunoni.* some; *Euphorbi.* some; *Vochysi.* all? (see Goodland, McGill Thesis, 1969, unpublished); *Polygal.* some; *Pentaphylac.* all, says Chenery; *Celastr.* some; *Icacin.* some; *Scytopetal.* some; *Geissolomat. Geissoloma marginatum*; *Viol.* some; *Crypteroni.* some; *Myrt.* some; *Melastomat.* some; *Rhizophor.* some; *Diapensi.* all, says Chenery. Hutchinson (1943) says: 'The entire family would appear to be characterized by marked aluminum accumulation, the genus *Shortia* in particular being rivaled, in this respect, only by certain species of *Symplocos* and the heterophyllous *Lycopodia*.'

Eric. Rhododendron; *Symploc.* all? Hutchinson says: 'it is reasonably certain that the specimens of *Symplocos* richest in the element [von Faber says up to 72,300 ppm in *S. spicata*!] contain more aluminum than do any other organisms, and that aluminum is probably exceeded in abundance only by hydrogen, oxygen and carbon in the elementary composition of such plants'.

Logani. some; *Gentian.* some; *Apocyn.* some; *Rubi.* some; *Lentibulari.* some; *Lili. Aletris*; *Rapate.* some; *Gram.* a few, at least; *Orchid.* at least one.

Antimony (Sb). Woody angiosperms have about 0·06 ppm (Bowen, 1966). It is moderately toxic to all organisms.

Argon (A, also Ar?). The atmosphere has about 0·8% *argon*. It is non-toxic to plants and animals in the presence of *oxygen*.

Arsenic (As). Woody angiosperms have an average of 0·2 ppm (Bowen, 1966). It is moderately toxic to plants. Soils in Argentina and New Zealand may have enough arsenic to make plants growing on them toxic to mammals.

[1] We may query this relationship.

Barium (Ba) may occur in plants from normal soils in amounts vary-ing from 0·5 to 40 ppm, and averaging about 10 ppm (Bowen and Dymond, 1955–6). Woody angiosperms have about 14 ppm. Some soils may have up to 3000 ppm, and plants growing in such soils (if they are poor in *calcium*) may have a much higher *barium* content than the average.

Ba is moderately toxic to plants. There is some evidence that it may be essential for mammals. It is said to be accumulated by:

    Legum.   *Astragalus* spp.

    Lecythid.   *Bertholletia excelsa* (to 4000 ppm in frt).

Beryllium (Glucinum) (Be, Gl) may occur in coal to 1000 ppm. Woody angiosperms have usually less than 0·1 ppm, but have more on volcanic and pegmatite soils (Bowen, 1966). It is toxic to animals and has been shown to inhibit the growth of *Phaseolus vulgaris*, affecting particularly the roots (Romney *et al.* 1962).

Bismuth (Bi) occurs in very small amount (0·06 ppm) in woody angiosperms. Plants growing in *thorium*-rich soils may contain 1-hour ^{212}Bi. Bi is said to be moderately toxic to plants.

Boron (B) may occur in soils in amounts sufficient to poison plants. It may also be so deficient in soils as to cause abnormal growth and death of plants.

Woody angiosperms have about 50 ppm. Some plants have been used as *indicators* for B: Cannon (1960) mentions the following:

    Chenopodi.   *Eurotia ceratoides, Salsola nitraria*

    Plumbagin.   *Limonium suffruticosum*

Is it coincidence that these families are considered by some to be related?

Plants that are *accumulators* include:

    Comp.   *Polymnia* spp.

Lee and Aronoff (1967) have considered the role of *boron*. They say: 'A biochemical syndrome of boron deficiency is the accumulation of phenolic acids; their excessive concentration appears to be the immediate cause of necrosis and ultimate death from this nutritional deficiency.'

Schütte (1964) says that some cereals, legumes, rubber, tea, and cocoa, have very low requirements for *boron* and readily show toxicity symp-toms when it is in excess.

Bromine (Br) occurs in sea-water in about 65 ppm but it is absorbed and concentrated by brown and red algae. These form organic *brom-phenols*, the chief of which, in the closely related red algae *Odonthalia* and *Rhodomela*, is *lanosol* (2,3-*dibromo*-4,5-*dihydroxy-benzyl alcohol*) (Webb, 1957).

Br occurs also in higher plants, about 15 ppm being present in woody angiosperms. It may be essential for mammals. Does it serve a useful purpose in angiosperms?

A few plants, members of the *Chenopodiaceae* and *Cucurbitaceae*, are said to have more than the average content of bromine. A careful study of these families might prove rewarding.

Cadmium (Cd) is present in minute amounts in fresh water but is said to be absorbed by freshwater plants (concentration-factor 1620). Woody angiosperms have about 0·64 ppm.

Attempts have been made to show its usefulness to higher plants. Thus Dobroliubskii and Slavvo (1958) sprayed grape-vines with $CdSO_4$, and obtained an increase in yield and sweeter, earlier-ripening grapes. Schroeder and Balassa (1963), however, say that vegetables that usually contain Cd can be grown in its absence. Cd is said to be moderately toxic.

Caesium (see Cesium).

Calcium (Ca) (see also *crystals, raphides, gypsum*). Ca is an essential element for higher plants, and woody angiosperms have about 18,000 ppm. Freshwater plants absorb it (concentration-factor about 265).

A discussion of its role in ecology would be out of place here but it is well known that some plants are found only on soils rich in lime, while others avoid it. There is undoubtedly material of chemotaxonomic value here.

Carbon (C). Many books have been written about *carbon* and its compounds, more than 500,000 of which are said to be known. It is, of course, one of the major components of plants, woody angiosperms having about 454,000 ppm.

Man is changing the C cycle—the amount of CO_2 in the atmosphere is said to have increased by 14% between 1900 and 1960. It has been said that living plants change the C_{12}/C_{13} ratio and that carbons of great age may be proved to be of biological origin by their increased C_{12}/C_{13} ratios. Bowen (1966) says that recent work has cast doubts upon this.

Most of this book deals with the carbon-compounds of higher plants!

Cerium (Ce) is accumulated somewhat by freshwater plants (concentration-factor 7100). Woody angiosperms have about 34 ppm. It is said to be *accumulated* by:

Jugland. Carya (320 ppm)

Cesium (Caesium, Cs) occurs to about 0·2 ppm in woody angiosperms. It is present in very small amount in fresh water but is concentrated somewhat by freshwater plants (concentration-factor 480).

It is relatively harmless to all organisms.

Chlorine (Cl) is an essential element for angiosperms. Woody angiosperms have about 2000 ppm.

Organochlorine substances, some of them antibiotic, are produced by fungi.

Sea-water has 19,000 ppm, and maritime and salt-desert plants may have much more Cl than the average.

Chromium (Cr). Woody angiosperms average about 0·23 ppm. Freshwater plants absorb and concentrate Cr (concentration-factor 695).

Cr may activate *phosphoglucomutase* and other enzymes.

I know of no *accumulators* among the angiosperms but the fern *Asplenium viride* is said to be one.

Cobalt (Co) is essential for nitrogen-fixation by free-living bacteria, blue-green algae, and symbiotic systems. Wilson and Nicholas (1967) have produced visible signs of *cobalt* deficiency in non-nodulated plants of *Trifolium subterraneum* and *Triticum durum*. It is organically bound in plants.

Woody angiosperms have about 0·48 ppm. Freshwater plants concentrate *cobalt* (concentration-factor 4425). The vitamin B_{12} (*cyanocobalamin*) is a *cobalt-porphyrin*.

Accumulators include:

Nyss. *Nyssa sylvatica* var. *biflora* (30·7 ppm)
Clethr. *Clethra alnifolia* (9·3 ppm, see below), *barbinervis*. Thus, Yamagata and Murakami (1958) say: 'The cobalt and nickel content of the ash [of lvs] of a variety of trees other than *Clethra* sp. ranged from less than 1·0 to 22·5 ppm and from 3·2 to 120 ppm, respectively. More than one hundred times as much cobalt and several times as much nickel were found in *Clethra* spp. as in other plant species.'

Columbium (Niobium, Cb, Nb). Woody angiosperms have about 0·3 ppm. Freshwater plants absorb *columbium* from the water around them (concentration-factor 7640).

Copper (Cu) is an essential element for angiosperms.

Bowen (1966) lists the following enzymes as containing Cu in the percentages indicated: *Phenol oxidase* (0·2), *tyrosinase* (0·195), *β-mercaptopyruvate trans-sulfurase* (0·17), *uricase* (0·056), *laccase* (0·22), *monoamine oxidase* (0·14), *ascorbic acid oxidase* (0·26), *ceruloplasmin* (0·32), *galactose oxidase* (0·055), *benzylamine oxidase, hyponitrite reductase, NO reductase, nitrite reductase type II*.

Solutions of Cu salts are very toxic but at least two species of fungi are said to be able to grow in saturated $CuSO_4$ solution! I have myself seen pellicles of mycelium growing *on* rather than *in* moderately strong solutions of $CuSO_4$ in laboratory reagent bottles.

Woody angiosperms have about 14 ppm.

Many plants have been used as 'copper-indicators' (Cannon, 1960). My notes include the following:

Bryophyta. 'copper-mosses' are well known. *Merkeya latifolia* is listed as an *indicator*.
Fag. *Quercus macrocarpa*. MacDougall (1899) says the wood of a

dead tree had almost 0·5 gm per kg (dry wt) of Cu, and that particles of the metal were visible in the cells!

Caryophyll. Gypsophila patrini, Polycarpaea spirostylis are *indicators.* MacDougall (1899) says that J. B. Skerthly 'has found that *Polycarpaea spirostylis* F. von Mueller occurs in such close connection with the copper deposits of North Queensland in such an invariable manner that it may be used as indication of copper deposits in the soil or in solution in the streams near by. On this account he has named it the "copper plant", and notes that in regions rich in copper it is the predominant member of the herbaceous flora.'

Silene inflata has Cu-tolerant types. Many others are *indicators.*

Papaver. Eschscholtzia mexicana (indicator)

Simaroub. Quassia gabonensis (grown on soils not rich in Cu, but may have 0·7%)

Myrt. Eucalyptus?

Plumbagin. Armeria maritima (may be an *indicator*)

Sapot. Sideroxylon?

Logani. Strychnos nux-vomica (sd, may have 0·24% Cu)

Lab. Acrocephalus roberti, Elsholtzia haichowensis, Ocimum homblei are *indicators.* (The last requires soils with not less than 100 ppm.)

Peisach, Aisen, and Blumberg have edited a recent (1966) monograph on the biochemistry of Cu.

Dysprosium (Dy) occurs only in minute amounts in most land-plants (Bowen, 1966, says < 0·02 ppm). It is said to be *accumulated* by

Jugland. Carya (Robinson *et al.*)

Erbium (Er) is said to be *accumulated* by

Jugland. Carya

Europium (Eu). Woody angiosperms have 0·021 ppm. It is said to be *accumulated* by

Jugland. Carya

Fluorine (F). 'Fluorosis' due to high concentrations of F in plants has been reported from N. Africa, Tanganyika, S. Africa, the U.S.A., and (worst of all) Madras.

Woody angiosperms have about 0·5 ppm. F has not been proven to be essential, though it has been much in the news in connection with the fluoridation of drinking water.

From the chemotaxonomic point of view the most interesting thing about *fluorine* is its occurrence in *fatty acids.*

Legum. Acacia georginae: seeds of this plant ('gidgie') are known to be toxic, and Oelrichs and McEwan (1961) have found them to contain *fluoroacetate. Gastrolobium grandiflorum* leaves have *fluoroacetate,* too.

Dichapetal. *Dichapetalum* was for long thought to be the only source of F-containing fatty acids. Seeds of *D. toxicarium* have *ω-fluoropalmitate* and *ω-fluorooleate*. *D. cymosum* leaves have *fluoroacetate*.

Rubi. *Palicourea marcgravii* is very toxic. Its leaves have been found (de Oliveira, 1963) to contain *fluoroacetate*.

Francium (Fr) is 'a natural isotope, occurring as the result of an alpha disintegration of actinium'. I have no record of it in plants.

Gadolinium (Gd) is said to be *accumulated* by
    Jugland. *Carya*

Gallium (Ga). Woody angiosperms have only 0·05 ppm. It has been thought to be essential for angiosperms but this is doubted.

Germanium (Ge). Coal has up to 3000 ppm. Tchakirian (1942) says that salts of Ge when added to soil may cause plants to show toxic symptoms.

Gold (Au) ordinarily occurs in very small amount in woody angiosperms (< 0·00045 ppm, says Bowen, 1966). In plants growing in gold-rich soils, however, much more may be present. Warren and Delavault (1950) report:
    Equisetum (0·03 to 0·075 ppm)
    Salic. *Populus tremuloides* (0·02 ppm), *Salix* sp. (0·023 ppm)

I seem to remember reading somewhere that *Equisetum* had been harvested for its gold content but I may be recalling inaccurately the following quotation (*Montreal Star*, 6 December 1951): 'Geologist Hans Lundberg said last night that gold-bearing plants—yielding as much as $400 an acre—soon may be grown commercially. He told of an area in Indiana with colloidal gold in the soil.

'When horsetail fern [*Equisetum*] was planted it absorbed as much as 9 oz. of gold in a ton of plant matter.'

Indicator-plants for gold are said to include:
    Mor. *Cecropia* spp.
    Typh. *Typha* spp.
    Zingiber. *Alpinia speciosa*

Hafnium (Hf). Land-plants have about 0·01 ppm?

Helium (He). I have no record of it in plants.

Holmium (Ho) occurs in igneous rocks. It is said to be *accumulated* by
    Jugland. *Carya*

Hydrogen (H) is one of the abundant constituents of all living things. Woody angiosperms have 55,000 ppm.

H_2 may be fixed by leaves of higher plants. Most of the compounds considered in this book contain *hydrogen*, often in large proportion.

Illinium (Il) is not even mentioned by Bowen (1966).

Indium (In). I have no record of it in plants.

Iodine (I). Sea-water has only about 0·06 ppm but it is concentrated (as is *bromine*) by diatoms and by brown algae (which last may have 1500 ppm). In seaweeds *mono-* and *di-iodo-tyrosine* and *thyroxine* are said to occur.

Woody angiosperms have about 0·4 ppm. Is *iodine* essential for some angiosperms? It is said to be *accumulated* by

    Myrt. Feijoa sellowiana

Iridium (Ir) occurs in land-plants in about 0·02 ppm (Bowen, 1966).

Iron (Fe) is an abundant element, ordinary soils having 30 to 300 ppm. It is concentrated by freshwater plants (concentration-factor about 4935). Woody angiosperms have about 140 ppm.

Iron is an essential element for green plants. It activates some *oxidases*, and it is a constituent of some *enzymes* (% Fe in brackets): *ferredoxin* from spinach (0·86), *pyrocatechase* (0·14), *metapyrocatechase* (0·04), *cytochrome oxidase, cytochrome C, peroxidase, catalase,* some *metalloflavin enzymes.*

Some plants are said to be *indicators* for Fe; others are *accumulators.*

    Betul. Betula sp. (*indicator* in Germany)
    Guttif. Clusia rosea (*indicator* in Venezuela)
    Rubi. Duroia longifolia (*accumulator*)
    Orchid. Epidendrum o'brienianum (*indicator* in Venezuela)

Krypton (Kr). I have no records of Kr in plants.

Lanthanum (La). Soils may have up to 5000 ppm. Woody angiosperms have 0·085 ppm. It is said to be *accumulated* by

    Jugland. Carya

Lead (Pb). Soils may have 200 ppm. Woody angiosperms average about 2·7 ppm. Some plants may serve as *indicators* for *lead*:

    Legum. Amorpha canescens
    Comp. Tussilago farfara (in Germany)
    Gram. Erianthus giganteus (Tennessee)

Lead is very toxic to most plants, but Bradshaw *et al.* (1965) say that strains of the grass *Agrostis tenuis* have developed great tolerance for *lead, copper, nickel* and *zinc*. The metals are absorbed but are not toxic to the adapted strains. *Festuca ovina* may also become *lead*-tolerant. There is some evidence for extremely rapid evolution of tolerance.

Lithium (Li) may replace *potassium* in cells. *Indicators* and/or *accumulators* include

    Ranuncul. Thalictrum (on soils from acid rocks, up to $1·5 \times 10^{-2}\%$ Li in ash)
    Solan. Lycium spp. and other solanaceous plants may have high Li contents.
    Comp. Cirsium spp. (on soils from acid rocks, to $3·3 \times 10^{-3}\%$ Li in ash)

Lutecium (Lu) is said to be *accumulated* by
  Jugland. Carya (4·5 ppm)

Magnesium (Mg) is a constituent of *chlorophyll*, and is an essential element for green plants. Its functions are said to be electrochemical, catalytic and structural. It is perhaps the commonest enzyme-activator. Bowen (1966) says that it 'probably holds ribosomes together'.

Limestones may have 47,000 ppm; soils may have up to 6000 ppm. Those derived from serpentinite, peridotite and dunite are rich in Mg and Fe and are said to be ultrabasic (ultramafic). Kruckeberg (1967) says: 'Ultramafic soils are highly infertile; they are deficient in calcium, nitrogen, and phosphorus, and often elicit other nutritional effects...As a consequence, such soils can have a pronounced exclusion effect on surrounding vegetation and yet often develop singular and even spectacular floras.'

Woody angiosperms have about 3200 ppm of Mg as a rule, but plants growing on serpentine, etc. may *accumulate* it. Baumeister (1958) says that in general *Leguminosae* have the highest and *Gramineae* the lowest *magnesium* contents.

Manganese (Mn) is an essential element for angiosperms. It is said to activate *phosphate transferases* and *decarboxylases* in the Krebs cycle. It is a constituent of *metalloflavin enzymes* such as *NADH nitroreductase* and *nitrite reductase*.

Woody angiosperms have about 630 ppm. Angiospermous families seem to differ significantly in their Mn contents (Bertrand and Silberstein, 1952; see Table 5).

Indicators and/or *accumulators* include
  Caryophyll. Stellaria holostea (950 ppm, dry wt)
  The. Thea sinensis
  Myrt. Eucalyptus crebra (ash to 1·5% Mn), *Melaleuca* spp. (have deposits of Mn compounds?)
  Trap. Trapa natans (*accumulator*)
  Scrophulari. Digitalis purpurea (*indicator*)

Manganese toxicity has been observed in coffee plantations in Africa.

Masurium (Ma). I have no information as to the occurrence of Ma in plants.

Mercury (Hg) occurs in small amount in soils (up to 0·3 ppm). Freshwater plants absorb and concentrate it (concentration-factor 5915). Woody angiosperms have about 0·015 ppm. *Mercury* is very toxic both to green plants and to fungi.

  Caryophyll. Arenaria setacea (an *indicator*)

Molybdenum (Mo). Some soils are deficient in Mo, while others may have so much as to yield toxic herbage (see below).

TABLE 5. Manganese in angiosperms (after Bertrand and Silberstein, 1952)

Family	Number of species studied	Average Mn content (ppm dry wt)
Polygon.	11	65
Caryophyll.	21	110
'Salsolaceae'[1]	11	39
Ranuncul.	23	103
Crucif.	26	44
Ros.	13	130
Legum.	25	77
Umbell.	14	64
Boragin.	10	68
Lab.	26	65
Solan.	11	65
Scrophulari.	12	471
Comp.	34	62
Other dicots.	81	109
Average for dicots.		98
Gram.	35	77
Other monocots.	36	126
Average for monocots.		99

[1] Chenopodi. ?

It is an essential element for angiosperms. It is a constituent of *metalloflavin enzymes* such as *aldehyde dehydrogenase, xanthine oxidase,* etc.

Woody angiosperms have about 0·9 ppm, but the seeds of some legumes are said to be rich in the element. Vinogradov (1964) gives the following (ppm dry wt): *Albizia julibrissin* (100), *Cercis siliquastrum* (6), *Cytisus* spp. (20 and 70), *Genista aetnensis* (100), *Gleditsia* spp. (7 to 10), *Laburnum* spp. (80 and 100).

Stewart and Leonard (1952) noted signs of Mo deficiency in *Citrus* and its cure by spraying and injections.

Mo accumulates in forage plants growing on granitic alluvial fans in Nevada. Concentrations as high as 300 ppm have been recorded, and the forage is then toxic to cattle.

Neodymium (Nd). Woody angiosperms have about 24 ppm. It is said to be *accumulated* by

Jugland.   *Carya* (460 ppm)

Neon (Ne). I have no information as to the occurrence of *neon* in plants.

Nickel (Ni). Serpentine soils may have up to 1000 ppm. Woody angiosperms have an average of 2·7 ppm, but accumulation is known. Sarosiek (1957) has studied the vegetation on 'mining–melting nickel heaps' poor in organic compounds but very rich in *nickel, iron, calcium* and *magnesium*. He found 3 accumulators of Ni. Winogradov (1964) found nickel-accumulating varieties of some species. We have as *accumulators*

> *Ranuncul.* *Anemone patens* (normal plant 7·8 ppm in ash; accumulating var. 310 ppm (Winogradov))
> *Crucif.* *Alyssum bertolonii*
> *Cunoni.* *Pancheria glabrosa*
> *Clethr.* *Clethra barbinervis* (140 ppm in ash)
> *Plantagin.* *Plantago lanceolata* (Sarosiek)
> *Campanul.* *Campanula rotundifolia* (a dwarfed form. Sarosiek)
> *Comp.* *Linosyris* (*Aster?*) *villosa* (Winogradov), *Tussilago farfara* (Sarosiek)

Ni is said to be very toxic to most green plants and to fungi.

Nitrogen (N) forms a large part of the atmosphere, and soils may have up to 2500 ppm. It is, of course, an essential element, a constituent of all living things, which occurs to the extent of about 33,000 ppm in angiosperms. It is surprising that although *nitrogen* in gaseous form is so abundant, most plants and all animals are unable to use it in that form. Plants in general, but not animals, can use simple inorganic salts of N.

Nitrogen-fixation—the transformation of gaseous *nitrogen* to combined forms—seems to be restricted to certain bacteria, some blue-green algae, and root-nodulated (bacteria-containing) higher plants. Stewart (1967) has published a brief review on nitrogen-fixing plants. He lists:

> *Casuarin.* *Casuarina*
> *Myric.* *Comptonia, Myrica*
> *Betul.* *Alnus*
> *Ros.* *Cercocarpus, Dryas, Purshia*
> *Coriari.* *Coriaria*
> *Rhamn.* *Ceanothus, Discaria*
> *Elaeagn.* *Elaeagnus, Hippophaë, Shepherdia* (i.e. all genera of this little family, see p. 1737)

Osmium (Os). I have no record of its occurrence in plants.

Oxygen (O) is, like C and H, a major constituent of all living organisms. Angiosperms are more than 40% *oxygen*. I have no records of angiosperms that are particularly rich or poor in the element.

Palladium (Pd) is said to be very toxic to fungi. I have no record of it in higher plants.

Phosphorus (P). Soils may have up to 650 ppm. Woody angiosperms have about 2300 ppm. P is, of course, an essential element. We have few special records:

> *Ranuncul.* Sosa-Bourdouil (1951) says that the P content of pollens of the genera parallel the classification.
> *Convolvul. Convolvulus althaeoides* has been used as an *indicator* plant for P in Spain (Cannon, 1960)

Platinum (Pt). I have no record of its occurrence in plants.

Polonium (Po). Igneous rocks have 2×10^{-10} ppm. ^{210}Po is an important α-emitter in regions of high rainfall. Plants have much higher α-activities than have animals.

Potassium (K). Soils may have up to 30,000 ppm.

Woody angiosperms average about 14,000 ppm. K is an essential element for angiosperms. It is known to activate a few *enzymes*. Some families seem to be richer than others in K. Guttler (1941) gives the following (an average might be 2·64% (dry wt)):

> *Caryophyll.* 3·87%
> *Primul.* 3·96%
> *Boragin.* 4·32%

Praseodymium (Pr) is said to be *accumulated* by

> *Jugland. Carya* (46 ppm)

Protoactinium (Pa). I have no record of it in plants.

Radium (Ra). Woody angiosperms have about 1×10^{-9} ppm, but Ra is said to accumulate in plants growing on *thorium*-rich soils.

Radon (Niton, Rn). I have no records of *radon* in plants.

Rhenium (Re). Wood and Harrison (1953) have studied the response of plants to *rhenium*. They noted darkening and abnormal growth with concentrations of from 5 to 50 mg/l. The symptoms appear to differ from those due to excess of *manganese* or of *phosphorus*.

Rhodium (Rh). I have no records of Rh in higher plants.

Rubidium (Rb) is probably present in all plants. Woody angiosperms are said to have about 20 ppm. Bertrand and Bertrand (1951) have studied its occurrence in the seeds of about 50 species. They found it in amounts ranging from 0·6 ppm (dry wt) in *Secale* to 45·7 ppm in *Coffea*. In adult plants values were from 1 or 2 ppm to 120 ppm. Grasses seem to have low values.

In excess Rb is toxic, but there is increased growth when *rubidium chloride* is added to some soils.

Ruthenium (Ru). Woody angiosperms average about 0·005 ppm. The concentration-factor for freshwater plants is about 1700.

Samarium (Sm) is said to be slightly toxic to plants. Woody angiosperms have about 0·0055 ppm. It is *accumulated* by

> *Jugland. Carya* (23 ppm)

Scandium (Sc). Woody angiosperms have only 0·008 ppm. Hutchinson (1943) discusses *scandium* and the other rare earths. He mentions records of it in *Carya* and *Betula* leaves, and says that *Symplocos tinctoria* has 'rather greater amounts'.

Selenium (Se) is an interesting element and much is known about its occurrence in plants. Woody angiosperms have on average about 0·2 ppm, but some plants have much more.

Selenium appears to be essential for some plants. It may activate *formic dehydrogenase*. It is a constituent of at least 6 *amino-acids—seleno-cysteine, selenocystine, selenomethionine, selenocystathionine, Se-methyl-selenocysteine,* and *Se-methyl-selenomethionine.*

It is said to occur in a plant wax as *dimethyl-selenide* and *ethyl-selenate.* In mammals it is said to function as an alternative to *vitamin E.*

Much of our knowledge of *selenium* in plants stems from the work of Beath and Eppson (1947), Trelease and Beath (1949), and Rosenfeld and Beath (1964). We may summarize briefly some of their findings.

Wheat grown on seleniferous soils may be toxic (the *gluten* may have 90 ppm Se). Rosenfeld and Beath say: 'The ability of widely distributed native plants of *Astragalus* to accumulate several thousand parts per million selenium explained the losses of livestock and the hitherto unknown cause of the disease known as blind staggers.' To contract blind staggers the animals must get the *selenium* from plants, presumably in organic form. Rosenfeld and Beath distinguish:

(*a*) Beath's selenium indicators—plants which are restricted to seleniferous soils, seem to need *selenium*, and are malodorous. These include

> Crucif. *Stanleya* (all spp. examined; *S. bipinnata* may have 700 ppm)
> Legum. *Astragalus* (*ca.* 24 species and vars), *Neptunia amplexi-caulis* (in Australia an *accumulator* and possibly an *indicator*)
> Rubi. *Morinda reticulata* (an *indicator* in Australia)
> Comp. *Haplopappus* (section *Oonopsis*), *Machaeranthera* (section *Xylorhiza*)

(*b*) Secondary selenium absorbers—capable of absorbing considerable quantities when growing on highly seleniferous soils, but not restricted to such soils. These include

> Santal. *Comandra pallida* (accumulates Se only when its roots are attached to a seleniferous host?)
> Chenopodi. *Atriplex canescens, nuttallii* (Se mostly as selenate)
> Scrophulari. *Castilleja* spp. (*accumulate* Se, even though they are root-parasites, through their own roots?)
> Comp. *Aster adscandens, coerulescens, commutatus, ericoides, glauc-oides, laevis* var. *geyeri, occidentalis* (Se in these is mostly in

selenates), *Grindelia* spp. (*G. squarrosa* has up to 102 ppm), *Gutierrezia diversifolia* (up to 723 ppm).

Silicon (Si) (see also notes under *silica* (SiO_2)).

Si is an extremely abundant element. Soils may have up to 350,000 ppm. Although sea-water has only about 3 ppm and river-water about 12 ppm, diatoms may accumulate SiO_2 in large amount.

Woody angiosperms have about 200 ppm. Silicon is possibly an essential element for some plants. *Accumulators* include

> Horsetails, ferns
> *Cyper.* many?
> *Gram.* many? *Pappophorum silicosum* (infl.). Si was supposed to increase the strength of grass-straws, but this has been denied.
> *Junc.* ?

Silver (Ag). Woody angiosperms have about 0·06 ppm, but plants growing near *silver* ores may have more.

> *Equisetum* 0·23 ppm even when in soils not evidently metalliferous.
> *Salic. Salix* sp. (0·28 ppm)
> *Polygon. Eriogonum ovalifolium* (has been used as an *indicator* of Ag in Montana, says Cannon, 1960).

Sodium (Na) is an abundant element. Woody plants have about 1200 ppm.

Na is said to be an essential element for some plants, at least, but this is difficult to prove. Deficiency symptoms have been noted, and enhanced growth has been obtained when Na is added to beet, spinach, celery, cotton, cabbage, oats, etc. It is believed to activate some *enzymes*. Halophytes and some other plants may accumulate *sodium*. Baumeister's book on *sodium* as a plant nutrient includes some of the following figures

> *Chenopodi.* some are *accumulators* (average for family 0·42 to 2·03% dry wt)
> *Legum.* Faboideae (0·007 to 0·84)
> *Crucif.* 0·02 to 0·39
> *Frankeni.* some are *accumulators*
> *Plumbagin.* some are *accumulators*
> *Solan.* 0·09 to 0·45
> *Potamogeton. Ruppia, Zostera* are *accumulators*
> *Gram.* 0·009 to 0·54

Strontium (Sr) almost always occurs with much *calcium*. It is said to be accumulated by brown algae in preference to calcium.[1] It may be essential to mammals.

---

[1] *Strontium*, including ⁹⁰Sr, is selectively absorbed by the alginates under experimental conditions. This may be of great importance in counteracting ⁹⁰Sr fallout.

Woody angiosperms have about 26 ppm, but there is great variation in plants. Bowen and Dymond (1955–6) say: 'The strontium content of plants grown on normal soils has been shown to vary between 1 and 169 p.p.m. with a mean value of 36 ppm for forty plants...Plants from strontium-rich [celestite] soils may contain the element in amounts up to at least 2·6% [dry wt].'

Grasses tend to be low in Sr (average for 6 species, 18 ppm). Some plants may be good indicators for Sr. Wolf and Cesare (1952) give evidence that a spray containing Sr cures chlorosis of peach.

Sulfur (S). Coal may have 10,000 ppm; soils may have up to 900 ppm, but 90% of it may be bound in humus and so unavailable.

It is an essential element, and many sulfur-compounds which occur in plants are discussed elsewhere in this book. Woody angiosperms average about 3400 ppm. A few figures, mostly from Baumeister (1958), include: 14 species of 'ordinary' plants, 0·16% (dry wt); 5 grasses, 0·16%; leaves of grasses near hot sulfur-springs, 2·62%; 5 halophytes, 1·2%.

Tantalum (Ta). I have no records of Ta in plants.

Tellurium (Te). Beath et al. (1935) report from 2 to 25 ppm in plants from Te-rich soils.

Terbium (Tb). Woody angiosperms are said to have less than 0·0015 ppm.

Jugland. Carya (is an accumulator, 14 ppm)

Thallium (Tl). Salts of Tl are poisonous to animals and are used to control rodents such as squirrels. They are said to be moderately toxic to plants, but increased growth has been observed when 0·1 ppm has been added to the nutrient medium in growth experiments. I have no records of the Tl content of plants.

Thorium (Th). Bowen (1966) says: 'In the majority of soils, [40]K contributes most of the radioactivity. There are, however, local regions [in Britain, Czechoslovakia, Russia, India, Africa, N. America, Brazil] where either uranium or thorium may be unusually abundant...The α-activity of land plants may be caused by either the uranium family or the thorium family or both.'

Thulium (Tm). Woody angiosperms have about 0·0015 ppm. Thulium is said to be accumulated by

Jugland. Carya (4·6 ppm)

Tin (Sn). Woody angiosperms average less than 0·3 ppm. The following are said to be indicator plants.

Crassul. Sempervivum soboliferum
Primul. Trientalis europaea
Comp. Pluchea quitoc

Titanium (Ti). Sea-water has only about 0·001 ppm but Ti is said to be accumulated by plankton. Woody angiosperms have only 1 ppm.

Increased growth of white mustard, pea and lucerne have been reported when Ti has been added to the soil.

Tungsten (Wolframium, W). Woody angiosperms are said to have 0·07 ppm. The growth of a *Penicillium* was stimulated by *tungsten* and there is some evidence that it stimulates growth of higher plants.

Uranium (U). Woody angiosperms have 0·038 ppm, but the amounts in plants generally may vary from 0·1 to 34 ppm.

> Legum.   *Astragalus* spp. are said to be *indicators* and may also be
> *accumulators* (Cannon, 1960).

Vanadium (V) is said to be essential for some lower organisms, in which it may activate *enzymes* concerned with N-fixation. Thus it plays an important role in fixation by *Azotobacter*, but it cannot replace *molybdenum* in fixation by *Anabaena*.

Reed (1965) deals with the biogeochemistry of *vanadium* and reports an extraordinary occurrence. In 1962–3 more than two dozen seedlings of *Cleome ornithopodioides* (*Capparid.*), a native of the Near East and not previously recorded in N. America, appeared on a pile of *vanadium* slag at Canton, Maryland. In the following year seedlings appeared again. Some, when transplanted to ordinary soils, made little growth, but grew rapidly when fine *vanadium* slag was added. A second species of *Cleome*, *C. integrifolia*, seems to accumulate *vanadium*, its ash containing 70 ppm. Reed considers that *vanadium* in small amount stimulates growth but in large amount is toxic to ordinary plants.

Virginium (Vi) is not mentioned by Bowen (1966) and I have no records of it in higher plants.

Xenon (Xe) is said to be harmless to plants.

Ytterbium (Yb). Woody angiosperms have less than 0·0015 ppm. It is said to be *accumulated* by

> *Jugland.   Carya* (23 ppm)

Yttrium (Y) is said to be *accumulated* by ferns and by

> *Jugland.   Carya* (up to 830 ppm)

Zinc (Zn). Woody angiosperms have 160 ppm.

Zinc is an essential element for higher plants. It occurs in *metalloprotein enzymes* (percentages in brackets) such as: bacterial *protease* (0·2), *carboxypeptidase* (0·18), *carbonic anhydrase* (0·25), *alkaline phosphatase* (0·17), etc.

Prasad (1966) has edited a volume on *zinc* metabolism.

Indicators and/or *accumulators* include

> Caryophyll.   *Minuartia verna* (*accumulator*), *Silene inflata* (has Zn-
> tolerant types?), others may be *indicators*.
> Crucif.   *Thlaspe alpestre* var. *calaminare* (may have > 3% Zn in
> ash)
> Saxifrag.   *Philadelphus* (*indicator*)

Rut.   indicators?

Aquifoli.   Ilex glabra (up to 61·5 ppm dry wt)

Viol.   Viola tricolor var. calaminare (accumulator), other species may have up to 2% Zn in ash.

Clethr.   Clethra alnifolia (to 127·5 ppm dry wt)

Plumbagin.   Armeria elongata (0·42% Zn in ash), maritima var. helleri (4·5% Zn in ash)

Comp.   indicators?

Zirconium (Zr). I have no records of zirconium in land plants, but freshwater plants are said to absorb it (concentration-factor 6230).

FATS AND FATTY-ACIDS

GENERAL

Fats and fatty-oils (which are fats liquid at 'room temperature') are esters of fatty-acids with the trihydric alcohol glycerol. Theoretically fatty-acids can form esters with monohydric alcohols—and they do, to form waxes; with dihydric alcohols such as ethylene glycol—and they seem not to do this;[1] with trihydric alcohols such as glycerol—and we have seen that they do, to form fats; and with alcohols which have more than three -OH groups—but I have no knowledge of any such compounds. It seems strange that Nature is so selective!

The fats are legion. They seem to occur in all living things, and in them in all living cells. We must distinguish between the universal 'body-fats', as they are called, and the more specialized 'depot-fats' which are stored (in plants) in some fruit-coats, in many seeds, and occasionally in other organs.

Body-fats

The 'body-fats' seem to vary rather little in composition. We have some information for leaf-lipids (Shorland, in Swain, 1963) which may be summarized here.

The total leaf-lipids amount to about 7% of the dry matter. Much of this consists of galactolipids, only a little of true fat. Shorland says that linolenic acid is a major or chief fatty-acid component. He also says: 'The information on the fatty acid composition of leaf lipids is not sufficiently detailed or extensive to have any great taxonomic value.'

There is some indication that although the leaf-lipids vary relatively

[1] But Varanasi and Malins (1969) have found what seem to be ethers of diols (like $H_{37}C_{18}$-O-$CH_2CH_2CH_2CH_2CH_2$-O-$C_{18}H_{37}$?) in lipids of porpoise jaw oils.

little as compared with seed-fats, they may in some cases reflect any unusual composition of the latter. Thus, quoting Shorland again:

The evidence suggests that the compositions of leaf and seed lipids are generally quite unrelated.

Instances may be found, however, where the occurrence of an unusual acid in the seed fat is reflected in the lipids of other parts of the plant. Thus the cyclopropene acids, malvalic and sterculic..., are found in both seed and leaf lipids of some species of Malvaceae and Sterculiaceae. Ximenynic acids, present in seed fats of certain members of the Olacaceae and Santalaceae, also occur as such, or in a related form, in other parts of the plant...the occurrence of an unusual acid both in the lipids of the seeds as well as in other parts of the plants, appears to have special taxonomic significance.

Fruit-coat fats

These were also discussed briefly by Shorland (loc. cit.). Some information was available to him from sixteen families: *Anacardi.*, *Burser.*, *Caprifoli.*, *Capparid.*, *Caryocar.*, *Celastr.*, *Cucurbit.*, *Elaeagn.*, *Euphorbi.*, *Laur.*, *Meli.*, *Myric.*, *Ole.*, *Palmae*, *Sterculi.* and *Valerian.*

Most fruit-coat fats have *palmitic, oleic* and *linoleic acids.* Shorland says: 'As with leaf lipids, fruit coat fats bear, as a rule, little resemblance to the seed fats from the same species.'

We may illustrate this from the families *Lauraceae* and *Palmae*. Most of the *Lauraceae* have seed-fats with much *lauric acid* and little *oleic acid*. *Laurus nobilis* seed-fat, for example, has about 42% *lauric acid* and about 36% *oleic acid* (unusually high for the family), while its fruit-pulp has 0 to 3% *lauric acid*, 20–24% *palmitic acid*, 56–63% *oleic acid*, and 14–22% *linoleic acid*. The fruit-coat of the avocado (*Persea gratissima*) has 17% *palmitic acid*, 68% *oleic acid* and 8% *linoleic acid*: no *lauric acid* was recorded.

In the *Palmae* most (all?) members have seed-fats very rich in *lauric acid* (35–50%) with lesser amounts of higher and lower members of the saturated series. In *Elaeis guineensis* fat is stored both in the seed (palm-kernel oil) and in the fruit-coat (palm oil). The former is typical of the seed-fats of palms, with 3–7% *capric acid*, 50–52% *lauric acid*, and 14–15% *myristic acid*. The latter has a quite different composition, with 32–47% *palmitic acid* and 40–52% *oleic acid*.

Seed-fats

These are of tremendous interest and importance. Much more work has been done upon them than upon body-fats and fruit-coat fats, few of which are of direct economic value. (Palm-oil, mentioned above, and olive-oil are exceptions. I have no very recent figures for either but over 200,000 tons of palm-oil and something like 1,000,000 tons of olive-oil are produced each year.)

The seed-plants are the dominant plants of the world and their seeds with few exceptions (such as those of orchids) contain massive food reserves for the use of the embryo when germination occurs. The food may be stored in the nucellus (perisperm), in the endosperm, and/or in the embryo. It may be largely as carbohydrate (cereals), as protein in part (legumes) and/or as fats and fatty-oils. Where the storage material is fat or oil it is usually, but by no means always, in the endosperm. Man makes use of fat-storing seeds on a hugh scale. Wolff (1966) says that more than 20,000,000 tons of vegetable fats and fatty-oils are produced annually, mostly from seeds.

A few examples of annual production will suffice here (not all the figures are recent):

Linseed oil (*Linum usitatissimum*)—6,000,000 acres in Argentina; 40,000,000 bushels from U.S.A.

Cottonseed oil (*Gossypium* spp.)—about 500,000 tons of oil.

Sesame oil (*Sesamum indicum*)—more than 3,000,000 acres.

Corn oil (*Zea mays*)—at least 100,000 tons of oil.

Olive-oil (*Olea europaea*)—about 1,000,000 tons.

Coconut oil (*Cocos nucifera*)—at least 500,000 tons of nuts.

Palm oil (*Elaeis guineensis*)—over 200,000 tons.

Palm-kernel oil (*Elaeis guineensis*)—at least 500,000 tons of kernels.

When fats are extracted for analysis from seeds we must remember that body-fats as well as depot-fats are included. In the case of seeds with *much* fat-storage the body-fats will be swamped and show up hardly at all in the analyses. In the case of seeds with quite low percentages of depot-fats the fatty-acids from the body-fats will loom large. One wonders how important this may be in interpreting the figures given for such seeds.

Plants are curiously selective in the fatty-acids which they use in seed-fats. It is true that they produce a very large number of fatty-acids —I have included nearly 150 in the lists which follow, and I have certainly omitted many—but a large proportion of these are rare or occur in small amount. The ones used commonly are surprisingly few in number. Hilditch (1956) has this to say:

Oleic and linoleic acids together probably account for about 80 per cent. or more of the total production of fatty acids in vegetable seed fats, whilst palmitic acid probably amounts to less than 10 per cent. of the total fatty acids produced in the world's seed fats. All other component fatty acids found in seed fats, unsaturated or saturated, together make up, therefore, a little more than 10 per cent. of the whole of the seed fats produced annually in the world...

Any complete theory of plant fat synthesis must account for the invariable appearance and overall predominance of oleic and linoleic acids, the invariable presence of palmitic acid, and for the occasional development in specific families or species of other acids, saturated or unsaturated, and also for the frequent constitutive resemblances between the rarer unsaturated acids and oleic acid.

Why, we might emphasize, are the commonest fatty-acids in most cases the C_{18} acids ? The following list shows this to be so (the numbers are those of my sections):

I. *Stearic acid*: in at least 80 families, though rarely in large amount.
II. *Oleic acid* (see above)
III. *Linoleic acid* (see above)
IV. *Linolenic acid* is one of the commonest of the fatty-acids with 3 double bonds.
V. Three out of four of the acids listed are C_{18}.
VI. None in plants ?
VII. Almost all of the *acetylenic acids* listed are C_{18}.
VIII. The two fatty-acids here are C_{18}.
IX. C_{18} acids seem to be the commonest.
X. All (?) C_{18} acids.
XI. Several C_{18} acids are prominent.
XII. *Chaulmoogric acid* (the C_{18} member of the series) is the most widely spread.
XIII. A methyl-C_{18} acid occurs.

Why, we might also ask, are virtually all fatty-acids of fats unbranched and with even numbers of C-atoms ? That there *are* exceptions shows that at least some plants can synthesize these oddities.

Why, too, do some members of families behave uncharacteristically ? Hilditch (1956) recognizes that this is the case:

It is curious to find, in a number of otherwise well-behaved botanical families, how here and there a quite extraordinary departure from the conventional seed fatty acids appears in isolated instances. Thus the monotony of the otherwise simple 'linoleic-rich' seed fats of the Compositae...is relieved by the appearance in the seeds of *Vernonia anthelmintica* of 'vernolic' (12,13-epoxy-octadec-9-enoic) acid...; *Sterculia foetida*, a member of a family which normally produces seed fats...rich in stearic as well as palmitic acid, and with little unsaturated acids other than oleic, yields a seed the fat in which contains a most unusual unsaturated acid of the structure

$$CH_3[CH_2]_7 . C{=}C . [CH_2]_7 . COOH.$$
$$CH_2$$

Quite probably, of course, other similar phenomena will continue to come to light as time goes on.

We shall see that the 'most unusual' structure shown above turns up in at least four families of the **Malvales** (section IX and p. 1458).

A paragraph or two on the composition of the triglycerides (fats) would seem to be in order here. We might expect that—given a number of molecules of different fatty-acids, and a number of glycerol molecules to form fats—the unions would be statistically random ones, the fat molecules having the different fatty-acids in the proportions expected. This is not the case: some plants, at least, seem preferentially to synthesize certain combinations. Thus *Laurus nobilis* seed-fat is said to have a higher percentage of *trilaurin* than would be expected from the fatty-acid mixture resulting from hydrolysis of the fat. The seed-fat of *Cuphea lanceolata* contains more *tridecanoin* than would be expected (Litchfield, Miller, Harlow and Resier, 1967). Wolff (1966) says that the *vernolic acid* of *Vernonia anthelmintica* is present almost entirely as *trivernolin*; while in *Euphorbia lagascae*, the seed-oil of which has 57% *vernolic acid*, there is only 18·5% *trivernolin*.

An interesting triglyceride is said to occur in *Sapium sebiferum*. It seems to have a tetra-ester constitution (see 8-*hydroxy-n-octa-5-6-dienoic acid*).

How well do we know the fats of plants? Scharapow (1958) says that one-third of all (higher?) plants store oil or fat. The first edition of Hilditch's *Chemical Constitution of Natural Fats* (1940) listed about 400 plant fats, the second (1947) about 450, the third (1956) about 600, and the fourth (by Hilditch and Williams, 1964) about 900. The number examined by this time will be much above this—Wolff (1966) says less than 1000—and there are obviously an enormous number that remain to be studied, the more so as a high proportion of the earlier analyses are suspect. We must remember how difficult it was, in the 'good old days' of plant biochemistry, to analyse fat, and how easy it was to overlook odd fatty-acids occurring in small amounts. Today the task is vastly easier and the numbers of papers appearing are so large that I, for one, have been quite unable to keep up with the literature.

We may still find much of chemotaxonomic interest in the lists that follow and may say with Shorland (in Swain, 1963):

In conclusion, although the data on the types and distribution of fatty acids do not provide an unequivocal guide to the classification of plants, many correlations of taxonomic significance have become apparent in spite of the small number of species examined up to now. It is believed that the results so far obtained justify more extensive investigations in this field and that the study of fats has a role in the chemical taxonomy of plants.

Classification of fatty-acids

As in so many of our chapters there is no completely satisfactory classification. Where does an acid with one -OH group and two double bonds belong, or an acetylenic acid with a cyclopropenyl group? When we know more of the biosynthetic pathways we may know the answers to such problems of classification. In the meantime the classification followed here is:

    I. Saturated fatty-acids: 15 listed
    II. Fatty-acids with one double bond
      1. Oleic acid series A and B: 14 listed
      2. Not in the oleic acid series: 19 listed
    III. Fatty-acids with two double bonds
      1. Linoleic acid series A and B: 3 listed
      2. Not in the linoleic acid series: 8 listed
    IV. Fatty-acids with three double bonds
      1. Linolenic acid series A and B: 2 listed
      2. Not in the linolenic acid series: 8 listed
    V. Fatty-acids with four double bonds
      1. With bond arranged $-(CH{=}CH)_4-$: 1 only
      2. With bonds arranged $-(CH{=}CH.CH_2)_4-$: 2 listed
      3. With bonds arranged otherwise: 1 only
    VI. Fatty-acids with five double bonds: none known from plants?
    VII. Fatty-acids with acetylenic linkages
      1. With one acetylenic linkage: 10 listed
      2. With two acetylenic linkages: 3 listed
      3. With three acetylenic linkages: 4 listed
    VIII. Fatty-acids with a keto group: 4 listed
    IX. Fatty-acids with a cyclopropenyl group: 4 listed
    X. Fatty-acids with an epoxy group: 4 listed
    XI. Fatty-acids with one or more -OH groups
      1. Saturated fatty-acids with an ω-OH group: 10 listed
      2. Saturated fatty-acids with an -OH group in the α- (or 2) position: 2 listed
      3. Saturated fatty-acids with an -OH group in other than the ω- or α- positions: 3 listed

4. Saturated fatty-acids with 2, 3, or 4 -OH groups: 6 listed
5. Unsaturated fatty-acids with 1 or more -OH groups: 9 listed

XII. Fatty-acids with a terminal cyclopent-2-enyl group (the chaulmoogric series): 9 listed

XIII. Branched-chain fatty-acids: 4 listed

Biosynthesis

Hendrickson (1965) says that the biosynthesis of fatty-acids is now well understood. They arise from acetate by carbon–carbon bond formation via an aldol-type condensation. This by repetition gives long chains with the characteristic even number of C-atoms. For details the reader is referred to chart 4 in Hendrickson's little book. We add a few further notes.

Wolff (1966) says that fatty-acids with cyclopropenyl and epoxy groups coexist with acetylenic acids 'in amounts and positions such as to suggest strongly that these various groups are related biosynthetically'.

Odd C-number fatty-acids are very rare in plants. The occurrence of large quantities of C-17 acetylenic acids in *Acanthosyris* is therefore of great interest. They coexist with C-18 acids and Wolff suggests that α-oxidation leads to loss of one C-atom. In the case of *sterculic acid* (odd-numbered) Wolff argues that it is 'undoubtedly formed by addition of 1 carbon to an even-numbered precursor' and that it gives rise to *malvalic acid* by α-oxidation.

Wolff's paper is full of intriguing suggestions, some supported by evidence, others biosynthetically plausible. There is no doubt that we shall know within a few years a great deal about the origins and inter-relationships of the fatty-acids. This will add enormously to the chemo-taxonomic usefulness of these substances.

Literature

The literature on fats and fatty-acids is so immense that we can afford to cite only a minute fraction of it. Many more particular references are scattered through my lists, or are cited when discussing the plants involved. We shall refer here only to a few general sources which we have used extensively.

A group of workers have been conducting a survey for new industrial fats and oils (Earle, Melvin, Mason, van Etten, Wolff and Jones, 1959; Earle *et al.* 1960; Earle, Wolff and Jones, 1960; Mikolajczak *et al.* 1961; Mikolajczak *et al.* 1962). Books on fats and oils include: Eckey (1954), *Vegetable Fats and Oils*; Gunstone (1958), *An Introduction to the Chemistry of Fats and Fatty Acids*; Hilditch (1940, 1947, 1956), *The*

Chemical Constitution of Natural Fats, editions 1, 2, and 3 and Hilditch and Williams (1964), edition 4; Jamieson (1944), *Vegetable Fats and Oils*, edition 2. Interesting surveys are those of Shorland (in Swain, 1963), and Wolff (1966).

I SATURATED FATTY-ACIDS

GENERAL

This series may be considered to begin with *formic acid* (H.COOH), and to proceed through *acetic acid* (CH_3.COOH), and *propionic acid* (CH_3.CH_2.COOH), to the higher members (CH_3.$(CH_2)_n$.COOH). The lower members occur as *esters* with *monohydric alcohols*; some higher members occur as *esters* of *long-chain alcohols* as *waxes*; members with *even* C-numbers from C_4 to C_{26} or higher occur as *esters* of the *trihydric alcohol glycerol* as the *fats* and *fatty-oils* of living creatures.

List and Occurrence

n-Tetranoic acid (Butyric acid; CH_3.$(CH_2)_2$.COOH) occurs in animal milk-fats. In plants it is found as *esters* in *essential oils*. I have no certain record of its occurrence in seed-fats. Does it occur (free?) in:

    Sapind. *Sapindus*
    Myrt. *Eucalyptus*
    Umbell. occurrence?

n-Hexanoic acid (Caproic acid; CH_3.$(CH_2)_4$.COOH) occurs in many fats but in small amount. We may note:

    Palmae. *Cocos nucifera* (endosperm, 1%), *pulposa* (2%)

n-Octanoic acid (Caprylic acid; CH_3.$(CH_2)_6$.COOH) rarely occurs in large amount in seed-fats.

    Ulm. *Ulmus* (several spp.), *Zelkova* (at least 1) have appreciable amounts; but *absent* (?) from *Celtis* (2), *Chaetacme*, and *Trema*.
    Lythr. *Cuphea hookeriana* (sd, 71%), *painteri* (sd, 78%)
    Palmae. probably in seed-fats of all. The records I have range from 10% (*Cocos pulposa*) to 1% (*Astrocaryum* spp.) or possibly 0% (*Roystonia*).

n-Decanoic acid (Capric acid; CH_3.$(CH_2)_8$.COOH) is a common constituent of seed-fats, but only in relatively few cases is it in large amount.

    Ulm. Early analyses seemed to support the split—*Ulmoideae* with and *Celtoideae* without large amounts of *capric acid*—but later figures cut across this. See *Ulmaceae* for discussion. We may note: *Ulmus* spp. (sds, to 72%), *Zelkova serrata* (73%).

Laur.   *Litsea zeylanica* (sd, 4%), *Neolitsea involucrata* (sd, 37%), *Sassafras albidum* (sd + endocarp, 59%)

Lythr.   *Cuphea hookeriana* (sd, 24%), *llavea* var. *miniata* (sd, to 83%!), *painteri* (sd, 20%)

n-Dodecanoic acid (Lauric acid; $CH_3.(CH_2)_{10}.COOH$) was first isolated from *Laurus*, and has subsequently been found to be characteristic of the seed-fats of *Lauraceae* and *Palmae*. It occurs in many other plant families but rarely in large amount.

Myristic.   members may average about 14% in seed-fats.

Laur.   *Actinodaphne* (sds, 90–96%), *Cinnamomum* (87–95%), *Laurus nobilis* (35–43%), *Litsea* (53–95%), *Neolitsea* (86%), *Umbellularia californica* (62%)

Simaroub.   *Irvingia* spp. (19–59%). Other genera have little?

Vochysi.   *Erisma calcaratum*? (one analysis reports 24%, another 0%!)

Salvador.   *Salvadora oleoides* (sd, 21–47%), *persica* (20%)

Palmae.   probably high in seed-fats of all.[1] *Acrocomia* (45%), *Areca* (17?–54%), *Astrocaryum* (42–49%), *Attalea* (44–46%), *Cocos nucifera* (44–51%), *Elaeis guineensis* (50–52%), *Hyphaene thebaica* (32%), *Manicaria saccifera* (47%)

n-Tetradecanoic acid (Myristic acid; $CH_3.(CH_2)_{12}.COOH$) seems to have been 'chosen' for the seed-fats of the *Myristicaceae*. Most fruit-coat fats, too, seem to have some *myristic acid*.

Myric.   the so-called 'wax' on fruits of *Myrica* is said to be a fat with large amounts of *myristic acid*. *M. cerifera* (33%), *cordifolia* (47–50%), *mexicana* (61%).

Myristic.   *Myristica fragrans* (sd, 60–77%), *irya* (67%), *malabarica* (39%); *Pycnanthus kombo* (57–62%); *Virola atopa* (73%), *bicuhyba* (67–73%), *surinamensis* (73%), *venezuelensis* ('much')

Simaroub.   *Irvingia* spp. (33–70%). Other genera much less?

Vochysi.   *Erisma calcaratum* (28–53%)

Salvador.   *Salvadora oleoides* (53%), *persica* (54%)

Palmae.   all or almost all seed-fats have from 9 to possibly 15% of *myristic acid*

n-Hexadecanoic acid (Palmitic acid; $CH_3.(CH_2)_{14}.COOH$). Hilditch (1952), writing of *oleic, linoleic*, and *palmitic* acids, says that all three occur, sometimes in small proportion, in all *seed-fats*. *Fruit-coat fats* may be very rich in *palmitic acid*.

Caryocar.   *Caryocar villosum* (sd-fat, 48%; frt-coat-fat, 41%)

Rut.   sd-fats average about 22%

Except *Rhopalostylis*? (p. 1875)

Bombac.   sd-fats average about 25%

Combret.   sd-fats average about 27%

Sapot.   Madhuca (sd-fat to 57%); other genera much less

n-Octadecanoic acid (Stearic acid; $CH_3.(CH_2)_{16}.COOH$) has been found in seed-fats of 80 families, says Karrer (1958). It is only rather seldom in large amount.

Menisperm.   Stephania (21%)

Dipterocarp.   Shorea robusta (44%), *stenoptera* (39–43%); *Vateria indica* (39–43%)

Guttif.   many, up to 62%

Capparid.   Courbonia (to 39%)

Burser.   Dacryodes rostrata (31–40%); *Canarium* spp. (much less)

Meli.   several genera to 24%

Anacardi.   Mangifera (to 42%); other genera much less

Sapind.   Nephelium (to 31%); other genera less

Sterculi.   Theobroma to 35%

Sapot.   many to 60%

Convolvul.   Cuscuta (30%)

In many of the genera with much *stearic acid* there is also *oleic acid*, and in the following genera the fatty-acids are almost entirely *stearic* + *oleic*: *Shorea, Vateria, Allanblackia, Pentadesma, Palaquium, Mimusops, Madhuca, Butyrospermum, Dumoria, Payena.*

Families with *very little stearic acid* in their seed-fats include: *Jugland., Betul., The., Crucif., Ros., Celastr., Bombac., Umbell., Solan., Lab., Palmae,* and *Gram.*

n-Eicosanoic acid (Arachidic acid; $CH_3.(CH_2)_{18}.COOH$) is widely distributed, but rarely in large amount in seed-fats.

Legum.   Abrus (5%), *Acacia* (to 2%), *Albizia* (to 11%), *Arachis* (hence the name, to 2%), *Butea* (6%), *Erythrina* (3%), *Pentaclethra* (to 5%), *Phaseolus* (to 3%), *Pongamia* (to 5%), *Tamarindus* (4%), *Trigonella* (to 2%), *Vicia* (1%)

Sapind.   many have much more than have the legumes. *Cardiospermum halicacabum* (10%); *Dodonaea viscosa* (6%); *Nephelium lappaceum* (35%), *mutabile* (22%); *Sapindus trifoliatus* (ca. 22%); *Schleichera trijuga* (*oleosa*) (20–31%)

n-Docosanoic acid (Behenic acid; $CH_3.(CH_2)_{20}.COOH$) was found in *oil of ben* (or *behen*) (*Moringa*). It is rare and usually present only in small amount in seed-fats.

Ochn.   Lophira alata (to 34%? Easily the largest percentage recorded), *procera* (21%)

Moring.   Moringa pterygosperma (*oleifera*) (1–7%)

Legum.   general (?), but never in very large amount. *Parkia biglandulosa* (8%, wrongly given as 39·4% in Karrer, 1958); *Pentaclethra eetveldeana* (14%), *macrophylla* (6%); *Xylia xylocarpa* (*dolabriformis*) (17%)

 Umbell. *Ammi visnaga* (some)

n-Tetracosanoic acid (Lignoceric acid; $CH_3.(CH_2)_{22}.COOH$)

 Aristolochi. *Aristochia indica* (root-oil has some)

 Legum. general (?) in small amount. Hegnauer (1956) says: 'Für die Leguminosen scheint nur das Trio Arachinsaure (C_{20}), Behensaure (C_{22}) und Lignocerinsaure (C_{24}) charakteristisch zu sein. Die Summe der drei genannten gesattigten Fettsauren schwankt in den meisten diesbezuglich untersuchten Leguminosen-olen zwischen 1 und 25% des Totals der Fettsauren.' A few examples (*arach.*: *behen.*: *lignocer.*; total) will illustrate Hegnauer's remarks.

 Abrus precatorius (5:5:3; 13%); *Adenanthera pavonina* (lignoceric 25%); *Butea frondosa* (6:6:4; 16%); *Cassia alata* (lignoceric 15%); *Dipteryx odorata* (total 13–15%); *Lupinus termis* (total 6%); *Pentaclethra eetveldeana* (5:14:3; 22%), *macrophylla* (4:6:11; 21%)

 Plantagin. *Plantago ovata* (1%)

 Other Karrer (1958) gives a list of fats from which *lignoceric acid* (presumably in small amounts) has been isolated.

n-Hexacosanoic acid (Cerotic acid; $CH_3.(CH_2)_{24}.COOH$) is known only from a few seed-fats. It seems likely that traces of it are present in those plants which produce *arachidic, behenic,* and *lignoceric acids,* since they obviously 'specialize' in long-chain saturated acids.

 The *waxes* of palms and other plants are said to have much *cerotic acid,* but Hilditch (1956) says: 'As already mentioned, "cerotic acid" of waxes is now recognized to be a mixture of several *n*-aliphatic acids of the even-numbered series, and is not solely *n*-hexacosanoic acid.'

 Olac. *Ximenia americana* (sd-fat, 2–15%)

n-Octacosanoic acid (Montanic acid; $CH_3.(CH_2)_{26}.COOH$) does not occur in *seed-fats?* It is present (1%) in *leaf-fat* of buckwheat? It occurs in the *wax* of *Copernicia* (*Palmae*).

n-Tricontanoic acid (Melissic acid; $CH_3.(CH_2)_{28}.COOH$) is not in *seed-fats?* It occurs in *waxes, leaf-fats,* etc., and has been reported from the *fruit-coats* of *Illicium* (*Illici.*) and *Oenocarpus* (*Palmae*).

n-Dotriacontanoic acid (Lacceric acid; $CH_3.(CH_2)_{30}.COOH$) has been reported to occur in carnauba wax.

II FATTY-ACIDS WITH ONE DOUBLE BOND

List and Occurrence

1. Oleic acid series may be divided into series A (*cis-9-enoic acids*) and series B (*cis-3-enoic, cis-5-enoic, cis-7-enoic acids*, etc.)

SERIES A

n-Dec-9-enoic acid (Caproleic acid; $CH_2=CH.(CH_2)_7.COOH$) occurs in milk-fat, but not in higher plants?

n-Dodec-9-enoic acid ($CH_3.CH_2.CH=CH.(CH_2)_7.COOH$) occurs in butter-fat, but not in higher plants?

n-Tetradec-9-enoic acid (Myristoleic acid;

$CH_3.(CH_2)_3.CH=CH.(CH_2)_7.COOH$) occurs in many animal fats.

In *seed-fats* it has been recorded from

    Myristic.   *Pycnanthus kombo* (24%); but *not* in other genera?
    Ochn.   *Lophira alata* (< 1%)
    Legum.   *Acacia cyclops* (9%)
    Malv.   *Gossypium* spp.?
    Cucurbit.   *Citrullus colocynthis* (< 1%)

n-Hexadec-9-enoic acid (Palmitoleic acid;

$CH_3.(CH_2)_5.CH=CH.(CH_2)_7.COOH$) is probably as widely spread as *oleic acid*, says Hilditch (1952), but usually in small amounts. He says it may be present in larger amounts in aquatics, but my records seem all to stem from land-plants!

    Prote.   *Embothrium coccineum* (23%), *Lomatia hirsuta* (23%), *Macadamia ternifolia* (20%); but *Guevina avellana* has *hexadec-11-enoic acid*!
    Guttif.   *Platonia insignis* (3%)
    Papaver.   *Argemone mexicana* (1–6%?); but *absent* from poppy-seed oil?
    Crucif.   in small amount in many?
    Legum.   *Acacia cyclops* (9%?), *giraffae* (8%)
    Malv.   *Gossypium herbaceum* (2%?)
    Cucurbit.   *Hodgsonia capniocarpa* (1%)
    Asclepiad.   *Asclepias syriaca* (10%)
    Bignoni.   *Doxantha unguis-cati* (64%!)
    Comp.   *Cynara cardunculus* (to 4%); other genera may have less
    Gram.   wheat-germ (2%)
    Palmae.   *Areca catechu* (8%?), *Cocos nucifera* (1%?), *Elaeis guineensis* (1%?)

n-Octadec-9-enoic acid (Oleic acid;

$CH_3.(CH_2)_7.CH=CH.(CH_2)_7.COOH$) seems to be present in all natural *fats* and *phosphatides*. Many *fatty-acids—linolenic*; *elaeostearic*; *parinaric*; *myristoleic*; *palmitoleic*; *n-eicos-11-enoic*; *erucic*; *docos-13,16-dienoic*; *ximenic*; *lumequic*—have one 'half' or the other of *oleic acid*. This must surely be of some significance. The amount of *oleic acid* in *seed-fats* of angiosperms varies enormously:

> *Jugland.* *Carya cordiformis* (72–88%), *illinoensis* (79%); other genera much less?
>
> *Betul.* *Corylus avellana* (56–91%)
>
> *Olac.* *Coula edulis* (95%!). Variable amounts in other members.
>
> *Ros.* *Crataegus oxyacantha* (81%); *Prunus amygdalus* (to 77%), *armeniaca* (to 79%), *laurocerasus* (73%) (table 68).
>
> *Caric.* *Carica papaya* (80–81%)

At the other end of the scale are families with very *low* percentages of *oleic acid*: *Salvador.*: *Salvadora oleoides* (5–12%), *persica* (5%); *Flacourti.*: *Caloncoba echinata* (2%), *welwitschii* (< 1%). Some *fruit-coat fats* are rich in *oleic acid*:

> *Myristic.* *Myristica fragrans* (ca. 80%)
>
> *Ole.* *Olea europaea* (70–85%)
>
> *Palmae* *Oenocarpus bataua* (79–81%)

n-Eicos-9-enoic acid (Gadoleic acid;

$CH_3.(CH_2)_9.CH=CH.(CH_2)_7.COOH$) occurs in the liver of the cod (*Gadus*). It may occur in small amounts in some seed-fats, but I have no records of it.

SERIES B

n-Hexadec-7-enoic acid ($CH_3.(CH_2)_7.CH=CH.(CH_2)_5.COOH$) has not been found in any plant fat?

n-Octadec-9-enoic acid (Oleic acid): above in Series A.

n-Eicos-11-enoic acid ($CH_3.(CH_2)_7.CH=CH.(CH_2)_9.COOH$) appears to be widely spread in dicotyledons. In *seed-fats* we may note:

> *Ranuncul.* *Delphinium hybridum* (18%; Chisholm and Hopkins, 1956)
>
> *Ochn.* *Lophira* (to 2%?)
>
> *Crucif.* general? Hilditch (1956) says: 'Eicos-11-enoic acid... has not so far been observed to exceed about 13 per cent. of the total acids in a Cruciferous seed fat. In the rape and mustard oils it rarely exceeds 5 or 6 per cent., but in some instances (Charlock and *Camelina*) in which it occurs in larger proportions it may actually exceed the amount of erucic acid which is also present.'

Legum. *Acacia* (to 2% ?), *Erythrina crista-galli* (9% ?)

Tropaeol. *Tropaeolum majus* (20%; Hopkins and Chisholm, 1953)

Sapind. *Cardiospermum halicacabum* (42%, 'unique among the true natural fats' say Chisholm and Hopkins, 1958). Other genera that probably have this acid are *Dodonaea* (4% ?), *Nephelium* (to 4% ?), *Sapindus* (to 22% ?)

The liquid *seed-wax* of *Simmondsia* is said to have much *eicos*-11-*enoic acid.*

n-Docos-13-enoic acid (Erucic acid;

$CH_3.(CH_2)_7.CH=CH.(CH_2)_{11}.COOH$) is the *cis*-form, and until recently it was thought that the *trans*-form (*brassidic acid*) did not occur. It has now been reported, with *erucic acid* (!), in the *perianth* of *Fritillaria camschatcensis* by Shibata and Takakuwa (1959).

Crucif. general? Ranging from 55% (*Brassica campestris*) to 3% (*Camelina sativa*) or even 0%? (*Hesperis matronalis*: has this been re-examined by modern methods?)

Limnanth. *Limnanthes douglasii* (13%) and other spp.; *Floerkea* (see discussion under family).

Tropaeol. *Tropaeolum majus* (69%), *minus*? (82%)

n-Tetracos-15-enoic acid (Selacholeic acid;

$CH_3.(CH_2)_7.CH=CH.(CH_2)_{13}.COOH$) seems, says Hilditch (1956), to be 'a characteristic component of the fats of many Elasmobranch fish...'. It is rare in *seed-fats.*

Olac. *Ximenia* spp. (in small amounts)

Crucif. *Lunaria biennis* (21%, Wilson *et al.* 1962)

n-Hexacos-17-enoic acid (Ximenic acid;

$CH_3.(CH_2)_7.CH=CH.(CH_2)_{15}.COOH$) is known only from *seed-fats* of

Olac. *Ximenia americana* (9 to 25%), *caffra* and var. (3 to 7%)

n-Octacos-19-enoic acid ($CH_3.(CH_2)_7.CH=CH.(CH_2)_{17}.COOH$) is, like *ximenic* (above) and *lumequic acids* (below), known only from *seed-fats* of

Olac. *Ximenia americana* and var. (to 12%), *caffra* and var. (5 to 10%)

n-Triacont-21-enoic acid (Lumequic acid;

$CH_3.(CH_2)_7.CH=CH.(CH_2)_{19}.COOH$)

Olac. *Ximenia americana* and var. (to 7%), *caffra* and var. (3 to 5%)

n-Dotriacont-23-enoic acid

($CH_3.(CH_2)_7.CH=CH.(CH_2)_{21}.COOH$)

Olac. *Ximenia* (in small amount?)

2. Not in the Oleic acid series

List and Occurrence

The possibilities here are very numerous but less than a dozen of these acids seem to occur in higher plants.

n-Dec-4-enoic acid (Obtusilic acid;
$CH_3.(CH_2)_4.CH=CH.(CH_2)_2.COOH$) occurs, with the related *linderic* and *tsuzuic* acids (below) in *seed-fats* of

Laur. *Lindera obtusiloba, umbellata* (*cis*-, 4%); *Litsea*?

n-Undec-10-enoic acid ($CH_2=CH.(CH_2)_8.COOH$) occurs in fungi and conifers, but not, I think, in angiosperms.

n-Dodec-4-enoic acid (Linderic acid;
$CH_3.(CH_2)_6.CH=CH.(CH_2)_2.COOH$) occurs in *seed-fats* of

Laur. *Lindera hypoglauca* (much?), *obtusiloba, strychnifolia* (little), *umbellata* (*cis*-, 47%!); *Litsea glauca* (much?)

n-Tetradec-2-enoic acid (?Macilenic acid;
$CH_3.(CH_2)_{10}.CH=CH.COOH$)

Myristic. *Myristica fragrans* (mace, in small amount?)

n-Tetradec-4-enoic acid (Tsuzuic acid;
$CH_3.(CH_2)_8.CH=CH.(CH_2)_2.COOH$ occurs in *seed-fats* of

Laur. *Lindera hypoglauca* (little?), *obtusiloba, umbellata* (*cis*-, 5%); *Litsea glauca, japonica*

n-Hexadec-3t-enoic acid ($CH_3.(CH_2)_{11}.CH=CH.CH_2.COOH$) has been reported from

Chenopodi. *Spinacia* (*leaf-fat*)

Scrophulari. *Antirrhinum* (*leaf-fat*)

Comp. *Helenium bigelowii* (*seed-fat*, 10%; Hopkins and Chisholm, 1964); *absent* from *H. hoopesii*? It is said to occur in at least 29 composites.

n-Hexadec-11c-enoic acid

Prote. one member

n-Hexadec-12-enoic acid (Tanacetum-oil acid;
$CH_3.(CH_2)_2.CH=CH.(CH_2)_{10}.COOH$) occurs in spores of *Lycopodium* and in

Comp. *Tanacetum vulgare* (flower-fat)

n-Octadec-3t-enoic acid

Comp. at least 7 species

n-Octadec-6c-enoic acid (Petroselinic acid;
$CH_3.(CH_2)_{10}.CH=CH.(CH_2)_4.COOH$) is one of several mono-unsaturated C_{18} acids occurring in Nature (see *oleic, petroselidic, elaidic, iso-oleic, cis-n-octadec-11-enoic*)

Euphorbi. *Mallotus japonicus* (seed-oil?)

Simaroub. *Picrasma quassioides* (seed-oil, in large amount)

> *Arali. Hedera helix* (seed-oil, 62%). The occurrence here is quoted as supporting relationship to *Umbelliferae*. I have no records of *petroselinic acid* in other members of the *Araliaceae*, however.
>
> *Umbell.* seed-fats of many

n-Octadec-6t-enoic acid (Petroselidic acid; Tarelaidic acid) is known only from

> *Umbell.* in small amounts with *petroselinic acid* (above).

n-Octadec-9t-enoic acid (Elaidic acid): note that the *cis*-form is *oleic acid* above. *Elaidic acid* is said to occur in fungi and rather doubtfully in

> *Ranuncul. Delphinium staphisagria* (seed-oil)
>
> *Zygophyll. Tribulus terrestris* (fruit-oil)
>
> *Solan. Physalis peruviana* (seed-oil)

n-Octadec-10-enoic acid (Iso-oleic acid) occurs in *seed-fats* and in *fruit-coat-fats*. It is recorded from

> *Ranuncul. Delphinium staphisagria* (seed-fat)
>
> *Ros. Cydonia* (seed-fat), *Malus* (seed-fat), *Pyrus* (seed-fat), *Rosa* (seed-fat)
>
> *Ole. Olea europaea* (fruit-coat-fat)
>
> *Arac. Pinellia tuberifera* (tuber)

n-Octadec-11c-enoic acid (Asclepic acid) has been found in horse-lipids, in fungi, and in

> *Asclepiad. Asclepias syriaca* (seed-fat, 15%; Chisholm and Hopkins, 1960)
>
> *Bignoni.* one member

n-Eicos-5c-enoic acid

> *Ranuncul.* in one member?
>
> *Limnanth. Limnanthes douglasii* (seed-fat, 65%), and at least 6 other spp. (see family)

n-Docos-5c-enoic acid

> *Limnanth. Limnanthes douglasii* (seed-fat, 7%), and at least 6 other spp. (see family)

III FATTY-ACIDS WITH TWO DOUBLE BONDS

1. Linoleic acid series

GENERAL

This group of unsaturated acids, with -CH=CH.CH$_2$.CH=CH-grouping, may be considered to belong to two series (A and B), corresponding to those noted above for the *oleic acid* series.

List and Occurrence

SERIES A

n-Hexadec-9c,12c-dienoic acid

$(CH_3.(CH_2)_2.CH=CH.CH_2.CH=CH.(CH_2)_7.COOH)$ seems to be rare.

 Legum. *Acacia giraffae* (seed-fat, some; but is it *cis*-, *cis*- ?)
 Asclepiad. *Asclepias syriaca* (seed-fat, 2%; probably *cis*-, *cis*-)

n-Octadec-9c,12c-dienoic acid (Linoleic acid;

$CH_3.(CH_2)_4.CH=CH.CH_2.CH=CH.(CH_2)_7.COOH)$ has, says Hilditch (1956): 'been observed, in small or (often) large proportions, in every vegetable fat so far examined; it is as ubiquitous as oleic acid or palmitic acid...'. Notably high amounts have been found in

 Jugland. *Juglans* spp. (to 76%); less in other genera?
 Ulm. *Celtis mississippiensis* (74%), *occidentalis* (77–78%); *Chaetacme microcarpa* (82%)
 Urtic. *Urtica dioica* (79%)
 Cucurbit. usually in fairly large amount
 Solan. *Atropa belladonna* (67%), *Hyoscyamus niger* (56–82%)
 Comp. usually in fairly large amount
 Agav. at least 13 species (in 5 genera) have 52–89%

SERIES B

n-Octadec-9,12-dienoic acid is *linoleic acid* (above).
n-Docos-13,16-dienoic acid
 Crucif. *Brassica campestris* (rape-seed-oil, in small amount)

2. Not in the Linoleic acid series

n-Deca-2,4-dienoic acid
 Euphorbi. *Sapium discolor* ? (seed-fat), *sebiferum* (seed-fat, 4–5%)
n-Dodeca-2,4-dienoic acid
 Euphorbi. *Sebastiana ligustrina* (seed-fat, 5%?)
n-Octadeca-5t,9c-dienoic acid
 Ranuncul. in one member
n-Octadeca-9t,12t-dienoic acid
 Bignoni. *Chilopsis linearis* (seed-fat, 15%; Chisholm and Hopkins, 1963)
n-Octadeca-10t,12t-dienoic acid
 Bignoni. *Chilopsis linearis* (seed-fat, 12%)

(−)-*n*-Octadeca-5,6-dienoic acid (Laballenic acid) is an allenic acid.
> *Lab.* *Leonotis nepetaefolia* (seed-fat). Probably of general occur-
> rence in the *Stachyoideae*. (It is in 53 spp. ?)
> *Comp.* (This acid ?) *Dicoma zeyheri* (with its methyl ester, up to
> 2·8% of dry wt)

n-Octadeca- ?, ?-dienoic acid: a *dienoic acid*, perhaps one of the three
above, has been reported from
> *Chrysobalan.* *Parinari*

n-Eicosa- ?, ?-dienoic acid
> *Ranuncul.* *Delphinium* (1%)

n-Docosa-5c,13c-dienoic acid
> *Limnanth.* *Limnanthes* spp. (seed-fats)—see family.

IV FATTY-ACIDS WITH THREE DOUBLE BONDS

1. The linolenic acid series

GENERAL

As with the *oleic acid* and *linoleic acid* series, we may distinguish two
series (A and B) having one 'end' or the other of *linolenic acid* itself.
They are all *cis,cis,cis-* ?

List and Occurrence

SERIES A

n-Octadeca-9,12,15-trienoic acid (Linolenic acid) seems to be the only
member of Series A to occur in higher plants. *Leaf-fats* may be rich in
linolenic acid, and Hilditch (1956) points out that horse depot-fats
have a considerable amount. He says: 'It may be concluded that
(like the pig...) the horse is capable of directly assimilating the
natural fats present in herbage or seeds which form major parts of its
food: pasture grass fats are rich in linolenic acid...'.
> *Jugland.* *Pterocarya* (sd-fat, probably fairly high—see family)
> *Ros.* *Rosa canina* (sd-fat, 14–32%), *rubiginosa* (sd-fat, 16%);
> *Filipendula ulmaria* (*Ulmaria palustris*) (sd-fat, 47%)
> *Lin.* *Linum usitatissimum* ('linseed-oil', 30–60%). Surprisingly, I
> have no records from other members of the family.
> *Euphorbi.* *Euphorbia calycina* (sd-fat, 60–66%), *erythraeae* (53%),
> *marginata* (45%); *Mercurialis perennis* (67%); *Tetracarpidium
> conophorum* (63–68%)

Lab. *Hyptis spicigera* (sd-fat, 60–66%); *Lallemantia iberica* (sd-fat, 53%), but *royleana* (none!); *Ocimum kilimandscharicum* (sd-fat, 61–65%); *Perilla ocymoides* (sd-fat, 63–70%); *Salvia hispanica* (sd-fat, 47–69%)

SERIES B

n-Hexadeca-7,10,13-trienoic acid
  Crucif. *Brassica napus* (leaf-lipids, but is it *cis, cis, cis-* ?)
n-Octadeca-9,12,15-trienoic acid is *linolenic acid* (above).

2. Not in the linolenic acid series

The acids known to occur are all C_{18} acids, i.e. they are isomers of *linolenic acid.*

n-Octadeca-9c,11t,13t-trienoic acid (α-Elaeostearic acid) occurs in large quantities in a few seed-fats.
  Ros. *Prunus yedoensis* (35%)
  Chrysobalan. *Cyclandrophora laurina* (30–34%), *Licania* spp. (to 17%), *Parinari* spp. (to 70%)
  Euphorbi. *Aleurites* spp. (47–81%), *Garcia nutans* (93–95%!), *Ricinodendron africanus* (49–53%), but *absent* from, or in very small amount in, some other genera.
  Cucurbit. *Momordica* spp. (seed-kernel, to 65%), *Telfairia occidentalis* (19%)
  Valerian. *Centranthus macrosiphon* (50%), *ruber* (43%); *Valeriana officinalis* (45%)
n-Octadeca-6,9,12-trienoic acid (γ-Linolenic acid) occurs in fungi and in the seed-fats of
  Mor. *Humulus lupulus*
  Onagr. *Oenothera biennis* (8–10%), *lamarckiana* (3–8%), *rhombipetala* (5%)
  Boragin. *Onosmodium occidentale* (8% ?)
  Lili. *Astelia banksii* (18%), *neo-caledonica* (22%), *solandri* (22%), *trinervia* (25%); *Collospermum hastatum* (14%), *microspermum* (12%) (Morice, 1967—see under *Liliaceae*).
n-Octadeca-8c,10t,12c-trienoic acid
  Bignoni. *Jacaranda ovalifolia* (30%)
n-Octadeca-8t,10t,12c-trienoic acid (Calendic acid) occurs in seed-fats of some composites: see Chisholm and Hopkins (1960, 1966).
  Comp. *Calendula officinalis* (47%), *stellata* (50%), and all (?) other species; *Osteospermum hyoseroides* (36%).

n-Octadeca-9t,11t,13c-trienoic acid

> *Bignoni.* *Catalpa ovata* (seed-fat, 40%), *speciosa* (present); *Chilopsis linearis* (sd-fat, to 25%)

n-Octadeca-9c,11c,13t-trienoic acid (Punicic acid; Trichosanic acid) occurs in seed-fats of

> *Cucurbit.* *Cayaponia grandifolia* (to 39%), *Cucurbita, Momordica* spp. (to 56%), *Trichosanthes*
> *Punic.* *Punica*

n-Octadeca-3t,9c,12c-trienoic acid is said to occur in

> *Comp.* *Calea* (this acid?) and at least 21 other species.

n-Octadeca-5t,9c,12c-trienoic acid

> *Ranuncul.* in at least 11 species.

V FATTY-ACIDS WITH FOUR DOUBLE BONDS

List and Occurrence

1. With bonds arranged -(CH=CH)$_4$-

n-Octadeca-9c,11c,13c,15c-tetraenoic acid (α-Parinaric acid)

> *Chrysobalan.* *Cyclandrophora* (*Parinari*) *laurina* (sd-fat, to 56%)
> *Balsamin.* *Impatiens balsamina* (sd-fat, 29–42%), *biflora* (*fulva*) (sd-fat, 51%), *holstii* var. (sd-fat, 13%), *noli-tangere* (sd-fat, 32%), *parviflora* (sd-fat, 46%), *roylei* (*glanduligera*) (sd-fat, 40–50%), *sultani* (sd-fat, 27%)

2. With bonds arranged -(CH=CH.CH$_2$)$_4$-

n-Eicosa-5,8,11,14-tetraenoic acid (Arachidonic acid): of doubtful occurrence?

> *Gram.* *Oryza sativa* (embryo?)
> *Typh.* *Typha angustata* (sd-fat?)

n-Octadeca-6c,9c,12c,15c-tetraenoic acid

> *Boragin.* *Anchusa azurea* (seed-fat, 3%?), *capensis* (sd-fat, 4%?); *Lappula echinata* (sd-fat, 19%?); *Myosotis arvensis* (sd-fat, 7%?); *Onosmodium occidentale* (sd-fat, 8%) (Craig and Bhatty, 1964)

3. With bonds arranged otherwise

n-Octadeca-3t,9c,12c,15c-tetraenoic acid

> *Bignoni.* *Tecoma Stans* (sd-fat, 19%)

VI FATTY-ACIDS WITH FIVE DOUBLE BONDS

GENERAL

Acids with five double bonds arranged $-(CH=CH.CH_2)_5-$ have been found in *brain phosphatides*. It would not be surprising to have them 'turn up' in plant lipids.

VII FATTY-ACIDS WITH ONE OR MORE ACETYLENIC (-C≡C-) LINKAGES (see also IX)

GENERAL

The list of *acetylenic compounds* occurring in higher plants is formidable (p. 85). Much of our information stems from the work of Sörensen and his coworkers, and Bohlmann *et al*. We deal here only with the *acetylenic fatty-acids* occurring in seed-fats. The chemotaxonomy of these is discussed under **Santalales**.

List and Occurrence

1. Acids with one acetylenic linkage

Docos-13-ynoic acid (Behenolic acid)
 Crucif. *Brassica* (rape oil)
n-Heptadeca-10t,16-dien-8-ynoic acid
 Santal. *Acanthosyris spinescens* (sd)
n-Heptadec-10t-en-8-ynoic acid (Pyrulic acid)
 Santal. *Acanthosyris*?, *Pyrularia pubera* (sd-oil)
7-Hydroxy-*n*-heptadeca-10t,16-dien-8-ynoic acid
 Santal. *Acanthosyris spinescens* (sd)
7-Hydroxy-*n*-heptadec-10t-en-8-ynoic acid
 Santal. *Acanthosyris spinescens* (sd)
8-Hydroxy-*n*-octadeca-11t,17-dien-9-ynoic acid
 Santal. *Acanthosyris spinescens* (sd)
8-Hydroxy-*n*-octadec-11t-en-9-ynoic acid
 Olac. *Ximenia caffra* (sd-fat; 3-4%)
 Santal. one member
9-Hydroxy-*n*-octadec-10t-en-12-ynoic acid (Helenynolic acid)
 Comp. *Helichrysum bracteatum* (sd)
n-Octadeca-9c,14c-dien-12-ynoic acid (14,15-Dehydro-crepenynic acid)
 occurs in fungi and
 Legum. *Afzelia quanzensis* (sd-oil)

n-Octadeca-11t,17-dien-9-ynoic acid
  Santal. *Acanthosyris spinescens* (sd)
n-Octadec-9c-en-12-ynoic acid (*cis*-Crepenynic acid)
  Legum. *Afzelia quanzensis* (sd-oil)
  Comp. *Crepis foetida* (seed-oil, 60%). Wolff (1966) says that it
  may be in 22 species of the family.
n-Octadec-11t-en-9-ynoic acid (Santalbic acid; Ximenynic acid)
  Olac. *Ximenia americana* var. *microphylla* (sd-fat, 22%), *caffra*
  (sd-fat, 24%); but *absent* from other genera?
  Santal. seems to be more or less general. See under **Santalales**.
n-Octadec-17-en-9-ynoic acid
  Santal. *Acanthosyris spinescens* (sd)
n-Octadec-6-ynoic acid (Tariric acid)—Hilditch (1956) says:

  Unsaturation commencing at the *sixth* atom of the C_{18} chain...is a
  well-marked characteristic of acids in the seed fats of a few botanical
  families. In the monoethenoid series it is confined to *petroselinic acid*,
  which, however, is a prominent component of all Umbelliferous
  seed fats and of one or two seed fats in other families (Araliaceae,
  Simarubaceae). The monoethynoid analogue *tariric acid* occurs in
  seed fats of some species of *Picramnia* (also a member of the Simarubaceae), whilst a third tri-ethenoid acid of analogous structure is (so
  far) uniquely represented in the seed fat of *Oenothera*...

    Simaroub. *Picramnia camboita* (sd-fat), *carpenterae* (sd-fat), *linden-
    iana* (sd-fat, 20%), *pentandra* (sd-fat, much), *sow* (sd-fat, 90%!),
    tariri (sd-fat) (Steger and van Loon, 1933); but *absent* from other
    members of the family?

n-Octadec-9-ynoic acid (Stearolic acid): this 'acetylenic analogue of the
  ubiquitous oleic acid' was found by Hopkins and Chisholm (1964) in
  Pyrularia.
    Santal. *Exocarpus cupressiformis* (sd-fat, 6%); *Pyrularia pubera*
    (sd-fat, 19%); *Santalum acuminatum* (sd-fat, 3%), *album* (sd-
    fat, 3%)
Sterculynic acid: see section IX.

2. Acids with two acetylenic linkages

8-Hydroxy-*n*-Octadec-17-en-9,11-diynoic acid (Bolekic acid; Isanolic
  acid)
    Olac. *Ongokea klaineana* (*gore*) (sd-fat, 15–50% in different
    analyses)
n-Octadec-13t-en-9,11-diynoic acid (Exocarpic acid)
    Santal. *Buckleya distichophylla* (seed-oil, 29%; Hopkins and
    Chisholm, 1966), *Exocarpus* spp. (rts)

n-Octadec-17-en-9,11-diynoic acid (Erythrogenic acid; Isanic acid; ?Ongokic acid) turns red in light or when heated, hence one of its trivial names.

    Olac.   *Ongokea klaineana* (*gore*) (seed-fat, 15 to 40% in different analyses)

3. Acids with three acetylenic linkages

n-Dec-2t-en-4,6,8-triynoic acid
    Comp.   *Tripleurospermum* (as methyl ester ?)
n-Dec-2c-en-4,6,8-triynoic acid
    Comp.   *Artemisia vulgaris*

VIII FATTY-ACIDS WITH A KETO GROUP
(see also XII)

List and Occurrence

Glyoxylic acid ($H.CO.COOH$) occurs free, says my former colleague G. H. N. Towers, in every plant. It occurs, too, as *ureides* in some plants. It is not a *fatty-acid*.

Iso-licanic acid is like α-licanic acid, but is *cis-, trans-, cis-*.
    Chrysobalan.   *Licania rigida* (seed-fat)

α-Keto-β-hydroxy-butyric acid ($CH_3.CH(OH).CO.COOH$)
    Eric.   *Vaccinium vitis-idaea* (frt)

α-Keto-γ-hydroxy-butyric acid ($CH_2(OH).CH_2.CO.COOH$)
    Eric.   *Oxycoccus quadripetalis* (frt), *Vaccinium vitis-idaea* (frt)

4-Keto-*n*-octadeca- ?9c,11t,13t-trienoic acid (4-Keto-α-elaeo-stearic acid; α-Licanic acid)
    Chrysobalan.   *Licania arborea* (sd-fat, 73–74%), *crassifolia* (sd-fat, 65% or more), *rigida* (sd-fat, 55–82%, different analyses), *venosa* (sd-fat, 50%); *Parinari annamense* (sd-fat, 22%), *corymbosum* ?, *laurina* ?, *sherbroense* (sd-fat, 35–48%)

Pyruvic acid ($CH_3.CO.COOH$) is not really a fatty-acid. It is said to occur (free ?) in
    Crassul.   *Kalanchoë* (lvs)
    Legum.   *Arachis* (sdlg), *Pisum*, *Trifolium*
    Euphorbi.   *Ricinus communis* (sdlg)
    Umbell.   *Daucus carota*
    Lab.   *Mentha piperita*
    Solan.   *Solanum tuberosum*
    Lili.   *Allium*, *Tulipa gesneriana* (bulb)

IX FATTY-ACIDS WITH A CYCLOPROPENYL GROUP

GENERAL

A few *fatty-acids* with a *cyclopropenyl* (—C=C—) group are known to
occur in seed-fats of higher plants. They seem to be restricted to the
Malvales (Table 44), providing a very good example of the use of fatty-
acids in taxonomy.

List and Occurrence

'Bombacic acid': a C_{18} acid with a cyclopropenyl group? It may be
identical with *malvalic acid* (below).

    Bombac.   *Ceiba pentandra*

2-Hydroxy-sterculic acid (2-Hydroxy-8(2-octyl-1-cyclopropenyl)-octa-
noic acid; fig. 107)

    Bombac.   *Bombacopsis glabra, Pachira insignis*

Malvalic acid (fig. 107) seems to cause the pinkish 'whites' of eggs from
hens eating malvaceous plants. It occurs in leaves and seeds?

    Tili.   *Tilia* sp. (sd-oil)

    Malv.   *Althaea rosea* (sd-oil, 4%), *Hibiscus syriacus* (sd-oil,
      14–16%), *Lavatera trimestris* (sd-oil, 6–8%), *Gossypium* sp.
      ('cottonseed', 1%). Some other members give the 'halphen test'
      and may have *malvalic acid.*

    Bombac.   *Bombacopsis glabra* (sd-oil, 3%), *Bombax* (*oleagineum*?)
      (sd-oil, 5%)

    Sterculi.   *Pterospermum acerifolium* (sd-oil, 16%), *Sterculia foetida*
      (sd-oil, trace to 10%)

Sterculic acid (fig. 107)

    Tili.   *Tilia* sp. (sd-oil, < 1%)

    Malv.   *Althaea rosea* (sd-oil, 1%), *Hibiscus syriacus* (sd-oil, 2–3%),
      Lavatera trimestris (sd-oil, < 1%), *Gossypium hirsutum* (cotton-
      seed, < 1%)

    Bombac.   *Bombax* (*oleagineum*?) (sd-oil, 22%), *Pachira aquatica*
      (sd-oil, some)

    Sterculi.   *Brachychiton*?, *Firmiana*?, *Pterospermum acerifolium* (sd-
      oil, some), *Sterculia foetida* (sd-oil, 70%), *parviflora* (sd-oil, much)

Sterculynic acid (8,9-Methylene-octadec-8-en-17-ynoic acid; fig. 107)
has been found by Jevans and Hopkins (1968) in

    Sterculi.   *Sterculia alata* (sd-fat, 8%)

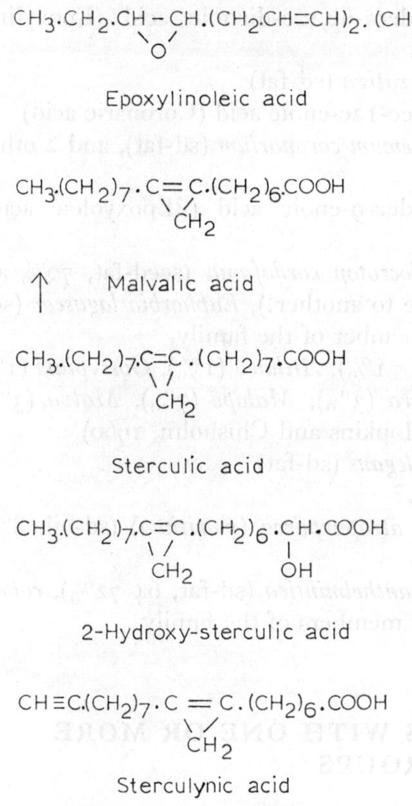

$$CH_3.CH_2.CH - CH.(CH_2.CH=CH)_2 . (CH_2)_7 \cdot COOH$$
$$\underset{O}{\diagdown \diagup}$$

Epoxylinoleic acid

$$CH_3.(CH_2)_7 \cdot C = C.(CH_2)_6.COOH$$
$$\underset{CH_2}{\diagdown \diagup}$$

Malvalic acid

$$CH_3.(CH_2)_7.C = C.(CH_2)_7.COOH$$
$$\underset{CH_2}{\diagdown \diagup}$$

Sterculic acid

$$CH_3.(CH_2)_7.C = C.(CH_2)_6.CH.COOH$$
$$\underset{CH_2}{\diagdown \diagup} \qquad \underset{OH}{|}$$

2-Hydroxy-sterculic acid

$$CH \equiv C.(CH_2)_7 \cdot C = C. (CH_2)_6.COOH$$
$$\underset{CH_2}{\diagdown \diagup}$$

Sterculynic acid

Fig. 107. Some epoxy- and cyclopropenyl- fatty-acids.

X FATTY-ACIDS WITH AN EPOXY GROUP

GENERAL

As recently as 1956 Hilditch wrote of *vernolic acid* (in *Vernonia*): '...so far this is the only known occurrence in nature of a higher fatty acid containing an epoxy group.'

We know today that several of these acids occur, and there is little doubt that others will be found.

List and Occurrence

trans-9,10-*n*-Epoxy-octadecanoic acid (Epoxy-stearic acid)
   Ole.   *Olea europaea* (fruit-coat oil)
      Comp.   one sp.?

cis-15,16-*n*-Epoxy-octadeca-9c,12c-dienoic acid (Epoxylinoleic acid; fig. 107)

    Crucif. *Camelina sativa* (sd-fat)

cis-9,10-*n*-Epoxy-octadec-12c-enoic acid (Coronaric acid)

    Comp. *Chrysanthemum coronarium* (sd-fat), and 2 other members of the family.

cis-12,13-*n*-Epoxy-octadec-9-enoic acid (?Epoxyoleic acid; Vernolic acid)

    Euphorbi. *Cephalocroton cordofanus* (seed-fat, 70% according to one report, none to another!), *Euphorbia lagascae* (sd-oil, 57%), and one other member of the family.

    Malv. *Abutilon* (< 1%), *Althaea* (1%), *Gossypium* (1%), *Hibiscus* (1–5%), *Lavatera* (3%), *Malope* (7%), *Malva* (3%), *Sidalcea* (5%) (sd-fats, Hopkins and Chisholm, 1960)

    Onagr. *Clarkia elegans* (sd-fat)

    Valerian. one sp. ?

    Dipsac. *Scabiosa atropurpurea* (*maritima*) (sd-oil, 8%), and one other.

    Comp. *Vernonia anthelmintica* (sd-fat, 64–72%), *colorata* (some), and seven other members of the family.

XI FATTY-ACIDS WITH ONE OR MORE HYDROXY GROUPS

1. Saturated acids with an ω-OH group

GENERAL

Few of these are constituents of *seed-fats*. Most of them have been found in *waxes*, but it is convenient to deal with them here.

List and Occurrence

2-Hydroxy-acetic acid (Glycollic acid; $CH_2OH.COOH$) does not occur in *fats*.

    Crassul. *Kalanchoë daigremontiana* (lvs)

    Euphorbi. *Ricinus communis* (sdlgs)

    Vit. *Vitis vinifera* (young frt)

    Sterculi. *Theobroma cacao* (lvs)

    Dichapetal. *Dichapetalum cymosum*

    Gram. *Saccharum officinarum*

12-Hydroxy-lauric acid (Sabinic acid) occurs as *polyestolides* in many conifer waxes. I have no record of it in angiosperms.

15-Hydroxy-pentadecanoic acid
  Umbell. *Angelica archangelica* (rt, as ester and lactone (*exaltolide*))
18-Hydroxy-stearic acid occurs in Carnauba wax
20-Hydroxy-arachidic acid in Carnauba wax
21-Hydroxy-heneicosanoic acid (Medullic acid) is said to occur as its
  lactone in Carnauba wax.
22-Hydroxy-behenic acid (Phellonic acid): in Carnauba wax and suberin.
24-Hydroxy-lignoceric acid; 26-Hydroxy-cerotic acid; 28-Hydroxy-
  montanic acid; and 30-Hydroxy-melissic acid are all reported from
  Carnauba wax.

2. Saturated acids with an -OH group in the α- (or 2-) position

List and Occurrence

2-Hydroxy-acetic acid: see above.
2-Hydroxy-propionic acid (Lactic acid) is common in plants, says
  Karrer (1955), but it does not occur in *fats.*
2-Hydroxy-arachidic acid (Macilolic acid)
  Myristic. *Myristica fragrans* (mace, in small amount?)

3. Saturated acids with an -OH group in other than the ω- or α-
  positions.

List and Occurrence

?-Hydroxy-tetradecanoic acid
  Phytolacc. *Phytolacca americana* (root-fat, < 1%)
  Umbell. *Angelica* (fruit, ess. oil)
  Lili. *Schoenocaulon officinale* (*Sabadilla*) (seed-oil)
11-Hydroxy-tetradecanoic acid (Convolvulinolic acid; 11-Hydroxy-
  myristic acid) is the aglycone of *convolvulinic acid* (?) from *Ipomoea*
  (*Convolvul.*).
(+)-11-Hydroxy-hexadecanoic acid (11-Hydroxy-palmitic acid; Jala-
  pinolic acid) is the aglycone of *jalapin, scammonium,* etc. from the
  Convolvulaceae.

4. Saturated acids with two, three, or four -OH groups

List and Occurrence

10,16-Dihydroxy-*n*-hexadecanoic acid (a Dihydroxy-palmitic acid)
  Ole. *Olea europaea* (lf-oil)
9,10-Dihydroxy-*n*-octadecanoic acid (Dihydroxy-stearic acid)
  Laur. *Actinodaphne hookeri* (sd-oil?, 7%)

Euphorbi.   Ricinus communis (sd-oil, to 1%)
Convolvul.   Ipomoea muricata (sd-oil, to 1%)
3,11-Dihydroxy-*n*-tetradecanoic acid (Dihydroxy-myristic acid; Ipuro-
lic acid)
Convolvul.   Pharbitis (in resin)
9,10,12,13-Tetrahydroxy-*n*-octadecanoic acid (Sativic acid; Tetra-
hydroxy-stearic acid) is said to occur in several places, but Karrer
(1958) thinks it may be secondary, arising from *linoleic acid.*
Vit.   Vitis vinifera (sd-oil)
Lili.   Zigadenus intermedius (lf-fat)
Gram.   Oryza sativa (embryo)
9,10,18-Trihydroxy-*n*-octadecanoic acid (a Trihydroxy-stearic acid;
Phloionolic acid) occurs in *cork* (2%), and in
Ole.   Olea europaea (lf-oil)
9,10,14-Trihydroxy-*n*-octadecanoic acid (a Trihydroxy-stearic acid;
Artemisic acid)
Comp.   Artemisia monogyna

5. Unsaturated acids with one or more -OH groups

List and Occurrence

Dihydroxy-myricinoleic acid is a C_{30} acid which is said to occur in
Euphorbi.   Pedilanthus (candelilla *wax*)
(+)-14-Hydroxy-*n*-eicos-11c-enoic acid (Lesquerolic acid)
Crucif.   Lesquerella spp. (seed-fats of 12 out of 14, in amounts of
from 45 to 75%. The two species lacking *lesquerolic acid* have
C_{18} and C_{16} hydroxy-acids; Mikolajczak *et al.* 1962.)
ω-Hydroxy-hexadec-7-enoic acid does not occur naturally. Is *ambretto-
lide* (of *Hibiscus abelmoschus*) its *lactone*?
?-Hydroxy-linoleic acid
Apocyn.   Wrightia annamensis (sd-fat, in small amount?)
9-Hydroxy-*n*-octadeca-10,12-dienoic acid (*cis, trans-* or *trans, cis-*)
Euphorbi.   Mallotus claoxyloides (sd-fat, 65%), *discolor* (sd-fat,
70%), *japonicus* (sd-fat), *philippinensis* (sd-fat, different analyses
give 26, 36, 58, and (Hatt, 1958) 75%!); *Trewia nudiflora* (39%).
8-Hydroxy-*n*-octa-5,6-dienoic acid
($CH_2(OH).CH=C=CH.(CH_2)_3.COOH$) is an *allenic acid.* It
occurs in a *tetra-ester triglyceride* in which *glycerol* seems to have it,
linoleic, and *linolenic acids* esterified with *dec-2,4-dienoic acid* as its
3 ester groups (Sprecher *et al.* 1965). See also (−)-*octadeca-5,6-
dienoic acid.*
Euphorbi.   Sapium sebiferum (sd-oil)

    Comp. Tragopogon porrifolius (sd-fat, totalling with the next
        acid below, 4%), and several other members of the family
        (Wolff, 1966)

12-Hydroxy-*n*-Octadec-9c,15c-dienoic acid
    Crucif. 5 spp. (Wolff, 1966)

13-Hydroxy-*n*-octadeca-9,11-dienoic acid (*cis, trans-* or *trans, cis-*)
    Coriari. Coriaria sp.
    Comp. 3 species

9-Hydroxy-*n*-octadeca-10t,12t-dienoic acid (Dimorphecolic acid)
    Comp. Dimorphotheca aurantiaca (sd-oil, chief constituent),
        Osteospermum ecklonis (sd-oil, 54%)

12-Hydroxy-*n*-octadec-9c-enoic acid (Ricinoleic acid) is said to be
widely distributed. Some of the following records, however, have
been questioned:
    Opili. Agonandra brasiliensis (sd-oil, 47–65%)
    Papaver. Argemone mexicana (sd-fat; one analysis says 10%,
        another 0%!)
    Legum. Cassia absus (sd-oil, 1–10%)
    Euphorbi. Cephalocroton cordofanus?; *Ricinus communis* (sd-oil,
        80–95%!), *zanzibarinus* (90%)
    Vit. Vitis vinifera (sd-oil? Probably *not*, says Hilditch, 1956)
    Apocyn. Wrightia annamensis (sd-fat, principal constituent?)
    Solan. Solanum dulcamara (sd-fat, some?)

9-Hydroxy-*n*-octadec-12-enoic acid
    Apocyn. Strophanthus sarmentosus (sd-fat, 7%), and in other
        species?

18-Hydroxy-*n*-octadeca-9c,11t,13t-trienoic acid (18-Hydroxy-α-elaeo-
stearic acid; Kamlolenic acid) *may* occur in part as polyesters or
condensation products (Hilditch, 1956).

XII ACIDS WITH A TERMINAL CYCLOPENT-2-ENYL GROUP (THE CHAULMOOGRIC SERIES)

GENERAL

My first paper in the field of chemotaxonomy (Gibbs, 1945) was
written when there was still considerable interest in the use of chaulmoogra oil in the treatment of leprosy. There had been a spate of
papers on the occurrence and chemistry of the fatty-acids of the
chaulmoogra series and I dealt rather fully with them. Interest has
waned and comparatively little further information has come my way.
The interested reader is referred to chapter 13 of Peattie's *Cargoes*

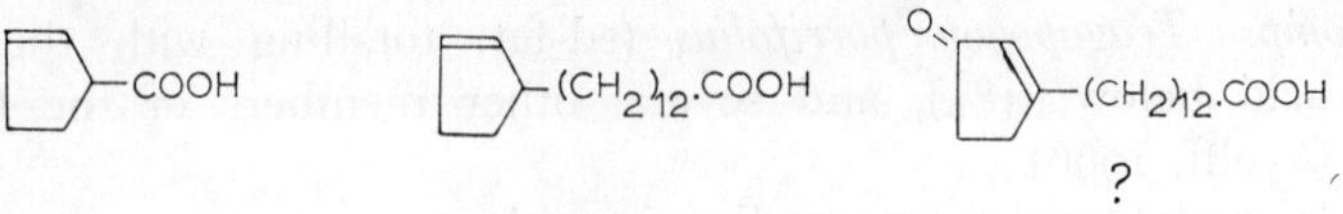

Fig. 108. Fatty-acids of the chaulmoogric series.

and Harvests (1932) and the paper by Rock, Fairchild and Power (1922).

It is comparatively easy to detect acids of the chaulmoogric series. They are strongly optically active and their presence may be inferred if the seed-oil is markedly dextrorotatory.

They seem to be confined to the *Flacourtiaceae* (q.v.).

List and Occurrence

1-Cyclopent-2-enyl-formic acid (Aleprolic acid; fig. 108)
  Flacourti. *Hydnocarpus* (sd-oil, in small amount)
3-Cyclopent-2-enyl-propionic acid: has not been found?
5-Cyclopent-2-enyl-pentanoic acid (Aleprestic acid)
  Flacourti. *Hydnocarpus* (sd-oil, in small amount)
7-Cyclopent-2-enyl-heptanoic acid (Aleprylic acid)
  Flacourti. *Hydnocarpus* (sd-oil, in small amount)
9-Cyclopent-2-enyl-nonanoic acid (Alepric acid)
  Flacourti. *Hydnocarpus* (sd-oil, in small amount)
11-Cyclopent-2-enyl-undecanoic acid (Hydnocarpic acid)
  Flacourti. *Asteriastigma?*, *Caloncoba* (3 spp., to 18%), *Carpo-troche* (probably in 3 spp., 45% in one), *Casearia?*, *Hydnocarpus* (several spp.; but *absent* from some?; to 68% in one?), *Laetia?*, *Lindackeria* (5 spp.?, to 11% in one), *Mayna*, *Samyda?*, *Tarakto-genos* (3 spp., to 35%), *Zuelania?*
13-Cyclopent-2-enyl-tridecanoic acid (Chaulmoogric acid; fig. 108) is probably in all members of the *Flacourtiaceae* which have optically active fatty-acids.
  Flacourti. *Asteriastigma*, *Buchnerodendron*, *Caloncoba* (3 spp., to possibly 94%!), *Carpotroche* (3 spp., to 24%), *Casearia?*, *Hydnocarpus* (several spp., to 90%), *Laetia?*, *Lindackeria* (5 spp., to 51%), *Mayna* (2 spp.?), *Samyda?*, *Taraktogenos* (3 spp., to 40%), *Zuelania?*
13-Cyclopent-2-enyl-tridec-6-enoic acid (Gorlic acid; Dehydro-chaulmoogric acid)
  Flacourti. *Caloncoba* (3 spp., to 17%), *Carpotroche* (to 15%), *Hydnocarpus* (2 spp., to 12%), *Taraktogenos* (to 23%)

11-Keto-cyclopent-2-enyl-undecanoic acid (Keto-hydnocarpic acid)
  Flacourti. Carpotroche brasiliensis (with *keto-chaulmoogric acid,* 4%)
13-Keto-cyclopent-2-enyl-tridecanoic acid (Keto-chaulmoogric acid; fig. 108)
  Flacourti. Carpotroche brasiliensis (with *keto-hydnocarpic acid,* 4%)

XIII BRANCHED-CHAIN ACIDS

Isovaleric acid (Isopropyl-acetic acid; $(CH_3)_2.CH.CH_2.COOH$) has been found in depot-fats of the dolphin and porpoise, but *not*, I think, in seed-fats. It does occur, free and as esters, in some plants.
2-Methyl-butyric acid ($CH_3.CH_2.CH(CH_3).COOH$)
  Convolvul. Ipomoea parasitica (as a constituent of *glycolipid?*)
16-Methyl-heptadecanoic acid ($(CH_3)_2.CH.(CH_2)_{14}.COOH$)
  Scrophulari. Antirrhinum majus (plt, which also has small amounts of similar acids from C_{12} to C_{24}?)
16-Methyl-octadecanoic acid ($CH_3.CH_2.CH(CH_3).(CH_2)_{14}.COOH$)
  Scrophulari. Antirrhinum majus (plt, which also has small amounts of similar acids from C_{13} to C_{21}?)

FLAVONOIDS

GENERAL

So numerous, and so important, are the *flavonoids* that whole books have been written about them (Geissman, 1962; Goodwin (ed.), 1965; Harborne, 1967).

Swain, in his recent review of these compounds (in Goodwin, 1965), says:

Nature as it surrounds us is predominantly green. It is not surprising therefore that plants, or parts of plants which are in bright contrast to this overwhelming greenness have always attracted man, and indeed other denizens of the animal kingdom. Although the various shades of yellow are pleasing to the majority of people, the most fascinating colours are those which make the deepest contrast to green, that is, various shades of red and blue. Almost all the brilliant colours of this type which are found in flowers and fruit are due to the presence of one or more of the groups of flavonoid compounds

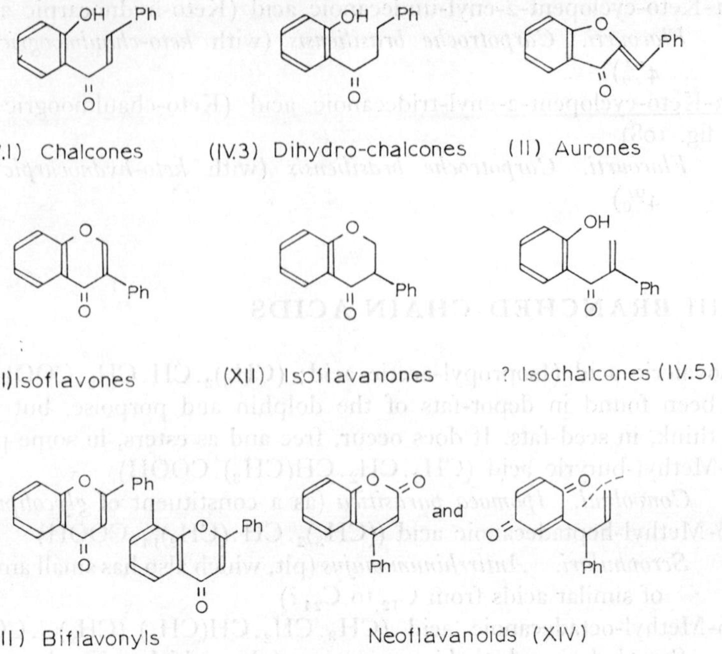

(IV.1) Chalcones   (IV.3) Dihydro-chalcones   (II) Aurones

(XIII)Isoflavones   (XII) Isoflavanones   ? Isochalcones (IV.5)

(III) Biflavonyls   Neoflavanoids (XIV)

Fig. 109. Flavonoids (our numbering in brackets).

known as anthocyanins. Other classes of flavonoid compounds are responsible for the yellow colour of certain flowers, although more usually this is due to the presence of carotenoid pigments. Yet other flavonoids account for the actual whiteness in most white flowers, which without them would perhaps appear almost translucent. Finally some of the brown and black pigments found in Nature are due either to the products of oxidation of flavonoid and related phenolic compounds, or to their chelates with metals.

The various classes of flavonoid pigments may be regarded as derivatives of *flavone*, which is usually numbered as shown in fig. 115. Unfortunately, different systems of numbering are used for some of the classes of *flavonoids* and this often leads to confusion.

Flavonoids may be considered to consist of two benzene rings A and B, linked by a C_3 section. This last may form a γ-pyrone ring, as in *flavone* itself. The classes of *flavonoids* (and we recognize a dozen or more, figs. 109 and 110) usually differ in the state of oxidation of this link.

Within each class of *flavonoids* individual compounds differ in the number and distribution of -OH and -OCH$_3$ groups. It might seem

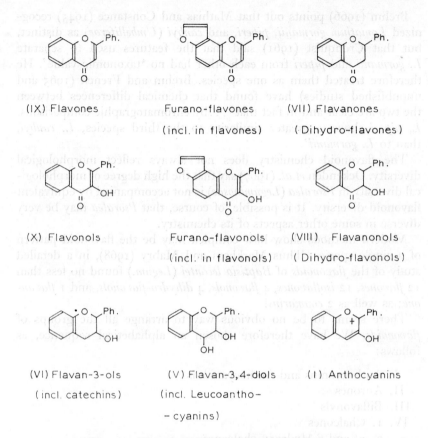

(IX) Flavones   Furano-flavones   (VII) Flavanones

(incl. in flavones)   (Dihydro-flavones)

(X) Flavonols   Furano-flavonols   (VIII) Flavanonols

(incl. in flavonols)   (Dihydro-flavonols)

(VI) Flavan-3-ols   (V) Flavan-3,4-diols   (I) Anthocyanins

(incl. catechins)   (incl. Leucoantho-

– cyanins)

Fig. 110. Flavonoids (our numbering in brackets).

to one newly introduced to these substances that Nature can place these anywhere. Actually there are definite patterns which are followed closely by most plants, and these patterns reflect the biogenetic pathways by which the compounds arise. Unusual groupings may be of great chemotaxonomic interest, and examples will occur in the pages which follow.

Many of the *flavonoids* seem to occur in the free state but often they are present as *glycosides* and are released during extraction.

Several different sugars are involved but only rarely are these unusual ones. The sugars are attached at preferred positions and with an -O-linkage in most cases. Some *C-glycosyl* compounds do occur, however, and these are sometimes of taxonomic interest.

We shall discuss chemotaxonomy of the groups of *flavonoids* as we deal with them, but a note or two may not be out of place here.

Brehm (1966) points out that Mathias and Constance (1945) recognized *Lomatium gormanii*, *piperi*, and *canbyi* (*Umbelliferae*) as distinct, but that Cronquist (1961) said that the features used to separate *L. gormanii* and *piperi* from each other had no 'taxonomic value'. He therefore treated them as one species. Brehm and French (1965 and unpublished studies) have found that chemical differences between the two are clear and in fact that '. . . by chromatographic comparisons, *L. piperi* shows a greater similarity to the third species, *L. canbyi*, than to *L. gormanii*'.

The flavonoid chemistry does not always reflect morphological diversity. Ockenden *et al.* (1967) say that the high degree of morphological diversity in *Psoralea* (*Leguminosae*) is not accompanied by equivalent flavonoid diversity. It is possible, of course, that *Psoralea* may be very diverse in some other aspects of its chemistry.

Modern methods show how complex may be the flavonoid pattern of a single species. Thus Markham and Mabry (1968), in a detailed study of the *flavonoids* of *Baptisia lecontei* (*Legum.*) found no less than 12 *flavones*, 12 *isoflavones*, 4 *flavonols*, 4 *dihydro-flavonols*, and 1 *flavanone*; as well as 2 *coumarins*!

There seems to be no obvious way to arrange all the groups of *flavonoids*. We have therefore chosen an alphabetical sequence, as follows:

   I. Anthocyanins and Anthocyanidins
  II. Aurones
 III. Biflavonyls
  IV. 1. Chalcones
      2. α- and β-Hydroxy-chalcones
      3. Dihydro-chalcones
      4. 2-Benzyl-2-hydroxy-coumaran-3-ones
      5. Isochalcones
   V. Flavan-3,4-diols and Leucoanthocyanins
  VI. Flavan-3-ols and Catechins
 VII. Flavanones (Dihydro-flavones)
VIII. Flavanonols (Dihydro-flavonols)
  IX. Flavones and Furanoflavones
   X. Flavonols and Furanoflavonols
  XI. Homo-isoflavones
 XII. Isoflavanones
XIII. Isoflavones
 XIV. Neoflavanoids

I ANTHOCYANINS AND ANTHOCYANIDINS

GENERAL

The *anthocyanidins* (figs. 111 and 112) are all derivatives of *2-phenyl-benzopyrilium*. There have been repeated reports of their occurrence in the free state but Harborne (1967) doubts the truth of these. He says:

Anthocyanidins have been reported from time to time to occur naturally in plant tissues *in the free state*, but to the author this seems unlikely, because of their great insolubility and general instability. Such reports are probably due to hydrolysis having occurred during extraction and isolation. Since acid-containing solvents are nearly always used for these purposes, it is practically impossible to avoid some hydrolysis during these procedures.

The *anthocyanidins* so far known number about 16. A few of these arise from *leucoanthocyanins*, the remainder occur as *glycosides* of the common sugars—*glucose, arabinose, xylose*, etc.—and are known as *anthocyanins*. These are water-soluble and occur in the cell-sap. They are responsible for many of the red, purple and blue colours of flowers and fruits. Since, in general, they are red in acid media and blue in alkali, one might suppose that the cell-sap of red tissue is acid in reaction and of blue tissue alkaline. This is not altogether true.

Recent papers by Jurd and Asen (1966) and Asen and Jurd (1967) are of interest in this connection. In 1966 they say:

Quercitrin, chlorogenic acid, and methyl gallate have no measureable effect on the color, spectra, or stability of cyanidin-3-glucoside [a typical *anthocyanin*] in aq. solutions at pH 3–6·5. In acetate buffer solutions (pH 5·45) containing aluminum salts, however, quercitrin and chlorogenic acid form highly colored co-ordination complexes with the anthocyanin (anhydro base). The chlorogenic acid complex is blue and insoluble in water.

In 1967 the same authors report the isolation of a blue pigment, *cyanocentaurin*, from the flowers of *Centaurea cyanus* and say that it 'must be an iron complex of 4 molecules of cyanidin-3,5-diglucoside and 3 molecules of a "bisflavone" glucoside'.

They say, too, that a blue pigment, *commelinin*, reported by others from the flowers of *Commelina communis*, has properties 'strikingly similar' to those of *cyanocentaurin*. Favreau *et al.* (1969) describe *actirubrine*, from *Actaea rubra*, as 'un complexe de cyanidine, d'acide caféique et d'aluminium...'.

528 CHEMOTAXONOMY OF FLOWERING PLANTS

It is clear from the above and from much other scattered information that the blue colours of flowers and fruits are not due to the alkalinity of the sap (measurements show that it is usually acid), but to complexes of *anthocyanins* with metals and other substances. Many blue-fruited plants are *aluminium-accumulators*, which may well be significant (p. 477).

It has long been known that some naturally occurring *anthocyanins* are acylated, but only recently has it been possible to determine the structures of such compounds. A paper by Harborne (1964) reports upon this subject. He says that 15 *acylated anthocyanins* gave in each case an *acylated sugar*; that the acyl groups were attached to the sugars in the 3-position; and that the acids involved are *p-coumaric, ferulic,* and *caffeic*. He found *no* evidence for the occurrence of *p-hydroxy-benzoic, sinapic,* and *malonic* acids (which had been thought to occur). We have included the *acylated anthocyanins* in our list below.

It is interesting to note that a number of *acylated flavonols* are now known.

I have found the sections on *anthocyanins* in Harborne's *Comparative Biochemistry of the Flavonoids* (1967) of great use in compiling this section.

Although so many kinds of *anthocyanins* have been discovered in the Angiospermae surprisingly few groups of flowering plants have been adequately studied for these compounds, and only a few notes on distribution will be included here.

(*a*) There seems to be little or no support for the splitting of the **Tubiflorae** as advocated by Hutchinson (1959). See p. 1796 for further discussion.

(*b*) One or two families which have been rather more fully investigated than others, notably the *Plumbaginaceae* and the *Gesneriaceae*, are characterized by unusual *anthocyanins*.

(*c*) The distribution of *anthocyanins* (and of *nudicaulin*) in *Papaver* parallels more or less Fedde's (1909) treatment of the genus (Harborne, 1967).

It is obvious that much remains to be done before we can make extensive use of *anthocyanins* in systematics.

List and Occurrence

Apigeninidin (Ap; Gesneridin; fig. 111) is a rare *3-deoxy-anthocyanidin*.
Apigeninidin-5-glucoside (Gesnerin)

> *Gesneri. Chrysothemis pulchella* (sepals), *Gesneria cuneifolia* (fl.), *Kohleria eriantha* (fl.), *Rechsteineria cardinalis* (fl.)
> *Gram. Sorghum vulgare* (lvs)

Apigeninidin-glucoside is probably *not* a *trigalloyl-glucoside*. Is it the 5-*glucoside*?

    Sterculi. *Chiranthodendron pentadactylon* (calyx)

Aurantinidin (Au; 6- or possibly 8-Hydroxy-pelargonidin)

    Balsamin. *Impatiens aurantiaca* (fl., free and as glycosides?)

Capensinidin (Cp; 3',5',5-Trimethoxy-delphinidin; fig. 111)

Capensinidin-3-rhamnoside (Capensinin)

    Plumbagin. *Plumbago capensis* (fl)

Carajurin (Cj; fig. 111) is a 3-*deoxy-anthocyanidin*.

    Bignoni. *Arrabidaea* (*Bignonia*) *chica* (lvs, free?)

Carexidin: a 3-*deoxy-anthocyanidin*? It has been found (probably free) in some of the *Cyperaceae* (Clifford and Harborne, 1969).

    Cyper. *Carex* (2), *Lepironia* (1), *Schoenus* (1), *Scleria* (1); but *absent* from several other members.

Columnidin (Co; fig. 111) is a 3-*deoxy-anthocyanidin*.

    Gesneri. *Columnea tulae* var. *flava* (fl., free?)

Columnin (Columnidin-5-glucoside?)

    Gesneri. *Alloplectus*, *Columnea* (7?), *Episcia* (3), *Koellikeria*, *Kohleria*, *Nauticalyx*, *Sinningia*, *Trichantha*

Cyanidin (Cy; fig. 111) is the commonest *anthocyanidin*. More than 30 different *glycosides* of it are known. Swain (in Goodwin, 1965) estimates that of all the plants producing anthocyanins 80% of the leaves, nearly 70% of the fruits, and 50% of the flowers have derivatives of *cyanidin*.

Cyanidin-3-arabinoside

    Sterculi. *Theobroma cacao* (frt)

    Eric. *Rhododendron* spp. (fls of red-flowered spp.), *Vaccinium* spp. (frt)

    Gram. *Hordeum vulgare* (husks), *Phalaris arundinacea* var. *picta* (rt), *Poa annua* (lvs, etc.)

Cyanidin-3-arabinoside-5-glucoside

    Eric. *Rhododendron* (*Azalea*) 'Red Wing' (fl.)

Cyanidin-3-(caffeoylglucoside)

    Orobanch. *Orobanche minor* (fl., st.)

Cyanidin-3-(caffeoylglucoside)-5-glucoside

    Lab. *Salvia splendens* (fl.)

Cyanidin-3-(caffeoylsophoroside)-5-glucoside

    Convolvul. *Ipomoea batatus* (tuber)

Cyanidin-3-(*p*-coumaroylglucoside) (Hyacinthin)

    Lili. *Hyacinthus orientalis* (bulb-scale)

Cyanidin-3-(*p*-coumaroylglucoside)-5-glucoside (Perillanin)

    Lab. *Perilla ocimoides* var. *crispa* (lvs)

    Lili. *Hyacinthus orientalis* (fl.), *Scilla non-scripta* (bulb, fl.)

Cyanidin-3-(*p*-coumaroylrutinoside)-5-glucoside (cyananin)
Viol.   *Viola* × *wittrockiana*
Solan.   *Solanum tuberosum*
Lili.   *Hyacinthus* (fl.)?
Cyanidin-3-(*p*-coumaroylsophoroside)-5-glucoside (Raphanusin-C)
Crucif.   *Brassica oleracea* var. *rubra* (lvs), *Raphanus sativus* (fl.,
frt, rt)
Cyanidin-3-(diferuloylsophoroside)-5-glucoside (Rubrobrassicin-C)
Crucif.   *Brassica oleracea* v. *rubra* (lvs)
Cyanidin-3,5-diglucoside (Cyanin) is a very common *anthocyanin*.
Caryophyll.   *Dianthus caryophyllus* (fl.)
Paeoni.   *Paeonia* spp.
Crassul.   *Kalanchoë blossfeldiana* (lvs, fl.)
Legum.   *Lupinus*?, *Phaseolus vulgaris* (sd)
Ros.   *Rosa*
Vit.   *Parthenocissus tricuspidata*
Eric.   *Rhododendron* (*Azalea*) 'Red Wing' (fl.)
Primul.   *Cyclamen* spp. (fl.)
Verben.   *Verbena* spp. (fl.)
Lab.   *Coleus blumei* cultivars (fl.), *Salvia splendens* (fl.)
Scrophulari.   *Digitalis purpurea* (fl.), *Linaria marocana* (fl.)
Comp.   *Centaurea scabiosa* and other spp.? (fl.), *Dahlia variabilis*
(fl.), *Helenium autumnale* (fl.), *Senecio formosus* (fl.), *Zinnia*
elegans (fl.)
Lili.   *Fritillaria* spp. (fl.), *Tulipa*?
Irid.   *Crocosma masonii* (fl.), *Gladiolus gandavensis* (fl.)
Gram.   *Oryza sativa* (lvs)
Orchid.   *Anacamptis pyramidalis* (fl.), *Orchis mascula* (fl.)
Cyanidin-3,7-diglucoside
Solan.   *Petunia hybrida* (fl.)
Cyanidin-3-(feruloylsophoroside)-5-glucoside (Raphanusin-D)
Crucif.   *Brassica oleracea* var. *rubra* (lvs), *Raphanus sativus* (fl.,
frt, rt)
Cyanidin-3-galactoside (Idaein)
Fag.   *Fagus sylvatica* var. ('copper' beech, lvs)
Polygon.   *Polygonum hydropiper* (sdlg)
Ros.   *Malus pumila* (frt), *Pyrus communis* (bk)
Legum.   *Lathyrus odoratus* (fl.)
Sterculi.   *Theobroma cacao* (frt)
Lythr.   *Lythrum salicaria*
Eric.   *Rhododendron* (*Azalea*) 'Red Wing' (fl.), *Vaccinium vitis-*
idaea, etc.
Myrsin.   *Ardisia crispa* (frt)

Cyanidin-3-gentiobioside
> *Primul.   Primula* spp. (st., fl.)
> *Rubi.   Rubia akane* (frt)
> *Solan.   Petunia hybrida* (fl.)

Cyanidin-3-glucoside (Asterin; Chrysanthemin) is one of the most widely distributed *anthocyanins*. It is recorded from
> *Salic., Mor., Polygon., Caryophyll., Calycanth., Magnoli., Ranuncul., The., Droser., Papaver., Crassul., Legum., Ros., Saxifrag., Euphorbi., Rut., Acer., Vit., Malv., Begoni., Myrt., Onagr., Eric., Primul., Plumbagin., Gesneri., Verben., Scrophulari., Orobanch., Caprifoli., Comp., Lili., Amaryllid., Gram., Lemn., Mus.*

Cyanidin-5-glucoside
> *Irid.   Crocosmia*

Cyanidin-3-glucosylglucoside
> *Ros.   Prunus*
> *Malv.   Hibiscus* (2)

Cyanidin-3-glucosylrutinoside
> *Begoni.   Begonia* spp. (lvs, fl.)

Cyanidin-3-(2^G-glucosylrutinoside)
> *Ros.   Prunus* (frt), *Rubus* spp. (frt)
> *Saxifrag.   Ribes* spp.

Cyanidin-3-lathyroside
> *Legum.   Lathyrus odoratus* (fl.)

Cyanidin-3-rhamnoside
> *Legum.   Lathyrus odoratus* (fl.)
> *Plumbagin.   Plumbago rosea* (fl.)

Cyanidin-3-rhamnoside-5-glucoside
> *Legum.   Lathyrus odoratus* (fl.), *Pisum sativum* (fl.)

Cyanidin-3-rhamnosylglucoside (?Cyanidin-3-rutinoside)
> *Irid.   Chasmanthe, Lapeirousia*

Cyanidin-3-rhamnosylglucoside-5-glucoside
> *Viol.   Viola* (acylated ?)

Cyanidin-3-rutinoside seems to be widely distributed.
> *Polygon.   Polygonum, Rheum*
> *Magnoli.   Magnolia* (fl.)
> *Ros.   Prunus* (frt), *Rubus* (frt)
> *Saxifrag.   Ribes* (frt)
> *Euphorbi.   Euphorbia pulcherrima* (bract)
> *Malv.   Abutilon insigne* (fl.)
> *Solan.   Cestrum, Nicotiana, Solanum*
> *Scrophulari.   Antirrhinum, Asarina, Digitalis, Mimulus* (2), *Misopates, Phygelius, Scrophularia*
> *Bignoni.   Campsis, Catalpa, Eccremocarpus, Incarvillea, Tecoma*

Gesneri. Chrysothemis, Episcia, Rhabdothamnus, Titanotrichum, Sinningia

Orobanch. Lathraea clandestina (fl.)

Rubi. Hoffmannia ghiesbreghtii

Comp. Cosmos, Haplopappus

Lili. Asparagus, Colchicum, Fritillaria (many), *Lilium, Tulipa*

Amaryllid. Clivia, Hippeastrum

Irid. Chasmanthe, Crocosmia, Lapeirousia

Gram. Oryza sativa (lvs)

Cann. Canna indica (fl.)

Mus. Musa velutina (bract)

Cyanidin-3-rutinoside-5-glucoside

Solan. Solanum

Gesneri. Streptocarpus

Irid. Crocosmia masonii (fl.)

Cyanidin-3-sambubioside

Ros. Rubus spp. (frt)

Saxifrag. Ribes spp.

Aquifoli. Ilex crenata (frt)

Begoni. Begonia (lvs, fl.; some spp.)

Caprifoli. Sambucus nigra (frt)

Gesneri. Aeschynanthus (4), *Jerdonia, Saintpaulia, Streptocarpus*

Scrophulari. Nemesia strumosa (fl.)

Amaryllid. Lycoris radiata (fl.)

Cyanidin-3-sambubioside-5-glucoside

Legum. Pisum sativum (frt)

Caprifoli. Sambucus nigra (frt)

Cyanidin-3-sophoroside

Papaver. Papaver spp.

Ros. Prunus (frt), *Rubus* (frt)

Saxifrag. Ribes (frt)

Malv. Hibiscus rosa-sinensis (fl.)

Begoni. Begonia (lvs, fl.)

Solan. Petunia hybrida (fl.)

Cyanidin-3-sophoroside-5-glucoside

Legum. Pisum sativum (frt)

Lili. Colchicum autumnale (fl.)

Cyanidin-3-sophoroside-7-glucoside

Papaver. Papaver?

Cyanidin-3-xylosylglucoside

Aquifoli. Ilex

Cyanidin-3-xylosylrhamnoside—or should it be *-rhamnosylxyloside*?

Lili. Fritillaria (1 sp. only)

Cyanidin-3-xylosylrutinoside
   Begoni. *Begonia* spp. (lvs, fl.)
Cyanidin-3-(2^G-xylosylrutinoside)
   Saxifrag. *Ribes* spp.
   Ros. *Rubus* spp. (frt)
Delphinidin (Dp; fig. 111) is, next to *cyanidin*, the commonest of *anthocyanidins*, about 20 *anthocyanins* having *delphinidin* as their aglycone. Harborne (1963) says:

> Delphinidin is noticeably absent from certain families, e.g. the Rosaceae, the Papaveraceae and the Orchidaceae. By contrast it is particularly abundant in other families, notably in the related group: Boraginaceae, Campanulaceae, Polemoniaceae and Hydrophyllaceae. There is here, of course, a strong correlation between the presence of delphinidin and blue flower colour. Only 10% of the blue-flowered species examined by Gascoigne *et al.* (1948) did not have delphinidin.

Delphinidin- ?-arabinoside
   Ranuncul. *Anemone coronaria* (pollen)
Delphinidin-3-arabinoside
   Eric. *Vaccinium* spp. (frt)
   Gram. *Hordeum* (aleurone)
Delphinidin-3-(caffeoylglucoside)
   Vit. *Vitis vinifera* (frt)
Delphinidin-3-(caffeoylglucoside)-5-glucoside
   Lab. *Salvia splendens* (fl.)
Delphinidin-3-(*p*-coumaroylglucoside)
   Vit. *Vitis vinifera* (frt)
Delphinidin-3-(*p*-coumaroylglucoside)-5-glucoside (Awobanin)
   Vit. *Vitis vinifera* (frt)
   Lab. *Hyssopus officinale* (fl.)
   Lili. *Hyacinthus orientalis* (fl.), *Scilla non-scripta* (fl., bu.)
   Commelin. *Commelina communis* (fl.)
Delphinidin-3-(*p*-coumaroylrutinoside)-5-glucoside (Delphanin)
   Viol. *Viola* × *wittrockiana*
   Solan. *Petunia hybrida* (fl.); *Solanum melongena* (frt-skin), *tuberosum* (fl.)
   Irid. *Iris* spp. and cultivars
Delphinidin-3-(di-*p*-coumaroylglucoside)-5-glucoside
   Solan. *Browallia speciosa* (fl.)
Delphinidin-3,5-diglucoside (Delphin)
   Ranuncul. *Delphinium ajacis*

Legum.   Medicago   sativa (fl.), *Phaseolus   vulgaris* (sd), *Pisum sativum* (fl.), *Wisteria* sp.
Vit.   Vitis vinifera (frt)
Punic.   Punica granatum
Primul.   Primula sp. (fl., st.)
Plumbagin.   Limonium sinuatum (fl.), and other spp. ?
Verben.   Verbena spp. (fl.)
Lab.   Salvia splendens (fl.)
Scrophulari.   Anarrhinum,   Antirrhinum,   Linaria,   Maurandia, Penstemon, Torenia
Bignoni.   Jacaranda acutifolia
Campanul.   Campanula sp. (fl.)
Irid.   Crocus spp. (fl.), *Gladiolus gandavensis* (fl.)
Delphinidin-3-galactoside (Empetrin)
Legum.   Lathyrus odoratus
Empetr.   Empetrum (2)
Eric.   Vaccinium spp. (frt)
Myrsin.   Bladhia sieboldii (fl.)
Plumbagin.   Ceratostigma plumbaginoides (autumn lvs)
Delphinidin-3-glucoside is widely distributed.
Nymphae.   Nymphaea var. (fl.)
Saxifrag.   Hydrangea macrophylla (fl.), *Ribes* (frt)
Legum.   Ononis spinosa (fl.), *Phaseolus vulgaris* (sd)
Malv.   Hibiscus manihot (fl.)
Rut.   Citrus sinensis (frt)
Passiflor.   Passiflora edulis (frt)
Vit.   Vitis vinifera
Myrt.   Eucalyptus sieberiana (lvs), *Metrosideros excelsa*
Eric.   Vaccinium spp. (frt)
Primul.   Cyclamen (fl.), *Primula* (fl.)
Plumbagin.   Limonium sinuatum (fl.), *Plumbago pulchella* (fl.)
Bignoni.   Jacaranda acutifolia (fl.)
Verben.   Verbena spp.
Gesneri.   Boea hygroscopica ?
Orobanch.   Orobanche elatior (fl.), *minor* (st., fl.)
Gentian.   Gentiana cashmerica (fl.)
Lili.   Tulipa spp. (fl.)
Mus.   Musa velutina (bract)
Delphinidin-3-glucosylglucoside
Ranuncul.   Clematis spp. (fl.)
Lin.   Linum grandiflorum var.
Solan.   Solanum melongena (frt)
Scrophulari.   Collinsia spp.

Delphinidin-3-rhamnoside
  Legum. *Lathyrus odoratus* (fl.)
  Plumbagin. *Plumbago coerulea* (fl.), *rosea* (fl.)
Delphinidin-3-rhamnoside-5-glucoside
  Legum. *Cicer, Lathyrus, Pisum, Vicia*
Delphinidin-3-rutinoside
  Saxifrag. *Ribes* spp. (frt)
  Solan. *Solanum* spp.
  Scrophulari. *Antirrhinum?*
  Orobanch. *Lathraea clandestina* (fl.)
  Mus. *Musa velutina* (bract), *Strelitzia regina* (fl.)
Delphinidin-3-rutinoside-5-glucoside
  Solan. *Petunia*
Delphinidin-3-sambubioside
  Daphniphyll. *Daphniphyllum macropodum* (frt)
Delphinidin-3-xyloglucoside (Daphniphyllin)
  Daphniphyll. *Daphniphyllum macropodum* (frt)
Delphinidin-3-xylosylgalactoside
  Legum. *Lathyrus odoratus*
Europinidin (Eu; 3′,5-Di-*O*-methyl-delphinidin?; fig. 111)
Europinidin-3-galactoside
  Plumbagin. *Ceratostigma plumbaginoides* (fl.), *willmottianum* (fl.)
Europinidin-3-glucoside
  Plumbagin. *Ceratostigma plumbaginoides* (fl.), *Plumbago europea* (fl.)
Fisetinidin (fig. 111): does not occur naturally? It arises with acid treatment from the *leucoanthocyanidin* known as *leucofisetinidin*.
Guibourtinidin is said to arise from *guibourtacacidin* (a *flavan-3,4-diol*).
Hirsutidin (Hs; fig. 111)
Hirsutidin-3,5-diglucoside (Hirsutin)
  Primul. *Primula* ('is almost universal to *Primula*').
  Apocyn. ? *Catharanthus roseus* is said to have a *hirsutidin glycoside*. Is it this one?
Luteolinidin (Lt; fig. 111)
Luteolinidin-5-glucoside
  Gesneri. *Alloplectus, Chrysothemis, Episcia, Gesneria, Hypocyrta, Kohleria, Rechsteineria*
  Gram. *Sorghum vulgare* (lvs)
Luteolinidin-glycoside: what is this?
  Gesneri. *Episcia melittifolia* (st.), *Sarmienta repens* (fl.)
Malvidin (Mv; Oenidin; Primulidin; Syringidin; fig. 111) is less common than some other *anthocyanidins*, but about 15 derivatives are known, a few of them being widely distributed.

Malvidin-3-arabinoside
  Eric. Vaccinium spp. (frt)
Malvidin-3-(caffeoylglucoside)
  Vit. Vitis vinifera (frt)
  Orobanch. Orobanche minor (fl., st.)
Malvidin-3-(*p*-coumaroylglucoside) (Coumaroyloenin)
  Vit. Vitis vinifera (frt)
Malvidin-3-(*p*-coumaroylglucoside)-5-glucoside (Tibouchinin)
  Vit. Vitis vinifera (frt)
  Melastomat. Tibouchina semidecandra (fl.)
Malvidin-3-(*p*-coumaroylrutinoside)-5-glucoside (Negretein)
  Solan. Brunfelsia calycina (fl.), *Petunia hybrida* (fl.), *Solanum
    tuberosum* (tuber)
  Irid. Iris spp. and cultivars (fl.)
Malvidin-3,5-diglucoside (Malvin)
  Crucif. Raphanus caudatus (frt)
  Legum. Lespedeza, Medicago, Phaseolus
  Vit. Parthenocissus (callus), *Vitis* (frt)
  Malv. Malva silvestris (fl.)
  Lythr. Cuphea ignea (fl.), *Lythrum salicaria* (fl.)
  Onagr. Clarkia elegans (fl.), *Epilobium hirsutum* (fl.), *Fuchsia* vars
    (fl.), *Godetia* (3, fl.)
  Eric. Rhododendron spp. (fl.)
  Primul. Cyclamen spp. (fl.), *Primula* spp. (fl., st.)
  Plumbagin. Armeria (7, fl.)
  Scrophulari. Torenia fournieri (fl.)
  Irid. Babiana stricta (fl.), *Gladiolus gandavensis* (fl.)
Malvidin-3-galactoside (Primulin; Uliginosin)
  Empetr. Empetrum nigrum (frt)
  Eric. Vaccinium uliginosum (frt)
  Primul. Primula polyantha (fl.), *sinensis*
  Myrsin. Bladhia sieboldii (fl.)
  Gram. Oryza sativa (lvs)
Malvidin-3-gentiobioside
  Primul. Primula spp. (fl., st.)
Malvidin-3-gentiotrioside
  Primul. Primula spp. (fl., st.)
Malvidin-3-glucoside
  Ranuncul. Anemone coronaria (pollen)
  Vit. Parthenocissus (callus), *Vitis*
  Myrt. Metrosideros excelsa (fl.)
  Eric. Vaccinium spp. (frt)
  Primul. Cyclamen (fl.), *Primula* (fl.)

Ole. *Ligustrum vulgare* (frt)
Solan. *Iochroma tubulosa* (fl.), *Petunia hybrida* (fl.)
Gram. *Oryza* (lvs)?
Irid. *Freesia* cultivars (fl.)
Malvidin-3-glucosylglucosylglucoside: is this *malvidin-3-gentiotrioside*?
Primul. *Primula*
Malvidin-3-rhamnoside
  Legum. *Lathyrus sativus* (fl.)
  Rhamn. *Ceanothus* cultivar (fl.)
Malvidin-3-rhamnoside-5-glucoside
  Legum. *Cicer, Lathyrus, Pisum, Vicia*
Malvidin-3-rutinoside-5-glucoside
  Gesneri. *Streptocarpus*
Malvidin-3-sophoroside-5-glucoside
  Crucif. *Raphanus* (acylated with *ferulic, p-coumaric,* and *caffeic acids*)
Nudicaulin has been stated to be an *anthocyanin*, but Harborne (1967)
says that it is probably not even a flavonoid. See *Papaver.*
Pelargonidin (Pg; fig. 111) is perhaps the third commonest of the
anthocyanidins. It is the aglycone of about 25 *anthocyanins.*
Pelargonidin-3-arabinoside
  Gram. *Hordeum* (aleurone), *Phalaris arundinacea* (rt)
  Lili. *Allium cepa* (bulb-scale)
Pelargonidin-3-(caffeoylglucoside)-5-glucoside (Salvianin)
  Lab. *Salvia splendens* (fl.)
Pelargonidin-3-(*p*-coumaroylferuloylsambubioside)-5-glucoside
  Crucif. *Matthiola incana* (fl.)
Pelargonidin-3-(*p*-coumaroylglucoside)-5-glucoside (Monardein)
  Polemoni. *Gilia coronopifolia* (fl.)
  Verben. *Holmskioldia sanguinea* (fl.)?
  Lab. *Monarda didyma* (fl.), *Salvia splendens* (fl.)
  Lili. *Hyacinthus orientalis* (fl.)
Pelargonidin-3-(*p*-coumaroylrutinoside)-5-glucoside (Pelanin)
  Solan. *Solanum tuberosum* (tuber)
Pelargonidin-3-(*p*-coumaroylsophoroside)-5-glucoside (Raphanusin-A)
  Crucif. *Raphanus sativus* (fl., frt, rt)
Pelargonidin-3,5-diglucoside (Monardin?; Pelargonin, Punicin?) is
very widely distributed.
  Caryophyll. *Dianthus caryophyllus* (fl.)
  Magnoli. *Magnolia*
  Saxifrag. *Bergenia crassifolia*
  Ros. *Rosa* (fl.)
  Legum. *Lupinus polyphemus* (fl.), *Phaseolus vulgaris* (sd)
  Gerani. *Pelargonium*

Balsamin.   Impatiens balsamina
Lythr.   Cuphea ignea (fl.)
Punic.   Punica granatum
Convolvul.   Convolvulus?, Ipomoea purpurea (fl.), *Pharbitis?*
Polemoni.   Phlox drummondi (fl.)
Verben.   Verbena sp. (fl.)
Lab.   Salvia splendens (fl.)
Comp.   Centaurea?, Dahlia variabilis (fl.)
Pelargonidin-3-(feruloylsophoroside)-5-glucoside (Raphanusin-B)
   Crucif.   Raphanus sativus (fl., frt, rt)
Pelargonidin-3-galactoside
   Fag.   Fagus sylvatica var. ('copper' beech, lvs)
   Legum.   Lathyrus odoratus (fl.)
Pelargonidin-3-galactoside-5-glucoside
   Legum.   Lathyrus odoratus (fl.)
Pelargonidin-3-gentiobioside
   Primul.   Primula spp. (fl., st.)
   Irid.   Tritonia cultivar (fl.)
Pelargonidin-3-gentiotrioside
   Primul.   Primula spp. (fl., st.)
Pelargonidin-3-glucoside (Callistephin) is one of the most widely
   distributed of *pelargonidin* derivatives.
   Caryophyll.   Dianthus caryophyllus (fl.)
   Ranuncul.   Anemone coronaria (fl., pollen)
   Papaver.   Papaver?
   Crucif.   Matthiola incana (fl.)
   Ros.   Fragaria (frt), *Rosa* (fl.), *Rubus* (frt)
   Legum.   Phaseolus vulgaris (sd)
   Euphorbi.   Euphorbia pulcherrima (bract)
   Primul.   Primula spp. (fl.)
   Verben.   Clerodendron splendens (fl.), *Verbena* spp. (fl.)
   Solan.   Iochroma coccinea (fl.)
   Scrophulari.   Verbascum phoeniceum
   Comp.   Callistephus chinensis (fl.)
   Lili.   Tulipa spp. (fl.)
   Irid.   Watsonia (3, fl.)
   Gram.   Zea mays (endosperm)
Pelargonidin-3-glucosylglucoside
   Passiflor.   Passiflora edulis
   Scrophulari.   Collinsia
Pelargonidin-3-(2G-glucosylrutinoside)
   Ros.   Rubus spp. (frt)
   Amaryllid.   Clivia miniata (fl.)

Pelargonidin-3-lathyroside
  Ranuncul. Anemone coronaria (fl.)
  Legum. Lathyrus odoratus
Pelargonidin-3-rhamnoglucoside
  Euphorbi. Euphorbia
  Gesneri. Gloxinia
Pelargonidin-3-rhamnoside
  Legum. Lathyrus odoratus (fl.)
  Plumbagin. Plumbago rosea (fl.)
Pelargonidin-3-rhamnoside-5-glucoside
  Legum. Lathyrus odoratus (fl.), *Pisum sativum* (fl.)
Pelargonidin-3-rutinoside
  Ros. Rubus (frt)
  Euphorbi. Euphorbia pulcherrima (bract)
  Solan. Cestrum purpureum (fl.), *Solanum* spp.
  Scrophulari. Antirrhinum (several), *Gambellia, Mimulus* (2),
    Phygelius, Verbascum
  Gesneri. Episcia (2), *Kohleria* (2), *Rhabdothamnus, Sinningia* cultivar
  Lili. Tulipa spp. (fl.)
  Amaryllid. Clivia miniata (fl.), *Hippeastrum* cultivars (fl.)
  Irid. Gladiolus gandavensis (fl.)
  Arac. Anthurium scherzerianum (spathe)
Pelargonidin-3-rutinoside-5-glucoside
  Gesneri. Achimenes ?, *Streptocarpus* ?
Pelargonidin-3-sambubioside
  Gesneri. Aeschynanthus obconicus (fl.), *tricolor* (fl.)
  Amaryllid. Nerine bowdenii (frt)
Pelargonidin-3-sambubioside-5-glucoside
  Gesneri. Agalmyla parasitica
Pelargonidin-3-sophoroside
  Papaver. Papaver spp.
  Ros. Rubus spp. (frt)
  Legum. Phaseolus multiflorus var. (frt)
  Tropaeol. Tropaeolum majus (fl.)
  Begoni. Begonia spp. (lvs, fl.)
  Rubi. Bouvardia spp. (fl.)
  Amaryllid. Cyrtanthus angustifolia (fl.)
  Irid. Watsonia (3, fls)
Pelargonidin-3-sophoroside-5-glucoside
  Irid. Gladiolus gandavensis (fl.)
Pelargonidin-3-sophoroside-7-glucoside
  Papaver. Papaver spp.
  Irid. Watsonia (3, fl.)

Peonidin (Pn; fig. 112) is one of the less common *anthocyanidins*, but about 15 derivatives are known.

Peonidin-3-arabinoside
  Eric.   Vaccinium spp. (frt)
  Gram.   Phalaris arundinaceae var. *picta*
Peonidin-3-(caffeoylglucoside)
  Vit.   Vitis vinifera (frt)
Peonidin-3-(*p*-coumaroylrutinoside)-5-glucoside (Peonanin)
  Solan.   Solanum tuberosum (tuber)
Peonidin-3,5-diglucoside (Paeonine, Peonin)
  Magnoli.   Magnolia
  Paeoni.   Paeonia spp. (fl.)
  Saxifrag.   Bergenia crassifolia
  Ros.   Rosa
  Gerani.   Pelargonium
  Balsamin.   Impatiens balsamina (fl.)
  Vit.   Vitis vinifera
  Onagr.   Fuchsia vars
  Primul.   Cyclamen spp. (fl.)
  Convolvul.   Pharbitis?
  Gesneri.   Streptocarpus?
Peonidin-3-galactoside
  Legum.   Lathyrus odoratus (fl.)
  Eric.   Vaccinium spp. (frt)
  Myrsin.   Ardisia crispa (frt)
Peonidin-3-galactoside-5-glucoside
  Legum.   Lathyrus odoratus (fl.)
Peonidin-3-gentiobioside
  Primul.   Primula spp. (fl., st.)
Peonidin-3-gentiotrioside
  Primul.   Primula spp. (fl., st.)
Peonidin-3-glucoside (Oxycoccicyanin)
  Magnoli.   Magnolia
  Ros.   Rosa (fl.)
  Vit.   Vitis vinifera
  Eric.   Vaccinium macrocarpon (frt)
  Primul.   Cyclamen (fl.), *Primula* (fl.)
  Solan.   Petunia hybrida (fl.)
  Scrophulari.   Verbascum phoenicium (fl.)
  Gesneri.   Streptocarpus
Peonidin-glucosylglucosylglucoside: is this *peonidin-3-gentiotrio-side?*
  Primul.   Primula

Peonidin-3-lathyroside
  Legum.   Lathyrus odoratus
Peonidin-3-rhamnoside
  Legum.   Lathyrus odoratus (fl.)
Peonidin-3-rhamnoside-5-glucoside
  Legum.   Lathyrus odoratus (fl.), *Pisum sativum* (fl.)
Peonidin-3-rhamnosylglucoside: is this *peonidin-3-rutinoside*?
  Irid.   Chasmanthe
Peonidin-3-rutinoside
  Magnoli.   Magnolia
  Lili.   Asparagus officinalis (shoot)
  Irid.   Chasmanthe aethiopica (fl.)
Peonidin-3-rutinoside-5-glucoside
  Magnoli.   Magnolia
  Gesneri.   Streptocarpus
  Irid.   Gladiolus gandavensis (fl.)
Peonidin-3-xylosylgalactoside
  Legum.   Lathyrus odoratus
Petunidin (Pt; fig. 112) is less common than *cyanidin* and *delphinidin*,
  but 15 or more *anthocyanins* yield it on hydrolysis.
Petunidin-3-arabinoside
  Eric.   Vaccinium spp. (frt)
Petunidin-3-(caffeoylglucoside)
  Vit.   Vitis vinifera (frt)
Petunidin-3-(*p*-coumaroylglucoside)
  Vit.   Vitis vinifera (frt)
Petunidin-3-(*p*-coumaroylglucoside)-5-glucoside
  Vit.   Vitis vinifera (frt)
  Solan.   Atropa belladonna (fl., frt)
Petunidin-3-(*p*-coumaroylrutinoside)-5-glucoside (Petanin)
  Solan.   Lycopersicum esculentum (lvs, st.), *Petunia hybrida* (fl.),
    Solanum tuberosum (tuber)
Petunidin-3-(dicoumaroylrutinoside)-5-glucoside (Guineesin)
  Solan.   Solanum guineense (frt)
Petunidin-3,5-diglucoside (Muscadinin?; Petunin)
  Legum.   Medicago sativa (fl.)
  Vit.   Vitis vinifera (frt)
  Primul.   Primula spp. (fl., st.)
  Boragin.   Anchusa italica (fl.)
  Scrophulari.   Torenia fournieri (fl.)
  Gesneri.   Streptocarpus?
Petunidin-3-galactoside
  Eric.   Vaccinium spp. (frt)

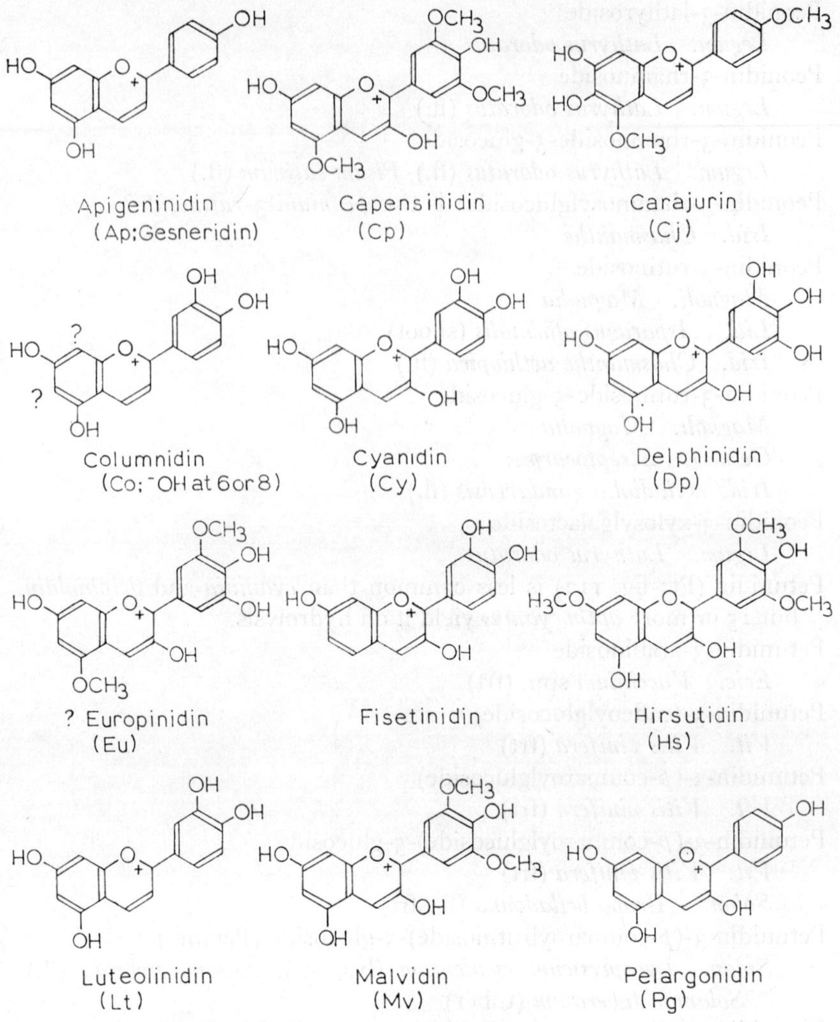

Fig. 111. Some anthocyanidins.

Petunidin-3-gentiobioside
   Primul.   *Primula* spp. (fl., st.)
Petunidin-3-gentiotrioside
   Primul.   *Primula* spp. (fl., st.)
Petunidin-3-glucoside
   Legum.   *Phaseolus vulgaris* (sd)
   Vit.   *Vitis vinifera* (frt)
   Eric.   *Vaccinium* spp. (frt)

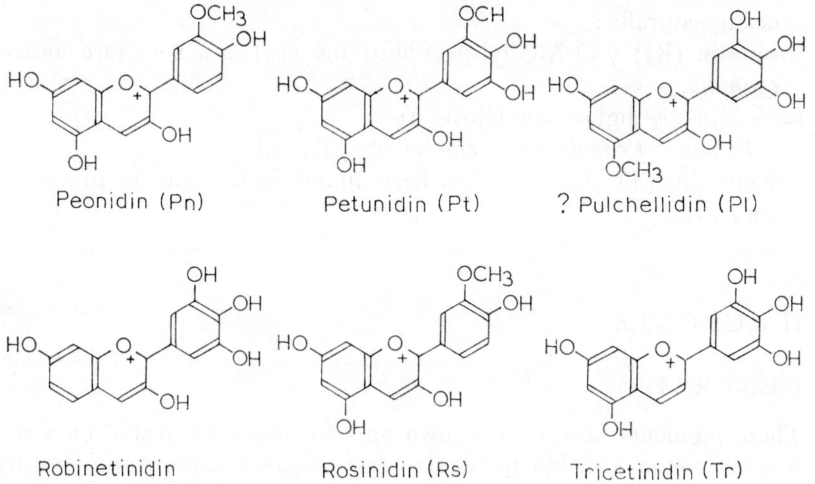

Peonidin (Pn)   Petunidin (Pt)   ? Pulchellidin (Pl)

Robinetinidin   Rosinidin (Rs)   Tricetinidin (Tr)

Fig. 112.   Some anthocyanidins.

Primul.   Cyclamen (fl.), *Primula* (fl.)
Solan.   Petunia hybrida (fl.)
Orobanch.   Orobanche minor (fl., st.)
Lemn.   Spirodela oligorrhiza (st.)
Petunidin-glucosylglucosylglucoside: is this *petunidin-3-gentiotrioside*?
   Primul.   Primula
Petunidin-3-rhamnoside
   Legum.   Lathyrus odoratus (fl.)
Petunidin-3-rhamnoside-5-glucoside
   Legum.   Cicer, Lathyrus, Pisum, Vicia
   Plumbagin.   Limonium (4, fl.)
Petunidin-3-rutinoside
   Solan.   Solanum spp.
Petunidin-3-sophoroside
   Gesneri.   Rhynchotechum parviflorum
   Solan.   Petunia hybrida (fl.)
Petunidin-5-xyloside is one of only 3 known monoxylosides says Sosa
   (1962).
   Lab.   Lavandula
Pulchellidin (Pl; 5-*O*-Methyl-delphinidin?; fig. 112)
Pulchellidin-3-glucoside
   Plumbagin.   Plumbago pulchella (fl.)
Pulchellidin-3-rhamnoside
   Plumbagin.   Plumbago coerulea (fl.)

Robinetinidin (fig. 112) arises from a *leucoanthocyanin*. It does not occur naturally?

Rosinidin (Rs; 7-O-Methyl-peonidin; fig. 112) is a very rare *anthocyanidin*.

Rosinidin-3,5-diglucoside (Rosinin)
    Primul. Primula rosea, clarkei, etc. (fl., st.)

Tricetinidin (Tr; fig. 112) has been found so far only in processed tea leaves.

II AURONES

GENERAL

These pigments have been known only for about 25 years. They are *benzalcoumaranones*, but the short name *aurones* has been proposed by Bate-Smith and Geissman (1951) and rather generally adopted. This latter names derives from the fact that they are often golden yellow. They may arise, in the laboratory, by oxidation of *chalcones*. Wong (1966), for example, found that he could obtain *hispidol* from the *chalcone isoliquiritigenin* (fig. 113) by oxidation with alkaline ferricyanide. Wong considers that his work on the biosynthesis of *hispidol* 'lends further support to the hypothesis that a chalcone is the common C_{15}-intermediate for the biosynthesis of all classes of flavonoids'. We have referred elsewhere to the relationship to the *2-benzyl-2-hydroxy-coumaran-3-ones* ('*hydrated aurones*').

Reviews of the chemistry and distribution of *chalcones* may be found in recent works by Harborne (1966, 1967). The numbering (again!) is somewhat different from that adopted for the *flavones* and *flavonols*.

Aurones with hydroxyls in the 3',4'-positions (corresponding to *quercetin*), and in the 3',4',5'-positions (corresponding to *myricetin*), are known. Writing in 1967 Harborne says that *aurones* with 4'-hydroxylation (corresponding to *kaempferol*) are not yet known. He predicts, however, that they will be found to occur since the equivalent 'hydrated aurone' *maesopsin* is known. *Hispidol* (fig. 113), which has 2 hydroxyls in the 4',6-positions, might be considered to fit the bill and be regarded as the deoxy-equivalent of *kaempferol*.

Flowers containing *aurones* turn bright orange-red when exposed to ammonia. I have made use of this in my *Aurone Test A (NH_3)* (p. 73).

List and Occurrence

Aureusidin (Cernuin; 4,6,3',4'-Tetrahydroxy-aurone; fig. 113) is the aglycone of at least two *aurone-glycosides*. It occurs free (Clifford and Harborne, 1969) in

Cyper.   *Eleocharis* (1), *Lepironia* (1), *Ptilanthelium* (1), *Remirea* (1), *Schoenus* (1), *Scirpus* (1). It was *not* found in: *Carex* (2), *Caustis* (1), *Cladium* (1), *Fimbristylis* (1), *Gahnia* (1), *Kyllinga* (1), *Lepidosperma* (1), *Schoenus* (1), *Scirpus* (1), *Scleria* (1).

Aureusidin-4-glucoside (Cernuoside)

Oxalid.   *Oxalis cernua*

Plumbagin.   *Limonium bonducelli*

Gesneri.   *Chirita micromusa, Cyrtandra oblongifolia* (fl.), *Didymocarpus malayanus* (fl.), *Petrocosmea kerrii*

Aureusidin-6-glucoside (Aureusin)

Oxalid.   *Oxalis cernua*

Scrophulari.   *Antirrhinum s. str.* (see Harborne (1963) and discussion under *Scrophulariaceae*), *Linaria maroccana* (fl.)

Bracteatin (4,6,3',4',5'-Pentahydroxy-aurone; fig. 113)

Bracteatin-4-glucoside (Bractein)

Comp.   *Helichrysum bracteatum* (yellow var.; Hänsel *et al.* 1962)

Bracteatin-6-glucoside

Scrophulari.   *Antirrhinum majus* (fl.), *nuttallanum* (fl.); *Linaria maroccana* (fl.)

Hispidol (4',6-Dihydroxy-aurone; fig. 113) has been found and studied by Wong (1966).

Legum.   *Glycine max* (sdlgs, free and as the 6-*glucoside*?)

Hispidol-6-glucoside has been obtained by Wong in biosynthesis experiments. Does it occur naturally in

Legum.   *Glycine max*?

Leptosidin (3', 4',6-Trihydroxy-7-methoxy-aurone; fig. 113)

Leptosidin-6-glucoside (Leptosin)

Comp.   *Coreopsis grandiflora* (fl.)

Maritimetin (3',4',6,7-Tetrahydroxy-aurone; fig. 113)

Maritimetin-6-glucoside (Maritimein)

Comp.   *Coreopsis maritima* (fl.)

Rengasin (Aureusidin-6-methyl ether; fig. 113): is this correct? Harborne (1967) has *aureusidin-4-methyl ether*.

Anacardi.   *Melanorrhoea* sp. ('Rĕngas' in Malay)

Sulphuretin (3',4',6-Trihydroxy-aurone; fig. 113) is the aglycone of *sulphurein*, and of *palasitrin*. It is said to occur free in Cotinus wood, whatever that is.

Legum.   *Acacia, Butea* (as glycosides?)

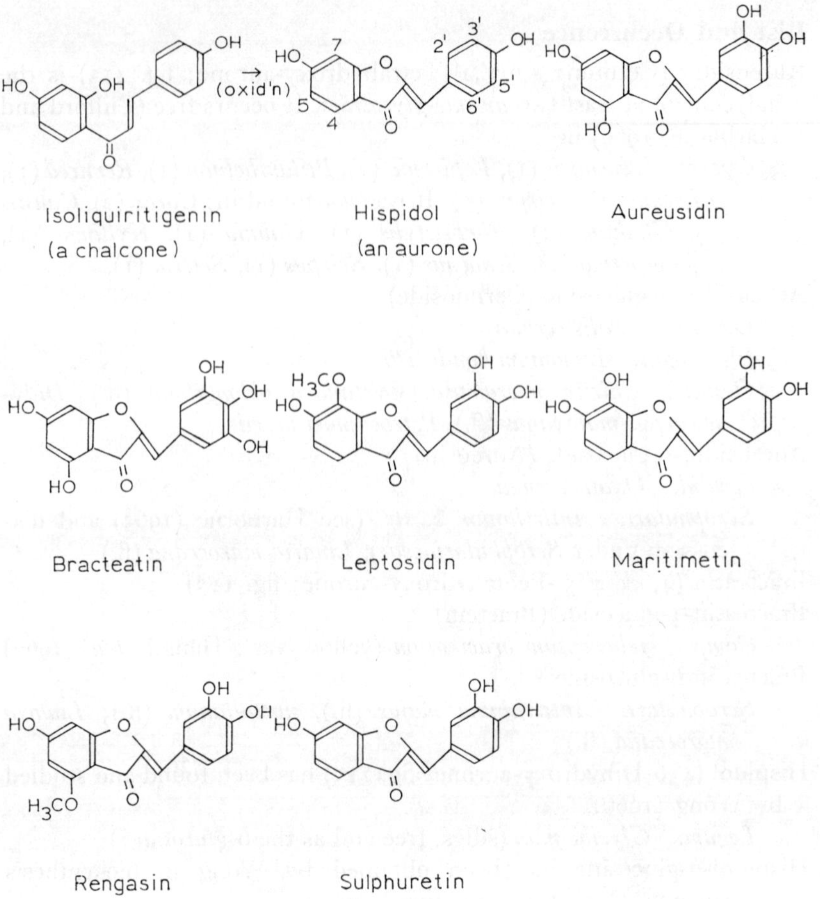

Isoliquiritigenin Hispidol Aureusidin
(a chalcone) (an aurone)

Bracteatin Leptosidin Maritimetin

Rengasin Sulphuretin

Fig. 113. Aurones.

Sulphuretin-6-diglucoside
  Comp. Dahlia
Sulphuretin-3',6-diglucoside (Palasitrin)
  Legum. Butea frondosa (fl.)
Sulphuretin-6-glucoside (Sulphurein)
  Comp. Cosmos grandiflora (fl.), *maritima* (fl.), *sulfureus* (fl.);
  Dahlia
Unidentified aurone
  An unidentified *aurone* is present in members of the *Restionaceae*
  (q.v.)

III BIFLAVONYLS

GENERAL

We have pointed out elsewhere how difficult it is to find consistent chemical differences between the major groups of plants. It looked at one time as if the *biflavonyls* might occur in *Selaginella* and in gymnosperms, but *not* in angiosperms. Several *biflavonyls—ginketin, isoginkgetin, sciadopitysin, kayaflavone, amentoflavone, hinokiflavone*, etc.— are widely distributed in the gymnosperms. Until comparatively recently none had been found in angiosperms. The discovery of *hinokiflavone* in *Casuarina*, a genus which was formerly considered to be a link between gymnosperms and angiosperms, was therefore a matter of great interest, and led Kariyone (1957) to write: 'It is of interest to know that estolide waxes and bisflavonoids [*biflavonyls*], which were taken to be peculiar to the Coniferae and some other gymnospermous plants, are now found in Casuarina, an angiosperm which in some systems closely follows the gymnosperms.'

We know now that *amentoflavone* occurs also in *Viburnum* of the *Caprifoliaceae*, and Harborne (1967) says of this last discovery: 'It appears to represent the retention of what is clearly a primitive flavone character in a relatively highly evolved plant family.'

I should argue differently and regard this as an independent development.

Since writing the above, I learn that more *biflavonyls* have been found (1967, 1970) in species of *Garcinia* (*Guttiferae*, far from *Casuarina* and *Viburnum*) and in *Xanthorrhoea* (a monocotyledon!). No doubt others will be discovered.

Close parallels to these *biflavonyls* are to be found in *ourateaproanthocyanidin-A, proanthocyanidin* (*Cola-nut*); and *procyanidino-(−)-epicatechin* (qq.v.).

List and Occurrence

Amentoflavone (fig. 114) occurs in *Selaginella*, in gymnosperms, and in
     Caprifoli. *Viburnum opulus* (bk), *prunifolium* (bk)
Hinokiflavone (fig. 114) is said to occur in all genera of the *Cupressaceae*
     and *Taxodiaceae*, in other gymnosperms, and in
     Casuarin. *Casuarina*
14-Hydroxy-xanthorrhone
     Xanthorrhoe. *Xanthorrhoea preissii* (resin of this sp. ?)
Morelloflavone is the first *biflavonyl* known to have a *flavone* and a
     flavanone unit.
     Guttif. *Garcinia morella* (htwd), *talboti* (rt)

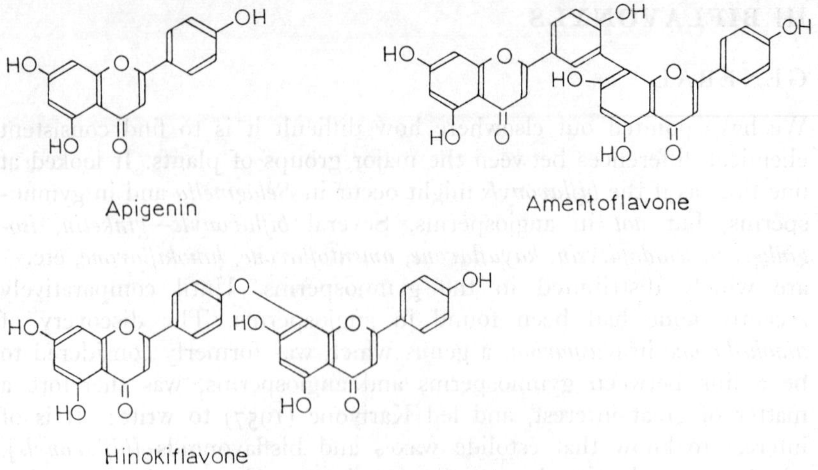

Apigenin   Amentoflavone

Hinokiflavone

Fig. 114. Apigenin and Biflavonyls.

Ouratea-proanthocyanidin-A can be hydrolysed to *ouratea-catechin* and *pelargonidin hydrochloride*.

    Ochn.   *Ouratea* sp. (rt)

Proanthocyanidin (Cola-nut)

    Sterculi.   *Cola acuminata* (frt)

Procyanidino-(−)-epicatechin yields on hydrolysis *cyanidin* and (−)-*epicatechin*.

    Hippocastan.   *Aesculus hippocastanum* (frt)

Talbotaflavone

    Guttif.   *Garcinia talboti* (rt)

4',5,7-Trihydroxy-3-(3',4',3,5,7-pentahydroxy-8-flavonyl)flavanone (GB-2)

    Guttif.   *Garcinia buchananii* (htwd)

4',5,7-Trihydroxy-3-(4',3,5,7-tetrahydroxy-8-flavonyl)flavanone (GB-1)

    Guttif.   *Garcinia buchananii* (htwd)

4',5,7-Trihydroxy-3-(4',5,7-trihydroxy-8-flavonyl)flavanone (GB-1a)

    Guttif.   *Garcinia buchananii* (htwd)

Xanthorrhone

    Xanthorrhoe.   *Xanthorrhoea preissii* (resin, of this sp. ?)

IV CHALCONES, α- and β-HYDROXY-CHALCONES, DIHYDRO-CHALCONES, 2-BENZYL-2-HYDROXY-COUMARAN-3-ONES, and ISOCHALCONES

GENERAL

The *chalcones* (sometimes '*chalkones*') and the *aurones* are often grouped as '*anthochlor pigments*'. We prefer to deal with them separately. In addition to the *chalcones* proper, we may include here α- and β-*hydroxy-chalcones*, *dihydro-chalcones*, *2-benzyl-2-hydroxy-coumaran-3-ones* and *isochalcones*.

Chalcone itself (fig. 115) does not, I think, occur free in Nature. It is a great pity that the numbering adopted for the *chalcones* differs from that used for the *flavones*. It is a pity, too, that because the A-ring can rotate the 2'- and 6'-positions are equivalent, as are the 3'- and 5'-positions.

Swain (in Goodwin, 1965) has given us a brief treatment of these compounds. Harborne (1966, 1967) has also dealt with them.

We are again faced with the problem of names. I have tried to follow a middle course as between the use of trivial and systematic names, probably pleasing no one in the process!

Harborne (1966) believes that *chalcones* are more 'primitive' than are the *aurones*, and uses their known distribution to support this view:

Chalcones occur in widely separated plant genera, being present in a fern (*Pityrogramma*), in a monocotyledon (*Xanthorrhoea*), in a primitive angiosperm genus such as *Paeonia* and in a highly advanced one such as *Coreopsis*. This distribution fits in with the biogenetic position of chalcones as primitive pigments. If a chalcone is the first C_{15} precursor to be formed in flavonoid synthesis as recent labelling experiments indicate, then this type of pigment would be expected to occur sporadically in high concentration in a wide range of plants ...the discovery of isosalipurposide [chalcononaringenin-2'-glucoside]...in four widely distant plant species, adds support to the hypothesis that chalcones are indeed C_{15} intermediates.

By contrast to the chalcones, aurones are found mainly in the Sympetalae (8 out of 12 genera) and particularly in one family, the Compositae, which is generally agreed to be very 'advanced'. If aurones are formed by a one-step enzymic oxidation from the corresponding chalcone, then the enzyme involved may be considered to have arisen by a 'gain' mutation at a fairly late stage in plant evolution. Aurones do appear to represent an 'advanced' type of flavonoid pigment in plants, but more investigation is needed to confirm this attractive phylogenetic hypothesis.

IV.1 Chalcones

List and Occurrence

Butein (2',4',3,4-Tetrahydroxy-chalcone; fig. 115) occurs chiefly as glycosides.

  Legum. Acacia mearnsii (bk), *Robinia pseudacacia* (htwd)

Butein-3,4'-diglucoside

  Legum. Butea frondosa (fl.)

Butein-4'-glucoside (Coreopsin)

  Comp. Baeria chrysostoma (fl.), *Bidens, Coreopsis* (5), *Cosmos sulphureus* (fl.), *Dahlia variabilis, Viguiera multiflora* (fl.)

Carthamin is the 6'-*glucoside* of 2',3',4',6',4-*pentahydroxy-chalcone.*

  Comp. Carthamus tinctorius

Carthamone (fig. 115) is a *quinone-glycoside* related to *carthamin.*

  Comp. Carthamus tinctorius

Chalcononaringenin (Isosalipurpol; fig. 115): see also *carthamone* and *xanthohumol.* This chalcone occurs in several combinations.

Chalcononaringenin-2',4'-dimethyl ether

  Piper. Piper methysticum (rt)

Chalcononaringenin-2'-glucoside (Isosalipurposide; Isosalipurpurin) is known, thanks to Harborne, to be rather widely distributed.

  Salic. Salix purpurea (bk)
  Caryophyll. Dianthus caryophyllus (yell. fl.)
  Paeoni. Paeonia trollioides (fl.)
  Acanth. Asystasia gangetica
  Gesneri. Aeschynanthus (3), *Cyrtandra pendula* (fl.)
  Comp. Helichrysum arenarium

Chalcononaringenin-4'-methyl ether

  Ros. Prunus (bk)

Chalcononaringenin-4-methyl ether-2'-glucoside (Neosakuranin)

  Ros. Prunus cerasoides

Chalcononaringenin-4',6',4-trimethyl ether

  Xanthorrhoe. Xanthorrhoea preissii (resin); but *not* in *X. resinosa* (resin)

2',4',6',3,4,5-Hexahydroxy-chalcone (fig. 115) occurs as glycoside(s).

2',4',6',3,4,5-Hexahydroxy-chalcone-2'-glucoside

  Comp. Helichrysum bracteatum

Isocarthamin (2',3',4',6',4-Pentahydroxy-chalcone-3'-glucoside) occurrence ?

Isoliquiritigenin (2',4',4-Trihydroxy-chalcone; fig. 113)

  Legum. Cicer arietinum (sdlg, free), *Glycine max* (sdlg, free ?)

Isoliquiritigenin-4-apiosylglucoside
  Legum.   Glycyrrhiza
Isoliquiritigenin-4'-diglucoside
  Legum.   Cicer arietinum (sdlg), *Ulex europaeus* (fl.)
  Comp.   Dahlia variabilis (yell. fl.)
Isoliquiritigenin-4',4-diglucoside
  Legum.   Ulex europaeus (fl.)
Isoliquiritigenin-4'-diglucoside-4-glucoside
  Legum.   Ulex europaeus (fl.)
Isoliquiritigenin-4-glucoside
  Legum.   Glycyrrhiza glabra (liquorice rt)
Isoliquiritigenin-4'-methyl ether
  Xanthorrhoe.   Xanthorrhoea australis (resin)
Iso-okanin is said to be a geometrical isomer of *okanin*. I find it listed,
  too, as 3',4',7,8-*tetrahydroxy-flavanone*.
  Legum.   Acacia salicina (spwd, as a *flavanone*), *Cylicodiscus*
Lanceoletin (Okanin-3'-methyl ether)
  Comp.   Coreopsis lanceolata (free ?)
Lanceoletin-4'-glucoside (Lanceolin)
  Comp.   Coreopsis lanceolata (fl.), *saxicola* (fl.)
Lonchocarpine (fig. 115) may be included here.
  Legum.   Lonchocarpus
Neoplathymenin (5'-Hydroxy-butein)
  Legum.   Plathymenia reticulata (htwd)
  Comp.   Coreopsis stillmanii (fl.) ?
Okanin (3'-Hydroxy-butein)
  Legum.   Cylicodiscus gabunensis (htwd)
  Comp.   Coreopsis?
Okanin-4'-glucoside (Marein)
  Comp.   Baeria chrysostoma (fl.); *Coreopsis gigantea* (fl.), *maritima*
    (fl.), *tinctoria* (fl.)
Olivin (fig. 115)
  Ole.   Olea europaea (lvs)
Pedicin (fig. 115) is a *quinol.*
  Gesneri.   Didymocarpus pedicellata (red deposit on lvs)
Pedicin-2',5'-dimethyl ether
  Gesneri.   Didymocarpus pedicellata (on lvs)
Pedicinin (fig. 115) is a *quinone.*
  Gesneri.   Didymocarpus pedicellata (on lvs)
Pedicinin-3'-methyl ether
  Gesneri.   Didymocarpus pedicellata (on lvs)
2',4',6',3,4-Pentahydroxy-chalcone-6'-glucoside
  Comp.   Helichrysum bracteatum

Robtein (2',4',3,4,5-Pentahydroxy-chalcone)
  Legum.   Acacia mearnsii (bk), *Robinia pseudacacia* (htwd)
Rottlerin (Mallotoxin; fig. 115) is a complicated derivative of *chalcone*.
  Euphorbi.   Mallotus philippinensis (*Rottlera tinctoria*) (frt-hairs)
Stillopsidin (2',4',5',3,4-Pentahydroxy-chalcone)
  Comp.   Coreopsis stillmanii (free ?)
Stillopsidin- ?-glucoside (Stillopsin)
  Comp.   Coreopsis stillmanii
Xanthohumol (fig. 116) is, according to Harborne, a derivative of
chalcononaringenin as shown. I have another formula for it.
  Mor.   Humulus lupulus

IV.2   α- and β-hydroxy-chalcones

GENERAL

α-*Hydroxy-chalcones* (fig. 116) are said not to occur in Nature since
they cyclize to 2-*benzyl-2-hydroxy-coumaran-3-ones* (fig. 116 and p. 552)
such as *alphitonin* and *maesopsin*.
  β-Hydroxy-chalcones (fig. 116) seem to be very rare.

List and Occurrence

Pongamol (Lanceolatin-C; fig. 116) is essentially a β-*hydroxy-chalcone*
  (or more accurately a *dihydro-chalcone*) in which methylation blocks
  cyclization.
  Legum.   Pongamia glabra, Tephrosia lanceolata

IV.3   Dihydroxy-chalcones

GENERAL

A few flavonoids occurring in higher plants are known to be derivatives
of *dihydrochalcone* (fig. 116). They have been found, too, in ferns.
  A recent review of the chemistry and occurrence of these substances
has been provided by Williams (in Swain, 1966).

List and Occurrence

Asebogenin (Asebogenol; Asebotol; fig. 116) is 2',6',4-*trihydroxy-*
  4'-*methoxy-dihydrochalcone*.

Asebogenin-6'-glucoside (Asebotin; Asebotoside)

> *Eric. Kalmia* (Williams (1966) says that *K. polifolia* has *no dihydrochalcones, angustifolia* has *asebotin,* and *latifolia* has 'in addition' [to *asebotin*?] another *dihydrochalcone*), *Pieris* (Williams says that *P. floribunda* has *no dihydrochalcones,* that *japonica* usually has *phloridzin,* and that *taiwanensis* usually has *asebotin*)

2',6'-Dihydroxy-4'-methoxy-dihydrochalcone

> *Salic. Populus balsamifera* (ess. oil)

Glycyphyllin (Phloretin-2'(6')-α-L-rhamnoside)

> *Lili. Smilax glycyphylla.* Williams has a most interesting discussion. Apparently *glycyphyllin* occurs in specimens of this Australian plant collected in New South Wales, but specimens from Queensland have *mangiferin* (a *xanthone*) instead!

3-Hydroxy-phloretin (2',4',6',3,4-Pentahydroxy-dihydro-chalcone)
3-Hydroxy-phloretin-6'-glucoside

> *Ros. Malus* spp. from E. Asia

Phloretin (2',4',6',4-Tetrahydroxy-dihydrochalcone; fig. 116)
Phloretin- ?-arabinoglucoside

> *Ros. Malus* (bk)

Phloretin-4'-glucoside (Trilobatin)

> *Ros. Malus trilobatus* (lvs) (Williams says this is the only sp. with *trilobatin.* It lacks *phloridzin*)

Phloretin-6'-glucoside (Phloridzin)

> *Ros. Malus* only? (Williams says the records of its occurrence in pear, plum and cherry are in error. In *Malus* it occurs in spp. from W. Asia)

Pongamol (Lanceolatin-C; fig. 116): should be here?

> *Legum. Pongamia glabra* (sd-oil), *Tephrosia lanceolata* (rtbk)

Sieboldin (fig. 116)

> *Ros. Malus* spp. (in most of Rehder's series *Sieboldianae,* says Williams)

IV.4   2-Benzyl-2-hydroxy-coumaran-3-ones

GENERAL

We have already seen that α-*hydroxy-chalcones* cyclize to 2-*benzyl-2-hydroxy-coumaran-3-ones* (fig. 116). Several of these compounds are known to occur in higher plants and they may be treated for convenience here.

They are closely related to the *aurones* and have been called '*hydrated aurones*'.

List and Occurrence

Alphitonin (fig. 116)

> *Rhamn.* *Alphitonia excelsa* (htwd)

2-Benzyl-3',4',6',2-tetrahydroxy-coumaran-3-one

> *Anacardi.* *Schinopsis balansae, lorentzii* (Quebracho tannin extract)

2-Benzyl-3',2,6-trihydroxy-4'-methoxy-coumaran-3-one

> *Anacardi.* *Schinopsis balansae, lorentzii* (Quebracho tannin extract)

Maesopsin is similar to *alphitonin*, but has one -OH group less.

> *Rhamn.* *Maesopsis eminii* (wd)

IV.5 Isochalcones

GENERAL

Just as one may have *flavones* (p. 568) and *isoflavones* (p. 612), so one may expect to meet with *chalcones* (p. 549) and *isochalcones*. Actually I know of but one substance, *angolensin*, which is essentially an *isochalcone*, but there may well be others. It is worth noting that two *isoflavones*, *muningin* and *prunetin*, occur with *angolensin*.

List and Occurrence

Angolensin (fig. 117) is essentially an *isochalcone*.

> *Legum.* *Pterocarpus angolensis* (htwd)

V FLAVAN-3,4-DIOLS AND LEUCOANTHOCYANINS

GENERAL

The 'parent' substance *flavan-3,4-diol* itself (fig. 118) has not, I think, been found in Nature, but some derivatives are known and these may be discussed briefly here.

Among the most interesting of these substances are the so-called *leucoanthocyanins* which have been much studied of late. It was thought until quite recently that *leucoanthocyanins* are glycosides which on hydrolysis yield sugars and *leucoanthocyanidins* which in turn are converted to *anthocyanidins*. It has become increasingly clear, however, that they are really 'condensed tannins' which yield under appropriate conditions the common *anthocyanidins—pelargonidin, cyanidin*, and

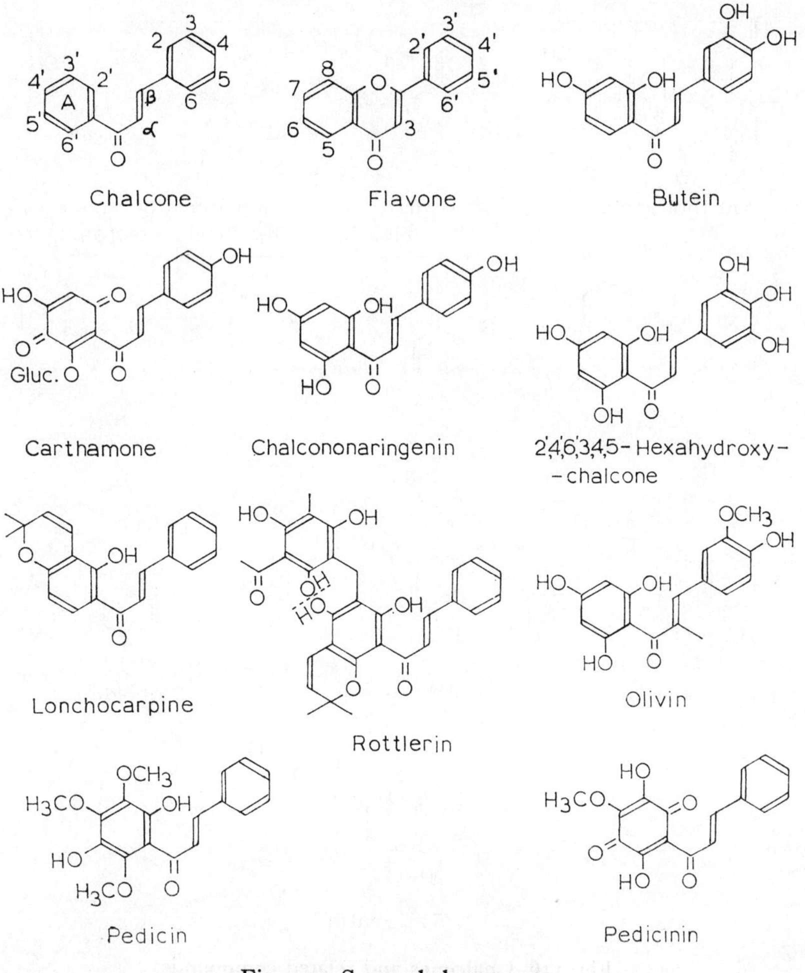

Fig. 115. Some chalcones, etc.

delphinidin (which *do* also occur naturally as glycosides—*anthocyanins*); and *fisetinidin, robinetinidin, 3,7,4'-trihydroxy-flavylium,* and *3,7,8,3',4'-pentahydroxy-flavylium* (which do *not* seem to occur also as glycosides). Because they are complex and difficult to work with we know much less about the chemistry of the *leucoanthocyanins* than we do about the simpler flavonoids.

It seems, however, that we have in these compounds dimers of a *flavan-3,4-diol* and a *flavan-3-ol* such as *leucocyanidin*; and polymers, the true 'condensed tannins'. These have been termed *flavolans*. Swain (1965) says that: 'the distinctive dark colour by which most

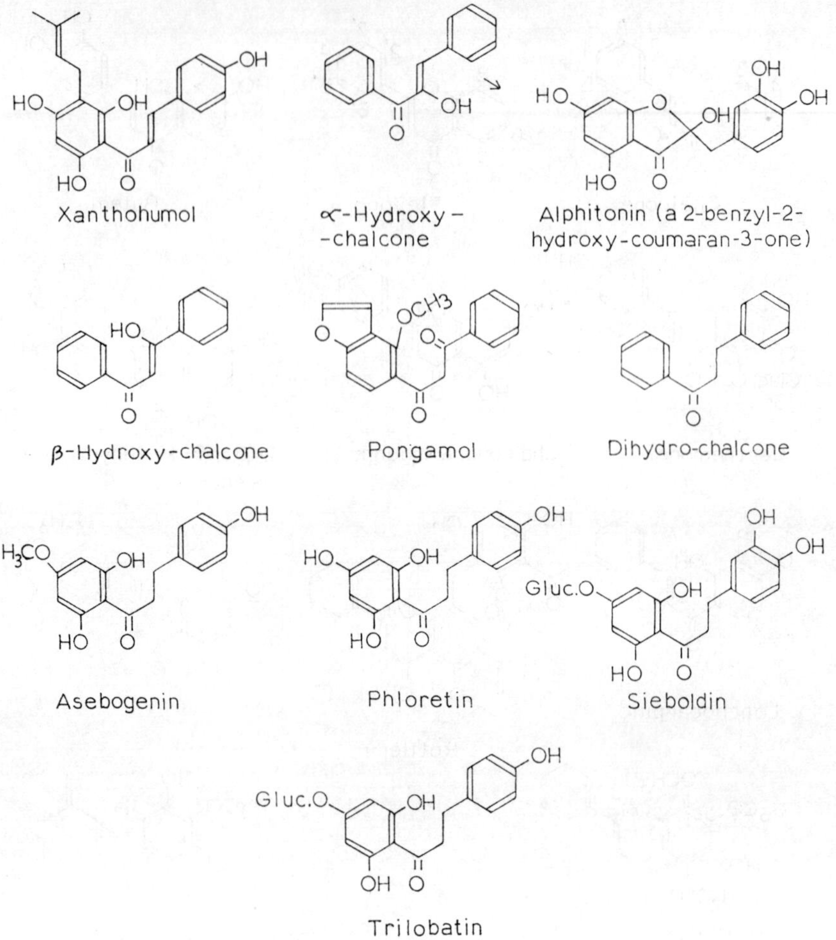

Xanthohumol   α-Hydroxy-chalcone   Alphitonin (a 2-benzyl-2-hydroxy-coumaran-3-one)

β-Hydroxy-chalcone   Pongamol   Dihydro-chalcone

Asebogenin   Phloretin   Sieboldin

Trilobatin

Fig. 116. Chalcones and related compounds.

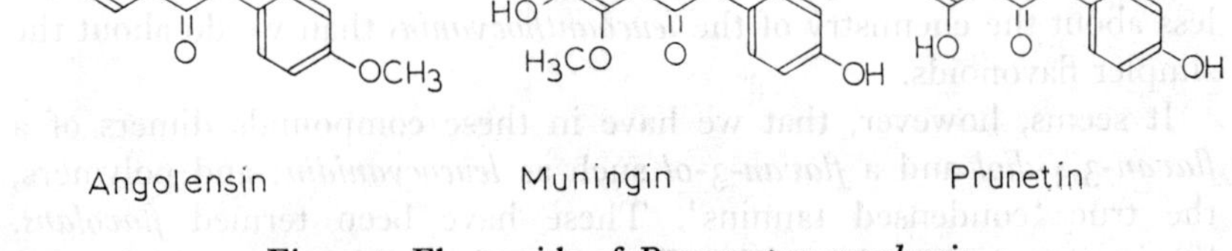

Angolensin   Muningin   Prunetin

Fig. 117. Flavonoids of *Pterocarpus angolensis*.

heartwoods are recognized is almost always due to the presence of flavolans'. They, with their oxidation products too, may be responsible in part at least for the browning of autumn leaves.

In view of this recent work one wonders how many of the substances listed below are correctly described.

Tissues containing *leucoanthocyanins*, when heated with 2N hydrochloric acid, give rise to *anthocyanins*. These, unlike the parent substances, are red in acid solution and may be extracted with amyl alcohol. This is almost certainly the basis of the '*leucoanthocyanin test*' —'*L.A. (test A)*'—which I have employed extensively and which is discussed elsewhere (p. 70).

List and Occurrence

(+)-Guibourtacacidin (4',7-Dihydroxy-flavan-3,4-diol; fig. 118)
    Legum. Guibourtia coleosperma (htwd)
Isomelacacidin is an isomer of *melacacidin*.
    Legum. Acacia melanoxylon
Isoteracacidin is an isomer of *teracacidin*.
    Legum. Acacia auriculiformis (htwd, (+)- and (−)-), *intertexta* (htwd)
Leucocyanidin (fig. 118) 'is by far the commonest of all leucoanthocyanidins...' (Harborne, 1967). It seems to be a dimer. See under individual families for distribution.
Leucodelphinidin (3',4',5',5,7-Pentahydroxy-flavan-3,4-diol; fig. 118) is of common occurrence, particularly in woody plants.
Leucofisetinidin (Gleditsin?; Mollisacacidin?; 3',4',7-Tri-hydroxy-flavan-3,4-diol)
    Legum. Acacia mearnsii (*mollisima*?); *Colophospermum mopane* (htwd), *Gleditsia japonica*?; *Guibourtia demensii* (htwd), *tessmannii* (htwd)
    Anacardi. Schinopsis
Leucoluteolinidin may be a *flavan-4-ol* (Bate-Smith and Swain, 1967). It has been found (mostly after hydrolysis) only in *Andropogoneae* of the *Gramineae*?
    Gram. Andropogon gerardii (lvs); *Bothriochloa* sp.; *Hyparrhenia* (*Andropogon*) *filipendula* (lvs), *hirta* (lvs); *Imperata cylindrica* (lvs); *Sorghum vulgare* (free); *Themeda triandra* (lvs)
Leuco-paeonidin (fig. 118) is of restricted distribution. Bate-Smith (1954) recorded it only from *Rosaceae* and *Leguminosae*.
Leucopelargonidin (4',5,7-Trihydroxy-flavan-3,4-diol) has been recorded from ferns and from
    Legum. Phaseolus vulgaris

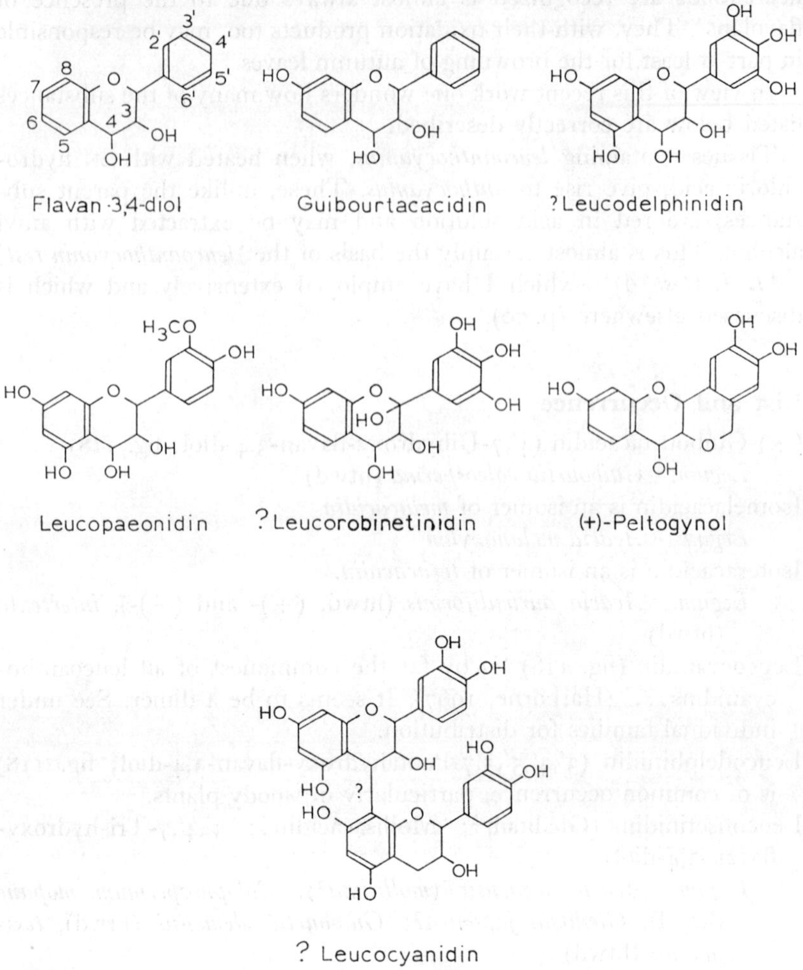

Flavan-3,4-diol   Guibourtacacidin   ?Leucodelphinidin

Leucopaeonidin   ?Leucorobinetinidin   (+)-Peltogynol

? Leucocyanidin

Fig. 118. Some flavan-3,4-diols, etc.

Connar.   *Connarus monocarpus* (rt)
Malpighi.   *Malpighia*
Rhizophor.   *Cassipourea*
Myrt.   *Eucalyptus calophylla* (gum)
Gram.   *Zea mays* (endosperm)
Mus.   *Musa acuminata* (sd), *balbisiana* (sd)—other parts have
   leucocyanidin and *leucodelphinidin*
Leucorobinetinidin (fig. 118)
   Legum.   *Acacia*

Melacacidin (3',4',7,8-Tetrahydroxy-flavan-3,4-diol)
  Legum. *Acacia excelsa, harpophylla, melanoxylon* (htwd)
(+)-Mopanol
  Legum. *Colophospermum mopane* (htwd)
(+)-Mopanol-B differs only spatially from *mopanol.*
  Legum. *Colophospermum mopane* (htwd)
(+)-Peltogynol (fig. 118)
  Legum. *Colophospermum mopane* (htwd), *Peltogyne porphyrocardia*
    (htwd)
(+)-Peltogynol-B differs only spatially from *peltogynol.*
  Legum. *Colophospermum mopane* (htwd)
(−)-Teracacidin
  Legum. *Acacia intertexta* (htwd)

VI FLAVAN-3-OLS AND CATECHINS

GENERAL

Flavan-3-*ol* itself (fig. 119) has not, I think, been reported from plants, but derivatives, which include the *catechins*, are important constituents of many species. Swain (1965) says: 'most of the brown pigments produced from flavonoids appear to be formed by the oxidation of catechins (flavan-3-ols...) and leucoanthocyanins (flavan-3,4-diols) and their oligomers and polymers (flavolans). Indeed these polymeric forms, which are in fact condensed tannins, are themselves coloured.'

List and Occurrence

Afzelechin (4',5,7-Trihydroxy-flavan-3-ol; fig. 119)
  Legum. *Afzelia*
  Myrt. *Eucalyptus calophylla* (kino-(−))
Arachidoside is said to be a glucoside of 4',5,7-*trihydroxy*-3'-*methoxy-flavan*-3-*ol.*
  Legum. *Arachis hypogaea* (sd)
Catechin (3',4',5,7-Tetrahydroxy-flavan-3-ol; fig. 119)
d-Catechin (*d*-Gambircatechin) is very widely distributed. I have records from
  Fag. *Castanea sativa* (young frt), *Quercus* (bk)
  Loranth. *Phrygilanthus flagellaris* (on *Acacia*), *Psittacanthus cuneifolius* (lvs)?
  Polygon. *Polygonum, Rheum*
  Ros. *Prunus yedoensis* (wd)
  Legum. *Acacia* (bk)

The.   *Camellia* (lvs)
Sapind.   *Paullinia cupana* (sd)
Krameri.   *Krameria argentea* (rts)
Sterculi.   *Cola* (frt or sd?)
Rubi.   *Uncaria acida, gambir*
Palmae.   *Areca catechu*

dl-Catechin (*dl*-Gambircatechin) occurs in small amount in all (?) the plants with *d-catechin.*

Legum.   *Acacia catechu*
Sapind.   *Paullinia cupana?*

l-Catechin (*l*-Gambircatechin)

Legum.   *Acacia catechu*

Epiafzelechin: how does this differ from *afzelechin?*

Legum.   *Afzelia* sp. (htwd, (−))

Epicatechin is a diastereomer of *catechin.*

d-Epicatechin (*d*-Acacatechin; Catechin-C)

Myrt.   *Angophora intermedia*; *Eucalyptus leucoxylon* (kino), *viminalis* (kino)
Rubi.   *Uncaria gambir*

dl-Epicatechin (*dl*-Acacatechin)

Myristic.   *Myristica malabarica* (kino)
Legum.   *Acacia catechu, Pterocarpus marsupium* (kino)
Myrt.   *Angophora intermedia*; *Eucalyptus* (3, kinos)

l-Epicatechin (*l*-Acacatechin, Kakaol; Teecatechin-I)

Myristic.   *Myristica malabarica* (kino)
Ros.   *Prunus spinulosa* (wd), *ssiori* (wd)
Legum.   *Acacia catechu* (wd), *Pterocarpus marsupium* (kino)
The.   *Camellia* (green tea)
Sterculi.   *Cola, Theobroma* (sd)
Vit.   *Vitis vinifera* (lvs, frt)
Myrt.   *Eucalyptus corymbosa* (kino)

l-Epicatechin-3-gallate (Tea-tannin)

The.   *Camellia* (green tea)

l-Epicatechin-3-glucoside

Legum.   *Gleditsia triacanthos* (sds)

(+)-Epifisetinidol

Legum.   *Colophospermum mopane* (htwd)

(−)-Epigallocatechin (3′,4′,5′,5,7-OH)

The.   *Camellia* sp. (lvs)
Legum.   *Acacia* sp. (bk)

Fisetinidol (3′,4′,7-Trihydroxy-flavan-3-ol)

Legum.   *Acacia dealbata* (−), *mearnsii* (*mollissima*) (−); *Afzelia xylocarpa* (+); *Colophospermum mopane* (htwd, (−))

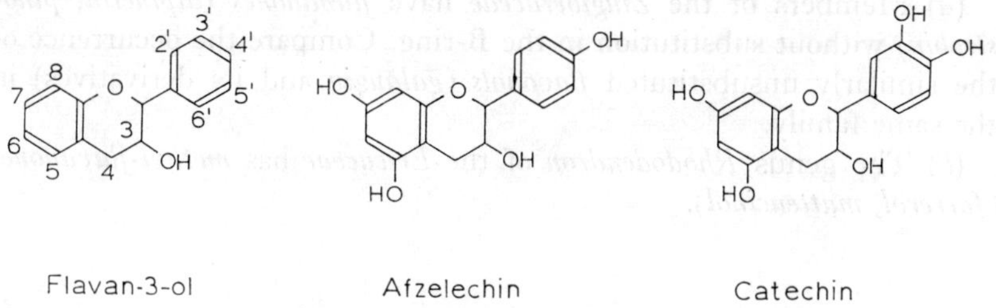

Flavan-3-ol   Afzelechin   Catechin

Fig. 119. Flavan-3-ols.

d-Gallocatechin (Casuarin; 3′,4′,5′,5,7-Pentahydroxy-flavan-3-ol)
  Fag. *Castanea* (bk), *Quercus* (bk)
  Legum. *Acacia* (bk)
  The. *Camellia* (lvs)
l-Gallocatechin (Delphinidol; *l*-Epigallocatechin; Tea-catechin-II)
  The. *Camellia* (green tea)
  Vit. *Vitis vinifera* (esp. sd)
l-Gallocatechin-3-gallate
  The. *Camellia* (green tea)
Quebrachocatechin (3′,4′,7-Trihydroxy-flavan-3-ol) occurs in *que-brachotannin.*
(−)-Robinetinidol (3′,4′,5′,7-OH)
  Legum. *Acacia* (bk), *Robinia pseudacacia* (htwd)
3′,5′,5,7-Tetrahydroxy-4′-methoxy-flavan-3-ol (Ouratea-catechin)
  Ochn. *Ouratea* sp. (rt)

VII FLAVANONES (DIHYDRO-FLAVONES)

GENERAL

Just as we have separated the *flavones* from the *flavonols*, so we may distinguish the *dihydro-flavones* or *flavanones* from the *dihydro-flavonols* or *flavanonols*.

The 'parent' substance, *flavanone* (fig. 120), has not I think been found in Nature, but many derivatives are known and these will be discussed briefly here.

It is thought that the *flavanones* arise from *chalcones* (qq.v.), and an extract from lemon-peel is said to catalyse the reaction. *Isoflavones* (qq.v.) can be prepared *in vitro* from *flavanones*.

The distribution of the *flavanones* has some points of interest. We may note:

(a) Members of the *Zingiberaceae* have *flavanones* (*alpinetin, pinostrobin*) without substitution in the B-ring. Compare the occurrence of the similarly unsubstituted *flavonols* (*galangin* and its derivatives) in the same family.

(b) The genus *Rhododendron* of the *Ericaceae* has *methyl-flavanones* (*farrerol, matteucinol*).

List and Occurrence

Alpinetin (7-Hydroxy-5-methoxy-flavanone; fig. 120) lacks substitution in the B-ring.
> *Zingiber. Alpinia chinensis* (sd), *Kaempferia pandurata* (rhiz.)

Aspalathin is a *C-glycosyl* derivative of *eriodictyol* (fig. 120) or it may be a *dihydro-chalcone*.
> *Legum. Aspalathus acuminata* (lvs)

Butin (3',4',7-Trihydroxy-flavanone)
> *Legum. Butea frondosa* (fl.)
> *Comp. Coreopsis drummondii, tinctoria; Cosmos sulphureus; Dahlia* (free and as glycosides in all?)

Butin-3',7-diglucoside (Butrin)
> *Legum. Butea frondosa* (fl.)
> *Comp.* ? see under *butin*

Citronetin (5,7-Dihydroxy-3'-methoxy-flavanone)
Citronetin-7-rhamnoglucoside (Citronin)
> *Rut. Citrus?*

Dihydro-wogonin (5,7-Dihydroxy-8-methoxy-flavanone); strangely enough *wogonin* itself occurs in *Scutellaria*—a labiate.
> *Ros. Prunus*

Eriodictyol (3',4',5,7-Tetrahydroxy-flavanone; fig. 120)
> *Ros. Prunus* (3), free and as glycoside
> *Legum. Lespedeza cyrtobotrya* (lvs)
> *Hydrophyll. Eriodictyon glutinosum* (lvs), and 2 other spp.
> *Comp. Dahlia variabilis, Helichrysum viscosum* var. *bracteatum* (plt, free)

Eriodictyol-glucoside(s)
> *Ros. Prunus*

Eriodictyol-7-rhamnoside (Eriodictin)
> *Rut. Citrus*

Farrerol (4',5,7-Trihydroxy-6,8-dimethyl-flavanone; fig. 120)
> *Eric. Rhododendron farrerae* (lvs)

Hesperetin (Hesperitin; 3',5,7-Trihydroxy-4'-methoxy-flavanone): does not occur free? Some glycosides are known.

Hesperetin- ?-glucoside (Persicoside)
    Ros. Prunus persica
Hesperetin-7β-neohesperidoside (Neohesperidin)
    Rut. Citrus aurantium, bigaradia (frt)
Hesperetin-7-rutinoside (Citrantin?; Hesperidin) has been said to be
    very widely distributed, but Karrer (1958) says that many of the
    records for 'hesperidin' are for hesperidin-like substances.
    Rut. Citrus spp.
    Scrophulari. Verbascum phlomoides (fl.)
Homoeriodictyol (Eriodictyonone; 4',5,7-Trihydroxy-3'-methoxy-flavanone)
    Hydrophyll. Eriodictyon glutinosum (lvs), and 2 other spp.
    Comp. Helichrysum viscosum var. *bracteatum* (plt, free)
Iso-pedicin (6-Hydroxy-5,7,8-trimethoxy-flavanone)
    Gesneri. Didymocarpus pedicellata
Iso-sakuranetin (Citrifoliol; Kikokunetin; 5,7-Dihydroxy-4'-methoxy-flavanone)
    Rut. several ?, as glycosides?
Iso-sakuranetin-7-glucoside (iso-sakuranin)
    Ros. Prunus
Iso-sakuranetin-7-rhamnoglucoside (Citrifolioside; Poncirin)
    Rut. Citrus, Poncirus trifoliatus
Iso-sakuranetin-7-rutinoside (Didymin)
    Lab. Monarda didyma (lvs)
Liquiritigenin (4',7-Dihydroxy-flavanone; fig. 120) is the aglycone of
    several *flavanone-glycosides*.
    Legum. Baptisia lecontei (lvs, free?), *Dalbergia latifolia* (free?)
Liquiritigenin-7-diglucoside
    Comp. Dahlia variabilis (fl.)
Liquiritigenin-4'-glucoside (Liquiritin)
    Legum. Glycyrrhiza
Liquiritigenin-7-glucoside
    Comp. Dahlia variabilis (fl.)
Matteucinol (Farrerol-4'-methyl ether) occurs, as the name implies,
    in *Matteucia* (a fern). It occurs also in
    Eric. Rhododendron simsii (lvs)
8 ?-Methoxy-butin
    Comp. Coreopsis
Naringenin (Naringetol; Salipurpol; fig. 120) is, if the following
    records are correct (some may be of glycosides, of which several are
    known), of wide distribution.
    Fag. Nothofagus dombeyi (htwd)
    Ros. Prunus

    Legum.   *Acacia, Ferreirea*
    Rut.   *Citrus*
    Myrt.   *Eucalyptus maculata*
    Comp.   *Dahlia, Helichrysum viscosum* var. *bracteatum* (plt, free)
Naringenin-6-*C*-glucoside (Hemiphloin)
    Myrt.   *Eucalyptus*
Naringenin-5-glucoside (Floribundoside; Helichrysin-B; Salipurpo-
    side?): Hänsel and Heise (1959) say that 'salipurposide' is an equi-
    molecular mixture of the 5-glucosides of the 2 diastereomers of
    naringenin.
    Salic.   *Salix purpurea*
    Legum.   *Acacia floribunda* (fl.)
    Comp.   *Helichrysum*
Naringenin-7-glucoside (Prunin)
    Ros.   *Prunus*
    Scrophulari.   *Antirrhinum majus* (yellow fl.)
Naringenin-7-rhamnoglucoside (Aurantiin; Isohesperidin; Naringin;
    Naringoside)
    Fag.   *Nothofagus dombeyi* (htwd)
    Ros.   *Prunus*
    Legum.   *Acacia*
    Rut.   *Citrus, Poncirus*
Pinocembrin (2,3-Dihydro-chrysin; 5,7-Dihydroxy-flavanone) occurs,
    as the name implies, in *Pinus.*
    Ros.   *Prunus ssiori* (wd)
    Xanthorrhoe.   *Xanthorrhoea preissii* (resin, of this sp.?)
Pinocembrin-?-rhamnoglucoside (Sarontoside)
    Legum.   *Cytisus (Sarothamnus?) commutatus*
Pinostrobin (5-Hydroxy-7-methoxy-flavanone) occurs in *Pinus* and
    Ros.   *Prunus avium* (htwd)
    Zingiber.   *Kaempferia pandurata* (rhiz.)
Plathymenin (fig. 120)
    Legum.   *Plathymenia reticulata* (with the corresponding *chalcone—*
    neoplathymenin)
Sakuranetin (4',5-Dihydroxy-7-methoxy-flavanone; fig. 120) occurs
    free (?) in
    Ros.   *Prunus avium* (htwd), *puddum* (bk)
Sakuranetin-5-glucoside (Sakuranin)
    Ros.   *Prunus* (at least 6 spp.)
Selinone (4'-*O*(3,3-Dimethylallyl) naringenin)
    Umbell.   *Selinum vaginatum* (rt)
3',4',7,8-Tetramethoxy-flavanone
    Comp.   *Coreopsis grandiflora* (fl.)

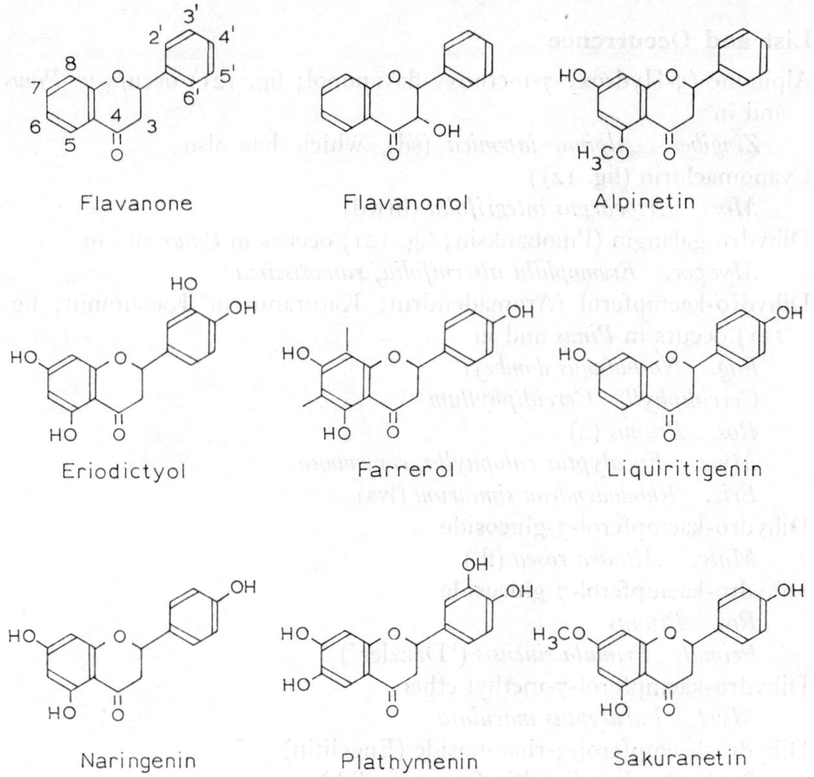

Fig. 120. Some flavanones (dihydro-flavones).

VIII FLAVANONOLS (DIHYDRO-FLAVONOLS)

GENERAL

The *flavanonols* (or *dihydro-flavonols*) are by no means numerous but they appear to be very widely distributed, occurring in gymnosperms, in several families of dicotyledons, and in at least one family (*Zingiber-aceae*) of the monocotyledons.

We may note:

(a) *Zingiberaceae* show, in at least one member of the family, *Alpinia japonica*, what may well prove to be a family character, the possession of flavonoids unsubstituted in the B-ring (see also *flavanones*).

(b) *Leguminosae* seem to be relatively rich in *flavanonols*.

(c) *Rosaceae*, which are considered to be closely related to the *Legu-minosae*, have at least one genus, *Prunus*, rich in *flavanonols*.

List and Occurrence

Alpinone (5-Hydroxy-7-methoxy-flavanonol; fig. 121) occurs in *Pinus* and in
    Zingiber. Alpinia japonica (sd), which has also
Cyanomaclurin (fig. 121)
    Mor. Artocarpus integrifolia (htwd)
Dihydro-galangin (Pinobanksin; fig. 121) occurs in *Pinus* and in
    Myopor. Eremophila alternifolia, ramosissima
Dihydro-kaempferol (Aromadendrin; Katuranin or Katsuranin; fig. 121) occurs in *Pinus* and in
    Fag. Nothofagus dombeyi
    Cercidiphyll. Cercidiphyllum
    Ros. Prunus (2)
    Myrt. Eucalyptus calophylla, corymbosa
    Eric. Rhododendron simiarum (lvs)
Dihydro-kaempferol-3-glucoside
    Malv. Althaea rosea (fl.)
Dihydro-kaempferol-7-glucoside
    Ros. Prunus
    Primul. Primula sinensis ('Dazzler')
Dihydro-kaempferol-7-methyl ether
    Myrt. Eucalyptus maculata
Dihydro-kaempferol-3-rhamnoside (Engelitin)
    Jugland. Engelhardtia formosana (bk)
    Myrt. Eucalyptus sideroxylon (lvs)
Dihydro-kaempferol-7-rhamnoside
    Santal. Exocarpos cupressiformis (lvs)
Dihydro-myricetin (Ampelopsin; fig. 121)
    Legum. Erythrophleum africanum (bk)
    Vit. Ampelopsis meliaefolia (lvs)
Dihydro-quercetin (Distylin; Taxifolin; fig. 121) occurs free and as several glycosides in conifers and in
    Hamamelid. Distylium racemosum
    Ros. Prunus campanulata (wd), *ssiori* (wd)
    Anacardi. Melanorrhoea
    Myrt. Eucalyptus
Dihydro-quercetin-4'-glucoside
    Solan. Petunia hybrida
Dihydro-quercetin-glycoside(s)
    Ros. Prunus
Dihydro-quercetin-3-glycoside(s)
    Eucryphi. Eucryphia milliganii (lvs)

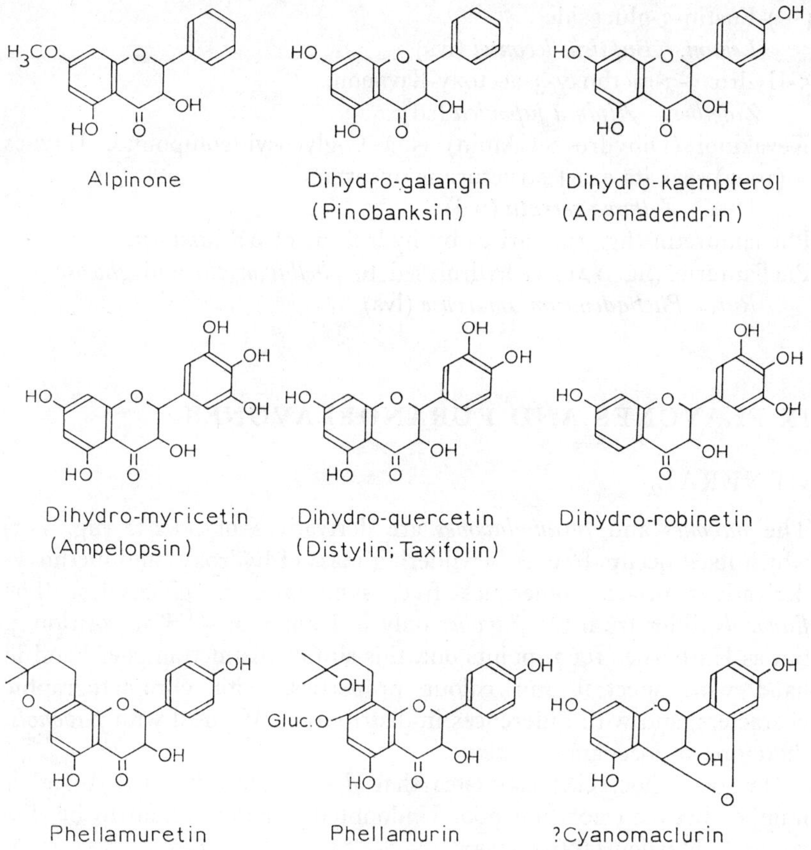

Fig. 121. Some flavanonols (dihydro-flavonols).

Dihydro-quercetin-3-rhamnoside (Astilbin)
    Laur.   *Litsea glauca* (lvs)
    Saxifrag.   *Astilbe odontophylla* (rhiz.), *thunbergii* (rhiz.)
Dihydro-robinetin (fig. 121)
    Legum.   *Robinia pseudacacia* (wd)
(+)-4',7-Dihydroxy-flavanonol
    Legum.   *Baptisia lecontei* (lvs)
(+)-4',7-Dihydroxy-flavanonol-3-glucoside (Lecontin)
    Legum.   *Baptisia lecontei* (lvs)
Fustins (Dihydro-fisetins) occur in (+) and (−) forms. It is not always
    clear from the records which form is present.
    Legum.   *Acacia* (+), *Baptisia lecontei* (lvs, +), *Gleditsia tri-
    acanthos* (htwd)
    Anacardi.   *Rhus* (−), *Schinopsis*

(+)-Fustin-3-glucoside
  Legum. Baptisia lecontei (lvs)
5-Hydroxy-7-methoxy-3-acetoxy-flavanone
  Zingiber. Alpinia japonica (sd)
Keyakinol (Dihydro-keyakinin) is a C-glycosyl compound. Haynes (1963) says its exact structure is uncertain.
  Ulm. Zelkova serrata (wd)
Phellamuretin (fig. 121) arises by hydrolysis of *phellamurin.*
Phellamurin (fig. 121) is hydrolysed to *phellamuretin* and *glucose.*
  Rut. Phelladendron amurense (lvs)

IX FLAVONES AND FURANOFLAVONES

GENERAL

The *flavones* and *furanoflavones* are derivatives of *flavone* (fig. 115) which itself occurs free. A bewildering mass of hydroxy- and methoxy-derivatives occur, sometimes free, sometimes as glycosides. The *flavonols* differ from the *flavones* only in having an -OH at position 3, but as Harborne (1967) points out, this simple distinction goes hand in hand with spectral and colour properties, with chromatographic characters, and with differences in distribution. We deal with *flavonols*, therefore, in a separate section.

Harborne (loc. cit.) estimates that *flavones* and *flavonols* together number between 200 and 300. Undoubtedly many remain to be discovered. Fowden (1965) says:

> Among the floral pigments, structures based on the flavone nucleus are now known that contain from 0 to 8 hydroxyl groups (see for example, flavone and digicitrin), all intermediate hydroxyl levels being represented. Who can then doubt that probably hundreds of flavones still remain to be characterized, for the range of structural variation is nearly infinite when one considers the possible ways in which intermediate numbers of hydroxyls may be attached to the basic carbon skeleton, and the fact that varying numbers of these groups may be either methylated or attached to sugar residues.

The *flavones* and *flavonols* contribute much less to colour in plants than do the *anthocyanins*, but many yellows in nature are due to them and they do modify colour when they occur with the *anthocyanins*.

Harborne points out the close correspondence between *flavones* and *anthocyanins* (or more strictly the *3-deoxy-anthocyanins*). The same types of glucosides occur, often together. Some of the *flavone glycosides,* however, are C-glycosyl compounds, which are rare or unknown among other flavonoids.

Here, more than in many groups, one is faced with a dilemma. Should one use trivial names, which are short and often in common use, or the more systematic names? I have, rather reluctantly, decided to do the former in many cases, including the systematic names as synonyms.

We shall discuss the chemosystematics of flavones in several places when considering particular groups of plants. A few notes are in place here.

(*a*) *Flavone* itself, and one or more simple hydroxy-derivatives occur as farina or meal on the surface of *Primula* and a few closely related members of the *Primulaceae*.

(*b*) *Methyl-flavones* are quite uncommon, but we have records of three —*eucalyptin*, *6-methyl-5-hydroxy-4',7-dimethoxy-flavone*, and *sideroxylin*—all from *Eucalyptus* spp.

(*c*) *Furanoflavones* occur only (?) in two genera of the *Leguminosae*.

(*d*) *Flavone-C-glycosides* are much commoner, and more widely spread, than we had supposed.

(*e*) Many of the *flavones* recorded in the following pages are known only from a single occurrence, others from but a few plants, and only a handful from many species. Since detailed investigations yield new flavones and new distributions in almost every case, we may expect that facts of chemosystematic significance will accumulate rapidly during the next few years.

List and Occurrence

Acacetin (5,7-Dihydroxy-4'-methoxy-flavone; Buddleoflavonol—but it is *not* a flavonol; Linarigenin; fig. 122) occurs (free?) in
    Legum.   *Robinia pseudacacia*
    Umbell.   *Ammi visnaga*
    Irid.   *Crocus laevigatus*
Acacetin-7-glucoside (Tilianin)
    Tili.   *Tilia japonica* (lvs)
Acacetin-8-C-glucoside (Cytisoside; 4'-O-Methyl-vitexin)
    Legum.   *Cytisus laburnum* (fl.)
Acacetin-7-glucosylrhamnosylxyloside
    Legum.   *Robinia pseudacacia* (lvs)
Acacetin-7-rutinoside (Acaciin; Buddleoflavonoloside; Linarin)
    Legum.   *Robinia*
    Rut.   *Fortunella* (fls of 3 spp.)
    Scrophulari.   *Linaria vulgaris* (fl.)

Buddlej. *Buddleja variabilis* (fl.)
Comp. *Chrysanthemum morifolium, Cirsium purpureum*
Acerosin (3′,5,7-Trihydroxy-4′,6′,8-trimethoxy-flavone)
Comp. *Iva acerosa*
Acrammerin (3′,4′,5′,5,7-Pentahydroxy-8-methoxy-flavone)
Legum. *Gleditsia triacanthos*
Apigenin (? Scutellarol; 4′,5,7-Trihydroxy-flavone; fig. 122) is, with
its many glucosides, of very wide distribution. It is the basis of all
(?) the *biflavonyls*. Are the following records all of *apigenin* in the free
state ?
  Resed. *Reseda luteola* (trace)
  Legum. *Baptisia lecontei* (lvs)
  Verben. *Verbena hybrida* (fl.)
  Solan. *Nicotiana* spp., *Solanum* spp.
  Gesneri. *Achimenes, Columnea, Kohleria, Rechsteineria, Smithi-
    antha, Streptocarpus, Trichantha*
  Comp. *Anthemis* (as glycoside), *Dahlia*
Apigenin-7-apiosylglucoside (Apiin)
  Legum. *Vicia hirsuta* (lvs)
  Umbell. *Apium graveolens* (sd), *Cuminum cyminum* (sd), *Petro-
    selinum crispum* (lvs, sd)
  Comp. *Dahlia?*
Apigenin-6-*C*-arabinosylglucoside
  Gram. *Avena sativa* (lvs)
Apigenin-6,8-*C*-diglycoside
  Gram. *Triticum dicoccum* (sd)
Apigenin-8-*C*-rhamnosylglucoside
  Gram. *Avena sativa* (lvs)
Apigenin-4′,7-diglucuronide
  Scrophulari. *Antirrhinum majus* (fl.)
Apigenin-4′-glucoside
  Comp. *Dahlia variabilis* (fl. of blue var.)
Apigenin-5-glucoside
  Legum. *Amorpha fruticosa* (lvs)
Apigenin-7-glucoside (Cosmetin; Cosmosiin) is one of the most
widely distributed of *apigenin-glucosides*.
  Mor. *Humulus japonicus* (lvs)
  Paeoni. *Paeonia arborea* (fl.)
  Ros. *Pyrus bretschneideri* (lvs), *galleryana* (lvs); but *not* in *lusi-
    tanica* (lvs)
  Legum. *Baptisia australis, lecontei* (lvs)
  Euphorbi. *Euphorbia* (2)
  Lab. *Lycopus virginicus*

Comp. *Achillea, Anacyclus, Anthemis, Bellis, Centaurea, Chrysanthemum* (4), *Cosmos, Dahlia, Echinops, Matricaria* (4), *Taraxacum, Zinnia*

Apigenin-7-glucuronide

Scrophulari. *Antirrhinum majus* (fl.), and in 6 out of 7 other species examined.

Comp. *Erigeron annuus*

Apigenin-7-neohesperidoside (Rhoifolin)

Anacardi. *Rhus succedanea* (lvs)

Rut. *Citrus paradisi* (lvs), *Poncirus, Pseudaegle*

Bombac. *Chorisia* (lvs of 4 spp.)

Comp. *Dahlia*

Apigenin-7-*O*-rhamnosylglucoside

Legum. *Baptisia lecontei* (lvs)

Apigenin-7-rutinoside

Urtic. *Boehmeria nipononivea* (lvs)

Paeoni. *Paeonia arborea* (fl.)

Rut. *Citrus* (2)

Anacardi. *Rhus succedanea*

Comp. *Dahlia variabilis*

Artocarpesin (fig. 122)

Mor. *Artocarpus heterophyllus* (htwd)

Artocarpetin (2′,4′,5-Trihydroxy-7-methoxy-flavone)

Mor. *Artocarpus?*

Artocarpin (fig. 122)

Mor. *Artocarpus*

Baicalein (5,6,7-Trihydroxy-flavone; Noroxylin; fig. 122) occurs free (?) in

Bignoni. *Oroxylum indicum* (bk)

Lab. *Scutellaria baicalensis* (rt)

Baicalein-6-glucoside (Tetuin)

Bignoni. *Oroxylum indicum* (sd)

Baicalein-7-glucuronide (Baicalin; Baicaloside)

Bignoni. *Oroxylum*

Lab. *Scutellaria* (4)

Bayin (5-Deoxy-apigenin-8-*C*-glucoside)

Legum. *Castanospermum*

Caesioside (Luteolin- ?-primeveroside)

Salic. *Salix caesia*

Chrysin (5,7-Dihydroxy-flavone; Chrysin acid; fig. 122) occurs free (?) and as a glucuronide. It occurs, too, as part of the unique alkaloids *ficine* and *isoficine*.

Salic. *Populus*

Ros. *Prunus* spp. (htwd)
Malv. *Malva*
Bignoni. *Dolichandrone, Oroxylum indicum* (bk)
Chrysin- ?-glucuronide
 Lab. *Scutellaria galericulata* (lvs)
Chrysoeriol (Scoparol; 4′,5,7-Trihydroxy-3′-methoxy-flavone; fig. 122)
 Bruni. *Nebelia paleacea* (lvs, hyd.), *Raspalia microphylla* (lvs, hyd.)
 Hydrophyll. *Eriodictyon*
 Comp. *Iva cheiranthifolia*
Chrysoeriol-7-apiosylglucoside (Graveobioside-B)
 Umbell. *Apium graveolens* (sd)
Chrysoeriol-7-glucuronide
 Legum. *Medicago sativa* (lvs)
 Scrophulari. *Antirrhinum majus* (fl.)
Cirsimaritin (4′,5-Dihydroxy-6,7-dimethoxy-flavone)
 Comp. *Helichrysum viscosum* var. *bracteatum* (plt)
Cirsimaritin-4′-glycoside (Cirsimarin)
 Comp. *Cirsium maritimum*
Cycloartocarpin (fig. 122) is obviously related to *artocarpesin* and *artocarpin.*
 Mor. *Artocarpus heterophyllus* (htwd)
3′-Demethoxy-sudachitin (4′,5,7-Trihydroxy-6,8-dimethoxy-flavone)
 Rut. *Citrus sudachi*
 Comp. *Hymenoxys scaposa* (lvs)
5-Deoxy-vitexin
 Legum. *Castanospermum australe* (htwd)
4′,7-Dihydroxy-flavone
 Legum. *Baptisia lecontei* (lvs), *Medicago sativa, Trifolium repens* (lvs)
5,8-Dihydroxy-flavone (Primetin)
 Primul. *Primula chionantha* (farina), *denticulata* (farina), *modesta*
4′,7-Dihydroxy-flavone-7-O-glucoside
 Legum. *Baptisia lecontei* (lvs)
4′,7-Dihydroxy-flavone-7-O-rhamnosylglucoside
 Legum. *Baptisia lecontei* (lvs)
5,7-Dihydroxy-2′-methoxy-flavone
 Lab. *Scutellaria*
5,7-Dihydroxy-2′-methoxy-flavone-7-glucuronide
 Lab. *Scutellaria epilobifolia* (lvs)
5,6-Dimethoxy-flavone
 Rut. *Casimiroa edulis* (rtbk)
Dinatin (Hispidulin; 4′,5,7-Trihydroxy-6-methoxy-flavone; fig. 122)

has, according to Harborne (1967), the formula given. This differs from earlier formulae.

Scrophulari. *Digitalis lanata* (lvs)
Comp. *Ambrosia hispida* (plt), *Gaillardia fastigiata* (plt)

Diosmetin (Hyssopin; 3',5,7-Trihydroxy-4'-methoxy-flavone)
Legum. *Cassia marilandica* (lvs) (with two 7-glucosides?)
Gesneri. *Columnea × banksii* (lvs, fl.)
Rubi. *Galium mollugo* (shoot)

Diosmetin-7-apiosylglucoside
Umbell. *Apium graveolens, Petroselinum?*

Diosmetin-7-rutinoside (Barosmin; Diosmin)
Crucif. *Capsella bursa-pastoris* (lvs)
Rut. *Barosma, Toddalia, Zanthoxylum* (2)
Umbell. *Conium maculatum* (lvs)
Scrophulari. *Linaria, Scrophularia*
Lab. *Hedeoma, Hyssopus, Mentha, Teucrium montanum* (fl.)
Comp. *Dahlia variabilis*

Echioidinin (2',5-Dihydroxy-7-methoxy-flavone)
Echioidinin-2'-glucoside
Acanth. *Andrographis echioides, wightiana* (lvs)

Eucalyptin (6,8-Dimethyl-5-hydroxy-4',7-dimethoxy-flavone; fig. 122) is an unusual *methyl-flavone* which occurs with other *methyl-flavones* in *Eucalyptus.*
Myrt. *Eucalyptus torelliana*

Flavone (fig. 115) occurs in the farina or meal on the surface of some members of the *Primulaceae*, but not elsewhere, so far as I know.
Primul. *Cortusa?*; *Dionysia* (3); *Primula* spp.

Gamatin is said to be a *furanoflavone.*
Legum. *Pongamia pinnata* (rtbk)

Genkwanin (Puddumetin; 4',5-Dihydroxy-7-methoxy-flavone)
Ros. *Prunus puddum* (and other spp?)
Thymelae. *Daphne genkwa*
Comp. *Artemisia sacrosum*

Genkwanin-5-glucoside (Glucogenkwanin)
Ros. *Prunus verekunda* (bk), and other spp.?

Homo-orientin (Lutonaretin; 8-C-Glucosyl-3',4',5,7-tetrahydroxy-flavone)
Polygon. *Polygonum orientale*
Legum. *Aspalathus*

Homo-orientin-7-glucoside (Lutonarin)
Gram. *Hordeum*

5-Hydroxy-4',7-dimethoxy-flavone
Betul. *Betula*

5-Hydroxy-flavone
  Primul.   Primula spp. (farina)
6-Hydroxy-luteolin (3',4',5,6,7-Pentahydroxy-flavone)
  Bignoni.   Catalpa (3), *Tecoma australis*
5-Hydroxy-3',4',5',7-tetramethoxy-flavone (Corymbosin)
  Rubi.   Webera corymbosa (lvs)
Hymenoxin   (Scaposin;   5',5,7-Trihydroxy-3',4',6,8-tetramethoxy-
  flavone; fig. 122)
  Comp.   Hymenoxys scaposa (lvs)
Hypolaetin (3',4',5,7,8-pentahydroxy-flavone) is the *flavone* analogue of
  gossypetin.
  Restion.   Hypolaena fastigiata
Iso-orientin (Luteolin-6-*C*-glucoside)
  Polygon.   Polygonum orientale (lvs)
  Legum.   Aspalathus linearis, Lespedeza capitata (lvs), *Psoralea*
    spp. (lvs), *Tamarindus indica* (lvs)
  Acer.   Acer palmatum (lvs)
Iso-orientin-7-methyl ether
  Gentian.   Swertia japonica
Iso-orientin-xyloside
  Ranuncul.   Adonis vernalis (lvs)
Iso-saponarin (4-D-Glucosyloxy-saponaretin)
  Lemn.   Spirodela
Iso-scoparin (Chrysoeriol-6-*C*-glucoside)
  Occurrence ?
Iso-vitexin (6-*C*-Glucosyl-apigenin)
  Legum.   Psoralea spp. (lvs), *Tamarindus indica* (lvs)
  Acer.   Acer palmatum (lvs)
  Malv.   Hibiscus syriacus (lvs)
  Combret.   Combretum micranthum (lvs)
Iso-vitexin-7-glucoside
  Caryophyll.   Saponaria officinalis (lvs)
Iso-vitexin-7-methyl ether
  Gentian.   Swertia japonica
Lanceolatin-B (7,8-Furano-flavone; fig. 123)
  Legum.   Tephrosia lanceolata (rtbk)
Lucenins-1 to -5 are 6,8-di-*C*-glucosyl derivatives of *luteolin.*
  Verben.   Vitex lucens
Lucidin(2)   (5,7-Dihydroxy-6,8-dimethoxy-3',4'-methylenedioxy-fla-
  vone)
  Laur.   Lindera lucida (rt)
  Gesneri.   Chrysothemis, Columnea, Episcia, Fieldia, Hypocyrta,

Jerdonia, Rechsteineria, Rhabdothamnus, Rhychotechum, Sarmienta, Titanotrichum

Caprifoli. *Lonicera*

Comp. *Bidens, Chrysanthemum* (as glycoside), *Coreopsis, Cosmos, Dahlia* (fl., free)

Lucidin (2)-dimethyl ether

Laur. *Lindera lucida* (rt)

Luteolin-7-apiosylglucoside (Graviobioside-A)

Umbell. *Apium graveolens* (sd), *Petroselinum crispum* (lvs, sd)

Luteolin- ?-arabinoside

Gram. *Arthraxon hispidus*

Luteolin-7-diglucoside

Comp. *Dahlia variabilis* (fl. of a blue var.)

Luteolin- ?-galactoside (Chaerophyllin)

Umbell. *Chaerophyllum*

Luteolin-3′-glucoside

Lab. *Dracocephalum thymiflorum*

Luteolin (Digitoflavone; 3′,4′,5,7-Tetrahydroxyflavone; fig. 123) is a very common flavone. It and its many glycosides are extremely widely distributed, but it is hard to be sure from the records how often it is present in the free state. Some of the following 'occurrences' may refer to glycosides.

Resed. *Reseda lutea*

Ros. *Prunus* spp.

Legum. *Baptisia lecontei* (lvs), *Erythrophleum, Galega officinalis* (fl., free), *Genista*

Bruni. *Raspalia microphylla* (lvs); but *absent* from some other members of the family.

Plumbagin. *Limonium sinuatum* (fl.)

Scrophulari. *Antirrhinum, Digitalis lutea* (lvs)

Bignoni. *Campsis radicans, Catalpa* (2), *Chilopsis saligna, Tecoma* (2)

Lab. *Lavandula, Lycopus, Mentha, Salvia, Stachys, Teucrium, Thymus*

Acanth. *Adhatoda, Andrographis, Asteracantha, Barleria, Justicia, Ruellia, Rungia, Thunbergia*

Luteolin-4′-glucoside

Ros. *Pyrus ussuriensis* (lvs)

Legum. *Spartium junceum* (fl.)

Acer. *Acer cissifolium* (lvs)

Comp. *Gnaphalium affine*

Luteolin-5-glucoside (Galuteolin) is said to be unusually acid-labile.

Legum. *Galega officinalis* (sd)

Umbell. *Chaetosciadium trichospermum* (lvs), *Torilis* spp. (lvs); but *absent* from many members of the family.

Comp. *Dahlia variabilis*

Luteolin-7-β-glucoside
Salic. *Salix gymnolepis* (lvs)
Mor. *Humulus japonicus* (lvs)
Ros. *Pyrus* (3)
Legum. *Baptisia australis, lecontei*; *Kummerowia striata* (lvs), *Microlespedeza striata* (lvs), *Sophora angustifolia* (lvs, fl.), *Spartium junceum* (fl.)
Ole. *Olea europea* (lvs)
Lab. *Lycopus virginicus, Thymus vulgaris*
Solan. *Solanum stoloniferum* (fl.)
Orobanch. *Orobanche minor* (plt)
Scrophulari. *Digitalis* (occurrence not confirmed)
Boragin. *Heliotropium tenellum*
Acanth. *Asystasia gangetica* (fl.)
Comp. *Carthamus, Cynara, Coreopsis, Dahlia, Elephantopus, Hieracium* (2), *Lactuca, Matricaria* (2), *Onopordon, Taraxacum*

Luteolin-8-*C*-α-D-glucoside (Epi-orientin)
Legum. *Parkinsonia aculeata* (lvs, fl.)

Luteolin-7-glucosylarabinoside
Salic. *Salix bakko* (lvs)

Luteolin-7-glucosylglucoside
Lab. *Thymus vulgaris*

Luteolin-7-glucosylglucuronide
Scrophulari. *Digitalis purpurea* (lvs)

Luteolin-7-glucuronide
Scrophulari. *Antirrhinum majus* (fl.), *Digitalis purpurea* (lvs)

Luteolin-7-rutinoside
Crucif. *Capsella bursa-pastoris* (lvs)
Legum. *Baptisia lecontei* (lvs)
Rut. *Citrus limon* (peel)
Caprifoli. *Lonicera japonica* (lvs)

Luteoloside is a glucoside of *luteolin*.
Resed. *Reseda lutea* (fl.)

Lutonarin-3′-methyl ether is a *C-glycosyl* compound.
Gram. *Hordeum*

Methoxy-apiin: what is this?
Umbell. *Apium*

6-Methyl-5-hydroxy-4′,7-dimethoxy-flavone
Myrt. *Eucalyptus torelliana*

Mikanin (5-Hydroxy-4',6,7-trimethoxy-flavone)
Comp.   Mikania cordata (lvs)
Nobiletin (3',4',5,6,7,8-Hexamethoxy-flavone)
Rut.   Citrus aurantium, nobilis, tankan (bk)
Nor-artocarpetin (Lotoflavin; 2',4',5,7-Tetrahydroxy-flavone)
Mor.   Artocarpus heterophyllus (htwd)
Orientin (Luteolin-8-*C*-glucoside)
Polygon.   Polygonum orientale
Legum.   Aspalathus linearis, Parkinsonia aculeata (lvs, fl.), *Psoralea*
spp., *Spartium junceum* (fl.), *Tamarindus indica* (lvs)
Oxalid.   Oxalis (2)
Gentian.   Swertia japonica
Gram.   Hordeum
Orientin-3'-methyl ether
Legum.   Sarothamnus scoparius (lvs)
Oroxylin-A (Baicalein-6-methyl ether)
Bignoni.   Oroxylum indicum (sd)
Parkinsonin-A (5-*O*-Methyl-luteolin-8-*C*-β-D-glucoside)
Legum.   Parkinsonia aculeata (lvs, fl.)
Parkinsonin-B (5,7-Di-*O*-methyl-luteolin-8-*C*-α-D-glucoside)
Legum.   Parkinsonia aculeata (lvs, fl.)
Paspaloside is said to be a glucoside of *luteolin*.
Gram.   Paspalum conjugatum
Pectolinarigenin (5,7-Dihydroxy-4',6-dimethoxy-flavone)
Comp.   Cirsium oleraceum (lvs, free ?)
Pectolinarigenin-7-rutinoside (?Neolinarin; Pectolinarin)
Legum.   Trifolium
Scrophulari.   Linaria japonica (lvs), *vulgaris* (fl.)
Comp.   Cirsium
Pedalitin (3',4',5,7-Tetrahydroxy-6-methoxy-flavone)
Pedali.   Sesamum indicum (lvs)
Pinnatin (fig. 123) is a *furanoflavone*.
Legum.   Pongamia pinnata (rtbk)
Ponkanetin (4',5,6,7,8-Pentamethoxy-flavone)
Rut.   Citrus
Pratol (7-Hydroxy-4'-methoxy-flavone)
Legum.   Cicer arietinum, Trifolium pratense (and other spp. ?)
Saponaretin (Homo-vitexin; Iso-vitexin) is a *C-glycosyl* compound and
probably an optical isomer of *vitexin*.
Polygon.   Polygonum
Verben.   Vitex
Saponarin is the *7-glycoside* of *vitexin* or of *saponaretin*. It was

originally described as 'soluble starch' because coloured blue by iodine!

Caryophyll. Saponaria
Malv. Hibiscus?
Verben. Vitex
Lemn. Spirodela
Gram. Hordeum vulgare

Scoparin (1) (Scoparoside; Chrysoeriol-8-*C*-glucoside)

Legum. Sarothamnus scoparius

Scutellarein (4′,5,6,7-Tetrahydroxy-flavone)

Lab. Scutellaria altissima (lvs, as glycoside)
Scrophulari. Digitalis lanata (lvs)
Bignoni. Millingtonia hortensis (fl.)

Scutellarein-5-galactoside

Bignoni. Millingtonia hortensis (fl.)

Scutellarein-7-glucuronide (Scutellarin)

Lab. Galeopsis; Scutellaria altissima (lvs, rt), *baicalensis* (lvs, rt), *galericulata* (lvs, rt); *Teucrium*

Scutellaroside: is an *apigenin-glucuronide*?

Comp. Centaurea

Sideroxylin (6,8-Dimethyl-4′,5-dihydroxy-7-methoxy-flavone)

Myrt. Eucalyptus sideroxylon

Sinensetin (3′,4′,5,6,7-Pentamethoxy-flavone)

Rut. Citrus sinensis (peel)

Sudachitin (4′,5,7-Trihydroxy-3′,6,8-trimethoxy-flavone)

Rut. Citrus sudachi

Swertiajaponin (7-*O*-Methyl-luteolin-6-*C*-glucoside)

Gentian. Swertia japonica?

Swertisin (Genkwanin-6-*C*-glucoside)

Gentian. Swertia?

Tangeretin (4′,5,6,7,8-Pentamethoxy-flavone)

Rut. Citrus deliciosa (*reticulata*), *jambhiri, paradisi, poonensis, sinensis*

Tectochrysin (Chrysin-7-methyl ether) occurs in *Pinus* spp. and in

Salic. Populus
Ros. Prunus spp. (htwd)

5,6,7,8-Tetramethoxy-flavone

Laur. Lindera lucida

5,6,7,8-Tetramethoxy-3′,4′-methylenedioxy-flavone

Laur. Lindera lucida

Tricin (4′,5,7-Trihydroxy-3′,5′-dimethoxy-flavone; fig. 123)

Legum. Medicago sativa

Orobanch. *Orobanche* (*Phelypaea*) *ramosa, arenaria* (but *not* in 8
   other spp.)
Irid. *Crocus cambessedesii* (and 2 other spp. ?)
Gram. *Triticum dicoccum* (lvs)
Tricin-5-diglucoside
Gram. *Triticum dicoccum* (lvs), and other spp.
Tricin-7-diglucuronide
Legum. *Medicago sativa* (lvs)
Tricin-5-glucoside
Gram. *Oryza sativa* (lvs), *Triticum dicoccum* (lvs)
Tricin-7-glucoside
Gram. *Oryza sativa* (lvs)
Tricin-glucosylglucoside: is this *tricin-5-diglucoside*?
Gram. *Triticum*
Tricin-7-glucuronide
Legum. *Medicago sativa* (lvs)
Tricin-7-rutinoside
Gram. *Oryza sativa* (lvs)
3′,5,7-Trihydroxy-4′,6-dimethoxy-flavone (3-Demethoxy-centaureidin)
Comp. *Centaurea nigrescens, phrygia* subsp. *pseudophrygia*
4′,5,7-Trihydroxy-3′,6-dimethoxy-flavone
Scrophulari. *Digitalis lanata* (lvs)
Comp. *Helichrysum viscosum* var. *bracteatum* (plt, free)
3′,4′,7-Trihydroxy-flavone
Legum. *Baptisia lecontei* (lvs), *Trifolium repens* (lvs)
3′,4′,7-Trihydroxy-flavone-7-glucoside
Legum. *Baptisia lecontei* (lvs)
5,7,8-Trihydroxy-flavone-7-glucuronide
Lab. *Scutellaria epilobifolia* (lvs)
3′,4′,7-Trihydroxy-flavone-7-rhamnosylglucoside
Legum. *Baptisia lecontei* (lvs)
2′,5,6-Trimethoxy-flavone
Rut. *Casimiroa edulis*
Vicenin (6,8-Di-*C*-glucosyl-apigenin)
Verben. *Vitex lucens*
Violaxanthin: is 4′,5,7-Trihydroxy-flavone-6,8-di-*C*-glucoside?
Viol. *Viola odorata, tricolor*
Vitexin (Apigenin-8-*C*-glucoside) seems to be quite widely distributed.
Polygon. *Polygonum orientale* (lvs)
Mor. *Humulus japonicus* (lvs)
Crucif. *Alliaria officinalis* (lvs)
Ros. *Crataegus*
Legum. *Psoralea* spp. (lvs), *Tamarindus indica* (lvs)

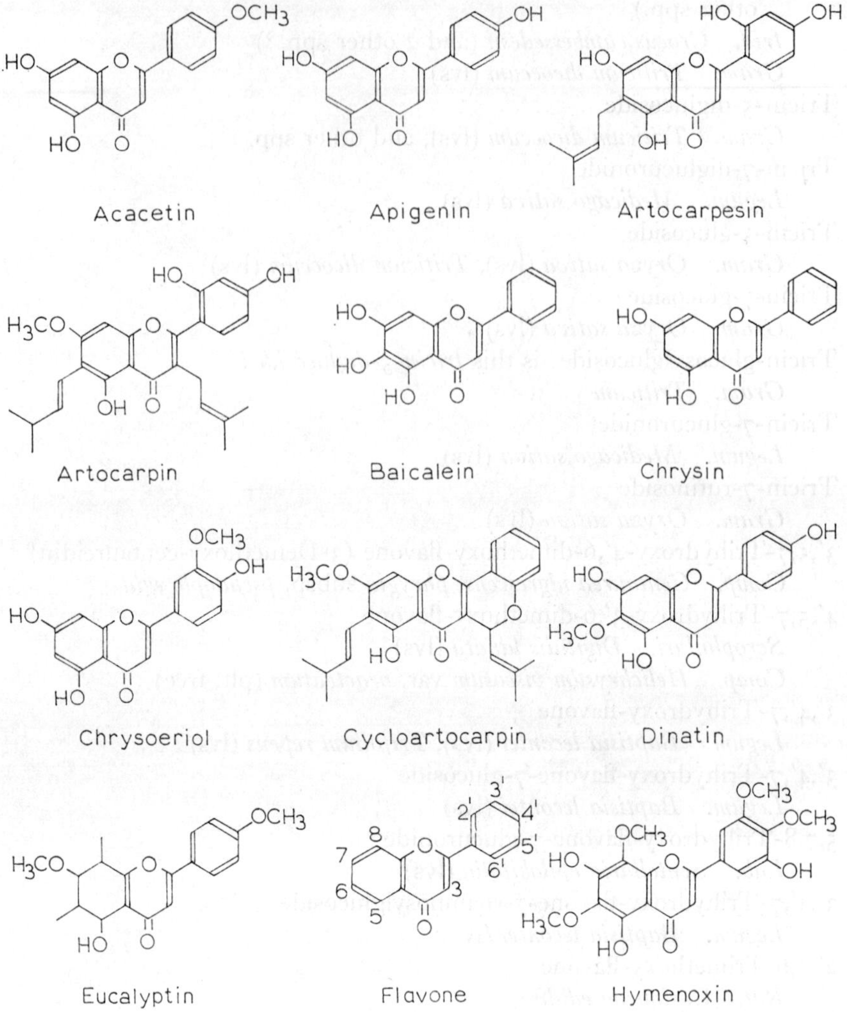

Fig. 122. Some flavones.

Acer. *Acer palmatum* (lvs)
Malv. *Hibiscus syriacus*
Combret. *Combretum micranthum* (lvs)
Verben. *Vitex* (8)
Vitexin-4-L-rhamnoside
    Ros. *Crataegus monogyna* (lvs), *oxyacantha* (lvs)
    Verben. *Vitex*?

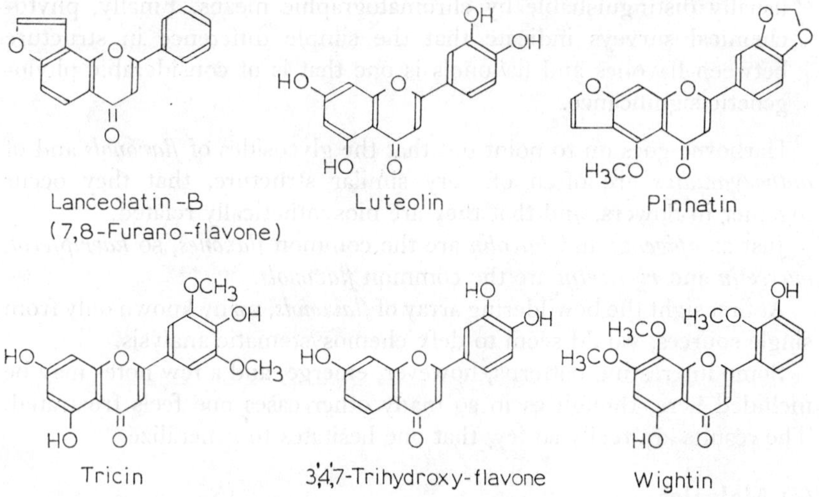

Fig. 123. Some flavones and turanoflavones.

Vitexin-?-xyloside
  Rut. Citrus spp. (frt)
Wightin (3′,5-Dihydroxy-2′,7,8-trimethoxyflavone; fig. 123): unique
  among *flavones* in having 2′,3′-oxidation?
    Acanth. Andrographis wightiana (st., rt)
Wogonin (5,7-Dihydroxy-8-methoxy-flavone)
    Lab. Scutellaria baicalensis (rt)
Xanthomicrol (4′,5-Dihydroxy-6,7,8-trimethoxy-flavone)
    Lab. Satureia douglasii

X FLAVONOLS AND FURANOFLAVONOLS

GENERAL

The *flavones* and *flavonols* have sometimes been grouped together as
anthoxanthins, reflecting the fact that they are often responsible for the
yellow colours of flowers. Harborne (1967) prefers to separate them,
saying:

> The distinction between flavones and flavonols is an arbitrary one,
> since flavonols are simply a class of flavone in which the 3-position is
> substituted by a hydroxyl group. It is a convenient division because
> such a large number of structures have been isolated. Furthermore,
> the two groups differ in their spectral and colour properties and are

usually distinguishable by chromatographic means. Finally, phyto-chemical surveys indicate that the simple difference in structure between flavones and flavonols is one that is of considerable phylo-genetic significance.

Harborne goes on to point out that the glycosides of *flavonols* and of *anthocyanidins* are often of very similar structure, that they occur together in flowers, and that they are biosynthetically related.

Just as *apigenin* and *luteolin* are the common *flavones*, so *kaempferol*, *quercetin* and *myricetin* are the common *flavonols*.

At first sight the bewildering array of *flavonols*, many known only from single sources, would seem to defy chemosystematic analysis.

Some interesting patterns, however, emerge, and a few notes may be included here, though as in so many other cases one feels frustrated. The results are really so few that one hesitates to generalize.

(a) **Malvales**

Within this order (7 families in *Syll.*12, 1964) we seem to have positive records from but 3 families: *Malvaceae* (5 genera out of about 75), *Sterculiaceae* (2 out of about 60), and *Tiliaceae* (*Tilia* only). Of the *Malvaceae* so far studied 3 genera are characterized by 8-*hydroxy* derivatives of *kaempferol*, *quercetin* and *myricetin* (*glycosides* of *herbacetin*, *gossypitin* and *hibiscetin*). Except for one record in the *Compositae* these particular *flavonols* seem to be confined to the *Malvaceae*, but other 8-substituted *flavonols* are to be found in *Ricinocarpos* (*Euphorbi.*, below). *Kaempferol* and/or *quercetin* glycosides (but not 8-hydroxy derivatives of these) occur in *Tilia* (*Tiliaceae*), and in *Guazuma* and *Firmiana* (*Sterculiaceae*).

(b) *Euphorbiaceae*

Few of the 300 or so genera of this big family have been reported to contain *flavonols*, but one of these, *Ricinocarpos*, has at least five 8-substituted *flavonols* similar to, but not identical with, those of the *Malvaceae*. They have been found in 2 of the 16 species of the genus. Have the others been studied?

(c) *Leguminosae*

This family is notable as containing several 5-*deoxy-flavonols* (which may also occur in the *Rutaceae*), such as *demethoxykanugin* (*Pongamia*), 4',7-*dihydroxy-flavonol* (*Baptisia*), *fisetin* (*Acacia*, *Baptisia*, *Butea*, *Gleditsia*), *fisetin-3-glucoside* (*Baptisia*), *fisetin-7-rhamnosylglucoside* (*Baptisia*), and 3',4',7,8-*tetrahydroxy-flavonol* (*Acacia*).

At least 2 *furano-flavonols* occur in the *Leguminosae*. These are *karanjin* and *pongapin* which are found in *Pongamia*. They are also 5-deoxy-flavonols. We have noted that *furanoflavones*, too, occur in the *Leguminosae*.

(d) Zingiberaceae

The presence of *flavonols* with *unsubstituted B-rings* seems to characterize the few members of this family that have been investigated. Thus, we have: *galangin* (*Alpinia officinarum*), also in *Datisca* of the *Datiscaceae*; *galangin-3-methyl ether* (*Alpinia officinarum*); and *galangin-7-methyl ether* (*Alpinia chinensis, japonica*).

(e) Melicope (Rutaceae)

Several *highly methylated flavonols* (*melibentin, melisimplexin, melisimplin, meliternatin, meliternin, ternatin,* and *wharingin*) seem to be characteristic of this genus. Again we must be cautious. My records show occurrences in but 3 of the 70 or more species of *Melicope*. On the other hand not one of this group of flavonols has been found elsewhere so far as I know.

(f) The 5-methoxy-flavonols and their glycosides

These have been discussed by Harborne in a very recent paper (1969). When chromatographed they give intensely fluorescent spots and so are easily detected. They seem to be quite restricted in their occurrence. He finds them to be abundant in the *Ericaceae*, but they occur also in *Juglandaceae, Lauraceae, Eucryphiaceae, Dilleniaceae, Leguminosae, Combretaceae, Plumbaginaceae* and *Scrophulariaceae*.

List and Occurrence

Amarbelin: a *trimethoxy-flavonol*?
    Convolvul. Cuscuta reflexa (sd)
Amurensin (Demethoxy-icaritin-7-glucoside)
    Rut. Phellodendron amurense (bk)
Arbusculoside is a *myricetin-galactoside*.
    Salic. Salix arbuscula (lvs)
Arbutoflavonols-A and -B: what are these?
    Eric. Arbutus
Artemisetin (Artemetin; 5-Hydroxy-3',4',6,7-tetramethoxy-flavonol-3-methyl ether)
    Comp. Artemisia
Auranetin (Aurantin; 4',6,7,8-Tetramethoxy-flavonol-3-methyl ether)
    Rut. Citrus aurantium

Ayanin (Quercetin-3',4',7-trimethyl ether)
Legum. Distemonanthus benthamianus (htwd)
Azaleatin (Quercetin-5-methyl ether; fig. 124) may occur free in some, at least, of the following:
Jugland. Carya pecan (htwd)
Dilleni. Tetracera akara, portobellensis
Eucryphi. Eucryphia cordifolia (lvs), *glutinosa* (lvs)
Eric. Cassiope cv 'Edinburgh' (lvs, fl.); *Daboecia azorica* (lvs, fl.), *cantabrica* (lvs, fl.); *Erica vagans* (lvs); *Kalmiopsis leachiana* (lvs); *Phyllodoce empetriformis* × *Phyllothamnus erectus* (lvs); *Rhododendron mucronatum* (fl., free and as glycoside), and many other spp.
Plumbagin. Plumbago (4, as glycosides?)
Azaleatin-3-arabinosylgalactoside
Eucryphi. Eucryphia cordifolia (lvs), *glutinosa* (lvs)
Azaleatin-3-diglucoside
Laur. Bielschmiedia miersii (lvs; this glycoside?)
Eucryphi. Eucryphia cordifolia (lvs), *glutinosa* (lvs)
Azaleatin-3-galactoside
Eucryphi. Eucryphia glutinosa (lvs)
Plumbagin. Ceratostigma plumbaginoides (lvs), *willmottianum* (lvs)
Azaleatin-3-rhamnoside (Azalein)
Eric. Erica vagans; but *not* in 6 other spp.; *Rhododendron mucronatum* (fl.), and in 43 other spp. out of 83 examined.
Plumbagin. Ceratostigma (2)?; *Plumbago capensis* (fl.), *pulchella* (fl.), *scandens* (fl.), *zeylanica* (fl.)
Caryatin (Quercetin-3,5-dimethyl ether)
Jugland. Carya pecan (htwd)
Eucryphi. Eucryphia cordifolia (lvs), *glutinosa* (lvs)
Eric. Cassiope; Phyllodoce; Rhododendron (12 spp., all of the subgenus *Eurhododendron*)
Casticin (Quercetagetin-3,4',6,7-tetramethyl ether)
Verben. Vitex agnus-castus (sd), *negundo, trifolia* (all Medit. or Africa); but *absent* from *megapotamica* (S. Am.), and *lucens* (N.Z.)
Centaurein is said to be the 7-*glucoside* of 4',6,8-*trihydroxy*-3',7-*dimethoxy-flavonol-3-methyl ether.*
Comp. Centaurea jacea
Chrysosplenetin (Quercetagetin-3',6,7-trimethyl ether)
Chrysosplenetin-3 or 5-glucoside (Chrysosplenin)
Saxifrag. Chrysosplenium japonicum
Datiscetin (2',5,7-Trihydroxy-flavonol; fig. 124)
Datiscetin-2'-methyl ether (Ptaeroxylol)

Datiscetin-2'-methyl ether- ?-diglucoside (Ptaeroxylosin) is said to occur in

    Meli.   *Ptaeroxylon obliquum* (bk)

Datiscetin- ?-rhamnoside (Datiscin): formerly described as a *rutinoside*?

    Datisc.   *Datisca cannabina* (rt)

    Paeoni.   *Paeonia*?

Demethoxy-icaritin (Nor-icaritin; fig. 124)

Demethoxy-icaritin-7-glucoside

    Rut.   *Phellodendron* (lvs)

Demethoxy-icaritin-3-rhamnoside- ?-glucoside

    Berberid.   *Epimedium macranthum* (rt)

Demethoxy-kanugin (fig. 124)

    Legum.   *Pongamia glabra* (bk)

Digicitrin (3',5-Dihydroxy-4',5',6,7,8-pentamethoxy-flavonol-3-methyl ether; fig. 124) is an extraordinarily heavily substituted compound!

    Scrophulari.   *Digitalis purpurea* (lvs)

4',5-Dihydroxy-7,8-dimethoxy-flavonol-3-methyl ether

    Euphorbi.   *Ricinocarpos stylosus* (plt)

4',7-Dihydroxy-flavonol

    Legum.   *Baptisia lecontei* (lvs)

3',5-Dihydroxy-4',7,8-trimethoxy-flavonol-3-methyl ether

    Euphorbi.   *Ricinocarpos muricatus* (lvs), *stylosus* (lvs)

Distemonanthin (fig. 124) may be regarded as a *flavonol* derivative and included here.

    Legum.   *Distemonanthus benthamianus* (htwd)

Erianthin (5-Hydroxy-3',4',6,7,8-pentamethoxy-flavonol-3-methyl ether)

    Comp.   *Blumea eriantha*

Europetin (Myricetin-7-methyl ether) occurs free (?) in

    Plumbagin.   *Plumbago europaea* (lvs), *pulchella* (lvs)

Europetin-3-rhamnoside

    Plumbagin.   *Plumbago europaea* (lvs)

Fisetin (Fustol; 3',4',7-Trihydroxy-flavonol)

    Legum.   *Acacia, Baptisia lecontei* (lvs), *Butea, Gleditsia*

    Anacardi.   *Rhus, Schinopsis* (as glycosides ?)

    Celastr.   *Celastrus*

Fisetin-3-glucoside

    Legum.   *Baptisia lecontei* (lvs)

Fisetin-4'-methyl ether

    Anacardi.   *Schinopsis lorentzii*

Fisetin-7-rhamnosylglucoside

    Legum.   *Baptisia lecontei* (lvs)

Flindulatin (5-Hydroxy-4′,7,8-trimethoxy-flavonol-3-methyl ether)
>   *Rut.   Flindersia maculosa* (lvs)

Galangin (5,7-Dihydroxy-flavonol; fig. 124) is very unusual in having no substitution in the B-ring. It is said to occur (free ?) in *Pinus* and in
>   *Datisc.   Datisca cannabina* (rt)
>   *Zingiber.   Alpinia officinarum* (rhiz.)

Galangin-3-methyl ether
>   *Zingiber.   Alpinia officinarum* (rhiz.)

Galangin-7-methyl ether (Izalpinin)
>   *Zingiber.   Alpinia chinensis* (sd), *japonica* (sd)

Garcinin (?Fukugetin) is an unusual *flavonol* for which I have more than one formula.
>   *Guttif.   Garcinia ovalifolia, spicata* (bk)

Gardenin (5-Hydroxy-3′,4′,5′,6,8-pentamethoxy-flavonol-3-methyl ether ?)
>   *Rubi.   Gardenia lucida*

Gossypetin (8-Hydroxy-quercetin) occurs chiefly as glycosides. See Harborne (1969).
>   *Crassul.   Sedum album*
>   *Legum.   Acacia constricta* (as a glucoside), *catechu* ?
>   *Malv.   Hibiscus esculentus* (fl.), *sabdariffa* (fl.), *vitifolius* (fl.): as glycosides in all ?
>   *Empetr.   Empetrum hermaphroditum* (lvs), *nigrum* (lvs) as glycosides.
>   *Primul.   Dionysia aretioides, Douglasia vitaliana* as glycosides.
>   *Plumbagin.   (?)*

Gossypetin-3-galactoside
>   *Legum.   Lotus corniculatus*
>   *Eric.   Erica arborea* var. *alpina* (lvs), *ciliaris* var. *aurea* (lvs); *Kalmia angustifolia* (lvs), *latifolia* (lvs); *Ledum columbianum* (lvs), *groenlandicum* (lvs), *palustre* (lvs); *Phyllodoce coerulea* (lvs), *nipponica* (lvs); *Phyllodoce empetriformis* × *Phyllothamnus erectus*; *Rhododendron* (lvs of 76, fls. of 10), *Rhodothamnus chamaecistus* (lvs)

Gossypetin-3-gentiotrioside
>   *Primul.   Primula* (fls. of 7 spp.)

Gossypetin-3-glucoside (Gossytrin)
>   *Malv.   Hibiscus sabdariffa* ?, *tiliaceus* (fl.)

Gossypetin-7-glucoside (Gossypitrin)
>   *Papaver.   Papaver nudicaule*
>   *Malv.   Gossypium arboreum* (fl.), *barbadense* (fl.), *herbaceum* (fl.), *neglectum* (fl.); *Hibiscus tiliaceus* (fl.)
>   *Comp.   Chrysanthemum segetum* (fl.)

Gossypetin-8-glucoside (Gossypin)
  Malv. *Gossypium indicum, Hibiscus* (2 ?)
Herbacetin (8-Hydroxy-kaempferol)—see Harborne (1969)—occurs free (?) in
  Malv. *Gossypium indicum* (fl.); *Thespesia populnea* (fl.)
Herbacetin-7-glucoside (Herbacitrin)
  Malv. *Gossypium herbaceum, indicum*
Hibiscetin (8-Hydroxy-myricetin) occurs free (?) in
  Malv. *Hibiscus sabdariffa* (fl.)
Hibiscetin-3-glucoside (Hibiscitrin)
  Malv. *Hibiscus cannabinus* (fl.), *sabdariffa* (fl.)
5'-Hydroxy-fisetin is unusual in lacking a hydroxyl in the 5-position.
  Legum. *Acacia*
5-Hydroxy-3',4',6,7-tetramethoxy-flavonol-3-methyl ether
  Verben. *Vitex negundo* (lvs)
5-Hydroxy-3',4',7,8-tetramethoxy-flavonol-3-methyl ether
  Euphorbi. *Ricinocarpos stylosus* (lvs)
5-Hydroxy-4',6,7,8-tetramethoxy-flavonol-3-methyl ether
  Rut. *Citrus aurantium* (peel)
5-Hydroxy-4',6,7-trimethoxy-flavonol-3-methyl ether
  Sapind. *Dodonaea lobulata*
Icaritin—see also *demethoxyicaritin* (fig. 124).
Icaritin-3-rhamnoside- ?-glucoside (Icariin)
  Berberid. *Epimedium macranthum* (lvs)
Incarnatrin (?Serotrin) is a *quercetin glucoside.*
  Legum. *Trifolium incarnatum* (fl.)
Isolimocitrol (3',5,7-Trihydroxy-4',6,8-trimethoxy-flavonol)
  Rut. *Citrus limon* (peel)
Isorhamnetin (Quercetin-3'-methyl ether; fig. 124) is said to be very widely distributed, but perhaps not all of the following records refer to the free flavonol.
  Cact. *Opuntia ficus-indica* (fl.)
  Ranuncul. *Caltha, Delphinium*
  Berberid. *Podophyllum*
  Crucif. *Cheiranthus* (fl.)
  Resed. *Reseda luteola*
  Legum. *Cassia* (2), *Trifolium*
  Bruni. *Brunia, Nebelia, Pseudobaeckea, Raspalia, Staavia* (lvs in all)
  Elaeagn. *Hippophaë*
  Myrsin. *Aegiceras*
  Plumbagin. *Limonium gmelinii* (rt)
  Comp. *Ambrosia artemisiifolia* (pollen)

Lili.   Lilium
Typh.   Typha
Isorhamnetin-3-4'-diglucoside (Dactylin)
   Crucif.   Matthiola incana (sd)
   Irid.   Crocus (pollen)
   Gram.   Dactylus glomerata (pollen), *Phleum pratense* (pollen)
Isorhamnetin-3,7-diglucoside
   Papaver.   Argemone mexicana
Isorhamnetin-3-dirhamnoside
   Monimi.   Peumus boldus (lvs)
Isorhamnetin-3-galactoside
   Cact.   Cactus grandiflora (plt), *Opuntia lindheimeri* (fl.)
Isorhamnetin-3-glucoside
   Cact.   Cereus grandiflorus
   Crucif.   Brassica napus, Sinapis arvense
   Papaver.   Argemone mexicana
   Ros.   Pyrus communis (frt-peel)
   Elaeagn.   Hippophaë rhamnoides (frt)
   Comp.   Calendula officinalis (fl.)
Isorhamnetin-7-glucoside
   Occurrence?
Isorhamnetin-?-glucoside (Typha-glucoside)
   Typh.   Typha
Isorhamnetin-3-glucoside-4'-rhamnoside
   Umbell.   Pastinaca sativa (frt)
Isorhamnetin-3-glucoside-7-rhamnoside (?Brassidine; Boldoside)
   Monimi.   Peumus boldus (lvs)
   Cruc.   Sinapis arvensis (lvs)
Isorhamnetin-3-glucosylglucoside-7-glucoside (Brassicoside)
   Cruc.   Brassica napus (lvs)
Isorhamnetin-3-KSO_3 (?Persicarin)
   Polygon.   Polygonum (*Persicaria*) *hydropiper* var. *vulgare* (lvs),
      thunbergii
   Umbell.   Oenanthe stolonifera
Isorhamnetin-3-rhamnosylgalactoside (or possibly -robinobioside).
   Cact.   Opuntia (fl.)
   Ros.   Pyrus communis (frt-peel)
   Lili.   Convallaria keiski
Isorhamnetin-3-rhamnosylglucoside
   Ros.   Pyrus communis (frt-peel)
Isorhamnetin-3-rutinoside (Narcissin)
   Caryophyll.   Herniaria glabra
   Cact.   Cactus grandiflora (plt), *Opuntia lindheimeri* (fl.)

Ros. Pyrus
Batid. Batis maritima
Elaeagn. Hippophaë rhamnoides (frt)
Umbell. Bupleurum multinerve
Comp. Calendula officinalis (fl.)
Lili. Lilium auratum (pollen)
Amaryllid. Narcissus tazetta (fl.)

Isorhamnetin-3-rutinosylgalactoside
Cact. Opuntia lindheimeri

Isorhamnetin-3-rutinosyl glucoside
Caryophyll. Herniaria glabra

Isorhamnetin-3-triglycoside yields *glucose, rhamnose,* and *galactose.*
Lili. Lilium candidum (pollen)

Kaempferol (Nimbicetin; Populnetin; Robigenin; Swartziol; Trifolitin; 4',5,7-Trihydroxy-flavonol; fig. 124) occurs free and as glycosides of many kinds in a wide variety of plants. Not all the following records refer to the free *flavonol*?

Polygon. Coccoloba, Polygonum, Rumex
Ranuncul. Delphinium (2)
Papaver. Meconopsis integrifolia (fl.)
Paeoni. Paeonia
Ros. Prunus
Legum. Acacia (2), *Afzelia, Cassia*
Bruni. said to be *absent*
Cunoni. Cunonia capensis; but *not* in other members of the family?
Rhamn. Rhamnus
Dipterocarp. Anisoptera, Hopea, Shorea
Myrt. Eucalyptus calophylla
Corn. Cornus
Plumbagin. several, but as glycosides?
Nolan. Nolana hemifusa (lvs)

Kaempferol-3-arabinoside
Jugland. Juglans regia (lvs)
Ros. Prunus spinosa (lvs), *Pyrus communis* (lvs)
Hippocastan. Aesculus hippocastanum (lvs, fl.)

Kaempferol-3-(p-coumaroylarabinoside)
Crassul. Bryophyllum daigremontianum (lvs)

Kaempferol-3-(p-coumaroylglucoside) (Tiliroside)
Ros. Rosa canina (frt)
Platan. Platanus occidentalis (lvs)
Tili. Tilia argentea (fl.)
Celastr. Celastrus orbiculatus (lvs)

Kaempferol-3-(*p*-coumaroylsophorotrioside)
   Legum.   *Pisum* spp.
Kaempferol-3-diglucoside (?Kaempferin)
   Legum.   *Cassia tora* (lvs)
   Comp.   *Helichrysum arenarium*
Kaempferol-3,7-diglucoside
   Ranuncul.   *Anemone alpina, Helleborus niger*
   Paeoni.   *Paeonia albiflora* (fl.), *arborea* (fl.)?
   Scrophulari.   *Antirrhinum majus* (fl.)
   Caprifoli.   *Viburnum opulus* (fl.)
Kaempferol-3,7-dimethyl ether
   Eucryphi.   *Eucryphia lucida* (lvs)
   Euphorbi.   *Beyeria* (lvs)
Kaempferol-3',7-dimethyl ether
   Rhamn.   *Rhamnus* (frt)
Kaempferol-3-dirhamnoside
   Santal.   *Exocarpos cupressiformis* (lvs)
Kaempferol-3,7-dirhamnoside (Kaempferitrin; Lespedin)
   Legum.   *Indigofera, Lathyrus, Lespedeza, Lotus*
   Tili.   *Tilia argentea* (fl.)
   Cucurbit.   *Trichosanthes cucumeroides*
   Celastr.   *Celastrus*?
   Comp.   *Tagetes erecta* (lvs)
Kaempferol-3-(feruloylsophoroside)
   Solan.   *Petunia hybrida* (fl.)
Kaempferol-3-(feruloylsophorotrioside)
   Legum.   *Pisum sativum* (lvs), and other spp.?
Kaempferol-3-galactoside (?Trifolin (1))
   Saxifrag.   *Hydrangea macrophylla* (sepal)
   Ros.   *Prunus persica* (fl.), *Pyrus communis* (lvs)
   Legum.   *Bauhinia variegata, Trifolium pratense* (lvs)
   Malv.   *Gossypium barbadense* (fl.)
   Menyanth.   *Menyanthes trifoliata*
   Convolvul.   *Calystegia hederacea* (lvs)
Kaempferol-3-galactosylrhamnoside)
   Solan.   *Atropa belladonna* (lvs)
Kaempferol-3-gentiobioside
   Primul.   *Primula sinensis* (fl.)
Kaempferol-3-gentiotrioside
   Primul.   *Primula sinensis* (fl.)
Kaempferol-3-glucoside (Astragalin) is very widely distributed.
   Fag.   *Fagus sylvatica* (lvs)
   Mor.   *Humulus lupulus*

Phytolacc. Phytolacca decandra (lvs)
Ranuncul. Anemone alpina
Paeoni. Paeonia albiflora (fl.)
The. Camellia sinensis (lvs)
Crucif. Sinapis alba
Hamamelid. many
Ros. Amelanchier, Pourthiaea, Prunus, Pyrus, Rosa
Legum. Astragalus sinicus (fl.), *Baptisia* spp., *Phaseolus, Pisum* spp.
  (lvs)
Platan. Platanus occidentalis (frt, ♂ fl.)
Hippocastan. Aesculus hippocastanum (lvs, fl.)
Vit. Vitis vinifera
Malv. Althaea rosea (fl.), *Hibiscus cannabinus* (lvs)
Tili. Tilia argentea (fl.)
Begoni. Begonia spp. (lvs, fl.)
Umbell. Daucus carota (fl.)
Primul. Cyclamen cultivars
Eben. Diospyros kaki (lvs)
Convolvul. Cuscuta reflexa (st.)
Solan. Nicotiana tabacum, Solanum spp.
Scrophulari. Antirrhinum majus (fl.)
Caprifoli. Viburnum opulus (fl.)
Comp. Arnica, Helichrysum, Solidago (3)
Kaempferol-4'-glucoside
Ros. Rosa spp. and cultivars
Kaempferol-7-glucoside (Populnin)
Malv. Gossypium?, *Thespesia populnea* (fl.)
Comp. Chrysanthemum
Kaempferol-3-glucoside-7-rhamnoside
Monimi. Peumus boldus (lvs)
Resed. Reseda luteola (fl.)
Tili. Tilia argentea (lvs, fl.)
Kaempferol-3-glucosylglucoside: is this the same as *Kaempferol-3-diglucoside*?
Fag. Fagus sylvatica (lvs)
Nymphae. Nelumbo nucifera
Kaempferol-3-(2^G-glucosylrutinoside)
Solan. Solanum tuberosum (fl.) and other spp.?
Kaempferol-3-glucuronide
Legum. Phaseolus vulgaris (lvs)
Euphorbi. Euphorbia cyparissias (lvs)
Kaempferol-7-glucuronide
Lili. Tulipa (fl.)

Kaempferol-3-lathyroside-7-rhamnoside
  Legum. *Lathyrus odoratus* (fl.)
Kaempferol-3-methyl ether
  Begoni. *Begonia* (lvs)
Kaempferol-4'-methyl ether (Kaempferide)
  Zingiber. *Alpinia officinarum* (rhiz.)
Kaempferol-5-methyl ether
  Dilleni. *Tetracera akara* (as glycoside), *portobellensis* (as glycoside)
  Eric. *Erica vagans* (lvs); *Gaultheria veitchiana* (lvs); *Kalmiopsis leachiana* (lvs); *Rhodothamnus chamaecistus* (lvs); *Rhododendron* (about 30 spp.)
Kaempferol-7-methyl ether (Rhamnocitrin)
  Rhamn. *Rhamnus cathartica* (frt)
Kaempferol-7-methyl ether-6-*C*-glucoside: is this *Keyakinin*?
  Ulm. *Zelkova serrata* (wd)
Kaempferol-3-rhamnoside (Afzelin) occurs in ferns and in
  Jugland. *Engelhardtia formosana* (bk)
  Fag. *Nothofagus fusca* (htwd)
  Hamamelid. many
  Legum. *Afzelia* spp. (wd), *Cassia javanica* (lvs), *Indigofera arrecta* (lvs), *Lathyrus odoratus* (fl.)
  Ros. *Prunus spinosa* (lvs), *Rosa* spp. and cultivars, *Rubus hirsutus*
  Hippocastan. *Aesculus hippocastanum* (lvs, fl.)
  Sterculi. *Guazuma tomentosa* (fl.)
  Tili. *Tilia argentea* (fl.)
  Myrt. *Eucalyptus sideroxylon* (lvs)
  Plumbagin. *Plumbago coerulea* (fl.), *rosea* (fl.)
  Menyanth. *Menyanthes trifoliata*
Kaempferol-7-rhamnoside
  Santal. *Exocarpos cupressiformis* (lvs)
  Lili. *Lilium regale* (fl.)
Kaempferol-3-rhamnoside-4'-arabinoside
  Ros. *Prunus spinosa* (lvs)
Kaempferol-3-rhamnosylarabinoside-7-arabinoside—or should it be -7-rhamnoside?
  Crucif. *Matthiola incana* (fl.)
Kaempferol-3-rhamnosyldiglucoside
  The. *Camellia* (lvs)
Kaempferol-3-rhamnosylgalactoside-7-galactoside
  Apocyn. *Vinca herbacea* (fl.), *major* (fl.), *minor* (fl.)
Kaempferol-3-rhamnosylglucoside (Nicotiflorin)
  The. *Camellia*
  Hippocastan. *Aesculus hippocastanum* (fl.)

Apocyn. Nerium
Convolvul. Calystegia
Solan. Nicotiana silvestris (fl.)
Lab. Hyptis capitata (lvs)
Kaempferol-3-robinobioside-7-rhamnoside (Robinin)
    Crucif. Cheiranthus cheiri (frt)
    Legum. Robinia pseudacacia (lvs, fl.); *Phaseolus angularis, trilobatus*
      (lvs); *Pueraria hirsuta* (lvs), *thunbergiana* (lvs); *Vigna angularis* (lvs)
    Apocyn. Acokanthera spectabilis (lvs, fl.); *Rauwolfia verticillata*
      (lvs); *Vinca herbacea, major, minor*
Kaempferol-3-rutinoside
    Mor. Humulus lupulus
    Magnoli. Magnolia spp. (fl.)
    Calycanth. Calycanthus occidentalis (lvs)
    Ranuncul. Anemone alpina (fl.)
    Papaver. Romneya coulteri (fl.)
    The. Camellia sinensis
    Ros. Pourthiaea villosa (fl.), *Pyrus communis* (lvs)
    Legum. Baptisia spp. (lvs), *Bauhinia variegata* (fl.), *Gliricidia*
      maculata, Phaseolus vulgaris (lvs)
    Hippocastan. Aesculus hippocastanum (lvs, fl.)
    Malv. Gossypium barbadense (fl.), *Hibiscus cannabinus* (lvs)
    Myrt. Eucalyptus sideroxylon (lvs)
    Arali. Acanthopanax pentaphyllus (fl.)
    Umbell. Ammi visnaga
    Apocyn. Nerium oleander (lvs)
    Convolvul. Calystegia japonica (lvs)
    Solan. Nicotiana tabacum, Solanum spp.
    Comp. Carthamus tinctorius (fl.)
Kaempferol-3-rutinoside-7-glucoside
    Ranuncul. Anemone alpina
    Solan. Nicotiana tabacum
Kaempferol-3-rutinoside-7-glucuronide
    Lili. Tulipa cultivars (lvs)
Kaempferol-3-sambubioside
    Ranuncul. Helleborus niger (fl.)
Kaempferol-3-sambubioside-7-glucoside
    Ranuncul. Helleborus niger (fl.)
Kaempferol-3-sophoroside (Sophoraflavonoloside)
    Ranuncul. Helleborus niger (fl.)
    Ros. Rosa cultivars (fl.)
    Legum. Cassia tora (lvs), *Pisum* spp. (lvs), *Sophora japonica* (frt)
    Solan. Petunia hybrida (fl.), *Solanum* spp.

Kaempferol-3-sophoroside-7-glucoside
Legum. Lathyrus vernus (lvs)
Solan. Petunia cultivars (fl.)
Amaryllid. Galanthus nivalis (fl.)
Kaempferol-3-sophoroside-7-rhamnoside
Solan. Solanum tuberosum (sd)
Kaempferol-3-sophorotrioside
Legum. Pisum sativum (lvs)
Kaempferol-3-sophorotrioside-7-rhamnoside
Solan. Solanum tuberosum (sd)
Kaempferol-triglucoside
The. Camellia (lvs)
Kaempferol-3-xylosylglucoside
Legum. Phaseolus vulgaris (sd)
Kanugin is, to me, of uncertain structure.
Legum. Pongamia
Karanjin (fig. 124) is a *furano-flavonol*.
Legum. Pongamia glabra (rt, sd-oil), *pinnata* (rtbk)
Limocitrin (4′,5,7-Trihydroxy-3′,8-dimethoxy-flavonol)
Rut. Citrus limon (frt-peel)
Limocitrol (4′,5,7-Trihydroxy-3′,6,8-trimethoxy-flavonol)
Rut. Citrus limon (frt-peel)
Melibentin (5,6,7,8-Tetramethoxy-3′,4′-methylenedioxy-flavonol-3-methyl ether) is one of an interesting group of *flavonols* occurring in the genus *Melicope*. The others are *melisimplexin, melisimplin, meliternatin, meliternin,* and *ternatin.*
Rut. Melicope broadbentiana
Melisimplexin (5,6,7-Trimethoxy-3′,4′-methylenedioxy-flavonol-3-methyl ether)
Rut. Melicope broadbentiana, simplex (bk)
Melisimplin (5-Hydroxy-6,7-dimethoxy-3′,4′-methylenedioxy-flavonol-3-methyl ether)
Rut. Melicope broadbentiana, simplex (bk)
Meliternatin (5-Methoxy-3′,4′,6,7-bismethylenedioxy-flavonol-3-methyl ether; fig. 124)
Rut. Melicope broadbentiana, simplex (bk), *ternata* (bk)
Meliternin (5,7,8-Trimethoxy-3′,4′-methylenedioxy-flavonol-3-methyl ether)
Rut. Melicope ternata (bk)
7-Methoxy-persicarin
Polygon. Polygonum hydropiper
Mollugo-flavonoloside: of undetermined structure ?
Mollugin. Mollugo

Mopanin is rather like *distemonanthin*.

   Legum.   Colophospermum mopane (htwd)

Morin ($2'$,$4'$,5,7-Tetrahydroxy-flavonol) is an isomer of *quercetin*.

   Mor.   Artocarpus integrifolia (htwd), *Chlorophora tinctoria* (wd), *Maclura pomifera* (wd), *Morus bambycis* (wd)

Multiflorin is said to be a *kaempferol-rhamnoglucoside*.

   Ros.   Rosa multiflora

Myricetin (Cannabiscetin; $3'$,$4'$,$5'$,5,7-Pentahydroxy-flavonol; fig. 125) is a very widely distributed *flavonol*, with many glycosides. The records which follow probably include some of glycosides, rather than of the free *flavonol*.

   Salic.   Salix
   Myric.   Myrica
   Betul.   Betula, Corylus
   Nymphae.   Nymphaea
   Cunoni.   Ackama rosaefolia; but *absent* or as a trace in other members?
   Legum.   Acacia, Haematoxylon, Intsia bijuga (wd), *Trifolium repens* (sd)
   Bruni. in traces only
   Coriari.   Coriaria
   Malv.   Hibiscus
   Dipterocarp.   Dipterocarpus, Dryobalanops, Hopea, Shorea, Vatica
   Anacardi.   Pistacia, Rhus
   Vit.   Ampelopsis
   Eric.   Arctostaphylos, Calluna
   Plumbagin.   Acantholimon, Aegialitis, Armeria spp., *Goniolimon, Limonium* spp., *Plumbago*
   Irid.   Crocus spp., *Iris*

Myricetin-3-arabinoside
   Eric.   Vaccinium macrocarpon (frt)

Myricetin-3-galactoside
   Salic.   Salix arbuscula (?*arbusculoside*)
   The.   Camellia sinensis (lvs)
   Onagr.   Oenothera lavandulaefolia (plt)

Myricetin-3-galactosylgalactoside
   Betul.   Betula pubescens, verrucosa
   Eric.   Vaccinium macrocarpon (frt)

Myricetin-3-glucoside
   Hamamelid. several
   Legum.   Acacia dealbata (pollen), *Phaseolus vulgaris* (sd)
   The.   Camellia (absent from *Stuartia*)

Vit.   Vitis vinifera (frt)
Primul.   Primula sinensis (fl.)
Plumbagin.   Plumbago coerulea (lvs), *pulchella* (lvs)

Myricetin-3'-glucoside (Cannabiscitrin)
Mor.   Cannabis indica
Malv.   Hibiscus abelmoschus (fl.), *cannabinus* (fl.)

Myricetin-3-methyl ether (Annulatin)
Plumbagin.   Aegialitis annulata (lvs)

Myricetin-5-methyl ether: occurs in at least some of the following as glycosides?
Eric.   Cassiope cv 'Edinburgh'; *Daboecia azorica* (lvs, fl.), *cantabrica* (lvs, fl.); *Gaultheria veitchiana* (lvs); *Rhododendron catawbiense, japonicum, obtusum,* and many other spp.
Plumbagin.   Plumbago europaea (as glycoside)

Myricetin-5-methyl ether-3-galactoside
Plumbagin.   Ceratostigma plumbaginoides (lvs)

Myricetin-5-methyl ether- ?-glycoside
Plumbagin.   Plumbago europaea (lvs)

Myricetin-3',4',5',3,7-pentamethyl ether (Combretol)
Combret.   Combretum quadrangulare (sd)

Myricetin-3-rhamnoside (Myricitrin)
Myric.   Myrica gale, nagi, rubra
Betul.   Betula?, Carpinus?, Corylus avellana (lvs)
Nymphae.   Nymphaea?
Hamamelid.   many
Saxifrag.   Astilbe odontophylla (lvs)
Legum.   Cercis siliquastrum (lvs), *Haematoxylon?, Lathyrus odoratus* (fl.)
The.   Camellia sinensis, Stuartia?
Sapind.   Xanthoceras ꞏorbifolia (lvs)
Anacardi.   Rhus?
Eric.   Calluna?
Eben.   Diospyros lotus (lvs)
Plumbagin.   Ceratostigma plumbaginoides (lvs), *Dyerophytum africanum* (lvs), *Limonium gmelinii* (rt) and other spp.

Myricetin-3-robinobioside-7-rhamnoside
Apocyn.   Vinca minor (fl.)

Myricetin-3-rutinoside (Myrticolorin)
The.   Camellia sinensis (lvs)
Plumbagin.   Limonium gmelinii (rt)
Solan.   Solanum soukupii (fl.) and other spp.

Myricetin-3-rutinoside-7-rhamnoside
Viol.   Viola (fl.)

Myricetin-4',5',3,7-tetramethyl ether
  Cist. Cistus monspeliensis (lvs)
Myricetin-4',3,7-trimethyl ether
  Euphorbi. Ricinocarpos (lvs)
Ombuin (Quercetin-4',7-dimethyl ether)
  Rhamn. Rhamnus (frt, as glycoside?)
Ombuin-3-rutinoside (Ombuoside)
  Phytolacc. Phytolacca dioica (lvs)
Oxyayanin-A: of unknown structure?
  Legum. Distemonanthus benthamianus (wd)
Oxyayanin-B: is 3',5,6-*trihydroxy*-4',7-*dimethoxy-flavonol*-3-*methyl ether?*
  Legum. Distemonanthus benthamianus (wd)
Patuletin (Quercetagetin-6-methyl ether; fig. 125)
  Legum. Leucaena
  Comp. Tagetes patula
Patuletin-3-glucoside
  Comp. Hymenoxys scaposa
Patuletin-7-glucoside (Patulitrin)
  Legum. Prosopis spicigera (fl.)
  Comp. Hymenoxys scaposa (fl.)
Patuletin-3-rutinoside
  Comp. Hymenoxys scaposa (lvs, fl.)
Pongapin (Pongamin; fig. 125) is a *furanoflavonol.*
  Legum. Pongamia pinnata (rtbk)
Pratoletin is said to be 4',5,8-*trihydroxyflavonol.*
  Legum. Trifolium pratense (fl.)
Prudomestin (5,7-Dihydroxy-4',8-dimethoxy-flavonol)
  Ros. Prunus domestica (htwd)
Quercetagetin (6-Hydroxy-quercetin; fig. 125) occurs free in
  Legum. Acacia catechu (wd), *Coronilla glauca* (fl.), *Leucaena glauca* (fl.), *Medicago sativa* (fl.)
  Comp. Tagetes (2, free?)
Quercetagetin-3,6-dimethyl ether
  Comp. Iva axillaris (plt)
Quercetagetin-3-gentiotrioside
  Primul. Primula vulgaris (fl.)
Quercetagetin-7-glucoside (Quercetagitrin)
  Papaver. Papaver nudicaule (fl.)
  Comp. Chrysanthemum (1), *Hymenoxys scaposa* (infl.), *Tagetes*
Quercetagetin-7-methyl ether
  Legum. Medicago
Quercetin (Ericin; Meletin; Sophorin; 3',4',5,7-Tetrahydroxy-flavonol;

fig. 125) is exceedingly common. Not all the records which follow are of the free flavonol.

Fag.   *Quercus*
Polygon.   *Polygonum*
Berberid.   *Podophyllum*
Illici.   *Illicium*
Saxifrag.   *Ribes*
Cunoni.   much, in all?
Ros.   *Crataegus, Fragaria, Prunus, Rosa*
Legum.   *Bauhinia, Trifolium*
Bruni.   in all?
Guttif.   *Hypericum*
Euphorbi.   *Euphorbia*
Dipterocarp.   *Dipterocarpus, Dryobalanops, Shorea*
Malv.   *Gossypium, Thespesia*
Rhamn.   *Helinus, Rhamnus*
Viol.   *Viola*
Hippocastan.   *Aesculus*
Onagr.   *Fuchsia*
Myrt.   *Psidium*
Arali.   *Fatsia*
Corn.   *Cornus*
Eric.   *Calluna, Vaccinium*
Plumbagin.   in many, but mostly as glycosides
Asclepiad.   *Marsdenia volubilis* (frt, hairs—free)
Nolan.   *Nolana humifusa* (lvs)
Comp.   *Aster, Cosmos, Erigeron, Solidago*
Lili.   *Allium*
Irid.   *Crocus* (some), *Iris* (some)
Gram.   *Zea*

Quercetin-3-arabinosides—there are 3 or 4 of these! Some records which are not specific are listed here.

Loranth.   *Loranthus parasiticus*
Ros.   *Filipendula ulmaria*; *Pyrus communis*
Umbell.   *Foeniculum vulgare* (lvs)
Eric.   *Rhododendron campyllocarpum* (fl.), *flavum* (lvs); *Vaccinium macrocarpon* (frt)

Quercetin-3-β-L-arabinoside (Polystachoside)

Polygon.   *Polygonum polystachyum*

Quercetin-3-α-L-arabofuranoside (Avicularin)

Loranth.   *Psittacanthus cuneifolius* (lvs)?
Polygon.   *Polygonum aviculare* (and others?), *Rumex salicifolius* (and others?)

Ros. Filipendula?, Malus?, Spiraea?
Eric. Vaccinium myrtillus (lvs)
Quercetin-3-α-L-arabopyranoside (Guaijaverin)
Myrt. Psidium guajava (lvs)
Quercetin-3-(caffeoylsophoroside)-7-glucoside
Ranuncul. Helleborus foetidus (fl.)
Quercetin-3-(*p*-coumaroyl-sophorotrioside)
Legum. Pisum sativum (lvs)
Quercetin-3-digalactoside
Droser. Drosera rotundifolia (rt)
Quercetin-3,3'-diglucoside
Hippocastan. Aesculus hippocastanum
Quercetin-3,4'-diglucoside
Lili. Allium cepa (bulb)
Quercetin-3,7-diglucoside
Legum. Baptisia spp., *Ulex europaeus* (fl.)
Quercetin-4',7-diglucoside
Lili. Allium cepa (bulb)
Quercetin-3,7-diglucuronide
Ros. Potentilla reptans (lvs)
Quercetin-3-diglycoside
Calycanth. Chimonanthus praecox (fl.)
Eucryphi. Eucryphia cordifolia (lvs), *glutinosa* (lvs)
Quercetin-3',3-dimethyl ether
Solan. Nicotiana tabacum (calyx)
Quercetin-3-dirhamnoside
Santal. Exocarpus cupressiformis (lvs)
Quercetin-3-(feruloyl-sophorotrioside)
Legum. Pisum spp.
Quercetin-3-galactoside (Hyperin; Hyperoside) is very common
  indeed:
Jugland. Juglans regia (lvs)
Betul. Alnus, Betula, Carpinus, Corylus, Ostrya
Polygon. Fagopyrum (3), *Homalocladium* (1), *Muehlenbeckia* (1),
  Oxyria (1), *Polygonum* (15), *Rheum* (8), *Rumex* (11)
Cact. Opuntia lindheimeri (fl.)
Ranuncul. Caltha palustris
Berberid. Podophyllum sikkimensis (rt, rhiz.)
Eucryphi. Eucryphia (3)
Guttif. Hypericum androsaemum (plt), *perforatum* (plt)
Ros. Crataegus, Filipendula (2), *Malus* spp., *Pyrus, Sorbus*
Legum. Acacia melanoxylon
Droser. Drosera rotundifolia (rt)

Platan.   Platanus occidentalis (fl.)

Euphorbi.   Euphorbia palustris (lvs)

Corn.   Cornus

Eric.   Arctostaphylos uva-ursi (lvs); *Ledum palustre* (lvs); *Rhodo-dendron* (4, and cultivars); *Vaccinium macrocarpon* (frt), *uligino-sum* (lvs), *vitis-idaea* (lvs)

Asclepiad.   Calotropis, Hemidesmus, Leptadenia, Marsdenia, Per-gularia, Telosma

Plumbagin.   Ceratostigma willmottianum (lvs)

Comp.   Nardosmia laevigata (lvs), *Solidago altissima* (fl.), *Tussilago farfara* (fl.)

Quercetin-3-galactoside-7-rhamnoside

Ranuncul.   Caltha palustris (fl.)

Quercetin-3-galactoside-7-xyloside

Ranuncul.   Caltha palustris (stamen)

Quercetin-3-galactosylarabinoside

Fag.   Quercus incana (lvs)

Quercetin-3-gentiobioside

Papaver.   Papaver somniferum

Primul.   Primula sinensis (fl.)

Quercetin-3-gentiotrioside

Primul.   Primula sinensis (fl.)

Quercetin-3-glucoside (Isoquercitrin; Isotrifoliin; Trifoliin) is a very common and widely dispersed glucoside:

Fag.   Fagus sylvatica (lvs)

Mor.   Humulus lupulus, Morus alba (lvs)

Polygon.   Polygonum

Phytolacc.   Phytolacca decandra (lvs)

Cact.   Opuntia dillenii (fl.)

Magnoli.   Magnolia spp. (fl.)

Saurur.   Houttuynia cordata (lvs)

Guttif.   Hypericum perforatum (lvs)

The.   Camellia sinensis (lvs), *Stuartia?*

Papaver.   Papaver somniferum

Hamamelid.   many

Saxifrag.   Ribes nigrum (frt)

Ros.   Malus, Prunus, Pyrus (2), *Rosa, Sorbus*

Legum.   Acacia, Baptisia spp., *Bauhinia, Cercis, Phaseolus, Pisum* spp., *Trifolium*

Euphorbi.   Sapium sebiferum (lvs)

Tropaeol.   Tropaeolum majus (lvs)

Vit.   Vitis vinifera

Hippocastan.   Aesculus

Malv.　*Althaea, Gossypium* (2), *Hibiscus*
Tili.　*Tilia argentea* (fl.)
Begoni.　*Begonia* spp. (lvs, fl.)
Myrt.　*Eucalyptus sideroxylon* (lvs)
Corn.　*Cornus controversa* (lvs)
Umbell.　*Ammi visnaga* (plt), *Pastinaca sativa* (frt)
Eric.　*Rhododendron?*, *Vaccinium* (3)
Primul.　*Cyclamen* vars
Apocyn.　*Holarrhena floribunda* (lvs)
Asclepiad.　*Hemidesmus, Leptadenia, Telosma*
Convolvul.　*Ipomoea* sp. (tuber)
Solan.　*Nicotiana tabacum* (lvs, fl.), *Solanum* spp.
Scrophulari.　*Antirrhinum majus* (fl.)
Comp.　*Ambrosia, Arnica, Baeria, Bidens, Cosmos, Liatris, Solidago*
Gram.　*Poa pratensis, Zea*

Quercetin-3'-glucoside
Malv.　*Gossypium* spp. (fl.)

Quercetin-4'-glucoside (Spiraeoside)
Hamamelid.　*Hamamelis japonica* (fl.), and other spp.?
Ros.　*Filipendula hexapetala* (fl.), *Rosa* spp. and cultivars, *Spiraea*?
Legum.　*Ulex europaeus* (fl.)
Hippocastan.　*Aesculus hippocastanum* (sd)
Lili.　*Allium cepa* (bulb)

Quercetin-5-glucoside is unusually acid-labile.
Lab.　*Lamium album* (fl.)?

Quercetin-7-glucoside (Quercimeritrin)
Nymphae.　*Nelumbo nucifera* (fl.)
Ros.　*Prunus* (3)
Legum.　*Baptisia* spp. (lvs), *Ulex europaeus* (fl.)
Malv.　*Gossypium* (3), *Hibiscus*
Solan.　*Nicotiana tabacum*
Comp.　*Chrysanthemum* (2), *Helianthus, Matricaria, Viguiera*
Gram.　*Andropogon sorghum* (frt)

Quercetin-3-glucoside-7-rhamnoside
Tili.　*Tilia argentea* (lvs, fl.)
Comp.　*Liatris spicata* (plt)

Quercetin-3-glucoside-7-rutinoside
Legum.　*Baptisia* spp.

Quercetin-3-glucosylglucoside (Meratin; Quercetin-3-diglucoside)
Calycanth.　*Chimonanthus (Meratia) praecox* (fl.)
Eric.　*Vaccinium myrtillus* (frt)
Ole.　*Forsythia suspensa* (fl.)

Quercetin-3-glucosylglucuronide
   Nymphae.   Nelumbo nucifera (lvs)
   Comp.   Cosmos bipinnatus (lvs)
Quercetin-3-(2^G-glucosylrutinoside)
   Solan.   Solanum tuberosum (fl.) and other spp. ?
Quercetin-3-glucuronide
   Salic.   Populus grandidentata (lvs)
   Legum.   Phaseolus vulgaris (lvs), *Vicia faba* (lvs)
   Euphorbi.   Euphorbia cyparissias
   Vit.   Vitis vinifera (frt)
   Eric.   Gaultheria miqueliana (lvs)
Quercetin-7-glucuronide (Quercituron)
   Legum.   Phaseolus vulgaris (lvs)
   Lili.   Tulipa (lvs)
Quercetin-3-methyl ether
   Bruni.   Berzelia, Brunia, Nebelia, Staavia (as glycosides in all ?)
   Plumbagin.   Aegialitis annulata (lvs)
   Solan.   Nicotiana tabacum (calyx)
Quercetin-3-rhamninoside
   Rhamn.   Rhamnus spp. (bk, frt)
Quercetin-3-rhamnoside (Quercitrin): some of the records here are
   probably errors for *rutin.*
   Jugland.   Engelhardtia formosana (bk)
   Loranth.   Psittacanthus cuneifolius (lvs)
   Fag.   Quercus (3)
   Mor.   Humulus lupulus
   Laur.   Neolitsea sericea (young lvs)
   Illici.   Illicium anisatum (bk, fl.)
   Cercidiphyll.   Cercidiphyllum
   Saurur.   Houttuynia cordata (lvs)
   Eucryphi.   Eucryphia (2)
   The.   Camellia sinensis, Stuartia?
   Hamamelid.   many
   Saxifrag.   Ribes spp. (frt)
   Ros.   Agrimonia?, Malus, Prunus (2), *Rosa* spp.
   Legum.   Bauhinia, Lathyrus, Vicia
   Euphorbi.   Aleurites cordata
   Hippocastan.   Aesculus hippocastanum
   Vit.   Vitis vinifera
   Tili.   Tilia argentea (fl.)
   Myrt.   Eucalyptus sideroxylon (lvs)
   Eric.   Rhododendron (3), *Vaccinium* (2)
   Ole.   Forsythia?, Fraxinus excelsior

Plumbagin.   *Ceratostigma, Plumbago* (3)
Solan.   *Lycopersicon esculentum* (lvs, frt-skin)
Rubi.   *Crusea calocephala* (lvs)
Comp.   *Erigeron* spp., *Solidago* spp. (lvs)
Quercetin- ?-rhamnoside (not -3-)
  Eric.   *Vaccinium myrtillus* (lvs)
Quercetin-3-rhamnosylarabinoside
  Crucif.   *Cheiranthus cheiri* (frt)
Quercetin-3-rhamnosyldigalactoside
  Rhamn.   *Rhamnus* (frt)
Quercetin-3-rhamnosyldiglucoside
  The.   *Camellia* (lvs)
Quercetin-3-rhamnosylgalactoside
  Ros.   *Crataegus monogyna* (lvs)
Quercetin-3-rhamnosylxyloside
  Tili.   *Tilia argentea* (lvs)
Quercetin-3-robinobioside-7-rhamnoside
  Apocyn.   *Vinca minor* (lvs)
Quercetin-3-rutinoside (Eldrin; Globulariacitrin; Melin; Myrticolorin; Osyritrin; Paliuroside; Rutin, Sophorin; Violaquercitrin). This compound, familiarly known as *rutin*, is probably the most frequent *flavonol-glycoside* found in plants. The following list is probably inaccurate and incomplete, but it gives some idea of the distribution of *rutin*.
  Salic.   *Salix triandra* (lvs)
  Betul.   *Betula humilis* (lvs)
  Mor.   *Ficus carica* (lvs)
  Urtic.   *Boehmeria* spp. (lvs)
  Prote.   *Grevillea?, Leucadendron?, Protea concinnum* (lvs)
  Santal.   *Osyris compressa* (lvs)
  Loranth.   *Phrygilanthus flagellaris* (on *Acacia aroma*)
  Polygon.   *Fagopyrum, Polygonum, Rheum*
  Phytolacc.   *Phytolacca*
  Caryophyll.   *Herniaria glabra* (lvs)
  Magnoli.   *Magnolia* spp. (lvs, fl.)
  The.   *Camellia sinensis* (lvs)
  Crucif.   *Brassica, Bunias, Capsella*
  Capparid.   *Capparis?*
  Papaver.   *Eschscholtzia californica* (fl.)
  Hamamelid.   *Fothergilla monticola* (lvs)
  Crassul.   *Bryophyllum?*
  Saxifrag.   *Hydrangea?*
  Ros.   *Crataegus* (2), *Pourthiaea, Prunus, Pyrus*

    Legum.   Acacia, Baptisia spp., *Bauhinia, Daviesia*?, *Phaseolus,*
       Sophora, Tephrosia?
    Platan.   Platanus occidentalis (lvs)
    Euphorbi.   Aleurites cordata (lvs)
    Rut.   Boenninghausenia, Ruta
    Hippocastan.   Aesculus hippocastanum (lvs, fl.)
    Malv.   Abutilon, Gossypium, Hibiscus
    Sterculi.   Firmiana platanifolia (lvs)
    Elaeagn.   Hippophaë rhamnoides (frt)
    Rhamn.   Paliurus
    Begoni.   Begonia spp. (lvs, fl.)
    Viol.   Viola arvensis (lvs), × *wittrockiana* (fl.)
    Myrt.   Eucalyptus (5)
    Arali.   Acanthopanax (2), *Hedera*?
    Umbell.   Ammi, Bupleurum (2), *Heracleum*?, *Oenanthe, Pastinaca*
    Eric.   Rhododendron
    Primul.   Cyclamen vars
    Plumbagin.   Limonium gmelinii (rt)
    Ole.   Forsythia
    Apocyn.   Nerium oleander (lvs), *Vinca herbacea* (fl.)
    Asclepiad.   Calotropis, Hemidesmus, Heterostemma, Leptadenia,
      Marsdenia
    Menyanth.   Menyanthes trifoliata
    Solan.   Atropa, Hyoscyamus, Lycopersicon, Nicotiana, Solanum spp.
    Boragin.   Caccinia glauca (lvs), *Lithospermum arvense* (plt)
    Globulari.   Globularia
    Lab.   Leonurus quinquelobatus
    Caprifoli.   Sambucus canadensis (fl.)
    Rubi.   Galium
    Comp.   Artemisia, Eupatorium, Liatris, Nardosmia, Senecio, Soli-
      dago (4), *Tussilago*
    Lili.   Asparagus?, *Tulipa* cultivars (fl.)
    Gram.   Festuca pratensis
    Palmae.   Phoenix
Quercetin-7-rutinoside
    Legum.   Baptisia spp.
Quercetin-3-rutinoside-7-glucoside
    Legum.   Baptisia spp.
    Solan.   Nicotiana tabacum
Quercetin-3-rutinoside-7-glucuronide
    Lili.   Tulipa cultivars (lvs)
Quercetin-3-rutinoside-7-rhamnoside
    Viol.   Viola × *wittrockiana* (fl.)

Quercetin-3-sambubioside-3'-glucoside
  Hippocastan. Aesculus hippocastanum
Quercetin-3-sambubioside-7-glucoside
  Ranuncul. Helleborus foetidus (fl.)
Quercetin-3-sophoroside
  Betul. Alnus cordata (pollen)
  Ros. Rosa spp. and cultivars, *Sorbus aucuparia* (fl.)
  Legum. Pisum spp. (lvs)
  Malv. Gossypium barbadense (fl.), *Hibiscus mutabilis* (fl.)
  Primul. Primula sinensis (fl.)
  Solan. Petunia hybrida (fl.), *Solanum* spp.
Quercetin-3-sophoroside-7-glucoside
  Solan. Petunia cultivar (lvs)
Quercetin-3-sophorotrioside
  Legum. Pisum sativum (lvs), and other spp. ?
Quercetin-triglucoside
  Caryophyll. Herniaria glabra
  The. Camellia (lvs)
Quercetin-3-triglycoside
  Eucryphi. Eucryphia moorei (lvs)
Quercetin-3-xyloside (Reynoutrin)
  Polygon. Reynoutria (Polygonum) japonica (lvs)
  Loranth. Psittacanthus cuneifolius (lvs)
  Ros. Malus pumila (bk, frt)
  Begoni. Begonia spp. (lvs, fl.)
Quercetin-3-(xylosylglucoside)-7-glucoside
  Ranuncul. Helleborus foetidus
Rhamnazin (Quercetin-3',7-dimethyl ether; fig. 125)
  Polygon. Polygonum (as sulfuric ester) ?
  Rhamn. Rhamnus?
Rhamnazin-3-rhamninoside
  Rhamn. Rhamnus spp. (bk, frt)
Rhamnetin (Quercetin-7-methyl ether; fig. 125)
  Rhamn. Rhamnus cathartica (frts, free ?)
Rhamnetin-glycoside
  Moring. Moringa oleifera (fl.)
Rhamnetin-3-rhamninoside (Xanthorhamnin)
  Euphorbi. Euphorbia hirta?
  Rhamn. Rhamnus spp. (bk, frt)
Robinetin (Norkanugin)
  Legum. Gleditsia monosperma (htwd), *Millettia stuhlmanni* (htwd),
    Robinia?

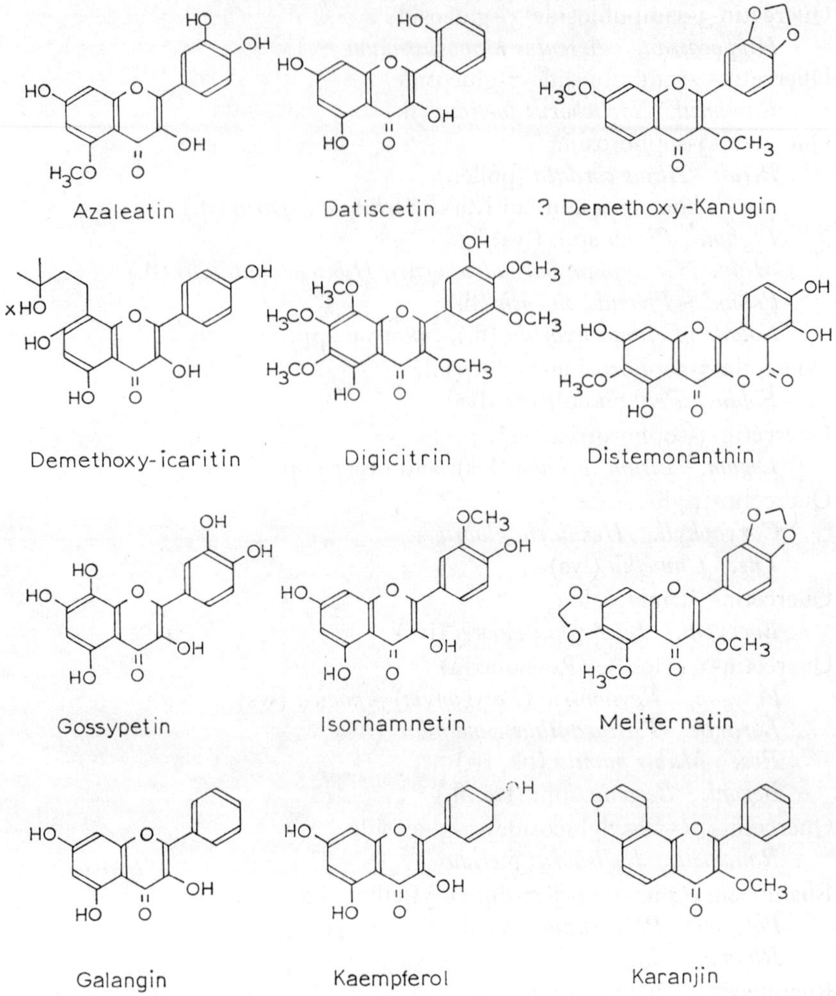

Azaleatin   Datiscetin   ? Demethoxy-Kanugin

Demethoxy-icaritin   Digicitrin   Distemonanthin

Gossypetin   Isorhamnetin   Meliternatin

Galangin   Kaempferol   Karanjin

Fig. 124. Some flavonols.

Sericetin (fig. 125) may have a slightly different formula from that
shown.

> Legum. *Mundulea sericea* (bk), which also has *mundulone* (an
> *isoflavone*) and *munduserone*

Serotrin may be identical with *incarnatrin*.

> Ros. *Prunus serotina*

Syringetin (Myricetin-3′,5′-dimethyl ether)
Syringetin-glycosides

> Legum. *Lathyrus pratensis*

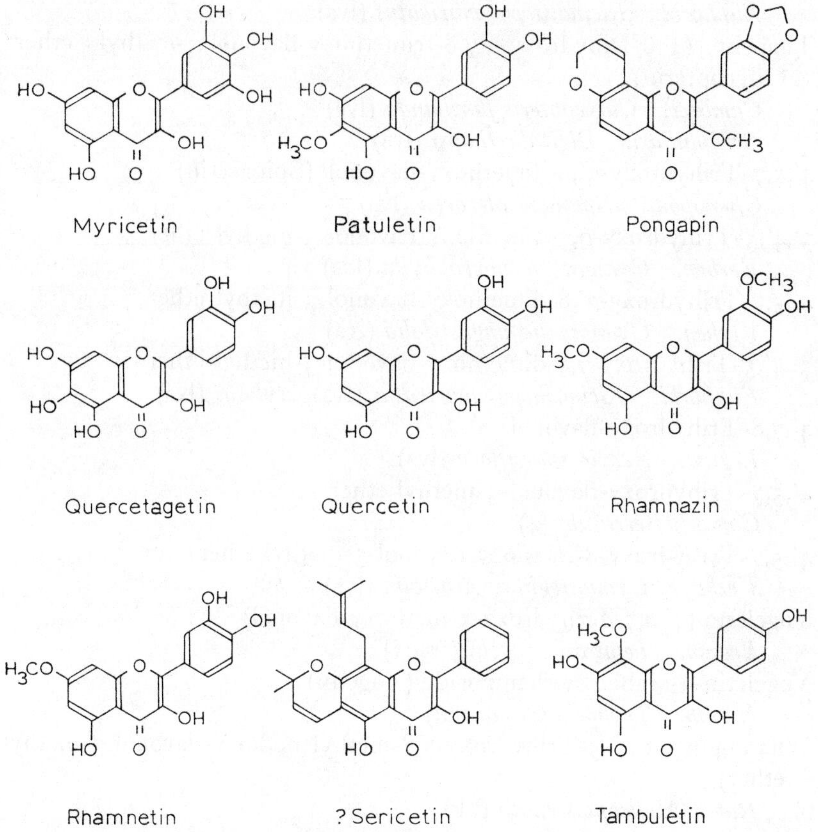

Myricetin   Patuletin   Pongapin

Quercetagetin   Quercetin   Rhamnazin

Rhamnetin   ? Sericetin   Tambuletin

Fig. 125. Some flavonols.

Tamarixetin (Quercetin-4'-methyl ether)
  Tamaric. Tamarix (lvs)
  Apocyn. Thevetia nereifolia (fl., as glycoside)
Tamarixetin-glycoside (Tamarixin)
  Tamaric. Tamarix troupii (lvs)
Tambuletin (8-Methoxy-kaempferol)
  Rut. Zanthoxylum acanthopodium (sd)
Tambuletin-4',7-dimethyl ether (Tambulin)
  Rut. Zanthoxylum acanthopodium (frt)
Ternatin (4',5-Dihydroxy-3',7,8-trimethoxy-flavonol-3-methyl ether)
  Rut. Melicope simplex (bk), *ternata* (bk)
3',4',7,8-Tetrahydroxy-flavonol
  Legum. Acacia melanoxylon (htwd)

3',4',5,7-Tetrahydroxy-8-methoxy-flavonol-3-methyl ether
    Euphorbi. *Ricinocarpos muricatus* (lvs)
Thapsin   (4',6-Dihydroxy-5,7,8-trimethoxy-flavonol-3-methyl ether;
  Calycopterin)
    Combret. *Calycopteris floribunda* (lvs)
    Scrophulari. *Digitalis thapsi* (lvs)
4',5,7-Trihydroxy-3',6-dimethoxy-flavonol (Spinacetin)
    Chenopodi. *Spinacia oleracea* (lvs)
3',4',5-Trihydroxy-6,7-dimethoxy-flavonol-3-methyl ether
    Verben. *Cyanostegia microphylla* (lvs)
4',5,7-Trihydroxy-3',8-dimethoxy-flavonol-3-methyl ether
    Verben. *Cyanostegia angustifolia* (lvs)
3',4',5-Trihydroxy-7,8-dimethoxy-flavonol-3-methyl ether
    Euphorbi. *Ricinocarpos muricatus* (lvs), *stylosus* (lvs)
4',7,8-Trihydroxy-flavonol
    Legum. *Acacia sparsiflora* (lvs)
4',5,7-Trihydroxy-flavonol-3-methyl ether
    Comp. *Serratula* (4)
4',5,7-Trihydroxy-8-methoxy-flavonol-3-methyl ether
    Verben. *Cyanostegia angustifolia* (lvs)
Vogeletin (4',6,7-Trihydroxy-5-methoxy-flavonol)
    Legum. *Tephrosia vogelii* (free?)
Vogeletin-3-arabinosylrhamnoside (Vogelin)
    Legum. *Tephosia vogelii* (sd)
Wharangin (3',4',5-Trihydroxy-7,8-methylenedioxy-flavonol-3-methyl
  ether)
    Rut. *Melicope ternata* (bk)

XI HOMO-ISOFLAVONES

GENERAL

Böhler and Tamm (1967) report the isolation of two substances, *eucomin* and *eucomol* (fig. 126), which they describe as the first of a new class of natural product, the *homo-isoflavones*. One feels that they should have been called 'homo-isoflavanones' (fig. 126).

List and Occurrence
Eucomin (fig. 126)
    Lili. *Eucomis bicolor* (bu.)
Eucomol (fig. 126)
    Lili. *Eucomis bicolor* (bu.)

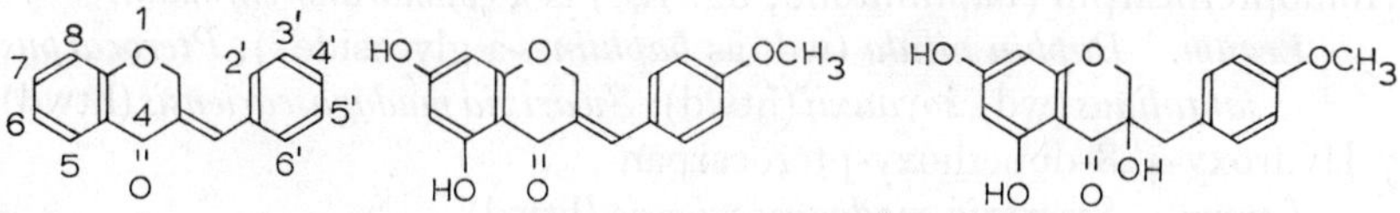

Fig. 126. 'Homo-isoflavone' and some related flavonoids.

XII ISOFLAVANONES

GENERAL

This small but interesting group of substances may be considered to be derived from *isoflavanone* (fig. 127), which does not, I think, occur as such in higher plants.

A few simple *isoflavanones* are known, but many—such as *rotenone* (fig. 127) and the 'rotenoids'—are quite complex. A few of these more complex substances are called *coumarano-chromans* by Ollis (in Geissman, 1962).

Because of their economic importance, the 'rotenoids'—which are confined (completely?) to the *Leguminosae*—have been much investigated, and that family has been found to contain many *isoflavanones*. Though some 'rotenoids' may occur in other families, they must be very rare or they would surely have been detected before this.

Note the occurrence of *isoflavanones* in *Swartzia*, which has been removed from the *Leguminosae* by some authors (see *Swartziaceae*), and in the *Rosaceae* (*Prunus*).

List and Occurrence

Deguelin (fig. 127)
    Legum. Derris, Lonchocarpus, Tephrosia (2)
7,8-Dimethoxy-3',4'-methylenedioxy-pterocarpan
    Legum. Swartzia madagascariensis (htwd)
Elliptone (Derrid; Elliptol?) is closely related to *deguelin*.
    Legum. Derris elliptica (wd), *malaccensis*
Ferreirin (2',5,7-Trihydroxy-4'-methoxy-isoflavanone; fig. 127)
    Legum. Ferreirea spectabilis (htwd)
Homoferreirin (5,7-Dihydroxy-2',4'-dimethoxy-isoflavanone)
    Legum. Ferreirea spectabilis (htwd), *Ougeinia dalbergioides* (htwd)

Homopterocarpin (Baphinitone; fig. 127) is a *coumarano-chroman*.
>   *Legum.*   *Baphia nitida* (wd, as *baphiin*—a glycoside?); *Pterocarpus santalinus* (wd), *soyauxii* (htwd); *Swartzia madagascariensis* (htwd)

7-Hydroxy-4′,8-dimethoxy-pterocarpan
>   *Legum.*   *Swartzia madagascariensis* (htwd)

7-Hydroxy-8-methoxy-3′,4′-methylenedioxy-pterocarpan
>   *Legum.*   *Swartzia madagascariensis* (htwd)

7-Hydroxy-4′-methoxy-pterocarpan
>   *Legum.*   *Andira inermis* (htwd); *Swartzia madagascariensis* (htwd)

?-Hydroxy-rotenone
>   *Legum.*   *Mundulea suberosa* (bk)

Inermin (Maackiain; fig. 127)
>   *Legum.*   *Andira inermis* (wd), *Maackia*, *Sophora*

Inermin-7-glucoside (Trifolirhizin)
>   *Legum.*   *Trifolium pratense* (rt)

Isomillettone is a 'rotenoid'.
>   *Legum.*   *Piscidia erythrina* (rt)

Isotephrosin
>   *Legum.*   *Lonchocarpus nicou* (rt)

Malaccol (5-Hydroxy-elliptone)
>   *Legum.*   *Derris elliptica* (rt), *malaccensis*

Millettone is a 'rotenoid'.
>   *Legum.*   *Millettia dura* (sd), *Piscidia erythrina* (rt)

Munduserone
>   *Legum.*   *Mundulea sericea* (bk)

Neotenone
>   *Legum.*   *Neorautanenia pseudopachyrrhizus*

Nepusidine: belongs here?
>   *Legum.*   *Neorautanenia pseudopachyrrhizus* (rts)

Ougenin (2′,4′,5-Trihydroxy-7-methoxy-6-methyl-isoflavanone)
>   *Legum.*   *Ougeinia dalbergioides* (htwd)

Pachyrhizone
>   *Legum.*   *Pachyrhizus erosus* (sd)

Padmakastein (Dihydro-prunetin) occurs free in
>   *Ros.*   *Prunus puddum* (bk)

Padmakastin is said to be a glycoside of *padmakastein*.
>   *Ros.*   *Prunus puddum* (bk)

Phaseollin is a *phytoalexin*.
>   *Legum.*   *Phaseolus vulgaris* (plt, when invaded by fungi)

Pisatin (fig. 127) is a *phytoalexin*.
>   *Legum.*   *Pisum sativum* (plt, when invaded by fungi)

Pterocarpin (Inermin-7-methyl ether)
>   *Legum.*   *Baphia nitida* (wd); *Pterocarpus* (3)

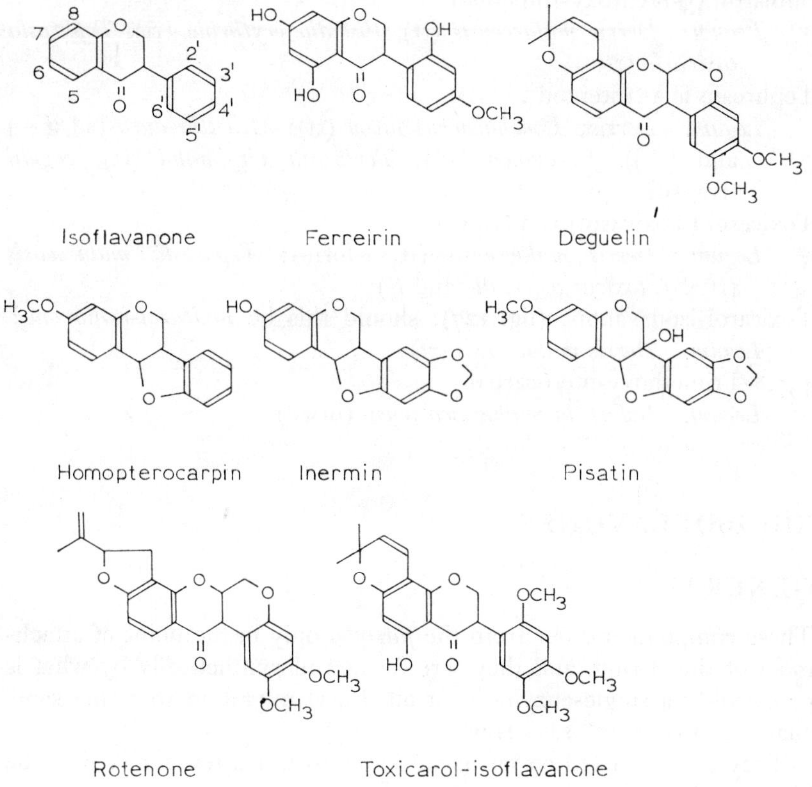

Fig. 127. Some isoflavanones.

Rotenone (Derrin; Tubotoxin; fig. 127) has been greatly studied, together with the other 'rotenoids', because of their importance as insecticides. According to Jones (1942) at least 65 legumes were known at that time to have 'rotenoids'. These included *Derris* (12), *Lonchocarpus* (12), *Millettia* (10), *Mundulea* (2), and *Tephrosia* (21). Jones says that the records of *rotenone* in *Paullinia*, *Polygonum*, and *Tillandsia* (all non-legumes) are probably erroneous. Harborne (1967) adds *Pachyrhizus*, *Neorautanenia*, *Piscidia*, and *Andira* to the list of plants containing 'rotenoids'. He gives reports of occurrence in *Myrica nagi* (*Myric.*) and *Verbascum thapsus* (*Scrophulari.*). Have these been thoroughly checked? My records for *rotenone* include

> *Legum.* *Derris* (4), *Lonchocarpus* (3), *Millettia* (2), *Mundulea*,
> *Pachyrhizus*, *Piscidia*, *Spatholobus*, *Tephrosia* (5)

Sophorol (2',7-Dihydroxy-4',5'-methylenedioxy-isoflavanone)

> *Legum.* *Sophora?*

Sumatrol (5-Hydroxy-rotenone)
> *Legum.   Derris malaccensis* (rt), *Piscidia erythrina* (rt), *Tephrosia*
> *toxicaria* (rt)

Tephrosin is a 'rotenoid'.
> *Legum.   Derris*; *Lonchocarpus nicou* (rt); *Millettia dura* (sd, (−)
> and (±)), *ferruginea* (sd); *Tephrosia virginiana* (rt), *vogelii*
> (lvs, sd)

Toxicarol (Toxicarin) is a 'rotenoid'.
> *Legum.   Derris malaccensis* (rt, *l*-form); *Tephrosia malaccensis*
> (rt, *l*-), *toxicaria* (rt, *dl*- and *l*-)

Toxicarol-isoflavanone (fig. 127): should this be *toxicarol-isoflavone*?
> *Legum.   Derris malaccensis* (rt)

4',7,8-Trimethoxy-pterocarpan
> *Legum.   Swartzia madagascariensis* (htwd)

XIII ISOFLAVONES

GENERAL

These compounds differ from the *flavones* only in the point of attachment of the B-ring, and they 'are formed biosynthetically by what is presumably a single-enzyme controlled aryl migration from the same chalcone precursor', says Harborne (1967).

They are restricted so far as we know to but a few families of the higher plants. Thus the *Leguminosae* have many, but restricted essentially to the *Faboideae* (p. 1663). The genus *Prunus*, of the related *Rosaceae*, has a few. The family *Moraceae* has a few *isoflavones* of unusual types. Finally the monocotyledonous family *Iridaceae* has some *isoflavones*.

List and Occurrence

Afrormosin (7-Hydroxy-4',6-dimethoxy-isoflavone) occurs free (?) in
> *Legum.   Afrormosia (Pericopsis) elata* (htwd), *Amphimas ptero-*
> *carpoides* (htwd), *Baptisia australis* (lvs, st.), *Castanospermum*
> *australe*, *Glycine*, *Myrocarpus fastigiatus* (wd), *Myroxylon*
> *balsamum* (wd), *Wisteria*

Afrormosin-7-glucoside
> *Legum.   Baptisia australis* (lvs, st.), *Wisteria floribunda* (fl.)

Baptigenin (3',4',5',7-Tetrahydroxy-isoflavone)
> *Legum.   Baptisia* (rt, free ?)

Baptigenin- ?-dirhamnoside (Baptisin)
> *Legum.   Baptisia*

Biochanin-A (Olmelin ?; Genistein-4'-methyl ether) occurs free (?) in
> *Legum.* *Andira inermis* (wd), *Cicer, Ferreirea, Gleditsia triacanthos* (frt, *olmelin*), *Trifolium* (2)

Biochanin-A-7-apiosylglucoside
> *Legum.* *Dalbergia lanceolata* (rtbk)

Biochanin-A-7-β-D-glucoside (Sissotrin)
> *Legum.* *Cicer arietinum* (lvs), *Dalbergia sissoo* (lvs)

Cabriuvin (3',4',7-Trimethoxy-isoflavone)
> *Legum.* *Myrocarpus fastigiatus* (htwd), *Myroxylon balsamum* (wd)

Calycosin (3',7-Dihydroxy-4'-methoxy-isoflavone) occurs free (?) in
> *Legum.* *Baptisia calycosa, lecontei* (lvs)

Calycosin-7-glucoside
> *Legum.* *Baptisia lecontei* (lvs)

Calycosin-7-rhamnosylglucoside
> *Legum.* *Baptisia lecontei* (lvs)

Caviunin (5,7-Dihydroxy-2',4',5',6-tetramethoxy-isoflavone)
> *Legum.* *Dalbergia nigra*

Daidzein (? Tatoin; 4',7-Dihydroxy-isoflavone; fig. 128) occurs free (?) and as several glycosides.
> *Legum.* *Baptisia lecontei* (lvs), *Cicer, Genista, Glycine, Psoralea, Pueraria* (as *puerarin*), *Trifolium*

Daidzein-7-glucoside (Daidzin)
> *Legum.* *Baptisia lecontei* (lvs), *Glycine*

Daidzein-7-rhamnosylglucoside
> *Legum.* *Baptisia lecontei* (lvs)

Dehydro-deguelin (fig. 128) is essentially an *isoflavone*.
> *Legum.* *Derris* sp. (rt), *Millettia dura* (sd), *Tephrosia vogelii* (sd)

Dehydro-millettone: belongs here?
> *Legum.* *Piscidia erythrina* (rt)

Dehydro-rotenone
> *Legum.* *Tephrosia virginiana* (rt)

Dehydro-toxicarol (Dehydro-toxicarin) differs only slightly from *dehydro-deguelin* and *dehydro-rotenone*.
> *Legum.* *Derris* sp. (rt)

4',5-Dihydroxy-6,7-dimethoxy-isoflavone (7-Methyl-tectorigenin)
> *Legum.* *Dalbergia sissoo* (fl.), *Pterocarpus angolensis* (htwd)

4',7-Dimethoxy-pterocarpen
> *Legum.* *Swartzia madagascariensis* (htwd)

Durlettone
> *Legum.* *Millettia dura* (sd)

Durmillone
> *Legum.* *Millettia dura* (sd)

Formononetin (Biochanin-B; Daidzein-4'-methyl ether; Ononetin) occurs free (?) in

> Legum. *Baptisia australis* (lvs, st.), *sphaerocarpa*; *Castanospermum australe*; *Cicer*; *Ononis spinosa*; *Trifolium*

Formononetin-7-glucoside (Ononin)

> Legum. *Baptisia australis* (lvs, st.), *Ononis spinosa* (rt), *Trifolium repens?*

Genistein (Genisteol; Prunetol; Sophoricol; fig. 128) occurs free or as glycosides in

> Ros. *Prunus*
>
> Legum. *Baptisia lecontei* (lvs), *Genista, Glycine, Lupinus, Sarothamnus, Sophora, Trifolium, Ulex*

Genistein-4'-glucoside (Sophoricoside)

> Legum. *Sophora japonica* (frt)

Genistein-7-glucoside (Genistin)

> Legum. *Genista, Glycine*

Genistein-5-methyl ether

> Legum. *Cytisus laburnum* (wd), *Genista hispanica*

Genistein-7-rutinoside

> Legum. *Baptisia sphaerocarpa*

Genistein-4'-sophorabioside (Sophorabioside)

> Legum. *Sophora*

6-Hydroxy-genistein (4',5,6,7-Tetrahydroxy-isoflavone)

> Legum. *Baptisia hirsuta* (plt)

6-Hydroxy-genistein-7-rhamnosylglucoside

> Legum. *Baptisia hirsuta* (plt)

Ichthynone

> Legum. *Piscidia erythrina* (rt)

Irigenin (3',5,7-Trihydroxy-4',5',6-trimethoxy-isoflavone; fig. 128)

> Irid. *Iris germanica* (rhiz.), *nepalensis*

Irigenin-7-glucoside (Iridin)

> Irid. *Belamcanda chinensis* (rt); *Iris kumaoensis, pallida*

Irisolidone (5,7-Dihydroxy-4',6-dimethoxy-isoflavone)

> Irid. *Iris nepalensis* (trace)

Irisolone (fig. 128)

> Irid. *Iris nepalensis* (rtstk)

Isoflavone (fig. 128), unlike *flavone*, does not, I think, occur in Nature.

Iso-osajin

> Mor. *Maclura?*

Iso-puerarin (Daidzein-6-C-glucoside)

> Occurrence ?

Jamaicin

> Legum. *Piscidia erythrina* (rt., bk)

Lisetin
> *Legum.* *Piscidia erythrina* (rt)

Maxima-substance-A (fig. 128)
> *Legum.* *Tephrosia maxima* (rt)

Maxima-substance-B
> *Legum.* *Tephrosia maxima* (rt)

Maxima-substance-C
> *Legum.* *Tephrosia maxima* (rt)

8-Methyl-genistein
> *Legum.* *Glycine max*

Milldurone
> *Legum.* *Millettia dura* (sd)

Mundulone
> *Legum.* *Mundulea sericea* (rtbk)

Munetone is said to be highly toxic to fish!
> *Legum.* *Mundulea suberosa*

Muningin (4′,6-Dihydroxy-5,7-dimethoxy-isoflavone)
> *Legum.* *Pterocarpus angolensis* (htwd)

Orobol (Norsantal; Santol; 3′,4′,5,7-Tetrahydroxy-isoflavone) occurs free (?) in
> *Legum.* *Baptisia lecontei* (lvs), *Lathyrus montanus* (*Orobus tuberosus*) (rt), *Pterocarpus*

Orobol- ?-glucoside (Norsantal; Oroboside)
> *Legum.* *Lathyrus macrorrhizus, montanus*

Orobol-7-rutinoside
> *Legum.* *Baptisia lecontei* (lvs)

Osajin (fig. 128) is closely related to *iso-osajin* and *pomiferin.*
> *Mor.* *Maclura pomifera* (frt)

Osajin-5-methyl ether
> *Legum.* *Derris scandens* (rt)

Piscerythrone
> *Legum.* *Piscidia erythrina* (rt)

Piscidone
> *Legum.* *Piscidia erythrina* (rt)

Pomiferin (3′-Hydroxy-osajin)
> *Mor.* *Maclura pomifera* (frt)

Prunetin (Prunusetin; Genistein-7-methyl ether)
> *Ros.* *Prunus*
> *Legum.* *Pterocarpus angolensis* (free ?)

Prunetin- ?-glucoside (Prunitrin; Prunitroside)
> *Ros.* *Prunus*

Pseudo-baptigenin (7-Hydroxy-3′,4′-methylenedioxy-isoflavone)
> *Legum.* *Baptisia lecontei* (lvs), *tinctoria* (rt); *Maackia amurensis*

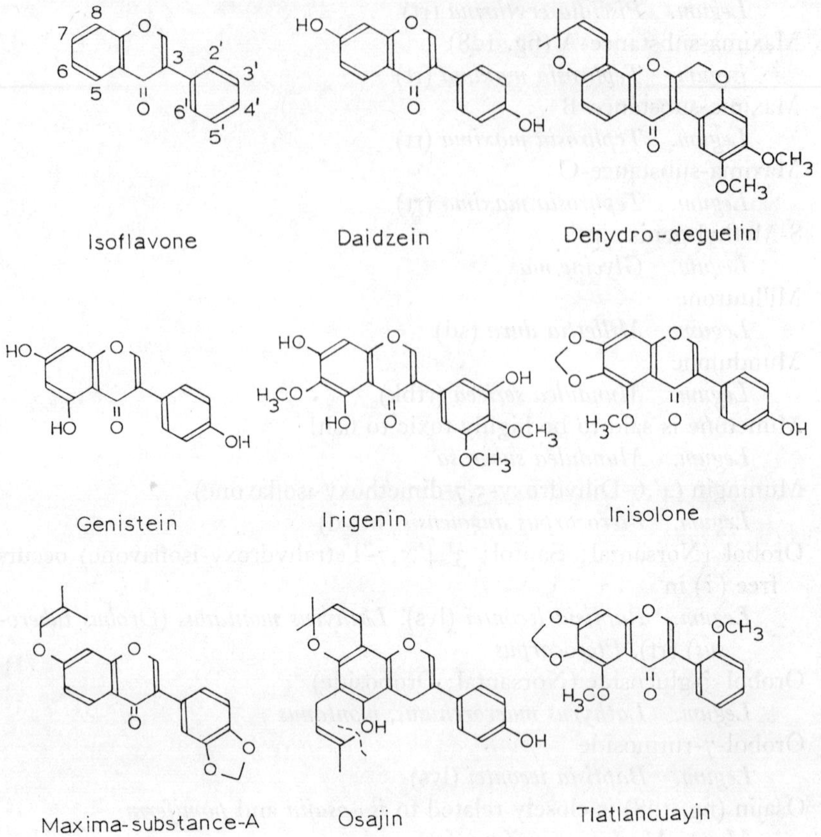

Fig. 128. Some isoflavones.

Pseudo-baptigenin-7-rhamnoglucoside
    Legum.   *Baptisia lecontei* (lvs), *tinctoria*
Puerarin (Daidzein-8-*C*-glucoside)
    Legum.   *Pueraria thunbergiana* (rt)
Puerarin-?-xyloside
    Legum.   *Pueraria thunbergiana* (rt)
Santal (Orobol-7-methyl ether)
    Legum.   *Baphia nitida, Pterocarpus santalinus* (wd)
Scandenone is an isomer of *osajin.*
    Legum.   *Derris scandens* (rt)
Sphaerobioside: belongs here?
    Legum.   *Baptisia lecontei* (lvs), *sphaerocarpa*

Tatoin may be *daidzein* or *4',5-dihydroxy-8-methyl-isoflavone* (I have both formulae from different sources).
    Legum. Glycine
Tectorigenin (4',5,7-Trihydroxy-6-methoxy-isoflavone) occurs free (?) or as glycosides in
    Legum. Baptisia (lvs), *Dalbergia sissoo* (fl.)
    Irid. Iris tectorum (rhiz.)
Tectorigenin-7-glucoside (Shekanin; Tectoridin)
    Irid. Belamcanda, Iris
Tlatlancuayin (fig. 129)
    Amaranth. Iresine celosioides (plt)
Toxicarol-isoflavone is closely related to *dehydro-deguelin*.
    Legum. Derris malaccensis (rt)
4',6,7-Trihydroxy-isoflavone
    Legum. Glycine max (sd)
3',5,7-Trihydroxy-4'-methoxy-isoflavone (Orobol-4'-methyl ether)
    Legum. Trifolium pratense

XIV NEOFLAVANOIDS

GENERAL

Eyton, Ollis, Sutherland, Gottlieb, Magalhães and Jackman (1966), in the first of a series of papers entitled 'The neoflavanoid group of natural products', point out that 2-, 3-, and *4-aryl-chroman* types of flavonoids may occur in Nature (fig. 129). They say: 'The dalbergiones represent a new class of natural quinones belonging to a group of natural products for which we suggest the general name neoflavanoids.'

The neoflavanoids have been found so far only in a few species of the closely related genera *Dalbergia* (which has about 300 species) and *Machaerium* (about 150), which are placed in *Faboideae–Dalbergieae–Dalbergiinae*; and recently (Sánchez-Viesca, 1969) in *Exostemma caribaeum* (*Rubiaceae*); but probably no detailed search has yet been made for them elsewhere.

It will be seen from the following list that only some of them are *quinones*. Others are *quinols*, and yet others *coumarins*.

List and Occurrence

Dalbergin (fig. 129) is a *coumarin*.
    Legum. Dalbergia latifolia, sissoo; *Machaerium scleroxylon* (spwd and htwd)
Dalbergione (fig. 129) is a *quinone*. The substance originally called

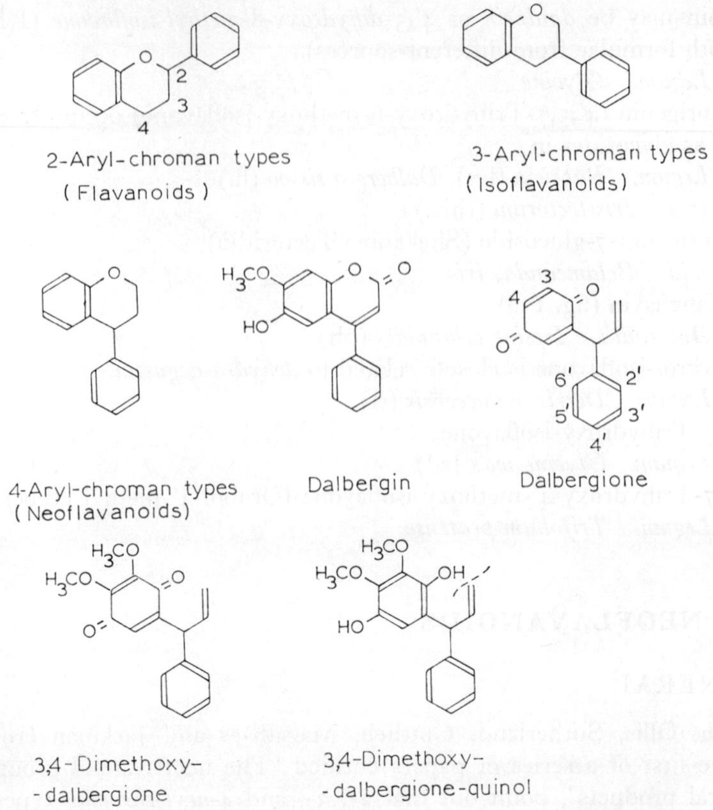

2-Aryl-chroman types
(Flavanoids)

3-Aryl-chroman types
(Isoflavanoids)

4-Aryl-chroman types
(Neoflavanoids)

Dalbergin

Dalbergione

3,4-Dimethoxy-
-dalbergione

3,4-Dimethoxy-
-dalbergione-quinol

Fig. 129. 2-,3-, and 4-aryl-chromans and some neoflavanoids.

'dalbergione' was the 4-methoxy-derivative. I have no record that *dalbergione* occurs free.

3,4-Dimethoxy-dalbergione (fig. 129)
    Legum.   *Machaerium scleroxylon* (htwd)
4,4′-Dimethoxy-dalbergione
    Legum.   *Dalbergia nigra* (htwd)
3,4-Dimethoxy-dalbergione-quinol (Machaerium-quinol; fig. 129)
    Legum.   *Machaerium scleroxylon* (htwd)
2′,5-Di-*O*-methyl-latifolin
    Legum.   *Dalbergia latifolia* (htwd)
Exostemin
    Rubi.   *Exostemma caribaeum*
4′-Hydroxy-4-methoxy-dalbergione
    Legum.   *Dalbergia nigra* (htwd), *violacea* (htwd, but with a different configuration)

Latifolin

   Legum.   *Dalbergia cochinchinensis* (htwd, R-form ?), *latifolia* (htwd, R- ?)

Latifolinone (2′,4-Dimethoxy-dalbergione) may arise by oxidation from the methyl ether of *latifolin*.

Melannein

   Legum.   *Dalbergia baroni, melanoxylon*

4-Methoxy-dalbergione was originally called 'dalbergione'.

   Legum.   *Dalbergia baroni* (wd, S-form), *latifolia* (htwd, R-), *violacea* (S-)

6-*O*-Methyl-dalbergin (Dalbergin-6-methyl ether)

   Legum.   *Dalbergia latifolia, sissoo*; *Machaerium scleroxylon* (spwd, htwd)

5-*O*-Methyl-latifolin

   Legum.   *Dalbergia cochinchinensis* (htwd, R-)

FURAN DERIVATIVES

GENERAL

Dean, who deals with these substances in chapters 1 and 5 of his *Naturally Occurring Oxygen Ring Compounds* (1963), says that they are known from insects (*Dendrolasius* has *dendrolasin*), from higher animals (the beaver has *castoramine*), from fungi, and from higher plants.

   Little is known of the biogenesis of these compounds, he says, but most of them are terpenoid and of patterns 1 to 3 (fig. 130).

   Several *furan derivatives* that have been described are believed to arise secondarily during extraction or other treatment of plant materials.

   As in so many other cases we are faced with difficulties in classification, and many *furan derivatives* have been discussed elsewhere in this book. We may note:

   Alkaloids   *nupharidine, nupharamine*
   Chalcones   *pongamol (lanceolatin-C)*
   Acetylenic compounds   *atractylodin, carlina oxide*
   Terpenoids   a fairly long list

   We may include here:

   I. *Furan* (fig. 130) and its derivatives—16 listed.
   II. *Benzofuran* (*Coumarone*; fig. 130) and its derivatives—7 listed.
   III. *Dibenzofuran* (*Diphenylene oxide*; fig. 130) and its derivatives— none occurring in higher plants?

I FURANS

List and Occurrence

α-Clausenane: a diene related to *perillene*?
  Rut.   Clausena willdenowii (leaf-oil)
β-Dehydro-elsholtzione (Naginata ketone)
  Lab.   Elsholtzia oldhamii (ess. oil), *Perilla frutescens*
4,5-Dimethyl-furan-3-aldehyde occurs in oil of cloves, but is an artefact?
Elsholtzione (fig. 130) was, says Dean (1963), the first *isoprenoid furan* to be investigated.
  Lab.   Elsholtzia cristata (leaf-oil), *oldhamii* (leaf-oil)
Furan (Furane; Furfurane; Tetraphenol; fig. 130) occurs in wood-oil, but secondarily? Does it ever occur naturally?
Furfural (Furfuraldehyde; Furole; Furfurole) has been found in many essential oils, but as an artefact. It is said to occur (naturally?) in
  Comp.   Atractylodes lancea (rhiz.)
α-Furfuryl alcohol is said to occur (secondarily?) in oils of cloves and of roasted coffee.
β-Furoic acid (Furan-β-carbonic acid) has been found in
  Legum.   Phaseolus multiflorus (rt)
  Celastr.   Euonymus atropurpureus (rt), *europeus* (sd)
  Solan.   Nicotiana (in tobacco)
  Myopor.   Myoporum acuminatum (ess. oil)
Ipomoeamarone is the optical antipode of *ngaione*. It occurs in diseased sweet potatoes (*Ipomoea*).
Ipomeanine accompanies *ipomoeamarone*.
5-Methyl-furfuraldehyde (5-Methyl-furfural; α-Methyl-furfural) is said to occur naturally (?) in green algae. It occurs secondarily in oil of cloves, etc.
Myoporone
  Myopor.   Myoporum bontioides (lvs)
Ngaione (fig. 130) is the optical antipode of *ipomoeamarone*.
  Myopor.   Myoporum acuminatum (lf-oil), *laetum* (lf-oil)
Perilla ketone (fig. 130)
  Lab.   Perilla frutescens (ess. oil)
Perillene (Perillone; fig. 130)
  Lab.   Perilla citriodora
Sylvan (Silvan; α-Methyl-furan) occurs in oils but secondarily in all (?) cases.

II BENZOFURANS

List and Occurrence

Benzofuran (Coumarone; fig. 130): does not occur free in Nature?
Egonol (fig. 130) is said to occur free and as a glycoside.
    Styrac. *Styrax americana* (sd-oil), *formosana* (sd-oil), *japonica*
      ('Egonoki', sd-oil), *obassia* (sd-oil)
Egonol glycoside yields *egonol* and 2 × *glucose.*
    Styrac. *Styrax formosana* (sd-oil?)
Euparin (fig. 130)
    Comp. *Eupatorium cannabinum* (rt), *purpureum* (rt)
Evodone (fig. 130)
    Rut. *Evodia hortensis* (lvs)
Furocoumarinic acid glucoside yields *psoralene* and *glucose.*
    Legum. *Coronilla glauca* (sd)
Melanoxin is a 2,3-*dihydro-benzofuran.*
    Legum. *Dalbergia melanoxylon*
Menthofurane (fig. 130) autoxidizes to *peperic acid*—which also occurs
  naturally?
    Lab. *Mentha piperita* (fl.-oil)

III DIBENZOFURANS

List and Occurrence

Several members of this group—*didymic acid, strepsilin, usnic acid,*
etc.—are found in lichens. I have no record of them from higher plants,
but they are likely to be found.
    Dibenzofuran (Diphenylene oxide; fig. 130) has not, I think, been
found in Nature.

GLYCOSIDES

GENERAL

Nearly twenty years ago McIlroy (1951) produced a little book called
The Plant Glycosides. In it he refers to general works on the subject, all
published yet twenty years earlier. There has not, I think, been a
recent work to compare with these.
    McIlroy recognized several groups of *glycosides*: those of *alcohols*

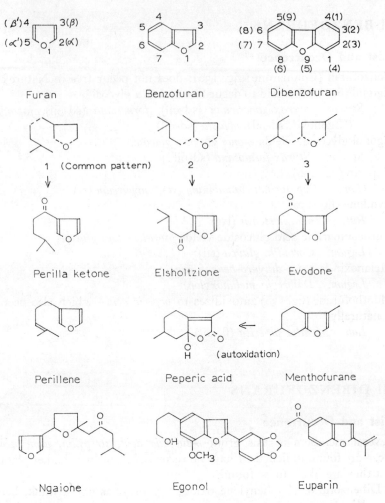

Fig. 130. Furan and furan derivatives.

and *phenols*, the *cyanogenic glycosides*, *thioglycosides*, some of the *flavo-noid glycosides* (which he called phenyl benzopyrone glycosides), *anthocyanins*, *coumarin glycosides*, *saponins*, *Solanum alkaloids*, *cardiac glycosides*, *anthraquinone glycosides*, *nucleosides*, and '*other*' *glycosides*. He was able to deal with these in less than one hundred pages!

Paris (in Swain, 1963) has reviewed the distribution of glycosides in plants. We may quote from him (italics mine):

Glycosides are organic compounds in which there is usually a semi-acetal linkage between the reducing group of a sugar and an alcoholic or phenolic hydroxyl group of a second molecule called an aglycone.

This link, being effected through oxygen, gives rise to the *O-glycosides* which are the most common in plants. These compounds are easily hydrolysed to the parent sugar and the aglycone by either enzymes or acids. The oxygen bridge of the sugar ring is retained, and thus one can have furanose or pyranose glycosides, the latter being the more common. Also, since the sugar moiety can exist in either α- or β-forms, one can obtain both α- and β-glycosides.

Two other groups of glycosides are known which involve a semi-acetal type of linkage. If the reducing group of the sugar is linked to a thiol, one obtains *S-glycosides* [e.g. *sinigrin*, fig. 166], which are less common than those mentioned above, and are somewhat restricted to particular families (Cruciferae, Tropaeolaceae, Resedaceae). The second group comprises the *N-glycosides*, which involve linkage to an amino-group... [e.g. *vicine* and *crotonoside*].

Several glycosides are known where the sugar moiety is not a true sugar, but a derivative such as uronic acid... [e.g. *glycyrrhizin*].

Finally, there is a group of compounds known as *C-glycosides*, which resist normal acid hydrolysis... [e.g. *aloin, vitexin, orientin, scoparoside*]... [and] which are distributed in many very different families of both monocotyledons and dicotyledons.

We may recognize yet another group of *glycosides*, the *sugar–sugar glycosides*. These include the *di-, oligo-,* and *polysaccharides*. We deal with these as *carbohydrates*, restricting ourselves in the present section to the sugar–aglycone group—the *heterosides*.

The sugars occurring in *heterosides* include: simple *hexoses*, of which D-*glucose* is the most common; *deoxy-hexoses*, of which *rhamnose* is very common; unusual sugars which seem to occur only in *cardiac glycosides* or other special types of glycosides; *disaccharides* such as *primeverose, rutinose* (common), *gentiobiose*, etc.; and *trisaccharides* such as *rhamninose, scillatriose, lycotriose*, etc.

The *aglycones* are of great diversity, and the glycosides are usually grouped according to the nature of their aglycones. We may note:

Alkaloidal glycosides: see *alkaloids*
Anthraquinone glycosides: see *quinones*
Aucubin-type glycosides: I of this section
Cardiac glycosides: see *steroids* (III)
Coumarin glycosides: see *coumarins*
Cyanogenic glycosides: II of this section
Diterpenoid glycosides: see *terpenoids* (IV) and *diterpenoid alkaloids*
Flavonoid glycosides: see *flavonoids* (I to XIV)
Glycolipids: IV of this section

Indoxyl glycosides: V of this section
Isothiocyanate glycosides: see sulfur compounds (V)
Phenolic glycosides: III of this section
Saponins: see *steroids* (IV) and *terpenoids* (V.1)

Glycosides may occur in any organ of the plant and individual ones may be restricted more or less to particular organs, as are some other groups of compounds. Paris (loc. cit.) gives as examples:

Leaf—*sennosides*
Bark—*aesculin* (in some cases only ?)
Root—*gentiopicrin*
Flower—*anthocyanins* (in some cases only)
Fruit—*flavanones* of *Citrus*
Seed—*sinigrin*

Glycosides have many functions in plants. Some of them, when once laid down, seem not to be used again, though one must be cautious before labelling any particular glycoside a 'waste product'. Others vary with the seasons and appear to function as 'reserve' materials. Yet others may be 'protective', giving bitter taste (to humans, at least), or poisonous properties, to the tissues in which they occur. Some perform useful biological functions in making tissues attractive, rather than repellent—the red and blue colours of many flowers, due to presence of *anthocyanins*, are examples.

The usefulness of glycosides in chemotaxonomy is obvious, but Paris (loc. cit.) was cautious: 'From the taxonomic point of view, glycosides appear to be interesting at the level of species or variety... and one can distinguish "chemical" races as described previously (p. 348)...But there are too many gaps in our knowledge, and if we wish to assess their importance to plant taxonomy further, we must continue to investigate their presence, structure, and function in the Plant Kingdom.'

I AUCUBIN GROUP

GENERAL

The most recent reviews available to me are those by Bate-Smith and Swain (in Swain, 1966) and Hegnauer (1966). In their introductions they discuss alternative names that have been given to the group. Because of the blue colour that results when *aucubin* or *asperuloside* (at least) are heated with dilute acid they have been called *pseudo-*

indicans. They have also been named *melampyrosides* and *iridoids*. The last derives from the simplest compound of this type, *iridodial* (fig. 131), which has been found in a meat ant (*Iridomyrmex*) and in *Myoporum*?

Bate-Smith and Swain would adopt the name *iridoid*, but I have preferred the older name. They include in their review some 'related substances' such as *oleuropein* and *swertiamarin*, which I deal with elsewhere.

Papers by Plouvier (1964) and by Wieffering (1966) have been of use in preparing the following list.

Wieffering has something to say about biosynthesis. He thinks these substances represent a biogenetically homogeneous group arising in the same way as *gentiopicrin* and similar substances, as the *monoterpenoid alkaloids* such as *actinidine* and *tecomanine*, and as some more complicated alkaloids such as *yohimbine* and *tubulosine*.

We have used a simple test, the *Ehrlich Test*, for aucubin-type glycosides, which is described elsewhere (p. 72). It has indicated the presence of these substances in some plants which have not yet been examined in detail. An example is *Phryma leptostachya* which is placed in an order, **Tubiflorae**, many families of which are known to contain *aucubin* and related substances.

An examination of the list which follows shows that these compounds have a fairly wide distribution among dicotyledons. Most of them occur in the **Tubiflorae**, but some are found in *Saxifragaceae* (*s.l.* of the **Rosales**); in *Cornaceae* and *Garryaceae* of the **Umbellales**; and in *Loganiaceae*, *Menyanthaceae*, *Apocynaceae*, and *Rubiaceae* of the **Gentianales**.

List and Occurrence

Agnuside is an acylated aucubin—with a *p-hydroxy-benzoic acid* group at position 10?
> *Verben.* *Vitex agnus-castus* (lvs, st.)

Asperocotillin (? fig. 131) is probably closely related to *asperuloside*.
> *Fouquieri.* *Fouquieria splendens* ('Ocotillo')

Asperuloside (Alstonin; Asperulin; Rubichloric acid; fig. 131) is rather widely distributed.
> *Hamamelid.* *Liquidambar styraciflua*?
> *Saxifrag.* *Escallonia* (all spp. ?); but *absent* from many other genera.
> *Daphniphyll.* *Daphniphyllum*
> *Apocyn.* *Alstonia constricta* ('alstonin')
> *Rubi.* *present* in many genera; but *absent* from many genera.
> *Globulari.* *Globularia* spp.

Aucubin (Aucuboside; Rhinanthin; fig. 131) is even more widely spread than is *asperuloside*, though some of the records are in doubt. I have

Eucommi. Eucommia ulmoides

Byblid. Byblis?

Hippurid. Hippuris vulgaris (plt)

Corn. Aucuba, Cornus

Garry. Garrya (4)

Apocyn. Thevetia neriifolia

Plantagin. Plantago (8)

Scrophulari. Melampyrum, Rhinanthus, Verbascum, Veronica, etc.

Orobanch. Lathraea; but *absent* from *Orobanche* spp. ?

Globulari. Globularia (4)

Buddlej. Buddleja (9)

Lentibulari. Utricularia

Martyni. Martynia?

Verben. Vitex agnus-castus (lvs, st.)

Callitrich. Callitriche sp.

Boschnialactone

Orobanch. Boschniakia rossica

Cardanthera-pseudoindican

Acanth. Cardanthera triflora (lvs)

Catalpinoside: is this distinct from *catalposide*?

Bignoni. Catalpa, Paulownia

Catalpol (fig. 131) coexists with *aucubin* in some plants. According to Wieffering (1966) it is rather widely distributed

Hippurid. Hippuris vulgaris (plt)

Buddlej. Buddleja (2)

Lentibulari. Pinguicula

Globulari. Globularia spp.

Scrophulari. Verbascum lychnitis (lvs), *Veronica* (3)

Callitrich. Callitriche sp.

Plantagin. Plantago

Catalpol-6-*O*-methyl ether

Buddlej. Buddleja

Catalposide (Catalpin)

Bignoni. Catalpa

Scrophulari. Veronica spp.

Globulari. Globularia spp.

Cephalarioside: of unknown structure?

Dipsac. Succisa pratensis

Deutzioside: of unknown structure?

Saxifrag. Deutzia longifolia (bk), *macrocephala* (bk), *mollis* (bk), *scabra* (lvs, bk, fl.), *schneideriana* (bk), *staminea* (lvs, bk), *taiwanensis* (lvs, bk)

β-Dihydro-plumericin
    Apocyn. Plumeria rubra v. *alba* (bk)

β-Dihydro-plumericinic acid
    Apocyn. Plumeria rubra v. *alba* (bk)

Fulvoplumierin
    Apocyn. Plumeria (2)

Genipin
    Rubi. Genipa americana

Harpagide (fig. 131)
    Pedali. Harpagophytum procumbens (rt)
    Lab. Ajuga reptans (plt), *Galeopsis* spp., *Melittis, Stachys* (3), *Teucrium montanum*

Harpagoside (8-*O*-Cinnamyl-harpagide)
    Pedali. Harpagophytum procumbens (rt)

Iridodial (fig. 131)
    Myopor. ?

Isoplumericin
    Apocyn. Plumeria rubra var. *alba*

Lamiol
    Lab. Lamium amplexicaule

Lamioside
    Lab. Lamium amplexicaule

Loganin (Meliatin; Meliatoside; fig. 131)
    Saxifrag. Hydrangea spp.
    Corn. Mastixia arborea (bk)
    Logani. Strychnos spp.
    Menyanth. Menyanthes trifoliata (rhiz.)
    Caprifoli. Lonicera spp.

Matatabilactone has been said to be identical with *iridomyrmecin* (from insects), but Bate-Smith and Swain give slightly different formulae for these two substances.
    Actinidi. Actinidia polygama (lvs)

Monotropein (fig. 131): Bate-Smith and Swain regarded the structure of this glucoside as sufficiently different from the other *aucubin glycosides* to make a separate sub-group. Believing it to occur only in *Pyrolaceae* they said: 'By assigning it provisionally to a group of its own, the botanically isolated position of the *Pyrolaceae* (in the Ericales) from all other irioid-containing families will be acknowledged.' Wieffering (1966), however, records *monotropein* from other sources, and we now have the following
    Hamamelid. Liquidambar styraciflua (bk)

> Pyrol.   Chimaphila sp., Monotropa hypopitys, Monotropastrum,
>   Pyrola rotundifolia
> Eric.   Vaccinium myrtillus
> Rubi.   Galium verum (plt)
> Globulari.   Globularia elongata (vulgaris), nudicaulis

Myodesertin (fig. 131) is very similar to aucubigenin.

> Myopor.   Myoporum deserti (In the essential oil of one race.
>   Another race has the corresponding dialdehyde (fig. 131), while
>   yet others have sesquiterpenes of the ngaione type. Personal
>   communication from M. D. Sutherland, 19 January 1967.)

Neo-nepeta-lactone

> Actinidi.   Actinidia polygama (lvs, galls)

Nepeta-lactones (fig. 131): two isomeric lactones, the second of which
has been called epinepetalactone, occur in oil of catnip. Eisner (1964)
says: 'Catnip (nepetalactone) is closely related chemically to certain
cyclopentanoid monoterpenes recently isolated from insects, and it
shares with some of these terpenes an ability to repel insects. It is
suggested that the adaptive function of catnip is to protect the plants
that produce it against phytophagous insects.' In a later paper,
Meinwald, Happ, Labows and Eisner (1966) say that the stick insect
Anisomorpha buprestoides and catnip (Nepeta cataria) produce
anisomorphal and nepetalactone respectively from the same precursors,
acetate and mevalonate.

> Lab.   Nepeta cataria (chiefly nepetalactone), citriodora, mussini
>   (chiefly epinepetalactone)

8-O-Acetyl-harpagide has an acetyl group at x in fig. 131.

> Lab.   Ajuga, Galeopsis ladanum var., Melittis, Stachys (3), Teuc-
>   rium

Plumericin is very closely related to isoplumericin.

> Apocyn.   Plumeria rubra var. alba

Plumieride

> Apocyn.   Plumeria (2)

Procumbide is said to resemble harpagoside.

> Pedali.   Harpagophytum procumbens (rt)?

Tetrahit-pseudoindican

> Lab.   Galeopsis tetrahit (lvs)

Unedoside seems to be closely related to catalpol.

> Eric.   Arbutus unedo (lvs, st.)

Verbenalin (Cornin; Verbenaloside; fig. 131)

> Corn.   Cornus florida (bk), Corokia cotoneaster (st.)
> Verben.   Verbena officinalis (plt)

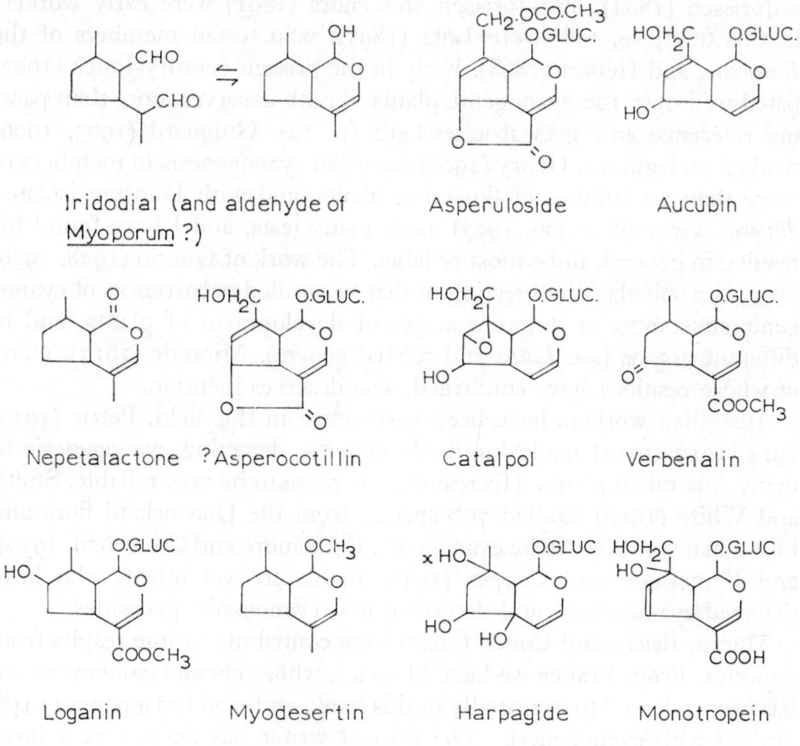

Fig. 131. Aucubin and some related compounds.

II CYANOGENIC GLYCOSIDES

GENERAL

It was recognized very early in the study of plant chemistry (p. 15) that some plants easily yield *hydrocyanic acid* (HCN) and that they may, at least under some conditions, be toxic to stock and other animals. Such plants are said to be *cyanogenic* (cyanogenetic). Most of the substances yielding HCN are *cyanogenic glycosides*, but see below.

The great ease with which HCN may be detected (p. 58) has led many authors to make tests for it. We have pointed out that it is easy, however, to get misleading results, and I am sure that many plants reported to be cyanogenic are, in fact, not so. We shall have more to say of this below.

We may list here some of those who have contributed to our knowledge of cyanogenesis: others are mentioned elsewhere.

Jorissen (1884), and Jorissen and Hairs (1891) were early workers in this field; so, too, were Lutz (1897), who tested members of the *Rosaceae*, and Hébert (1898). Early in the present century Jouck (1902) listed well over 100 cyanogenic plants. Treub deserves more than passing reference and gets it elsewhere (p. 12). Guignard (1905, 1906) worked on legumes. Henry (1906) recorded cyanogenesis in members of more than 20 families of flowering plants, and with Dunstan isolated *dhurrin*. Greshoff (1906, 1907) made many tests, and I have found his results, in general, to be most reliable. The work of Guérin (1928, 1929, 1930) is particularly interesting in that he studied occurrences of cyanogenic substances at different stages of development of plants, and in different organs (see *Lotus* and related genera). Mirande (1913), many of whose results I have confirmed, also deserves mention.

Australian workers have been very active in this field. Petrie (1913, 1914, 1917, 1920) made hundreds of tests, detecting cyanogenesis in many Australian plants. His results, too, seem to be very reliable. Smith and White (1918) studied 700 species from the Queensland flora and found many of them to be cyanogenic. Finnemore and Cox (1929, 1930), and Finnemore and Cooper (1936, 1938), are yet others who have detected cyanogenesis and described new cyanogenic glycosides.

Moran, Briese and Couch (1940) have contributed some results from America. From France we have Plouvier, whose chemotaxonomic work has been referred to repeatedly in this book, and who has a paper (1948) dealing with cyanogenesis. The present writer has made a very large number of tests (p. 60) and has discussed the distribution of cyanogenesis in several papers (1945, 1954, 1961, 1963). At his suggestion Honeyman (1956) studied the *Cruciferae* for occurrence of HCN. Many works on poisonous plants, such as that of Gardner and Bennetts (1956), have references to known cyanogenic plants and to others suspected, because of toxicity, to yield HCN. Finally, in this brief review, we must refer to the work of Hegnauer (1958, 1959*a* and *b*, 1960, 1961*a*, 1963, 1964, 1966), who has discussed the chemotaxonomy of cyanogenesis.

In his 1960 paper Hegnauer calls attention to the large number of plants in the Philippine Islands listed as cyanogenic by Quisumbing (1951). Like myself he feels that many of these results are not to be trusted. He says:

Die Liste umfasst 310 Arten aus 72 Familien und basiert auf Untersuchungen von D. D. Herbert, H. M. Kalaw und F. M. Sacay, F. DePeralta, J. B. Juliano, und J. B. Juliano und M. Guerra. Leider haben diese Untersucher nur den Guignard-Mirande-Test verwendet, und zwar in einer Modifikation, die seine Spezifität stark beeintrachtigt: 10 Gramm zerkleinertes Pflanzenmaterial wurden in 100 ml alkalische Pikratlösung mit etwas Chloroform gebracht; die Beurteilung erfolgte nach einer Stunde. Meiner Meinung nach bedürfen diese Befunde der Bestätigung. In der folgenden Ubersicht sind deshalb nur diejenigen Arten aufgefuhrt, für welche starke bis sehr starke Reaktion beobachtet wurde.

It is obvious that some cyanogenic glycosides are very stable. We have obtained definitely positive reactions for HCN from herbarium material of plants of *Lotus* spp. collected by John Ball (1818–89) and by R. H. Middleton (78 years in the herbarium!). Finnemore, Reichard and Large (1937) report similar results with *Phyllanthus gastroemii* collected nearly 30 years before testing. They say, however, that plants of *Goodia lotifolia* lose their ability to yield HCN when dried. Hegnauer (1960) points out that the cyanogenic glycoside of *Goodia* is unique in structure. He calls it a 'labile' glycoside. It seems that we may get clues as to the types of glycosides present by comparing stability.

We noted above that a few non-glycosidal substances may yield HCN Among these we may note:

Benzyl-cyanide (fig. 132) which seems to occur in
   Gyrostemon. Codonocarpus cotinifolia (lvs)
   Crucif. Lepidium sativum (plt)
   Tropaeol. Tropaeolum majus (plt)
   Rubi. Leptactina senegambica (fl.)
Mandelonitrile (fig. 132)
   Ros. Prunus persica (buds, free? They also have *prunasin*)
Girgensohnine: see under *pyridine alkaloids*.

Cyanogenesis is not completely restricted to plants. Eisner, Eisner, Hurst, Kafatos and Meinwald (1963) have described the cyanogenic glandular apparatus of a millipede (*Apheloria corrugata*) and say: 'The discharged secretion...contains benzaldehyde and hydrogen cyanide, but no free sugar...this suggests that the cyanide precursor in the reservoir is mandelonitrile...and it was shown that mandelonitrile is indeed present in the secretion...'.

It will be evident from a perusal of the following list that the distribution of cyanogenic glycosides is wide but not universal. I have tried to summarize my own results and those known to me of others in Tables 1 to 3. Here, as in other cases, our knowledge, though extensive, is still far from adequate. The problem is intensified by the many results that are dubious.

The chemotaxonomic value of our body of information is considerable. It is discussed to best advantage, I think, in our section on orders, so we shall give no details here.

List and Occurrence

Acacipetalin (fig. 132) was described by Rimington (1935). It yields *glucose, HCN* and *isobutyric acid*.

　　Legum. Acacia lasiopetala, stolonifera (hebeclada) (lvs)

Acalyphin was isolated by Rimington and Roets (1937).

　　Euphorbi. Acalypha indica. I have confirmed this, but I have not been able to detect HCN in other species, including *tricolor (wilkesiana)* which has been reported to have it.

Amygdalin (Amygdaloside; Glucoprunasin; D-(−)-Mandelonitrile-β-gentiobioside; fig. 132) was named by Roubiquet and Boutron-Charlard (1830). It yields $2 \times glucose, HCN$ and *benzaldehyde*.

　　Ros. Cydonia, Eriobotrya, Prunus, Pyrus

　　Sapot. Calocarpum (Lucuma) mammosum (sd)?—see *Lucumin.*

Corynocarpin may not be a cyanogenic glycoside. According to Greshoff (1906) it was found by Easterfield and Aston (1903).

　　Corynocarp. Corynocarpus laevigata

Dhurrin (β-D-Glucopyranosyloxy-L-*p*-hydroxy-mandelonitrile; fig. 132) was found by Dunstan and Henry (1902). Towers, McInnes and Neish (1964) have established its absolute configuration. See also *phyllanthin.*

　　Gram. Panicum maximum, muticum; Sorghum (Andropogon) vulgare (lvs)

p-Glucosyloxy-mandelonitrile (fig. 132) has been identified by Abrol, Conn and Stoker (1966). They say that their compound may be similar to that found by Finnemore and Large (1937) and thought to be *p-hydroxy-mandelonitrile glucoside* (below).

　　Ranuncul. Thalictrum aquilegifolium (lvs, etc.)

　　Berberid. Nandina domestica (lvs)

p-Glucosyloxy-mandelonitrile-β-glucoside

　　Ranuncul. Thalictrum aquilegifolium (lvs, etc.)

Gynocardin (fig. 132) was found by Power and Gornall (1904). Zechner (1966) gives the formula shown.

　　Flacourti. Gynocardia odorata (sd), *Pangium edule* (lvs, sd)

p-Hydroxy-mandelonitrile glucoside (Goodia-glycoside), found by Finnemore and Large (1937). It may be identical with *p-glucosyloxy-mandelonitrile* (above).

　　Legum. Goodia lotifolia

Isolinamarin is the α-anomer of *linamarin.* Does it occur in Nature?

Jamesia-glycoside is *prunasin*?

　　Saxifrag. Jamesia americana (lvs)

Linamarin (Acetone-cyanohydrin-β-glucoside; Manihotoxin; Phaseolunatin; fig. 132) was found and named by Jorissen and Hairs (1887, 1891). It is definitely the β-anomer. See also *lotaustralin*.

Ranuncul. *Thalictrum*

Legum. *Lotus arabicus, arenarius, corniculatus, creticus, edulis, maroccanus, parviflorus, tenuis* (sdlgs in all); *Phaseolus lunatus* (lvs, sd); *Trifolium repens* (lvs)

Lin. *Linum catharticum, grandiflorum* (sdlg), *narbonense* (sdlg), *perenne* (sdlg), *usitatissimum* (plt)

Euphorbi. *Hevea brasiliensis* (sd); *Manihot carthaginensis* (rt), *utilissima (esculenta)* (tuber)

Comp. *Dimorphotheca barberiae* (lvs), *ecklonis* (lvs), *spectabilis* (lvs); *Osteospermum jucundum* (lvs)

Lotaustralin (fig. 132) was discovered by Finnemore and Cooper (1938). It is almost always present in plants which have the closely related *linamarin* (Butler, 1965).

Legum. *Lotus arabicus, arenarius* (very little), *corniculatus, creticus, edulis, maroccanus, parviflorus, tenuis* (sdlgs in all); *Phaseolus lunatus* (sd); *Trifolium repens* (lvs)

Lin. *Linum grandiflorum, narbonense, perenne, usitatissimum* (sdlgs in all)

Euphorbi. *Manihot carthaginensis* (rt)

Comp. *Dimorphotheca barberiae* (lvs, trace), *ecklonis* (lvs, trace); *Osteospermum jucundum* (lvs, trace)

Lotusin probably does not exist. Hegnauer (1960) says: 'Bis zur Wiederauffindung dieser Verbindung möchten wir aber annehmen, dass Lotusin ein mit Lotaustralin verunreinigtes Quercetinglykosid war.'

Lucumin (Lucuminoside; fig. 132) is a *cyanogenic glycoside*, say Bachstez, Prieto and Gaja (1948), yielding 1 or 2 × *arabinose, benzaldehyde*, and *?HCN*. Hegnauer (1961) gives the formula shown. Jamieson and McKinney say that *Lucuma* has *amygdalin*.

Sapot. *Lucuma (Calocarpum) mammosa* (sd). Other species of *Lucuma* yield *HCN*.

Phyllanthin (1) (β-D-Glucopyranosyloxy-D-*p*-hydroxy-mandelonitrile; Taxiphyllin; fig. 132) was named by Finnemore, Reichard and Large (1937), who thought it might be *dhurrin*. Towers, McInnes and Neish (1964), however, have shown that *phyllanthin* and *dhurrin* are configurationally distinct. Towers *et al.* prefer the name *taxiphyllin* (the glycoside occurs also in *Taxus*) because a 'bitter principle' of *P. niruri* has been called 'phyllanthin'.

Euphorbi. *Phyllanthus gastroemii* (lvs)

Prulaurasin (Amorphous amygdalin; *dl*-Mandelonitrile-D-glycoside;

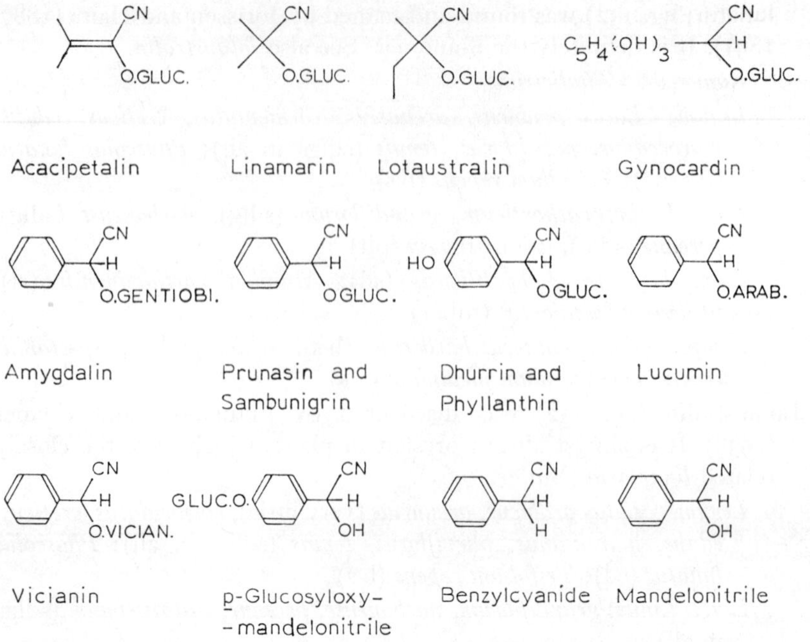

Fig. 132. Cyanogenic substances.

Laurocerasin) was mentioned very early by Winckler?, by Simon (1839), and named by Hérissey (1905).

    Ros. Cotoneaster (at least 23 species?); *Prunus laurocerasus* (lvs), *padus* (bk)

Prunasin (*d*-(−)-Mandelonitrile-D-glucoside; fig. 132) was first isolated by Hérissey (1907). It seems to be widely distributed.

    Saxifrag. Jamesia americana (lvs?)

    Ros. Photinia serrulata (lvs), *Prunus laurocerasus* (lvs), *macrophylla* (lvs), *padus* (lvs, st.), *serotina* (bk, lvs)

    Myrt. Eucalyptus corynocalyx (*cladocalyx*)

    Scrophulari. Linaria repens (*striata*)

    Myopor. Eremophila maculata (lvs)

Sambunigrin (*l*-(+)-Mandelonitrile-D-glucoside; fig. 132) was named by Bourquelot and Danjou (1905).

    Olac. Ximenia americana (lvs)

    Legum. Acacia cheelii (lvs), *glaucescens* (lvs)

    Caprifoli. Sambucus nigra (lvs, fl.)

Triglochinin (*O*-[β-D-Glucopyranosyl]-1-cyano-1-hydroxy-4,5-dicarboxy-1,3-pentadiene)—Eyjólfsson (1970).

    Juncagin. Triglochin maritimum (fl.)

Vicianin (*l*-Mandelonitrile-vicianoside; fig. 132) was found by Bertrand (1906).

  Legum.   *Vicia angustifolia* (sd), *macrocarpa*, *sativa* (very little)

Zierin (*m*-Hydroxymandelonitrile-β-glucoside) was found by Finnemore and Cooper (1936).

  Rut.   *Zieria laevigata* (aerial pts). Some other spp. are cyanogenic and so are some other genera of the family.

III PHENOLIC GLYCOSIDES

GENERAL

It will be clear from the following list that our knowledge of *phenolic glycosides* is extremely patchy. Recent papers by Thieme (1965, 1967), and by Binns, Blunden and Woods (1968) have thrown considerable light on the chemotaxonomy of the *Salicaceae*. On the other hand we have several glycosides known to me only from single records. Examples are: *p-coumaric acid*-D-*fructoside*, *echinacoside*, *furcatin*, *glycosmin*, *linocinnamarin* and *xylosmoside*. Are these really so restricted in their distribution?

  Certain families—such as the *Salicaceae* (as mentioned above), the *Rosaceae*, and the *Ericaceae*—seem to be particularly rich in *phenolic glycosides*, and more detailed investigations of these and of related families will undoubtedly prove to be of chemotaxonomic interest.

List and Occurrence

Acertannin is said to yield 2 × *gallic acid* and *polygalitol*.

  Acer.   *Acer*

Arbutin (Arbutoside; Ericoline; Vacciniin; 1,4-dihydroxy-benzene-1-glucoside; fig. 133) seems to be rather restricted in its distribution (to judge from the many records of absence).

  Prote.   *Grevillea, Hakea, Persoonia*

  Saxifrag.   *Bergenia* (2); but *not* in *Deutzia, Philadelphus*

  Ros.   *Pyrus calleryana, communis, sinensis*; but *not* in *Amygdalus, Cydonia, Malus, Prunus, Sorbus*

  Legum.   *Lathyrus niger* (plt); but *not* in *Caragana, Lupinus, Robinia, Sophora*

  Eric.   in many. Karrer (1958) says 'A. kommt fast in allen Ericaceen vor...'.

  Pyrol.   *Chimaphila maculata, umbellata* ('ericoline'); *Pyrola rotundifolia* (lvs, st.)

Comp.   Serratula (3); but *not* in *Achillea, Taraxacum*
It is *not* in: *Jugland (Carya, Juglans)*; *Myric (Myrica)*; *Salic.*
(*Populus, Salix*); *Betul.* (*Alnus, Betula*); *Fag.* (*Fagus, Quercus*);
Ulm. (*Zelkova*); *Eucommi.* (*Eucommia*); *Mor.* (*Humulus, Morus*);
Urtic. (*Urtica*); *Loranth.* (*Viscum*); *Polygon.* (*Polygonum, Rumex*);
Caryophyll. (*Stellaria*); *Chenopodi.* (*Beta*); *Magnoli.* (*Magnolia*);
Annon. (*Asimina*); *Schisandr.* (*Schisandra*); *Calycanth.* (*Calycan-
thus*); *Laur.* (*Lindera*); *Euptele.* (*Euptelea*); *Cercidiphyll.* (*Cercidi-
phyllum*); *Ranuncul.* (*Caltha*); *Berberid.* (*Berberis*); *Lardizabal.*
(*Akebia*); *Aristolochi.* (*Aristolochia*); *Actinidi.* (*Actinidia*); *Gutt.*
(*Hypericum*); *Papaver.* (*Chelidonium, Eschscholtzia*); *Crucif.*
(*Brassica*); *Hamamelid.* (*Liquidambar*); *Platan.* (*Platanus*); *Gerani.*
(*Erodium*); *Tropaeol.* (*Tropaeolum*); *Euphorbi.* (*Euphorbia, Secur-
inega*); *Rut.* (*Evodia*); *Simaroub.* (*Ailanthus*); *Anacardi.* (*Rhus*);
Acer. (*Acer*); *Hippocastan.* (*Aesculus*); *Aquifoli.* (*Ilex*); *Celastr.*
(*Euonymus*); *Staphyle.* (*Staphylea*); *Bux.* (*Buxus*); *Rhamn.*
(*Rhamnus*); *Vit.* (*Vitis*); *Tili.* (*Tilia*); *Thymelae.* (*Daphne*);
Elaeagn. (*Hippophaë*); *Stachyur.* (*Stachyurus*); *Tamaric.* (*Myri-
caria*); *Davidi.* (*Davidia*); *Corn.* (*Cornus*); *Arali.* (*Acanthopanax,
Hedera*); *Umbell.* (*Aegopodium*); *Primul.* (*Primula*); *Plumbagin.*
(*Armeria*); *Eben.* (*Diospyros*); *Ole.* (*Fraxinus, Syringa*); *Asclepiad.*
(*Periploca*); *Convolvul.* (*Convolvulus*); *Lab.* (*Elsholtzia, Lamium*);
Solan. (*Lycium, Solanum*); *Bignoni.* (*Catalpa*); *Plantagin.*
(*Plantago*); *Caprifoli.* (*Lonicera, Sambucus*); *Lili.* (*Asparagus*);
Irid. (*Iris*); *Lemn.* (*Lemna*); *Gram.* (*Phragmites*); *Typh.*
(*Typha*)

Betuloside (fig. 133) is a glucoside of *betuligenol.*
   Betul.   *Betula alba* (bk), *platyphylla* (bk)
   Eric.   *Rhododendron chrysanthum* (lvs)
Caffeoyl-calleryanins (*cis-* and *trans-*)
   Ros.   *Pyrus calleryana* (lvs)
Coniferin (Abietin; Coniferoside; Laricin; 4-Glucoside of coniferyl
alcohol) occurs in conifers and in
   Chenopodi.   *Beta vulgaris*
   Styrac.   *Styrax*
   Ole.   *Fraxinus quadrangulata* (bk)
   Comp.   *Scorzonera hispanica*
   Lili.   *Asparagus*
   Orchid.   *Vanilla planifolia*
Corilagin is said to yield *glucose* and 3 × *gallic acid.*
   Legum.   *Caesalpinia coriaria*
   Myrt.   *Eucalyptus gigantea*
   Combret.   *Terminalia chebula* (frt)

p-Coumaric acid-D-fructoside (Pajaneelin)

    Bignoni. Pajanelia rheedii (bk)

Coumarinic acid-β-glucoside

    Legum. Dipteryx (Coumarouna) odorata (frt, sd; Haskins and Gorz, 1963), *Melilotus alba*?

Digalloyl-glucose

    Combret. Terminalia (?myrobalan tannin)

    Plumbagin. Plumbago rosea (fl.)

3,4-Dihydroxybenzyl alcohol-4-glucoside (Calleryanin; fig. 133)

    Ros. Prunus lusitanica (lvs), *Pyrus calleryana* (lvs)

Echinacoside   yields 2 × D-*glucose*, L-*rhamnose, caffeic acid* and β-(3,4)-*dihydrophenyl)-ethyl alcohol.*

    Comp. Echinacea angustifolia (bk)

Fragilin is a glycoside of 6-*acetyl-salicin*.

    Salic. Salix alba (lvs), *babylonica* (lvs), *callicarpaea (arctica)* (lvs), *calodendron* (lvs), *fragilis (decipiens)* (lvs), *incana* (lvs), *nigricans* (lvs), *phylicifolia* (lvs), *viminalis* (lvs) but *not* in some other species.

Furcatin is the 6-*apiosyl-glucoside* of *p-vinylphenol.*

    Caprifoli. Viburnum furcatum

l-Galloyl-β-D-glucose (Glucogallin; fig. 133)

    Polygon. Rheum officinale

    Plumbagin. Plumbago rosea (fl.)

p-Galloyl-oxyphenyl-β-D-glucoside

    Saxifrag. Bergenia cordifolia (lvs), *crassifolia*

    Eric. Arctostaphylos uva-ursi (lvs)

Gein (Geoside; Eugenol vicianoside)

    Ros. Geum coccineum, rivale, urbanum (rt)

Glucovanillin (Vanillin-4-glucoside)

    Gram. Agropyron (Triticum) repens (rt, sd), *Avena sativa*

    Orchid. Vanilla planifolia (frt)

Glycosmin is a veratroyl derivative of *salicin.*

    Rut. Glycosmis pentaphylla

Grandidentatin

    Salic. Populus alba (lvs), *grandidentata* (but *not* in *candicans* (lvs, bk), *nigra* (lvs, bk), *tremula* (lvs, bk), *tremuloides* (lvs, bk), *trichocarpa* (lvs, bk)); *Salix alba* (lvs), *americana* (?lvs), *babylonica* (?lvs), *callicarpaea (arctica)* (?lvs), *calodendron* (?lvs), *daphnoides* (?lvs), *fragilis (decipiens)* (bk, lvs), *incana* (lvs), *pentandra* (bk, lvs), *phylicifolia* (lvs), *purpurea* (bk, lvs), *repens* (?lvs), *triandre* (?bk, lvs), *viminalis* (?lvs) (but *not* in *aurita* (bk), *caprea* (bk, lvs), *cinerea* (bk, lvs), *myrsinifolia* (?*nigricans*) (lvs, bk)).

Hamameli-tannin can be hydrolysed to 2 × *gallic acid* and *hamamelose.*

    Hamamelid. Hamamelis virginiana (rt)

Helicin is said to be a *salicylic aldehyde glucoside* which *may* be identical with *spiraein*.

  Ros. Spiraea?

Homo-arbutin (2-Methylquinol-4-β-D-glucoside)

  Pyrol. Pyrola incarnata (rt)

p-Hydroxybenzoyl-calleryanin

  Ros. Prunus lusitanica (lvs), *Pyrus calleryana* (lvs)

Linocinnamarin is a *glucoside* of *p-coumaric acid methyl ester.*

  Lin. Linum usitatissimum (sd)

Lusitanicoside (Chavicol-β-rutinoside; 4-Allylphenol-rhamnoglucoside)

  Ros. Prunus lusitanica (lvs)

Melilotoside (Melilotin; *trans-o-*Coumaric acid-2-glucoside)

  Legum. Melilotus altissima (fl.), *arvensis* (fl.)

Methoxy-hydroquinone-glucoside

  Gram. Triticum sativum (sdlg)

Methyl-arbutin (1-Hydroxy-4-methoxy-benzene-1-glucoside)

  Illici. Illicium verum

  Ros. Pyrus communis (some vars)

  Pyrol. Pyrola secunda (lvs)

  Eric. Arctostaphylos uva-ursi (lvs, some plts)

Monotropitoside (Gaultherin; Monotropin; Monotropitin) is the *primveroside* of *methyl-salicylate.*

  Betul. Betula lenta (bk), *Ostryopsis davidiana* (bk)

  Ros. Spiraea spp.

  Polygal. Securidaca longepedunculata (rt)

  Pyrol. Monotropa hypopithys

  Eric. Gualtheria cumingiana (lvs), *procumbens* (lvs, etc.)

6-*O*-Acetyl-arbutin (Pyroside)

  Ros. Pyrus communis (lvs)

  Eric. Vaccinium vitis-idaea (lvs)

2-*O*-Caffeoyl-arbutin

  Eric. Vaccinium vitis-idaea (lvs)

2-*O*-Galloyl-arbutin

  Saxifrag. Bergenia cordifolia (lvs), *crassifolia* (lvs)

  Eric. Arctostaphylos uva-ursi (lvs)

6-*O*-Galloyl-arbutin

  Saxifrag. Bergenia cordifolia (lvs), *crassifolia* (lvs)

  Eric. Arctostaphylos uva-ursi (lvs)

Orcinol (5-Methyl-resorcinol) has been found in leaf-hydrolysates of some *Ericaceae* by Harborne and Williams (1969). Is it always present as glycoside?

Orcinol-β-D-glucoside

  Eric. Erica arborea v. *alpina* (lvs)

Orobanchoside (Orobanchin) yields *caffeic acid*, D-*glucose* and L-*rhamnose*. It is said to be involved in the blackening of *Orobanche* spp. Harborne (in Swain, 1966) gives most of the following as unpublished

    Ole. present

    Logani. present

    Verben. present

    Scrophulari. present

    Bignoni. present

    Acanth. present

    Gesneri. present

    Orobanch. *Orobanche cruenta, minor, rapum*

Phlorin is a *β-glucoside* of *phloroglucinol*. Does it occur naturally? (It is synthesized by leaves of *Malus* and other plants fed *phloroglucinol* and *glucose* (Hutchinson, Roy and Towers, 1958). They obtained other synthetic *phenolic glucosides.*)

Picrorhizin is a *glucoside* of *vanillic acid.*

    Ros. *Prunus lusitanica* (lvs)?

    Scrophulari. *Picrorhiza kurroa* (rhiz.)

Populin (6-Benzoyl-salicin)

    Salic. *Populus nigra, pyramidalis, tremula* (lvs, bk); *Salix callicarpaea* (?*arctica*) (lvs), *daphnoides, fragilis* (*decipiens*) (lvs), *incana* (lvs), *pentandra* (lvs?), *purpurea* (lvs); but *not* in some other species.

Primveroside (Primverin) is the 2-*primveroside* of 4-*methoxy-methyl salicylate.*

    Primul. *Primula kewensis* (rt), *officinalis* (rt), *viscosa* (rt)?

Primulaveroside (Primulaverin) is the 2-*primveroside* of 5-*methoxy-methyl salicylate.*

    Primul. *Primula acaulis, officinalis* (rt)

Protocatechuic acid-3-β-D-glucoside

    Ros. *Prunus lusitanica* (lvs), *Pyrus calleryana* (lvs)

Protocatechuoyl-calleryanin

    Ros. *Prunus lusitanica* (lvs), *Pyrus calleryana* (lvs)

o-Pyrocatechuic acid-3-glucoside

    Apocyn. *Vinca minor* (lvs)

Pyrolatin (Pirolatin; Pyrolagenin-glucoside) is a *hydroquinone* derivative.

    Pyrol. *Pyrola* (*Pirola*) *japonica* (lvs, 1·3%): what is this?

Salicin (fig. 133) is the 2-*glucoside* of *salicyl alcohol*. Should the occurrences outside the *Salicaceae* be queried?

    Salic. *Populus alba* (lvs, etc.), *balsamifera* (lvs, bk), *candicans* (lvs, bk), *nigra* (lvs, bk), *tremula* (lvs, bk), *tremuloides* (lvs, bk), *trichocarpa* (lvs, bk); *Salix alba* (lvs, bk), *americana* (lvs), *aurita* (bk), *babylonica* (lvs), *callicarpaea* (?*arctica*) (lvs), *calodendron* (lvs), *caprea* (lvs, bk), *cinerea* (lvs), *daphnoides*, *fragilis* (?*decipiens*) (lvs, bk), *helix* (?*purpurea*) (bk), *incana* (lvs), *myrsinifolia* (?*nigricans*) (lvs, bk), *pentandra* (lvs, bk), *phylicifolia* (lvs), *purpurea* (lvs, bk), *repens* (lvs, bk), *triandra* (lvs, bk), *viminalis* (lvs, bk)

Ros.   Spiraea (I have no details)
Caprifoli.   Viburnum prunifolium (bk)

Salicortin is a *glycoside* of *salicyl-salicin*.

Salic.   *Populus alba* (lvs, bk), *candicans* (lvs, bk), *nigra* (lvs, bk), *tremula* (lvs, bk), *tremuloides* (lvs, bk), *trichocarpa* (lvs, bk); *Salix alba* (lvs, bk), *americana* (lvs), *aurita* (bk), *babylonica* (lvs), *callicarpaea* (?*arctica*) (lvs), *calodendron* (lvs), *caprea* (lvs), *cinerea* (lvs), *daphnoides*, *fragilis* (?*decipiens*) (lvs), *incana* (lvs), *myrsinifolia* (?*nigricans*) (lvs, bk), *pentandra* (lvs, bk), *phylicifolia* (lvs), *purpurea* (lvs, bk), *repens* (lvs, bk), *triandra* (lvs), *viminalis* (lvs)

Salicyl-populin

Salic.   Populus tremula

Salicyl-tremuloidin

Salic.   Populus grandidentata, tremuloides

Salidroside (4-Hydroxyphenylethanol-β-D-glucopyranoside)

Salic.   *Salix alba* var. (lvs), *americana* (lvs), *babylonica* (lvs), *calliparpaea* (?*arctica*) (lvs), *calodendron* (lvs), *caprea* var. (lvs), *cinerea* (lvs), *daphnoides*, *fragilis* (?*decipiens*) (lvs), *incana* (lvs), *nigricans* (lvs), *pentandra* (lvs), *phylicifolia* (lvs), *purpurea* (lvs), *triandra* (lvs, bk), *viminalis* (lvs)

Salireposide

Salic.   *Populus alba* (bk, *not* lvs), *candicans* (bk, *not* lvs), *tremula* (bk, *not* lvs), *tremuloides* (bk, *not* lvs), *trichocarpa* (lvs, bk); *Salix purpurea* (bk), *repens* (bk), *triandra* (?bk); but *not* in some species.

Spiraein *may* be identical with *helicin*.

Ros.   Spiraea

Syringic acid-glucoside is said to be hydrolysed to *glucose* and *methyl-syringate*.

Legum.   Robinia
Myrsin.   ?*Aegiceras* has *syringic acid*

Syringoside (Ligustrin; Lilacin; Syringin): see the '*Syringin* (1:1 H_2SO_4) *test*'. It is reported from

Loranth.   Viscum album (on *Fraxinus*?)
Legum.   Robinia pseudacacia (bk)
Ole.   ± general—see discussion under the family
Caprifoli.   Lonicera arborea (bk), *myrtilloides* (bk ?), *pyrenaica* (bk ?), *ruprechtiana* (bk), *tatarica* vars. (bk), *thibetica* (bk) (all Plouvier, 1951)

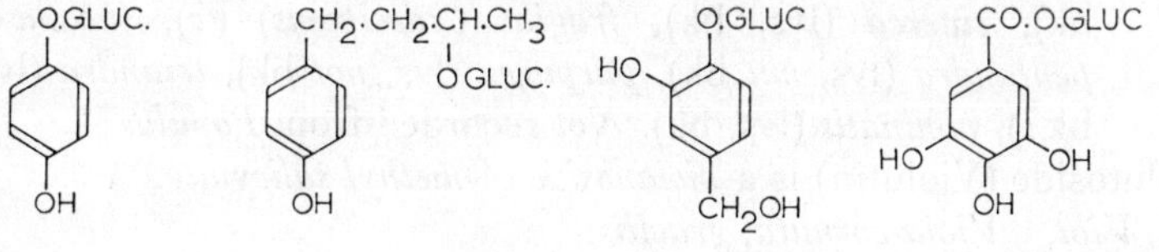

Arbutin   Betuloside   3,4-Dihydroxy-   1-Galloyl-β-
-benzyl alcohol-4-   -D-glucoside
-glucoside (Calleryanin)

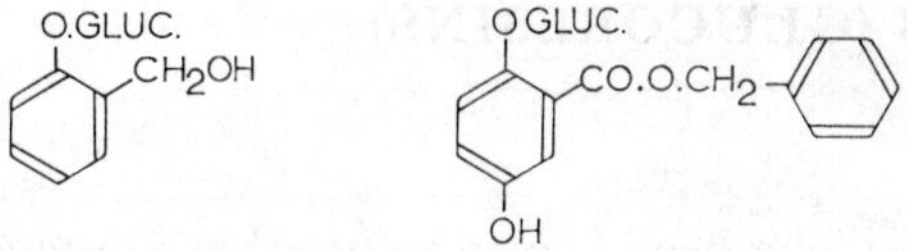

Salicin   Trichocarpin

Fig. 133 Some phenolic glycosides.

Tremulacin

Salic. Populus alba (lvs, bk), *tremula* (lvs, bk), *tremuloides*
(lvs, bk), *trichocarpa* (lvs): but *not* in some spp.; *Salix—not*
found?

Tremuloidin (2-Benzoyl-salicin)

Salic. Populus alba (lvs, *not* bk), *tremula* (lvs, *not* bk), *tremuloides*
(lvs, *not* bk), *trichocarpa* (lvs, bk), but *not* in some species;
Salix alba (lvs), *babylonica* (lvs), *callicarpaea* (?*arctica*) (lvs),
fragilis (lvs), *incana* (lvs), *nigricans* (lvs), *pentandra* (lvs), *purpurea*
(lvs), *triandra* (lvs): but *not* in some species

Triandrin (4-Hydroxy-cinnamyl alcohol-β-D-glucopyranoside)

Salic. Salix alba (bk), *aurita* (bk), *babylonica* (lvs), *callicarpaea*
(?*arctica*) (lvs), *calodendron* (lvs), *caprea* (bk, *not* lvs), *cinerea* (lvs),
daphnoides var., *fragilis* (?*decipiens*) (lvs, bk), *myrsinifolia* (?*nigri-*
cans (bk), *pentandra* (lvs, bk), *purpurea* (lvs, *not* bk), *triandra*
(lvs, bk), *viminalis* (lvs, bk): but *not* in some species. *Not*
recorded from *Populus*?

Trichocarpin (fig. 133)

Salic. Populus candicans (lvs, bk), *balsamifera* (lvs, st.), *trichocarpa*
(lvs, bk): but *not* in some species. *Not* recorded from *Salix*?

Vanillyl alcohol-4-glucoside

Orchid. Vanilla (green frt)

Vimalin (4-Methoxy-cinnamyl alcohol-β-D-glucopyranoside)

Salic. Salix alba (lvs, *not* bk), *americana* (lvs?), *babylonica* (lvs),
callicarpaea (?*arctica*) (lvs), *calodendron* (lvs), *caprea* (lvs, *not*

bk), *cinerea* (lvs, bk), *fragilis* (*?decipiens*) (?), *incana* (lvs), *pentandra* (lvs, *not* bk), *purpurea* (lvs, *not* bk), *triandra* (lvs, *not* bk?), *viminalis* (lvs, bk). *Not* recorded from *Populus*?

Violutoside (Violutin) is a *vicianoside* of *methyl salicylate*.

 Viol. Viola cornuta, gracilis

Xylosmoside is an α-*glucoside* of *gentisic acid* (or should it be *alcohol*?).

 Flacourti. Xylosma apactis (*Apactis japonica*) (bk)

IV GLYCOLIPIDS (GLUCORESINS)

GENERAL

The *Convolvulaceae* have long been known to produce substances such as jalapin, scammonium and scammony-resin, which are chemically and physiologically of considerable interest. They consist, in part at least, of *glycolipids* which yield, when subjected to alkaline hydrolysis, short-chain *aliphatic acids* and *glycosidic acids*. The latter, on acid hydrolysis, give *hydroxylated fatty-acids—jalapinolic acid, convolvulinolic acid*—and *dihydroxy* derivatives of *tetradecanoic, pentadecanoic?, hexadecanoic* and *octadecanoic acids*; plus *sugars* such as D-*glucose*, D-*fucose*, L-*rhamnose* and 6-*deoxy*-D-*glucose* (D-*quinovose*).

Writing about these *glycolipids*, Smith, Niece, Zobel and Wolff (1964) say: 'Evidently it has not been recognized that certain glycolipid bacterial metabolites that have been discovered comparatively recently are strikingly similar to the glycosides of the Convolvulaceae in their general makeup.'

The *glycolipids*, or the mixtures in which they occur, are so complicated that I find it difficult to get the reports in the literature disentangled. Synonymy, too, in the plants involved is hard to straighten out. For these reasons I am afraid that the list which follows is far from satisfactory.

List and Occurrence

Convolvulin (Rhodeoretin) is the glycoside of jalap. It is hydrolysed to *glucose, rhodeose* and *convolvulinic acid*.

 Convolvul. Exogonium purga (Vera Cruz jalap)

Convolvulinic acid is formed by the partial hydrolysis of *convolvulin* (above). It can be itself hydrolysed to *convolvulinolic acid* (usually said to be 11-*hydroxy-tetradecanoic acid*, but also reported to be a *hydroxy-pentadecanoic acid*) and 5 × *glucose*. Does it occur free?

Jalapin (Orizabin, Scammonin) is a strong purgative and fish-poison.

It is hydrolysed to *jalapinolic acid*, D-*glucose*, *rhodeose*, a *methyl-tetrose*, and perhaps something else.

 Convolvul. *Convolvulus orizabensis, scammonia* (rt)

Turpethin: belongs here? It is a constituent of *turpethum* resin. It yields on hydrolysis D-*fucose* and ?.

 Convolvul. *Operculina (Turpethum) turpethum* (resin)

V INDOXYL GLYCOSIDES

GENERAL

At least two naturally occurring substances seem to be *glycosides* (or one a near-glycoside) of *indoxyl*. They may be treated here for convenience.

List and Occurrence

Indican (Indoxyl-β-D-glucoside) yields, under suitable conditions, the once-important dye *indigo*. It is possible that not all the reported occurrences are of *indican*.

 Polygon. *Polygonum tinctorium* (plt)
 Crucif. *Isatis lusitanica (aleppica)* (but see below)
 Legum. *Crotalaria cunninghamii* (lvs), *incana* (lvs), *retusa* (lvs), *turgida* (lvs); *Indigofera argentea (articulata)*, *arrecta* (lvs), *hirsuta, leptostachya* (lvs), *longiracemosa* ?, *suffruticosa, sumatrana* (lvs), *tinctoria* (lvs); *Robinia pseudacacia* (lvs)
 Polygal. *Polygala tinctoria*
 Apocyn. *Echites religiosa* (latex), *Wrightia (Nerium) tinctoria* (plt)
 Asclepiad. *Asclepias (Gymnema) tingens* (a doubtful record)
 Orchid. *Bletia* sp. (lvs, fl.); *Calanthe (Limodorum) veratrifolia* (lvs, fl.), *vestita* (lvs, fl.); *Epidendrum difforme* (lvs, fl.); *Phaius grandi-folius* (lvs, fl.), *indigoferus* (lvs, fl.)

Isatan-B is said to be the indigo precursor in 'woad'. It can be hydrolysed to *indoxyl* and 5-*ketogluconic acid*, so it is *not* a true *glycoside*.

 Crucif. *Isatis tinctoria* (plt—'woad')

GUMS, MUCILAGES AND RESINS

GENERAL

These are not, or are only rarely, single chemical entities. They are almost always complex and often variable mixtures of compounds, themselves often complex. They are difficult to work with, are sometimes contaminated as they become available on the market, and all too often the botanical sources are obscure.

Nevertheless it is clear that some groups of plants produce *gums*, others *mucilages* and yet others *resins*, and that the types of materials may be highly characteristic of the plant groups producing them.

In the case of the conifers, for example, some genera—such as *Pinus*—form resins so individual to the species that they may be used in identification (Mirov, 1961). Among the angiosperms some families are known for their resins—the *Dipterocarpaceae* come to mind—while others seem to be utterly devoid of them.

The seeds of some plants have mucilaginous coats and the chemistry of the *mucilage* may be characteristic in at least some families. We have made no attempt to collect in detail information on this, but we *have* attempted to record presence or absence of mucilage as reported in the literature, and we have tried to observe presence or absence for ourselves, particularly when carrying out *HCN* (*Test A*).

It would be nice to have some quick and simple test for *mucilage*, comparable with our tests for *tannins*, *saponins* and so forth. I know of none, but Flück (1963) mentions measurement of viscosity as a possible test.

An outstanding example of a group rich in *mucilage* is the order **Malvales**.

Difficulties are compounded in the case of the *gums*. Many plants which seem not to produce gums when uninjured are subject to 'gummosis' under some conditions—as when wounded or infected. It is often hard to decide whether the host plant or the infecting agent produces the *gum*. Apparently there is some disagreement about the pathology of *gums* and *mucilages*. Onslow (1931) and Steele (1949) said respectively: 'Both gums and mucilages are abnormal products of the cell-wall.' and: 'The mucilages are normal constituents of plants, but the gums are mostly produced under pathological conditions.'

There seems, indeed, to be no hard and fast line to be drawn between *gums* and *mucilages*. The former are acidic substances which swell to form gels, or viscous sticky solutions: the latter merely swell in water. Both are largely carbohydrate, yielding *simple sugars* and *uronic acids*.

A recent treatment of the chemistry of these substances is that of Aspinall (1969). He says that the most common type of *exudate gum* is the *galactan type*, including gum arabic and other *Acacia* gums and mesquite gum. In these there seems to be a core of *galactopyranosyl* units linked (1 → 3 and 1 → 6); residues of D-*glucuronic acid* and/or its 4-*methyl ether*; and outer chains of L-*arabinofuranosyl* residues or L-*rhamnopyranosyl* residues.

The members of the *gluconomannan group* have basal chains of alternating 4-*O*-substituted D-*glucuronic acid* and 2-*O*-substituted D-*mannosyl* residues. Here belong gums of *Anogeissus latifolia* and *leiocarpus* (*schimperi*)—and of *Prunus* spp. ?

The *galacturonorhamnan group* includes gums with interior chains of D-*galacturonic acid* and L-*rhamnosyl* residues. *Tragacanthic acid* from gum tragacanth, and the khaya gums from *Khaya grandifolia, ivorensis* and *senegalensis* seem to be of this type; as do the *Sterculia* gums and the gum from *Cochlospermum gossypium* (very similar though from unrelated plants).

The *xylan group* includes gums of sapote (*Achras zapota*) and *Watsonia*.

The *xyloglucan group* includes gums from several groups of plants: *Tamarindus* (sd), white mustard, sycamore, etc.

Aspinall deals only briefly with matters of chemotaxonomy. He says that relationship is particularly evident in the case of the *Acacia* gums. Tookey and Jones (1965), who studied *seed-gums* from 300 spp., belonging to 139 genera and 31 families, would agree. They say that all the gums from the 20 legumes considered are of *galactomannan* type. They found seeds of the *Caesalpinioideae* to be richer in gum than those of *Mimosoideae* and *Faboideae*.

Hirst (1951), too, says: 'The plant gums are indeed so highly specific in their chemical structure that some workers believe that a knowledge of the chemical nature of a particular gum would enable the species and perhaps even the variety of the parent to be identified.'

Gums and mucilages may be found in all, or almost all organs of the plant. Under *mucilage* I have in my records: seeds—*Plantaginaceae* (*psyllium*), *Linaceae* (linseed), *Cruciferae*; bark—*Ulmaceae* (slippery elm); tubers—*Amaryllidaceae*; bulbs—*Liliaceae*; pseudobulbs—*Orchidaceae*; raphide-sacs—many plants.

Among the publications most useful in this field we may note Howes, *Vegetable Gums and Resins* (1949), Mantell, *The Water Soluble Gums* (1947), and Smith and Montgomery, *The Chemistry of Plant Gums and Mucilages* (1959).

The *resins* are included here for convenience. Chemically they are quite distinct from the *gums* and *mucilages*, being essentially terpenoid in character and soluble in organic solvents rather than in water. As they occur in Nature, however, they may be mixed with gums. A distinction is sometimes made between true *resins*, which are usually transparent and brittle; the *gum-resins*, which are mixtures of true *gums, essential oil* and a large proportion of *resin*; and the *balsams*, which are usually obtained by wounding the plant, 'when the injured cambium layers of cells develop a pathological secretion'.

Resins are of frequent occurrence in the gymnosperms, but some families of dicotyledons have resin-canals much like those of the conifers, while others have cells with 'resiniferous' contents. The following list, compiled largely from Metcalfe and Chalk (1950), shows how widespread these may be. It should be remarked that in some cases no true resins may be present.

Jugland. *Jugland.* (in at least 1 sp., McNair, 1930)

Fag. *Betul.* (in at least 1 sp., McNair, 1930)

Urtic. *Mor.* (*Artocarpus* has much resin in latex)

Magnoli. *Schisandr., Gomorteg.* and *Tetracentr.* (have cells with resiniferous contents)

Ranuncul. *Berberid.* (*Podophyllum*)

Guttifer. *Paeoni.* (*Paeonia* has resins); *Dipterocarp.* (resins in *Dipterocarpoideae*, but *not* in *Monotoideae*); *Marcgravi.* (oleo-resin in *Souroubea*; cells with resiniferous contents in others); *Guttif.* (resins in all?)

Ros. *Hamamelid.* (*Altingia, Liquidambar* has storax); *Myrothamn.* (in 1 sp., McNair, 1930); *Pittospor.* (secretory-canals, which have been described as schizogenous resin-canals, are 'a constant and characteristic feature of the family...in stem, roots, and leaves'); *Bruni.* (cells with resiniferous contents); *Legum.* (in at least 39 spp., McNair, 1930. Copals, balsams, resins).

Gerani. *Zygophyll.* (in at least 2 spp., McNair, 1930); *Lin.* (*Humiria*, at least 2 spp., McNair, 1930); *Euphorbi.* (cells with resiniferous contents)

Rut. *Rut.* (cells with resiniferous contents); *Simaroub.* (*Ailanthus* yields medicinal resin); *Burser.* (elemi, frankincense, myrrh. Resins in at least 35 spp., McNair, 1930); *Meli.* (cells with resiniferous contents. *Cedrela* has resins).

Sapind. *Anacardi.* (resin in 15 spp., McNair, 1930); *Sapind.* (in at least 1 sp., McNair, 1930. The stigma of *Koelreuteria* is said to secrete resin).

Juliani. *Juliani.* (*Juliania* has cells with resiniferous contents)

Rhamn. *Rhamn.* (resin in at least 2 spp., McNair, 1930)

Thymelae. *Thymelae.* (*Aquilaria* has resin)

Viol. *Flacourti.* (*Hydnocarpus, Zuelania*); *Cist.* (resins in at least 3 spp., McNair, 1930); *Cochlosperm.* (Are said to have cells with resiniferous contents, but McNair, 1930, says there is *no* tannin or resin present.)

Cucurbit. *Cucurbit.* (*Bryonia* has resin)

Myrt. *Myrt.* (*Eugenia*, '*Spermolepis*': should this be *Arillastrum*?)

Umbell. *Arali.* (in 1 sp., McNair, 1930); *Umbellif.* (gum-resins in many. McNair, 1930, says 14 spp.)

Eben.   *Styrac.* ('Balsamic resin')

Ole.   *Ole. (Olea* has gum-resin)

Gentian.   *Asclepiad.* (resin in latex); *Rubi.* (Cells with resiniferous contents. Resin in 6 spp., McNair, 1930)

Tubiflorae.   *Convolvul.* (Glucoresins. McNair, 1930, in 6 spp.); *Verben.* (*Tectona*); *Lab.* (*Salvia sclarea*); *Solan.* (*Capsicum* has oleo-resin?); *Myopor.* (*Myoporum* has oleo-resin)

Dipsac.   *Caprifoli.* (resin in 1 sp., McNair, 1930)

Campanul.   *Comp.* (in 6 spp., McNair, 1930)

Lili.   *Lili.* (in 3 spp., McNair, 1930); *Xanthorrhoe.* (acaroid resin); *Agav.* (*Dracaena*).

Gramin.   *Gramineae* (an 'oily, resinous secretion' in one)

Principes   *Palmae* (resin in 4 spp., McNair, 1930)

Spathiflorae   *Ar.* (*Philodendron*)

Scitamineae   *Zingiber.* (*Zingiber*)

Microspermae   *Orchid.* (*Vanilla*)

Resins are chemically quite complex. In them, or arising from them, have been found *sesquiterpenes*; *diterpenes*; *resin-acids* such as *abietic acid*, and *l-* and *d-pimaric acids*; *resin-esters* such as *benzyl benzoate* (dragon's blood), *cinnamyl cinnamate* (storax), esters of *ferulic* and *umbellic acids* (asafoetida), and so on; *resenes* (myrrh, dammar, mastic—resulting, perhaps, from polymerization); and *triterpenes*.

Few families have been adequately studied for their resins. The *Dipterocarpaceae* (q.v.) is an exception, with papers by Diaz, Ourisson and Bisset (1966), Bisset *et al.* (1966), and Bisset *et al.* (1967).

HYDROCARBONS

GENERAL

We may recognize three major classes of hydrocarbons:

I. Aliphatic or Acyclic Hydrocarbons, which are mostly dealt with here.

This group includes:

1. The normal saturated *alkanes* or *paraffins* ($CH_3.(CH_2)_n.CH_3$; C_nH_{2n+2})

2. The branched-chain saturated *alkanes*—iso-($CH_3.CH(CH_3).(CH_2)_n.CH_3$) and anteiso- ($CH_3.CH_2.CH(CH_3).(CH_2)_n.CH_3$)

3. The unsaturated *alkenes*, a few of which are included here. *Acetylenic* members are dealt with elsewhere (p. 88). Branched-chain *alkenes* may be *terpenoid,* and such are dealt with elsewhere.

II. Alicyclic Hydrocarbons include some of the *carotenoids* and other *terpenes* and are dealt with elsewhere.

III. Aromatic Hydrocarbons. *Naphthalene* and some *acetylenic compounds*, are dealt with elsewhere. *Styrene* belongs here.

I ALIPHATIC OR ACYCLIC HYDROCARBONS

GENERAL

These are usually called nowadays *alkanes* (saturated) and *alkenes* (unsaturated). In plants the *alkanes* occur most abundantly in the cuticle 'waxes' on leaves and stems; and those with an odd number of C-atoms seem to predominate in most species. Much of the earlier work has been shown to be erroneous. Chibnall *et al.* (1934), for example, found that *triacontane* (C_{30}) had been 'identified' many times in the literature. In every case the sample was shown to be a mixture, mostly of the very common C_{29} and C_{31} alkanes. They concluded that most plant (and insect) 'waxes' have odd-C-number *n-alkanes* ranging from C_{25} to C_{37}. Some even-numbered members do occur, however, and Kranz *et al.* (1961) claim to have found the *n-alkane* $C_{62}H_{126}$!

In addition to the unbranched *n-alkanes* ($CH_3.(CH_2)_n.CH_3$), some *iso*-($CH_3.CH(CH_3).(CH_2)_n.CH_3$) and *anteiso*-forms ($CH_3.CH_2.CH(CH_3).(CH_2)_n.CH_3$) have been found.

The odd-C-number *alkanes* are thought to arise from the next-higher even-C-number *fatty acids* by decarboxylation:

$$CH_3.(CH_2)_n.CH_2.COOH \rightarrow CH_3.(CH_2)_n.CH_3$$

(where *n* is odd).

It is clear that we know far too little about these substances to get much of chemotaxonomic interest out of them. We may note a few suggestive facts, however.

(*a*) If we plot the numbers of families in which each of the saturated normal hydrocarbons occur against the C-numbers (fig. 134), it is clear, even from my very incomplete records, that the commonly occurring members are C_{23}–C_{35}. The occurrence in a plant of any of these hydrocarbons would be of limited interest. The less commonly occurring members (below C_{23} and above C_{35}) might well be of great interest.

(*b*) In the **Tubiflorae** a few analyses are available from 6 of the 26 families. All the hydrocarbons recorded lie between C_{24} and C_{35}, i.e. none is unusual.

(*c*) In the *Scrophulariaceae* (**Tubiflorae**) a few records of leaf-waxes from *Bacopa*, *Digitalis* and *Hebe* are interesting. Eglinton, Hamilton and

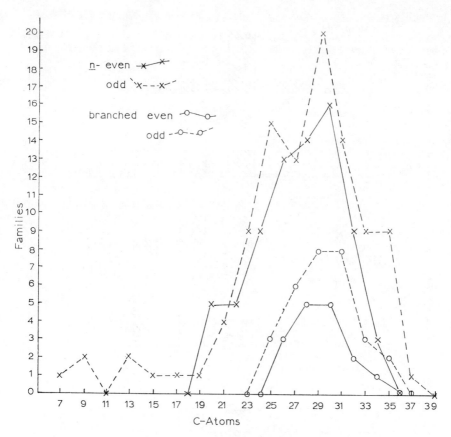

Fig. 134 Frequency of occurrence of *n*- and branched alkanes.

Martin-Smith (1962) found that normal hydrocarbons with odd-C-numbers predominated in *Hebe* but: 'within the genus *Hebe* the major constituent is C_{29} in *H. odora*, C_{31} in *H. parviflora* and *H. diosmifolia*, and C_{33} in *H. stricta*, thus giving an immediate chemotaxonomic distinction'.

The analysis of *Bacopa monnieri* is very similar to that for *Hebe parviflora* (fig. 135). At least one species of *Digitalis* has the C_{30} hydrocarbon, which is in *Bacopa* and in *Hebe* (4 spp.) in small amount.

(*d*) In *Solanum* (Mecklenburg, 1966) all the 20 species examined had both normal (C_{25} to C_{31}) and branched (C_{25} to C_{32}) *alkanes* in their inflorescence waxes. Mecklenburg concluded that: 'In general, the results of this work tend to confirm relationships between species thought to exist on the basis of morphological, cytogenetic, and inter-fertility data.'

22

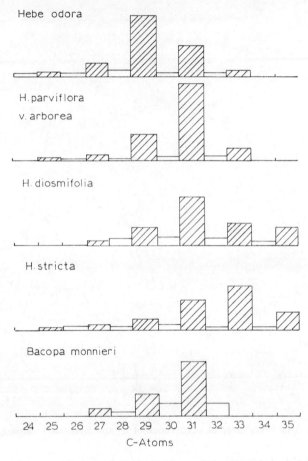

Fig. 135 *n*-Alkanes of the leaf-waxes of the *Scrophulariaceae*
(Eglinton *et al.* for *Hebe*)

(*e*) The *Crassulaceae* have been relatively fully investigated by
Eglinton *et al.* (1962) and Herbin and Robins (1968). The members
have normal and branched hydrocarbons from C_{25} to C_{35}, with C_{29},
C_{31} and C_{33} in largest amounts. See fig. 135 for *Kalanchoë*.

(*f*) More than 60 species of the genus *Aloë* of the *Liliaceae* have been
studied by Herbin and Robins (1968). They found leaf-cuticular waxes
(entered in my list) to show species specificity in composition. The
perianth-wax alkanes proved even better chemotaxonomically. Branched
alkanes were found in one leaf-wax. *Alkenes* were found in two perianth
waxes and in all style and filament waxes.

(*g*) If we plot the alkanes of *Eucalyptus* (19 spp.), *Agave* (19 spp.),

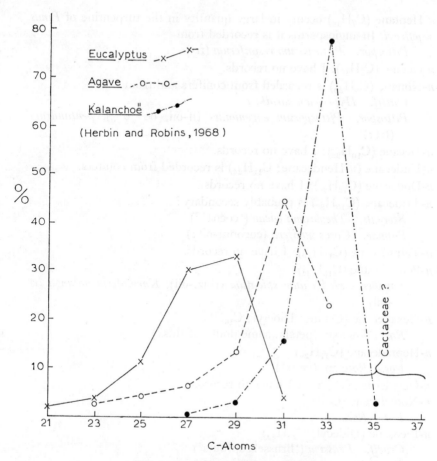

Fig. 136 *n*-Alkanes of some plants.

and *Kalanchoë* (5 spp.) we see that the patterns are quite distinct (fig. 136).

The unsaturated hydrocarbons, *alkenes*, seem to be few in number and of little taxonomic value. *Olea* (*Oleaceae*) seems to have several, but its product olive-oil has been much investigated.

List and Occurrence

1. Normal Alkanes

The first few members of the series are gases, the next liquids, and only with the C_{16} member do we come to a solid.

I have no record of any of these *alkanes* below C_7.

22-2

n-Heptane (C_7H_{16}) occurs in large quantity in the turpentine of *Pinus jeffreyi*. In angiosperms it is recorded from
>Pittospor. *Pittosporum resiniferum* (frt)

n-Octane (C_8H_{18}): I have no records.

n-Nonane (C_9H_{20}) is recorded from conifers and from
>Guttif. *Hypericum sarothra*
>Pittospor. *Pittosporum eugenioides* (lf-oil, 60–70%), *pentandrum* (frt ?)

n-Decane ($C_{10}H_{22}$): I have no records.

n-Undecane (n-Hendecane; $C_{11}H_{24}$) is recorded from conifers.

n-Dodecane ($C_{12}H_{26}$): I have no records.

n-Tridecane ($C_{13}H_{28}$) is probably secondary ?
>Sterculi. *Theobroma cacao* ('cocoa' ?)
>Palmae. *Cocos nucifera* (coconut-oil ?)

n-Tetradecane ($C_{14}H_{30}$): I have no records.

n-Pentadecane ($C_{15}H_{32}$)
>Zingiber. *Hedychium spicatum* (rhiz.-oil), *Kaempferia galanga* (rt -oil)

n-Hexadecane (Cetane; Dioctyl; $C_{16}H_{34}$)
>Ros. *Rosa* sp. (petals: some doubt of this ?)

n-Heptadecane ($C_{17}H_{36}$)
>Ros. *Rosa* sp. ('wax')

n-Octadecane ($C_{18}H_{38}$): I have no records.

n-Nonadecane ($C_{19}H_{40}$)
>Ros. *Rosa* sp.

n-Eicosane (Didecyl; $C_{20}H_{42}$)
>Crucif. *Brassica* ('Brussels sprouts')
>Ros. *Rosa* sp. ?
>Legum. *Acacia farnesiana* (fl.)
>Comp. *Artemisia* sp.
>Lili. *Aloë* (lvs of 1, 1%)

n-Heneicosane ($C_{21}H_{44}$) is said to occur in green algae and in
>Ros. *Rosa* sp. ?
>Myrt. *Eucalyptus* (lvs of 10, to 1%)
>Lili. *Aloë* (lvs of 26, to 4%)
>Agav. *Agave* (lvs of 4, tr.)

n-Docosane ($C_{22}H_{46}$)
>Ros. *Rosa* sp. ?
>Rhamn. *Rhamnus* sp.
>Myrt. *Eucalyptus* (lvs of 15, to 2%)
>Lili. *Aloë* (lvs of 33, to 7%)
>Agav. *Agave* (lvs of 6, tr.)

n-Tricosane ($C_{23}H_{48}$)

    Betul.   *Corylus avellana* (pollen)

    Crassul.   *Crassula* (lvs of 1, tr.), *Echeveria* (lvs of 1, tr.), *Kalanchoë* (lvs of 1, tr.)

    Ros.   *Malus* (apple, tr.), *Rosa* sp. ?

    Gerani.   *Geranium macrorrhizum* (ess. oil)

    Myrt.   *Eucalyptus* (lvs of 17, to 8%)

    Arali.   *Nothopanax simplex* (ess. oil)

    Scrophulari.   *Hebe* (lvs)

    Lili.   *Aloë* (lvs of 54, to 8%)

    Agav.   *Agave* (lvs of 14, to 1%)

n-Tetracosane ($C_{24}H_{50}$)

    Crassul.   *Crassula* (lvs of 2, to 2%), *Echeveria* (lvs of 1, tr.), *Kalanchoë* (lvs of 1, tr.)

    Myrt.   *Eucalyptus* (lvs of 19, to 19%)

    Ole.   *Olea europaea* (olive-oil)

    Scrophulari.   *Hebe odora* (lf-wax, little)

    Comp.   *Chrysanthemum indicum* (fl.)

    Lili.   *Aloë* (lvs of 57, to 7%)

    Agav.   *Agave* (lvs of 15, to 1%)

    Palmae.   *Attalea excelsa* (wax)

    Gram.   *Avena*

n-Pentacosane ($C_{25}H_{52}$)

    Salic.   *Populus* (2)

    Crassul.   *Aeonium* (lvs of 18, to 2%), *Crassula* (lvs of 3, to 4%), *Echeveria* (lvs of 2, tr.), *Kalanchoë* (lvs of 4, to 1%; petals of 2, tr.), *Sedum* (lvs of 1, tr.)

    Ros.   *Acaena anserinifolia* (lvs and st.), *Malus* (apple, tr.), *Rosa* sp.

    Legum.   *Ferreirea*

    Rut.   *Citrus* (2)

    Thymelae.   *Pimelea prostrata* (lvs and st., 3%)

    Myrt.   *Eucalyptus* (lvs of 19, to 33%)

    Arali.   *Nothopanax simplex* (ess. oil)

    Eric.   *Gaultheria* (lvs and st. of 2, to 4%)

    Solan.   *Mandragora, Nicotiana, Solanum* spp. (infl.)

    Scrophulari.   *Hebe* (lvs of 3)

    Lili.   *Aloë* (lvs of 62, to 25%)

    Agav.   *Agave* (lvs of 19, to 7%)

    Gram.   *Arundo conspicua* (lvs, 4%)

    Typh.   *Typha*

n-Hexacosane ($C_{26}H_{54}$)

    Crassul.   *Aeonium* (lvs of 19, to 1%), *Aichryson* (lvs of 1, tr.), *Crassula* (lvs of 3, to 4%), *Echeveria* (lvs of 2, tr.), *Greenovia* (lvs of 3 or more, tr.), *Kalanchoë* (lvs of 3, to 1%), *Monanthes* (lvs of 4, tr.), *Sedum* (lvs of 1, tr.)

Ros. *Acaena anserinifolia* (lvs and st., 1%), *Rosa* sp. ?

Euphorbi. *Euphorbia* (5, to 2%)

Myrt. *Eucalyptus* (lvs of 19, to 15%)

Ole. *Olea europaea* (olive-oil)

Solan. *Solanum* spp. (infl.)

Scrophulari. *Hebe* (lf-waxes of 3)

Comp. *Chrysanthemum indicum* (fl.)

Lili. *Aloë* (lvs of 62, to 13%), *Phormium tenax* (rhiz., 4%)

Agav. *Agave* (lvs of 19, to 7%), *Cordyline australis* (rhiz., 2%), *Dracaena draco* (5%)

Gram. *Lolium multiflora* (1%)

n-Heptacosane ($C_{27}H_{56}$) occurs in ferns and in

Crassul. *Aeonium* (lvs of 22, to 8%), *Aichryson* (lvs of 1 or 2, to 1%), *Crassula* (lvs of 4, to 3%), *Echeveria* (lvs of 2, to 1%), *Greenovia* (lvs of 2 or more, to 1%), *Kalanchoë* (lvs of 5, to 1%; petals of 2, to 4%), *Monanthes* (lvs of 7, to 1%), *Sedum* (lvs of 3, to 1%)

Ros. *Malus* (apple, 1%)

Euphorbi. *Euphorbia* (6, to 51%)

Thymelae. *Pimelea prostrata* (lvs and st., 2%)

Myrt. *Eucalyptus* (lvs of 19, to 56%)

Arali. *Nothopanax simplex* (ess. oil)?

Eric. *Gaultheria* (lvs and st. of 2, to 3%)

Ole. *Olea europaea* (olive-oil)

Solan. *Solanum* spp. (infl.)

Scrophulari. *Bacopa monnieri*; *Hebe* (lf-waxes of 4)

Lili. *Aloë* (lvs of 62, to 50%)

Agav. *Dracaena draco* (12%)

Palmae. *Copernicia* (wax)

Gram. *Lolium multiflora* (7%)

n-Octacosane ($C_{28}H_{58}$)

Crassul. *Aeonium* (lvs of 19, to 2%), *Aichryson* (lvs of 1, tr.), *Crassula* (lvs of 4, to 4%), *Echeveria* (lvs of 2, to 2%), *Greenovia* (lvs of 1 or more, tr.), *Kalanchoë* (lvs of 5, to 1%; petals of 2, tr.), *Monanthes* (lvs of 4, tr.), *Sedum* (lvs of 2, to 1%)

Ros. *Acaena anserinifolia* (lvs and st., 2%), *Rosa* sp.

Euphorbi. *Euphorbia* (6, to 3%)

Tili. *Tilia europea* (fl.)

Malv. *Malva rotundifolia*

Thymelae. *Pimelea prostrata* (lvs and st., 3%)

Myrt. *Eucalyptus* (lvs of 19, to 8%)

Eric. Gaultheria (lvs and st. of 2, to 3%)

Solan. Solanum spp. (infl.)

Scrophulari. Bacopa monnieri, Hebe (lf-waxes of 4)

Comp. Antennaria dioica (fl.)

Lili. Aloë (lvs of 63, to 18%), Phormium tenax (rhiz., 3%)

Agav. Agave (lvs of 19, to 11%), Cordyline australis (rhiz., 3%), Dracaena draco (7%)

Gram. Arundo conspicua (lvs, 5%), Lolium multiflora (1%)

n-Nonacosane ($C_{29}H_{60}$)

Salic. Populus

Caryophyll. Cerastium

Crucif. several, often in very large amount

Crassul. Aeonium (lvs of 25, to 12%), Aichryson (lvs of 2 or 3, to 2%), Crassula (lvs of 4, to 12%), Echeveria (lvs of 3, to 9%), Greenovia (3 or more, to 2%), Kalanchoë (lvs of 5, to 1%; petals of 2, to 12%), Monanthes (lvs of 7, to 1%), Sedum (lvs of 3, to 9%)

Ros. Acaena anserinifolia (lvs and st., 11%), Malus (apple-peel wax, in *very* large amount)

Legum. 'bean', Gleditsia, Spartium

Euphorbi. Euphorbia (6, to 25%)

Rut. Citrus

Thymelae. Pimelea prostrata (lvs and stem, 65%)

Myrt. Eucalyptus (lvs of 19, to 70%)

Onagr. Chamaenerion, Epilobium

Corn. Cornus

Arali. Nothopanax simplex (ess. oil)

Eric. Gaultheria (lvs and st. of 2, to 26%)

Asclepiad. Cryptostegia grandiflora

Solan. Solanum spp. (infl.)

Scrophulari. Bacopa monnieri, Hebe odora (chief hydrocarbon) and 3 others

Lili. Aloë (lvs of 63, to 63%), Phormium tenax (rhiz., to 47%)

Agav. Agave (lvs of 19, to 35%), Cordyline australis (rhiz., 15%), Dracaena draco (22%)

Gram. Lolium multiflora (40%), Zea

n-Triacontane ($C_{30}H_{62}$)

Caryophyll. Cerastium

Crassul. Aeonium (lvs of 21, to 2%), Aichryson (lvs of 2 or 3, to 4%), Crassula (lvs of 4, to 3%), Echeveria (lvs of 3, to 1%), Greenovia (lvs of 1 or more, tr.), Kalanchoë (lvs of 5, to 1%; petals of 2, to 1%), Monanthes (lvs of 2, to 3%), Sedum (lvs of 3, to 2%)

Ros. Malus, Rosa

Gerani.   Geranium macrorrhizum (ess. oil)
Euphorbi.   Cluytia, Euphorbia (5, to 3%)
Hippocastan.   Aesculus
Thymelae.   Pimelea prostrata (lvs and st., 2%)
Myrt.   Eucalyptus (lvs of 18, to 2%)
Eric.   Gaultheria (lvs and st. of 2, to 3%)
Hydrophyll.   Eriodictyon glutinosum (lvs)
Solan.   Solanum spp. (infl.)
Scrophulari.   Bacopa monnieri (little), *Digitalis, Hebe* (lvs of 4, in small amounts)
Comp.   Achillea, Anthemis, Arnica, Carpesium
Lili.   Aloë (lvs of 62, to 14%), *Phormium tenax* (rhiz., to 3%)
Agav.   Agave (lvs of 19, to 10%), *Cordyline australis* (rhiz., 3%), *Dracaena draco* (6%)
Gram.   Lolium multiflora (1%)

n-Hentriacontane ($C_{31}H_{64}$)
Crucif.   'mustard leaf-wax', more than 50%
Crassul.   Aeonium (lvs of 24, to 79%), *Aichryson* (lvs of 2 or 3, to 17%), *Crassula* (lvs of 4, to 77%), *Echeveria* (lvs of 3, to 55%), *Greenovia* (lvs of 3 or more, to 9%), *Kalanchoë* (lvs of 5, to 30%; petals of 2, to 32%), *Monanthes* (lvs of 7, to 52%), *Sedum* (lvs of 3, to 80%)
Ros.   Acaena anserinifolia (lvs and st., 59%), *Malus* (apple, tr.)
Legum.   'bean leaf-wax', 48%
Euphorbi.   Euphorbia (5, to 70%), *Pedilanthus pavonis* (wax)
Thymelae.   Pimelea prostrata (lvs and st., 13%)
Myrt.   Eucalyptus (lvs of 19, to 10%)
Eric.   Arbutus, Gaultheria (lvs and st. of 2, to 56%)
Apocyn.   Ervatamia wallichiana (lvs, bk)
Solan.   Solanum spp. (infl.)
Scrophulari.   Bacopa monnieri (chief hydrocarbon), *Hebe* (chief hydroc. of 2) and 2 others
Lili.   Aloë (lvs of 62, to 96%), *Phormium tenax* (rhiz., to 8%)
Agav.   Agave (lvs of 19, to 80%), *Cordyline australis* (rhiz., 10%), *Dracaena draco* (31%)
Gram.   Arundo conspicua (lvs, 12%), *Leptochloa digitata* (chief hydroc. of stem-wax), *Lolium multiflora* (40%)

n-Dotriacontane (Dicetyl; $C_{32}H_{66}$)
Crassul.   Aeonium (lvs of 21, to 5%), *Aichryson* (lvs of 2 or 3, to 4%), *Crassula* (lvs of 4, to 7%), *Echeveria* (lvs of 3, to 4%), *Greenovia* (lvs of 3 or more, to 3%), *Kalanchoë* (lvs of 5, to 5%; petals of 2, to 3%), *Monanthes* (lvs of 7, to 2%), *Sedum* (lvs of 3, to 5%)

Ros.   *Acaena anserinifolia* (lvs and st., 2%), *Alchemilla vulgaris*
Euphorbi.   Euphorbia?
Eric.   Gaultheria (lvs and st. of 2, to 4%)
Lab.   Mentha
Myopor.   Myoporum laetum (this, or $C_{34}H_{70}$)
Lili.   Aloë (lvs of 52, to 8%), *Phormium tenax* (rhiz., 2%)
Agav.   Agave (lvs of 19, to 5%), *Dracaena draco* (1%)
Gram.   Arundo conspicua (lvs, 2%)

n-Tritriacontane ($C_{33}H_{68}$)
    Cact.   Opuntia sp.
    Crassul.   Aeonium (lvs of 23, to 80%), *Aichryson* (lvs of 2 or 3, to
        62%), *Crassula* (lvs of 4, to 57%), *Echeveria* (lvs of 3, to 46%),
        Greenovia (lvs of 3 or more, to 82%), *Kalanchoë* (lvs of 5, to
        87%; petals of 2, to 51%), *Monanthes* (lvs of 7, to 94%), *Sedum*
        (lvs of 3, to 47%)
    Ros.   Acaena anserinifolia (lvs and st., 19%), *Malus* (apple,
        tr.)
    Euphorbi.   Euphorbia (4, to 18%), *Pedilanthus pavonis* (wax)
    Eric.   Gaultheria (lvs and st. of 2, to 7%)
    Asclepiad.   Cryptostegia grandiflora (lvs)
    Lili.   Aloë (lvs of 47, to 58%)
    Agav.   Agave (lvs of 19, to 67%), *Dracaena draco* (4%)
    Gram.   Arundo conspicua (lvs, 3%), *Lolium multiflora* (3%)

n-Tetratriacontane ($C_{34}H_{70}$)
    Crassul.   Aeonium (lvs of 17, to 3%), *Aichryson* (lvs of 2 or 3, to
        2%), *Crassula* (lvs of 3, to 3%), *Echeveria* (lvs of 3, tr.), *Greenovia*
        (lvs of 3 or more, to 12%), *Kalanchoë* (lvs of 5, to 1%; petals of 1,
        tr.), *Monanthes* (lvs of 5, to 1%)
    Scrophulari.   Hebe (lvs and st. of 2, to 1%)
    Myopor.   Myoporum laetum (this, or $C_{32}H_{66}$)

n-Pentatriacontane ($C_{35}H_{72}$)
    *Cact.   at least one
    Papaver.   Fumaria officinalis
    Crassul.   Aeonium (lvs of 22, to 13%), *Aichryson* (lvs of 2 or 3, to
        6%), *Crassula* (lvs of 3, to 30%), *Echeveria* (lvs of 3, to 1%),
        Greenovia (lvs of 3 or more, to 14%), *Kalanchoë* (lvs of 5, to 5%;
        petals of 1, 1%), *Monanthes* (lvs of 6, to 4%), *Sedum* (lvs of 1,
        tr.)
    Pittospor.   Pittosporum undulatum (frt)
    Malv.   Gossypium sp.
    Asclepiad.   Gymnema sylvestre
    Hydrophyll.   Eriodictyon glutinosum (lvs)
    Verben.   Vitex lucens (lvs)

Scrophulari.   Hebe (lvs and st. of 2, to 16%)

n-Hexatriacontane ($C_{36}H_{74}$): I have no records.

n-Heptatriacontane ($C_{37}H_{76}$)
   Cact.   Opuntia sp.

n-Dohexatriacontane ($C_{62}H_{126}$)
   Gram.   Leptochloa digitata (stem-wax, in small amount)

2. Saturated Branched-chain Hydrocarbons

I have listed these as iso-, but some of the records may be of anteiso-
forms.

Iso-pentacosane ($C_{25}H_{52}$)
   Crassul.   Aeonium (lvs of 1, tr.)
   Solan.   Solanum spp. (infl.)
   Lili.   Phormium tenax (rhiz.)

Iso-hexacosane ($C_{26}H_{54}$)
   Crassul.   Aeonium (lvs of 1, tr.)
   Solan.   Solanum spp. (infl.)
   Lili.   Phormium tenax (rhiz.)

Iso-heptacosane ($C_{27}H_{56}$)
   Crassul.   Aeonium (lvs of 8, to 2%), Greenovia (lvs of 3, tr.),
      Monanthes (lvs of 1, tr.)
   Euphorbi.   Euphorbia (2, to 1%)
   Solan.   Solanum spp. (infl.)
   Scrophulari.   Hebe (lvs and st. of 1)
   Lili.   Phormium tenax (rhiz., 2%)
   Agav.   Cordyline australis (rhiz., 1%)

Iso-octacosane ($C_{28}H_{58}$)
   Crassul.   Aeonium (lvs of 6, to 2%)
   Ros.   Alchemilla alpina
   Euphorbi.   Euphorbia (1, tr.)
   Solan.   Solanum spp. (infl.)
   Lili.   Phormium tenax (rhiz.)

Iso-nonacosane ($C_{29}H_{60}$)
   Crassul.   Aeonium (lvs of 17, to 16%), Aichryson (lvs of 2, to 2%),
      Greenovia (lvs of 1, 2%), Monanthes (lvs of 5, to 1%)
   Ros.   Acaena anserinifolia (lvs and st., 1%)
   Euphorbi.   Euphorbia (2, to 1%)
   Thymelae.   Pimelea prostrata (lvs and st.)
   Solan.   Solanum sp. (infl.)
   Scrophulari.   Hebe (lvs and st. of 3)
   Lili.   Phormium tenax (rhiz., to 4%)
   Agav.   Cordyline australis (rhiz., 1%)

Iso-triacontane ($C_{30}H_{62}$)
  Crassul. *Aeonium* (lvs of 8, to 1%)
  Ros. *Acaena anserinifolia* (lvs and st., 1%)
  Euphorbi. *Euphorbia* (1, tr.)
  Solan. *Solanum* spp. (infl.)
  Lili. *Phormium tenax* (rhiz.)
Iso-hentriacontane ($C_{31}H_{64}$)
  Crassul. *Aeonium* (lvs of 24, to 30%), *Aichryson* (lvs of 3, to 7%),
    Greenovia (lvs of 4, to 2%), *Monanthes* (lvs of 2, to 1%)
  Ros. *Acaena anserinifolia* (lvs and st., 1%)
  Euphorbi. *Euphorbia* (1, tr.)
  Thymelae. *Pimelea prostrata* (lvs and st.)
  Solan. *Solanum* spp. (infl.)
  Scrophulari. *Hebe* (lvs and st. of 3)
  Lili. *Phormium tenax* (rhiz., 3%)
  Agav. *Cordyline australis* (rhiz., 1%)
Iso-dotriacontane ($C_{32}H_{66}$)
  Crassul. *Aeonium* (lvs of 14, to 3%), *Aichryson* (lvs of 2, to 7%)
  Solan. *Solanum* spp. (infl.)
Iso-tritriacontane ($C_{33}H_{68}$)
  Crassul. *Aeonium* (lvs of 20, to 39%), *Aichryson* (lvs of 3, to 14%),
    Greenovia (lvs of 3 or more, to 3%), *Monanthes* (lvs of 5, to 2%)
  Ros. *Acaena anserinifolia* (lvs and st.)
  Scrophulari. *Hebe* (lvs and st. of 2, to 1%)
Iso-tetratriacontane ($C_{34}H_{70}$)
  Crassul. *Aeonium* (lvs of 5, to 1%), *Aichryson* (lvs of 1, 2%)
Iso-pentatriacontane ($C_{35}H_{72}$)
  Crassul. *Aeonium* (lvs of 16, to 6%), *Aichryson* (lvs of 2 or 3, to
    3%), *Greenovia* (lvs of 1, or 2, to 2%)
  Scrophulari. *Hebe* (lvs and st. of 1, 1%)

3. Some Unsaturated Hydrocarbons

This is a heterogeneous group of substances which I have arranged
alphabetically.
Arachidene ($C_{19}H_{38}$)
  Legum. *Arachis hypogaea*
Butylene ($CH_2{=}CH.CH_2.CH_3$ or $CH_3.CH{=}CH.CH_3$; C_4H_8)
  Crucif. *Diplotaxis tenuifolia* (lvs)
Diallyl ($CH_2{=}CH.CH_2.CH_2.CH{=}CH_2$; C_6H_{10})
  Comp. *Ormenis multicaulis*
Ethylene ($CH_2{=}CH_2$; C_2H_4) is evolved by ripening fruits, etc. Fading
  flowers of *Vanda* (*Orchid.*) are said to produce > 3400 μl per kg per hr.

Gadusene ($C_{18}H_{32}$)
  Gram. wheat-germ
Hexadecadiene ($C_{16}H_{30}$)
  Ole. Olea europaea
Hypogene ($C_{15}H_{30}$)
  Legum. Arachis hypogaea
2-Methyl-5,12-tetradecadiene ($C_{15}H_{28}$)
  Comp. Echinacea angustifolia (rt)
2-Methyl-6,12-tetradecadiene
  Comp. Echinacea angustifolia (rt)
Nonadecadiene ($C_{19}H_{36}$)
  Ole. Olea europaea
Nonylene (C_9H_{18})
  Burser. Bursera delpechiana (oil)
Octacosatetraene ($C_{28}H_{50}$)
  Ole. Olea europaea
Octylene ($CH_3 . (CH_2)_5 . CH=CH_2$; C_8H_{16})
  Guttif. Hypericum?
Tricosatriene ($C_{23}H_{42}$)
  Ole. Olea europaea
Tridecadiene ($C_{13}H_{24}$)
  Ole. Olea europaea

II ALICYCLIC HYDROCARBONS are dealt with as *terpenes*

III AROMATIC HYDROCARBONS

Styrene (Cinnamene; Cinnamol; Cinnamomin; Phenylethylene; Styrol; Styrolene; Vinyl-benzene)
  Hamamelid. Liquidambar orientalis (storax, styrax)
  Xanthorrhoe. Xanthorrhoea hastilis (resin)

KETONES

GENERAL

This is probably an unnatural group, biosynthetically speaking, even though we have excluded *monoterpenoid ketones, acetylenic ketones, keto-sugars, keto-fatty-acids, furan derivatives, chalcones* and other *flavonoids*, and the *quinones* (which may be called *diketones*).

We are left with:

I. Aliphatic ketones
II. Aromatic ketones
   1. Acetophenones
   2. Benzophenones
   3. Other aromatic ketones
III. Other cyclic ketones

I ALIPHATIC KETONES

GENERAL

We have excluded from this section *monoterpenoid ketones* (see *monoter-penoids*), *acetylenic ketones* (see *acetylenic compounds*), and the *keto-sugars* (see *carbohydrates*).

(*a*) It is clear that the *Rutaceae* are rich in these ketones.

(*b*) In the **Magnoliales** we have a few records from *Annonaceae* (1), *Schisandraceae* (2), *Lauraceae* (3 in 2 genera). We have no records from **Ranunculales**.

(*c*) In the **Tubiflorae** the closely related *Verbenaceae* (1) and *Labiatae* (3 in 3 genera) have aliphatic ketones.

List and Occurrence

Acetone (Dimethyl-ketone; Propanone) is, says Karrer (1958), often a secondary product formed during distillation of essential oils, etc. I have a few records for what they are worth.
   Legum. *Phaseolus*
   Euphorbi. *Hevea, Manihot*
   Erythroxyl. *Erythroxylum*
   Umbell. *Coriandrum*
   Lab. *Pogostemon*

Butan-2,3-dione (Diacetyl; $CH_3.CO.CO.CH_3$) is often produced secondarily in the extraction of essential oils. It seems, however, to be responsible for the odours of some flowers.
   Annon. *Polyalthia canangoides* var. *angustifolia* (fl.)
   Logani. *Fagraea racemosa* (fl.)

But-2-ol-3-one (Acetoin; Acetyl-methyl-carbinol;
$CH_3.CH(OH).CO.CH_3$)
   Ros. *Fragaria*?, *Rubus*?
   Legum. 'bean leaves'
   Gram. *Zea mays* (lvs)

Decan-2-one (Methyl-octyl-ketone; $CH_3.CO.(CH_2)_7.CH_3$)
  Rut.   *Ruta graveolens* (oil), *montana* (oil)
Hentriacontan-22-ol-16-one (22-Hydroxy-palmitone)
  Santal.   *Santalum album* (lf-wax)
Hentriacontan-16-one (Aethalone; Palmitone;
  $CH_3.(CH_2)_{14}.CO.(CH_2)_{14}.CH_3$) occurs in bacteria and in
  Santal.   *Santalum album* (lf-wax)
  Comp.   *Tagetes grandiflora* (fl., probably)
Heptacos-14-one (Myristone; $CH_3.(CH_2)_{12}.CO.(CH_2)_{12}.CH_3$)
  Legum.   *Medicago sativa* (not confirmed?)
Heptan-2-one (Methyl-*n*-amyl-ketone)
  Laur.   *Cinnamomum zeylanicum* (oil)
  Rut.   *Ruta montana* (oil, trace)
  Myrt.   *Eugenia caryophyllata* (cloves)
2-Methyl-hept-2-en-6-one
  Urtic.   *Urtica dioica*
  Gerani.   *Pelargonium*
  Rut.   *Citrus?*
  Sterculi.   *Theobroma cacao*
  Lab.   *Ocimum canum*
  Verben.   *Lippia citriodora*
  Comp.   *Artemisia scoparia*
  Gram.   *Andropogon citratus, nardus*
  Zingiber.   *Zingiber officinale*
Nonacosan-15-one (Dimyristyl-ketone; Di-*n*-tetradecyl-ketone)
  Crucif.   *Brassica* (lf-wax)
Nonan-2-one (methyl-*n*-heptyl-ketone)
  Rut.   *Boronia ledifolia* var., *Phellodendron* sp., *Ruta chalepensis*,
    and other spp.
  Myrt.   *Eugenia caryophyllata* (cloves)
  Palmae.   *Cocos nucifera* (oil)
Octan-2-one (Methyl-*n*-hexyl-ketone; 2-Octanone)
  Rut.   *Ruta montana* (oil, trace)
Octan-3-one (Ethyl-*n*-amyl-ketone; 3-Octanone)
  Lab.   *Lavandula vera* (oil); *Mentha*
Pentan-2-one (Methyl-*n*-propyl-ketone)
  Bromeli.   *Ananas sativus* (frt, trace)
Tridecan-2-one (Methyl-*n*-undecyl-ketone)
  Schisandr.   *Schisandra nigra* (lf-oil, to 15%)
Undecan-2-one (Enodyl; Luparone; Methyl-*n*-nonyl-ketone)
  Mor.   *Humulus lupulus* ('*luparone*')
  Schisandr.   *Schisandra nigra* (ess. oil)
  Laur.   *Litsea odorifera* (lf-oil)

Saurur.   *Houttuynia cordata* (oil)

Legum.   *Glycine max* (soy-bean oil)

Rut.   *Boronia ledifolia* (lf-oil); *Citrus limetta* (frt-peel-oil); *Fagara
xanthoxyloides* (frt-peel); *Phellodendron amurense* (frt-oil); *Ruta
bracteosa* (oil, much), *chalepensis* (oil, much), *graveolens* ('*enodyl*'),
montana (much)

Palmae.   *Cocus nucifera* (oil), *Elaeis guineensis* (palm-kernel oil)

Undec-1-en-10-one $(CH_2=CH.(CH_2)_7.CO.CH_3)$

Laur.   *Litsea odorifera*

II AROMATIC KETONES. 1 Acetophenones

List and Occurrence

Acetophenone (Hypnone; Methyl-phenyl-ketone; fig. 137) seems to be
widely distributed.

Salic.   *Populus balsamifera* (buds)

Urtic.   *Urtica dioica*

Prote.   *Stirlingia latifolia*

The.   *Camellia* (green tea, trace)

Tili.   *Corchorus olitorius*?

Cist.   *Cistus creticus, ladaniferus*

Irid.   *Iris*

Acetovanillone (Apocynin; 3-Methoxy-4-hydroxy-acetophenone; fig.
137) seems to be very widely distributed.

Cact.   *Echinocereus engelmannii, Mammillaria runyonii, Neolloydia
texensis*

Apocyn.   *Apocynum androsaemifolium* (rt), *cannabinum* (rt,
apocynin)

Amaryllid.   *Buphane disticha* (bulb)

Irid.   *Iris*

Acetovanillone-glucoside (Androsin; Gluco-acetovanillone)

Cact.   *Neolloydia texensis* (plt)

Apocyn.   *Apocynum androsaemifolium* (rt, '*androsin*')

Acetovanillone-4-β-primveroside (?Neolloydosin)

Cact.   *Neolloydia texensis* (plt, '*neolloydosin*')

Acetoveratrone (3,4-Dimethoxy-acetophenone)

Irid.   *Iris*

3,4-Dihydroxy-acetophenone occurs in a conifer (*Picea*), but not (?) in
angiosperms.

2-Hydroxy-acetophenone (*o*-Hydroxy-acetophenone)

Rubi.   *Chione glabra* (wd, bk)

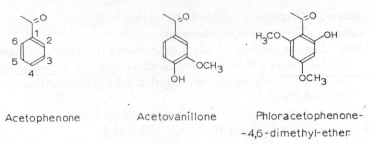

Acetophenone   Acetovanillone   Phloracetophenone-
                                              -4,6-dimethyl-ether

Fig. 137 Some acetophenones.

4-Hydroxy-acetophenone (Ameliarol; Piceol; *p*-Hydroxy-acetophenone)
is the aglycone of *salinigrin*.
  Salic.   Populus trichocarpa (buds)
2-Hydroxy-5-methoxy-acetophenone
  Primul.   Primula acaulis (rhiz.; as glycoside)
2-Hydroxy-6-methyl-acetophenone
  Elaeocarp.   Elaeocarpus polydactylus (lvs)
6-Methoxy-paeonol
  Xanthorrhoe.   Xanthorrhoea arborea, preissii, reflexa, tateana (these
    occurrences have been questioned by later workers)
4-Methyl-acetophenone (Oryzanone) is an attractant for the rice stem
borer.
  Gram.   Oryza sativa
Paeonol (Peonol; 2-Hydroxy-4-methoxy-acetophenone)
  Paeoni.   Paeonia moutan (rtbk)
  Primul.   Primula auricula (rt-oil, as glucoside?)
  Xanthorrhoe.   Xanthorrhoea arborea (resin), *reflexa* (resin)
Paeonol-glucoside (Gluco-paeonol)
  Paeoni.   Paeonia arborea (rt)
Phoracetophenone (2,4,6-Trihydroxy-acetophenone)
  Rut.   Zanthoxylum alatum, aubertia
Phloracetophenone-4,6-dimethyl ether (Brevifolin; Xanthoxylin; fig.
  137)
  Euphorbi.   Hippomane mancinella (lvs)
  Rut.   Fagara arenaria (lvs, frt); *Geijera parviflora, salicifolia*;
    Zanthoxylum (*Xanthoxylum*) *alatum* (sd), *aubertia* (sd), *rhetsa*
    (frt)
  Myrt.   Eucalyptus bakeri (lvs, oil)
  Comp.   Artemisia brevifolia (plt, 'brevifolin'), *Blumea balsamifera*
    (ess. oil)
Phloracetophenone-2,4,6-trimethyl ether
  Amaryllid.   Lycoris radiata (bulb)

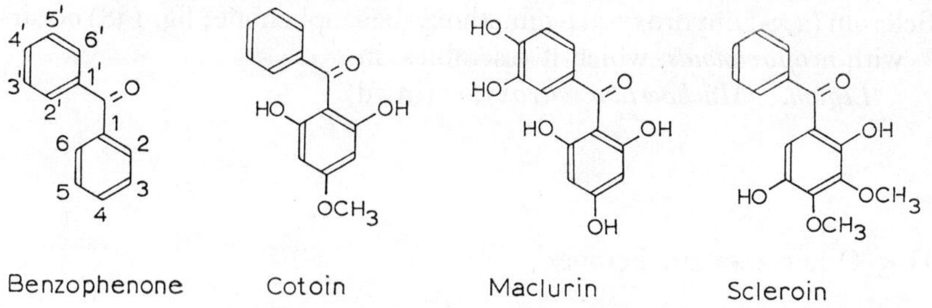

Fig. 138 Some benzophenones.

Salinigrin (Ameliaroside; Picein; Pungenin?; Salicinereine; 4-Hydroxy-acetophenone-β-D-glucopyranoside) occurs in a conifer (*Picea*) and in
  Salic.   *Salix cinerea* (bk), *nigra*; *Populus*?
  Ros.   *Amelanchier vulgaris* (bk, '*ameliaroside*')
  Verben.   *Clerodendron trichotomum* (bk)

II.2 Benzophenones

List and Occurrence

Benzophenone (Diphenyl-ketone; fig. 138): does not occur as such?
Cotoin (2,6-Dihydroxy-4-methoxy-benzophenone; fig. 138) occurs in
  'coto-bark'. Is this from *Nectandra coto* (*Laur.*) or from *Rudgea* (*Rubi.*)?
Hydro-cotoin (6-Hydroxy-2,4-dimethoxy-benzophenone) occurs in
  'para-coto-bark' (*Nectandra* or *Rudgea*?).
4-Hydroxy-benzophenone (*p*-Hydroxy-benzophenone)
  Magnoli.   *Talauma mexicana* (lvs)
Maclurin (Laguncurin; 2,4,6,3',4'-Pentahydroxy-benzophenone; fig. 138)
  Mor.   *Chlorophora* (*Maclura*, *Morus*) *tinctoria*
  Legum.   *Acacia* sp.
  Combret.   *Laguncularia racemosa* (bk, '*laguncurin*')
Methyl-hydro-cotoin (2,4,6-Trimethoxy-benzophenone) occurs in
  'para-coto-bark' (*Nectandra* or *Rudgea*?) and in
  Rhamn.   *Rhamnus purshiana* (bk)
Methyl-protocotoin (Oxyleucotin; 2,4,6-Trimethoxy-3',4'-methylene-dioxy-benzophenone) occurs in 'para-coto-bark' (*Nectandra* or *Rudgea*?).
Protocotoin (6-Hydroxy-2,4-dimethoxy-3',4'-methylenedioxy-benzophenone) occurs in 'para-coto-bark' (*Nectandra* or *Rudgea*?).

Scleroin (2,5-Dihydroxy-3,4-dimethoxy-benzophenone; fig. 138) occurs
with *neoflavanoids*, which it resembles, in
  Legum.   Machaerium scleroxylon (htwd)

II.3 Other aromatic ketones

GENERAL

Again we have difficulties in classification. By no means all of the
compounds listed here are biogenetically related. Some seem to be
terpenoid, some are derivatives of *phenolic acids*.

It is obvious that the large and much-investigated family *Myrtaceae*
has many of these substances. An interesting group occurs in *Humulus*.
Another group of related ketones occurs in the *Zingiberaceae*.

List and Occurrence

Adhumulone is an isomer of *humulone*.
  Mor.   Humulus lupulus
Angustione (fig. 139) was the first natural *biketone* (or *triketone*) to be
  described.
  Myrt.   Backhousia angustifolia (lvs)
Anise-ketone (Anise-acetone; Anisyl-ketone; *p*-Methoxy-phenyl-acet-
  one)
  Illici.   Illicium verum (frt-oil)
  Umbell.   Foeniculum vulgare (oil), *Pimpinella anisum* (oil)
Aristolone: may be a *sesquiterpene*?
  Aristolochi.   Aristolochia debilis (rt)
Aritasone: may be a *diterpene*?
  Chenopodi.   Chenopodium ambrosioides (ess. oil)
Baeckeol (fig. 139)
  Myrt.   Baeckea crenulata (lf-oil?), *frutescens* (ess. oil), *gunneana*
    var. *latifolia* (lf-oil); *Darwinia grandiflora*
Bis(*p*-hydroxycinnamoyl)-methane
  Zingiber.   Curcuma longa
Cohumulone—see *humulone*.
  Mor.   Humulus lupulus
Colupulone—see *humulone*.
  Mor.   Humulus lupulus
Conglomerone is very like *baeckeol*.
  Myrt.   Eucalyptus conglomerata (lf-oil)

Cryptone (fig. 139) occurs in *Pinus* and
>   *Rut.* *Zanthoxylum rhetsa* (frt-oil, *l*-)
>   *Myrt.* *Eucalyptus cneorifolia* (oil, *l*-), *dumosa* (*l*-), *hemiphloia* (*l*-).
>   *micrantha* (oil, *l*-), *polybracteata* (oil, *l*-), *viridis* (*l*-)
>   *Umbell.* *Oenanthe phellandrium* (oil, *d*-)
Curcumin (Diferuloyl-methane; fig. 139)
>   *Zingiber.* *Curcuma aromatica* (rt?), *longa* (rhiz.), *tinctoria*,
>   *xanthorrhiza* (rhiz.)
Dehydro-angustione is said to be toxic in soil.
>   *Myrt.* *Backhousia angustifolia* (lvs), *Eucalyptus rariflora*
Dihydro-ionone
>   *Comp.* *Saussurea lappa* (rt-oil, *cis*-)
Eugenone is very like *baeckeol*.
>   *Myrt.* *Eugenia caryophyllata* (wild form)
Flavesone (fig. 139)
>   *Myrt.* *Eucalyptus decorticans* (ess. oil), *Leptospermum flavescens* (ess. oil)
Humulone (fig. 139) is one of a group of related substances occurring in the much-investigated hops.
>   *Mor.* *Humulus lupulus* (resin)
p-Hydroxy-cinnamoyl-feruloyl-methane
>   *Zingiber.* *Curcuma longa*
p-Hydroxy-propiosyringone may be a 'building brick' of *lignins*, particularly of angiosperms.
p-Hydroxy-propiovanillone may be a 'building brick' of *lignins*.
d-α-Ionone (fig. 139)
>   *Rut.* *Boronia megastigma* (ess. oil)
>   *Lythr.* *Lawsonia inermis* (fl.-oil)
>   *Comp.* *Saussurea lappa* (rt-oil)
β-Ionone (Boronione)
>   *Rut.* *Boronia megastigma* (ess. oil)
>   *Lythr.* *Lawsonia inermis* (fl.-oil)
>   *Comp.* *Saussurea lappa* (rt-oil)
α-Irone is closely related to the *ionones*.
>   *Irid.* *Iris florentina* (rt), *germanica*, *pallida* (rt)
β-Irone
>   *Irid.* *Iris germanica*
γ-Irone
>   *Irid.* *Iris* spp.
Leptospermone (Leptospermol; fig. 139): is this also a *sesquiterpene*?
>   *Myrt.* *Eucalyptus*?; *Leptospermum flavescens* (lf-oil), *scoparium* (ess. oil)

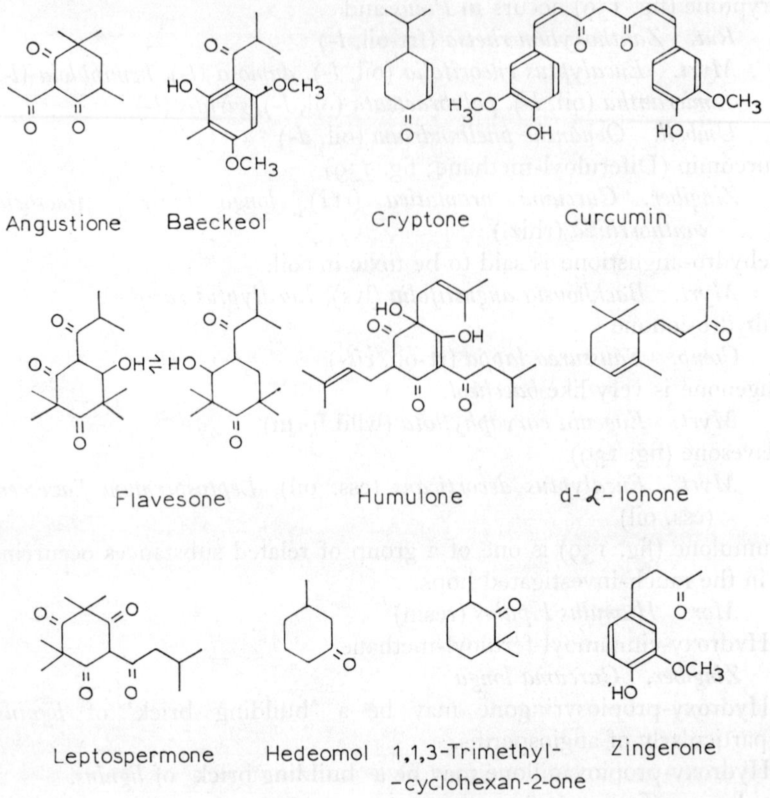

Angustione   Baeckeol   Cryptone   Curcumin

Flavesone   Humulone   d-ℓ-Ionone

Leptospermone   Hedeomol   1,1,3-Trimethyl-   Zingerone
                             -cyclohexan-2-one

Fig. 139 Some aromatic ketones.

Lupulone—see *humulone*.
    Mor.   Humulus lupulus
d-1-Methyl-cyclohexan-3-one (Hedeomol; fig. 139)
    Lab.   Hedeoma pulegioides (ess. oil), *Mentha canadensis?* (ess. oil)
    Gram.   Andropogon nardus (oil)
Methyl-gingerol
    Zingiber.   Zingiber officinale (rhiz.)
1-Phenyl-butan-3-one (Methyl-β-phenyl-ethyl ether)
    Pandan.   Pandanus odoratissimus (fl.-oil)
Santenone (π-Nor-camphor): should be placed among the *monoterpenes*?
    Santal.   Santalum album
Shogaol
    Zingiber.   Zingiber officinale (rhiz.)
Tasmanone
    Myrt.   Eucalyptus risdoni

1,1,3-Trimethyl-cyclohexan-2-one (fig. 139)
    Cist.   *Cistus creticus* (oil), *ladaniferus* (oil)
Zingerone (fig. 139)
    Zingiber.   *Zingiber officinale* (rhiz.)

III OTHER CYCLIC KETONES

GENERAL

A few *ketones* have *cyclopentane* or *cyclopentene* rings, and these may be considered briefly here.

Some of them, at least, are effective when used against insects. Is this of biological significance for the plants producing them?

List and Occurrence

Calythrone (fig. 140)
    Myrt.   *Calythrix tetragona* var. A (ess. oil), *virgata* (ess. oil)
Cinerin-I (fig. 140) is an active principle of '*pyrethrum*'. Does it occur as such?
Cinerin-II is very like *cinerin-I*. It, too, is said to be an active principle of '*pyrethrum*'. Does it occur as such?
Cinerolone is derived from *pyrethrin-I*. Does it occur as such?
Cyclopentan-1-one (fig. 140) has been found in wood-oil, but secondarily?
3-Isopropyliden-1-acetyl-cyclopent-5-ene (fig. 140): should this be treated as a *monoterpene*?
    Myrt.   *Eucalyptus globulus* (ess. oil)
3-Methyl-2-pentenyl-cyclopent-2-en-1-one (Jasmone)
    Rut.   *Citrus* (fl. oil)
    Ole.   *Jasmimum grandiflorum* (fl.-oil, *cis-*)
    Lab.   *Mentha piperita* (oil)
Pyrethrin-I (fig. 140) is a constituent of '*pyrethrum*'.
    Comp.   *Chrysanthemum cinerariaefolium* (fl.) (and other spp. ?)
Pyrethrin-II is a constituent of '*pyrethrum*'.
    Comp.   *Chrysanthemum cinerariaefolium* (fl.) (and other spp. ?)
Pyrethrolone is derived from '*pyrethrum*'. Does it occur as such?
'Pyrethrum' is, says Hill (1952), of at least 3 sources: *Chrysanthemum cinerariaefolium* (Dalmatian insect flowers), the most important; *C. coccineum* (Persian ditto); and *C. marschallii* (Caucasian ditto). 'Pyrethrum' is one of the most effective of natural products for use

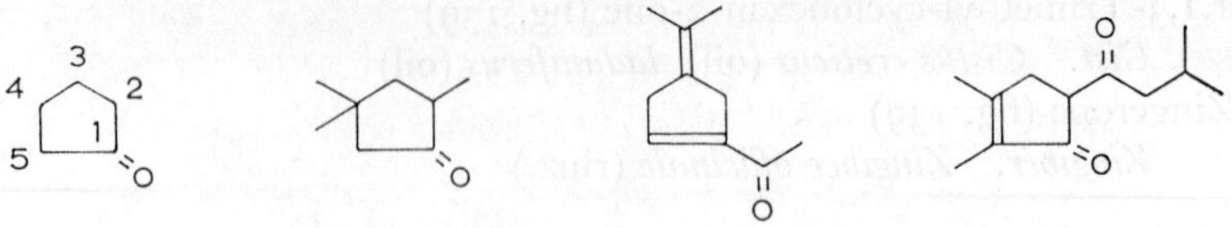

Cyclopentan-   2,4,4-Trimethyl-   3-Isopropyliden-   Calythrone
-1-one   -cyclopentan-1-   -1-acetyl-cyclo-
                   -one   pent-5-ene

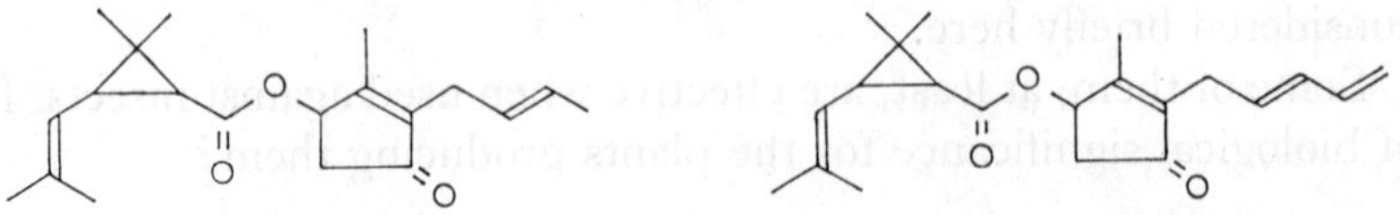

Cinerin-I   Pyrethrin-I

Fig. 140 Some cyclic ketones.

against insects. It is not toxic to man. Some, at least, of its active ingredients have been listed above.

2,4,4-Trimethyl-cyclopentan-1-one

    Lab.   *Mentha pulegium* (ess. oil)

LACTONES

GENERAL

As in so many other cases classification is difficult. We include here a number of *lactones* with five-membered heterocyclic rings. Many lactones with six-membered rings, however, are α-*pyrones* and we have treated them as such. A few are obviously derived from *hydroxy-fatty acids*. Some *alkaloids*, such as those of *Stemona*, are *lactones*. Many *sesquiterpenes* are *mono-* or *di-lactones*. At least one *acetylenic lactone* is known, and it is treated with its parent as an '*acetylenic compound*'.

Many fungal products which are antibiotic are *lactones*, and a few of the *lactones* of higher plants are said to be antibiotic, too.

Note the occurrence of ten or more *phthalides* in the *Umbelliferae*.

List and Occurrence

Anemonin (fig. 141) is a dimer of *protoanemonin*.

>*Ranuncul. Aconitum napellus* ?; *Anemone pulsatilla* (and other spp.); *Clematis* (2); *Ranunculus* (several spp.)

Biglandulinic acid

>*Euphorbi. Euphorbia biglandulosa* (as a calcium salt in latex)

3-*n*-Butyl-phthalide (fig. 141)

>*Umbell. Apium graveolens* (sd-oil), *Levisticum officinale* (rt-oil), *Ligusticum acutilobum* (rt-oil)

Cnidilide

>*Umbell. Cnidium officinale* (rt)

'Cnidium-lactone': a mixture?

>*Umbell. Cnidium officinale* (rt)

Cuscutalin: what is this?

>*Convolvul. Cuscuta*

Eleutherol (fig. 141) is a *naphthalide*.

>*Irid. Eleutherine bulbosa* (bulb)

Grantianic acid—the *necic acid* of *grantianine*—is a *lactone*.

Hibiscic acid (?Hibiscus acid; (+)-Allo-oxycitronic acid-lactone)

>*Malv. Hibiscus sabdariffa* (lvs, fl., fruiting-calyx)

Holigarna-lactone is, says Karrer (1958), of uncertain structure. He has '*holygarna-lactone*'.

>*Anacardi. Holigarna arnottiana* (sd)

3-Isobutylidene-3α,4-dihydro-phthalide

>*Umbell. Apium graveolens* (odorous constituent)

3-Isobutylidene-phthalide (fig. 141)

>*Umbell. Apium graveolens* (odorous constituent)

3-Isovalidene-3α,4-dihydro-phthalide

>*Umbell. Apium graveolens* (odorous constituent)

3-Isovalidene-phthalide

>*Umbell. Apium graveolens* (odorous constituent)

Junceic acid—the *necic acid* of *junceine*—is a *lactone*.

Leucodrin (Proteacin; Protexin; fig. 141): belongs here? It occurs (always?) as *leucoglycodrin*.

Leucoglycodrin (*p*-Glucosyl-leucodrin)

>*Prote. Leucadendron adscendens* (lvs), *concinnum* (lvs), *stokoei* (lvs)

Ligusticum-lactone (3-Butylidene-phthalide; fig. 141)

>*Umbell. Levisticum officinale* (rt-oil), *Ligusticum acutilobum* (frt-oil)

Ligustilide (fig. 141)

>*Umbell. Cnidium officinale* (rt), *Ligusticum acutilobum* (rt)

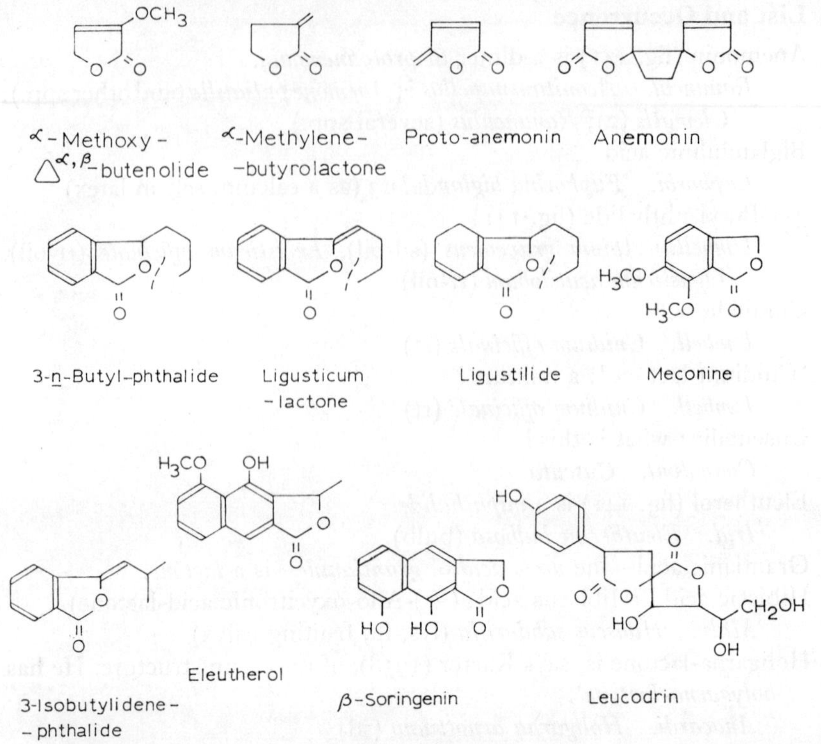

α-Methoxy- $\Delta^{\alpha,\beta}$-butenolide   α-Methylene- -butyrolactone   Proto-anemonin   Anemonin

3-n-Butyl-phthalide   Ligusticum -lactone   Ligustilide   Meconine

Eleutherol

3-Isobutylidene- -phthalide   β-Soringenin   Leucodrin

Fig. 141 Some lactones.

Meconine (6,7-Dimethoxy-phthalide; Mekonin; Opianyl; fig. 141) is the 'bottom' of a *phthalide-isoquinoline alkaloid*.

    Ranuncul.   Hydrastis canadensis (rt)

    Papaver.   Papaver somniferum

α-Methoxy-$\Delta^{\alpha,\beta}$-butenolide (fig. 141)

    Lili.   Narthecium ossifragum (infl.)

α-Methylene-butyrolactone (fig. 141) is said to be bacteriostatic.

    Lili.   Erythronium americanum (chiefly as a glycoside?)

Monocrotalic acid, a *necic acid*, is a *lactone* (but not in the alkaloid *monocrotaline*?).

Neocnidilide

    Umbell.   Apium graveolens (frt-oil), *Cnidium officinale* (rt)

Peperic acid is said to be an autoxidation product of *mentho-furan*, but it also occurs naturally in

    Lab.   Bystropogon mollis (oil)

Protoanemonin (fig. 141) is the aglycone of *ranunculin*. It is said to be antibiotic.

Ranuncul. Anemone pulsatilla, Caltha?, Clematis (8), *Ranunculus* (several)

Ranunculin is a glycoside of *protoanemonin*.

Ranuncul. Ranunculus acris, arvensis, bulbosus, sceleratus

Sceleranecic acid—a *necic acid*—is a *dilactone*?

'Sedanolide' is a mixture of *neocnidilide* and *n-butyl-phthalide*.

Umbell. Apium graveolens (sd-oil)

Sedanonic acid anhydride

Umbell. Apium graveolens (sd-oil)?, Cnidium officinale (rt), *Levisticum officinale* (rt-oil)

α-Sorigenin is a *naphthalide*. It is the aglycone of α-*sorinin*.

β-Sorigenin (fig. 141) is the aglycone of β-*sorinin*.

Rhamn. Rhamnus japonica (bk, free?)

α-Sorinin is α-*sorigenin-5-primveroside*.

Rhamn. Rhamnus japonica (bk)

β-Sorinin is β-*sorigenin-5-primveroside*.

Rhamn. Rhamnus japonica (bk)

LIGNANS

GENERAL

Haworth (1937), writing of 'natural resins', pointed out the importance of the union of two C_6–C_3 units in the formation of certain components of the resins. He proposed, because of their frequent occurrence in wood, the generic name 'lignane'. The name, but without the final 'e', seems to have been adopted, and we now speak of *lignans* as a class.

Some of the *lignans* are, at the same time, *lactones*.

Erdtman (in Todd, 1956), has much to say of *lignans* in connection with conifer taxonomy. He says (p. 474):

The lignans must be considered to be typical examples of secondary constituents. They form a rather large group of substances of varying structure in which, however, there are two easily recognizable C_6–C_3 units condensed together at the β-carbon atom of the side chains. It seems out of the question that such compounds could be synthesized in Nature except from primary C_6–C_3 compounds...In the laboratory, one can in fact prepare compounds of lignan type by the dehydrogenation of, for example, isoeugenol (to an analogue of conidendrin), ferulic acid (to an analogue of pinoresinol), and coniferyl alcohol (to dl-pinoresinol).

Hearon and MacGregor, at about the same time (1955), say:

> In relationship to other non-carbohydrate plant constituents the lignans would represent a dimer stage intermediate between monomeric propyl-phenol $[C_6-C_3]$ units and lignin[s]. Naturally occurring trimers and tetramers have not been reported.

Some of the *lignans* found in wood may be due to pathogenic factors. Thus Erdtman (in Swain, 1963) says that Hasegawa and Shirato found large amounts of the lignan *iso-olivil* (which occurs 'normally' in the resin of an olive, *Olea cunninghamii*) in the wood of a *Prunus* suffering from attack by a fungus. The *lignan* is said not to occur in the fungus or in the *Prunus* when alone. We may wonder about this, however. I believe some of the *depsides* produced by lichens—and which were said not to be formed by either of the lichen partners alone—are, in fact, formed by the fungal partners when grown under appropriate conditions in pure culture.

Although *lignans* appear to be widely distributed in higher plants our records from angiosperms are still too few for many generalizations. We may note a few suggestive facts, however.

(*a*) I have no records at all from monocotyledons. Are *lignans* indeed absent from that great group?

(*b*) A disproportionate number of records come from **Magnoliales**, **Ranunculales**, **Piperales** and **Aristolochiales**, orders which are considered to be closely related. Thus we have (numbers of *lignans* present in brackets):

Magnoliales

1. *Magnoli.*   *Liriodendron tulipifera* (1)
3. *Himantandr.*   *Galbulimima baccata* (2), *belgraveana* (1)
7. *Myristic.*   *Myristica otoba* (3), *Virola* (1)
14. *Monimi.*   *Piptocalyx moorei* (1)
17. *Laur.*   *Eusideroxylon zwageri* (1); *Ocotea usambarensis* (1), *veraguensis* (1)
18. *Hernandi.*   *Hernandia ovigera* (4)

Ranunculales

2. *Berberid.*   *Diphylleia grayi* (1); *Podophyllum emodi* (6), *peltatum* (6), *sikkimensis* (1)

Piperales

2. *Piper.*   *Piper cubeba* (1), *lowong* (1), *peepuloides* (1)

Aristolochiales

1. *Aristolochi.*   *Asarum blumei* (1), *sieboldii* (1)

List and Occurrence

Arctigenin (fig. 142) is the aglycone of *arctiin*.
>   *Comp. Arctium lappa* (frt)

Arctiin was the first *lignan-glucoside* to be discovered.
>   *Comp. Arctium lappa* (frt)

Asarinin is a stereoisomer of *sesamin*.
>   *Aristolochi. Asarum blumei* (l-)
>   *Rut. Acronychia muelleri* (lvs, d-); *Zanthoxylum carolinianum* (bk, l-), *clava-herculis* (bk, l-)

Calopiptin
>   *Monimi. Piptocalyx moorei*

Cicutin is the C_3-epimer of *deoxy-podophyllotoxin*.
>   *Umbell. Cicuta maculata* (rt)

Collinusin
>   *Euphorbi. Cleistanthus collinus* (lvs)

Cubebin
>   *Piper. Piper cubeba* (frt)

Dehydro-podophyllotoxin
>   *Berberid. Podophyllum peltatum*

Demethylenedioxy-deoxy-podophyllotoxin
>   *Hernandi. Hernandia ovigera* (sd-oil)

4'-Demethyl-podophyllotoxin (fig. 142)
>   *Berberid. Podophyllum emodi* (resin), *peltatum*

4'-Demethyl-podophyllotoxin-glucoside (fig. 142) has *glucose* at x.
>   *Berberid. Podophyllum emodi* (rhiz.)

Deoxy-podophyllotoxin (Anthricin; Hernandion; Silicicolin) occurs in conifers and in
>   *Hernandi. Hernandia ovigera* (sd-oil)
>   *Berberid. Podophyllum peltatum* (resin), *pleianthum*
>   *Umbell. Anthriscus silvestris* (rt)

Diaeudesmin
>   *Piper. Piper peepuloides* (frt)

Diphyllin
>   *Berberid. Diphylleia grayi* (rt)
>   *Euphorbi. Cleistanthus collinus* (lvs)

l-Eudesmin (Pinoresinol dimethyl ether)
>   *Myrt. Eucalyptus hemiphloia* (Kino)
>   *Convolvul. Humbertia madagascariensis* (wd)

Eusiderin
>   *Laur. Eusideroxylon zwageri* (wd)

d-Forsythigenol (d-Pinoresinol-methyl ether; Phillygenin; Phillygenol) is the aglycone of *forsythin*.

Forsythin (Phillyrin; Philyroside) is dimorphic.
>*Ole.* Forsythia (3), *Olea*?, *Phillyrea* (3)

Galbacin
>*Himantandr.* Galbulimima baccata (bk)

Galbulin (fig. 142)
>*Himantandr.* Galbulimima sp. (bk)

Galcatin
>*Himantandr.* Galbulimima baccata (bk)

Galgravin
>*Himantandr.* Galbulimima belgraveana (bk)

Gmelinol
>*Verben.* Gmelina leichhardtii (wd)

l-Guaiaretic acid (fig. 142)
>*Zygophyll.* Guaiacum officinale (resin)

Hydroxy-otobain
>*Myristic.* Myristica otoba (frt-oil), *Virola cuspidata* (bk)

d-Iso-olivil
>*Ros.* Prunus (diseased wd)
>*Ole.* Olea cunninghamii (resin)

Iso-otobain
>*Myristic.* Myristica otoba (frt-oil)

Justicidin-A (Diphyllin-methyl ether) (but the formula I have seems not to be that of *diphyllin-methyl ether*).
>*Rut.* Cneoridium dumosum (plt)
>*Acanth.* Justicia hayatai var. *decumbens*

Justicidin-B
>*Acanth.* Justicia hayatai var. *decumbens*

Liriodendrin is a diglucoside of *lirioresinol*.
>*Magnoli.* Liriodendron tulipifera (bk)

Lirioresinol is a stereoisomer of *syringaresinol*. How does it differ from (−)-*lirioresinol-C*?
>*Salic.* Populus sp.

(−)-Lirioresinol-C
>*Apocyn.* Aspidosperma marcgravianum (wd)

Lyonia-xyloside ((+)-Dimethoxy-isolariciresinol-xyloside; fig. 142)
>*Betul.* Alnus glutinosa
>*Ros.* Sorbus
>*Eric.* Lyonia sp.

Nordihydro-guaiaretic acid
>*Zygophyll.* Larrea cuneifolia, divaricata (lvs), *nitida*

Olivil
>*Ole.* Olea europaea (wd)

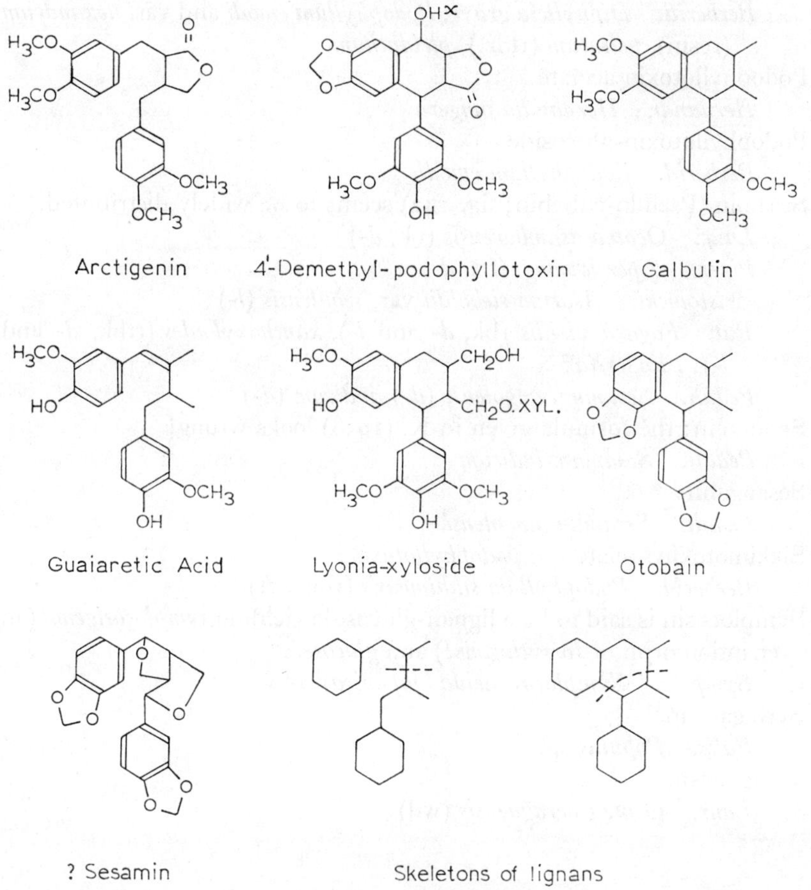

Arctigenin   4'-Demethyl-podophyllotoxin   Galbulin

Guaiaretic Acid   Lyonia-xyloside   Otobain

? Sesamin   Skeletons of lignans

Fig. 142 Some lignans.

(+)-*O,O*-Dimethyl-lirioresinol-B
 Apocyn. Aspidosperma marcgravianum (wd)
Otobain (fig. 142)
 Myristic. Myristica otoba, Virola cuspidata
α-Peltatin
 Berberid. Podophyllum peltatum (rt)
α-Peltatin-glucoside
 Berberid. Podophyllum peltatum
β-Peltatin
 Berberid. Podophyllum peltatum (rt)
Picropodophyllin, Picropodophyllin-acetate, etc., are artefacts?

Podophyllotoxin occurs in conifers and in

　　Berberid.　Diphylleia grayi; *Podophyllum emodi* and var. *hexandrum*
　　(resin), *peltatum* (rhiz.), *pleianthum*

Podophyllotoxin acetate

　　Hernandi.　Hernandia ovigera

Podophyllotoxin-glucoside

　　Berberid.　Podophyllum emodi

Sesamin (Pseudo-cubebin; fig. 142) seems to be widely distributed.

　　Laur.　Ocotea usambarensis (bk, *d-*)
　　Piper.　Piper lowong. (frt, *d-*)
　　Aristolochi.　Asarum sieboldii var. *seoulensis* (*l-*)
　　Rut.　Fagara viridis (bk, *d-* and *l-*), *xanthoxyloides* (rtbk, *d-* and
　　l-); *Flindersia*?
　　Pedali.　Sesamum angolense (*d-*), *indicum* (*d-*)

Sesamolin: the formula given in K. (1958) looks wrong!

　　Pedali.　Sesamum indicum

Sesangolin

　　Pedali.　Sesamum angolense

Sikkimotoxin: related to *podophyllotoxin*?

　　Berberid.　Podophyllum sikkimensis (rhiz., rt)

Symplocosin is said to be a lignan-glucoside yielding *symplocosigenol* (an
enantiomorph of *forsythigenol*) and *glucose*.

　　Symploc.　Symplocos lucida (*japonica*) (bk)

Syringaresinol

　　Salic.　Populus sp.

Veraguensin

　　Laur.　Ocotea veraguensis (wd)

LIGNINS

GENERAL

Botanists have recognized for a very long time that certain tissues of
vascular plants—xylem, bast-fibres, sclereids of various kinds and
distribution, pith (sometimes), and even (but rarely) stomata—may be
'lignified'. Such tissues react differently from 'unlignified' tissues to
stains and some reagents, and the relative constancy of these differences
has led botanists until comparatively recently to think of an entity,
lignin, which conveys the character of 'woodiness' to lignified tissues.

Yet seventy years ago Mäule showed that in general the woods of
gymnosperms and angiosperms differ in their colour reaction when
chlorinated and then treated with ammonia (p. 75). This has suggested

to some investigators the possibility that more than one kind of *lignin* exists, and that groups of plants may be characterized by their lignins.

But lignins have proved refractive and we cannot, even today, use lignin chemistry to any great extent in chemotaxonomy. I have been involved a little in this problem. In the 1940s Hibbert and others were subjecting woods to alkaline oxidation and were obtaining quite large yields of *vanillin* and *syringaldehyde* (fig. 143). When Hibbert told me that he got *syringaldehyde* from maple, but not from spruce wood, I suggested that Mäule's reaction (mentioned above) might be due to presence of the syringyl grouping in the one but not in the other. We were able to show (Creighton, Gibbs and Hibbert, 1944) that this was indeed the case. Creighton also found that some monocotyledons seemed to have a third grouping in their lignin, yielding *p-hydroxy-benzaldehyde* (fig. 143) in addition.

Already it had been shown by others that at least one species of *Podocarpus* (a gymnosperm) is unusual in giving a positive Mäule reaction like an angiosperm. We were able to demonstrate that this (and some other) species of *Podocarpus*, *Tetraclinis articulata* (of the gymnospermous *Cupressaceae*), members of the gymnospermous (?) **Gnetales**, and perhaps all cycads, give positive Mäule reactions and that their lignins yield syringaldehyde.

An important observation was that the ratio syringaldehyde:vanillin is about 3:1 for most angiosperms. Some 'primitive' angiosperms seemed to have lower ratios, and this is correlated with a weaker Mäule reaction (Towers and Gibbs, 1953). We also amassed evidence suggesting the separation of *Negundo* from *Acer*.

There is some reason, then, to believe that there is not one lignin, but several; or that lignin varies in its exact structure from species to species, or even during the development of a single plant. Alston and Turner (1963) see some hope for further use of lignin(s) in chemotaxonomy: 'Lignin is a plant product which potentially is of great systematic value, especially if technical advances occur which provide a method of analysing the sequential linkages of the building units and their cross linkages.'

There is abundant evidence that C_6–C_3 units such as *coniferyl alcohol* (fig. 143) are the building blocks of lignin(s). It has been shown, for example, that C^{14} *coniferin* (the glucoside of *coniferyl alcohol*) is very efficiently incorporated into spruce lignin. Freudenberg and others have postulated a polymeric structure for lignin(s), and some dimers such as the *lignans* (see our preceding section) are known, and have even been synthesized enzymatically.

The relationship of the C_6–C_3 units involved in lignin(s) to the *flavonoids* is clear. Bate-Smith (1963) even goes so far as to say that

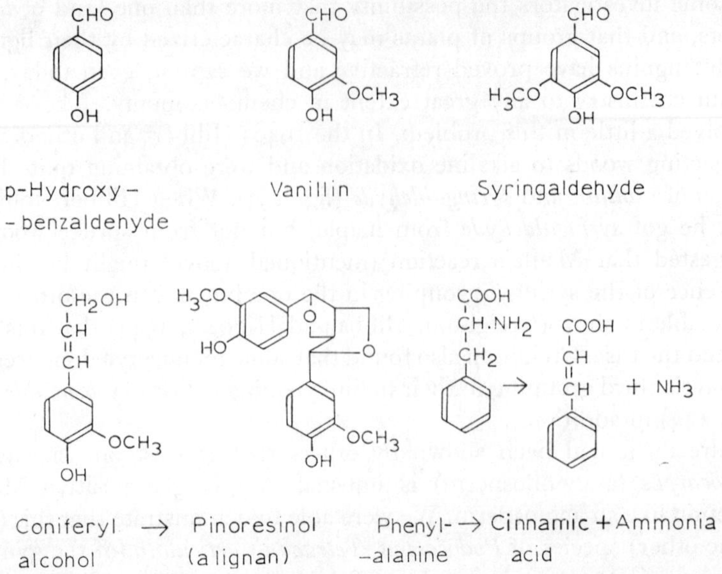

Fig. 143 Substances believed to be involved in lignin(s).

lignins may 'be regarded as flavonoids in the wider sense', and that: 'the presence of leucoanthocyanins, flavonols and hydroxy acids in the leaves is associated with the uninhibited deposition of lignin [hence woodiness] whereas the presence of flavones and methoxy acids in leaves is associated with a tendency for suppression of lignification'.

Harborne (1966) enlarges on this and says: 'The relative wealth of flavone production in some herbaceous plants, e.g. members of the Compositae, may represent a means of avoiding a build-up of lignin precursors.'

Some, at least, of the 'lignin-precursors' are said to arise from one of the 'protein' amino-acids, *phenyl-alanine* (fig. 143).